A LIBRARY OF LITERARY CRITICISM

A Library

MODERN

Volume III
P-Z

Fourth enlarged edition

of Literary Criticism

AMERICAN LITERATURE

Compiled and edited by
DOROTHY NYREN CURLEY
Coordinator of Adult Services
Brooklyn Public Library

MAURICE KRAMER
Assistant Professor of English
Brooklyn College, The City University of New York

ELAINE FIALKA KRAMER

Frederick Ungar Publishing Co., New York

Copyright © 1960, 1961, 1964, 1969 by Frederick Ungar Publishing Co., Inc.
Printed in the United States of America
Library of Congress Catalog Card No. 76-76599
ISBN 0-8044-3046-2 Set
0-8044-3047-0 Vol. I
0-8044-3048-9 Vol. II
0-8044-3049-7 Vol. III

Second Printing, 1970

Selections in these volumes
are quoted with the approval of the copyright owners
and may not be quoted elsewhere without their consent.
For acknowledgments see page 469 in Volume III.

AUTHORS INCLUDED

Authors added in the fourth edition are marked (†)

VOLUME III

Parker, Dorothy
Parrington, V. L.†
Patchen, Kenneth
Percy, Walker†
Porter, Katherine Anne
Pound, Ezra
Powers, J. F.
Pynchon, Thomas†
Rahv, Philip†
Ransom, John Crowe
Rawlings, Marjorie Kinnan†
Reed, John†
Rexroth, Kenneth
Rice, Elmer
Rich, Adrienne†
Richter, Conrad
Roberts, Elizabeth Madox
Roberts, Kenneth
Robinson, Edwin Arlington
Roethke, Theodore
Rölvaag, Ole†
Roth, Henry†
Roth, Philip
Rourke, Constance†
Rukeyser, Muriel
Runyon, Damon†
Salinger, J. D.
Sandburg, Carl
Santayana, George
Saroyan, William

Sarton, May
Schisgal, Murray†
Schulberg, Budd
Schwartz, Delmore
Scott, Winfield Townley
Sexton, Anne†
Shapiro, Karl
Shaw, Irwin
Sherwood, Robert
Simon, Neil†
Simpson, Louis†
Sinclair, Upton
Snodgrass, W. D.†
Sontag, Susan†
Stafford, Jean
Steele, Wilbur Daniel†
Steffens, Lincoln†
Stegner, Wallace
Stein, Gertrude
Steinbeck, John
Stevens, Wallace
Stickney, Trumbull†
Styron, William
Swados, Harvey†
Tarkington, Booth†
Tate, Allen
Taylor, Peter
Thomas, Augustus†
Thurber, James
Torrence, Ridgely†

Trilling, Lionel

Twain, Mark

Updike, John

Van Doren, Mark

Van Druten, John

Veblen, Thorstein†

Viereck, Peter

Wallant, Edward Lewis†

Warren, Robert Penn

Welty, Eudora

Wescott, Glenway

West, Nathanael

Wharton, Edith

Wheelock, John Hall

Wheelwright, John Brooks

White, E. B.†

Whittemore, Reed†

Wilbur, Richard

Wilder, Thornton

Williams, Tennessee

Williams, William Carlos

Wilson, Edmund

Winters, Yvor

Wolfe, Thomas

Wouk, Herman†

Wright, James†

Wright, Richard

Wylie, Elinor†

Young, Stark†

PERIODICALS USED

Where no abbreviation is indicated, the magazine references are listed in full.

	Accent
AHR	American Historical Review
AJHQ	American Jewish Historical Quarterly
AJS	American Journal of Sociology
AL	American Literature
Am	America
AM	American Mercury
AmQ	American Quarterly
AnR	Antioch Review
	Arizona and the West
AS	American Scholar
ASR	American Sociological Review
At	Atlantic Monthly
Bkm	Bookman
BkmL	Bookman (London)
	Book World
BNYPL	Bulletin of the New York Public Library
	Carleton Miscellany
	Century
	Chimera
CC	Christian Century
CE	College English
CF	Canadian Forum
	Christian Scholar
Cmty	Commentary
	Columbia University Forum
Com	Commonweal
CR	Chicago Review
Crit	Criterion
	Critic

	Criticism
	Critique
CS	Chicago Sun Book Week
CSM	Christian Science Monitor
CW	Catholic World
	Denver Quarterly
	Dial
DR	Dublin Review
DS	Drama Survey
EJ	English Journal
ELH	English Literary History
	Encounter
	English Studies
ER	Evergreen Review
ETJ	Educational Theatre Journal
	Forum
Fm	Freeman
	Griffin
	Georgia Review
Harper	Harper's Magazine
HdR	Hudson Review
HR	Hopkins Review
	Horizon
IJE	International Journal of Ethics
	Independent
IW	Independent Woman
JEGP	Journal of English and Germanic Philology
JF	Jewish Frontier
JHI	Journal of the History of Ideas
JP	Journal of Philosophy
JSS	Jewish Social Studies
	Judaism
KR	Kenyon Review
	Library Chronicle
	Life
LJ	Library Journal
LM	London Mercury
Lon	London Magazine
LR	Literary Review
LtR	Little Review
MD	Modern Drama
MFS	Modern Fiction Studies
MinnR	Minnesota Review

MLQ	Modern Language Quarterly
	Midstream
	Modern Age
MP	Modern Philology
MR	Massachusetts Review
NAR	North American Review
	Nation
	National Review
NC	Nineteenth Century
	Nineteenth Century Fiction
NDQ	North Dakota Quarterly
NEQ	New England Quarterly
NL	New Leader
NMQ	New Mexico Quarterly
NR	New Republic
NSN	New Statesman and Nation, later Statesman and Nation
Nwk	Newsweek
NWW	New World Writing
NY	New Yorker
NYEP	New York Evening Post Book Section
NYHT	New York Herald Tribune Book Section
NYHTts	New York Herald Tribune Theater Section
NYR	New York Review of Books
NYT	New York Times Book Section
NYTd	New York Times Daily Newspaper
NYT mag	New York Times Magazine Section
NYTts	New York Times Theater Section
OM	Overland Monthly
	Outlook
Per	Perspectives U. S. A.
	Phylon
PMLA	Publications of the Modern Language Association
	Poetry
PR	Partisan Review
PS	Pacific Spectator
QJS	Quarterly Journal of Speech
Ren	Renascence
	Reporter
	Salmagundi
SAQ	South Atlantic Quarterly
	Science
Scy	Scrutiny
SLM	Southern Literary Messenger

SoR	Southern Review
	Southern Folklore Quarterly
Spec	Spectator
SR	Saturday Review of Literature, later Saturday Review
	Survey
SwR	Sewanee Review
SWR	Southwest Review
TA	Theatre Arts
TC	Twentieth Century
TCL	Twentieth Century Literature
TDR	Tulane Drama Review, later The Drama Review
	Theatre Magazine
	Time
	Tri-Quarterly
TSL	Tennessee Studies in Literature
UKCR	University of Kansas City Review, later University Review
UR	University Review
UTQ	University of Toronto Quarterly
VQR	Virginia Quarterly Review
WHR	Western Humanities Review
WLB	Wilson Library Bulletin
	Works
WSCL	Wisconsin Studies in Contemporary Literature, later Contemporary Literature
YR	Yale Review

PARKER, DOROTHY (1893–1967)

Dorothy Parker runs her little show as if it were a circus; she cracks her whip and the big elephant joke pounds his four legs in glee and the pink ladies of fantastic behavior begin to float in the air like lozenges. . . . Mrs. Parker has begun in the thoroughly familiar Millay manner and worked into something quite her own. . . . Miss Millay remains lyrically, of course, far superior to Mrs. Parker. . . . But there are moods when Dorothy Parker is more acceptable, whiskey straight, not champagne.

Genevieve Taggard. *NYHT*. March 27, 1927. p. 7

Here is poetry that is "smart" in the fashion designer's sense of the word. Mrs. Parker need not hide her head in shame, as the average poet must, when she admits the authorship of this book. For in its lightness, its cynicism, its pose, she has done the right thing; she is in a class with the Prince of Wales, the Theatre Guild, Gramercy Park, and H. L. Mencken. And these somewhat facetious remarks are not intended as disparagement. It is high time that a poet with a monocle looked at the populace, instead of the populace looking at the poet through a lorgnette.

Marie Luhrs. *Poetry*. April, 1927. p. 52

In verse of a Horatian lightness, with an exquisite certainty of technique, which, like the lustre on a Persian bowl, is proof that civilization is itself a philosophy, Dorothy Parker is writing poetry deserving high praise. . . . I suspect that one should quote Latin rather than English to parallel the edged fineness of Dorothy Parker's verse. This belle dame sans merci has the ruthlessness of the great tragic lyricists whose work was allegorized in the fable of the nightingale singing with her breast against a thorn. It is disillusion recollected in tranquillity where the imagination has at last controlled the emotions. It comes out clear, and with the authentic sparkle of a great vintage.

Henry Seidel Canby. *SR*. June 13, 1931. p. 891

More certain than either death or taxes is the high and shining art of Dorothy Parker. . . . Bitterness, humor, wit, yearning for beauty and love, and a foreknowledge of their futility—with rue her heart is laden, but her lads are gold-plated—these, you might say, are the elements of the

1

Parkerian formula; these, and the divine talent to find the right word and reject the wrong one. The result is a simplicity that almost startles.

Frankin P. Adams. *NYHT*. June 14, 1931. p. 7

To say that Mrs. Parker writes well is as fatuous, I'm afraid, as proclaiming that Cellini was clever with his hands. But it's fun to see the lamented English language rise from the Parisian boneyard and race out front with the right jockey in the saddle, and I cannot help attempting to communicate to others my pleasure in the performance. . . . The trick about her writing is the trick about Ring Lardner's writing or Ernest Hemingway's writing. It isn't a trick.

Ogden Nash. *SR*. Nov. 4, 1933. p. 231

Drunk or sober, angry or affectionate, stupid or inspired, these people of Mrs. Parker's speak with an accent we immediately recognize and relish. Mrs. Parker has listened to her contemporaries with as sharp a pair of ears as anyone has had in the present century, unless, to be sure, Lardner is to be considered, as he probably is, without a rival in this field. Mrs. Parker is more limited than Lardner; she is expert only with sophisticates. . . . But she does her lesser job quite perfectly, achieving as she does it a tone half-way between sympathy and satire. . . . Again it is only Ring Lardner who can be compared with her in the matter of hatred for stupidity, cruelty, and weakness.

Mark Van Doren. *EJ*. Sept., 1934. pp. 541–2

One comes back to Mrs. Parker's light verse with the greatest pleasure; with its sharp wit, its clean bite, its perfectly conscious—and hence delightful—archness, it stands re-reading amply. Here her high technical polish has great virtue. . . . But what, of course, is more important is the sense of personality that converts what might otherwise be merely a witty idea into a dramatic, however cockeyed, situation; a sense of personality that gives us not cynicism in the abstract but laughter applied to an objective. There is no one else in Mrs. Parker's special field who can do half as much.

Louis Kronenberger. *NYT*. Dec. 13, 1936. p. 28

Men have liked her poems because of the half-bitter, half-wistful tribute to their indispensability and their irresistible, fatal charms. A different kind of lover, the lover of light verse, has admired her extraordinary technical competence and the way in which her verse constantly veers over into the domain of genuinely lyric poetry. The wits of the town have been delighted to see a Sappho who could combine a heart-break with a wisecrack.

Irwin Edman. *Nation*. Dec. 19, 1936. p. 737

The urbanity of these stories is that of a worldly, witty person with a place in a complex and highly-developed society, their ruthlessness that of an expert critical intelligence, about which there is something clinical, something of the probing adroitness of a dentist: the fine-pointed instrument unerringly discovers the carious cavity behind the smile. . . . Mrs. Parker may appear amused, but it is plain that she is really horrified. Her bantering revelations are inspired by a respect for decency, and her pity and sympathy are ready when needed.

William Plomer. *Spec.* Nov. 17, 1939. p. 708

Mrs. Parker's published work does not bulk large. But most of it has been pure gold and the five winnowed volumes of her shelf—three of poetry, two of prose—are so potent a distillation of nectar and wormwood, of ambrosia and deadly nightshade, as might suggest to the rest of us that we all write far too much. Even though I am one who does not profess to be privy to the intentions of posterity, I do suspect that another generation will not share the confusion into which Mrs. Parker's poetry throws so many of her contemporaries, who, seeing that much of it is witty, dismiss it patronizingly as "light" verse, and do not see that some of it is thrilling poetry of a piercing and rueful beauty.

Alexander Woollcott. *The Portable Woollcott*
(Viking). 1946. pp. 181–2

. . . in her own stories her acidity bit most often into the gilt and brass of a certain type of American personality, the self-absorbed female snob. This happened to be a type she knew best in its middle-class manifestations. . . . Miss Parker invites comparison with [Ring] Lardner in her focus on the female companion of Lardner's idle middle-class man, also in her frequent use of the diary form, the monologue, and trivial dialogue. Sometimes her idle, middle-class females are smug and aggressive; sometimes they are pathetic like Lardner's "victims"; sometimes both. Occasionally they are more amusing than anything else.

(K)   Norris W. Yates, *The American Humorist* (Iowa
State). 1964. p. 266

In print and in person, Miss Parker sparkled with a word or a phrase, for she honed her humor to its most economical size. Her rapier wit, much of it spontaneous, gained its early renown from her membership in the Algonquin Round Table, an informal luncheon club at the Algonquin Hotel in the nineteen-twenties, where some of the city's most sedulous framers of bon mots gathered. . . .

Her lifelong reputation as a glittering, annihilating humorist in poetry, essays, short stories and in conversation was compiled and sustained brickbat by brickbat. One of her quips could make a fool a celebrity, and vice versa. She was, however, at bottom a disillusioned romantic, all the fiercer because the world spun against her sentimental nature. She truly loved flowers, dogs and a good cry; and it was this fundamental sadness and shyness that gave her humor its extraordinary bite and intensity.

(K)   Alden Whitman. *NYTd*. June 8, 1967. pp. 1, 38

See *The Portable Dorothy Parker* (poetry and prose).

PARRINGTON, V. L. (1871–1929)

Now it appears that Mr. Parrington is about to start an unheaval in American literary criticism. He has yanked Miss Beautiful Letters out of the sphere of the higher verbal hokum and fairly set her in the way that leads to contact with pulsating reality—that source and inspiration of all magnificent literature. No doubt, the magpies, busy with the accidence of Horace, the classical allusions of Thoreau, and the use of the adverb by Emerson, will make a big outcry, but plain citizens who believe that the American eagle could soar with unblinking eyes against the full-orbed noonday sun if he had half a chance will clap their hands with joy and make the hills ring with gladness. . . . Our author has traced American political, economic, and social development in broad strokes and has sought to relate letters and opinion to the forces "anterior to literary schools and movements," revealing the substance from which literary culture springs. In carrying out his project he has written a truly significant book; according to signs on every hand, a work that promises to be epoch-making, sending exhilarating gusts through the deadly miasma of academic criticism.

Charles A. Beard. *Nation*. May 18, 1927. pp. 560–2

Within its limits the book [*Main Currents*] has real merits. It makes clear how much American literature can reveal to the open-minded historian; it gives deserved attention to some writers little remembered today, particularly some nineteenth-century Southerners; and it is especially useful in its contributions to an understanding of certain aspects of "the colonial mind." There should be hearty agreement with Professor Parrington's protest against the narrowness implicit in the purely aesthetic point of view from which most of our colonial literature is seen as uninteresting. Many of his biographical and critical sketches of the writers by whom he charts intellectual currents are admirable; and in some of them the application of new tests to supposedly familiar figures brings real revelation.

Kenneth B. Murdock. *YR*. Jan., 1928. p. 382

In his *The Colonial Mind* [*Main Currents*, Vol. 1], Professor Vernon Louis Parrington discusses the Puritans and Pilgrims of early Massachusetts from a rather unusual point of view. . . . Briefly, Professor Parrington's contention seems to be this: that, among the Puritans of the Massachusetts Bay colony, Calvinist theology and political aristocracy went hand in hand, whereas, among the Pilgrims of Plymouth Plantation, Lutheran theology and political democracy were equally inseparable.

This attitude, especially since it is accompanied by the acceptance of the theory that the Puritan aristocrats finally acceded to Separatist democratic ideals, places an uncommon emphasis upon Lutheranism as a force in the development of colonial Massachusetts. To explain this interpretation, Professor Parrington makes a brief survey of European religious and political movements relevant to Puritanism and Separatism; and, since the value of such a treatment depends upon its validity as history, it seems natural to expect definite references to the investigations of recognized authorities. It may be assumed that Professor Parrington's reading on the subject has been comprehensive, but the works listed in his bibliography do not seem to bear out the theory that the Pilgrims were Lutheran democrats whose influence prevented the Puritans from imprinting upon America a lasting Calvinistic aristocracy.

Esther E. Burch. *AL.* May, 1929. p. 115–6

Precisely because the book [*Main Currents*] reveals Parrington as such a vital personality, delicate in perception and felicitous in expression as well as robust of faith in the better possibilities of human life, there is real danger in a conception of literature so hazy as to allow the utilitarian to crowd out the artistic or to let that which is useful merely as a means suppress that which is delightful in itself as the heart's desire. Public issues are of undoubted importance, but serious students must not forget that great literature is concerned also with those vital realities of our inner personal life and those enrapturing superpersonal cosmic vistas compared with which the issues of public life are pale and relatively inconsequential.

Professor Parrington's politico-economic progressiveness not only befogs his conception of literature but also prevents him from fully realizing what is involved in any attempt to write of the main currents of thought of any period. For one thing, he did not sufficiently inform himself to do justice to the history of American thought in religion, science, art, education, or even law.

Morris Raphael Cohen. *NR.* Jan. 28, 1931. p. 303

It is characteristic, to cite but one example, that in a book dealing with "critical realism" in American literature the author should practically ignore literary ideals and critical theory, that Henry George—who "did more than any other man to spread through America a knowledge of the law of economic determinism"—is given six times as much space as Henry James. The latter is given a scant two pages out of over four hundred, and is rather bitterly derided by the defender of *Jurgen* and *Beyond Life* as representing "The Nostalgia of Culture." The central question which students of literature will have to face is this: have not many contemporary literary scholars, of whom Mr. Parrington is the most gifted spokesman, tended to confuse social history and literature? Everywhere, as a disciple of Taine, Mr. Parrington considers books on the basis of whether or not they represent the "honest voice" of their generation in dealing with local and ephemeral topics such as, for example, the Greenback issue.

Harry Hayden Clark. *Bkm.* Feb., 1931. p. 654

A kind of environmental or sociological interpretation of literary movements had already been gaining favor. He sharpened it, gave it point, by making it definitely economic, because of his desire to reveal the motivating interests and real direction of specific works of literature. Thus his method was part of his general intention. It is inconceivable that he would have investigated with such firmness the social ties of individual writers or been so eager to expose the sectional and class issues underlying the ideological tendency which each writer represented, if his sympathies had not been lower-class. Nowadays "class-angling" is not a sport of kings.

Radical—not just liberal or progressive—is the word. He had none of that amiable tolerance which comes of cynicism, nor was he the kind of optimist whose buoyancy is based upon an Olympian idealism. He was partisan from the start—passionately so.

Bernard Smith in *Books That Changed Our Minds,*
edited by Malcolm Cowley and Bernard Smith (Kelmscott). 1939. p. 186

Parrington, then, deals with literature only in so far as literature is a matter of fragmentary ideas clearly visible to the innocent eye; furthermore, he deals only with a limited range of ideas, and relegates the rest to the region of illusion. Had Parrington written, as he seems to imply that he meant to write, a history of Jeffersonian liberalism, and neglected all matter irrelevant to his subject, he might have been more or less successful. But he unquestionably did not do so: he wrote what purports to be a history of American literature, but treated wholly in terms of what he conceives to be the development of Jeffersonian liberalism.

The result could easily have been forecast. His frame-work of ideas has no serious relationship to most of the great writers, and, since he thus has no way of understanding them, his treatment of them is almost purely impressionistic.

Yvor Winters. *In Defense of Reason* (Swallow). 1947.
p. 560. [1943]

The work [*Main Currents*] did not appear until 1927 and became a powerful influence only in the nineteen-thirties. But it represents the most ambitious single effort of the Progressive mind to understand itself, and can be understood only in reference to the idealism, prejudices, and characteristic sentimentality of that mind—all of which Parrington sought almost unwittingly, in the drive of his great idea, to impose upon intellectual history in America. For though Parrington often seemed to go beyond the diverse rebellions of the period, he was astonishingly loyal to them all, and often simultaneously. It was the grass-roots radical, the Populist, the Jeffersonian liberal, even the quasi-Marxist in him, that combined to make him so outstanding a Progressive intellectual. His culture seems to have been wider than that of the others, his education less pedestrian; but these did not show in the indifference to literary values which his book displayed.

Alfred Kazin. *On Native Grounds* (Reynal). 1942. p. 155

Vernon L. Parrington, one of our few serious cultural historians, furnishes an interesting contrast in method to Constance Rourke on [*Davy*] Crockett. While she is chiefly interested in the charm of the legends themselves and anxious to deny any evidence she thinks might detract from them, his effort is to place the Crockett legends in terms of political genesis and function. In a withering analysis in *Main Currents of American Thought* he strips the legendary hero down to the real Crockett: a rather pathetic figure, ignorant, boastful, and ambitious; built up as an American symbol by skilled Whig publicists who wanted a coonskin hero to oppose to Jackson; used by the Whigs as long as he was usable; and then when his backwoods constituents repudiated his voting record of uninterrupted support for Eastern banking interests, tossed aside by his Whig friends. Parrington shows how the legend was built step by step, conjectures shrewdly as to who ghosted each of the books, shows the constant anti-Jackson propaganda smuggled into their comedy, and at the end shows Crockett, like so many mythologized real heroes, coming to believe the legends himself.

Stanley Edgar Hyman. *The Armed Vision* (Knopf). 1948. p. 139

In *Main Currents in American Thought* two tendencies are fused. The brilliant individual characterizations, enriched by affirmative or damaging quotations, the seeking out of a *qualité maîtresse* in a writer, as when Parrington says of Samuel Sewell: "In his religious life he was the same prudent, plodding soul, that stowed away in his strongbox deeds to ample possessions during his pilgrimage"—these devices remind us that this historian is heir of a tradition stretching back through Moses Coit Tyler and Taine to Sainte-Beuve. But he is also a child of the eighteenth century, which was his spirit's home. His ideals are lucidity, order, a scrupulous and efficient prose. He builds as Gibbon or Voltaire built books—orderly paragraphs marching to schematized ideas. The table of contents to the unfinished third volume is a debater's outline, a lawyer's brief, and shows us how he worked, for his aim is not merely the right word in the right place but also the right author under the right subhead of an argument developed with mathematical rigor. Moreover, his theories of human nature likewise descend from the Enlightenment, or at least from utilitarianism. Because men are supposed to know and follow their best interests, the duty of the writer in America is to persuade and convince, to clarify, defend, and denounce, but not to charm, to astonish, to enrich the soul.

Howard Mumford Jones. *The Theory of American Literature* (Cornell). 1948. pp. 142–3

Parrington did not regard his task as a judicial one or pretend to be objective, impartial, or aloof. He interpreted American intellectual history as a struggle between the forces of freedom and of privilege, and he deliberately took sides in that struggle.

Indeed this fastidious scholar, himself so aloof from controversy, so remote from the hurly-burly of public affairs, lived all his life in the midst of battle. His splendid pages pulse and glow with passion and excitement, resound with the clash of arms and echo with the rallying cries of chieftains. He was a veritable Creasy, and all the decisive battles of American history were fought out anew in his volumes: the struggle between theocracy and Independency, Old World tyranny and New World liberty, federalism and republicanism, slavery and freedom, frontier and seaboard, agrarianism and capitalism, labor and industry. All his heroes were warriors; those who somehow did not fit into the neat scheme were passed over or made to do service in a civilian capacity, as it were.

What emerged from all this was an identification of democracy with Americanism. The great tradition of American thought, Parrington insisted, was the tradition of liberalism and revolt; and they were the most American who spoke with the accent of radicalism—the word he originally used instead of the weaker "liberalism."

Henry Steele Commager. *The American Mind* (Yale). 1950. pp. 300–1

It is possible to say of V. L. Parrington that with his *Main Currents in American Thought* he has had an influence on our conception of American culture which is not equaled by that of any other writer of the last two decades. His ideas are now the accepted ones wherever the college course in American literature is given by a teacher who conceives himself to be opposed to the genteel and the academic and in alliance with the vigorous and the actual. And whenever the liberal historian of America finds occasion to take account of the national literature, as nowadays he feels it proper to do, it is Parrington who is his standard and guide. Parrington's ideas are the more firmly established because they do not have to be imposed—the teacher or the critic who presents them is likely to find that his task is merely to make articulate for his audience what it has always believed, for Parrington formulated in a classic way the suppositions about our culture which are held by the American middle class so far as that class is at all liberal in its social thought and so far as it begins to understand that literature has anything to do with society. . . .

Yet he had after all but a limited sense of what constitutes a difficulty. Whenever he was confronted with a work of art that was complex, personal and not literal, that was not, as it were, a public document, Parrington was at a loss. . . . It does not occur to Parrington that there is any other relation possible between the artist and reality than this passage of reality through the transparent artist; he meets evidence of imagination and creativeness with a settled hostility the expression of which suggests that he regards them as the natural enemies of democracy.

Lionel Trilling. The Liberal Imagination (Viking).
1951. pp. 3–5

America's intellectual history, thought Parrington, fell into the three broad phases of Calvinistic pessimism, romantic optimism, and mechanistic pessimism.

Although much of his material on this last period had a deep gloom, Parrington never failed to strike the courageous note that was a tocsin to a drooping liberalism. No longer were the theologians, political philosophers, industrial masters, or bankers "the spokesmen of this vibrant life of a continent, but the intellectuals, the dreamers, the critics, the historians, the men of letters, in short; and to them one may turn hopefully for a revelation of American life." To the end, Parrington held out Jeffersonian democracy as a hopeful ideal.

There was thrilling writing in these volumes [Main Currents] that called a wayward America back from the drab reality of a business civilization to the day-dream of an agrarian democracy. Parrington never escaped the influence of that arch foe of industrialism, William Morris.

M. Kraus. The Writing of American History
(Oklahoma). 1953. pp. 354

A product of the Progressive era, he shared to a large extent the indictment of the great American fortunes held by Gustavus Myers and the arraignment of business and politics offered by the muckraker. His strictures on capitalism were not, as is obvious, those of the socialists, but of an obsolete agrarianism. Greatly outweighing his faulty economics were his flashes of insight into American writers and political leaders. He was ever alert to the impact of European upon American culture, and he brought to light in all his volumes many a neglected poet, novelist, essayist, critic, and seminal thinker, whose contribution to belles-lettres was small but who offered great insights into the American mind.

H. Wish. *The American Historian* (Oxford). 1960. p. 303

In 1927 appeared the single most important book written by a historian of the frontier tradition, Vernon Louis Parrington's *Main Currents in American Thought*. . . . the greatness of the book as a concluding testament to a dying tradition rests on the manner in which it clarifies the roots of this tradition in the eighteenth-century Enlightenment and ultimately in seventeenth-century Puritanism. Parrington's book is truly a summary of the main currents of American thought and the fatal impasse these currents had reached by the 1920's. . . . And this is the fundamental significance of Parrington: his was a voice crying out to his people to return to the ways of their ancestors, to reform, to purify themselves before it was too late. *Main Currents* must be seen as a great expression of that peculiar Puritan theological literary form, the Jeremiad. As the Puritan preachers had warned their people at the end of the seventeenth century that they were straying from their special relationship to God as a chosen people and must face disaster if they did not turn back from corruption to live by the national covenant, so Parrington, in the 1920's, warned his people that they must experience the terrors of history unless they too returned to the national covenant expressed by Thomas Jefferson—a covenant which promised the faithful that they might live in harmony as long as they followed nature's principles. But his was a despairing voice from the wilderness because Parrington was not able to offer any hope that the covenant could be fulfilled in urban-industrial America.

D. W. Noble. *Historians Against History* (Minnesota). 1965. pp. 98–9

See *Main Currents in American Thought* (essays).

PATCHEN, KENNETH (1911–   )

At their worst his poems are like the dream compositions of a leftist editorial writer, repeating class sentiments with a strange syntactical or structural distortion. . . . Patchen's word-pour may be praised as creative vitality

or condemned as artistic debauchery, but in either case it is more weari-
some than interesting.

Robert Fitzgerald. Poetry. Sept. 1936. p. 342

Mr. Patchen has the high scorn of a certain type of young man, and the
determination to use certain words that poetry has eschewed. This does
not make his poetry any better. Neither does certain snarling and scram-
bled invective. But you have to give the man his head, because he can
write desperately and movingly at times, and his era is responsible for
him. Mr. Patchen is trying to talk as the tough-minded talk in the street
and at the same time write poetry. It is not an easy assignment.

William Rose Benét. SR. Nov. 25, 1939. p. 16

Beyond any book of poems I have encountered First Will and Testament
gives a lively sense of what it is to be a young man in America in a time
when, for more of the young than we like to think, living and dying have
lost all meaning. Kenneth Patchen is sure of his vocation as a poet, somewhat less sure of his craft. But he is able and eloquent, witty and strong.
And what he is trying to do in this book is through poetry to recover meaning. . . . His poetic speech is contemporary and close to the streets; but he
has held to nothing he has heard in the streets unless it has its own vigor
to recommend it.

John Peale Bishop. Nation. Dec. 2, 1939. p. 620

Whatever the idealogy of the earlier poems was, the poems themselves
had a hard beauty, an imaginative frenzy abstracted out of reality, a
moving sad terror. And there was a quality of bewilderment that got into
the poems. In his new book (The Dark Kingdom) all of those qualities
seem to be there, but they are there only as masquerades, larger, vaster in
scope, but with less weight. . . . I believe Patchen to be one of the finest
talents in America today. He has depth, imagination, and resourcefulness.
He is "endowed" lyrically, but he appears a little contemptuous of it.

Harvey Breit. Poetry. June, 1942. pp. 160, 162

Here (in The Dark Kingdom) is proof, if proof is needed, that Mr.
Patchen is a poet. But he is also a seer, and there seems to be some
danger that the seer will eat up the poet. It is possible that the seer has
already taken a chunk out of the poet. What is left is, however, interesting
enough. . . . There is a wealth of exciting images and sharp phrases, sometimes splendid, sometimes horrible, always violent and apocalyptic. . . .
He affirms his world too vehemently, too wholeheartedly. The seer cannot
wait on the slow process of poetic exploration. And this means that though

there is poetry in the book there are few poems with a recognizable structure.

Robert Penn Warren. Nation. July 4, 1942. p. 17

Mr. Patchen has and habitually uses the naive vision of life. . . . But to have the naive vision and nothing else is to be a child. . . . It must be granted that Mr. Patchen knows this; the signs of his departure from the childlike approach are manifold, and include the elaborate and evasive technique of the drawing-and-type poem . . . along with other practices. . . . And these devices are to an extent successful, for they generate interesting and even brilliant effects to which the naivete then becomes contributory. Finally, however, I feel that the poems . . . do not "satisfy"; and I trace this dissatisfaction to the poet's lack of a body of sharp and empirically genuine ideas—of perhaps a political and psychological nature.

E. S. Forgotson. Poetry. Feb., 1944. p. 280

A representative chunk of Patchen will contain references to immortality, God and death of the gods (à la Nietzsche), capitalism, anarchism, and pacificism, sex, murder, and blood-guilt, and any number of generally unacknowledged leanings toward and derivations from psychoanalysis. . . . The fact that the tradition in which Patchen writes depends to such a large extent on surrealistic maneuvers deprives it of a good deal of the power and wisdom it claims for itself. It has staked all on a sleight-of-hand, a trick of symbolism that actually throws out the deeper human context that it is supposed to provide for literature. Patchen's politics, for example, a kind of anarcho-pacificism, uncompromisingly opposed to capitalism and war, is the nearest thing to an escape from politics that can be contrived in political language.

Isaac Rosenfeld. NR. Dec. 3, 1945. pp. 773–4

Faced with the problems of our complex and chaotic world, Mr. Patchen, in regarding them, is not serene in the knowledge of invisible realities, nor does he project a better world of the imagination, neither has he a program of revolt; he goes to pieces. . . . There is but one remedy—to hide his face on the breast of his beloved. . . . While he may, as his admirers claim, possess a real spark of genius, his talent is inadequate, thus far, consistently to catch this spark and blow it to a flame.

Jean Starr Untermeyer. SR. March 22, 1947. pp. 15–6

There is no denying the compelling power of his poetry at its best . . . nor the tremendous vitality of the personality from whence it flows. Moreover the coupling of his name with Whitman is in a way inevitable, since the compulsion which drove Whitman to utter his "barbaric yawp" in nonmetrical verse is the same which urges Patchen to the audacities of his own free technique; and what transpires from the poetry of both is the sense of a "fullness of being" too ebullient to be confined to the sophisticated and severely disciplined modalism of regular versification.

But while Whitman in spite of his "barbarism" achieved a kind of Olympian dignity, there is about Patchen a faint aura of darkness which betrays him as a sort of minor chthonian deity, at the same time a little above and a little below the merely human.

Frajam Taylor. Poetry. Aug., 1947. pp. 270–1

Kenneth Patchen writes with much more violence (than William Carlos Williams), with a Celtic turbulence and humor, and passion for and against. . . . His descriptions are accurate, sharp with color, sounds, and tastes; and his anger can be cool and the passion turn to a love song of surprising delicacy. . . . There is much of death and graves in the poetry, the rollicking dead under beer cans, the dead of history and legend, all of them envious of those alive, however evil their lot may be.

Eugene Davidson. YR. Summer, 1949. p. 725

Much of Patchen's work is conceived in the limbo of nightmare, in a world where the humor is worse than the horror. Frenzy rules here; phantasmagoria triumphs in slapstick satire, casual killings, and sinister obscenity. But there is more to Patchen than his power to evoke ugliness, violence, and nonchalant treachery. . . . The tone is savage disillusionment, but not apathy; it is rebellious and ribald, indignant and desperate, but clean-cut even in its fury.

Louis Untermeyer. Modern American Poetry
(Harcourt). 1950. p. 642

It is Patchen who extends the vision of (Henry) Miller and Céline to the farthest stretches of sanity and by the agility and poetry of his language brings their wail to full throat. Patchen, whose basic message, after all the variations, is no more than this:

WE BELIEVE IN YOU. THERE IS NO DANGER. IT IS NOT GETTING DARK. WE LOVE YOU.

He tells you again and again: "I must tell you what I have said is not true. This is all a damn lie." But we still remember what we wanted to see, what we wanted to hear. We must milk dry the doubt he provides us with. It is all he leaves us to combat the terrors he has made rise in us. But one senses, in a stunned way, that it is a very valuable thing to have.

Hugh McGovern. NMQ. Summer, 1951. p. 195

See *First Will and Testament, The Dark Kingdom,* and *Red Wine and Yellow Hair* (poetry); also *The Journal of Albion Moonlight* (novel).

PERCY, WALKER (1916–   )

The truth is that for Binx, the bewildered but amiable hero of Walker Percy's polished first novel [*The Moviegoer*], these neighborhood movie houses are oases of reality in an unreal world. . . . Ultimately, Binx breaks out of his own shell by having to face the far more desperate problems of his beautiful cousin, Kate Cutrer. As Kate sinks deeper within herself, only Binx can talk to her. And in the end, when Kate hits bottom, only Binx can save her. He does so by making decisions, taking risks, and opening himself to suffering—in other words by accepting reality. . . . Nothing is stated; everything is implied. The reader gets fragments of meaning and occasional glimpses of deep-rooted causes. Yet so expertly are these fragments fitted together and these glimpses sustained that Binx and Kate grow steadily in character throughout the book. . . .

These revelations take place against a background of New Orleans in Mardi Gras. The flavor, the spirit and the dialogue of this extraordinary American city are reproduced with marvelous accuracy.

Robert Massie. *NYT*. May 28, 1961. p. 30

Walker Percy has made his novel [*The Moviegoer*] of oblique angles, all smoothly fitted together, and all finally, despite his unwillingness to push or even nudge an effect, making its points and creating one form that reflects and illuminates all the scenes and characters. The retroactive effect: the best novels have it. And he gets just right the color and shape of the world of "everydayness": a neat styrene identification card; his landlady, Mrs. Schexnaydre, "a vigorous pony-size blond who wears sneakers summer and winter"; a girl who can't help overplaying her part when she meets children, "squatting down and hugging her knees like Joan Fontaine visiting an orphanage."

Edwin Kennebeck. *Com*. June 2, 1961. pp. 261–2

During the Thirties critics talked a lot about modern man's fragmented image. . . . This subject was illuminated in fiction in the middle of the Nineteenth Century by Dostoevsky in his remarkable expository novel: *Notes from Underground*—though few there were then who grasped his light. In a novel of remarkably similar form, the poet-novelist Albert Camus re-examined the theme in 1956: *The Fall*. And now it has been done, in the milieu of the post modern barbarians, by Walker Percy in *The Moviegoer*—in like form and comparably sharp illumination.

The formal similarity of these three novels is marked and, I think, significant. Each presents a narrator-hero who reveals himself to be a villain —or, more exactly, a damned man seeking salvation. They report on humanism, however, at different points in its history. In *Notes from Underground* scientific humanism is first *exposed*. In *The Fall* it is recognized for what it is, but through pride that apes humility, still clung to. In the world of *The Moviegoer,* however, it has already been abandoned and our hero stumbles amid its shards and glimmering confusion toward a clear but distant candle.

Brainard Cheney. SwR. Autumn, 1961. p. 691

There are flaws in *The Moviegoer,* certainly. One character, Sam Yerger, a figure of superhuman wisdom who imitates Amos 'n' Andy, is preposterous from start to finish, and a mistake. Sometimes Jack's philosophy, as when he meditates on "the genie-soul," is just blather. There are occasional pretentious attempts to make Jack's search seem not neurotic but deeply spiritual, along the lines of Percy's unfortunate statement on receiving the National Book Award that his novel shows Judaeo-Christian man as "a wayfarer and a pilgrim." These are minor failings in a considerable success. I think that *The Moviegoer* is a better novel than the work it most readily brings to mind, Albert Camus' *The Stranger*. It is patronizing and ridiculous to say of a 46-year-old man who has been late publishing his excellent first novel that he shows "promise." Walker Percy shows performance.

Stanley Edgar Hyman. New Leader. April 30, 1962. p. 24

Though the prose [of *The Last Gentleman*] is capable of the subtlest modulations of thought and expression, it maintains a certain lyrical opacity; it never ceases to arrest and fascinate. This is a novel alive with ideas and one in which every detail is beautifully perceived. . . . *The Last Gentleman* is a haunting novel, and there is no way out of it. There is no reconciliation possible between immanence and transcendence, between being a fornicator and being a gentleman. The book ends as it ends, quite literally in suspended animation, at precisely that point beyond which any further action is unthinkable.

Stephen Donadio. PR. Summer, 1966. pp. 451–2

He avoids [in *The Last Gentleman*] plain narrative as if it were poison ivy. Everything is prismatic, discrete, a matter of half-conveyed hints; the reader has to work so hard to sort out what is going on that after a while he begins to congratulate himself: This isn't just any old novel, but a novel written for very alert people. Important questions of motivation are consistently varnished with irony until they become too slick to take hold of. All the characters are lightly brushed with satire, including the central character himself, so that at any given moment it is quite impossible to tell whether Mr. Percy is entirely behind what he is telling us or slightly to one side of it—and if the latter, which side. And—it goes without saying, in this kind of novel—central plot episodes are presented in so glancing a fashion, because of the author's holy dread of straightforward narrative exposition, that the reader, glued to the page in the effort to decipher the story, cannot muster the energy to feel moved.

There is, of course, nothing accidental about this. Mr. Percy is a breath-takingly brilliant writer, and it is part of his brilliance that, having taken one's breath, he hands it back with a smile of ironic knowingness.

John Wain. *NYR*. July 28, 1966. p. 23

Up to the second half of the last chapter [*The Last Gentleman*] is the work of a highly sophisticated artist, with intellect and moral pride and courage; and then suddenly everything goes soft and the air is full of bank-lobby music. Percy is a liberal Southerner who lives in the South—a very diffi-cult thing; I am a liberal Southerner who lives in the North—a much easier thing; and I feel an embarrassment in criticizing him; but that doesn't change the fact that his hero's ultimate decision is delusory. . . . There are several startling coincidences *ex machina,* but the prose is so uncommonly clean and good, the use of modern techniques of simultaneity is so un-obtrusively skillful, the characters are so concretely visible, their speech and mannerisms are so true, and their adventures are so full of detail of Southern life, that I wish I could believe that Williston will maintain his hard-won integrity against the heavy odds he has chosen to face.

J. Mitchell Morse. *HdR*. Autumn, 1966. p. 510

See *The Moviegoer, The Last Gentleman* (novels).

PORTER, KATHERINE ANNE (1894–   )

Miss Porter's mind is one of those highly civilized instruments of percep-tion that seems to have come out of old societies, where the "social trend" is fixed and assumed. The individual character as the product of such a background also has a certain constancy of behavior which permits the writer to ignore the now common practice of relating individual conduct to some abstract social or psychological law; the character is taken as a fixed and inviolable entity, predictable only in so far as a familiarity may be said to make him so, and finally unique as the center of inexhaustible depths of feeling and action. In this manner Miss Porter approaches her characters, and it is this that probably underlies many of the very specific virtues of her writing.

Allen Tate. *Nation*. Oct. 1, 1930. pp. 352–3

It is to Miss Porter's high credit that, having fixed upon the exceptional background and event, she has not yielded, in her treatment of them, to queerness and forced originality of form. . . . Miss Porter has a range of effects, but each comes through in its place, and only at the demand of her material. She rejects the exclamatory tricks that wind up style to a spurious intensity, and trusts for the most part, to straightforward writing, to patience in detail and to a thorough imaginative grasp on cause and character.

Louise Bogan. NR. Oct. 22, 1930. p. 277

Katherine Anne Porter moves in the illustrious company headed by Hawthorne, Flaubert, and Henry James. It is the company of story-tellers whose fiction possesses distinct esthetic quality, whose feelings have attained harmonious expression in the work. . . . Each of the narratives maintains its own tone—in the sense of effects of color and modulation and accents appropriate to the expression of its individual sentiment. And each of the poignant little dramas represented by them unfolds continually and unpredictably, never betraying its ultimate turns, which arrive as shocks and surprises. Ideal beauty, a fugitive poetry, again and again flashes through the substance of the narrative. But the tone, too, invariably is unemphatic and quiet.

Paul Rosenfeld. SR. April 1, 1939. p. 7

Emphasis on her style should not obscure the fact that Miss Porter has other attributes of a good fiction writer. At her best she has mastered narrative pace and narrative construction; her dialogue is colloquial and at the same time graceful and dignified: she has observed with minuteness a variety of locales and ways of living; her people are speaking likenesses; she has wit; and there is a shrewd modern intelligence, if not an extremely original or forceful one, dominating the story from some little distance.

Philip Blair Rice. Nation. April 15, 1939. p. 442

Miss Porter has no genius but much talent. Her average level is high, and she doesn't let you down. She is more fundamentally serious than Katherine Mansfield, less neurotic, closer to the earth. She is dry-eyed, even in tragedy: when she jokes, she does not smile. You feel you can trust her. . . . Having praised so much, I pause and wonder just what it is that prevents me from uttering the final, whole-hearted hurrah. . . . She is grave, she is delicate, she is just—but she lacks altogether, for me personally, the vulgar appeal. I cannot imagine that she would ever make me cry, or laugh aloud.

Christopher Isherwood. NR. April 19, 1929. pp. 312–3

Among her Southern contemporaries in short prose fiction Miss Porter has few peers. She lacks the social emphasis of Mr. Erskine Caldwell, but she also lacks his sensationalism. She has nothing of Mr. William Faulkner's hypnotic quality, his violent power, or his flair for abnormal psychology; but neither has she any of his obliquity. At her best she is superior as a craftsman to both. At any point in her art she is one of the most talented of living American writers.

Lodwick Hartley. *SwR*. April, 1940. p. 216

Both in conception and execution her work seems to me to bear the relation to prose that the lyric bears to poetry. Her intelligence is extraordinary, but it is akin to that of a poet rather than that, say, of a novelist like Henry James, who was also interested in the thumb-print but had both the strong desire and the capacity for broad formulation which the long flight requires.

Margaret Marshall. *Nation*. April 13, 1940. p. 474

The exquisite rightness of this author's art has been commented upon by many; and these sketches and tales reveal to the vague tribe, the discriminating reader, what fundamental brainwork goes into the creating of episodes that, on the surface, seem hastily thrown together. To be sure, this deftness is bought at a price, and the careful casualness of Miss Porter's approach sometimes reminds one of a cat stalking its prey with unnecessary caution. If some of these narratives were told in the straightforward narrative manner formerly characteristic of the short story, they might not lose in delicacy and might gain in dramatic power.

Howard Mumford Jones. *SR*. Sept. 30, 1944. p. 15

Miss Porter's thematic statements are given their extraordinary power through a rich and complex characterization. Four or five outstanding personality traits are usually boldly established, and these are used as reference points from which to thrust with the quick image and the loaded phrase into the spaces of modifying qualification. The qualification made, she retires for a moment to the centre, waits calmly, and then stabs again —this time either farther in the same direction or in a new direction. In the end, though the characters are typical, recognizable types, they are also particular flesh and bones—somewhat fluid, unpredictable, elusive, contradictory.

Charles Allen. *AQ*. Summer, 1946. p. 93

The important thing to notice is that in all cases Katherine Anne Porter's characters possess qualities which have some point of similarity with her own experience. If they are Irish or Mexican, they are also Roman

Catholic—or they are political liberals. They are usually Southerners. I don't mean to suggest this as a serious limitation, but it may help to account for the consistently high level which her work represents, a level probably unsurpassed by any writer of her time.

Ray B. West, Jr. *HR*. Fall, 1952. p. 19

Katherine Anne Porter is conventionally praised for her humanity and warmth and for the stoic virtues which her people show in the face of life's hardships. It is true that she sets up the stoic as the best of behavior. It is also true that the dignity and compassion of her characters are strikingly apparent. But Miss Porter's world is a black and tragic one, filled with disaster, heartbreak, and soul-wrecking disillusionment. The most noble of her characters . . . must submit in the nature of things to sorrows which are not ennobling but destructively abrasive of joy, love, and hope; all of them end with a bleak realization of the Everlasting Nay. They are confronted by the thing "most cruel of all," which in its enormity transcends all other sorrows—the obliteration of hope. The tiny particle of light must always be snuffed out in the depths of the whirlpool.

James William Johnson. *VQR*. Autumn, 1960. p. 611

[*Ship of Fools*] is a vast portrait gallery, with portraits of all sizes hung here and there on the wall, high and low; and some of the portrayed ones seem to dance down out of their frames; some tumble out, some fight their way out, with fearful vitality. I can think of only one possible reason for anyone's not liking this book: just at the start the characters are almost too strong, one shrinks from them a little. No, you may say, I do not wish to spend another page with this smug glutton, or this hypochondriac drunkard, or this lachrymose widow; no, not another word out of that girl in the green dress! But presently, having read a certain number of pages, you feel a grudging sympathy with one and all, or a rueful empathy, or at least solidarity, as a human being.

Glenway Wescott. *At*. April, 1962. p. 48

Her contemptuous and morbid attitude toward human sexuality plays a large part in deflecting her sensibility to its incessant quarrel with human nature and in leading it by inevitable stages to a vision of life that is less vice and folly than a hideously choking slow death. For Miss Porter's versions of political action, artistic creation, religious belief, teaching, and so forth are no less skewed and embittered than her versions of copulation. Further, this clammy connection between sex and evil appears to rule out any feeling toward her characters other than a nagging exasperated irony, and to remove the possibility of any struggle toward deeper insight. As a result, the consciousness that is operating in the book, for all its range of view, is standing, so to speak, on a dime, and has little contact with the sources of imaginative vitality and moral power that renew a long work of fiction.

Theodore Solotaroff. *Cmty*. Oct., 1962. p. 286

Life—which to Miss Porter means personal relationships—is a hazardous affair, however cautiously we try to live it. We walk a tightrope, never more than a step away from possible disaster, so strong and so intimately connected with our need for other people are the primitive impulses of violence and egoism and so thin is the net of civilized behavior that is between us and the pit. Indeed, if in trying to civilize ourselves we have been trying to make order out of chaos, Miss Porter seems to be saying that we have succeeded only in becoming more systematically and efficiently, though less directly violent; the more definite and clear-cut the code by which we live and expect others to live, the more clearly even our ordinary actions reflect the violence that is only imperfectly submerged and that many erupt savagely and nakedly at any time.

Marjorie Ryan. *Critique*. Fall, 1962. p. 94

Innovation in the modern novel is often mere trickiness: to eliminate plot, to eliminate time, even, as in some recent French fiction, to eliminate characters, Katherine Anne Porter in *Ship of Fools* has used no tricks that were not contained in the workbag of George Eliot. Her innovations, however, are still fundamental. Her book not only contains no hero or heroine; it contains no character who is either the reader or the author, no character with whom the reader can "identify." Nor is there anywhere in the book any affirmation of the basic striving upwards or even courage of mankind, always considered essential to a "great" novel. To have put it in would have begged the very question the novel asks. And, finally, despite all of Henry James's warnings, Miss Porter has eschewed her "native pastures." Not only does the action take place at sea, between the ports of countries other than the United States, on a German boat, but the American characters are less vivid than the German and Spanish, are even a bit pale beside them. Mrs. Treadwell seems less of a born New Yorker than the Captain seems a Berliner.

Yet the experience of reading *Ship of Fools* is still an exhilarating rather than a somber or depressing one, because Miss Porter has reproduced the very stuff of life in reproducing those twenty-seven days on the *Vera*, and her novel sparkles with vitality and humor.

(K)   Louis Auchincloss. *Pioneers and Caretakers*

(Minnesota). 1965. p. 151

She has constantly dealt with the chaos of the universe and with the forces within man and within society which have led to man's alienation. Her probings of the human condition are deeply personal and yet, because of the constant play of irony in everything she writes, impersonal also.

Her often and justly praised style is never mannered, is perfectly adaptable to her material, and is characterized by clarity. She has consciously avoided stylistic characteristics or peculiarities which would make it instantly recognizable. No skeleton keys are needed to unlock her stories or her style. She learned from Sterne, Mrs. Woolf, Joyce, James, and others; but she set out not to imitate them but to write simply and clearly, flowingly and flawlessly. She used her admirable style to create characters of complexity, characters which grip the imagination: María Concepción, Braggioni, Miranda, Stephen, Homer T. Hatch, Papa Müller, to name only a few. She also re-created with authority the social backgrounds of Mexico, of turn-of-the-century Texas, of Denver during wartime, of immigrant Irish in the slums.

(K)   George Hendrick. *Katherine Anne Porter* (Twayne).
1965. p. 154

Miss Porter's imagination is statuesque, not dynamic: it does not see life in dramatic terms as the grinding of past and present. She does not think at all in terms of action. In her best stories, to exist is to remember: this is the source of their identity, their stability. (Unamuno says somewhere: "Intelligence is a terrible thing, it tends to death as memory tends to stability.") When Miss Porter cares about her characters, she gives them a past dense enough and a memory searching enough to ensure their stability. But she feels a force only when it has fixed its object in position in its frame; and then she probes it by retrospection. A dynamic imagination works differently; as in John Crowe Ransom's poems, for instance, where actions speak louder than words or pictures.

(K)   Denis Donoghue. *NYR*. Nov. 11, 1965. p. 18

She knows, we are forced to believe, that if one is to try to see "all," one must be willing to see the dark side of the moon. She has a will, a ferocious will, to face, but face in its full context, what Herman Melville called the great "NO" of life. If stoicism is the underlying attitude in this fiction, it is a stoicism without grimness or arrogance, capable of gaiety, tenderness, and sympathy, and its ethical point of reference is found in those characters who, like Granny Weatherall, have the toughness to survive but who survive by a loving sense of obligation to others, this sense being, in the end, only a full affirmation of the life-sense, a joy in strength.

(K)   Robert Penn Warren. *YR*. Winter, 1966. p. 290

The anger that speaks everywhere in the stories would trouble the heart for their author whom we love except that her anger is pure, the reason for it evident and clear, and the effect exhilarating. She has made it the tool of her work; what we do is rejoice in it. We are aware of the compassion that guides it, as well. Only compassion could have looked where she looks, could have seen and probed what she sees. Real compassion is perhaps always in the end unsparing; it must make itself a part of knowing. Self-pity does not exist here; these stories come out trenchant, bold, defying; they are tough as sanity, unrelinquished sanity, is tough.

Despair is here, as well described as if it were Mexico. It is a despair, however, that is robust and sane, open to negotiation by the light of day. Life seen as a savage ordeal has been investigated by a straightforward courage, unshaken nerve, a rescuing wit, and above all with the searching intelligence that is quite plainly not to be daunted. In the end the stories move us not to despair ourselves but to an emotion quite opposite because they are so seriously and clear-sightedly pointing out what they have been formed to show: that which is true under the skin, that which will remain a fact of the spirit.

(K)   Eudora Welty. *YR*. Winter, 1966. p. 269

What is most striking about all her stories is their air of indestructible composure. Their elements seem admirably balanced and fitted, like parts of a machine. No energy is wasted here; and it is true that when, in stories like *Noon Wine,* the characters confront each other head-on, there is sudden power in the encounter. (Mr. Hatch and Mr. Thompson remain vivid because they are singular; the power of the representation derives from its incisive, unrelenting specificity.) More often, however, the author does not succeed in perceiving particulars with an intensity which would lend them the force and weight of general statement; instead, inventing circumstances which contain foregone conclusions, she elaborates general statements with appropriate details. . . .

. . . if one excludes *Noon Wine* and "The Jilting of Granny Weatherall" (a nicely executed *tour de force* of less than major interest), her most memorable stories—"Flowering Judas," *Pale Horse, Pale Rider,* and *The Leaning Tower*—are those in which the central characters are forced to test themselves against "other minds and other opinions and other feelings." In general, these stories deal with the attempts of individuals to resist everything in their experience which does not fit their own sense of themselves, to protect and preserve the secret myths enabling them to keep their lives in order.

(K)   Stephen Donadio. *PR*. Spring, 1966. pp. 279, 281

See *Collected Stories; Ship of Fools* (novel).

POUND, EZRA (1885–   )

He is like a man who goes hunting hedgehogs with bare feet—and finds his prey all prickles; to vary and mix the metaphor, he sits on his little hill in Kensington as if it were Olympian, casting forth winged words which, like boomerangs, are returned unto him an hundred-fold! In the melee his work is disloyally attacked, his least errors are exposed with a malignant triumph; his sensitiveness, which hides under a cover of bluster, is denounced as conceit; his fineness of perception is misunderstood as triviality. His scholarship, with its rather overwhelming pretension, is suspect; his polemics verge on hysteria. His fault is that he is an anachronism. With the enthusiasm of a Renaissance scholar, one of those whose fine devotion but faulty learning revealed to the fifteenth-century world the civilization of Greece, he lives in an age which looks at literature as a hobby, a freak, a branch of education; but never as a life study, a burning passion.

Richard Aldington. Poetry. July, 1920. p. 214

Given a mind that is not averse to labouring, provided that a kernel lies beneath the hard shells, you can reach the purpose of these poems. They contain the subconscious matter deposited by years of reading and observation in one man's mind, and in their residence in this sub-conscious state they have blended into the man's mental and emotional prejudices and undergone a metamorphosis, in which they become his visualization and interpretation of past men's events. Legendary heroes, kings, dukes, queens, soldiers, slaves, they live again as this man would have them live, and speak words that are partly his and partly their own, in the manner of ubermarionettes. Their fragmentary and often tangled existence—quick appearances and vanishings—is a distinctive feature of the subconscious state that enclosed them before they were extracted from the poet.

Maxwell Bodenheim. Dial. Jan., 1922. p. 91

When a man has written poetry as good as the best of Pound, it is impossible to dismiss him, however much the conservative mind may so desire. It is there now and poetry-lovers will be sure to find it. Its qualities are individual and they are compact of color, brilliant and flashing phrasing, and the subtle marriage of mood and manner. These things, I should say, are its distinguishing characteristics. There is always the creation of an atmosphere, always the melody of phrasing, always the quick ear for the shy felicities of beautiful words, always the varying of form to suit the emotional content.

Herbert S. Gorman. NAR. June, 1924. pp. 864–5

There are many so-called educators in our over-instructed world, but few inspired teachers. Ezra Pound is one of the few. . . . His method has been fiercely destructive of rooted prejudices, but magically encouraging to every green shoot of new growth. His mind, being imaginatively creative, presented examples as well as precept, offered beautiful poems to the world. . . . Whether or not he ever offers us more songs, his best work has already the completeness of adequate beauty. As a leader, a revolutionist in the art, he will have a place in literary history; as a poet he will sing into the hearts and minds of all free-singing spirits in the next age—and perhaps in the ages beyond much of our prophecy.

Harriet Monroe. *Poetry*. May, 1925. pp. 94–7

Pound talks like no one else. His is almost a wholly original accent, the base of American mingled with a dozen assorted "English society" and Cockney accents inserted in mockery, French, Spanish, and Greek exclamations, strange cries and catcalls, the whole very oddly inflected, with dramatic pauses and *diminuendos*. It takes time to get used to it, especially as the lively and audacious mind of Pound packs his speech—as well as his writing—with undertones and allusions.

Iris Barry. *Bkm*. Oct., 1931. p. 159

Some would say the facing in many directions of a quadriga drawn by centaurs, that we meet in the Cantos, puts strain on bipedal understanding; there is love of risk; but the experienced grafting of literature upon music is very remarkable—the resonance of color, allusions, tongues, sounding each through the other as in symphonic instrumentation. Even if one understood nothing, one would enjoy the musicianly manipulation. . . . Mr. Pound, in the prose that he writes, has formulated his own commentary upon the Cantos. They are as an armorial coat of attitudes of things that have happened in books and in life; they are not a shield but a coat worn by a man, as in the days when heraldry was beginning.

Marianne Moore. *Poetry*. Oct., 1931. pp. 48–50

The cantos are a sort of *Golden Ass*. There is a likeness, but there is no parallel beyond the mere historical one: both books are the production of worlds without convictions and given over to a hard secular program. Here the similarity ends. For Mr. Pound is a powerful reactionary, a faithful mind devoted to those ages when the myths were not merely pretty, but true. And there is a cloud of melancholy irony hanging over the cantos. He is persuaded that the myths are only beautiful, and he drops them after a glimpse, but he is not reconciled to this aestheticism: he ironically puts the myths against the ugly specimens of modern life that have defeated them. . . . He understands poetry and how to write it.

This is enough for one man to know. And the thirty cantos are enough to occupy a loving and ceaseless study—say a canto a year for thirty years, all thirty to be read every few weeks just for tone.

Allen Tate. *Nation*. June 10, 1931. pp. 633–4

When we consider this devotion to literature, we come upon the essential characteristic of the Cantos: their philological discussions, their translations, their textual references, their peculiar and unceasing interest in how things are said, not to speak of the various dialects and slangs which are introduced, and the habitual quotation of letters, codices, and other documents. . . . Pound has been the pure literary man, the complete man of letters; the concern with literary things, with the very look of print upon the page, is at the center, the source of his writings. . . . Pound fits one of his own categories: he has been a great inventor in verse, and we know how few can be supposed to know the satisfaction of fulfilling their own canons of excellence.

Delmore Schwartz. *Poetry*. March, 1938. pp. 326–39

But what is Pound's class, and how can it be described without contemptuousness in the description and without giving the effect of anything contemptible in the class; for it is an admirable class and ought to be spoken of with admiration. Essentially it is the class of those who have a care for the purity of the tongue as it is spoken and as it sounds and as it changes in speech and sound, and who know that that purity can only exist in the movement of continuous alternation between the "fawn's flesh and the saint's vision," and who know, so, that the movement, not the alternatives themselves, is the movement of music. . . . Poets like Pound are the executive artists for their generation; he does not provide a new way of looking . . . but he provides the *means* of many ways of looking.

R. P. Blackmur. *Poetry*. Sept., 1946. pp. 344–5

The opinion has been voiced that Pound's eventual reputation will rest upon his criticism and not upon his poetry. (I have been paid the same compliment myself.) I disagree. It is on his total work for literature that he must be judged: on his poetry, *and* his criticism, *and* his influence on men and on events at a turning point in literature. In any case, his criticism takes its significance from the fact that it is the writing of a poet about poetry: it must be read in the light of his own poetry, as well as of poetry by other men whom he championed. . . . Pound's great contribution to the work of other poets (if they choose to accept what he offers) is his insistence upon the immensity of the amount of *conscious* labor to be performed by the poet. . . . He . . . provides an example of devotion to "the art of poetry" which I can only parallel in our time by the example of Valéry.

T. S. Eliot. *Poetry*. Sept., 1946. pp. 331–8

Pound's cantos are the words of a man for whom the thing given has, in general, the upper hand over deliberation, a man whose long isolation in Rapallo and unfretful assurance as to his own technical power have allowed unusual freedom in moving here or there, up or down, forward or backward (like a swimmer in clear water) among verbal or substantial intimations and seizing them, putting them down, when a more hesitant— or sluggish—artist would have left them in the air. . . . In perception or vision he would mount to a *paradisio* as his master, Dante did. . . . Well, the moral universe of the *Divine Comedy* was orthodox, graded, and public, firmly conceived to its uttermost corner; and this of Pound's is quite a different thing. But at their least valuation I submit that these cantos in which light and air—and song—move so freely are more exhilarating poetic sketch-books, *Notes from the Upper Air,* than can be found elsewhere in our literature.

Robert Fitzgerald. *NR*. Aug. 16, 1948. pp. 21–3

The Cantos are like a tremendous tapestry in which certain designs predominate, or like a great fugue with recurring motifs, or like a modern Commedia, with the stenches from hell more often than not climbing up to smother purgatory and hover cloudily on the sill of paradise. . . . Pound uses . . . stories, some legendary, some apocryphal, some true, to symbolize or exemplify the cruelties of usury, and to point up his fury with those "who set money lust before the pleasures of the senses," those responsible for the mutilation of men and of art. In his rage he sometimes gets out no more than a stuttered curse or lashes blindly at the innocent, but I do not think even Dante has more powerfully set down the hideousness of corruption, and the fewest lyricists have equaled Pound's gift for evoking particulars of breath-taking delicacy and luster.

Babette Deutsch. *NYHT*. Aug. 22, 1948. p. 7

Pound was one of the most opinionated and unselfish men who ever lived, and he made friends and enemies everywhere by the simple exercise of the classic American constitutional right of free speech. His speech was free to outrageous license. He was completely reckless about making enemies. His so-called anti-Semitism was, hardly anyone has noted, only equaled by his anti-Christianism. It is true he hated most in the Catholic faith the elements of Judaism. It comes down squarely to anti-monotheism. . . . Pound felt himself to be in the direct line of Mediterranean civilization, rooted in Greece. . . . He was a lover of the sublime, and a seeker after perfection, a true poet, of the kind born in a hair shirt—a God-sent disturber of the peace in the arts, the one department of human life where peace is fatal.

Katherine Anne Porter. *NYT*. Oct. 29, 1950. p. 4

I could never take him as a steady diet. Never. He was often brilliant but an ass. But I never (so long as I kept away) got tired of him, or, for a fact, ceased to love him. He had to be loved, even if he kicked you in the teeth for it (but that he never did); he looked as if he might, but he was, at heart, much too gentle, much too good a friend for that. And he had, at bottom, an inexhaustible patience, an infinite depth of human imagination and sympathy. Vicious, catty at times, neglectful, if he trusted you not to mind, but warm and devoted—funny, too, as I have said. We hunted, to some extent at least, together, and not each other.

William Carlos Williams. *Autobiography* (Random). 1951. p. 58

Because the poet is still there one cannot pity Pound—he has retained an integrity as a poet which can be admired without reluctance. It is clear that he will go on now to the end of the Cantos regardless of what is done for him or about him, in Saint Elizabeth's because he happens to be there, but with equal vigor in prison, or back at Rapallo, or anywhere else. He will go on blasting usury and preaching Social Credit, praising Mussolini and damning Roosevelt, as long as he has a voice and a listener. And however wrong-minded we may think all this is in a citizen of a democracy, we must, I think, admire it, however grudgingly, in the uncompromising poet.

Sam Hynes. *Com*. Dec. 9, 1955. p. 254

Certainly Ezra Pound can be read and understood in depth only with a detailed explication of his references in the other hand. . . . Yet the fact remains that even a reader who drives through these Cantos at full gallop will see that the poem is epic in intent, that its subject is the history of modern man's consciousness, and that the telling occurs in a kind of perpetual present, a sort of reverie of the racial consciousness. . . . A book, I propose, becomes a good book when it creates a world one can enter credibly in imagination and a perception of a life one can live vicariously. A good book becomes a great book when that world achieves a magnitude and that life-perception a depth that not only satisfies the imagination but enlarges it beyond all expectation. The final measure of the Cantos lies, I believe, in the fact that they do offer such an enlargement to a willing reader.

John Ciardi. *NYT*. June 24, 1956. pp. 4–5

Pound should be credited with having weighed the perils of the method he elected. It pays the reader the supreme compliment of supposing that he is seriously interested: interested, among other things, in learning how to deploy his curiosity without being a dilettante. . . . His utility enters its second phrase when disparate materials acquire, if only by way of his personality, a unity of tone which makes them accessible to one another. . . . In his third phase of utility . . . the poet instigates curiosity: how many people in the last thirty years have read the *Odyssey* on account of Joyce, or Donne at the encouragement of Mr. Eliot, or Dante and Confucius thanks to Pound? . . . And he would consider that he was performing his maximum service for the fourth kind of reader, the one with the patience to learn and observe, within the poem, how exactly everything fits together and what exactly, page by page and canto by canto, the fitting together enunciates.

Hugh Kenner. *Poetry.* July, 1957. pp. 240–1

Certainly, *Propertius,* like *Mauberley,* is also an ironic survey of Pound's own time and place; in it the Roman becomes curiously modern. . . . It is this that gives [Pound] that resilience and intelligent sense of proportion which reminded Dr Leavis of the seventeenth-century poets; they too were soaked in classical literature. The difference is that Pound does not, as most modern poets might, get at the Latin through the seventeenth century. He seems to work directly through the foreign language. And this is the essence of his best writing. It owes its freshness and economy to this power of using words as if he had just coined them. His language has no literary incrustations. He is the only poet in the last three hundred years to write English as though he had never read Shakespeare. . . . When I suggested this to him, he replied that his literary ancestor was Dante.

(K)   A. Alvarez. *Stewards of Excellence* (Scribner).
1958. pp. 54–5

The hardest thing in art is to get the emotion right and at the same time keep the artist's shadow from dimming out the picture. Pound's poetry at its best is a poetry of absolute distinction, the rhythmic units cleanly defined and vibrant, the voice at once intense and removed, and everything subordinated to the form of the poem itself. . . .

Pound overdoes—no question of it. But it is the excess of a man with more than enough to say. Even though one could wish he might spend the second seventy-five years of his life condensing and reorganizing the *Cantos,* one must recognize the poem for what it is: a gigantic work-in-progress of a new kind, the boldest experiment in poetry of the twentieth century, the continuous expression through more than half his lifetime of one of the most gifted of modern poets.

(K)   M. L. Rosenthal. *Nation.* April 23, 1960. p. 368

Perhaps he will turn out to have been the Ossian of the twentieth century.
. . . As Whitman's love for himself would drive him to transforming all
other selves into aspects of himself in order that he might love them, so
Pound's love for himself would drive him to destroy all other selves whose
existence his idea of love will prevent him from loving. Whitman's and
Pound's means to making an American epic are thus diametrically opposed, but they have at least this in common: they ask that their poetry
lead to a totally unifying sacramentalism. To know, is for Whitman, to
become; for Pound, to become or be destroyed.

(K)   Roy Harvey Pearce. *The Continuity of American*
                              Poetry (Princeton). 1961. pp. 100–101

. . . the whole point of the *Homage* [*To Sextus Propertius*] is the defense
of the individual poet's right to make poetry as his own artistic principles,
and not as the age, demanded. Love in itself is not Pound's concern here,
but the right to produce love poetry and not propaganda. This comparative
lack of interest in the subject for its own sake is indicated by the comparatively low temperature of those sections of the *Homage* which were intended to reproduce Propertius' very genuine amorous fire. And this, it
might be argued, is a fault, for it underrates the devotion of Propertius to
Cynthia *qua* mistress and not *qua* subject for writing poetry. It stresses a
more doctrinaire and more literary attitude, which is of course there in
Propertius' artistic concern, but does not fit Propertius so much as Pound
("*il miglior fabbro*").

(K)   J. P. Sullivan. *KR*. Summer, 1961. pp. 476–7

Fortunately there are kinds of humanism other than those represented by
Irving Babbitt and Ezra Pound. To the democratic humanist a number of
Pound's attitudes are offensive. The poet's long standing aristocratic bias,
his fascist ideals of order, and his crass anti-Semitism are obtrusive faults
and limiting features of his poetry and cannot be thought of as simply the
aberrations and personal opinions of Pound the man. The meanings of
literature are among its most conspicuous formal aspects, and an analysis
of the ideas and values in a poem cannot be set apart, as a function distinct
in kind, from criticism concerned with its patterns of sound, syntax, and
imagery. To attempt to do so, as the Bollingen committee did in awarding
a prize to *The Pisan Cantos* for aesthetic or technical considerations, apart
from the opinions expressed, is to assume an untenable form-content distinction. A writer's work is assessed for the quality of its ideas and values,
as well as for the quality of the other formal elements with which they are
interrelated.

To say this is not to damn Pound or deny his achievement. It is too easy
to do so self-righteously. The image of the alienated artist which he pro-

jected as the caged poet of *The Pisan Cantos* stands as a counter-indictment of the world against which he had recoiled in so extreme a fashion—a world which has in many ways been inimical to the human values (for Pound *has* his humanities) and the creative freedom he has championed for half a century.

(K)   Walter Sutton. Introduction to *Ezra Pound: A Collection of Critical Essays,* edited by Walter Sutton (Prentice). 1963. p. 8

This claim for Pound—that he recovered for English verse something lost to it since Campion or at least since Waller—may get more general agreement than any other. And [Charles] Olson is surely right to point to this achievement as rooted in something altogether more basic and less conspicuous than, for instance, the luxurious orchestration of the choruses in *Women of Trachis.* It is something that has to do with the reconstituting of the verse-line as the poetic unit, slowing down the surge from one line into the next in such a way that smaller components within the line (down to the very syllables) can recover weight and value. When Pound is writing at his best we seem to have perceptions succeeding one another at unusual speed at the same time as the syllables succeed one another unusually slowly. But succession, in any case, is what is involved—succession, sequaciousness.

(K)   Donald Davie. *Ezra Pound: Poet as Sculptor* (Oxford). 1964. p. 246

The suggestion worked out in this book is that Pound's tragedy as a man of letters was in being born into a world which could offer him nothing to offset the extravagance of his mind: no system of thought worthy of the name, and no faith beyond a gentlemanly faith in the inevitable 'progress' of man. Pound accepted much of this world and at the same time revolted against it, but only in its own terms, so that his thought and work is, in a way, the plight of the modern Romantic incarnate.

(K)   Noel Stock. *Poet in Exile: Ezra Pound* (Barnes and Noble). 1964. p. x

Originally, Pound thinks, the Chinese sign for man was a stylized picture of a man; the sign becomes a quasi-pictorial representation of a concept. An Imagist poem is likewise a quasi-pictorial presentation of what we may call a poetic moment, the moment when, as Pound has suggested, an outward thing darts inward: the presentation of a moment of total perception —visual, visceral, emotional. But the brevity and simplicity which gave Imagist poems their impact also restricted their expressive possibilities. Pound made it possible to preserve the intensity of Imagistic presentation and yet escape its miniaturistic brevity when to the almost exclusively stylistic "rules" of Imagism he added the notion of the meaningful juxta-position of analogous or contrasting images, so that . . . the meaning of the resultant ideogram arises from the relationships among its components. This is the method of the *Cantos*.

(K)   Thomas H. Jackson. *ELH*. June, 1965. p. 239

A poet's anti-Semitism, a poet's eugenics, may therefore connect him not only with the debased pragmatism of men he ought to despise, but with a crude primitivism of the sort he would never consciously regard as relevant to his own more refined regress. Pound's radio talks were no doubt the work of a man who had lost some of the sense of reality; but above all they represented a failure of what I have called clerical skepticism, and a be-trayal rather than a renovation of the tradition which, it is assumed, lies under the threat of destruction by corrupt politics, economics and language.

(K)   Frank Kermode. *PR*. Summer, 1966. pp. 350–1

Underneath all his restive search for a satisfying literary environment, T. S. Eliot wrote of Pound in 1946, "the future of American letters was what concerned him most." The American literature for which he con-tended, however, was primarily not an autochthonous expression but rather a redemptive agent in the preservation of the finest values evolved by Western civilization. Rooted as his mind was basically in the cultural premises of the eighteenth century and the Enlightenment, he continued to project the axiomatic belief of such Americans as John Adams and Crèvecœur that the arts traveled Westward with empire, and that America was destined to complete the great circle. Like the eighteenth century, too, he inclined to construe literature not in a merely narrow belletristic sense but as an expression of the full intellectual scope of man. The arts, said Pound during the First World War, must be placed ahead of the church and scholarship as the "acknowledged guide and lamp of civilization."

(K)   Benjamin T. Spencer. *PMLA*. Dec., 1966. p. 459

. . . when I see Ezra Pound's example appropriated exclusively by one or another group of poets, it seems to me that this is a diminution of his place in our world and that I must do what I can to correct it; for in respect to Pound several possibilities should be borne in mind. First, the possibility of preferring—and preference is not dogma—the poems of *Lustra, Cathay, Propertius,* and *Mauberley,* which Pound wrote at the same time as his influential prose statements of theory and criticism, to much of the *Cantos,* which he wrote at a considerably later period. Second, the possibility that Pound by himself re-invented the poetic line as the unit of poetry, variable and end-stopped, that his concept of modern verse measure was clearer and more workable than anyone else's, and that he came to it long before [William Carlos] Williams conceived his notion of the variable foot. Third, the possibility—indeed, it is much more—that Pound was as closely associated with Eliot as with Williams *throughout their lives,* that on the other hand he damned London as heartily as he did Concord, and that his immense influence has descended *equally,* though no doubt differently, through the entire conspectus of Anglo-American writing to the present day. . . .

(K)   Hayden Carruth. *Poetry.* May, 1967. p. 104

See *Personae, The Cantos* (poetry); *The Classic Anthology Defined by Confucius* (translation); *Collected Letters; ABC of Reading* (essay).

POWERS, J. F. (1917–   )

Even though the expert technique of these stories is as unemotional and photographic as the later Hemingway, consisting mainly of placing the model in a good clear light and shooting, the collection as a whole leaves one with the impression that the author has a disciplined distaste for materialism and bullying, and that he believes that these two traits account for most of the frustrations and woes of contemporary man, whether in the church or out of it.

Eunice S. Holsaert. *NYT.* May 4, 1947. p. 20

He avoids the stereotyped two-dimensional layout, the affected obliquity which keeps everything on the same level, and the colorless neutrality which makes such an obvious pretense of "objectivity." He is unabashedly inside his story, focusing on objects, catching nuances for us, and heightening the volume when he wishes. . . . His perceptions are interesting not only for their acuteness but for the mass of dense particulars which they penetrate.

Henry Rago. *Com.* Aug. 22, 1947. pp. 457–8

Of all modern writers known to me who have dealt with Catholic religious life J. F. Powers . . . is far and away the best. He has his own peculiar technique for handling the subject. Unlike the sentimentalists and satirists, he rarely glances at religion itself, as though it were a light too strong for his eyes. He is interested mainly in the pettiness and vulgarity of a mechanical civilization. . . . After the darkness of so much American fiction this book (*The Presence of Grace*) produces a peculiar shock of delight. Having lived with Mr. Power's first book, *Prince of Darkness,* for some years, I can testify that it is not a delight that disappears as the shock diminishes. Powers is among the greatest of living storytellers.

Frank O'Connor. *SR*. March 24, 1956. p. 22

Competitiveness is central in Powers's work, whether he is using the secular world or the tight world of the Church. . . . The competitive agitation leads to a distinctive developmental pattern in Powers's stories. Most typical is a centripetal movement that begins on the outskirts of things, with the inconspicuous, literal, mundane detail, and slowly whirls in toward a still point of revelation that in a sense negates all hierarchies. The protagonist is at least temporarily freed of the compulsion to maintain self, sees himself and others as victims of a condition endemic to humanity, glimpses and responses to a motivation that operates as an antidote—that is, there is a release from the pressure of self-interest, with the concomitant experiencing of compassion and even of love.

George Scouffas. *Critique*. Fall, 1958. p. 42

What made these stories so remarkable was maturity. American fiction is always striking an attitude or being "psychological" or just reporting the violence of some unusual experience. Mr. Powers's work was about a *world;* it constantly yielded literary vanity to the truth and depth of this world. He was subtle, funny, precise, and always unexpected. The book seemed to come out of a longer background than most young American writers of fiction ever own. . . . I admire Mr. Powers very much—story after story is worked out to the finest possible point; this is work that manages by fusing intelligence and compassion, to come out as humor. There is real love in his heart, but he knows that the *heart* does not write short stories, and that the beauty of grace can appear only against the background of the horrid daily element, which is gravity.

Alfred Kazin. *Contemporaries* (Little). 1962. pp. 223–5

In this novel (*Morte D'Urban*), as in many of his best-known short stories, Powers writes about the Catholic Church with an air of great authority. He writes as an insider, though certainly not *for* insiders. The Order of St. Clement may be his invention, but it is as real as Yoknapatawpha County. Having created a little world of his own, with its particular beliefs and customs, he can write a comedy of manners. There are no dramatic incidents and no large issues, but we do have a quiet, steady revelation of character, a revelation superb in its subtlety and depth. . . . His faith permits him to look with tolerance on the foibles of good men and to recognize the virtues of bad ones.

Granville Hicks. *SR*. Sept. 15, 1962. p. 21

It seems pretty generally agreed that Satire Is Dead. I'm delighted to inform you that you must revise your opinion, because J. F. Powers has written a book (*Morte D'Urban*) which is satire in the pure sense—not a symbolic action in the manner of Joyce or Kafka, not a psychological comedy in the manner of Kingsley Amis or Peter de Vries, though all these can be turned to critical ends—but a pure satire which will nevertheless please the most sophisticated literary tastes. Powers has done something quite remarkable: he has revived the satire of the Great Age —from Erasmus to Swift, let's say, reverting to tradition—within a modern context of style and attitude. In fact, the stylishness almost—but not quite—obscures the point that his book is a classical satire against mankind based on the exploitation of types.

Hayden Carruth. *NR*. Sept. 24, 1962. p. 24

From the start, nearly twenty years ago now, when his writing began to excite the admiration of the readers of *Accent,* it was evident that the stories of J. F. Powers had a very special quality, a rare richness of theme and perception; and, for all their liberal zeal and satirical intent, often an even rarer gentleness of tone. . . . Powers's theme remains truly haunting; it is one that might be framed as a question: how can the spirit express itself in nature without compromise, without debasement, since one is so distant from the other, and each one is obedient to different laws? Again: can a mind manipulate its work in the world without becoming completely worldly itself? . . . Powers has found the formula for his fiction in all this. He regularly sees the priest in a worldly role. The necessity of this role makes Powers's satire kind. The contradictions implied make his irony deep.

William H. Gass. *Nation*. Sept. 29, 1962. pp. 182–3

The characters in *Morte D'Urban* have the tangibility that real people have for us in those rare moments when the fog of abstraction and self-absorption lifts, and they come illuminated out of the fog with Powers's rare combination of irony, sympathy and humor. . . . Yet the novel is not simply a gallery of memorable portraits; characters are revealed in action and interaction. Few writers today have as acute a sense of the drama of interpersonal relations as Powers has. . . . *Morte D'Urban* is not simply an anecdotal display of a central character by a writer whose ear for American speech is as good as O'Hara's; in it character and theme are dramatized in a significant complex. . . . It is Powers's version of that most Christian of ironies: the Fortunate Fall.

John P. Sisk. *Critique*. Winter, 1962–3. pp. 101–2

Powers's is a world of the living all too living, and only in such a world can the ethical consideration bear much weight. For the purposes of fiction, he effects a divorce between faith and morals. The question is not whether faith, in the measure his characters have it, makes them greatly better or greatly worse than those outside the fold. The question is whether those inside the fold can sustain the moral life at the level of average good will, self-respect, and taste. If this approach is necessary to Powers as a moral realist, it is also congenial to him as a story teller; and his love of narration in all shapes, sizes and degrees of seriousness is obvious. Stories within stories, ranging from rectory-table anecdotes through biblical parables to scraps of radio serials caught from the airwaves, thicken the fictional atmosphere. Each sentence tends to be an event; yet every event, like every firm but fluent sentence, is an open door into the next half-expected, half-shocking encounter. Thus does J. F. Powers coax stories out of the shabby rectories of his not altogether mythical Minnesota.

F. W. Dupee. *PR*. Spring, 1963. p. 114

The Prince of Darkness and *The Presence of Grace,* necessary preliminaries to *Morte D'Urban,* have few faults and present less of the big world than Powers's novel. *Morte D'Urban* is not woven tightly; it overuses narrative bridges; it hurries its concluding section; it sometimes exhibits an overindulgence in clever ambiguities; its experiments with the play form within a novel achieve the partial success that calls attention to technical dexterity rather than to the heart of the matter. Yet these faults seem slight flaws as I think back over the experiences of reading the novel. Err though he may, Powers *has* gone on from the smaller provinces where a cat whimsically evaluates or outwits a priest, even beyond the short importance of a good Franciscan's death with his "will amenable to the divine," beautiful though it may be. Here is J. F. Powers's large world, fully peopled with the Clementines he invented and those they contend against and try to tend and live with. Here, fully imagined, is the tragic and comic world where Father Urban lives within, above, and beneath his own and the Order's scheme of values, forgetting and remembering and learning about the God who gives him rein and pulls him to heel.

Harvey Curtis Webster. *KR*. Winter, 1963. p. 167

See *The Prince of Darkness* and *The Presence of Grace* (short stories); and *Morte D'Urban* (novel).

PYNCHON, THOMAS (1936–   )

The book [*V*.] reads like a literary hoax, a parody of the quest romance and tale of international intrigue. We are made to witness violent happenings in Cairo, Florence, and Malta, explorations of the Antarctic and crocodile hunts in the sewers of New York. The fantastic web of events spans three generations, moving back and forth through space and time at will. The characters, as the author puts it, are mostly yo-yos. The style is elliptic and cockeyed, studded with zany names and improbable locutions. The whole novel gives an impression of studied confusion, a mood that expresses both the futility and vitality of human life.

Ihab Hassan. *SR*. March 23, 1963. p. 44

The trouble, however, goes deeper than this broad, youthful, self-conscious humor with its fatiguing brightness, its bad jokes, and toneless prose. It resides in the fact that Pynchon is an extremely facile writer of caricature. If Virginia Woolf, Gide, Borges, Proust, and Lawrence Durrell, for example, turn up in *V.,* they do so not as "influences" but as taking-off points. It is very much as if Pynchon's talent can only work given the springboard of pastiche, as if he can deal with his characters only on the condition that they are isolated and qualified by some literary or psychological tongue-in-cheek. Thus he has great difficulty in stabilizing his characters and in getting them to talk to one another, for they are constantly being defaced by the universal solvent of Pynchon's archness, which functions like some hidden second thought of the writer, something he knows that his characters don't know: that he is the only deviser and player of the pinball game through which they spin.

Irving Feldman. *Cmty*. Sept., 1963. p. 259

V. is, among other things, a novel about, among other places, New York. In contrasting scenes of shifting time and place, Mr. Pynchon creates a bizarre mosaic of modern events against which his characters seek their personal destinies. Herbert Stencil, an Englishman committed to solving the mystery of V. in his father's life, and Benny Profane, a "schlemihl" committed to keeping himself alive in a chancy universe, are Mr. Pynchon's *alter egos:* one quixotically pursuing the past in order to find the key to the future and the other doggedly holding on to the present, willing to let the future take care of itself.

V. is rich and inventive, wide and various, overlong and uneven—and in a strange way highly eclectic. It seems, in fact, the apotheosis of the mid-century American novel: one of those loose, baggy monsters that have dominated our post-war fiction.

Paul Levine. *HdR*. Autumn, 1963. p. 459

Thomas Pynchon's first book, *V.,* published in 1963, established him as a *virtuoso* performer in fiction. There seemed to be nothing he could not render, no style he could not imitate. He had the structural gift as well, and an impressive command over the language of science and historiography. Part of *V.* took place at carefully imagined moments of crisis in European history. Part of it took place in contemporary New York Bohemia. Both parts dovetailed brilliantly into an allegory about how the search for the symbolic meaning of the past can "animate" the mind even as the mind's world becomes progressively "inanimate" or dead. Maybe *V.* lacked the most important thing—some simple center of sincere feeling to cry out for a piece of us and want to be believed. But in 1963 one ignored this lack in favor of the novelist's sheer inventive and structural power.

In *The Crying of Lot 49,* Pynchon's theme and method remain essentially what they were in *V.,* though the recent book is shorter, more deliberately whimsical, and somewhat less substantial. . . . As an exercise in epistemology, *Lot 49* is not without theoretical value. And, at times, Pynchon's speculative prose attains the dense suggestiveness of verse. . . . But verbal density and theoretical value are not enough to make a good novel.

Arthur Gold. NYHT. April 24, 1966. p. 5

The first novel, *V.,* was a designed indictment of its own comic elaborateness. The various quests for "V." all of them substitutes for the pursuit of love, are interwoven fantastically, and the coherence thus achieved is willfully fabricated and factitious. Pynchon's intricacies are meant to testify to the waste—a key word in *The Crying of Lot 49*—of imagination that first creates and is then enslaved by its own plottings, its machines, the products of its technology. . . .

Gestures of warmth are the most touching in his novels for being terrifyingly intermittent, shy and worried. . . . Efforts at human communication are lost among Pynchon's characters, nearly all of whom are obsessed with the presumed cryptography in the chance juxtaposition of Things, in the music and idiom of bars like the V-Note or The Scope, or merely in the "vast sprawl of houses" that Oedipa [in *The Crying of Lot 49*] sees outside Los Angeles, reminding her of the printed circuit of a transistor radio, with its "intent to communicate."

Richard Poirier. NYT. May 1, 1966. p. 5

The focus of *The Crying of Lot 49,* Thomas Pynchon's new novel, moves feverishly between Southern California's shot-up cities and their indistinguishable environs. It is a desperately funny book, conceived and executed with an awesome virtuosity. The novel's tone and pace are characterized by their absolute intensity, and Mr. Pynchon's essential technique is suggested most simply by his descriptions, which invariably cut from one layer of the culture to another. . . . The ironies are intricate, the prose composed in styles varying from scholarly exposition to parodies of

Jacobean tragedy to TV commercialese; but Mr. Pynchon does not lose control. His primary observation remains central, and it is one which our current foreign policy only seems to confirm: that paranoia is the last sense of community left us.

Stephen Donadio. *PR*. Summer, 1966. pp. 449–50

The great cultural polarity in *The Education* [*of Henry Adams*] was of course the Virgin (or Virgin-Venus) and the Dynamo. Pynchon too postulates cultural alternatives, but they are never so sharply defined or as clearly polarized. His single central image is abstract, the letter "V.," which subsumes multiple meanings (including one roughly comparable to the Virgin-Venus concept) and undergoes a number of transformations in the course of the narrative. His other recurrent image is both prosaic and ominous. It is of all things the well-known yo-yo, that toy with the simple, repetitive motions. For Adams, the dynamo embodied powerful industrial, technological energies. Pynchon's yo-yo, in various metaphorical forms, comes to characterize a mechanistic and meaningless society: it is his *reductio ad absurdum*.

Don Hausdorff. *WSCL*. Autumn, 1966. p. 259

See *V., The Crying of Lot 49* (novels).

RAHV, PHILIP (1908–   )

It occurs to me that there may be only two main types of literary critic—one oriented to prose, the other to poetry. Each type has its own special skill. If the second excels in close verbal analysis, the first is usually superior at picking out leading ideas and analyzing the structure of lengthy and complex works of literature.

Mr. Rahv is what one may call a pure example of the first type. Not one of the fourteen essays before me [*Image and Idea*] is concerned with poetry; even when he writes of William Carlos Williams, Mr. Rahv confines himself to that writer's short stories. . . . As a critic, he possesses the specific virtues of his type. The witty simplicity with which he divides all American writers into two groups—Palefaces and Redskins—is only the most striking example of a real gift for sane and striking generalization.

Vivian Mercier. *Com.* July 22, 1949. p. 369

What one admires most in Philip Rahv's essays is the determination to search among our modern cultural closures and total ideologies for "the cultural forms of dissidence and experiment." And what one admires about Rahv's critical method is his abundant ability to use such techniques as Marxism, Freudian psychology, anthropology, and existentialism toward his critical ends without shackling himself to any of them. . . . Rahv is above all a political critic, in the sense that his criticism takes literature to be involved in the upshot of history and the practical transactions of men and public ideas. His skill in handling a complex criticism, which is only infrequently allowed to vanish away into the rigidities of a narrow technique, places these essays [*Image and Idea*] among the very best written by the leftist critics of the 1940's.

Richard Chase. *Nation.* July 23, 1949. p. 89

Though they were published in a number of magazines over a period of some ten years, and deal with such apparently diverse writers as Hawthorne, Henry James, Tolstoy, Dostoevsky, Kafka, Virginia Woolf, Henry Miller, William Carlos Williams, Arthur Koestler and Bernard DeVoto, these fourteen extremely intelligent essays [*Image and Idea*] have a unity of conception and concern which makes it possible to read them as interrelated chapters of a single work. The key to this unity is in the term alienation. It is an alienated age which Philip Rahv is brilliantly analyzing

39

here, and it is an alienated age to which the magazine *Partisan Review,* edited by Rahv and William Phillips since its beginning in 1936, has given such influential and representative expression. . . . .

Rahv's writing lacks the connotative precision, the rich immersion in the medium which he admires in James, and it has a little of the journalistic flair for striking simplifications which he criticizes in Koestler. But the way in which he has tried to comprehend his own very representative political and ethical evolution through a reassessment of American and European writers has made *Image and Idea* one of the most clarifying of recent books of criticism.

Robert Gorham Davis. NYT. Aug. 14, 1949. p. 6

The specific literary judgments and helpful criticism in this volume [*Image and Idea*] are found almost haphazardly, and frequently in unexpected links and parallels. From a really wide reading, the critic illuminates a writer or a book or a relevant situation by juxtaposition or comparison. Again, a telling judgment may occur in a reference to a writer's background or experience; for example, with deceptive casualness he really puts the finger on Henry Miller when he says that "the final impression we have of his novels is that of a naturally genial and garrulous American who has been through hell." The range of Rahv's taste is extraordinary; characteristic is a balanced and generous estimate of Virginia Woolf. And common sense is indistinguishable from brilliance in an essay called "Notes on the Decline of Naturalism."

John Farrelly. NR. Sept. 26, 1949. p. 24

Another version of the story adds some interesting additions. It begins in 1932, when "an obscure boy from the Bronx" mailed an essay on Plekhanov to *The New Masses.* Joseph Freeman read it, liked it, and invited its author, Philip Rahv, to send him more. A year or so later, Rahv and his friend William Phillips, both active in the New York City John Reed Club, came to Freeman with the complaint that *The New Masses* was too political. They urged the creation of a literary magazine. Freeman not only agreed, but also helped them to start *Partisan Review* and wrote the opening editorial statement. In substance, the editors promised to publish the best work of the New York John Reed Club members and sympathetic nonmembers; to maintain the viewpoint of the working class, to struggle against war and fascism, and to defend the U.S.S.R.; and to combat "the decadent culture of the exploiting classes," narrow-minded sectarianism, and "debilitating liberalism."

Was *Partisan Review,* then, founded in opposition to *The New Masses*? On the contrary, it has been argued, it never would have appeared without the active support of *The New Masses* editors and writers, some of whom appeared in its pages as late as October 1936.

Daniel Aaron. *Writers on the Left* (Harcourt). 1961.
pp. 298–9

Rahv's title [*The Myth and the Powerhouse*] suggests, in his rejection of both its terms, a strong moral view of literature. It applies to only a few of the essays explicitly, and to some others implicitly. We already know Rahv for his *Image and Idea* (1949) and for his editing and reviewing in various places. That he can be a first-rate critic is demonstrated by the two essays on Dostoevsky, both of them marvels of close reading, philosophical inference and useful knowledge. But Rahv's principal thesis, that modern critics are allowing us to be self-indulgent by substituting myth for a genuine "orthodoxy" is, at best, presented here too late to be relevant.

Frederick J. Hoffman. *Nation*. Nov. 8, 1965. p. 334

The essays in Rahv's first book, *Image and Idea,* were pioneering studies, many of them, in Kafka, in Henry James, in the new re-appraisal of American literature such as his famous alignment of Paleface and Redskin, and in a re-appraisal of Russian literature and Marxism. Among these novelties, Rahv was sensible, solid, and weighty. He still is, and he still has his large Johnsonian gift for reality. But the object of his criticism in this collection [*The Myth and the Powerhouse*] is, necessarily, often criticism itself. . . . Rahv's conception of literary criticism is, sensibly, that it mediates between literature and the great world, that in fact criticism should aid literature to reach out, to locate and struggle with "experience." But except for a few eloquent passages of invocation, and one or two specific references to the past, there is little reaching out here. There is only comment on literature, on literary fads, on literary books.

John Thompson. *NYR*. Dec. 9, 1965. p. 36

Mr. Rahv . . . deals with the biggest corporate enterprises: Dostoevsky, Gogol, Chekhov, James, Eliot, Joyce, Hemingway, history, Hegel, Tillich, the *Zeitgeist,* God. Mr. Rahv's "powerhouse" is history. . . . To give the *Zeitgeist* its due, one must grant that an occasional literary subject is able to penetrate the underbrush of Mr. Rahv's style and preoccupations. He writes intelligently, and even in bearable English, about Dostoevsky, for instance; as if Dostoevsky is political enough to free Mr. Rahv from the compulsion to question everybody else's timeliness and credentials. But his lapses are rare.

Marvin Mudrick. *HdR*. Winter, 1965–66. p. 596–7

See *Image and Idea, The Myth and the Powerhouse* (essays).

RANSOM, JOHN CROWE (1888–   )

Poetry

I suppose that if I were set to fill in a literary passport to send Ransom to Parnassus, I should include in a summary of his Ransomness first, a humorous turn of speech, including a sweetening scepticism; second, a muscular quality of both metre and thought, and third, the periodic detonation of most unlikely and effective phrases.

Robert Graves. SR. Dec. 27, 1924. p. 412

The poet cannot solve his problem (the relation of the artist to the ordered, or disordered society in which he happens to live) by an act of will, but he can attempt to work out some sort of equilibrium that may permit him, even though at odds with himself, to continue the practice of his art without violating his own honesty. Analysis will show that most of Ransom's poems are objectifications of this little interior drama. . . . These poems are not mere commentary, however witty, on the nature and conduct of the external world.

Robert Penn Warren. Poetry. May, 1930. p. 111

No pavilioned clipper ships appear on his horizon; no peculiarities, human or zoological, except the actors in an occasional allegory; no flashing tropical color nor tinkling lilt or harlequinade enter his theater. He reflects sombrely on the inexorable duality of things, the gulf between the senses and the intellect, the body and head; between the life of actuality and the life of contemplation; between scientific knowledge and imaginative vision; between the joys of childhood and adult self-torment. His irony is the most important single element in his poetry. It dictates the subdued key which is so much more susceptible of subtle economics of tone-change than a larger volume would be. It restricts his language to the simple, lucid forms which take on a special sheen and sharpness when an oddity is dropped in their midst or a film of archaism passed over them. It infuses humor into his philosophic reflections and tempers his occasional solemnities.

Elizabeth Drew. Directions in Modern Poetry
(Norton). 1940. pp. 77–8

Without making a fetish of the Old South, Ransom is the last notable poet to express its more enduring and engaging qualities. . . . Ransom is quite capable of sympathy with the modern world, yet above all is heir of the best spirit of a fatherland dearer to its sons because of its heroic distrusts, so that a delicate irony pervades his verses. . . . The many parallels between the wit and irony in Ransom's verse and in the Elizabethans are again due to the history and mental climate of the South.

Henry W. Wells. The American Way of Poetry
(Columbia). 1945. pp. 161, 171

To be a Ransom in Tennessee is something more precious than it is easy to say. . . . Mr. Ransom's poems are composed of Tennessee. . . . He drew a picture of it, many pictures of it, in his book. The greater the value he set on it, the dearer it became, the more closely he sought out its precise line and look, the more it became a legend of things as they are when they are as we want them to be, without any of the pastiche of which the presence vulgarizes so many legends and possibly everything legendary in things, not as they are, but as we should like them to be.

Wallace Stevens. SwR. Summer, 1948. pp. 367–9

Ransom's production is small—his selected poems take up only seventy-four pages. . . . It is the work of a lifetime. When I reread it, I marveled at its weight—few English poets have written so many lyrics that one wants to read over and over again. . . . There is the language; it's a curious mixture of elaboration and bluntness; courtesy and rudeness. . . . To appreciate the language in Ransom's poems, you must realize that it is the language of one of the best talkers that has ever lived in the United States. . . . There is the unusual structural clarity, the rightness of tone and rhythm, the brisk and effective ingenuity, the rhetorical fire-works of expository description and dialogue; but even more: the sticking to concrete human subjects—the hardest; and a balance, control, matureness, nimbleness, toughness, and gentleness of temperament.

Robert Lowell. SwR. Summer, 1948. pp. 374–6

To my mind the most striking thing about John Crowe Ransom's poems is their elegance. . . . Elegance, in this connection, is a means to a precision of statement, more especially a means to the control of tone: it implies manners, or style. . . . The attitude I seek to distinguish has much to do with irony. . . . The emphasis of the poems is for the most part clearly on intellect and brilliance; the vocabulary is more than usually exotic, the rhymes are witty and boldly slanted, the poet's attitude and stance are in the main remote, often amused.

Howard Nemerov. SwR. Summer, 1948. pp. 417–22

Instead of listening to him through the hands, with closed eyes, as one is sucked deeper and deeper into the maelstrom, one listens with one's eyes wide open and one's head working about as well as it usually works. Most writers become over-rhetorical when they are insisting on more emotion than they actually feel or need to feel; Ransom is just the opposite. He is perpetually insisting, by his detached, mock-pedantic, wittily complicated tone, that he is not feeling much at all, not half as much as he really should be feeling.

Randall Jarrell. *Poetry and the Age* (Knopf). 1953. pp. 98–9

Ransom has a special sympathy for his deluded characters. The fact that he knows they are deluded and they do not, does not make him satiric because it is only by perceiving their delusion that he realizes, by its inevitability, the vanity of his own efforts. The very elements which make the situations of Ransom's poems susceptible to objective and ironic mockery, allow the softening of its effect with personal feeling.

(K)   G. R. Wasserman. *UKCR*. Winter, 1956. p. 155

A number of Ransom's poems concern themselves with knightly combat, an amusing metaphor for the intellectual jousting of literary life. He makes mocking use of such archaic and scholarly words as "ogive" (pointed arch), "thole" (endure), "pernoctated" (passed the night), and "diuturnity" (something lasting). Other poems are as far from the domestic and the homely as one can get. "Armageddon" is an amazing account of the final battle between Christ and Antichrist, seen as an odd kind of chivalric ballet. "Antique Harvesters" harvests history in what appears to be a corner of Kentucky, with everything so numinous that even the fox pursued by spectral hunters becomes a "lovely ritualist." "Painted Head" starts as a description of a portrait and in the course of nine quatrains manages to create an esthetics, a metaphysics, and an ethics. . . . As a poet, Ransom remains an original. One can see the faint influence of John Skelton in such a poem as "Somewhere Is Such a Kingdom," of John Donne in "The Equilibrists," of Thomas Hardy in "Puncture" and "Master's in the Garden Again" (the latter dedicated to him), of Wallace Stevens in "Prometheus in Straits" and "Prelude to an Evening." One can see other poems from which Robert Graves has learned, or Robert Lowell, or Howard Nemerov. But in a deeper sense John Crowe Ransom's poetry seems to be without ancestry and descendants, to spring up timeless and beautiful like Indian pipes in deep woods, to delight our minds and refresh our hearts.

(K)   Stanley Edgar Hyman. *NL*. August 5, 1963. p. 18

Throughout his poetry and prose is an awareness of the radical difference between what men yearn for and what they get. It informs the elements which make up his double vision of man: the "fury against abstractions," the conception of the modern mind as divided and at war with itself; the mistrust of monistic philosophies and sciences; the image of a pluralistic universe and the belief that the arts offer the most comprehensive mode of representing it; the argument in support of an agrarian culture; and the irony of his delivery. Only in death, where the difference seems most immense, does it end. . . .

Balancing opposing forces within a harmonious and unified order is the fundamental principle of Ransom's style and the communication of his unique vision of man. When reading one of his mature poems we have a sense of radical diversity, of complicated lines of stress, of collisions among the elements. At the same time we feel threading among these strong filaments which bind the poem together, and in the end we are left with a satisfying impression of wholeness. If, as usually happens, we are offered two views of and attitudes toward the subject, we find on finishing the poem that they have preserved their separate identities. The opposition has not been resolved though it has been assimilated into the total statement of the poem, which itself affects us as a single entity.

(K)   John L. Stewart. *The Burden of Time: The Fugitives and Agrarians* (Princeton). 1965. pp. 206, 228–9

Conventional poetry about love follows the easy routes: it assumes that outward Nature is the harmonious ally of inward feeling, provides embellishment by lush, sensuous description of interiors, uses emotional overstatement, the grandiose adjective. In scorning these transparent devices and concentrating on formal audacity, Ransom becomes like his equilibrists, caught between a poet's necessity to deal with emotion and a self-conscious modernist's preoccupation with subtle technical execution. His major weakness seems to be that he often settles for a sophisticated execution without emotional power or the clear lyric line: he frequently incurs more disadvantages than he can transcend through a strict fidelity to his principles. His impotent poems about love ("Spectral Lovers" for one) are skeletal reflections of his fatal obsession with technique. Sometimes his poetry seems like a deliberate, narcissistic cerebral amusement rather than an adventure in the brave encompassing of life. Only in "The Equilibrists," a flawed masterpiece, does he extract an overwhelming passion from his uncompromisingly meager poetics. But the devices sometimes announce themselves and the passion is intellectual; it is not an aesthetic ecstasy. To achieve that, he has to permit feeling to be first.

In "Winter Remembered" all of Ransom's important principles are not only intact, but they are amenable to an unobtrusive sophisticated power. The very indirection is a source of excitement when it works so quietly to unleash emotion. Our awe at discovering that the emotion of love can be intensified by the bizarre image of frozen parsnips is the best authentication of Ransom's singular control. This reclamation of unpoetic resources is the highest pitch of Ransom's monastic ecstasy.

(K)   Thornton H. Parsons. *MLQ*. Dec., 1965. p. 585

In both cases [of genteel virtue and mythology] Ransom's regret is mostly for the loss of a world in which such virtues, such myths, such learning were relevant, not as things in themselves, although he does concede their value. To continue to practice the virtues or to insist that people should learn classical myths—unless they can be tricked into learning them, as we have noted—seems to strike him as absurd. Ransom has presented a case history of absurdity in the gyrations and activities of his Captain Carpenter, a ridiculous, yet grotesquely splendid figure, who is quixotic, but also fully aware of where his folly is leading him, and persistent in that folly as a way of insisting upon the values by which he lives. I mention this element of grotesquerie qualified by a certain splendor, in turn destroyed almost by its own absurdity, because it seems so typical of so many of Ransom's characters.

(K)   Samuel H. Woods. *CE*. Feb., 1966. pp. 411–12

Criticism

His chief criterion of literary excellence is metaphysical poetry. According to him it is the best poetry of the past, and poetry like it should be the poetry of the present. It is the finest way to express that concentration on the particular moment of experience which is the business of art as opposed to the less human, less adult business of science, which concentrates on the abstract.

Theodore Spencer. *NR*. Aug. 10, 1938. p. 27

Mr. Ransom . . . comes through as a kind of enlightened reactionary. He is too well-informed to be lumped with the ivory-tower school and too cynical to be lumped with any liberal one. . . . He has qualities of acumen and wit to which not very many critics of today can lay claim. But the problem of poetry today can hardly not be linked to the problem of human culture, which is plainly being menaced.

Louis Kronenberger. *Nation*. Aug. 13, 1938. pp. 161–2

He began by excoriating naturalism and positivism, yet ended by affirming that the analysis of the "structural properties" of poems were the main business of criticism. . . . This new criticism, based on a vicarious orthodoxy and textual analysis of advanced poetry, seemed . . . the only answer to the havoc of the times. . . . What one saw in the work of critics like Ransom and Tate, Blackmur and Yvor Winters, was the use of form as a mysterious ultimate value, form as a touchstone, a kind of apotheosis in a void.

Alfred Kazin. *On Native Grounds* (Reynal). 1942.
pp. 429–31

His major contribution to American criticism has been made through the *Kenyon Review,* which he has edited since 1939. . . . It is as a critic that Ransom is best known and most influential. He is the founder and leader of the Kenyon School—literally a school where the most distinguished critics have come to teach and lecture, and, less literally, that phase of contemporary criticism, usually designated as the "New Criticism," which seeks to study poetry in terms of its structure (the logic of the poem) and its texture (the detail of the poem), quite apart from its historical and social contexts.

Stanley J. Kunitz. *Twentieth Century Authors.*
First Supplement (Wilson). 1955. p. 814

. . . my interest here is not in the "truth" of Ransom's speculations, but in their illustration of where the search for a suitable theory of poetry as knowledge is likely to lead when the knowledge is not to be prose knowledge—either scientific or, in the words of a critic of the New Critics, "common knowledge, of things that everyone incipiently knows, or has overlooked, or forgotten." Even if you begin as Ransom did with a respect and a love for particulars, you seem to get drawn in the footsteps of Aristotle, Plato, the Hegelians—and of course the great Romantic poets and theorists of the last century—where in the beginning you may have especially wanted *not* to go: "higher," or "further," or "behind"—or even, like Blackmur, "below."

(K) Richard Foster. *The New Romantics* (Indiana).
1962. p. 144

Ransom sees the poem as developing from a determination of the poet, who knows what he wants to say or how he wants the poem to sound, or both, before writing the poem. The poet starts, then, with a determinate meaning, a determinate sound, or both. But language cannot be mastered so completely; the meaning will not fit into the emergent verse pattern, so it changes until it becomes something the poet did not foresee—indeterminate meaning. Nor will the language bear both the sound and the meaning the poet wanted, so indeterminate sound enters. Here, incidentally, Ransom's theory is far superior to most others we have examined. What happens, Ransom urges, is that the medium in which the poet works is obstinate; it forces him to admit effects of sound and sense which he did not intend and for which he is not entirely responsible. Hence, presumably, arises the "tissue of irrelevance" which Ransom considers the peculiar property of poetry.

(K)   Lee T. Lemon. *The Partial Critics* (Oxford).
                                                          1965. pp. 119–20

A great deal of Ransom's criticism has been actively concerned with limiting the field of aesthetics and making explicit its divorce from the work of the "moralist." His defence of the poem's autonomy, his insistence on ruling out its effect on the critic as reader, his discussion of technique without reference to its function as a medium of communication or expression (denying indeed that this is its function), his analysis of poetic quality only in terms of a texture irrelevant to what moral substance the poem's logical core may possess: all these can be seen as facets of Ransom's dissociation of himself from the moralists whom he evidently considers as his chief opponents.

(K)   Andor Gomme. *Attitudes to Criticism* (Southern
                                                          Illinois). 1966. p. 22

See *Selected Poems* and *The World's Body* (criticism).

RAWLINGS, MARJORIE KINNAN (1896–1953)

South Moon Under is laid in a country far removed from the violences of the depression, the Florida scrub. It is a slow, old-fashioned novel, carefully and sometimes beautifully written, beginning with the coming of the Lantrys to the wilderness and ending with the flight of the lost generation to wilderness still deeper. There is a great deal of factual information packed away unobtrusively in the novel, information on such unfamiliar subjects as the making of corn liquor, on the ways of hunting wildcats, or the methods of rafting logs down the river. . . . And if the characters are sometimes a little misty, and seem mere passive agents for observing the multiple details of wild life, they at least always observe clearly.

                              Robert Cantwell. *NR*. March 8, 1933. p. 108

There comes a moment everywhere when ceasing to be a boy may be a tragedy like dying. But the story of that moment has never been more tenderly written than by Marjorie Kinnan Rawlings in this novel [*The Yearling*] of Jody, the boy of the Florida hammock country, and Flag, the faun, who grew together out of a frolicking youngness to the bitter realities of maturity.

It is a story sad enough; one, indeed, which might easily fall into the bathos of youth's own humorless seeing of its incomparable despair. But

Mrs. Rawlings wisely has not written in the solemn terms of tragedy. Rather her book of the Baxter family is crowded with comedy of character, with full-bodied folk wisdom, and with the silence and the excitement, the ultimate noise and accumulated natural history of the backwoods hunt.

Jonathan Daniels. *SR*. April 2, 1938. p. 5

If the reader can survive the many "fragile clusters of lavender bloom," "white tufted sky," "pale green earth," "golden sunlight," and finally an "arched rainbow" of the first chapter [of *The Yearling*], he has a real treat in store for him, for Mrs. Rawlings writes with a sincere and unusual beauty. Her Cracker dialect is interesting and never becomes tiresome; her characterization is excellent; and her leisurely method of unfolding her plot fascinates the reader to the end of the book.

Philip Hartung. *Com*. April 29, 1938. p. 24

Writing fiction for adults about a child in a child's world is a delicately difficult literary undertaking. . . . Marjorie Kinnan Rawlings has succeeded where so many have failed, and *The Yearling* is a distinguished book. Her Jody Baxter lives, a person in himself, within the boundaries of his own years and his own world. One-third intuition, one-third knowledge, one-third perception, the boy moves through the Florida river country, and the chronicle of his year is unforgettably written. . . . Even a Thoreau cannot report on the world outdoors as a child might. The naturalist sees only those things which concern his informed eye. To a child the barn and the woodshed are as much a part of the natural workable landscape as the lizard under the log. Mrs. Rawlings has done a small miracle in that she knows this, never stops to interpret, never once steps outside Jody's perceptions, never mars her great skill by pausing to explain. She has captured a child's time sense, in which everything lasts forever and the change of season takes him always unawares.

Frances Woodward. *At*. June, 1938. n.p.

Few other contemporary American novelists exhibit so marked a detachment from the problems, the currents of opinion, the pressures and tensions which characterize American life today. So complete is her detachment from the specifically contemporary and the transient as, occasionally, to perplex her readers. . . . In the case of so intelligent and meticulous a craftsman as Mrs. Rawlings, it is absurd to suppose that this detachment, and the rigorous exclusions which it imposes, are purely accidental. They are obviously dictated by a personal perception of life, by a concern for ultimate rather than relative values, and by an intention to present experience in its most simple and enduring forms.

To make this point is merely to suggest that Mrs. Rawlings is essentially a classicist, writing at a moment when the dominant accent of our fiction is romantic. Her work more closely resembles Miss Cather's *My Antonia,* or Mrs. Wharton's *Ethan Frome,* than it does the novels of Ernest Hemingway or Erskine Caldwell. But, although a classicist in her perception of life, she is a romantic in her literary endowment. Sensibility is its most impressive element, and imparts to Mrs. Rawlings's writing certain qualities more familiar in poetry than prose fiction.

Lloyd Morris. *NAR.* Autumn, 1938. p. 180

There is a deceiving simplicity about *Cross Creek,* a book of pleasant reminiscences of "a bend in a country road" by the sharply perceptive author of *The Yearling.* By the time you finish it you realize that it is more than the story of the people and flora and fauna of a backwoods community: it is a way of life—a way that smacks of Thoreau, without Thoreau's asceticism, for the author, while believing that nature possesses the secret of happiness, loves all sorts of people, and records their peculiarities of temper and dialect with zest and humor.

"I do not understand," she writes, "how anyone can live without some small place of enchantment to turn to." She herself has found her small place among the colored folk, the white folk, the magnolia trees, the hogs, and the waters of the "Yearling" country, and in this narrative of her sojourn there she reveals herself again as an extremely sensitive observer, who sees much that others do not and feels keenly about everything. It is as if color and sound and happiness and sorrow were all heightened for her, and she translates this brightness and sharpness for the reader.

Louis B. Salomon. *Nation.* March 21, 1942. p. 346

Cross Creek is in a sense an unclassifiable book. It is not a "local color" book. Nor would it fit into, although it might nudge the category of "Florida, Flora, and Fauna." It is not even a good sociological report. The Floyd family negate that possibility. No competent sociologist would admit into his records the fact that the Floyds thoroughly enjoyed belonging to the underprivileged class. Rather, and for the lack of anything better, Cross Creek would seem to be pure Marjorie Kinnan Rawlings. It's an autobiography. And for the sake of the record, it is necessary to add that Mrs. Rawlings does not make herself out either quaint, or amusing, or gay, or tragic. In *Cross Creek* she reveals herself as a good cook and an artist. That is an accomplishment, indeed, for one woman.

Carroll Munro. *SR.* April 4, 1942. p. 6

One does miss the lift of *The Yearling.* It was as if the earlier book were written out of the heart because the author *had* to write it. There are moments in *The Sojourner* which read like so many novels that appear today—as if the author felt that he must go ahead and finish it. Do not let me mislead you. Mrs. Rawlings is a skilled and able writer, and she has a good story to tell. The characters are, as they say, "well drawn," although at times one feels that she is laying on the whimsy a bit thick.

Louis Bromfield. *SR*. Jan. 3, 1953. p. 10

It is perhaps the author's joy in her work which carries through to the reader so strongly the vitality of the characters and the gusto one feels in their hard and dangerous lives. There is much hardship and sorrow and tragedy in the book [*The Yearling*], but here, possibly more than in any other of her books, Marjorie Rawlings has conveyed the quality of these people who drew her sympathy—their gallantry, their grace of spirit and the joy in living that they find in lives which appear, in the facts, to be merely bitter struggles for survival. . . .

It is clear that the scrub and the hammock and, above all, their inhabitants, the Florida Crackers, were the well-spring of Marjorie Rawlings' inspiration and the lodestone of her writing talent. The best of her writing is that which is close to this land and to these people whom she understood so deeply because of her love for them. Through her they have gained a place in the literature of their country, and through them that literature has been enriched by the achievement of an outstanding writer.

Julia Scribner Bigham. Introduction to *The Marjorie Rawlings Reader* (Scribner). 1956. pp. xviii–xix

See *The Yearling* (novel); *Cross Creek* (autobiography).

REED, JOHN (1887–1920)

Reed's real chance came when the Metropolitan Magazine sent him to Mexico. All his second-rate theory and propaganda seemed to fall away, and the public discovered that whatever John Reed could touch or see or smell he could convey. The variety of his impressions, the resources and color of his language seemed inexhaustible. . . .

Reed has no detachment, and is proud of it, I think. By temperament he is not a professional writer or reporter. He is a person who enjoys himself. Revolution, literature, poetry, they are only things which hold him at times, incidents merely of his living. Now and then he finds adventure by imagining it, oftener he transforms his own experience. He is one of those people who treat as serious possibilities such stock fantasies as shipping before the mast, rescuing women, hunting lions, or trying to fly around the world in an aeroplane. He is the only fellow I know who gets himself pursued by men with revolvers, who is always once more just about to ruin himself.

Walter Lippmann. NR. Dec. 26, 1914. p. 15

He is content to let the narrative [of *Ten Days That Shook the World*] flow on naturally and quietly, welded together by the hammer of relevant fact after relevant fact, in short paragraphs which frequently end in a tiny row of dots, a happy incorporation of the technique of Wellsian suggestiveness. Often he includes proclamations of the various parties and statements and speeches of the party leaders in the text itself, although the more important of the documentary material is included in an appendix which historians of the future will find as invaluable as the living observers of today. The story does not lack emotional thrill because of this deliberately chosen method of unemphatic presentation. If anything, it gains. Mr. Reed has taken only ten days of the Bolshevik Revolution—the vital ten days—with short glimpses before them and few after. Consequently there is some inevitable repetition. But the effect is cumulative. A picture of the state of mind which made the Bolsheviki uprising inevitable emerges gradually, with the outlines of the picture becoming sharper and sharper, until finally it stands forth etched with unforgetable definiteness.

Harold Stearns. Dial. March 22, 1919. p. 302

No ray of sunshine, no drop of foam, no young animal, bird, or fish, and no star, was as happy as that boy was. If only we could keep him so, we might have a poet at last who would see and sing nothing but joy. Convictions were what I was afraid of. I tried to steer him away from convictions, that he might play; that he might play with life; and see it all, love it all, live it all; tell it all; that he might be it all; but all, not any one thing. And why not? A poet is more revolutionary than any radical. Great days they were, or rather nights, when the boy would bang home late and wake me up to tell me what he had been and seen that day; the most wonderful thing in the world. Yes. Each night he had been and seen the most wonderful thing in the world.

He wrote some of those things. He became all of those things. He fell head over heels in love with every single one of those most wonderful things: with his job; with his friends; with labor; with girls; with strikes; with the I.W.W.; with socialism; with the anarchists; with the bums in the Bowery; with the theatre; with God and Man and Being.

Lincoln Steffens. The World of Lincoln Steffens,
edited by Ella Winter and Herbert Shapiro (Hill
and Wang). 1962. p. 236. [1920]

John Reed was so active in radical politics as to have too little time left for poetry; but in this place it is proper to record that his neglect of the art was accident and not intention. Like Jack London, he was always dreaming of tomorrow's masterpiece. Knowing himself for a poet, he hoped to prove his vocation by many poems worthy to endure; but life was so exciting, and the social struggle in these States and Mexico, in Finland, Russia—everywhere—so tempting to a fighting radical, that poetry had to wait for the leisure which—alas!—never came.

Harriet Monroe. *Poetry.* Jan., 1921. pp. 208–9

The glorious Jack turned his poetry into action, and died in the Russia which has honored him with a monument his own land should have erected. Most of our radicals seem pale pamphleteers and parlor intellectuals in comparison. It was Reed's secret ambition to return to poetry after the battle. He went down at a time when some of his Manhattan allies, wistfully yearning for freedom, began writing popular novels and Hollywood scenarios.

Alfred Kreymborg. *Our Singing Strength* (Coward-McCann). 1929. p. 469

Jack Reed I began to know for the first time; he had been away much of the four years I had been in New York. He was a great, husky, untamed youth of immense energies and infantine countenance, who had helped Elizabeth Gurley Flynn and Arturo Giovannitti organize the Paterson strike, had been arrested and jailed there, and then had organized the magnificent Paterson Strike Pageant in Madison Square Garden; he had been a war-correspondent with Villa in Mexico, and then in Europe reporting the World War, and then in Russia. Along the way he tossed off beautiful poems, and poetic plays, and stories full of a profound zest for life. He was adventurer and artist, playboy and propagandist.

Floyd Dell. *Homecoming* (Farrar and Rinehart). 1933. p. 397

It is no wonder that *Ten Days That Shook the World* is a great book. John Reed knew how to use his eyes: *Insurgent Mexico* had shown that. He knew all the tricks that a good newspaperman knows, and could think in terms of headlines as well as in terms of color and romance. And he had learned, slowly and resistingly, the value of accuracy and documentation, learned it at Ludlow and Bayonne and in the fight against war. He was perfectly trained for the task of reporting a revolution. But there was something more than that: he was a participant as well as an observer, and his book was a weapon as well as a report, all the more effective for its restraint and precision. In those three months that he spent bent over a typewriter, surrounded by his great piles of papers and pamphlets, he knew what he was doing: the world must be shaken again and again. . . .

Wherever Reed spoke to radical groups, he found that *Ten Days* was regarded as a kind of handbook of revolution. What did he care if Charles Edward Russell damned it in the New York *Times?* Passed from hand to hand, and read till the pages fell apart, the book was what he had wanted it to be—a weapon. "You are correct," he said, in his letter to the *Times,* "when you call information about Russia Bolshevik propaganda, for the great majority of persons who learn the truth about Russia become convinced Bolsheviki." The statement may have been extravagant, but it would not be easy to compute the number of persons whose interest in Communism dates from the reading of *Ten Days That Shook the World.*

Granville Hicks. *John Reed* (Macmillan). 1936.
pp. 325–6, 341

John Reed . . . was a swell bourgeois kid in a pioneering, well-to-do family out in young Portland, Oregon. He had a grandmother who indulged an aristocratic waywardness; and as we all know now, a brilliant socialite father who was an idle dude till called by a muckraker to a real job. He sent his boy, the revolutionary-to-be, to swell schools and to Harvard; the very worst. And the boy was not a "good student" except where his mind was interested and his muscles engaged. Then he became a pretty good sport and an eager student in a few lines, all for social success in the exclusive clubs, in the swell sets. When he came to New York, Jack was nothing but a bundle of fine nerves, bulging energy, overweening vanity and trembling curiosity, with an egotistical ambition to distinguish himself as a poet.

Lincoln Steffens. *Lincoln Steffens Speaking* (Harcourt).
1936. p. 309

Superficially Jack seemed the playboy *in excelsis.* . . . Only a few of us knew the slowly maturing man. This was the other Jack Reed, the sensitive young night-wanderer, the interpreter of Bowery dives and bread-lines, who wrote, "It didn't come to me from my books that the workers produced all the wealth of the world, which went to those who did not earn it." This was the probing realist, the disciple of Lincoln Steffens, who gave Jack his first assignment on a periodical with a national circulation; it was the propagandist off-guard, the recorder of heroic defeats, the poet. . . .

That was the Jack Reed I knew—at least that was part of him. The boisterousness and the quiet passion for truth, the insurgency and the integrity, never quite fused until his last phase (the real, not the romantic, revolutionist) when he wrote his masterpiece *Ten Days That Shook the World.*

Louis Untermeyer. *From Another World* (Harcourt).
1939. pp. 58, 62

We were carrying realism so far in those days that it walked us right out of our books. We had a certain scorn of books. We wanted to live our poetry. Jack Reed did especially. His comradeship with Louise Bryant was based on a joint determination to smash through the hulls of custom and tradition and all polite and proper forms of behavior, and touch at all times and all over the earth the raw current of life. It was a companionship in what philistines call adventure, a kind of gypsy compact. And that will to live, to be themselves in the world, and be real, and be honest, and taste the whole tang of it, was more to them than any writing. It was more to them than any particular practical undertaking, even a revolution. It was as though they had agreed to inscribe at least two audacious, deep, and real lives in the book of time and let the gods call it poetry.

Max Eastman. Heroes I Have Known (Simon). 1942. p. 213

Reed was elated when the Bolsheviki, activated by their determined and dominating leader Lenin, struck for political power. He tried to be everywhere at once, and shuttled between the two opposing forces in his wish to observe every move on both sides. He was being educated fast in the making of a revolution—by the only method he was able to assimilate: concrete action. When Lenin refused to compromise at a time when concession seemed inevitable, Reed was quicker to grasp his great generalship than many of the seasoned Bolsheviki. . . . Aware that the revolution was shaking the whole world, he assiduously collected data, figures, leaflets, newspapers, reports—every scrap of documentary evidence which recorded the progress of the epochal event. He was determined to record the greatest social cataclysm in modern history so faithfully and factually as to preclude any hostile attempt at distortion. That he was successful in his undertaking became evident after the publication in 1919 of *Ten Days That Shook the World*—still the best one-volume account of the Bolshevik Revolution.

Charles Madison. Critics and Crusaders (Holt). 1942.
pp. 521–2

Would he have been able to survive the fierce rivalries and intrigues in Moscow? Four years after his death, the work that was his greatest monument, *Ten Days That Shook the World,* became one of the storm centers in the struggle between Stalin and Trotsky. On one point in connection with the Bolshevik uprising of 1917, Trotsky had found confirmation in Reed's book. Stalin counter-attacked by charging that Reed had been "remote" from the Bolshevik party, that he had picked up hostile gossip from enemies, and had spread one of their "absurd rumors." It is hard to imagine Reed rallying to the defense of Stalin, who was virtually unknown to him in 1920 and who was moreover allied with Zinoviev in

1924 against Trotsky, whom Reed knew intimately and had portrayed as one of the greatest heroes of the Russian Revolution.

Death took him prematurely, not only as a human being but as a political symbol. The mystery of John Reed is what he would have done in the last act of his own life's drama. No one really knows, and everyone has written it differently in his or her own image.

Theodore Draper. *The Roots of American Communism*
(Viking). 1957. pp. 292–3

His sketches and stories written between 1913 and 1918—scenes from the Mexican revolution, New York Bowery life, the war in the Balkans—are sharply observed (he had a wide-ranging and retentive reporter's eye) and set down in the impressionistic or expressionistic manner of Stephen Crane. If they lack Crane's precision, his "long logic" and sad irony, and if they are sentimental and romantic where Crane is not, they reveal a sensitive and generously impulsive young man who sympathizes with the down-and-out. A touch of O. Henry can be detected here, a touch of the young Dos Passos. Reed, the gifted and upper-class young man has not yet identified himself completely or unself-consciously with the proletariat. He is still luxuriating in the colors and the paradoxes of the big city. His bums, prostitutes, revolutionaries, capitalists, Mexicans, Serbs are still "materials" to be exploited for their journalistic possibilities.

Daniel Aaron. *Writers on the Left* (Harcourt). 1961. p. 39

In fact, the outstanding pieces of writing in the book [*Echoes of Revolt: The Masses 1911–1917*] are John Reed's story of the famous textile strike in Paterson and his funny accounts of his run-ins with the cops. If only to remind us of what a first-rate journalist John Reed was, *The Masses* would be worth resurrecting, particularly since the conservatism of the last few decades has tended to bury not only the radical ideas but the radical figures of the past.

William Phillips. *NYR*. March 9, 1967. p. 8

See *Insurgent Mexico, Ten Days That Shook the World* (reporting).

REXROTH, KENNETH (1905–   )

At his best, he is a simple-minded man, with a liking for outdoors, in particular the high Sierra, and a decent reverence for nature and the stars. Of these he writes well; his observation is direct and immediate, leading him to the true line—"The stone is clean as light, the light steady as stone." . . . Mr. Rexroth's other aspect, the erudite indoor ponderer over

many and difficult texts is less deserving of encouragement. . . . For his
poetry's sake he would be well advised . . . to beat out of his head the
idea that . . . abstractions, whether simple or involute, are the serviceable
material of poetic art.

Rolfe Humphries. NR. Aug. 12, 1940. p. 221

Rexroth owes a great deal to the early Ezra Pound. Imagism, D. H.
Lawrence . . . and the Chino-Japanese lyricists are other discernible influences. . . . Which is not to say that Rexroth is not Rexroth. He has made
a style, and an instantly recognizable one, out of the most tenuous elements. But its classicism, the rather self-conscious sensuality expressed in
an equally self-conscious avoidance of rhetoric, is not what makes the
poetry come to life. This spark is provided by observation, the delight in
what used to be called Nature, and the choice of the appropriate word to
express that delight.

Selden Rodman. NYHT. May 7, 1950. p. 22

Rexroth is one of the leading craftsmen of the day. There is in him no
compromise with the decayed line of past experience. His work is cleanly
straightforward. The reek of polluted Shakespeare just isn't in it, or him.
. . . As verse, reading them through, the plays (in *Beyond the Mountain*)
are a delight to me for the very flow of words themselves. The pith is there,
don't mistake me, and there with a jolt to it (in the very line, I want to
make it clear) that goes well below the surface. But the way of the writing
itself is the primary attraction. It palls, at times, I acknowledge it, but that
is the defect of the method. It does not falsify. It is a feat of no mean proportions to raise the colloquial tone to lines of tragic significance.

William Carlos Williams. NYT. Jan. 28, 1951. p. 5

Anything Kenneth Rexroth writes is worth reading. He has a directness,
a virile imaginative power, a seeming self-sufficiency rare among contemporary poets. As it does upon all men so the law of compensation
operates upon him, and Rexroth's virtues as poet are liable also to exhibit
overdoses of flat prosiness, traces of immature exhibitionism in the virile
power, and occasional slapdash carelessness in the self-sufficiency. But
take him by and large, he is one of our contemporary poets whose work
is always interesting to read. (If that sounds like mild praise, such is not
my intention: consider how seldom one can apply it.)

Winfield Townley Scott. NYHT. Feb. 1, 1953. p. 8

It is as though in Rexroth we had a Mark Twain who had grown up; who,
without yielding an iota of his sense of the absurd and the pitiful, had
discarded the clown's motley for the darker dress of the comic philos-

opher; and who had miraculously been endowed with the power of making poetry. This account (*The Dragon and the Unicorn*) of Rexroth's travels in England, Wales, France, Italy, and so on operates on many levels of which the surface one—narrative, anecdote, description—though the most entertaining, is the least ponderable. It is an indictment of society. It is an indictment of—well, not so much what America is doing to Europe, as what the whole of Western civilization is doing to itself. The *J'accuse!* is unanswerable.

Dudley Fitts. NR. Feb. 9, 1953. p. 19

Rexroth has invented a form with some help from Pound and Williams of short lines without rhyme. It is hard as prose and lithe as lyric. The combination, with an individualistic and controlled rhythm, makes it possible for the author to sustain his matter indefinitely.

The perfection of this new medium is striking. It enables Rexroth to express his most subtle philosophical generalizations, his strongest passions, the multifarious nature of his ideas with a kind of absolute accuracy. The lines are hard and clear, precise and lean, with continuous tensile strength and nothing fuzzy.

Richard Eberhart. NYT. Feb. 15, 1953. p. 25

I, for one, no longer object to this kind of plain, tight metrical practice as much as I did when discovering the great verbal musicians of our age. It has a good deal of variety of its own and is as essential a medium for his feeling as Cummings' syntactical whoopla for his, or Stevens' whimsical extravagance for his. If Rexroth sells short the more elaborate traditions, he does so consciously, and with a born affinity for other traditions no less important to the health of poetry. Rexroth's California, like Winters' and Jeffers', is a tradition in itself, a well-loved fastness from which a poet can hurl transcontinental thunderbolts at anything and everything that gets between him and the sun.

R. W. Flint. NR. Feb. 18, 1957. p. 19

The poetry of self-exploration, which usually comes early, came late in Rexroth's writing career. It is retrospective in character. . . . Elegies and epistles. Memories of his first wife, Andrée, who died young. Reliving their love in memory, trying to bridge the sense of separation with unmailable letters. . . . Trying to relate the personal experience to the social experience. . . . Trying to convince himself that in abandoning the "social" poem . . . or the "public speech" . . . he was still performing the function of the social poet. . . . And arriving at the "religious anarchism" which he would have us believe has been "the point of view . . . in all my work" from the beginning.

Lawrence Lipton. Poetry. June, 1957. pp. 173–4

Kenneth Rexroth is the strongest of the West Coast anarchist poets because he is a good deal more than a West Coast anarchist poet. He is a man of wide cultivation and, when he is not too busy shocking the bourgeois reader . . . , a genuine poet. If fate had made Rexroth a Mormon or a Rhode Island Republican lawyer, he would still be able to write excellent poems. . . . Almost everything I have ever read by Rexroth has been worth reading, even when he was indulging himself, even when the piece was only half-finished, and even when he was both wrong and wrongheaded.

M. L. Rosenthal. *Nation.* Sept. 28, 1957. pp. 199–200

The fineness of Kenneth Rexroth's *In Defense of Earth* depends on several virtues which are rare in this year but which are apparent in almost every one of the Rexroth poems: a lyric-minded-ness that has been prepared by many disciplines to summon up its music; a learning that eats the gifts of the world, knowing . . . how many cultures must be drawn on to make human fare; and that quality which has been talked about so much in speaking of Kenneth Rexroth and of those he has known in San Francisco: rage. . . . There is little enough control around anywhere this year, and less commitment. The sound of commitment comes through as the voice of anger. . . . Kenneth Rexroth is dealing with the plans of women and men in these magnificent poems, which are harsh, full of grace and certainty and grief: poems of the mountain nights.

Muriel Rukeyser. *SR.* Nov. 9, 1957. p. 15

Rexroth's poetry is in a much older tradition than that of American individualist ecstasy, which he shares in to some extent with Whitman, Hart Crane, and William Carlos Williams. His main tradition is a less provincial one than that, a less strident and ambitious one than that, and one much less prone to artificial supercharging of the sort given it recently by the so-called "Beat" poets. I don't know quite how to name it, except to call it the *personal* or *humane* tradition of lyric poetry—from the tragedy and passion and humor of the late Roman and Mediaeval lyric poets to the pathos and sweetness and dignity of the classic Japanese. Perhaps I am only saying that Rexroth is a fine universal lyric poet whose work has affinities with much of the best lyric poetry of the past. He is no barbaric yawper, as I had always believed. . . .

Perhaps the truly essential Rexroth is found in the love poems. Almost all of his good poems could be said to be love poems. From the sweetly reserved translations of Chinese and Japanese poems, to Rexroth's own intense, free-flowing poems, the theme is love. Love—the recognition of mortality, the turning of the seasons and the great, silently commentative drift of the constellations overhead, and the stepping forth into full, intense, imaginative reality of mortal persons, lover, wife, child, and friend.

(K)   Richard Foster. *MinnR*. Spring, 1962. pp. 378, 381

We are likely to approach this book [*An Autobiographical Novel*] thinking of Rexroth as "the last of the great Bohemians," associating him with the new apology for jazz and its marriage to poetry, remembering his splendid renderings of Japanese and Chinese short poems as part of the revival of Zen, even considering him a kind of uneasy father to the post-1955 Beat Renaissance—in short, to regard him not only as a veteran swinger but as a contemporary, whatever his nominal age. Yet the forces that cut him off from certain key experiences of his own generation have left him utterly disapproving of, if not entirely isolated from, the contemporary scene. . . .

For whatever the blindnesses of *An Autobiographical Novel,* it is a fascinating record of a world which, even if it once existed, can scarcely be credited any more: the world of the isolated provincial Bohemia where the second-rate, embarrassed by no great talents, can live out the parable of the freedom of art, in a way that it is hard to live it out in great centers or in the presence of the supremely gifted.

(K)   Leslie Fiedler. *NYHT*. March 6, 1966. p. 10

Being a skeptical and conservative fellow, I couldn't help wondering whether Mr. Rexroth was laying it all on a bit thick [in *An Autobiographical Novel*]. So, as we happen to live in the same town, I called on him and asked him bluntly if he was a liar. He said no, he wasn't, and went on to tell me several stories that he'd left out of the book. During an evening of delightful and rambling conversation, he told me several things about my home town in England which I didn't know, including the name of the family who ran the place back in Tudor times and some details about the rood screen in the cathedral. On the basis of this and other aspects of our conversation, I was obliged to conclude that Mr. Rexroth did experience all the events he describes. He himself maintains that the variety was only possible because the social structure in the West was then so open and because it was easy to drift into what would now be much more tightly guarded groups.

As an account of that free-swinging period, Rexroth's reminiscences make valuable social history. One reviewer has castigated him for arrogance, but I consider that unfair. Writing as one of nature's onlookers, I salute him for his energy, for the catholicity of his interests, and for his formidable memory.

(K)   Sarel Eimerl. *Reporter*. May 19, 1966. p. 62

Reading through all of Kenneth Rexroth's shorter poems is a little like immersing oneself in the literary history of the last 40 years; for Rexroth experimented with almost all of the poetic techniques of the time, dealt, at least in passing, with all of its favorite themes.

One moves through imagist lyrics, Chinese and Japanese forms, surreal constructions, poems intended to be read against the improvisations of jazz combos, other poems intended to be sung to the tune of folk ballads, poems influenced by Apollinaire and poems that influenced, one assumes, Ferlinghetti, Ginsberg and Corso. In a great many of the poems, Rexroth makes clear just how he stands on social issues. . . .

And yet to read Rexroth in this way is to miss the heart of the man. For in spite of all of his restless literary experimentation and his obvious concern with the way of the world, he finds very early a technique that he returns to again and again—a rather flat statement, usually in short lines and very often in short poems; and a subject matter that can belong to no one else: himself and the women he has loved—his mother, his wives and, in recent poems, his daughters.

(K)   John Unterecker. *NYT*. July 23, 1967. p. 8

See *Signature of All Things, The Dragon and the Unicorn, In Defense of Earth, Natural Numbers* (poetry); *Behind the Mountain* (verse plays); *Bird in the Bush, Assays* (essays); *An Autobiographical Novel*.

RICE, ELMER (1892–1967)

Plays

Mr. Rice's vision of the world may infuriate you. . . . You cannot miss it; you cannot withdraw yourself from its coherence and completeness. Examine his plays (*The Adding Machine*) scene by scene, symbol by symbol. The structure stands. There are no holes in its roof. It gives you the pleasure of both poetry and science, the warm beauty of life and love, the icy delight of mathematics. I am aware of the fact . . . that my profound sympathy with Mr. Rice's substance necessarily colored my reaction to his play. Not, however, to its form, not to the heartening fact that here is an American drama with no loose ends or ragged edges or silly last-act compromises, retractions, reconciliations. The work, on its own ground, in its own mood, is honest, finished, sound.

Ludwig Lewisohn. *Nation*. April 4, 1923. p. 399

Street Scene is, at bottom, conventional in form. Yet the swift, accurate, quickly changing manner of its acting, the finely adopted setting which shadows it and gives it an exciting unity, and the genius of the direction—Mr. Rice did this job himself—make it as new as even the very best of the downright stylized experiments. *Street Scene* proves what many of us have long suspected, that a new form in itself may not be a creation at all, that a traditional form, hammered and polished and fused in a white heat of imagination . . . will glow with as new a light as the wildest expedition into constructivism, expressionism, or any other rebellion born in the travail of dramatic experiment in Berlin or Moscow.

Robert Littell. *TA*. March, 1929. pp. 164–5

In everything he has written—melodrama, smart drama, expressionist drama, realist drama, he has shown himself a perfect technician. . . . With this equipment, and the gradual deepening of purpose which is evident through his writing, it is not idle to expect that Elmer Rice's major work in the theatre is yet to be done. The least that he can give is a chronicle of American scenes done in an American way, a procession of characters whose externals of manner and speech are perfectly reproduced. . . , but in his latter plays he has given evidence that he has the power to quicken these characters with the kind of life that makes "pure music" out of "program music."

Meyer Levin. *TA*. Jan., 1932. p. 62

In contrast to *Street Scene* which was universal, Elmer Rice's latest play, *We, the People,* is of a particular day and mood. It is vibrantly of the present moment, almost hysterically so at times. It is a play of angry and ironic protest against the broader aspects of social injustice in times like these and against special and particular forms of injustice and hypocrisy. Hot fury runs through it like a fever, the more so because delusions are often mixed with realities and half truths with honest statements of fact. The delusions and half-truths concern chiefly the inner motives of some of the leading characters. The honest facts relate to happenings recorded with tragic monotony in every edition of every newspaper. . . . The play provides a stirring experience, and makes an appeal, no matter how prejudiced it may seem, to the fires of self-examination which are slowly kindling beneath the agony of our day.

Richard Dana Skinner. *Com*. Feb. 8, 1933. p. 411

As art *We, the People* has now and again precisely the limitations that Mr. Rice's plays have often had. I am surprised that so many judgments of the new piece have turned on the talking, the haranguing, the raw statement of causes and thoughts. This is what Mr. Rice did in *Street Scene* and in *The Left Bank,* though the love story and the various esthetic considerations eased the tedium of a lack of creation in the dramatist. . . . This talk without creation appeared and heavily, in the young heroine's long speech in the last act of *Street Scene,* and almost constantly in *The*

Left Bank. As a matter of fact, the new play has less of it, what with the push of the many scenes to be presented.

Stark Young. NR. Feb. 15, 1933. p. 19

With *Two on an Island* Mr. Rice, I think, resumes his place among the best of our comic writers, along with the Messrs. Behrman, Barry, and Kaufman. . . . Neither the comic insight nor the wit of Mr. Rice is like that of any of the others, and it rests, one might say, on a broader base, derives from the spirit of a larger mass of people. It is not merely that his favorite characters are landladies, taxi drivers, and the like, persons whose knowingness is combined with an innocent unsophistication. It is also that the whole flavor of his writing is more robust, more earthly, less narrowly local, and less highly specialized in spirit if not in manner. Of the four he is the most inclusively American, and without him the quartet would represent far less completely than it does the comic spirit of this nation.

Joseph Wood Krutch. Nation. Feb. 3, 1940. p. 136

Elmer Rice is a heavy-set man with reddish hair who does not look anywhere near fifty-one. A serious, conscientious person, he still has a lot of humor—the wry, understated kind—and his quietness makes it hard to imagine him ever blowing up about anything. Nevertheless he has always been mixed up in controversies; he is a great man for taking a stand about anything, from the destructive influence of the critics on the theatre to world problems of today. . . . Politically Elmer Rice has always been firmly and vocally to the Left. Which is consistent, because it would be odd if a man who has always been a persistent experimentalist in art forms should turn out to be, ideologically, a conservative.

Elizabeth R. Valentine. NYT mag. Sept. 12, 1943. p. 15

Elmer Rice in *Dream Girl* has broken away from his usual preoccupation with the state of the nations to contemplate fondly, and at great length, the naive charms of a sweet young thing as she wrestles with her adolescent problems. . . . Mr. Rice plays exclusively with the surface of this young girl's mind. She is not asleep; she is merely indulging in the kind of futile and entirely volitional day dreaming to which we are all prone. She fancies herself in all sorts of heroic attitudes—a prisoner in the dock, a prostitute, a great actress reciting the "quality of mercy" speech. As a result the play is a tour-de-force in quick changes and continuous action but it lacks psychological and emotional content.

Rosamond Gilder. TA. Feb., 1946. pp. 78–9

In the half-bakery of Broadway, the belated recognition of the science of psychiatry usually results in a kind of convention of disorder the moment the faculty of imagination (healthy or otherwise) is summoned by one or other members of a cast. Immediately, enormous, unidentifiable, tenanted, visions—often in the form of ballets—are sprung out of nowhere and swirled and swooped for no discernible reason other than ART, one supposes, or POETRY, or some equivalent miscalculation. In his depiction of a heroine who spends a long day largely dreaming it, while Mr. Rice has given himself almost unlimited opportunities for flight and figment, he has, I think, got off on the right foot. Beginning with *character,* his fantasies are naturally ordered: the dreams fit into the day so to speak; there are no figurations too alarming, interesting, or expensive for the size of the figurer; all the shadows are owned. If the case-history seems somewhat simple, nevertheless it is true, and its people are alive.

Kappo Phelan. *Com.* Feb. 15, 1946. p. 457

In his middle years Mr. Rice was such a generative force in so many aspects of the theater that now it is difficult to remember that for 15 years Broadway did not take him seriously. In 1914 when he was in his early 20's and had just passed a civil service examination in proofreading, he wrote a courtroom play, *On Trial,* that told its story in terms of flashbacks. The technique was new. Much to the surprise of an inexperienced young man, the play was produced and became a fabulous success.

Mr. Rice assumed that he had become part of an established trade, but nine years went by before he had his second success—*The Adding Machine,* his first serious play and now a classic; and his most famous play, *Street Scene,* was rejected by most of Broadway's producers before William Brady accepted it in 1929. The director had so little faith in it that he deserted during the rehearsals and Mr. Rice had to direct it himself. It was the first of his many jobs as director. His play won the Pulitzer Prize for that season. After 15 years he had compelled Broadway to accept him on his own terms.

(K)   Brooks Atkinson. *NYTd.* May 9, 1967. p. 1

Novels

Here in a satire (*Voyage to Purilia*) which is both nimble-witted and pervasive, and which at times attains the implacable complexity of a nightmare, the author of *Street Scene* pays his respects to that planet known to astronomers as Purilia, where life is so utterly different from that of earth as to be almost incomprehensible. Not since Merton of the Movies announced that his wife was his best pal and his severest critic has there been anything as detached and scarifying as this excursion into the unplumbed vacuity of the celluloid. This is satire of a high order, so high that it at times suggests the Golden Ass of Apuleius.

John Carter. *NYT.* March 23, 1930. p. 2

Mr. Elmer Rice's *Voyage to Purilia* is an amusing satire on the American film. It is a short book, gracefully and gaily written. Mr. Rice, according to his diary, sets off in an aeroplane for the undiscovered country, known to no terrestial map, where cinema scenarios come into being. From the first moment when he gets among the "soft, pink mists" and the unceasing sentimental music that surround the new planet, until the moment when his Purilian bride, much to his disappointment, dissolves on the altar steps in the Nirvana of a fade-out, there is no experience known to humanity, and yet there is no situation or sentiment that is not an admired commonplace of the movies.

Hubert Griffith. NSN. Sept. 27, 1930. p. 764

The theatre novel is traditionally a bête noir. . . . Now, in *The Show Must Go On,* Elmer Rice has done very well with the subject. And what could be more appropriate, for he can write as one in authority and not as the scribe. This makes his story, apart from its other qualities, as complete and clinical a primer of how our American theatre runs in its every aspect as any aspirant thereto could desire. It reveals, also, the lofty concept of the theatre artist's obligation to his craft that has always distinguished Mr. Rice and made him one of the most constructive, as well as gifted, people in it. . . . He does not write a distinguished prose but in most other respects, such as characterization and dialogue and story sense, his talents as dramatist carry over into the narrative medium.

Edmund Fuller. SR. Oct. 15, 1949. p. 15

His least friendly contemporaries—and Mr. Rice has had his share of them, his temperament being what it is—never accused him of failing to say what was on his mind. Nor will they charge him with changing his ways in this autobiography [*Minority Report*] to which he turned as he neared the age of 70. Well, yes, he may be somewhat mellower now than he was in his frequently embattled prime. He says as much toward the end of his chronicle: he wishes that he might have been "less egotistical, less opinionated, less caustic, less irritabie, less impatient, less intolerant." He surely means this, but it is not so certain that he would have been the valuable citizen and artist if he had been less opinionated, less caustic, etc.

(K)   John K. Hutchens. *NYHT*. Aug. 18, 1963. p. 5

Rice has produced a remarkable body of work—large, varied, experimental, and honest. It ranges from frivolous entertainment to intense seriousness, from irony to pathos, from photographic realism to stark stylization. The best of it truthfully documents almost fifty years of American life; it castigates the follies, it expresses the confusions; and it suggests the remedies for many of the ills which have beset free men of good will in the twentieth century. In a theatre whose most currently prominent voices are the negative ones of a Williams or an Albee, the affirmations of Rice may be unpopular, but they will also be valuable.

(K)   Robert Hogan. *The Independence of Elmer Rice*
(Southern Illinois). 1965. p. 150

See *The Adding Machine, Street Scene, Counsellor-at-Law, Dream Girl* (plays); *Voyage to Purilia, The Show Must Go On* (novels); *Minority Report* (autobiography).

RICH, ADRIENNE (1929–   )

Miss Rich at 21 is a poet thoroughly trained by masters of verse whom she echoes at times but never slavishly. Thanks to her search for perfection she has composed her poems with an almost flawless perception and sound ear. While one might say that she belongs to an age in which youth is skeptical of a world unmade by tottering elders, she is clearly aware of the artist's place in society, and this without special pleading or self-defenses. She is, in short, the kind of neo-classic poet who relies on true form. In this she resembles another young poet, somewhat older than herself, the perfectionist Richard Wilbur.

Alfred Kreymborg. *NYT*. May 13, 1951. p. 27

Adrienne Cecile Rich is distinguished by her uncanny ability to write. Again and again her poetry communicates the peculiar excitement of exactness. Young poets of talent generally have one of two flaws; either they are afflicted with every kind of clumsiness, and must have their poems weeded clear of dead metaphors, extra feet, clichés, and dishonest rhetoric; either that, or they are gifted with easy competence and are plagued by not always sounding quite like themselves. Adrienne Cecile Rich falls into the second category, but she does not fall far. It is easy to greet several of her poems with familiarity: "How do you do, Mr. Frost? And you, Mr. Auden?" But even if one should decide to dismiss these poems (which would be foolish), there would be many left to which one could attach no name but the author's own.

The Diamond Cutters is Miss Rich's second volume, and it is superior to *A Change of World*. The earlier book was sometimes tame, and even a little smug about its ability to keep experience away from the door. In the second book, the wolf is inside and is busy writing poems about its successful campaign.

Donald Hall. *Poetry*. Feb., 1956. p. 301

Everybody thinks young things young, Sleeping Beauty beautiful—and the poet whom we see behind the clarity and gravity of Miss Rich's poems cannot help seeming to us a sort of princess in a fairy tale. Her scansion, even, is easy and limpid, close to water, close to air; she lives nearer to perfection (an all-too-easy, perfection, sometimes—there are a few of Schubert's pieces that are better the first time than they ever are again, and some of Miss Rich's poems are like this) than ordinary poets do, and her imperfections themselves are touching as the awkwardness of anything young and natural is touching. The reader feels that she has only begun to change; thinks, "This young thing, who knows what it may be, old?" Some of her poems are very different from the others, some of her nature is very far from the rest of it, so that one feels that she has room to live in and to grow out into; liking her for what she is is a way of liking her even better for what she may become.

Randall Jarrell. *YR*. Autumn, 1956. p. 100

Lynn Fontanne is said to speak our tongue without accent—neither British nor American, but "standard" English. Even so Adrienne Rich, and as in Miss Fontanne's case, there is nothing dull about decorum, nothing impersonal about propriety (indeed, the word means ownership), nothing weak about womanliness. The earlier work in *Snapshots of a Daughter-in-law,* fabricated on the careful loom responsible for the poems in Adrienne Rich's first two books, interest me most, though I can see that in the later pieces she is doing something new, generating a tenser tone, beyond cosiness, and the energy of this reaching style must stand surrogate for the knowingness of her past poems that seemed to be possessed of an effortless control. Naturally such ease is the triumph of hard work, a kind of verbal topiary, and its reward, as in the two most ambitious pieces of this collection, the title poem and "Readings of History," is a freedom, a sense of possibility apparently unhampered by even the strongest awareness of personal limitation.

Richard Howard. *Poetry*. July, 1963. pp. 258–9

. . . Adrienne Rich's *Snapshots of a Daughter-in-Law* . . . makes it evident that she is more than the able and delicate poetess some of her neat poems have implied. She has a hard vision and restlessness in the confines of her forms which save her from the monotony sometimes resulting from rather neutral language and standard versification. She hasn't the elegance of, say, Richard Wilbur in managing her stanzas and rhymes, nor the vitality and surprise of May Swenson. But she is more relentless than either in working at ragged human feelings, in catching the quality of our senseless isolation as we ride the random tide of history.

Judson Jerome. *SR*. July 6, 1963. p. 31

Adrienne Rich has grown steadily more interesting from book to book and now in her fourth work, *Necessities of Life,* this advance, tortuous and sometimes tortured as it has been, is an arrival, a poised and intact completion. . . .

From the beginning, there was a yearning, a straining onward, a sense of disproportion between the life of looking and the life of living, tremors of discontent running through a style perhaps too beautiful and contented. After the perfection of *The Diamond Cutters* her work became in *Snapshots of a Daughter-in-law* more reckless. The opening poems are gnarled, sketchy and obscure. They read like jottings in a notebook, and looked like frayed threads in a spider web. Sometimes we seemed to be watching the terrible and only abstractly imaginable struggle of a beetle to get out of its beetle shell and yet remain a beetle.

Robert Lowell. *NYT*. July 17, 1966. p. 5

The dominating quality of Adrienne Rich's work, the quality which knits all, sound, syntax, and sense, into a marvelous unitary structure, is what she herself calls "fierce attention." . . . Other words have been used for it—compression, concern, concentration—and none is exactly right; but the poetry shows what it is: a need not simply to confront experience—in this book [*Necessities of Life*] the experience, disconcerting enough, of a woman who is an artist—not simply to exclaim over it, to apostrophize it (one thinks of Sylvia Path), but to *solve* it; to make it come right. This is a small book, but compact. There is not a glib word in it, nor a wasted breath. The poems stand like the stones of Arizona, singly and distinct, some taller than others, all eroded; but with the natural resolution—balance, place, hardness—of stone.

Hayden Carruth. *Poetry*. Jan., 1967. p. 267

See *A Change of World, The Diamond Cutters, Snapshots of a Daughter-in-Law, Necessities of Life* (poems).

RICHTER, CONRAD (1890–1968)

Mr. Richter, unmoved by the stormier phases of frontier life, is attracted by small authenticities, by the unaffected kindliness of simple people who face life with bare hands, by a sort of temperature refinement which is characteristic of isolated people, by a romanticism which sees something vague and incomprehensible in the daily walk, by the pathos which hangs about those who play a lone hand.

It must be a careless reader who fails to realize that here is an admirably trained intellect with fine perception of character reproducing impressions of life; not the life of today, but of a past neglected by historians and enshrined in forgotten newspapers.

Charles J. Finger. *SR*. Aug. 8, 1936. p. 7

Though there is a slight element . . . of sententious platitudinizing . . . there is much more than that. There is research, sincerity, imagination and beauty of writing. It is escape literature of a high-class sort . . . that is, it sets the mind free and refreshes it with images and figures from an innocent, half legendary world; a world as far removed from us as if it were another planet, but real all the same, and comforting as rain in a parched land. . . . Richter makes skilful use of his evidently profound historical studies, and the picture of pioneer life he builds up is extraordinarily concentrated, detailed and vivid.

Rosamond Lehmann. *Spec*. May 17, 1940. p. 694

Mr. Richter has hoarded up every savorous and homely detail of the life of the early nineteenth century . . . and now pours them out. The result is as American as goldenrod or Indian pudding. . . . (His novels are) written with infinite care to make the atmosphere and background authentic and convincing. The furniture and utensils in the cabin, the phrases of the dialogue, the hymns sung at the prayer meeting—all seem just right. But one might admire Mr. Richter for his exactitude on these points and still not count him a good novelist. However he does succeed in making the stuff of life flow in the veins of most of the people who inhabit these careful settings of his.

Theodore M. Purdy. *SR*. April 13, 1946. p. 72

In his handling of the past Conrad Richter is an artist in prose. His short, compact novels demonstrate the fact that story-telling need not be subordinated to documentation of history, for reality of the imagination can be made more compelling than the appearance of fact. To him a story is always a record of human experience, regardless of time or setting. In short, he has been writing novels while other and more popular writers were turning out sword-and-musket romances or historical theses dressed up as fiction.

Dayton Kohler. *EJ*. September, 1946. p. 364

Conrad Richter has been steadily piling up a record for solid and distinguished achievement. His writing is distinguished and poetic both as to character and image. It is intensely atmospheric and backed in the case of the historical novels on sound research. Moreover he has the supreme gift of novelists in creating a world of utter reality in which the reader is able to lose himself completely after the first page or two.

Louis Bromfield. *NYHT*. April 23, 1950. p. 5

In 1928 Conrad Richter, thirty-eight years old and all his novels yet unwritten, moved from Pennsylvania to New Mexico. The Southwest was not wholly new to him; from early boyhood he had heard tales of New Mexico from relatives who had lived there in territorial times. And having moved two thousand miles away, he did not forget his ancestral country. As a writer he found himself inhabiting both backgrounds and looking back to a vanished past: to the late eighteenth century in the Allegheny frontier and to the late nineteenth century in New Mexico. The two lands, so unlike to the senses, he found alike in their demands upon the people who would possess them and in the opportunity they offered for bold, far-reaching actions. . . . To both his eastern and western frontier settings Conrad Richter brings a chivalrous respect. The great forest and the high plains are the frontiersman's adversaries, and at the same time they are his magnificent birthright.

Walter Havighurst. *SR*. May 25, 1957. p. 14

. . . Richter's New Mexico books are not as big as the Ohio novels; they are deliberately smaller in compass and design. In each separate novel of the Ohio trilogy there is a strong, free, natural flow of life. The Southwestern novels are problem stories, tighter, more complicated, less reflective. Yet they are always lyrical, evoking the moods of the land and the commitments of its people. . . . To both his eastern and western frontier settings Conrad Richter brings a chivalrous respect. The great forest and the high plains are the frontiersman's adversaries, and at the same time they are his magnificent birthright.

(K)   Walter Havighurst. *SR*. May 25, 1957. p. 14

. . . his trilogy of the Pennsylvania-Ohio border—*The Trees, The Fields,* and *The Town*—has few parallels as a fictional record of early establishment, and the magnificently drawn pioneer heroine of these books, Sayward Luckett Wheeler, is challenged only by O. E. Rolvaag's Beret Holm. . . .

But although his historical trilogy is his most distinguished work to date, he is limited neither by one region nor by one fictional type. The three novels about middle western settlement are specific, documentary, and detailed, although their canvas is rather small. But his fiction about the Southwest is atmospheric, dramatic, and episodic. His four books of stories about his adopted environment are as authentic and vivid as his studies of Pennsylvania and Ohio life, yet they are different in tone and even technique. Remembering Hawthorne's distinction [between novel and romance], one is tempted to call them romances despite the fact that the old term is now obsolete.

(K)   John T. Flanagan. *SWR*. Summer, 1958. pp. 189–90

So John Donner [in *The Waters of Kronos*] moves on the edges of a life long since gone, seeing people and scenes as they were and not as memory would have them, probing deeply into "the dream that others called reality." The climax of John Donner's awareness comes when he solves the perennial father-son antagonism, the myth of rebellion and hatred: it is that the fear of the father is one's instinctive fear of "the older self to come."

The Waters of Kronos is a brilliantly evocative treatment of past and present, sensitive and reflective. Mr. Richter begs off a bit at the end when it comes to a final reconciling of the literal and figurative. Perhaps he merely pushes that reconciliation to the page just after the last one, the page that every reader of this book will write for himself.

(K)   Riley Hughes. *CW*. July, 1960. p. 254

Indeed, [*A Simple Honorable Man*] is hardly a novel in the conventional sense at all, but rather a loosely sketched portrait of the truly spiritual man; a man not without faults, who yet achieves a large measure of the grace of God. We see in him, perhaps, a reflection of the recent past, where such achievement was easier, rather than a guide to a future in which the conditions for moral survival are complex and sophisticated.

This "frontier quality" of the American past is the mine that Richter has worked in all his books, and while he has not glorified it beyond recognition, he does select those aspects which we like to think of as representing the best in our heritage. Simplicity and honor are certainly among them.

(K)   •   David Dempsey. *SR*. April 28, 1962. p. 19

What is not clearly evident in these early stories, but what is an important aspect of all of his thinking, is his nostalgia for his ancestors and his own youth, and with this, a nostalgia for America's past. It is easy to see the basis for this interest in a time and race gone by. Even ordinary people who have died take on a somewhat heroic stature in our memories. Through story and research he uncovered in the American past a breed of giants that satisfied his deep desire for an image of man as hard working and persevering, as a force which triumphed over adversity. . . . In the work of Conrad Richter, choosing the more difficult way always leads to success. . . . Conrad Richter has never written a novel which does not have as one of its themes the American pioneer's struggle and resultant strength.

(K)   Marvin J. LaHood. *UR*. Summer, 1964. p. 313

Richter is one of America's most autobiographical writers. Whether he is writing of his own time or of the past, he draws largely on personal experience—either that of himself or of his family and other persons he has known. But for his historical fiction he has added to materials obtained from these oral sources those gleaned from old documents, letters, newspapers. The use of the familiar, of course, is not inherently meritorious. To the contrary, it can result (as occasionally it does for Richter) in a tendency toward sentimentality. Too, it can lead (as it does not for Richter) toward didacticism. The real significance of Richter's dependence on the familiar is that it has turned him toward an introspection that prompts his works to veer more often than generally recognized toward the mystical and mythical.

Again, the indulgence in mysticism and myth, especially for the mere sake of esotericism, fails to distinguish a writer. What does merit acclaim is the successful attempt to utilize mysticism and myth to find new forms for the novel and new concepts of man and history. But to suggest that Richter has thus succeeded would be to misrepresent his accomplishment. For the mysticism and myth with which he works are not new but conventional: the alienation from the earthly and Spiritual fathers and the subsequent search for reconciliation, and the assumption of guilt; and the myths of the making of the American racial unconscious; and time and individual identity.

(K)   Edwin W. Gaston. *Conrad Richter* (Twayne).
                                                                    1965. p. 153

The Trilogy—The Trees, The Fields, The Town

Mr. Richter's indubitable learning is worn so lightly that one has no sense at all that this is a "historical" novel or that its people are playing character parts in a costume play. You feel them as individuals, some of whom lived by the forest; others, to subdue it; and still others to be killed by it. In a setting so alien that it is hard for city folks to realize it, he shows movingly what were those other ways in which these Americans found joy, terror, and satisfaction in living, in which they earned their livelihood, showed their love of family and home.

                                    Mary Ross. *NYHT*. March 3, 1940. p. 2

Mr. Richter saw his trilogy, both structurally and humanly, in the shape of one of those trees, the fate which symbolizes the entire progress in Sayward's mind. *The Trees,* in which Sayward must turn mother and father to her brothers and sisters in their forest hut, is a kind of trunk to the whole, a direct and simple tale of a life narrow and strong and dark. In *The Fields,* with the coming of neighbors and clearings, and the development of Sayward's own life as wife and actual mother, there is a branching out of purposes and interests and a brightening of atmosphere.

And now, in *The Town,* the longest and most complex story of the three, comes the leafing out of the many who flourish better in the sun of man's laws than in the primeval gloom of nature's.

Walter Van Tilburg Clark. *NYT.* April 23, 1950. p. 4

Like all good works of fiction Conrad Richter's fiction means different things to different people. Simply stated, his trilogy is the story of the realization of the great American dream. In the time between the Revolution and the Civil War a port of timber by a river grew to be Americus, a prosperous town with a waterfront, many churches, and a railroad; and in this town there was a fine house where died a rich old woman who remembered the green twilight of the great forest and how it was to live from the woods with neither bread nor salt. The pioneers have conquered everything—trees, Indians, loneliness, mud, distance, ignorance, poverty —for some everything is conquered except ambition, death, fear of change, and such things as ugliness and the smell of the waterfront.

Harriette Arnow. *SR.* May 16, 1953. p. 13

See *Sea of Grass, The Trees, The Fields, The Town, Always Young and Fair, The Lady, The Waters of Kronos, A Simple, Honorable Man, A Country of Strangers* (novels).

ROBERTS, ELIZABETH MADOX (1886–1941)

Again and again of course she returned (and still returns) to Kentucky; I never saw her there. But wherever she is, it evidently underlays the outbranching experience, folded shadowily into the typical scenes of an author's life—an immense territorial ghost. Its past, still animated in her imagination, accompanied the present. One who knew her but had never traveled to Louisville and beyond was always aware of it, as vivid in her talk, her shepherdess's far-sighted gaze, the archaic foldings of her hands, as on the most evocative pages; in her company one never seemed to be altogether where one was in reality, with that spiritual landscape in the air! And with herself, though always keeping in character, it also underwent impressive changes.

Glenway Wescott. *Bkm.* March, 1930. p. 13

Miss Roberts' work is free of sentimentality, but its realism, like that of Chaucer, is permeated with romance, with glamour. This is possible because she has discarded the poor old worn-out duality of body and mind from which the sordidness of realism springs. Her leading characters, to whom she entrusts the task of directly or obliquely conveying her idea, experience life with their whole bodies indivisible, think with their whole bodies. This extraordinary sensitiveness not only enriches common experience, but establishes also a community of living between the character and the grasses, the cows, the birds, amidst which she works.

J. D. Robins. *CF*. Nov., 1930. pp. 66–7

Her language, it should be said at once, is in itself a thing of perpetual delight—taut with wit as well as languorous with longing for certitude. It is the mixture of these elements in it that accounts for its pre-eminence over the language of other southern novelists today who try perhaps to do the same thing Miss Roberts is doing. They fail because they lack her complexity of mind which, after everything else is said, is the thing we come back to when we are explaining the excellence of a novelist or artist of any kind. Her language is the language of her own mind; and so is everything in her novels typical of her own character.

Mark Van Doren. *EJ*. Sept., 1932. p. 528

The time is ripe, I think, to evaluate the work of Elizabeth Madox Roberts in the novel. Let me say at the outset that I consider her to be a writer of genius, one who at her best has written scenes which stand with the finest in the history of fiction. I draw no qualifications to this— I say the finest and I mean the finest, whether in the Russian, French, or English novel. I think that this occasional mastery of hers has not yet received its due recognition, and I think too that her work as a path-breaker in the art of fiction has not yet been fully understood. At the same time I am equally of the opinion that her shortcomings have not been adequately discussed. She has received high praise which was not high enough; but also, along with some very invalid adverse criticism, there has been insufficient mention of certain weaknesses which have kept Miss Roberts from reaching her potential stature as a creative artist. . . . They are in part the product, it seems to me, of a too great turning inward—an ever present danger to the mystically inclined mind. The very habits of thought which give depth and power to her work are also those which obscure it. . . . Her style, as everyone who knows her work is aware, is extraordinarily perceptive, rich in the power of suggestion, and sustained by subtle and very beautiful rhythms. But it is sometimes and, I think, increasingly, indirect and tenuous.

J. Donald Adams. *VQR*. Jan., 1936. pp. 80–90

The critical neglect of Elizabeth Madox Roberts during the last few years of her life and since her death in 1941 is indeed hard to account for. . . . Though Miss Roberts did not write so much as Cather, her four best novels are on the whole quite as good as the four best of Cather; in fact, in some ways, especially in her poetic imagination and her gift for penetrating satire, Miss Roberts is decidedly superior to Cather. Indeed Miss Roberts' poetic imagination, or what E. M. Forster in reference to D. H. Lawrence has called "the rapt bardic quality," makes her best work worthy of comparison in this respect with the best of Lawrence and Faulkner.

Harry Modean Campbell. SWR. Autumn, 1954.
p. 337

The Time of Man

I have compared this novel to Reymont's tetralogy and, putting the relative smallness of the scale aside, Miss Roberts' book does not suffer much from the comparison. Like Reymont, Miss Roberts seems absolutely saturated in her material and capable of using it with a freedom which suggests rather an intimate experience than any laborious documentation. Moreover she seems to owe little to any of the schools of fiction which have hitherto busied themselves with the treatment of American provincial life. Her mood is original, powerful, and without ever verging upon sentimentality, tender.

Joseph Wood Krutch. SR. Aug. 28, 1926. p. 69

Poetry

Miss Roberts's art consists most often in juxtaposing simple physical details of a landscape or situation in such a way that they act upon and limit each other definitely and minutely, without being at any point similar or parts of each other. They are simply carefully ordered parts of a whole, and bear in every case an intimate relationship to the sound movement. . . . Occasionally she lets a rhythm that has already been used in this manner carry over its emotion as a sort of superimposed comment upon lines, the content of which is too far removed from the physical to fuse with sound.

Yvor Winters. Poetry. April, 1923. p. 47

Miss Roberts's most characteristic invention is a poem of the following kind. . . : a combination of an impulsive feeling, somewhat indeterminate in its object—longing, the sense of being haunted—with an objective and even minute picture of agricultural activity. The feeling is given especially in the lilting rhythm, either moderately lilting, as with anapests among iambs, or strongly lilting, breaking down ordinary double-meters into amphimacer and amphibrachs, to the point of song. . . . At her best, Miss Roberts is deep in the forty years of the American Renascence, drawing on both its inspiration of expressing feeling by pictures and feeling and thought by actuality.

Paul Goodman. *Poetry*. Oct., 1940. pp. 43–5

See *The Time of Man, My Heart and My Flesh, The Great Meadow*, and *Black Is My True Love's Hair* (novels); also *Under the Tree* and *Song in the Meadow* (poetry).

ROBERTS, KENNETH (1885–1957)

Surely in these novels the reader enjoys a remarkable visualization of place and incident. One never loses touch with the people or their story. The secret of this power is probably in the apt use of a vast store of historical details gathered through years of study. This power of keeping the object clearly before the reader is also, I believe, a direct result of Mr. Roberts' years of experience as a newspaperman. Journalism is a good training for a novelist, for it teaches him to get the necessary details for a clear view of an incident and for a coherent story. One also enjoys knowing that in Roberts' novels the specific details of history are the authentic results of sound research.

Chilson H. Leonard. *Kenneth Roberts* (Doubleday).
1936. p. 16

His earlier books, the stories of Arundel and the two sea stories, are conventional historical narratives, traditionally romantic in outline but original and realistic in detail, unreflective, rapid, and usually superficial in their feeling for history. By superficial I do not mean to derogate from Mr. Roberts' rich inventiveness nor to deny that he has a fine eye for the characteristic, the picturesque, and the historically appropriate; I mean that he has been indifferent to the energies and movements of which the events he describes were a specific expression, that he has not bothered about their relation to the age.

Bernard DeVoto. *SR*. July 3, 1937. p. 5

For something like twenty years Kenneth Roberts has been reminding Americans of their heritage—how once men discovered that this was a mighty continent, a land of untold wealth for hardy people, with huge forests to be turned into homes, fertile lands to till, great rivers for fish and traffic, abundance of wild life and mountains full of metals. The hardy men came, his romances report, from several nations, to fight and scheme against one another and the original possessors, and against the wily boys from home with an eye to their own main chance. In spite of his Saturday

Evening Post background of affiliations and ideas, Kenneth Roberts has written some good novels about this country; the black and white demarcations of his pamphleteering shade off into the lighter and darker grays of reality in his best fiction.

B. E. Bettinger. *NR*. July 14, 1937. p. 287

One of my numerous and heretical opinions is that Kenneth Roberts has no particular talent for writing fiction. As a novelist he gets by, I think, as in the Arundel series and in *Northwest Passage,* wholly because he is primarily a most excellent nonfiction writer. . . . He gets some fire and force into his yarns out of pure resentment against the myths handed down from one to another, by the academic historians. . . . If we decide we are going to have history and put it into books, let it be history, not legend. Roberts feels that way about it, and I'm for him.

The thing that makes him good in this respect, of course, is the thing that militates against his being a very good writer of fiction. Fiction . . . is not concerned with facts or even with minor truths: it is concerned with the universal truths.

Burton Rascoe. *Nwk*. June 20, 1938. p. 31

Mr. Roberts' . . . best talents lie in the swift narration of some tale of heroic exertions or resistances. Nobody better than he can bring a battle, a siege, a toilsome march, a wrestle with overmastering moral and material forces, vividly before us. He has a fine power of visualization, an even finer faculty for enlisting the reader in the ardors and endurances of some embattled body of men. When it comes to the presentation of gentler scenes, whether in drawing rooms, courts, or congresses, he is much less effective. Nor is he skilled in the integration of a far-reaching and highly varied piece of fiction.

Allan Nevins. *SR*. Nov. 23, 1940. p. 5

He is a hater of shams, pretensions, self-deceptions, fallacies; and he particularly hates the persistent distortion of history. In what would be for him the best possible world, every history would be written with a fine impartiality and by a neutral party. He is tireless in hunting out proof that Colonials during the Revolutionary period were (a) dauntless heroes, or (b) blovalating politicians and self-seekers; the choice depending on which misconception he is at the moment engaged in setting right. He is equally tireless in proving that all British and Tories were (a) cultivated and intelligent gentlemen abused by the Colonials, or (b) tyrannical rascals abusing the Colonials.

For Ken, who expects from the historian a remote impartiality, himself always has a thesis to demonstrate. His thesis is the unrecognized truth;

and he will with the most laborious research write a book to prove that on a given subject everyone who believes that everyone else believes is wrong!

Ben Ames Williams. Introduction to *The Kenneth
Roberts Reader* (Dutton). 1945. p. ix

I wish Mr. Roberts had a clearer idea of what to eliminate from his first drafts. His novels, even the best of them, have a tendency to sprawl, and in this case (*Lydia Bailey*), as in *Northwest Passage,* there are a beginning, a middle, and an end, and then without pause for breath, another beginning and middle and end. It adds up to too much, and in the protraction, in the constant shift from one background to the next, the main characters lose their orientation, they become flat rather than forceful, the victims of romance rather than of a reality.

Edward Weeks. *At.* Feb. 1947. p. 130

Kenneth Roberts is a big, hearty, vital, opinionated, hasty-tempered man. He hates politicians, hypocrisy, corruption, cowardice, and tyranny. He loves food, action, valor, independence, and the very stuff of history itself. All this is plain as a pikestaff in his books. He is uninterested in, or incapable of, the subtleties of fiction as an art. His plots are crude and clumsy, his virtuous characters only stilted puppets. But he is a superb chronicler of violence, battle, massacre, rape, flight, and pursuit. He is wonderfully effective in his portraits of picturesque, eccentric, lusty men of action. And always his enormous relish for the life of the past endows his work with a living background of interest in itself.

Orville Prescott. *YR.* Spring, 1947. p. 573

Though his novels . . . suffer from unnecessary repetitions and occasional lags, they have a definite advantage over most other period novels, and this is the unobstrusive introduction of a fundamental human problem— namely the clash of the attitude of loyalty with independent pragmatic judgment in one and the same person. . . . It is true that this conception does not appear to be strong enough to lift these novels to the plane of an irrational and feverish search for some kind of non-pragmatic values as, say, in Thomas Wolfe's novels, but it carries enough weight to keep the intelligent reader's attention and sympathy through the stories.

Heinrich Straumann. *American Literature in the
Twentieth Century* (Hutchinson). 1951. p. 67

This "implacable detestation of false men and evil measures," this moral impatience which he attributes to America, severely cripples Mr. Roberts' imagination. No doubt his intolerance is well grounded in reason and experience, and it will be as Richard Wilbur puts it, that "In a time of continual dry abdication/ And of damp complicities" Mr. Roberts' narrow rectitude is the proper tonic. I doubt it, though.

Thomas E. Curley. Com. Feb. 10, 1956. p. 496

See *Arundel, Boon Island, Captain Caution, Lively Lady, Northwest Passage,* and *Oliver Wiswell* (novels).

ROBINSON, EDWIN ARLINGTON (1869–1935)

He has an ascetic hatred for the trite word, the facile phrase, the rhetorical cadence. His individual idiom—as clearly marked as John Donne's, whom he resembles in many ways—was apparent from the first. . . . The thought it packed very tight, except in the humorous diffusion and willful Wordsworthian flatness of occasional passages in the monologues. The athletic sparseness of epithet, the suppression of climaxes, the projection of the planes of the poem beyond the lines of the poem itself—these are Robinsonian characteristics that will continue to repel some readers as certainly as they fascinate the adepts.

Bliss Perry. NYT. Dec. 21, 1919. p. 765

Robinson had discovered that simply by making a plain statement of certain important things, he achieved a poetic effect unlike anything known to poetry except possibly the ballad. . . . Robinson wrote in the old meters. He often employed stock poetic phrases. But all the stanza forms he used resolved themselves to the level of the ballad statement of fact, and stock poetic phrases were an ironic reflection on the poverty of a life of which the phrase was the sole grandeur.

Samuel Roth. Bkm. Jan., 1920. pp. 507–8

Now Mr. Robinson is a dyed-in-the-wool New Englander, and that must never be forgotten. His tenacity of purpose is thoroughly New England, so is his austerity and his horror of exuberance of expression. His insight into people is pure Yankee shrewdness, as is also his violent and controlled passion. He is absolutely a native of his place, the trouble was that he was not a native of his time. He was twenty years ahead of his time, and that advance has set the seal of melancholy upon him; or, to speak in the cant of the day, it has wound him in inhibitions which he has been unable to shake off.

Amy Lowell. Dial. Feb., 1922. p. 133

Mr. Robinson, even in youth, was a poet of failure and regret. He was preoccupied with New England in decay. In the moonlight of an eternal autumn he sat brooding on the poor ghosts of men—brooding sadly rather than in grief. . . . And since Mr. Robinson began in autumn he has never had his rightful spring. He was old from the very first. When his time came for him to be really old, his trees were doubly bare.

Edmund Wilson. *Dial*. May, 1923. p. 516

If the psychology of failure, or of that uncertain middle ground between spiritual success and failure, is Robinson's recurrent motive, it may be interesting to study his attitudes and his methods in presenting that motive in art. It is heroic, not ignoble, struggle that engages him, or if not heroic, at least the struggle of highly strung, sensitive souls to fulfil their manifest destiny; ending either in acceptance of compromise, or in tragic spiritual revolt that induces some kind of dark eclipse. The form is usually narrative, with the poet as the narrator, under some assumption of friendship or at least neighborliness; but in the longer poems we have, as a rule, monologue and dialogue, the characters unfolding their perplexities, or recording their action upon each other, in long speeches which are not talk, as talk actually ever was or could be, but which are talk intensified into an extra-luminous self-revelation; as if an x-ray, turned into the suffering soul, made clear its hidden structural mysteries.

Harriet Monroe. *Poetry*. Jan. 1925. p. 210

Robinson's portrait of the American failure (a failure arrived at through the misapplication of New England pragmatism) is so complete, that the fact many of his books became best sellers must be a source of quiet amusement to him. There lies the irony more profound than anything Robinson has written. He remains, as always, the most unshaken, the most unmoved of America's critics, his clinical finger piercing an open wound. He has made his one discovery, has patented it; sometimes the statement produces poetry, sometimes merely words, but there it is; and it would take another reincarnation of Robinson to deny it.

Horace Gregory. *Poetry*. Dec., 1934. pp. 160–1

His artistry has much of the Yankee in it: on the one hand, its laconic, word-sparing quality and its tendency to understatement; on the other, its gift for circumlocution when this device will either conceal or veil what the Yankee has in mind or what is in his mood. . . . Moreover, it is this trait of expressing by indirection that makes Robinson seem more exclusively intellectual than he actually is. The man who does not wear his heart on his sleeve is not therefor heartless, but he is bound sometimes to produce that impression. And the man who on occasion talks by indirec-

tion or . . . so curtly that he throws away everything but the meaning—
and keeps that to himself, does not always suffer from a tertian ague of
tongue-tiedness and verbosity.

> Percy H. Boynton. *Literature and American Life*
> (Ginn). 1936. pp. 804–5

His lyric perceptions, like his human values, are rooted in the known and
possible—the capacities of a man which survive even in his sorriest condition of stultification and confusion. . . . He is a realist not only in conscience but in style and diction; in *milieu* as much as in imagery; and this
gives him his license to explore the problems of abstract casuistry and
moral contradiction which he filed down into that style of attenuated rumi-
nation, impassioned hair-splitting, and bleak aphorism which will always
remain unmistakably his own.

> Morton D. Zabel. *Literary Opinion in America*
> (Harper). 1937. p. 405

Edwin Arlington Robinson personified winter. Abandoning New England,
he had carried to New York an aura of blight, desolation, decay, and
defeat. His view of the world was wintry,—so was his life,—and his style
and his personality were bleak and bare. Had there ever been a poet who
loved life less or found so little joy in the turning of the seasons? In the
down-east phrase, Robinson was "master chilly."

> Van Wyck Brooks. *New England: Indian Summer*
> (Dutton). 1940. pp. 490–1

Because his own poetry was based so firmly on his personal and sensitive
appreciation of what was unchanging and available in the poetry of the
past, Robinson was finally able to contemplate the future with some equanimity. Subsequent revolutions in taste have somewhat impared the reputation he finally won toward the end of his career, but these revolutions
have also shown that some of Robinson's poetry did attain the stature at
which he aimed and that it will not be quickly forgotten. There can be
little doubt that his best work is now part of the ideal order by which he
always wished to be measured.

> Edwin S. Fussell. *Edwin Arlington Robinson*
> (California). 1954. p. 186

The fact is that he *likes* people. Shy, austere, fastidious, distressed by the
taste of the general public ("as for the democratization of art, there ain't
no such animal"), and distrustful of its intelligence (as he makes plain in
Dionysus in Doubt), with no capacity or desire to be a "popular" poet,
he nevertheless distinguishes the person from the mob; and piercing the

armor of apparent nonentity, he finds a human being like himself and lends an attentive ear to his unique variant, comic or tragic, of the story common to mankind.

(K)   Ellsworth Barnard. *Edwin Arlington Robinson*
(Macmillan). 1952. p. 179

It is a village world, to be sure, but a village world whose sense of community has been destroyed. Most of its inhabitants are failures: sometimes resigned to their failure, sometimes unresignedly crushed by it. They have no means of declaring directly their sense of themselves; if such a sense exists, we are given to know it only inferentially, as, putting himself in the position of the inevitable outsider, Robinson can make us know it. They are in and of themselves not expressive; they have lost the power, if they have had it, of direct communication. . . . Even the relative successes like Flammonde cannot communicate. Still, whatever their degree of failure or success, they are as persons meaningful to us. For they signify something important in the nature of the modern psyche—even if it is only as they are made to recall, in their inability to communicate directly, a condition and a time when such a thing as self-reliance (in any of its various forms) was a radical possibility for all men. In them, Robinson pushes to an outer limit a sense of the exhaustion, perhaps the bankruptcy, of the simple, separate person. Tilbury Town is the underworld of Walden and Paumanok.

(K)   Roy Harvey Pearce. *The Continuity of American*
Poetry (Princeton). 1961. p. 258

Although strongly influenced by Balzac, Zola, Henry James, Crabbe, Browning, and at first by Kipling, he soon found his own authentic voice. He did not rebel against, but pointedly ignored, the traditional distinction between poetic and unpoetic matter. He wrote interesting poetry about the disintegrated inner life of contemporary civilized men, using the language and word order of sophisticated conversation. His style, quite devoid of unction and afflatus, was remarkable for its coolness and dry precision. Many of his most serious poems were tinged with ironic wit. Best of all, he had the precious gift of ambiguity: it was often hard to see what he was driving at.

There are several reasons why these facts have largely been forgotten. Robinson's traditional verse patterns make him seem old-fashioned even when he is most original. He reacts against Tennysonianism not by attempting to create a new poetic language but by writing poetry in good though sometimes tortuous prose. This prose is essentially discursive: feeling and thinking are related in a structure of statements, not fused in symbolic images. The surface dramatic impersonality does not conceal the fact that he is usually talking about himself. He makes no attempt to heal the dissociation of sensibility by shaping an autotelic poem-world. More important for us, however, is the fact that under close inspection this sophisticated, ironic, disenchanted man so often proves to be embarrassingly "inspirational." As with his master Browning, his simplicities undermine his complexities.

(K)   Hoxie Neale Fairchild. *Religious Trends in English*
                       Poetry, vol. V (Columbia). 1962. pp. 238–9

Robinson's characters . . . are on the periphery of things—either voted in the high-school year book as the most popular, the most likely to succeed, or altogether at the time ignored and forgotten. It does not follow, however, that Tilbury Town is a town of peripheral people, intended to be quite different from other towns. The population is obviously composed mostly of those whom Robinson does not write about at all. And these emerge from the poetry, rather obliquely, as a group of austere, uncommunicative New Englanders who are unaware of, and unresponsive to, the people around them. It is possible to conclude, in fact, that Robinson's characterizations are far less an *evocation* of Tilbury Town than they are a message *to* it. The poet himself, a kind of outcast from Gardiner, Maine, creates with his poetry a bond of sympathy with humanity that he feels too few of us share. Indeed, Robinson's poetry is also evidence of his own inner light that the home town folks evidently never believed was burning within him.

(K)   Robert N. Hertz. *MinnR.* Spring, 1962. p. 349

Altogether, what Robinson called his "idealism" was nothing of the sort. It made no attempt to define exclusive reality, it set up no archetypes, no ultimates. It was no more than an assertion of his preference for the life of the mind within "thought's impenetrable mail," the contemplation by his outer conscious self of his inner unconscious self whose subsensuous activity was a mood, a mood of universal clairvoyance composite of being, perceiving, and loving. This mood possessed Robinson more completely and continuously than it does most people, even most artists, and his delight in it was the "joy" of "idealism" for which he was willing to forego "all those pleasures which are said to make up the happiness of this life." Variously accoutered with the materials of outer experience, the clairvoyant mood motivated his poetry and his "philosophic" notions. Its universal love gave him his concern for all individuals. Its identity with all Being gave him his religion.

(K)   Chard Powers Smith. *Where the Light Falls: A Portrait of*
                       Edwin Arlington Robinson (Macmillan). 1965. p. 290

. . . although there can be no doubt that Robinson means himself when he uses the first person singular in such poems as the "Octaves" and "Credo," the vision in these poems and in *Captain Craig* is as exaggeratedly exalted as the vision in "The Night Before" is anguished. "The Night Before" and *Captain Craig* present, in fact, the two poles of Robinson's experience. The circumstances of their heroes are identical in the respect that they are men who have been scarred by life and who are now at the point of death; but Craig has won his way to love, truth, and light, whereas the condemned man has sunk too deeply into passion and darkness to attain more than a liberating glimpse of what Craig sees. As man and poet, Robinson had ideas about what he wanted to see and what he ought to see; but actuality —what he did see—was something else again.

(K)   James G. Hepburn. *PMLA*. June, 1965. p. 268

Robinson's sense of conscience shares much with Thoreau's but with a difference. Both want, in a way and to a degree, to protest against the narrowing of conscience to the Anglo-Saxon, Protestant, village code. Good writing is as much a matter of conscience as good ploughing or honest shopkeeping. But Robinson *seems*—and I think was—more troubled than Thoreau: his periodic alcoholism was one symptom.

New England standards had deteriorated in the period after the Civil War, and [Henry] Adams, Henry James, and Robinson could no longer live there. I see something in common between all three which is partly, but only partly, prefigured in Thoreau. . . .

There is yet one more thing to add: Conscience requires utmost veracity with oneself and with others. This shows itself even in syntax: and *The Man Against the Sky* shows its cerebral structure in the repeated, and structurally located, conjunctions and conjunctive adverbs—the alternative possibilities of interpretation: "or," "again," "or maybe," "may have," "if," "or."

New England once had, in its intellectuals, dogmatic assurance. By the times of Adams and Robinson, such dogmatic assurance is no longer possible to the lettered. But one can keep himself from feigning an assurance he no longer feels and from uttering dogmas all too plainly subjective.

(K)   Austin Warren. *The New England Conscience*
(Michigan). 1966. pp. 190, 193

Unlike his contemporaries . . . Robinson had a great deal of success in accomplishing a meaningful movement from dark or gray or dead gods to light and color and life. Perhaps this is because his genius separated him from them in nothing more clearly than in its depriving him of his youth. Not only did he serve out his apprenticeship in greater geographical isolation than did they, not only did he live a celibate's life, but he also had the stamina to deny himself a young man's outlook on the world. His was a dramatic imagination, and, somewhat like Sarah Jewett, he was able to see himself in older people and to check his impatience at the darkness ahead by seeing that it was ahead only because he was young; that, in point of fact, it was behind for many, and, because they had experienced it, it was not all darkness. He could project a drama involving this perception so completely that his assertions of the light glimmering somewhere were validated by the felt experience set forth in the poem, since a life had been lived there, rather than sounding, as in the poems of his contemporaries, like the pronouncements of youthful bravado.

(K)   Larzer Ziff. *The American 1890s* (Viking).
                                                    1966. pp. 330–1

There are two kinds of alienation, however, and they serve to separate the characters in Robinson. One class is made up of those who have seen the truth about themselves and cannot get it out of their minds. These characters, the realists, have two choices: they may commit suicide (Barnard counts fourteen suicides in E. A. Robinson) or they may silently withdraw from life. The second class, the romantics, is made up of those who have made a covenant with themselves not to see the truth. With the aid of their illusions, they survive, but they are rejected by their fellow men, who find their illusions either contemptible or laughable. . . . If there is a message in Robinson's best poetry, it is that we are probably happier if we remain ignorant of the hell that is life on earth, but that any such happiness is necessarily hollow and meaningless.

(K)   Scott Donaldson. *AL*. May, 1966. p. 225

Robinson's heroes were bound to be antiheroes, like Captain Craig (or his heir, John Crowe Ransom's "Captain Carpenter") and the scores who followed him out of Tilbury Town or those in the Arthurian cycle—misfits and alienated men whose moral heroism is paradoxically made possible by the fact of their irredeemable failure. "I shall never be a Prominent Citizen," Robinson wrote in 1895, "and I thank God for it, but I shall be something just as good perhaps and possibly a little more permanent." Exploring personal alienation and social failure, he achieved success; setting forth the actuality of despair, he secured hope ("I suppose I'm the damnedest optimist that ever lived," he wrote in 1913); dramatizing the reign of the antihero, he defined and made relevant a hero for the modern world.

(K)   Jay Martin. *Harvests of Change* (Prentice). 1967.
                                                    p. 155

The center of Robinson's region is a town; he usually deals with town-dwellers, while Frost and Hardy usually deal with countrymen. Furthermore, Robinson's speakers, unlike those of Frost and Hardy, are seldom outsiders looking in. They are not city-dwellers regarding the country, or country people regarding the ways of the town, or people with a sense of the past regarding the present. Rather, they almost always participate exclusively in the social and moral milieu which they examine. They may sense weaknesses in that milieu, but their points of view seldom provide larger contexts from which the situation can be more accurately assessed. By implication, such contexts exist; but readers must find them for themselves, or find them on the basis of very limited hints in the poetry.

(K)   Paul Zietlow. *NEQ*. June, 1967. p. 191

Shorter Poems

Mr. Robinson's shorter poems are many and various, and the perfection they reach is remarkably many-sided. In blank verse, in talkative rhyme, in suave epigram, in running eloquence he has found his forms; in men of all conditions and characters he has found his material. But he is still consistent . . . in his presentation of the problem which existence is. A little light in a great deal of darkness, a wisp of music in a universe of irregular and ominous drums—it is in such images that he tells . . . of man's never wholly vain struggle for self-respect.

Mark Van Doren. *Edwin Arlington Robinson*
(Literary Guild). 1927. pp. 49–50

As with the passage of time their quality stands out from the bulky later work that tends to hide them, as the nation in maturing, gains in respect for the intellectual and contemplative virtues and sees behind material satisfactions the tragedy of human condition and feels the glory of art that in accepting tragedy transcends it, Robinson's figure will grow.

Emery Neff. *Edwin Arlington Robinson* (Sloane).
1948. p. 259

See *Collected Poems*, also *Selected Poems; Triangulated Stars* (letters).

ROETHKE, THEODORE (1908–1963)

A good poet can be recognized by his tense awareness of both chaos and order, the arbitrary and the necessary, the fact and the pattern. . . . By such a test Mr. Roethke is instantly recognizable as a good poet. . . . Many people have the experience of feeling physically soiled and humiliated by life; some quickly put it out of their mind, others gloat narcissistically on its unimportant details; but both to remember and to transform the humiliation into something beautiful, as Mr. Roethke does, is rare.

W. H. Auden. *SR*. April 5, 1941. pp. 30–1

Theodore Roethke uses flowers, wind, water, and such materials of art and nature to express his views of them and of larger issues. . . . These serve him as images often presented with the clear sharp colors of the objects and then are transformed into symbols of human struggle or contemplation. . . . Mr. Roethke does evoke the turbulent anxieties of a young man and the return of a hard-won equilibrium with many lines of considerable talent.

Eugene Davidson. *YR*. Summer, 1948. p. 747

What Roethke brings us . . . is news of the root, of the minimal, of the primordial. The sub-human is given tongue; and the tongue proclaims the agony of coming alive, the painful miracle of growth. Here is poetry immersed in the destructive element.

Stanley Kunitz. *Poetry*. Jan., 1949. p. 225

He meets, in his way, the problem which Eliot met in another by expanding his poetry to encompass theological doctrine, and thereby including a terminology which, within the Roethke rules, would be ungainly (unless used ironically—and children don't take to irony). Eliot added winds of doctrine. Roethke "regressed" as thoroughly as he could, even at considerable risk, toward a language of sheer intuition.

Kenneth Burke. *SwR*. Jan., 1950. p. 102

With many a writer who affects to plumb the depths of his own unconsciousness, one feels that after he has dived into the bathysphere, he is only too apt to emerge with nothing but the bathetic—or the banal—and that if he comes up with something rich and strange, or only grotesque, one cannot feel sure but that he has planted his deep-sea bucket in advance with a few specimens of starfish and sea-urchins, not to mention an old boot or two, just to make it look better. Mr. Roethke is more convincing; he has established, and this is a matter of technique as surely as feats of prosody, avenues of communication to his own unconsciousness. . . . Adept at breathing, so to speak through his gills, Mr. Roethke seems to me a little less sure of himself when it is time to use his lungs.

Rolfe Humphries. *Nation*. March 22, 1952. p. 284

By the controlled restriction of his theme, the intense hyperbolical sexual wit, the almost perceptual level of his language, Roethke asks of us the most delicate reading even for sympathetic appreciation, let alone an evaluation. He has launched a brilliant and to a large degree victorious assault upon deadening abstractions in poetry.

Frederick Brantley. *YR*. Spring, 1952. p. 476

Roethke's work is his own. His shorter poems are distinguished not so much by their matter . . . but by their tone. He manages to escape the pedestrian flatness of some of his fellows and the strained intellectualism of others. He has as much to say of the interior landscape as of that without, and writes with particular acuteness of the nameless malaise of the spirit. His work gains from the fact that his childhood was intimately bound up with the life of a Michigan greenhouse, which physically and otherwise, was to afford the material for some of his best lyrics. . . . Shifting cadences and homely images taken from childhood memories of the floriculturist's world, meanings as evasive as some secretive animal and equally frightening, produce unusual and powerful effects. These poems are an account of the journey through the dark wood—here symbolized by stagnant water, among other forms of death—into the light that clothes the visible in the garments of eternity.

Babette Deutsch. *Poetry in Our Time* (Holt). 1952.
pp. 182–3

Roethke's is the poetry of therapy; it dances its way from madness (symbolized by the wet riot of vegetable roots and the grossness of flesh) to a reflective calm (winter and distance). It is the richness and variety of Roethke's rhythm together with the shock and clarity of his broken phrases that persuades. Roethke slams into his dance, arms in air and ranting like a sibyl. His style seems most nearly founded on Christopher Smart, Blake, the Elizabethan rant, and the backwoods brag, all scattering free, but always with a sense of breaking through a tremendous formal control. Roethke's strength is that he never talks about his subject matter but enters and performs it. The best measure of his achievement is that there are now a subject, a rhythm, and a kind of perception that are specifically Roethkean.

John Ciardi. *Nation*. Nov. 14, 1953. p. 410

Mr. Roethke has accepted the evolutionary story as a chart for his poetic voyage. And derived much joy from this newly-discovered closeness to the rest of earth's creatures. . . . Indeed, one of the striking things about Mr. Roethke's poetic stance is this very joyousness. . . . There is considerable experimentalism, the odd originality of the child . . . which, however, is at least partially backed by a symbolism more than childlike.

Gerard Previn Meyer. *SR*. Jan. 16, 1954. p. 19

A very good poet is Theodore Roethke. From the precise statements of *Open House* (1941) through the sensuous wilderness of *Praise to the End* (1951) he has arrived at the wild precision of his most recent verse. . . . Never, in Roethke's "free verse," is there a hint of the arbitrary; every line is glued in place, as fixed as in his regular forms. . . . He is more accomplished outside conventional forms than any poet since Wallace Stevens.

Donald Hall. *NWW* 7. 1955. pp. 236–7

It is sufficiently clear by now that Theodore Roethke is a very important poet. . . . These poems appear, at first glance, to be uncontrollable and subliminal outcries, the voices of roots, stones, leaves, logs, small birds; and they also resemble the songs in Shakespearean plays, Ophelia's songs perhaps most of all. This surface impression is genuine and ought not to be disregarded. But it is only the surface, however moving, and as such it can be misleading or superficial. The reader who supposes that Roethke is really a primitive lyric poet loses or misses a great deal. . . . Throughout his work, Roethke uses a *variety* of devices with the utmost cunning and craft to bring the unconsciousness to the surface of articulate expression.

Delmore Schwartz. *Poetry*. June, 1959. p. 203

Roethke is an intensely introspective poet. His chief subject is himself, but the poems range from his childhood to his maturity, from his frustrations to the freeing himself from these frustrations, from almost crippling inner tensions to the achievement of a balanced maturity with his emotional and intellectual faculties in equipoise, from a mistaken to a positive self-knowledge. His poetry has been of value to him and is to us because of its analysis in depth. Technically, he is both conservative and revolutionary. His most successful device is his use of symbols drawn from his close and intimate association with nature, not only as he has lived with it along the streams, marshes, stagnant pools, forests in and near the "thumb" district of Michigan, but as he has encountered it in the forcing area of a greenhouse. He has, it is true, written several poems Frostian in quality, and he has looked so steadily and perceptively at the minutiae of nature that his symbol-free early descriptions in the light of his later work assume a symbolic quality. He has, too, written some moving poems on death. Basically, however, death, nature, and love are only a few of the subjects which have helped him rid himself of his inner tensions. Roethke is not a prolific poet, and understandably so when the reader is aware of the intensity of his concentration on isolated moments.

(K)   James G. Southworth. *CE*. March, 1960. pp. 326–7

There was something of a cry in each of Roethke's lines: a cry of astonishment at finding the thing—tree, stone, shell, woman—*really* there, and himself also there at the same time: a cry of affirmation at knowing some-how that he and it *would* be there. This may account for the fact that there is some mindless, elemental quality in the sound of his voice, something primitive and animistic, something with the wariness and inhuman grace of the wild beast, and with it another thing that could not be and never has been animal-like. His poems are human poems in the full weight of that adjective: poems of a creature animal enough to enter *half* into unthink-ing nature and unanimal enough to be uneasy there, taking thought at what the animal half discerns and feels. This position, which at times seems triumphantly an extraordinary kind of wholeness impossible to ani-mals and possible to men only at rare times, is the quality that Roethke has caught in his best poems.

(K)   James Dickey. *Poetry*. Nov., 1964. pp. 120–1

I am myself too much influenced and shaped by Roethke's use of language to be at the moment a good critical judge of his work. I know that what he does involves a great deal of daring, because it includes opening the word to its broadest areas of connotation, admitting and controlling the most formidable body of possibility. Often one may begin discussing a Roethke poem in terms of limited reference: it is *about* religious experience or *about* madness. But in the end one discovers that "about" is the wrong word, that what Roethke has done is to abandon abouts, and to try instead to deal with central patterns and motions of human experience, patterns which recur, are relevant, in terms of religious experience or madness, but which are really larger than any one of their limited manifestations sug-gests. The effort of Roethke's poetry is an incredible effort; it wants to admit everything. What is even more incredible is the fact that it does, it succeeds.

(K)   William Dickey. *HdR*. Winter, 1964–65. p. 596

More reliable than reason, for instance. In his search for a viable and live order, Roethke used his mind for all it was worth, but he would not vote for reason. He did not believe that you could pit the rational powers against the weeds of circumstance and hope to win. When he spoke of reason, it was invariably Stevens' "Reason's click-clack," a mechanical affair. In one poem Roethke says, "Reason? That dreary shed, that hutch for grubby schoolboys!" Indeed, reason normally appears in his poems, at least of-ficially, as a constriction. Commenting on his poem "In a Dark Time," Roethke said that it was an attempt "to break through the barriers of ra-tional experience." The self, the daily world, reason, meant bondage: to come close to God you had to break through; these things were never the medium of one's encounter with God, always obstacles in its way. For such encounters you had to transcend reason; if you managed it, you touched that greater thing which is the "reason in madness" of *King Lear*.

The good man takes the risk of darkness. If reason's click-clack is useless there remains in man a primitive striving toward the light. Nature, seldom a friend to man, at least offers him a few saving analogies; one being that of darkness and light.

(K)   Denis Donoghue in *Theodore Roethke: Essays on
the Poetry*, edited by Arnold Stein (Washington).
1965. p. 151

His poems controlled, they sympathized. They only began, at the end, fully to give. They controlled the wide and deep areas of the personal, the widest and deepest, I am persuaded, in the work of any contemporary American poet. And they demonstrated again and again how we have access to those areas only through sympathy—the power of human sympathy as it at first derives and then differentiates itself from the power which maintains the natural order of things. Roethke began to learn, and to make poems which teach, that out of the power of sympathy there comes the power to give, thus to be given to. He began to comprehend the full range of the other, that chain of being which moves from the minimal to God.

The poems in *The Far Field* indicate the distance he had come. Many of the love poems are centered on the consciousness of woman, an "I" different enough from the center of consciousness of the earlier love poems to manifest not only the power of sympathy but of identity with another.

(K)   Roy Harvey Pearce in *Theodore Roethke: Essays
on the Poetry*, edited by Arnold Stein (Washington).
1965. p. 190

In his poems, Roethke seems often to be dancing. This is not the dance transcended and purified in the poetry, the entry into a metaphysical pattern of theological joy of Auden or Eliot, nor is it the tragic dancing on the graves of the dead of Yeats—it is simply Roethke incredibly and almost against his will dancing. He is the boy who is waltzed round by his father of the whiskeyed breath; the sensual man swaying toward the woman swaying toward him; the dying man dancing his way out of his body toward God.

There was never, one might say, such ungainly yet compulsive dancing, as in Roethke. . . .

(K)   Stephen Spender in *Theodore Roethke: Essays on the
Poetry*, edited by Arnold Stein (Washington). 1965. p. 5

Roethke's passionate and near-microscopic scrutiny of the chemistry of growth extended beyond "the lives on a leaf" to the world of what he termed "the minimal," or "the lovely diminutives," the very least of creation, including "beetles in caves, newts, stone-deaf fishes, lice tethered to

long limp subterranean weeds, squirmers in bogs, and bacterial creepers."
These are creatures still wet with the waters of the beginning. At or below
the threshold of the visible they correspond to that darting, multitudinous
life of the mind under the floor of the rational, in the wet of the subconscious.

Roethke's immersion in these waters led to his most heroic enterprise,
the sequence of interior monologues which he initiated with the title poem
of *The Lost Son,* which he continued in *Praise to the End* (1951), and
which he persisted up to the last in returning to, through a variety of
modifications and developments. . . .

The protagonist, who recurrently undertakes the dark journey into his
own underworld, is engaged in a quest for spiritual identity. The quest is
simultaneously a flight, for he is being pursued by the man he has become, implacable, lost, soiled, confused. In order to find himself he
must lose himself by reexperiencing all the stages of his growth, by re-
enacting all the transmutations of his being from seed-time to maturity.
We must remember that it is the poet himself who plays all the parts. He
is Proteus and all the forms of Proteus—flower, fish, reptile, amphibian,
bird, dog, etc.—and he is the adversary who hides among the rocks to
pounce on Proteus, never letting go his hold, while the old man of the
sea writhes through his many shapes until, exhausted by the struggle, he
consents to prophesy in the *claritas* of his found identity.

(K)   Stanley Kunitz. *NR.* Jan. 23, 1965. p. 24

As a poet, Roethke was involved in still another quest: for the best means
of presenting that direct expression of human experience. Beginning with
the intellectuality of the metaphysical school, with discourse and analysis,
he moved inexorably toward the sensuous, the symbolic, the organic
metaphor. Extending the doctrine of correspondences, he did not merely
speculate about, but, in the greenhouse poems, actually entered the world
of the subhuman and the prerational; and he used the techniques developed there for brilliant explorations of the growth of the psyche in
Praise to the End! From the private world of psychology, Roethke's concern with death, and the meaning of life, brought him to the more public
realms of philosophy and religion, and therefore to an appropriately more
formal lyric. But even here, Roethke attempted to be less sophisticated,
and more direct, than the poetic tradition he had assimilated. And the
new sequences of meditations, more discursive versions of the "primary
process" patterns of *Praise to the End!,* derive much of their power from
a system of evocative correspondences between inner and outer, primitive
and adult, worlds.

(K)   Karl Malkoff. *Theodore Roethke: An Introduction
to the Poetry* (Columbia). 1966. p. 221

I am not sure how well Roethke's memory was served by his very uneven last poems, which he had been readying for the press when he died in August 1963. The poems are touching in at least two ways. First, they refer to his illness and seem aware of imminent death, though he was only fifty-five or younger when they were written. Second, behind their assumption of an achieved, transcendent quietude lies a deeper impression of inability to cope with the old, still unresolved hysteria, which Roethke had unloosed in his earlier work, and of a consequent resort to the stock cosmic pieties of sagedom from Chuang-tzu on down.

(K)   M. L. Rosenthal. *The New Poets* (Oxford). 1967.

p. 113

See *Collected Poems; On the Poet and His Craft: Selected Prose.*

RÖLVAAG, OLE (1876–1931)

Does Rölvaag's work belong legitimately to Norwegian or to American literature? The problem has unusual and interesting features. The volume before us deals with American life, and with one of the most character-istically American episodes in our history. It opens on the western plains; its material is altogether American. Yet it was written in Norwegian, and gained its first recognition in Norway. Whatever we may decide, it has already become a part of Norwegian literature. Rölvaag's art seems mainly European; Rölvaag himself, as I have said, is typically American. His life and future are bound up in the New World; yet he will continue to write in a foreign language. Had he been born in America, would his art have been the same? It seems unlikely. On the other hand, had he remained in Norway—had he accepted the boat that fine, clear day in Nordland—how would his art have fared?

Lincoln Colcord. Introduction to *Giants in the Earth* by
Ole Rölvaag (Harper). 1927. pp. xxii–xxiii

Giants in the Earth is a great and beautiful book that suggests the wealth of human potentialities brought to America year after year by the peasant immigrants who pass through Ellis Island and scatter the length and breadth of the land. Written in Norwegian, and stemming from a rich old-world literary tradition, it is at the same time deeply and vitally American. The very atmosphere of the Dakota plains is in its pages, and it could have been written only by one to whom the background was a familiar scene. The artist has lived with these peasant folk; he is one of them, and he penetrates sympathetically to the simple kindly hearts hidden to alien eyes by the unfamiliar folk ways. To gather up and preserve in letters these diverse folk strains before they are submerged and lost in the common American *mores,* would seem to be a business that our fiction might undertake with profit.

Vernon L. Parrington. Introduction to *Giants in the Earth* by Ole Rölvaag (Harper). 1927. pp. xviii–xix

[*Giants in the Earth*] is probably the best novel that has yet been written about the American pioneer. That romanticized American is here viewed, not through the spectacles of prosperous descendants, but by a man who has been one and can still remember the experience through European eyes. . . .

The book records the partial conquest of the American prairie by the pioneer, and the partial conquest of the pioneer's heart and mind by the prairie. It would be untrue to say that either had completely won over the other—and Rölvaag above all else is distinguished as a truth teller. . . . Before the novel ends, every joy and sorrow, hope and terror that can come to the heart of the frontier is set down in the course of Per Hansa's story and that of his wife. There is much fierce courage, hope, and joyful accomplishment packed into the book, though in the end the prairie with something of the fierceness and fatality of the sea takes its toll of the pioneer settlement.

Charles R. Walker. *Independent.* July 9, 1927. p. 44

The prairie filled with excitable wrangling men [in *Peder Victorious*] doesn't excite us as did the prairie empty except for that preposterous little band from Nordland [in *Giants in the Earth*]. The prairie itself was the hero of that magical book, and on it there appeared a tiny maggot in the form of the ingenious and whimsical Per Hansa, who refused to be daunted by its silence or its winds, its vastness or its cold; who thought up the most incredible ways to evade it, and ultimately to tame it. The prairie got him at last, but his children spread over it, breaking up its rich virgin sod, building ugly little towns and ugly little houses.

What they did to it we like too little to sympathize greatly with their exertions in the doing. What Per Hansa might have done to it died with him. We are faced in the story, as in contemporary life, with the fact that the second generation, which built our Western towns, is far less interesting than the first, which drove its rickety covered wagons through the pathless grass of the prairies. *Giants in the Earth* was a fairy tale, one of the most wistful, the saltiest, the most prodigious of all fairy tales. *Peder Victorious* is an ordinary story of ordinary beings like you and me, engaged in discovering their toes.

Alice Beal Parsons. *Nation.* March 13, 1929. p. 317

Giants in the Earth is presented in two parts. I have tried to suggest the essentials of the former in terms of primitive ethnology: man and nature in their eternal conflict; man as part of the tide of human life inexorably certain of success; man, the individual, ephemeral as the grass of the field. In "The Land Taking" [the second part] the conflict is presented, the sentence is pronounced alike on human strength and human weakness, but Peder Victorious is born. Man falls in the taking of the land, but his seed survives for the founding of the kingdom. . . .

The concluding picture in *Giants in the Earth* is of Per Hansa in the horrid dissolution of death, struck down by the Monster of the Plain. The concluding scene in *Peder Victorious* is of mother Beret bending to the inevitable. Her son, promise of the future, is advancing to meet it, speaking the alien tongue of a new land, marrying an alien immigrant from another land, their son to be American-born of American-born. For her it is either estrangement or surrender, and the final choice is inevitable. Once more and in another way the pioneer is overcome, even while in the act of creating a new America.

Percy H. Boynton. EJ. Sept., 1929. pp. 539–40

Beneath the appalling wreck of amiable Lars Houglum's life [in *Pure Gold*], with all his simple aspirations swept away by the flame-like greed of his wife's thoroughly mean nature, even as she burned their house to ashes, there is the ancient tragedy of farm life—its meagreness, isolation, suspicion, its monotony, cruel toil and rare fulfillment.

Professor Rölvaag, one of the most interesting literary phenomena of our day, progresses unerringly toward his objective. There is something better than realism in his work—he has found within his breast that "crucible" wherein, according to Benedetto Croce, "the certain is converted into the true." Like many of the great Scandinavians, Rölvaag has genuine moral force and he has also that understanding of lives lived close to the soil, which is the essence of Hamsun's genius.

Outlook. Feb. 12, 1930. p. 267

As a piece of literature *The Boat of Longing* is noteworthy for its combination of two widely dissimilar strains, the mystical folktale and the realistic novel. On one page we read of an ecstatic vision followed by a mysterious disappearance; on the next, of a confidence game in a Y.M.C.A. Strangely enough, it is in the latter vein that Rölvaag is most authentic. When he writes in the manner of the old legends he is transparently the professor; it is too literary to grip us. But when he sets down simply the adventures of his hero in the New World he makes a real contribution. What is more, it is then that he is most Scandinavian, for the blood of the ancient Norsemen seems to prefer to show itself, not in romantic imitation of the sagas, but in the humdrum and commonplace of a Minneapolis alley.

Gerald Sykes. *Bkm*. March, 1933. pp. 302–3

The problems that arise from pioneering are discussed in *Giants in the Earth*. The problems that come from pioneers contrasted with new settlers, age versus youth, the coming into manhood and womanhood of the sons and daughters of the pioneers are discussed in *Peder Victorious*. The problems that the children of the pioneers, now the leaders of the community, have to face are expressed in *Their Father's God*. Besides this general progressive theme there are three other important themes that run through the trilogy: language and customs, shall they be given up? religion —first the lack of church organization, then the division of the church, and then inter-religious marriages, the social and political revolt of the youth of the settlement, and the conflict between age and youth. . . . The characters are, paradoxical as it may seem, both types and individuals in the novels of Rölvaag. As types they are used as symbols to express one of the main themes of the novel. For example, Per is the full embodiment of the spirit of adventure. He has deliberately chosen to come to the west to wrestle a living from nature. The elements are strong against him, the loneliness of the country sinks into his soul, discouragements array themselves before him, but he is possessed of that spirit which dares and fights to the end.

George Leroy White. *Scandinavian Themes in American Fiction* (Pennsylvania). 1937. p. 100

The transformation in the character of the pioneer, as described by [F. J.] Turner, is revealed in the two leading characters of the novel [*Giants in the Earth*], Per Hansa and his wife Beret, and to a lesser degree in the minor figures. Through the use of a mixed point of view and a modified stream-of-consciousness technique. Rölvaag ably demonstrates the varying results of the influence of the frontier upon the Norse. Per Hansa and Beret are case studies in frontier personality; their psychological natures cause them to react in startingly opposite ways to the stimuli of the prairie and its challenge. And, ironically, their fates are in inverse proportion to their attitudes: Per, stubborn, strong, resourceful, and optimistic, dies in a blinding blizzard; Beret, only partially recovered from her recurrent insanity, ascends to a plateau of serenity—the malignant prairie can no longer harm her.

Robert C. Steensma. *NDQ*. Autumn, 1959. p. 101

But if one is asked to select the most famous or the best South Dakota novel, he is likely to name Ole Rölvaag's masterful *Giants in the Earth*

(1927). Rölvaag's trilogy of early life in Dakota Territory and South Dakota has been largely ignored by historians and critics of American literature (he is given three scanty paragraphs in the *Literary History of the United States*). It may be true that *Peder Victorious* (1929) and *Their Father's God* (1931) do not measure up to the earliest novel, but the fact that Rölvaag, limited as his literary production might have been, has been given a back seat to such intellectual and artistic mediocrities as Dreiser, Farrell, Dos Passos, and, in certain respects, Sinclair Lewis, is a sad reflection on American criticism. The reasons for this eclipse are obvious. Some still think of Rölvaag as a Norwegian writer. While it is true that his books often made their first appearance in Norwegian, the translations were also his own work except for certain suggestions made by his close friends, among them Lincoln Colcord and Nora Solum. And there is also the possibility that Rölvaag was foolish and idealistic enough to write about pioneers in an age which was far more interested in jazz, gin, and the Charleston, both in its daily life and its fiction.

Robert C. Steensma. NDQ. Spring, 1962. p. 41

See *Giants in the Earth, Peder Victorious, Their Father's God, Pure Gold, Boat of Longing* (novels).

ROTH, HENRY (1906–   )

So much for the preparation; we know the story. But one is soon aware that this [*Call It Sleep*] is not merely a human document. Three levels of language are used to tell that story: one is the language of the narrator, another a direct translation of Yiddish into English, another a dialect that is neither English nor Yiddish but a transition between the two, at first a difficult and awkward tongue, ugly and harsh, yet slowly gaining speed and flexibility. Through the medium of these three levels a set of characters emerge: David the boy, his father, his mother, Aunt Bertha, and Rabbi Yidel Pankower, who is master within the whitewashed walls of a cheder. The technical device that Henry Roth employs reveals the various levels of experience in which his characters participate, and through the eyes of David we share something of that complex world: its transition between hope and fear, between fantasy and reality, between dreams of the old world left behind and the poverty-stricken terror of the new.

Horace Gregory. Nation. Feb. 27, 1935. p. 255

Although poverty . . . is the all-embracing, brutally dominating fact in slum tenement life, its climate, so to say, and its very soil, the author in his depiction almost completely ignores its role. What also helps to make the novel [*Call It Sleep*] seem unreal as a transcript of life is the author's injection of passages and chapters of stylized writing in the ultramodern tradition.

But the distortion of the picture—for, by and large, his picture is distorted—must be laid to the author's temper, which casts over familiar scenes and people a hectic light and creates an atmosphere in which human beings could not long survive. Mr. Roth's east side is an extremely violent and febrile world; rarely a moment of peace there, a breath of respite; nothing but poisonous life goes on. . . . There is much, to be sure, that is true in Mr. Roth's novel; he has a sensitive ear for speech; his characters speak from character and in the idioms of their land; he remembers amazingly and reports photographically; still, let me repeat, the book in part and as a whole does violence to the truth.

Joseph Gollomb. SR. March 16, 1935. p. 553

Since Michael Gold's *Jews Without Money* is likewise concerned with life in the East Side Ghetto at roughly the same historical time, it is instructive to compare his book with *Call It Sleep*. Though Gold's intentions were— to be fair—somewhat different from Roth's, the comparison shows the difference in result between the operations of the Coleridgian "fancy" and "imagination." Gold's book is that of a man with strong impulses and sympathies, but without, as the very sketch form of the book suggests, the capacity for sustained artistic vision. Roth's impulses and sympathies are strong also, but he has the ability, essential for the first-rate writer, to express them fully while simultaneously remaining in control of them, shaping them into the most effective form for transmission to the reader. Though the presence of an actual plot in *Call It Sleep* may seem contrived to some, the real force of the author is revealed in the intricate strength of his symbolic pattern. Both men, moreover, write with respect for their characters, even the hopelessly twisted ones; but Gold's people are simplified literally into sketches, while Roth's are given all the tangled complexity of human beings. Gold's pictures of the Ghetto are frequently blurred by a warm rush of sentiment or jarred out of focus by a kind of hysteria; Roth's view of the same life has the dizzying intensity of the mystic who sees all things at once, even the most minute, in utter clarity.

Walter Rideout. The Radical Novel in the United
States (Harvard). 1956. pp. 187–8

No book insists more [than does *Call It Sleep*] on the distance between the foulness man lives and the purity he dreams; but none makes more clear how deeply rooted that dream is in the existence which seems to contradict it. It is, perhaps, this double insight which gives to Roth's book a Jewish character, quite independent of the subject matter with which he happens to deal. . . .

It is possible to imagine many reasons for Roth's retreating to childhood from adult experience; for retreat it does seem in the light of his second withdrawal, after the publication of a single book, into the silence in which he has persisted until now. To have written such a book and no other is to betray some deep trouble not only in finding words but in loving the life one has lived enough to *want* to find words for it. A retreat from all that 1935 meant to Roth: from the exigencies of adult sexuality and political commitment alike—this is what *Call It Sleep* seems to the retrospective insight of 1960.

Leslie Fiedler. *Cmty.* Aug., 1960. p. 105

The scenes [in *Call It Sleep*] in the cheder, or Hebrew school, are both realistic and idealistic. The aggravated melamed, or teacher, is irritated and frustrated. The children of the New York immigrant Jews want to tear themselves away from their religious studies, but they fear their teacher. He uses a stick on them, shouts at them, but is delighted when one of them shows an aptitude for study. David is a good boy; he is willing to learn. The letters of the Hebrew alphabet come to him easily, and the blessings and prayers trip from his youthful lips. The teacher likes him for that. But the moment David becomes daring in class, or does something he shouldn't, the teacher—to whom Torah is of paramount importance —becomes a scourge and a tormentor. There is violence in these sketches, but the novelist writes out of love and understanding—and knowledge.

These are elements which have for a long time been missing in American Jewish writing. Where there is knowledge, there too frequently appears cynicism. And love and understanding are usually absent.

Harold U. Ribalow. *WSCL.* Fall, 1962. p. 11

Nineteen thirty-four began with a major event in publishing, the first American edition of Joyce's *Ulysses.* When *Call It Sleep* was published eleven months later, reviewers were struck by similarities between the two novels. Comparison of the two is inevitable: both make massive use of stream-of-consciousness; both are "noisy," their authors fascinated by the sheer clamor of interior and exterior experience. There are certain similarities of characterization. The placid femininity of Genya Schearl relates her to Molly Bloom; there are moments when the rabbi Yidel Pankower conjures up the alienated Leopold.

Certainly both can be called—using the term loosely—Freudian novels, novels based upon the assumption that total character can be revealed only when overt acts and speech are presented in relation to the freely associative flow of psychic experience. Roth's technical handling of this assumption is often highly Joycean: one might guess that both the Sirens and Circe chapters of *Ulysses,* in particular, exercised a strong influence on

Roth's presentation of the events in Chapter XXI of *Call It Sleep,* where young David Schearl runs through a wild storm of exterior and interior experience surrounding the climactic act of the novel.

Call It Sleep, however, is technically far less elaborate than *Ulysses,* and it is therefore surprising to find that the experience of reading it is somewhat more intense. . . . We have little choice but to rediscover ourselves in David Schearl; all the terrors, all the joys of childhood seem to dwell in his consciousness. In a very real sense, reading *Call It Sleep* is a psychoanalytic experience, capable of producing an unusual degree of emotional discomfort in the reader.

Sidney A. Knowles. MFS. Winter, 1965–66. p. 396

The imagination does not literally create, it transforms, and what it transforms are the very materials which Roth has transfigured in *Call It Sleep* —the fears, the anguish, the pain, and the ugliness of life—here a young boy's life on the Lower East Side. The important point, though, is that Roth has transfigured his raw materials without distorting them out of recognizable shape. For the myths of redemption and rebirth are implicit in the story of David Schearl, and both are rendered largely by means of a symbolic image pattern that is part of David's own conscious awareness and that is viewed symbolically by his own fertile imagination as well as by the reader. Such a fusion of myth, symbol, and profound realism does more than raise *Call It Sleep* far beyond the level of most of the proletarian fiction that once obscured it. It makes Roth's novel one of those too rare works of fiction that we can both live and admire, simultaneously.

William Freedman in The Thirties, edited by Warren
French (Everett Edwards). 1967. p. 114

See *Call It Sleep* (novel).

ROTH, PHILIP (1933–   )

It's not far from Newark to Short Hills—or from the Bronx to Westchester —but the gap is sometimes unbridgeable, no matter how steep a toll one is prepared to pay. It is about the middle-class Jewish residents of both these worlds that Philip Roth writes in his first book, *Goodbye, Columbus.* . . . Philip Roth surveys the role of the Jew in modern American society with keen perception. Underlying his stories is the Jews' century-old tragic sense of life, leavened with warmth and humor, and with compassion. There are no excesses of sentimentality or bitterness: his characters cannot be typed as either Molly Goldbergs or Sammy Glicks.

If there is any doubt in my mind, it concerns the validity of these stories for the non-Jewish, or even the non-Eastern, reader. For so much depends on a familiarity with the peculiarly parochial surroundings and the subtle speech inflections.

Arnold Dolin. SR. May 16, 1959. p. 31

In some ways Jews may be thin-skinned and sensitive but in others they have a capacity to mock themselves mercilessly. That is why there are so many superb comedians among them. That is also why their best writers have written of them with an awareness of the thin line between the ludicrous and the pathetic, the comic and the tragic. Among those who have recently exploited this vein is Bernard Malamud. Now Philip Roth joins this company with a short novel and five short stories . . . marked by a comic, almost a caricaturist's, view of character, and effects that are at once funny and dreadful. At his most serious he has an original and most disturbing capacity for converting farce into nightmare.

Milton Rugoff. NYHT. May 17, 1959. p. 3

What many writers spend a lifetime searching for—a unique voice, a secure rhythm, a distinctive subject—seem to have come to Philip Roth totally and immediately. At 26 he is a writer of narrow range but intense effects. He composes stories about the life of middle-class American Jews with a ferocity it would be idle to complain about, so thoroughly do they pour out of his own sense of things.

   Mr. Roth's stories do not yield pleasure as much as produce a squirm of recognition: surely one feels, not all of American Jewish life is like this, but all too much is becoming so. Anyone who might object to these stories insofar as they are "reports" about a style of life cannot do it on the ground that Mr. Roth is hard-spirited—for given his material what else can he be?—or that he is unskilled—for, like so many other young writers these days, he has quickly absorbed the lessons of modern crafts-manship, perhaps a bit too quickly. If one is to object to these stories on non-literary grounds, out of a concern for the feelings or reputation of middle-class American Jews, it can be done only by charging that, in effect, Mr. Roth is a liar. And that, I am convinced, he is not.

Irving Howe. NR. June 15, 1959. p. 17

Goodbye, Columbus is a first book but it is not the book of a beginner. Unlike those of us who came howling into the world, blind and bare, Mr. Roth appears with nails, hair, and teeth, speaking coherently. At twenty-six he is skillful, witty, and energetic and performs like a virtuoso. His one fault, and I don't expect all the brethren to agree that it is a fault, is that he is so very sophisticated. Sometimes he twinkles too much. The New York Times has praised him for being "wry." One such word to the wise ought to be sufficient. Mr. Roth has a superior sense of humor (see his story "Epstein"), and I think he can count on it more safely than on his "wryness."

Saul Bellow. *Cmty*. July, 1959. p. 77

The best of the *New Yorker* story writers, like John Cheever, always make me feel that, keen as they are, there is a whole side to their observations of American society that is entirely fantastic, imaginative, almost visionary, and so belongs to themselves alone. Roth, though emphatically not tailored to the *New Yorker,* involuntarily fits it because of a certain excess of intellectual theme over the material. There are too many symbols of present-day society, too many quotable bright sayings; the stories tend too easily to make a point. . . . I admire the edge and fierceness of Mr. Roth's mind, but his book (*Goodbye, Columbus*) leaves me worried about his future. For he has put so much of himself into being clear, decisive, straight, his stories are consciously so brave, that I worry whether he hasn't worked himself too neatly into a corner. He shows himself too anxious in each story not only to dramatize a conflict but also to make the issue of the conflict absolutely clear.

Alfred Kazin. *Contemporaries* (Little). 1962. pp. 261–2

That Roth is a careful observer and has a good ear is known to every reader of *Goodbye, Columbus,* but these gifts can be abused, and in the novel (*Letting Go*) Roth has abused them. Line by line the writing is fine, but that does not save long stretches from being unpardonably dull and quite superfluous. . . . What the book seems to demonstrate is not that contemporary civilization is a disaster but that many people manage to mess up their lives—which isn't news. . . . Let me make it clear that Roth is still a figure to be reckoned with. This is the kind of bad book that only a good writer could have written. But, after *Goodbye, Columbus,* with its vitality and sureness of touch, *Letting Go* is a disappointment.

Granville Hicks. *SR*. June 16, 1962. p. 16

Letting Go is not just a book that displays the virtues of *Goodbye, Columbus* at far greater length. It is also a deliberate and almost too fully achieved realization of the sense of life that Mr. Roth shares to a large extent with his whole generation and in very obvious ways with such writers as Saul Bellow, Harvey Swados, and William Styron (and with Jack Kerouac, too, who provides an unintentional parody of it). This sense of life is oddly self-conscious and limited, despite the talent and insight of these writers, as if they had spent more of their lives with the *Paris Review* crowd or in Iowa City or some similar "creative writing" center than was good for them as writers. It is almost exclusively personal. There is a great deal about the public life in these writers, but they always see that life as an unjustifiable, inexplicable—if immovable—obstacle to the realization of the private self, which is inexhaustibly queried, analyzed and suffered over by everyone in their books, as it might be in some incredibly brilliant soap opera or undergraduate short story.

Arthur Mizener. NYT. June 17, 1962. p. 1

If there is any fault with this novel (*Letting Go*), it is that Mr. Roth is too lavish with his gifts. His talent for swift and concise characterization is such that he tends to bring minor characters unnecessarily into the foreground of the action. The result is that the book becomes too diffuse. In a few remarkable pages near the beginning he has given us Paul and Libby to the life; we know the kind of history they will have, and we hardly need the remorseless accumulation of detail with which Mr. Roth follows their fortunes. Complex as their personalities are, their life together is too threadbare and starveling to carry the weight of a saga.

William Barrett. At. July, 1962. p. 111

Perhaps it would have been as well for Philip Roth if he hadn't been cited again and again as a leading member of the new school of American-Jewish novelists. Without so portentous a label hung round his neck, he might never have been lured into writing such tawdry, incoherent stuff. . . . Writers like Bellow and Malamud derive their blend of warmth and irony both from the intensity of the past, and from their ambiguous relationship with that past. From Jewish experience they abstract a metaphor for 20th century man: rueful, displaced, tragi-comic. Mr. Roth has borrowed a few externals from this tradition, but his high-gloss prose suggests another line of descent. He really belongs with a very different group of American-Jewish writers, the slick professionals like Irwin Shaw, Jerome Weidman, or even Herman Wouk.

John Gross. NSN. Nov. 30, 1962. p. 784

What grieves Roth most is the awareness that normalcy has, like a Procrustes' bed, truncated the range of life, excluding on the one hand the embrace of aspiration, the exhilaration of wonder, and on the other the acceptance of suffering. From this sadness grows Roth's ferocity, directly mainly against those who deny life, against the cowards who fear it, against all who would reduce it to safe insignificance, against all who flee from self and suffering—to seek repose is a travesty of all the realities of life and the potential of man. Roth is committed to his unheroic heroes who yearn and aspire, who want to climb out of the morass "up the long marble stairs that led to Tahiti."

Joseph C. Landis. MR. Winter, 1962. p. 261

Whatever the faults, "Goodbye, Columbus" is a rich and deeply moving story, provocative in many directions. It marks the successful working out of a significant theme: the rejection of Jewish life, not because it is too Jewish, but because it is not Jewish enough, because it is so dominated by and infused with the American ethos that it partakes of the same corruption, offering no significant alternative.

(K)   Dan Isaac. *CR*. 1964. p. 90

American society as a whole has developed many ways in which personal confrontation can be avoided, and in a story such as "Eli, the Fanatic" Roth himself recognizes this and extends his criticism beyond the Jews. But if the avoidance of confrontation, indeed the willful escape from all that it involves, is not limited to the Jew, it is nonetheless, as seen in Roth's stories, the dominant Jewish problem. Perhaps it is here that the Jew is becoming Americanized, and that we can see the assimilation of which Roth's reviewers speak. Still, the author's focus on the need for relationship is a specification of something more than becoming American or middle-class; it is both a sign of Roth's intense involvement in Judaism's deepest values, and a criticism of both the Jew and the middle-class in terms of a problem that is not so much sociological as it is spiritual and fundamentally human.

(K)   Norman Leer. *Christian Scholar*. Summer, 1966. p. 134

Philip Roth's *When She Was Good* is a strange book disguised as a conventional one. . . .

All this has the sadness and the authenticity of a small-town graveyard. The simple effort to make a simple life can be tragic. Simple small-town people, who are nicknamed "Blondie" and who think this "corny," can go mad with despair. They aspire only to Fort Kean College for Women, and for a family; but are their vocabularies too vulgar even for this? Is it inadequate perhaps even to aspire to a family, to be American, to live in a small town? Why is the author so meticulously absent? Scarcely does he even mock them, as Sinclair Lewis used to do; he does not seem to wish them well, as Sherwood Anderson did, nor to connect them with human fate, as Peter Taylor does. Only once is he really savage, and this is exactly about the inadequacy of their vocabularies, of the vocabulary in which the story is so subtly told. . . . One can only wonder why the author, from whatever height he has concealed himself upon, has watched these people with a gaze so long and pitiless and blank.

(K)   John Thompson. *NYR*. June 15, 1967. pp. 15–16

The deadness at the corner of *When She Was Good* is no accident. It is the deliberate result of Philip Roth's cold persecution of his characters. And a certain ugly power gets generated when a highly gifted writer so relentlessly denies sympathy to his own creations. . . . After a dilly-dallying beginning, Mr. Roth's execution of this subject is straightforward, fast and appallingly flat. At first I took the two-dimensionality as Pop Art, but soon the malice behind the comic-strip simplifications became too audible to ignore. The caricatures are recognizable but Mr. Roth's feeling about them seems privately motivated, to the point where he can do nothing but say it all over and over again. Nothing in what Lucy does, nothing in the people she tortures, deepens our understanding of her or increases our sense of her importance. Rather the opposite—we are moved to protect her. And it seems also to be chiefly Mr. Roth who is victimizing her husband.

With this character, however, it becomes possible to place the quality of Mr. Roth's motive and emotion more accurately. I recognize Roy Bassart—or rather, I recognize my feelings about the type. Roy Bassart brings to mind words I haven't used much since high school, words like "jerk" and "schnook."

(K)   Robert Garis. *HdR*. Summer, 1967. p. 328

In the same year as [Donald Barthelme's] *Snow White* Philip Roth has published *When She Was Good,* which is in effect a posthumous Dreiser novel, with much family-album verisimilitude ("Edward's bronchitis had lingered nearly three weeks") and some acutely observed American domesticity. Roth continues, clumsily and anachronistically, to be gnawed —as he was in that underrated novel, *Letting Go*—by the problem of sin and responsibility. Why do destructive people behave as they do? How do they persuade themselves that they are good? How does it *feel* to be bad? Roth cares about such questions, stumbling along in the burlap sack of his prose. . . .

When She Was Good is, most of it, hopelessly old-fashioned, and it is an interesting novel. Why not? The novel, of all artifacts, remains the one least divisible from its artificer, whose idiosyncrasies and judgments may prevail over the demands of the genre itself. Roth's mind, besieged by archaic American dreariness, is more interesting than Barthelme's or [William] Burroughs'. Novels are too long, the novelist can't get away with gimmicks or momentary flashes; he has to disclose substance and continuity somewhere, perhaps in himself.

(K)   Marvin Mudrick. *HdR*. Autumn, 1967. pp. 485–6

See *Goodbye, Columbus* (stories); *Letting Go, When She Was Good* (novels).

ROURKE, CONSTANCE (1885–1941)

Certainly these five figures dealt in words: Lyman Beecher and Henry Ward, the preachers, Harriet Beecher Stowe, the novelist who helped make a war, Horace Greeley, incessantly pouring forth words, and often very picturesque words, in his Tribune, and Barnum, the first of the advertisers and persuaders of the mob to believe in miracles.

They had in them a kind of greatness of vision coupled often enough with an inadequacy of thought. Yet they spoke for their time, and the time heard. [In *Trumpets of Jubilee*] Miss Rourke gives solid three-dimensional portraits of these symbols. She is none too gentle with their pretense and their ultimate thinness, but she understands how they molded and also voiced their generation. . . . This volume is not one of debunking, but of de-mything. These so-called giants are caught out of their official poses and stripped of the legends that have helped to make them great. Yet within them resided something of greatness, much of courage, and vast reservoirs of tumultuous energy and democratic faith in mere size that we find missing from our present quiet, but less exciting day.

Leon Whipple. *Survey*. July 1, 1927. p. 390

Here [*Troupers of the Gold Coast*] is a story of the theatre written as such a story should be. The gold-rush days of California in the fifties and sixties were an exuberant, changing pattern of comedy, tragedy, farce, and melodrama, and, strangely enough, a vigorous theatre flourished at the same time and in the same mood. The excitement and color of both, Miss Rourke manages to capture within the pages of her book. Tent-shows, saloon halls, lavish buildings housed these productions in San Francisco, Sacramento, Sonora. The troupers travelling mule-back from mining camp to mining camp played under any roof available. Those were the days of child actors, minstrels, satires, burlesques, varied at times with large quantities of Shakespeare, and increasingly with ballads, jigs, hornpipes, and cruel imitations of rival productions. Those were the days also of audiences who plunged headlong into the spirit of the performance themselves, hurling comments, choruses, bags of nuggets, or missiles with equal extravagance; and of companies led by such actors as Edwin Booth, Laura Keene, Caroline Chapman, Lola Montez.

Vera Kelsey. *TA*. Nov., 1928. p. 844

It is a mighty subject, this of American humor: a subject one conceives of as approachable from ever so many unsuspected angles; and it could hardly have fallen, for the moment, into better hands than Miss Rourke's. For one thing, it is not easy to think of many writers capable at once of her industry and of her skill, of her patience in research and her lucidity in exposition; in a word, of her balanced competence. *American Humor* is an erudite book: it is chock full of what are called "materials"; but among a thousand such it is the one book that stands on its own legs, and allows you, in spite of everything, to see the wood as well as the trees.

But this is not all, or indeed the best, that one can say of it. Literary competence is one thing, and gifted insight is another; and what chiefly gratifies a reader of Miss Rourke's is her sense of the many dimensions in her subject, the free play of her mind over more than a few of its aspects: particularly, her recognition that the problem must be constantly referred to psychology and constantly posed against a background of social history. Humor not simply as a formal entity, a literary mode, but humor envisaged dynamically as the product of personal needs and social conflicts, the expression of a whole people's ambitions and disappointments and joy in achievement: such is the subject of her book as Miss Rourke apprehends it.

Newton Arvin. NR. April 22, 1931. p. 278

This interpretation of the American character—which, by the way, has a malapropos title [*American Humor*] that conveys both too little and too much—embodies the results of what a politician would call a fishing expedition. For what Miss Rourke has done is to throw her hook into all the waters of the American spirit in the hope of pulling something to the surface with each cast; and she has let what she has fished up dictate her conclusions. There is therefore no air of preconception about her brilliant study; and if she has let one or two fish get away from her, that is because mortal arms are not as strong as Paul Bunyan's or Davy Crockett's or Mike Fink's. Her lucid style is admirably adapted to skirting the abysses of the human spirit without falling in and calling it mysticism; and she makes tenuous matters seem solid as headlands.

Miss Rourke begins with American mythology and ends with the more conscious literature of Henry James, Ring Lardner, Sinclair Lewis, and Willa Cather. She has tried to uncover national characteristics as revealed by what American story tellers have conceived their countrymen to be in various places and at various times. The first clear figure in our mythology is that of the Yankee, the man "lank as a leafless elm" from down east (originally from Yorkshire?), who always got the better of a bargain, whether on the coast of the China seas or in swapping a horse on Gus Longstreet's Georgia frontier. . . . Meanwhile in the West, a rival myth was springing up. This was the myth of the gamecock of the wilderness, the man who could whip his weight in wildcats.

John Chamberlain. Forum. June, 1931. pp. vi–vii

The first hundred and thirty-seven pages [of *American Humor*] trace the rise of the Yankee cult in the East, the Backwoodsman in the West, and the "long tail'd blue" tradition in the South. The trinity of American mythology reveals the fundamental characteristics of the native humor—both folk and professional—: an innate love for masquerade; a perverted self-consciousness; story-telling by means of a monologue which borders on soliloquy; a prepossession for the homely and 'natural'; and an obsession for size, strength, scale, power (cf. the "tall tale")....

American Humor is in many ways a study of profound value. It would be if it did nothing except call attention to the importance of native influences on our writers, often overlooked, especially in the criticism on Poe. But many of the characteristics which Miss Rourke identifies as American comic traditions may just as accurately be attributed to foreign sources. For example, reverence for the homely and 'natural' is merely a phase of European romanticism; the monologue bordering on soliloquy is found in the Bible, among other places; and since it is usually admitted that practically all the Kentucky ballads are simply paraphrases and adaptations of the original three hundred and six English and Scottish ballads, is it not likely that most of our folk legends have been transported and transmuted from Europe?

Gay Wilson Allen. SwR. Jan.-Mar., 1932. pp. 112–13

Davy Crocket is designed for younger readers, but the simplicity of style and of treatment that Miss Rourke has achieved results not from vulgarization or condescension but from a complete mastery of her material and a scholarship thorough and discriminating. Miss Rourke is steeped in the psychological atmosphere of the American West: she neither interprets nor criticises, but recreates as a dramatist recreates character. *Davy Crockett* has the saltiness, the homely realism, the gusto, and the energy that made *American Humor* one of the notable books of recent years; though a far less ambitious work than the earlier one, the Crockett volume is no less successful. Miss Rourke is, properly, just as concerned with the Crockett myth as with Crockett himself, and she has not sought to distinguish the two with irrelevant precision.

Henry Steele Commager. YR. June, 1934. pp. 846–7

The old question "Can the artist work in America?" is the underlying subject of this book [*Charles Sheeler, Artist in the American Tradition*]. And in telling the story of Charles Sheeler's career as an American artist Miss Rourke makes an affirmative answer that both convinces the mind and excites the imagination. The question is of such long standing that, as Miss Rourke points out, it has itself functioned as part of the American tradition; and the doubt it expresses, combined with the further assumption that American art is merely the offshoot of European art, has served to limit both the possibilities and the self-assurance of many an artist. It has, moreover, tended to discourage the realization of our native cultural past by its implication that the past is so scanty as not to be worth the trouble. It is Miss Rourke's thesis, on the contrary, that we have a cultural past, particularly in the arts, far richer than we are wont to assume—witness our early portraiture, wall paintings, water colors—and that one of the principal tasks of criticism is to gather it in, give it usable shape, and make it part of the national consciousness—if we are ever to produce a full-blown and distinctively American culture.

Margaret Marshall. Nation. Sept. 17, 1938. p. 270

She was equally at home in music, literature, painting, drama, and the crafts; and she would run down an obscure picture, ferret out a local tale, or rummage through heaps of faded letters with the relentless patience that marks the useful spadeworker. But she had what few ordinary field workers have: a sense of relative values; so that all her special items gained value by their relevance to the greater whole she carried in her mind. . . .

American culture, as Constance Rourke conceived it, had its roots in the folk and emanated from their fresh experience in a new land. Even when it made use of European techniques or materials, it transposed the European notes into another key and another measure. Indians, Negroes, Moravian peasants, Puritans, Shakers, farmers, merchants, miners, lumbermen, cowboys, all had made their contributions to our rich cultural compost: they had never been so materialistic, so preoccupied with the mere urgencies of physical survival, as a more utilitarian interpretation had supposed. What had seemed a lapse of culture in one generation often turned out to be only a lapse of memory in the generation that succeeded it.

Lewis Mumford. SR. Aug. 15, 1942. p. 3

Constance Rourke's first book of genuine folk criticism was *Charles Sheeler,* published in 1938. In Sheeler she found a serious artist (although not so good a one as she believed) who had discovered an American folk tradition for himself, the functional form of the Shaker artisans, and who had consciously grounded his work in it, to the work's great benefit. Looking at Sheeler's paintings and photographs (many of them reproduced as evidence in the book), she discovered the basic principle that had eluded previous popularizers of the folk tradition, that a tradition is not in subject but in *form,* that the secret does not lie in painting a hillbilly building a silo, but in painting *as* a hillbilly builds a silo. (This was the key realization that helped her to such later insights as that the writers who said we had no native theatrical tradition were wrong. They hadn't known where to look. She looked in the public ceremonial of the Indian treaty, in the dialectic play of the Calvinist sermon, and found it.)

Stanley Edgar Hyman. The Armed Vision (Knopf).
1948. p. 130

Her interests reached beyond the bellestristic and included the arts of all kinds, however humble, so long as they were indigenous and representative of the ongoing life of the American people. She directed research and selected material for the *Index of American Design,* making as complete a record as was then possible of the arts and the role they played in American life. This indeed is the sustaining spirit and animating purpose behind her work; she sought to render explicit and give proper emphasis to the organic connection between folk traditions, many of which actively survive, and national art. She set herself the monumental task of assembling and interpreting all the material of this sort that still remained so that the native roots of our culture might be widely known and serve to call forth the best in the creative workers of our land. Unfortunately she died before carrying out her ambitious plan to compose a three-volume *History of American Culture,* but she had succeeded in discovering and making available an American folk tradition that American writers and artists could put constructively to use. This is her most distinctive contribution to the field of American criticism.

> Charles Glicksberg. *American Literary Criticism, 1900–1950* (Hendricks House). 1951. pp. 498–9

The march of our [American] experience has been so dominantly expansive, from one rapid disequilibrium to the next, that we have neglected to see what Constance Rourke, among others, has now pointed out so effectively: that notwithstanding the inevitable restlessness of our long era of pioneering, at many stages within that process the strong counter-effort of the settlers was for communal security and permanence. From such islands of realization and fulfilment within the onrushing torrent have come the objects, the order and balance of which now, when we most need them, we can recognize as among the most valuable possessions of our continent. The conspicuous manifestation of these qualities, as [Horatio] Greenough already knew, has been in architecture as the most social of forms, whether in the clipper, or on the New England green, or in the Shaker communities. But the artifacts of the cabinet maker, the potter and the founder, or whatever other utensils have been shaped patiently and devotedly for common service, are likewise a testimony of what Miss Rourke has called our classic art, recognizing that this term "has nothing to do with grandeur, that it cannot be copied or imported, but is the outgrowth of a special mode of life and feeling."

> F. O. Matthiessen. *American Renaissance* (Oxford). 1954. p. 172

See *Trumpets of Jubilee, Troupers of the Gold Coast, Davy Crockett, Audubon, Charles Sheeler* (biographies); *American Humor, The Roots of Culture* (essays).

RUKEYSER, MURIEL (1913–   )

Theory of Flight is one of those rare first volumes which impress by their achievement more than by their promise. It is remarkable poetry to have been written by a girl of twenty-one, and would do credit to most of her elders. . . . Here is a well-stored, vigorous mind attempting to bring its world into some kind of imaginative and human order. . . . Miss Rukeyser's poems are among the few so far written in behalf of the revolutionary cause which combine craftsmanship, restraint, and intellectual honesty.

Philip Blair Rice. Nation. Jan. 29, 1936. p. 134

Miss Rukeyser's first book is remarkable for its self-confidence and lack of hesitation. At twenty-one, she has already covered much of the technical ground of modern American verse, and has learned how to pick up everything she feels capable of consolidating into a poem. . . . Miss Rukeyser's verse, however, unlike that of the immediately preceding generation of modernists, does not emanate from the decorative or phenomenalistic fascination alone; it contains a moral will, a will to make itself useful as statement, and a will to warm itself against the major human situations of our day. Thus the subjective, rarely quieted in her, is redirected towards recurrent themes of class-oppression, death, the historical background, revolution.

Harold Rosenberg. Poetry. May, 1936. pp. 107–8

Though at first consideration she seems typical of our young class-conscious poets, she will be found to transcend them in nearly every respect. Her materials, like her contemporaries', is every-day life. . . . Her viewpoint, like theirs, has the clearness and objectivity of a photograph. But she is far more aware what an adaptable instrument the camera is, and achieves effects the poetic realist of the past never dreamed of. . . . Where her confreres tend to grasp only broad social phenomena, or only isolated examples, she captures both the general meaning and the specific detail, plays one against the other, thereby reaching a truer, more moving analysis.

Kerker Quinn. NYHT. Feb. 20, 1938. p. 12

There are moments in *US 1* that are pretty dull, but that's bound to be the character of all good things if they are serious enough: when a devoted and determined person sets out to do a thing he isn't thinking first of being brilliant, he wants to get there even if he has to crawl on his face. When he is able to—whenever he is able to—he gets up and runs. . . .

(But) I hope Miss Rukeyser does not lose herself in her injudicious haste for a "cause," accepting, uncritically, what she does as satisfactory, her intentions being of the best. I hope she will stick it out the hardest way, a tough road, and invent! make the form that will embody her rare gifts of intelligence and passion for a social rebirth the chief object of her labors.

William Carlos Williams. *NR*. March 9, 1938.

pp. 141–2

What most distinguishes Muriel Rukeyser's third book, *A Turning Wind,* from her earlier work is an extension of method and point of view, which has greatly enriched her poetry and at the same time introduced a corresponding, though not, I believe, a necessary obscurity.

The extension of viewpoint may best be described in simplification as a shift of emphasis from the concrete to the abstract, from the immediate concern with evidence of social decay and its remedies to the more speculative concern with its causes, particularly psychological. . . . One reason, I believe, for the occasional failure to communicate is that Miss Rukeyser has not yet been wholly successful in extending her method to keep pace with the extension of viewpoint and subject matter.

Philip Horton. *NR*. Jan. 22, 1940. p. 123

What is exciting about Miss Rukeyser's work is the vitality and largeness of her ideas and feelings, and the amazing but controlled originality of her methods of expressing them. . . . Hers is an original and startling talent for the bright and expanding image, the concrete phantasy, the magical reality of a world of machines, cities, social forces, and nervous complexities. . . . Even when one cannot put his words on what all her "sources of power" are, one feels she has power. Beauty and thought are tremendously exciting even when we cannot measure their height, or compass their horizons.

Mildred Boie. *At*. Feb., 1940. Unpaged

If Muriel Rukeyser is—as I believe she is—the most inventive and challenging poet of the generation which has not yet reached thirty, it is because of her provocative language fully as much as because of her audacious ideas. . . . *Theory of Flight* announced a new symbolism as well as a new speech. The style was swift, abrupt, syncopated; it matched the speed of the strepitant post-war world, the crazy energy of murderous machines, the "intolerable contradiction" of flight. . . . For her the images of war and industry are all too natural. . . . It is the "agonies of decision" which Miss Rukeyser expresses for more than her own generation. . . . In the midst of desperate remedies and clamoring negatives, she affirms the life of people and the life of poetry—the life of the spirit giving all processes and inventions, the creative life which is the double answer to living slavery and to the wish for quick escapes, comforting death.

Louis Untermeyer. *SR*. Aug. 10, 1940. pp. 11–3

One of the most interesting phases of the transformation of the social poet in years of stress is the change in his use of language. In the case of Muriel Rukeyser, it moves from that of simple declarative exhortation, in the common phrases of the city man, to that of a gnarled, intellectual, almost private observation. In her earlier usage, images are apt to be simple and few; the whole approach is apt to be through the medium of urban speech. In the latter work, images become those of the psychologist, or of the surrealist, charged with increasing complication of symbols; the first are public, the last, even though they may represent universal issues, are privately conceived and privately endowed.

John Malcolm Brinnin. *Poetry*. Jan., 1943. p. 555

The dilemma of conflict rising from an unresolved dualism in view-point has characterized Muriel Rukeyser's recent work. . . . Hers is a poetry of confusion in a confused world—a poetry which submits to that confusion—falls back upon the non-rational: the myth, the dream, the supernatural; or selects as its mouth-pieces a "drunken girl," a "madboy," a "child." By so doing, the poet seemingly justifies lack of organization, disassociated images, abrupt shifts in person and tense, and enigmatical meaning. . . . It seems to me her poems are much more effective when she forgets myth, symbol and dream . . . and turns to factual events or experiences common to the majority of men and women today.

Ruth Lechlitner. *NYHT*. Dec. 31, 1944. p. 4

Muriel Rukeyser is a forcible writer with a considerable talent for emotional rhetoric, but she has a random melodramatic hand and rather unfortunate models and standards for her work—one feels about most of her poems pretty much as one feels about the girl on last year's calendar. . . . One feels, with dismay and delight, that one is listening to the Common Siren of our century, a siren photographed in a sequin bathing suit, on rocks like boiled potatoes, for the week-end edition of PM, in order to bring sex to the deserving poor. . . . Yet all the time the poem keeps repeating, keeps remembering to repeat, that it is a *good* girl—that it is, after all, dying for the people; the reader wanders, full of queasy delight, through the labyrinthine corridors of the strange, moral, sexual wish-fantasy for which he is to be awarded, somehow, a gold star by the Perfect State.

Randall Jarrell. *Nation*. May 8, 1948. pp. 512–3

In a time of shrinking poets and shrinking critics here, at any rate, is one capable in both poetry and criticism, who expands and embraces. . . . Miss Rukeyser disowns little or nothing. With her poet's knack of seeing the symbolic meanings in events and the connections latent in them, and with various and deep reading she adduces and enriches from every quarter of contemporary life, from punctuation to the blues, from Fenellosa to Leadbelly. . . . Yet I have a disturbing sense that in these recent poems Miss Rukeyser's motile, ringing energies are becoming over-agitated. Frenetic is too harsh a word, but her images and rhythms, like Shelley's, seem humid and driven by a general passion behind and so external to all particular items of our experience.

James R. Caldwell. *SR*. March 11, 1950. p. 26

Non-fiction? Fiction? A poem? Miss Rukeyser tells us in her foreword: "It is a book, a story, and a song." The bookmaking is beautiful, the story is Wendell Willkie's, and power (public and private) is the song.

One Life is episodic, dissonant, fragmented, and explosive—as Willkie's life was and as his country still is. Indeed, the temptation to condescend to Willkie's human failures, to faint-praise his history, is part of a reader's temptation to faint-praise Muriel Rukeyser's rhetoric, and to condescend to the faults of this book. Yet this is perhaps the most ambitious attempt since *Let Us Now Praise Famous Men* to define a segment of America, and for that it deserves any reader's praise. . . . The wonder, in all such history, is that Miss Rukeyser doesn't heroize Willkie; she sees, rather, heroic dimensions in his search for identity and in his capacity for growth. He becomes, somehow, a kind of political Sisyphus, in the act of failure succeeding most—all in the amorphous America for which Miss Rukeyser, too, risks so greatly.

(K)   Philip Booth. *SR*. August 3, 1957. p. 12

Of her one does not use the word elegant; rather, primordial. She is long-swept Whitmanian without rhyme. She is not didactic. She has a love of life and sings of people and things. Her love and care for mankind are evident in every poem. The strength of her convictions coupled with her integrated conception of the world probably makes for the originality of her style, which is uncompromising in its difference from that of other poets and is always fresh, vibrant, profound.

Poetry is a personal thrusting and stance of being. It is thrown into the relations of mankind. It cannot exist without communication and is thus profoundly allied to society. Miss Rukeyser exemplifies these tenets. Hers is the great insolence of poetry and its great love. Never a cultist, never given to this fad or that, or labeled with the mark of only one decade, she submits her vision to art as a strong personal force and her delighting power to a lifetime of concentrated effort in a unitary plane. It is this striding vigor that I find most American. She is not a jewel-maker but a fire-thrower. It is the heavy brunt of meaning that we take on every page and in which many readers rejoice.

(K)   Richard Eberhart. *NYT*. Sept. 9, 1962. p. 4

Muriel Rukeyser has published a large body of work since her first collection, *Theory of Flight,* appeared when she was only twenty-one. It immediately marked her as an innovator, thoroughly American, Whitman-like in method and scope. Characteristic of her poetry, of which we now have a survey in *Waterlily Fire* (Poems 1935-1962), is the big canvas, the broad stroke, love of primary color and primary emotion. Her method is the opposite of the designer's, her vision is never small, seldom introverted. Her consciousness of *others* around her, of being but one member of a great writhing body of humanity surging out of the past, filling the present, groping passionately toward the future, is a generating force in her work. She celebrates science as much as nature or the restless human heart. . . . Another main fulcrum of her work is psychological, even mystical (but it never departs from a physical, in fact a sexual base), and exploration of being and becoming and then of re-becoming, growing out of her interest in Eastern philosophy as well as Western primitivism.

(K)   May Swenson. *Nation*. Feb. 23, 1963. p. 164

In *The Orgy,* the poet and biographer Muriel Rukeyser has written a book that is less a conventional novel than a record of the experience of Puck Fair as felt through a thoroughly modern sensibility steeped in the literature of anthropology and psychology. It is hard, even, to guess to what extent this record is fiction; the otherwise unidentified narrator is addressed at one point as "Muriel," and there are a number of other references to well-known persons. Miss Rukeyser herself describes the book as a "free fantasy" on a real event, and the evidence at hand would appear to indicate that this is a precise and well-chosen term. . . . The narrator and her friends, responding to the dimly understood mysteries of the old, pagan religion, provide on one level a counterpoint of psychoanalysis and comparative anthropology, while on another level they are caught up in the orgiastic spirit of the fair, their partings and rejoinings seeming to have become powerfully infused with new and rather disturbing meanings.

This is a poet's book in a real sense—distilled, allusive, with more suggested than is in plain sight. I read it with great interest, with enthusiasm even, and still feel somewhat under the brooding influence of its dark and troubling beauty.

(K)   Kenneth Lamott. *NYHT*. Feb. 28, 1965. p. 20

In a brief preface [to *The Orgy*] Miss Rukeyser's very knowledgeable book is stated to be a free fantasy on the event [Puck Fair in Ireland]. The goat, the fair and the orgy are real. Nevertheless there is so much dropping of actual names throughout her account that it is difficult to avoid regarding it as autobiographical. . . . The book itself is both exciting and intriguing. It is written in an unusual style that might, perhaps, be described as verse, under the disguise of free prose, rather than the more usual prose in the form of free verse. This method has many of the allusive qualities of poetry, together with its concomitant disregard for continuity, and some occasional doubts as to who or what the writer is referring. . . . Miss Rukeyser's technique also has a strong resemblance to that of the documentary cinema—a montage in which the writer piles up a catalogue of visual images, untrammeled on the whole by verbs, in the course of which, like the camera, she is able to focus the attention not on the scene as a whole but on some special element that impresses her. . . . One may perhaps wonder whether so subjective a method is suited to so extrovert an occasion—assuming, of course, that Puck Fair is the actual point of the book.

(K)   Denis Johnston. *Nation*. March 15, 1965. pp. 202–3

See *Waterlily Fire* (poems); *Life of Poetry* (criticism); *One Life, Willard Gibbs* (biographies); *The Orgy* (novel).

RUNYON, DAMON (1880–1946)

Damon Runyon's stories are spiked with sentiment and served with Broadway hard sauce. Here [*Damon Runyon's Blue Plate Special*] are thirteen characteristic dishes, already approved by the palate of the magazine public, including a lively murder mystery called "What, No Butler?" and a tear-jerker, entitled "Little Miss Marker," which has been recently perpetuated in enduring celluloid. Chorus girls, cheap sports, race track hustlers and other specimens of Broadway hangers-on comprise Mr. Runyon's cast of characters. He is familiar with their language, their habits and their minds. His fables are fluent, ingenious, first-rate entertainment.

Lisle Bell. *NYHT*. Aug. 5, 1934. p. 8

In Our Town, a collection of twenty-seven anecdotes, though bereft of the vocabulary and much of the historical present of *Guys and Dolls, Money From Home, Blue Plate Special*, is still the Runyon of old.

The cynical humor that spoofs at stuffed-shirtism, the simplicity of style, the sympathy for the underdog and the plots that break like a fast curve—they're all here. Moreover, there is none of the maudlin nostalgia that frequently cramps works of elderly writers in search of happy youth. Runyon is still master of the art of anonymity in the first person. There is a quality of the good vignette to these tales, which, in sum, gives a better picture of small-town life and pace than many weightier, sociological tomes.

Murray Schumach. *NYT*. June 2, 1946. p. 27

Another controversy stewed over whether the real Broadwayites talk in the present tense slanguage used by the fictional Runyon guys and dolls. The controversy was taken seriously in England where the Runyon stories were as popular as they were here. Do guys and dolls really talk like that?

Unser Fritz' English was mangled like a shirt in a same-day laundry, yet in "All Horse Players Die Broke" he speaks pure Broadwayese, or more correctly, Runyonese. What escapes most who claim Runyon reported what he had heard is that in his stories an anonymous "I" tells the tales. It is he who speaks in the present tense even when he is quoting someone like Unser Fritz. The anonymous "I," of course, is Runyon.

It is true that some Broadwayites, especially in the Lindy's set, fall into the present tense in their gabble. . . . However, even those to whom the present tense comes naturally usually mix in the past tense, too. In the Runyon stories this present tense was pure, carried out to every word, and it was laborious writing to make it read smoothly. If anyone talks like that along the Big Street they come after the fact, or rather fiction.

Damon Runyon, Jr. *Father's Footsteps* (Random). 1954. pp. 112–13

Although Runyon did not lack appreciation of his craftsmanship, he lacked confidence in his ability to produce longer works. He thought he could not write a novel and rejected proposals that he work on one. Yet he maintained interest in the Turps, My Old Man, and another, unnamed, character of his through hundreds of thousands of words—more than the average novel contains. The unnamed character is the narrator of the Broadway Guys and Dolls stories who tells us, "names make no difference to me, especially on Broadway, because no matter what name a man has, it is not his square moniker," and offers us no square moniker, or any shape moniker at all, for himself—one of the most artfully delineated characters in modern literature.

Clark Kinnaird. Foreword to *A Treasury of Damon Runyon* (Random). 1958. pp. xiv–xv

With the teachers of American literature, Damon Runyon stood and stands nowhere. Critics often dismiss his characters and plots because they are simple, stylized, and sentimental; they pass over the mawkish nature of underworld society, and until 1963 some of them were inclined to believe that such a society did not really exist. It existed and exists, and Damon Runyon came closer than any other man to becoming the social historian of the underworld.

Damon Runyon's Broadway stories, far from his first published fiction, were the outcome of a deep-seated quarrel with society. When he began writing the Broadway stories in the 1920's he had ceased to take any personal responsibility for society's conduct. He was the expatriate whose sensitivity to the wrongs committed in his own country drives him to live abroad among strangers, whose immoralities leave him guilt-free. Damon's retreat was to move into the world of guys and dolls, a world that was real and as exciting to him as the world of the Western gunmen and Indian fighters he had admired as a boy. He said as much in a column he wrote in the third person, analyzing the writing of one Damon Runyon. "By saying something with a half-boob air, by conveying an air of jocularity, he gets ideas out of his system on the wrongs of this world." Short-story writer Runyon was not a humorist as such, columnist Runyon said, but more of a dramatic writer who did not have the moral courage to protest aloud.

Edwin P. Hoyt. *A Gentleman of Broadway*
(Little). 1964. pp. 6–7

See *A Treasury of Damon Runyon.*

SALINGER, J. D. (1919–   )

J. D. Salinger's writing is original, first rate, serious and beautiful. . . . He has the equipment for a born writer to begin with—his sensitive eye, his incredibly good ear, and something I can think of no word for but grace. There is not a trace of sentimentality about his work, although it is full of children that are bound to be adored. He pronounces no judgments, he is simply gifted with having them passionately. . . . What this reader loves about Mr. Salinger's stories is that they honor what is unique and precious in each person on earth.

Eudora Welty. NYT. April 5, 1953. p. 4

Salinger is an extreme individualist with a pleasing disregard for conventional narrative form and style. . . . Above all Salinger appears to be ravenously interested in human beings, whom he depicts with an understanding, without either sentimentality or condescension, something unusual in so young a writer. Even his weaker stories are peopled with memorable minor characters, people who appear on stage for a few moments only, but who are endowed with lives of their own.

William Peden. SR. April 11, 1953. pp. 43–4

The special quality of Mr. Salinger's stories is humaneness. He engages the reader's civilized sympathies for the puzzled and troubled individuals whose sensibilities civilization has injured. There is little perception of the tragedy of life or, as Faulkner has put it, of the human heart in conflict with itself. Mr. Salinger's is the tradition of Chekhov applied to middle-class niceties and influenced by the standards of The New Yorker. . . . What he does do, he does well, but the scope of these stories is strictly limited. They are more concerned with a slice of life, an impression of it, than with life itself. For the most part, one discovers the problem of sensibility isolated, misdirected, misunderstood, and at last interpreted in a flash of insight.

Gene Baro. NYHT. April 12, 1953. p. 6

J. D. Salinger's closest resemblance is to F. Scott Fitzgerald—that is, close in one sense. Salinger is at home with the details of upper middle-class life, and, like Fitzgerald, there is much grace, lightness of touch, and bitter-sweet emotion in his stories. But since Salinger is his own man, and hardly an

119

imitation, the analogy with Fitzgerald ends at a certain point; there is a bitterness and intensity of the young writer's work which is subtly wedded to the charm, and the combination makes Fitzgerald seem romantically old-fashioned by comparison. But both writers have that particular poignance which results from a lyrical identification with subject matter set off by a critical intelligence; they are both lovers, so to speak, who are forced to acknowledge that they have been "had," and this gives their work the emotion of subtle heartbreak.

Seymour Krim. Com. April 24, 1953. p. 78

Salinger's fiction convicts us, as readers, of being deeply aware of a haunting inconclusiveness in our own, and in contemporary, emotional relationships—members all of the lonely crowd. His characters exist outside the charmed circle of the well-adjusted, and their thin cries for love and understanding go unheard. They are men, women, and adolescents, not trapped by outside fate, but by their own frightened, and sometimes tragicomic awareness of the uncrossable gulf between their need for love and the futility of trying to achieve it on any forseeable terms.

Salinger's short stories are all variants on the theme of emotional estrangement.

David L. Stevenson. Nation. March 9, 1957. p. 216

In January, 1953, after a year and a half of literary fame and literary silence, Salinger published in the New Yorker a story called "Teddy," which began his latest phase. It reads <i>methodically;</i> as if the impulse had first been to write something that was not a story. It has dialogue of a kind then new to his work but now his standard: no longer seducing our belief and lighting up characters with things we had heard but not listened to, but expounding an ordered set of ideas as plainly as can be done without actually destroying the characters into whose mouths they are put. The ideas are mostly Zen.

In the stories Salinger has published since then . . . poignant, beautifully managed philosophic dialogues, really—the doctrine is developed, sometimes in the language of Christian mysticism (after Meister Eckhart) and sometimes as a rather high-flying syncretism.

Donald Barr. Com. Oct. 25, 1957. p. 90

What Salinger has seen in American life is the extraordinary tension it sets up between our passion to understand and evaluate our experience for ourselves and our need to belong to a community that is unusually energetic in imposing its understanding and values on its individual members. Whatever one may think of Salinger's answer to the problem, this view of American life is important; it has a long and distinguished history.

But Salinger's achievement is not that he has grasped an abstract idea of American experience, important as that idea may be in itself; it is that he has seen this idea working in the actual life of our time, in our habitual activities, in the very turns of our speech, and he has found a way to make us see it there, too.

Arthur Mizener. *Harper*. Feb., 1959. p. 90

For the college generation of the Fifties, Salinger has the kind of importance that Scott Fitzgerald and Ernest Hemingway had for the young people of the Twenties. He is not a public figure as they were; on the contrary, his zeal for privacy is phenomenal; but he is felt nevertheless as a presence, a significant and congenial presence. There are, I am convinced, millions of young Americans who feel closer to Salinger than to any other writer.

In the first place, he speaks their language. He not only speaks it, he shapes it, just as Hemingway influenced the speech of countless Americans in the Twenties. . . . In the second place, he expresses their rebellion.

Granville Hicks. *SR*. July 25, 1959. p. 13

There are many writers, like J. D. Salinger, who lack strength, but who are competent and interesting. He identifies himself too fussily with the spiritual aches and pains of his characters; in some of his recent stories, notably "Zooey" and "Seymour: An Introduction," he has overextended his line, thinned it out, in an effort to get the fullest possible significance out of his material. Salinger's work is a perfect example of the lean reserves of the American writer who is reduced to "personality," even to the "mystery of personality," instead of the drama of our social existence. . . . The delicate balances in Salinger's work, the anxious striving, inevitably result in beautiful work that is rather too obviously touching.

Alfred Kazin. *Harper*. Oct., 1959. p. 130

He has always been open, of course, to the charge of being soft-centered. To youth and laziness he promises a release into the utopia where every difficulty and agony is understood to be a result of the barbaric insensitivity of Others; at the heart of his myth lies the conviction that no one of merit ought to *work,* that all truly decent folk spring full-brained from the womb and therefore need only to master a few great texts of anti-knowledge—weapons with which to belabor knaves and scholars. Putting it another way: the world of most Salinger stories connects (in its assumptions) not with the general world but with those odd communities that grow up around conservatories and museum schools—societies in which youngsters who haven't read a word of Shakespeare or Spinoza argue violently about Wilhelm Reich or Edmund Begler, M.D., pleasingly pleased with themselves.

Benjamin DeMott. *HdR*. Winter, 1961–2. pp. 626–7

Salinger offers no difficult visions; he's guaranteed not to disturb. He permits his reader to eat his cake and have it too—secure in the knowledge that he deserves better cake, but there is none to be had. Salinger is not concerned with genuine (or at least, possible) alternatives to the values and life-styles he deplores. His technique for handling the individual vs. society situation is simply to divide the world between the sensitive few and the vulgar many. You, my reader, he assures us, belong to an elite —not because you want to live differently, but because you are sensitive. You have religious experiences, you have special affinities with little girls, you can't stand phonies, you *understand*. You are so sensitive it's a wonder you go on. In fact, Salinger implies, *you are a hero and your heroism is not based on heroic action but on mere existence.*

Jeremy Larner. *PR*. Fall, 1962. p. 597

Before the present volume (*Franny and Zooey*), Salinger had always presented madness as a special temptation of males; perhaps because, in the myth he was elaborating, it is a female image of innocence that, at the last moment, lures his almost-lost protagonists back from the brink of insanity: a little girl typically, pre-pubescent and therefore immune to the world's evil, which, in his work, fully nubile women tend to embody. The series which begins with "Esme" goes on through "A Perfect Day for Bananafish," where the girl-savior appears too late to save Seymour, oldest of the Glass family; and reaches an appropriate climax in *Catcher in the Rye,* where the savior is the little sister and the myth achieves its final form. It is the Orestes-Iphigenia story, we see there, that Salinger all along has been trying to rewrite, the account of a Fury-haunted brother redeemed by his priestess-sister; though Salinger demotes that sister in age, thus downgrading the tone of the legend from tragic to merely pathetic.

Leslie Fiedler. *PR*. Winter, 1962. p. 130

How did Salinger get hung up on the idea that the Glass menage had to produce a Messiah? It's not really his line of work at all. His concern from the first was with the incoherently, callowly genuine; and with this theme he made excellent fun. But to be a prophet in the wilderness, Saint Salinger Cornishhensis, he simply isn't equipped; he's got nostalgia, he's got confusion, but he has neither faith nor the structured intellect which properly produces it. Having promised a revelation for so long, he's more or less bound to oblige; and the sort of mouse his mountains are liable to yield may be guessed from the wretched rodent that squeaks forth at the end of *Seymour, an Introduction.*

Robert M. Adams. *PR.* Spring, 1963. p. 129

The marvel of "Seymour," which appeared in 1959 [as a short story], is that Salinger confronts himself. It is a chronicle of the confrontation between the writer and the saint, and he hardly bothers to pretend it is a fiction. How disingenuous it was of all those critics and reviewers to have spoken of the piece as though it were a story, and how heartless it was of them who had loved him so much to have rapped him on the knuckles because he, the emperor, was the first to point out that he was wearing no clothes, had in fact been naked for years. "Seymour" is a courageous act, a much more personal display than having photographs published or signing books in department stores or making public appearances. And having given himself totally to those who had been lusting after him ever since *The Catcher,* all they did was respond by crying, "Shame!"

Yes, of course, "Seymour" is mannered and self-conscious and boring, but so were the other Glass pieces—and they were in addition dishonest, except for "Franny"—even though Salinger managed to keep these things hidden from his readers, if not from himself. What he says in "Seymour" is that he cannot live without Seymour, that he cannot give up writing about Seymour even though he *cannot* write about Seymour, that there is no Seymour and he must construct him piece by piece, feature by feature. And in the process of saying so, all the literary pretensions and affectations and mannerisms are knitted into a hair-shirt which he is going to wear because that is the Way he has chosen for himself.

(K)   Alfred Chester. *Cmty.* June, 1963. p. 474

The Glass family stories make it increasingly apparent that Salinger is no longer content to produce what it is generally agreed he can do so well— the short sharp fiction, the narrowly constructed *tour de force* dramatizing the desiccating effects of life without meaning. Like the late Eliot, he is now more concerned with the solution than with a reiteration of the problem. Agreeing with Fitzgerald's best vision of the sadness of a shallow, meretricious society—Buddy says that in his youth *The Great Gatsby* was his "Tom Sawyer"—Salinger ultimately refuses to accept a naturalistic world in which the American dream has turned into nightmare. Seeing the world as it is, the Glasses wholly commit themselves to leading a meaningful life in it. . . . Neither the Jesus Prayer nor expatriation nor even the way of Zen is offered as a sufficient formula. However at least part of the answer is suggested by the moral and aesthetic emphasis which Salinger places on character instead of action, on being rather than event, on awareness rather than status.

(K)   Sam S. Baskett. *WSCL.* Winter, 1963. p. 61

Like all of Salinger's fiction, *Catcher in the Rye* is not only about innocence, it is actively for innocence—as if retaining one's childness were an
existential possibility. The metaphor of the title—Holden's fantasy-vision
of standing in front of a cliff and protecting playing children from falling
(Falling)—is, despite the impossibility of its realization, the only positive
action affirmed in the novel. It is, in Salinger's Manichean universe of
child angels and adult "phonies," the only moral alternative—otherwise
all is corruption. Since it is spiritually as well as physically impossible to
prevent the Fall, Salinger's idealistic heroes are doomed either to suicide
(Seymour) or insanity (Holden, Sergeant X) or mysticism (Franny), the
ways of sainthood, or to moral dissolution (Eloise, D. B., Mr. Antolini),
the way of the world.

(K)   Jonathan Baumbach. *MLQ*. Dec., 1964. p. 462

Salinger's long silence after the appearance of "Seymour: An Introduction" in 1959 was ended in 1965 with the publication of another chapter
in the Glass saga, "Hapworth 16, 1924." This story did nothing to reassure those who hoped for a return to the earlier brilliance of *Catcher in
the Rye*. Indeed, it tended to accentuate those characteristics of the later
work which most readers found disturbing—a tedious length, a humor
often self-consciously cute, a muting of narrative in favor of philosophical
asides. But in spite of its apparent defects, the story was an important addition to the life of Glasses, particularly as it shed new light on the remarkable character of Seymour. . . .

Seymour's unusual knowledge of the past and insight into the future
derive from "two, tantalizing, tiny portals" in his mind which have opened
involuntarily and which give him foresight not only of his own life but
also of the lives of others. At one point he has a "stunning glimpse" of
Buddy, "quite bereft" of Seymour's "dubious, loving company," busily at
work writing stories on his "very large, jet-black, very moving, gorgeous
typewriter." The effect of such passages is difficult to describe or assess.
They seem both preposterous and ironic.

(K)   James E. Miller. *J. D. Salinger* (Minnesota).
                                                        1965. pp. 42–3

The most unusual aspect of Salinger's liberated Glasses is that change
comes by way of a verbal flow of abstraction. This may be a contradiction-
in-terms, for to experience the liberation of Zen by a second-hand conscious verbal overflow is not the usual way of deriving enlightenment. But
in Salinger's highly self-conscious world, this is the means by which his
characters attain a twentieth century American form of enlightenment. In
this enlightened state the Glass children become freed of their critical
tendencies, become freed of their highly separate selves, become one with

the Fat Lady or the Christ in each that makes for universal empathy. Perhaps Salinger is the keenest social critic of our time. He has, we feel, focused on a major problem in the modern world, on the last stronghold of the sacred, for an atomized self is disastrous.

(K)   Bernice and Sanford Goldstein. *MFS.* Autumn, 1966.

p. 324

Buddy's understanding of the Glass saga will always be incomplete. The important fact, however, is the development of that understanding. This is shown most dramatically in his changing attitudes toward Seymour. "A Perfect Day for Bananafish" recreates Seymour's suicide with the perspective which Buddy had in 1948. How much of the story is "factual" we do not know, and perhaps will never know; it is conceivable, though unlikely, that Buddy could have got most of the facts from the "witnesses," as he did with "Zooey." But the most important witness is his own. In the bananafish story we see a Seymour who is conscious of his own superiority, yet who expects as much of others as he does of himself. But in the later stories a different Seymour emerges each time, until in "Hapworth" we have Buddy discovering a Seymour who was, at seven, conscious of being unstable, but also of being "gloriously normal." Buddy's developing insight is a brilliant narrative device; it functions, like the multiple narrators in Faulkner's fiction, to suggest the multiplicity and elusiveness of final truth.

(K)   Howard M. Harper. *Desperate Faith* (North
Carolina). 1967. p. 93

See *Catcher in the Rye* (novel), *Nine Stories,* also *Franny and Zooey* and *Raise High the Roof Beams, Carpenters* (each two stories).

SANDBURG, CARL (1878–1967)

The free rhythms of Mr. Carl Sandburg are a fine achievement in poetry. No one who reads *Chicago Poems* with rhythm particularly in mind can fail to recognize how much beauty he attains in this regard. But the more arresting aspect of Mr. Sandburg's achievement is, for myself, the so-called imagistic aspect. . . . At first these poems may seem too innocent of self-interpretation to mean anything, too impressionistic to compel the name of beauty—to give that completion which has no shadow and knows no end beyond itself. But such exquisite realization of the scenes that gave Mr. Sandburg the mood of beauty is in itself a creation of the beautiful.

Francis Hackett. *Horizons* (Huebsch-Viking). 1918.

pp. 304–5, 309

The "natural rhythms of a manly life" that Plato insisted upon . . . just as they tumble roughly along in Mr. Sandburg's vibrant verse, beat out from the very unpoetic look of this poet. And when he talks—there is no jabber nor gesticulation nor studied modulation in his talk—and when his eyes burn out their black fire, your attention is gripped by that same honest man-to-man sincerity which he is able to put into the grinding, crashing, angular words of his unrhymed free-rhymed verses, and you can understand more clearly why his verse must be unrhymed, free-rhymed, unfettered. . . . Mr. Sandburg's poems are Mr. Sandburg. They are powerful, live, brutal, gentle, and human—and so is he.

Walter Yust. *Bkm.* Jan., 1921. pp. 286, 290

There must be some powerful principle of life in the man, that he can make one feel so much. There must be some rocky strength, some magnetic iron in him, that compels, despite coatings of muck and dust, and draws iron to iron. For Sandburg is an almost rudimentary artist. His successful effects are almost sparks of fire out of a chaos, sudden tongues of flame that leap out of smoking matter and subside as suddenly again. He appears to be as nearly unconscious as an artist can be and still remain a creator; it is well-nigh in spite of his technique that he manages to communicate.

Paul Rosenfeld. *Bkm.* July, 1921. p. 393

Buried deep within the He man, the hairy, meat eating Sandburg there is another Sandburg, a sensitive, naive, hesitating Carl Sandburg, a Sandburg that hears the voice of the wind over the roofs of houses at night, a Sandburg that wanders often alone through grim city streets on winter nights, a Sandburg that knows and understands the voiceless cry in the heart of the farm girl of the plains when she comes to the kitchen door and sees for the first time the beauty of prairie country.

The poetry of John Guts doesn't excite me much. Hairy, raw meat eating He men are not exceptional in Chicago and the middle west.

As for the other Sandburg, the naive, hesitant, sensitive Sandburg—among all the poets of America he is my poet.

Sherwood Anderson. *Bkm.* Dec., 1921. p. 361

Sandburg is alien to most of the Anglo-Saxon elements in American life. Its aspects which he chooses to describe are those precisely which distinguish it from life in England. . . . He avoids the language along with everything else that is English. He never wrote an American dictionary, but he does something even more hazardous and exciting: he writes American. With earlier authors American was a dialect; it was the speech of the comedian and the soubrette; the hero, when serious, declaimed his Sunday-best Oxford. The case is opposite with Sandburg. . . . Sandburg writes American like a foreign language, like a language freshly acquired in which each word has a new and fascinating meaning.

Malcolm Cowley. Dial. Nov., 1922. pp. 565–6

Sandburg, for all his strength, is not without his weakness. . . . In giving way to a program of mysticism, Sandburg gives the unconscious an absolutely free hand; he lets it dictate its unfettered—and, one might almost add, its unlettered—fantasies. There are times, more frequent than one might wish, when he completely fails to guide the current of his thought; it directs or misdirects him so that he follows blindly what, too often, is merely a blind alley. . . . But though the meaning is not always clear, there is no mistaking the emotion. It is implicit in every line; a concentrated exaltation, rich in its sweeping affirmations, rich in suggestive details.

Louis Untermeyer. American Poetry since 1900
(Holt). 1923. pp. 86–7

Sandburg's profoundest belief about the world is that the universe is mainly cruel and capricious, that meaning is given it only by the lives of men—pitiful and noble lives which are continually being thwarted by death or disease or the facts of the social order. . . . As Sandburg, because he sets so high a value on men, is continually brought to the thought of death, so, like other mystics, he prizes silence above noise, introspection above activity. . . . He feels keenly that ideas are frail, values are fragile, language is inadequate.

Howard Mumford Jones. VQR. Jan., 1927. pp. 112,
116, 121

Of tenderness, of human feeling, of generous and robust sentiment, there is notoriously a great deal: of strong, sharp and ardent emotion, of the specific passion and intensity of poetry, there is singularly little. This verse, you feel, is the work of a man whose emotional nature, like his intellectual life, has never found the earth and air in which it could develop freely and expansively. His strength has laid in his closeness to the people, but they are a people whose impulses and affections have been nipped and stunted . . . like wild flowers on a stock farm; and of so cramped an emotional existence this too cool, too inexpensive, too phlegmatic poetry— this poetry of half-lights and understatement and ironic anti-climaxes—is the inevitable expression.

Newton Arvin. NR. Sept. 9, 1936. p. 120

Sandburg's poetic instrument is exactly fitted to his purposes: it simply happens that those purposes are too vaguely poetic to make the instrument become anything more than the loose, amorphous, copious, semi-prose medium that it still remains after twenty-five years of use. And one may suppose that if he had exerted more labor on the task of filing and concentrating his verse, giving one phrase or anecdote the pith now thinned out over twenty, he would have arrived at something more fixed and specific in his social beliefs. . . . The potentialities of an epic judgement lie in Sandburg's materials, but he has not realized them.

Morton D. Zabel. *Poetry*. Oct., 1936. pp. 43–4

Carl Sandburg petered out as a poet ten years ago. I imagine he wanted it that way. His poems themselves said what they had to say, piling it up, then just went out like a light. He had no answers, he didn't seek any. Without any attempt at the solace which the limitations of art (as with a Baudelaire) might bring the formlessness of his literary figures was the very formlessness of the materials with which he worked. That was his truth. That was what he wanted truthfully to make plain, that was his compulsion. That form he could accept but at a terrible cost: failure deliberately invited, a gradual inevitable slackening off to ultimate defeat.

William Carlos Williams. *Poetry*. Sept., 1951. p. 346

In all his poetry a single effort was represented—that of refounding his derived romanticism, its vision and imaginative ecstasy upon the common realities of a labor and populist experience. This latter remained for him a fixed element, one he would not place in perspective and seemingly could not alter. . . . Consequently, the only mobile or adaptable part of his work lay in its other half—the essentially rhetorical and willful exercise of fancy to embellish and stage impressively his obdurate poetic matter. Like the other midwesterners, Sandburg was a poet of subject. Where his subject was itself arresting, moving, and satisfying, his poem likewise could achieve these qualities.

Bernard Duffey. *The Chicago Renaissance in
American Letters* (Michigan State). 1954. pp. 216–7

Increasingly Sandburg disregards the metaphor for direct statement. Now poetry of statement may be very great poetry, as Dryden and Pope have shown us, but it must by its nature be a poetry diamantine in its hardness and brilliance. Sandburg lacks any technique in this sense, and consequently his late ideological poetry fails. . . . Early or late, however, wherever the metaphor of itself exercises absolute control of the poem—as in "Chicago," "The Harbor," "Fog," "Cool Tombs," and "Grass"—Sandburg attains technical success. It is an extremely limited success as an imitator of Whitman and as one of the Imagists.

Nicholas Joost. *Com*. Jan. 16, 1958. p. 382

Everybody loved Carl Sandburg in our town. Nobody knows where he went. . . . Compare "I Am the People, The Mob" with *The People, Yes.* It's enough to make you weep. In the early poem you see so clearly behind the abstraction the stark individuals of the other poems in *Chicago Poems.* Behind the second *People* is only mush. . . . It is a terrible pity, but after about 1925 there is nothing of value. Since most of the prose comes after that, Sandburg the historian, novelist, autobiographer, writer of children's stories simply does not exist for literature. I suppose the last thing was the *Songbag.*

Kenneth Rexroth. Nation. Feb. 22, 1958. pp. 171–2

He realizes that many folk with homely virtues and skills are far superior to both lettered and unlettered blockheads, and their society healthier and stabler than a parasitic one where men prey on men.

Sandburg, then, has a basic content which can be summed up in the word Man and which can nourish the mind of the young in the best traditions of Western Civilization. The next question to be raised is, Is what Sandburg writes poetry, and, if so, how good is it?

Sandburg . . . was not sure that he was writing poetry. He was trying to communicate to an audience which was not sophisticated verbally, to whom the connotations of words are very closely related to their denotations, to whom literary allusion and subtle metaphor are meaningless. He has been an exponent of Wordsworth's "man talking to men." But this use of a *lingua communis* carries with it its own trap, as Coleridge pointed out. The language of prose and the language of metrical composition are two different entities. Thus Sandburg's work quite often degenerates into a pedestrian prosaism summed up by the word "talk."

(K)   Michael Yatron. *EJ.* Dec., 1959. p. 527

He loves "facts," and has made a career of collecting them to be used in journalism, speeches, biography, a novel, and poetry. Yet he is in no sense a pedant; his facts (when they are facts and not prejudiced supposition) are alive and pertinent, and he is usually willing to let them speak for themselves. "What is instinct?" he asks in "Notes for a Preface" (and the title itself is characteristic). "What is thought? Where is the absolute line between the two. Nobody knows—as yet." He is still, he says, a "seeker." He might be called a pragmatic humanist. Certainly he is not a Naturalist, who believes that human nature is simply animal nature; or a supernaturalist, who has an equally low opinion of mankind. Among his new poems is a satire on a contemporary poet, probably Eliot, who believes that "The human race is its own Enemy Number One." There is no place for "original sin" in Sandburg's theology.

From first to last, Sandburg writes of man in the physical world, and he still regards the enemies of humanity as either social or political. Man's salvation, he thinks, is his instinctive yearning for a better world; in the practical sense: idealism, the "dream."

(K)   Gay Wilson Allen. *SAQ*. Summer, 1960. p. 318

America is an urban and highly materialistic culture today and the Lincoln ideas have long been submerged by the exigencies of crisis government and politics by advertising. While Sandburg embodies that part of the past, he also embodies the victory won by the union men in the bitter labor wars and the successful fight the immigrant waged against entrenched privilege. This is a fight not completely over. When Congress applauds Sandburg on Lincoln's birthday, the Representatives and Senators may be trying to convince themselves they are applauding what they *were,* but down deep perhaps they know they are also applauding what they are. It is not for nothing that Sandburg's parents were immigrants and that Sandburg, long before he undertook the Lincoln biography, described in eloquent poetry the terrible adjustments of immigrants and farmers to an industrial society.

(K)   Harry Golden. *Carl Sandburg* (World). 1961. p. 29

We should always be grateful to Sandburg as a pioneer liberator of American poetry from the genteel tradition. Even regardless of historical considerations, here is still a body of poetry in which the old America of the frontier and the new America of the industrial city are imaginatively synthesized by a loving, lofty spirit. And yet it must be said that Sandburg is never a great and seldom even a very good poet. He abounds in potentially poetic feeling, but he is not sufficiently interested in writing poems. Too often he is the victim, too seldom the master, of tender emotions which liquefy his desire to seem hard and tough. He loves real people and real things but does not look at them intently enough to make his images of them come alive: his impressionism saps his realism. His free verse is merely free; he adopted it because it seemed the most unrestricted way of pouring out his feelings and because he mistakenly supposed it to be closer to the natural poetic heart of the folk than rhyme and meter. His formal and spiritual indebtedness to Whitman, though far from slavish, is too obvious to permit us to think of him as a genuine innovator. Like his master, he is more limited than enfranchised by his lack of saturation in European culture.

Beneath the regional and documentary surface of his work, beneath its relative modernity of matter, form, and diction, one discerns the wish to be a quite old-fashioned poet-prophet. His "message" is inseparable from a religiosity which is never clearly formulated.

(K)   Hoxie Neale Fairchild. *Religious Trends in English Poetry,* vol. V (Columbia). 1962. pp. 499–500

Though he may not have a blueprint for the future, he does show strength in his expression of the minutiae of life. He is a poet to be read not *in toto* nor even in great slabs, but at short sittings. He is what might be called a "spare-minute" poet, for his intimate glimpses, his brief expressions of mood, idea, longing, his landscapes and personal etchings, are pleasing— even stimulating—for a limited reading. His talkiness and his tendency to all inclusiveness make the search for the penetrating line, the memorable observation, and the occasional fresh combination of images sometimes, quite frankly, a tiring one. What Sandburg needs more than anything else is a sympathetic but severe editor.

(K)   Richard Crowder. *Carl Sandburg* (Twayne). 1964. p. 109

See *Complete Poems* and *The New American Songbag;* also *Always the Young Strangers* (autobiography) and *Abraham Lincoln* (biography).

SANTAYANA, GEORGE (1863–1952)

To him no ties are morally binding but those of common thoughts and purposes. Instead of allowing the accident of family, country or profession to dictate his affection and his future, he has followed his affinities and aspirations. Even the age he has chanced to live in has not kept him from communing with the ancients he admires. . . . He seems to know all that is worth knowing, to feel everything that touches the human heart. He writes with the calm of an ancient philosopher, the passion of a mystic poet, the insight into eternal and intimate things which belongs to the great dead. He writes as if he had lived a long time ago and were writing for all time to come.

Van Meter Ames. *Proust and Santayana* (Willett). 1937.
pp. 50, 80. Used by permission of Harper and Brothers

Without prejudicing in the least the question of the respective validities of the ways of thought and action idealized in the *Life of Reason* and the *Realms of Being,* one cannot ignore the fact that the period in which the second work was written witnessed the disintegration of the world whose stability seemed so assured during the years when he composed that philosophic masterpiece, the *Life of Reason.* He has experienced not so much a metaphysical conversion as a moral revulsion before the tremendous changes in the world he once knew. The situations that are difficult to master when approached as tasks and challenges he has forever settled, in his own mind, by converting them into spectacles.

Sidney Hook. *Nation.* Nov. 2, 1940. p. 424

He was not, as he says in a well-known sonnet, "born to be beatified by anguish," but "to stand perplexed aside from so much sorrow." Still, there are many cherished writers who experienced neither anguish nor joy but something in the middle ground that helped them to ruminate on life and on the symbols that have been evolved for the explanation of it, writers who often seem to be more knowledgeable, less dense, for the limitation of their experience. Santayana, not only by temperament but by his own plan of life, seems to have been destined for the middle way. Anyhow, he has gone that way and has brought out of it a curious wisdom, something that is a combination of the mundane with the disinterestedly spiritual. His mind has never been distorted by the strain of too intense feeling or by impetuosity, by too much work or a too imprudent sense of duty.

Mary M. Colum. *SR*. April 21, 1945. p. 8

Although a materialist, Santayana considers himself devout and worship-ful. He loves the rites and ceremonies of the Catholic Church. He loves its dogmas, knows them to the last detail, and dwells on them with un-reserved emotion. But he does not think they are true. He thinks they express in a symbolic way ideals that are needful to spirits in finding their way through a material world. . . . I do not think going through the motions of religion without genuine belief is a peculiarly Catholic phenomenon—or even a peculiar phenomenon. The peculiar thing about Santayana is his candid confession, or rather bold celebration, of it. He makes a sincerity of being insincere. He is devout with no object of devotion. He is religious without any religion.

Max Eastman. *AM*. Nov., 1951. p. 38

The dominating interest of Santayana, throughout his whole repertory of writings, is psychological. His consistent concern is with the events that occur in the human psyche and in the human spirit. . . . Santayana's moral system, as developed in *The Life of Reason* and in the other volumes which cluster around *The Life of Reason,* seems precisely to accomplish the post-Lockean goal of delineating the structure of human nature, with the added security of an assumed material world as the sum of the existing. Thus, it satisfies at once the demands of a modern faith and those of a humane sensibility. Among philosophical systems of the century, it is uniquely acceptable to persons whose taste may be described as literary and traditional, and whose religion is scientific naturalism. Its aesthetic is marked by unconcern for fashionable, arbitrary, or occult doctrines of poetry and fine art.

Charles T. Harrison. *SwR*. Spring, 1953. pp. 209, 212

It can hardly be said that Santayana writes like one inspired, or like one with a zeal for either understanding or reforming the world. . . . His style reminds one more of the soliloquy of a dreamer who has never taken the world or even the facts of human life and achievement with intense serious- ness or been overly disturbed by the prospect and actuality of catastrophes that have threatened human happiness and existence. The acute observa- tions of, and the definite reactions to, the most crucial problems of living (which form a large part of his contribution to philosophy) are expressed in prose that seems so effortless and such a delight in itself that often one must, as Kant said of Rousseau's writings, read his essays and books sev- eral times in order to give attention to the matter rather than to the beauty of the style.

> Willard E. Arnett. *Santayana and the Sense of Beauty*
> (Indiana). 1955. pp. 202–3

It was not Santayana's abstract "message" that explains his magic. It was not even the limpid and epigrammatic prose in which he stated it. It was the mixture of irony and sympathy he brought to his great theme, the unrelenting standards combined with the unillusioned acceptance of men as they are; it was the glinting wisdom, and the literary imagination which evoked the inner experience of men living in the most disparate moral climates. Most of all, it was the expression of a frankly relativistic moral outlook that was nevertheless Dantesque in its stringent declaration of preferences, its comprehensiveness, and its consistency. Here was a man with the sobriety of Aristotle writing with the poetry and excitement of Plato on the only things which give anything else meaning—human ideals.

> Charles Frankel. *SR*. Jan. 7, 1956. p. 11

Santayana's peculiar genius is comprehensiveness. This fact, along with the delight provided by the texture of his writing, accounts for the unique interest he has inspired—if not in professional philosophers, at least in the cultivated laity whom he professes to address. Every student of Santa- yana's works has observed and discriminated some of the several elements in the Santayanan synthesis. Familiarly, these include materialism and transcendentalism: thus his philosophy serves, at once, the two most im- perative of modern intellectual masters—however mutually antipathetic they may immediately appear. Beyond these, and of equally familiar recog- nition, is the "Platonism" which finds value only in intuited essences, non- existent denizens of the realm which commanded Santayana's ultimate ex- ploration. But I should like to signalize a fourth element. I am not sure that this is, strictly, an element in Santayana's system, though I am convinced of its high importance in the substance of his discourse. It, too, is a Pla- tonism (or Aristotelianism), which seems to forget the embarrassed meta-

physical status of the essences and which assumes the dignity, the persistence, and the universality of primary ethical and aesthetic forms.
(K)   Charles T. Harrison. *SwR*. Winter, 1957. p. 141

A spiritual vocation, as Santayana stated in the preface to *The Last Puritan,* can be a devastating thing, putting one at odds with life. More than once Santayana or one of his characters points out that one of Oliver's mistakes [in the novel] was attempting to lead an ordinary life. . . . The Lucifer [of Santayana's play, *Lucifer*] . . . could not countenance a world of partiality and illusion and therefore rebelled. He returned to dally with the world, as Oliver did, but both found in the end that the ways of the world were not for them. Lucifer withdrew in bitterness. Oliver, having no refuge to turn to, merely waited for the end. He "petered out," as his author said. . . . To be sure, Santayana was firmly of the opinion that this predicament need not paralyze, as it did in the case of Lucifer and Oliver. . . . The paradigm of the spiritual life for Santayana was of course not Lucifer but Christ, who possessed among other virtues that of piety. He did not come into the world to rail at it or regulate or reject it but to love it for what it aspired to and thus to be a model of the spiritual life. . . .
(K)   Frederick W. Conner. *AL*. March, 1961. pp. 16–17

In setting down the history of this portion of his life many years later, Santayana undoubtedly had a tendency to describe his Harvard years in a somewhat abstract or even allegorical fashion: persons and places had become for him merely the materials of a spiritual drama. . . . Any writer's autobiography is a "deception" in the sense of its being in some ways as much an imaginative artifact as his professedly literary works. Santayana, in particular, seems to have enjoyed playing the role of the disillusioned philosopher living always in the eternal. And even at the end —faithful, it would seem, to Yeats's idea of the tragic nobility of the artist. . . , Santayana maintained his part in the play.
(K)   Joel Porte. *NEQ*. Sept., 1962. p. 345

This change-over, from the tears of things to laughter at them, has more and more impressed me as the vital focus of Santayana's secret and private, his "poetic," his personal, philosophy. Some of his readers may account for such shifts as they discern in his reflections upon value and existence by invoking a clash between his Spanish derivation and his Yankee education; others may attribute the shifts to a disregard for logical consistency, heedless of fitting into each other conflicting insights and divergent utterances; still others will argue that his mind was not professionally philosophical at all, only the mind of a sage who was a bit of a poet, and thought in images and tropes; and still others declare him preeminently a man of letters and a critic of letters. . . .

. . . His design for living was a harmonization of the psyche's impulses into a life of reason, and he appraised this harmony as the topmost reach of an aspiration destined to tragedy, of an accident in a universe of accidents where the reason it achieved was the only reason this universe contained; of a contingency doomed, soon or late, blindly to be destroyed even as it was blindly created. To survive, to postpone, to avert, the doom, man's reason shaped itself a citadel of illusions wherein it could feel at home and safe.

(K)   Horace M. Kallen. *JP*. Jan. 2, 1964. pp. 23–4

What [Wallace] Stevens found in Santayana, then, was a theory of knowledge and of the imagination which was extremely hospitable to aesthetic values and aesthetic experience, which would in fact serve as a justification for poetry and point the way toward a poetic idea, the Supreme Fiction and its hero. The implications of this philosophy in the realm of poetry did not have to be inferred; attached as he was to experience in its aesthetic dimension, Santayana, a poet himself, wrote a great deal about poetry and its possibilities. He was a demanding critic. Even his three philosophical poets, Dante, Lucretius, and Goethe fall short in some respects; they are being measured against the highest and most rigorous standard, against the ideal possibilities of a philosophical poetry. . . . In ideal terms, poetry and religion are nearly identical; both exist in "the sphere of significant imagery, of relevant fiction, of idealism become the interpretation of the reality it leaves behind."

(K)   David P. Young. *Criticism*. Summer, 1965. pp. 276–7

He had above all an acute sense of man's impotence to control the course of civilization. The material world, progressing or not, could at any stage outstrip the ideals which sponsored it, without in fact making a chaos. There was a conflict, so to speak, between brain and brain-child such as transcendentalism could never preclude or conceal. He separated the ideal from the institution, and advocated a lively, developing sense of the material world. In his opinion, transcendentalism was a shady, illogical way of admitting that the world didn't always come up to expectations. What he proposed to substitute was an ideal of integration such that, whatever the world produced, the product could be assimilated without its destroying the coherent identity of an individual: such identity constituting for him the most enduring and most sensible achievement possible in the flux.

(K)   Paul West. *The Wine of Absurdity* (Pennsylvania
                                             State). 1966. p. 192

The Last Puritan

His attitude to the world of ideas no less than of the senses has always seemed to be an artist's rather than a philosopher's, and this, while no doubt making him an object of suspicion to his fellow thinkers, makes his philosophical writings enjoyable to the layman. It is notable, too, that he has (again unlike a philosopher) a sensitiveness to literature that has produced first class literary criticism. . . . His novel is therefore really a novel, not an arrangement of mouthpieces for philosophic speeches; the moral tensions he is interested in arise of themselves from the fable and call for little explication; and in his handling of them one is aware only of the (duly self-effacing) artist. The social fable is extended in all directions by the frequent symbolic implications, and behind the overt action one may sense an allegory of the moral life of man.

Q. D. Leavis. *Scy.* Dec., 1935. p. 322

Unashamedly old-fashioned in its method, and in its quiet thoroughness, *The Last Puritan* makes the average contemporary novel, even the best, look two-dimensional by contrast. It has the solidarity of a *Tom Jones* or *Clarissa Harlowe,* does for the New England scene, or a part of it, what those novels did for eighteenth-century England, and with the same air of easy classic competence. Nor is it quite fair to call it old-fashioned: for Santayana's employment of a kind of soliloquy-dialogue is an extremely interesting invention technically, and very skillfully done.

But the whole book is a delight, so richly packed with perceptions and wisdom and humans, not to mention poetry, that it can be read and re-read for its texture alone.

Conrad Aiken. *NR.* Feb. 5, 1936. p. 372

The characters are seen only from certain aspects, and are seldom physically vivid. And the dialogue is like none heard in the novel for a generation. It is an exchange of soliloquies or finished essays; it is full of unblushing self-explanation or exposition, not for the benefit of the person ostensibly addressed, but for the reader; and nearly always it is much too intelligent and clairvoyant. . . . These long, explicit, uninterrupted speeches are a device of compression: we come to assume that what is said in one long speech by a character is the meat of what he really said over the course of a whole evening or a week; and the unnatural intelligence and articulateness of everyone is a refreshing relief from the current convention of laconic obtuseness or incoherent stream of consciousness.

Henry Hazlitt. *Nation.* Feb. 26, 1936. p. 255

Readers must approach this book with a tolerance of fancy. The epicurean wisdom of Peter Alden, the emotionalism and naïveté of Fraulein Irma, the fervid Catholicism of Caleb Wetherbee—these must be accepted as significant on their own account and not merely as supplementary to the narrative, because it is these elements which the author has either fused in his thought or systematically excluded from it. The import of this novel is primarily philosophical—of greater value to many readers than its author's abstract works, being as Mario says, a picture painted, and "all the truer for not professing to be true." Mr. Santayana has here realized imaginatively a suggestion he made in a paper over twenty years ago— that one way for a philosopher to justify his system would be for him to acknowledge its personal basis. The proponent, if such he could be called, of any system would merely set forth his cognitive and moral experience, imparting to others that kind of knowledge which any keen observer might arrive at.

Justus Buchler. *NEQ*. June, 1936. p. 282

Except for William James . . . Santayana's thought would never have taken just the turn it did. . . . It is true that, from Santayana's point of view, America had a merely negative and astringent value for him, and a deep-rooted American will not feel that either *The Last Puritan* or *Persons and Places* does justice to what was most creative in America. . . . American readers of these books can make their own reservations, mainly in silence, and meanwhile there is much to be learned from them. No one but Santayana could have seen what he saw in the New England of the Age of Howells: his memories of those decades have a fictional sharpness, a precision of imagery, a piercing psychological quality that one finds in few comparable American autobiographies.

Newton Arvin. *Nation*. Jan. 29, 1944. p. 133

The Last Puritan analyzes a failure in American culture. The life of Oliver Alden illustrates a serious but ineffectual attempt by sensitive young American intellectuals of the early twentieth century to provide a culture commensurate with the achievements of a mechanized society. Possessing the legacy of puritanism themselves, they were dissatisfied with its precipitant, the genteel tradition. But the conditions of that legacy prevented them from uniting with the vital American Will and redirecting that Will from preoccupation with the control of matter to reflection on the consequences of its control. In a "mechanized democracy" content with its physical successes, there was no function for young intellectuals who inherited the "agonized conscience" of their forebears. Santayana saw the atavistic puritan as a tragic figure—full of noble intentions but lacking the vigor to effect them.

(K)   James C. Ballowe. *AmQ*. Summer, 1966. p. 132

Poetry

The world has scarcely any objective existence for him. Though in weaving his similitudes he uses the traditional apparatus of flowers and stars, mountains, rivers, and the sea, these things are pure ideas to him, divested of all material attributes. . . . The pageantry of life means little or nothing to him. He has no vision for external nature, but only for the summaries, essences, abstracts of phenomena, recorded in the concave of his soul. . . . Theoretically, this characteristic ought to imply a serious defect in Mr. Santayana's work; practically I find it no defect at all, but rather a source of distinction. It is a relief, for once in a way, to escape from the importunate details of the visible world into a sphere of pure thought and pure melody.

William Archer. *Poets of the Younger Generation* (John Lane). 1902. pp. 373–4

The joy of his verse is not so much its delicacy as its brilliance and the temper of its strength. His manner is the manner of swordsmanship, and the blade, though daintily raised, bites in. He is an exquisite in thrust and parry and a master of the subtle feints of fence, but there is more than swordplay in his skill. There is sometimes a desperate courage in the stab of a phrase as though he drove against a shadowy antagonist always at point to strike and overwhelm. . . . But for all its intensity the poetry of George Santayana never fails of a fine restraint and an unobtrusive mastery of form. His glimpses of reality are labored into closely articulated epigrams, and his phrases of wonder or of doubt or grief are inevitable unities, perfect to the uses of his will.

Archibald MacLeish. *Bkm.* Oct., 1925. pp. 188–9

Among philosophical personalities the most urbane and humanistic since Socrates may well be Mr. Santayana. I imagine he is what Emerson might be if Emerson had had a philosophical instead of a theological background; in other words if his Harvard had been the Harvard of today or yesterday. As an Emerson disturbs the theologians, a Santayana disturbs the philosophers—an admirable function. Each speaks luminously, and that dismays his professional colleagues and drives them to speak primly; and each pours out an incessant gnomic wisdom, so that the colleagues look a little innocent or empty. The likeness goes further: each possesses the technical accomplishment of verse. But here the report is not so favorable. Emerson was too much the theologian to be quite released by poetry, and Mr. Santayana is imprisoned with all his graces in the net of his intellectualism. They do not command the freedom of poets.

John Crowe Ransom. *The World's Body* (Scribner). 1938. p. 304

One must of course be attuned to the sensitiveness of such a temperament as Santayana's to detect the emotion which the sonnets and certain of the other more personal verses reveal. One must share his aesthetic responsiveness, his sincere deference in the presence of beauty, his delight in quiet contemplation, his high seriousness. Santayana's Muse asks no plaudits of the crowd, desires no throng of admirers or followers. His poetry is personal and aloof, the discourse of a man with his soul, a soliloquy hardly more than a whisper, or perhaps a prayer.

George W. Howgate. *George Santayana*
(Pennsylvania). 1938. p. 85

In the pessimism of the eighties and nineties, especially in that of Schopenhauer, Santayana found a mood that tallied with his own and a philosopher with a sense of beauty in art and life. Together with Leopardi and Musset, Byron and Shelley—all early favorites—Schopenhauer taught Santayana that man must rise above the chaos and suffering which threaten him in the world of will, to a salvation through sublime contemplation. Indeed, Schopenhauer's thought was not the passing infatuation Santayana has suggested it was. Schopenhauer provides the basic philosophical structure for almost all of the poetry Santayana wrote in the nineties. The emotional force of the sonnets rises from the tension between the demands of will and the recurrent desire for detachment from the world of will through contemplation of the permanence of dream.

(K)   Maurice F. Brown. *NEQ*. June, 1960. p. 158

Disillusioned with life and what it offered a young man so unfortunately situated as he was, Santayana came at the age of thirty to view the world in a new perspective. Just as the poet discovers, in the second sonnet sequence, that physical love, which promises so much, is a transitory and unsatisfying experience, so Santayana discovered that youth and the warm fellowship is afforded him, were transitory and irretrievable. His relationship with his sister was seriously altered by her marriage; his father was dead; his religion had proved false. But a shift in perspective, in the way of assigning value to things, "separated the inner self from the outer." The outer self belonged to the temporal flux of experience, but the inner, myth-making, idealizing self could be attuned to the realm of the eternal. This separation, in which both elements are reconciled, provided Santayana with a tenable vision of experience, focused in such a way as to see all things "under the form of eternity." This "re-adjustment," as I have been calling it, this *metanoia*, expressed by the highly stylized conventions of his second sonnet sequence, goes a long way toward explaining the origin and nature of the aloofness and detachment which Santayana's critics have long noted in his work.

(K)   Douglas L. Wilson. *NEQ*. March, 1966. p. 25

See *The Sense of Beauty* and *The Life of Reason* (philosophy); also *Poems* and *The Last Puritan* (novel).

SAROYAN, WILLIAM (1908–   )

Mr. Saroyan is excited, eager, clever, honestly introspective, . . . narcis-sistic, wistful, humane, tender and the very reverse of naïve while affecting naïveté. He is an original. I see no traceable influence upon him except that of Sherwood Anderson, the untutored, homely honesty of whose early writings Mr. Saroyan has apparently absorbed. . . . There is evidence . . . that a new, refreshing, and interesting talent is in the first experimental stages of creation. . . . It is an apollonian and eager talent, entertaining us and leaving us expectant.

Burton Rascoe. NYHT. Oct. 21, 1934. p. 9

It is obvious . . . that Saroyan is not what is called "a good writer"; people who smack their lips over good writing will never come within smacking distance of him. But it's equally obvious that what he's shouting about is not just his bumptious Armenian self but something vital. The rub comes in deciding whether he's a blasphemer or a buffoon. Or, perhaps, neither. . . . A good deal of Whitman's writing was promissory, a great deal of it sheer brag. The professors have mummified him into a literary figure, but he was better than that. He could hardly write his name in their language; but he made his mark. William Saroyan is the same sort of fellow.

T. S. Matthews. NR. March 18, 1936. p. 172

Saroyan takes you to the bar, and he creates for you there a world which is the way the world would be if it conformed to the feelings instilled by drinks. In a word, he achieves the feat of making and keeping us boozy without the use of alcohol and purely by the action of art. . . . These magical feats are accomplished by the enchantment of Saroyan's tempera-ment, which induces us to take from him a good deal that we should not take from anyone else. With Saroyan the whole thing is the temperament: he hardly ever tries to contrive a machine. The good fairy who was present at his christening thus endowed him with one of the most precious gifts that a literary artist can have, and Saroyan never ceases to explain to us how especially fortunate he is.

Edmund Wilson. NR. Nov. 18, 1940. p. 697

My Name Is Aram, in its highly original way, has linked itself to one of the most fertile lines of the American literary tradition; while at the same time adding a new element of the utmost importance for an imaginative study of America as America is. It is an Armenian book, charged with the Christianized orientalism of the Armenians, rich in the highly humor-ous contrasts of their ideal of living in California environment, written with the naïve blend of spirituality and realistic cynicism that one finds in Arabic popular literature. And at the same time it is intensely American. . . . I should vote, indeed, for this story of an Armenian boyhood as the most truly American book of the year.

Henry Seidel Canby. SR. Dec. 28, 1940. p. 5

Someone soon will have to make an analysis of his very personal style, for though one might say of it that it is in the Hemingway tradition, there is something added, or is it taken away? For the art is most definitely one of subtraction, of shearing away the trimmings; it becomes an art of inarticulateness, where the silences say more than the words. . . . The writer, of course, has to fill in the significance of the silences, and that is where the art comes in; and he has to manage the business without your noticing what he is after. Mr. Saroyan knows how to do it.

Bonamy Dobrée. Spec. March 28, 1941. p. 354

He can be charming, he can be vastly amusing, he can be tender and innocent and even sometimes, as if by accident or inspiration, profound, but he can never be quite satisfying. Mr. Saroyan is a complete romantic. His fancifulness, his ecstatic love and admiration for children and even half-wits, his enthusiasm, his delight, his wonder at everything and anything, his faith in the promptings of the heart over those of the head . . . , his conviction that good always drives out sickness and evil and that love conquers all, makes him difficult to argue with. One can only disagree.

Wallace Stegner. NYT. Feb. 28, 1943. p. 7

No one in any serious sense believes in him any longer as a major prophet.

Saroyan might well have been one. He arrived on the American literary scene at a time when the public was tired of the destructive and cynical dicta of post-war novelists. He tried to affirm by his puckish humor, his Armenian folk-tales, his fables and his naive emotionalism that nothing mattered in the world except love and being true to yourself. He failed because a depression followed the war and another world war followed the depression. . . . We look today at Saroyan's men and women. . . . We love their primitive honesty, but . . . feel . . . that he is a gifted teller of fairy-tales, or parables, which have little relation to a world faced with continual revolution, starvation, and the threat of another war.

Harrison Smith. SR. June 1, 1946. pp. 7–8

At best Saroyan's fiction gives expression to a philosophy of life which is typically Californian, and also is central to the American transcendental tradition. Unlike the muckraking and socialistic writing of Upton Sinclair, Saroyan has no axe to grind, no gospel to preach. Unlike the naturalistic and sociological fiction of John Steinbeck, Saroyan treats human nature and social injustice without violence and anger. But because he rejects the utopian socialism of Sinclair and the revolutionary violence of Steinbeck, Saroyan does not adopt the pessimistic nihilism of Robinson Jeffers. Rather he reaffirms the old American faith of Emerson and Whitman, who, skeptical both of social reformers and of prophets of doom, proclaimed that the world could be reformed only by reforming the individual, and that this could not be accomplished by social compulsion and physical violence but only by personal freedom and loving tolerance.

Frederic I. Carpenter. *PS*. Winter, 1947. p. 96

Unlike his contemporaries of the late Nineteen Thirties he was given neither to political ranting nor to standardized thinking. In virtually everything he wrote—and he was astonishingly prolific—there was a curious twist of poetry and flashes of genuine humor and imagination. He was almost completely original, seeming to derive from no one at all, and the naïveté that was part of his style contained a winning charm that reflected the pleasant egoism of youth. In addition, he had mastered the integrate art of playwriting from the beginning, a technical feat at which many a fine novelist failed.

Thomas Quinn Curtiss. *NYT*. Nov. 20, 1949. p. 5

Saroyan's concept of goodness, once synonymous with love and gratitude, has become linked with man's tenacity, his will to live. And because this new optimism has a firmer basis in fact and bears out a dramatic element in life, his plays, with all their fantasy, have grown in plausibility. . . . Saroyan's outlook seems to have taken a Shavian turn (and not surprisingly, since Shaw is the one writer he admires). But with one important difference, that Saroyan's faith in the Life Force does not stem from dialectic but from his intuitive feeling of the ultimate meaning of things and events.

Nona Balakian. *NR*. Aug. 7, 1950. p. 20

I should say that Saroyan at his best turns out a peculiar literary version of schizophrenia. He writes of a world of strangers and loose ends in which there is no real human contact; it is a world in motion, but the laws of motion are suspended and none of the common patterns persists. Ordinary human feelings, such as hunger and loneliness—the two with which he is most often preoccupied—are presented in a minimum of setting, a social void, in which they are laid bare of the usual association. The attention is concentrated on the isolated action or emotion, which is, in turn, distorted, blown out of its common proportions, by being projected out of context. . . . The distortion heightens the expressive effect, and what comes through . . . represents a perception which is frequently absent in the more crowded "realistic" view of the universe. . . . But "human kind cannot bear very much reality," and Saroyan can't stand even his own. He is in constant flight from it.

Isaac Rosenfeld. *NR.* Dec. 8, 1952

He has not merely, by some august fortuity, happened, chanced or blundered upon a public; he may be said to have charmed one into existence and, by his blend of oddity with persuasive strength, bound his readers to him along his way. . . . Probably since O. Henry nobody has done more than William Saroyan to endear and stabilize the short story, as it were, to guarantee it, to rescue it from its two extremes of possible disrepute—that of being purely esthetic, divorced from life, or purely commercial, divorced from virtue. Also, does not this writer tilt against the deadening uniformity of society, constituting himself the spokesman of the odd man out, the champion of the misfit, the chronicler of the bum? Herein may lie some part of his fascination for those who do not dare deviate, but might wish to. Here, one may infer is a tempting, disturbing, repeated manifestation of innocence, on the part of somebody who has never sold out—the inspired, sometimes flamboyant alien, for whom nothing is yet quite normal in the American scene, and who flutters and dips in Americanism, like a bird in a bird-bath, without being in any way processed by it.

Elizabeth Bowen. *NR.* March 9, 1953. p. 18

The story of William Saroyan's amazing success and rapid decline is, in microcosm, a history of American optimism. Saroyan rose in mid-Depression as a bard of the beautiful life, a restorer of faith in man's boundless capacities; he has declined as a troubled pseudo-philosopher, forced to acknowledge man's limitations, yet uncomfortable in the climate of Evil. Indeed, he has come to dwell on Evil in order to deny its reality, reasserting, blatantly and defensively now, the American Dream of Unlimited Possibilities and Inevitable Progress. As a self-styled prophet of a native resurgence—believing in the virtue of self-reliant individualism, in the innate goodness of man and the rightness of his impulses—he has followed the tradition of American transcendentalism. (One critic has quite seriously called Saroyan the creator of "the new transcendentalism.") But it need hardly be said that Saroyan is no Emerson, either by temperament or by talent. The extent to which his later work has failed reflects, in one sense, the inadequacy of his equipment for the task he set himself. Yet it is also true that Saroyan is the representative American of the mid-twentieth-century, a man baffled at the failure of the Dream but unwilling to give it up; incapable of facing his dilemma frankly or of articulating it meaningfully.

(K)   William J. Fisher. *CE*. March, 1955. p. 336

I wish that more attention had been paid to the vivacity of his affirmations and even his sentimentalities. Saroyan's characters maintained their integrity in a humdrum, practical world that Saroyan took delight in turning topsy-turvy. He was acute enough to know how to confound the workaday, philistine world in such pieces as *My Heart's in the Highlands, The Time of Your Life,* and *The Beautiful People.* A sharp gamin's intelligence played behind the mask of his naïveté and behind the sentimentality of his protestations of brotherly love. In those days Saroyan conquered the commonplace world with a perverse kind of reasoning; he used even his own commonplaces for that purpose. There was a measure of provocative impudence in his gospel of brotherly love which pulled down the mighty. His sentimentality, the element in his work most frequently deplored, sometimes concealed and sometimes flaunted a cutting edge that both his admirers and detractors tended to overlook.

(K)   John Gassner. *Theatre at the Crossroads* (Holt).
1960. p. 150

Saroyan is not easy to write about, though his plays are simplicity itself. One cannot speak critically, for instance, of "Talking With You" (the first play on the bill) or of "Across the Board on Tomorrow Morning" (the second) without seeming sappy. Saroyan writes deliciously, but if you quote his plays you risk making him appear infantile or pretentious—and he is neither.

There *is* naïveté: a naïveté so genuine that it dissolves all other faults—including the embarrassment of a certain awkward sophistication. Saroyan has the spirit of a healthy child, trapped in a world far too chaotic and burdensome for him to be at ease. The "child" is really sad, but frisks about, smiles, does little tricks, tries to rouse us to play with him and to reassure us that neither he nor we need feel too bad.

(K)   Harold Clurman. *Nation*. Dec. 2, 1961. p. 460

William Saroyan is probably the freest man in captivity. In fact he is so free it hurts. It hurts the income tax collectors, to whom he still owes $29,000. It hurts Saroyan, who at the age of fifty-two says he hasn't yet picked up the pieces of his life to discover who he is. And it hurts audiences who sit through Saroyan plays with the feeling that each of them could and should be better than it is. . . .

Mr. Saroyan's theory is right, provided the works written with this ease *do* win a horde or even half a horde. The unfortunate fact is that most of his works have not done so, and there seems to be not the slightest chance of ever persuading him either to reorganize and develop or to let someone else reorganize and develop the almost always exciting material he has achieved with such ease.

(K)   Henry Hewes. *SR*. Dec. 23, 1961. p. 30

As a writer Saroyan is a primitive or a natural, and he has always relied on improvisation, often brilliant, to bring off his effects. He is in the tradition of Walt Whitman, with whom he shares, as this book [*Not Dying*] makes clear, a capacity for mysticism and intuitive insight, a warm feeling for the importance of each man and the unity of all men. He is also in the tradition of Mark Twain, with whom he shares, in the spirit of the raconteur, a gay neglect of esthetic form and a desperate need to find material to pad out his manuscript to book-length: *Not Dying* often seems to be a patchwork of irrelevancies.

But Whitman and Twain contributed to the tradition of nineteenth-century innocence. Saroyan is a twentieth-century man. His father came to America from Europe, from the Old World to the New, to seek a life of hope that was implicit in the promise of America as nineteenth-century optimism had framed that promise. The largest meaning of this book, for our culture and for the writer, is that it shows Saroyan returning to the Old World and the old life. The journey to the East represents the symbolic abandonment of that optimism and hope. It is the journey toward death.

(K)   Chester E. Eisinger. *SR*. Aug. 31, 1963. p. 46

Saroyan's sense of irony, one of the identifying marks of his early fiction, was compounded of this awareness of death and of an intensified responsiveness to life. It made possible the incongruous but enormously effective metaphor of his title [*The Daring Young Man on the Flying Trapeze*], and it imparted an indefinable charm to this first book. The Preface closes with the assertion that one must learn to breathe deeply, to taste, and even to sleep with as much zest and responsiveness as one's capacities permit: "Try to be alive. You will be dead soon enough." For those who knew the privations of the depression, this plea to make the most of life's simple joys struck a responsive note, and they welcomed this new writer as one who seemed to possess a poet's instinct to express what they themselves had come to feel.

(K)   Howard R. Floan. *William Saroyan* (Twayne). 1966.
                                                                              p. 22

Since the early 40s the familiar Saroyan stories have continued to flow, a few novels have appeared and been variously received; and plays both produced and unproduced, with seemingly tireless admonitory prefaces, have been published—all reminders that Saroyan is not only still around but that he is still the same old Saroyan. And, except for the tone of his non-dramatic work, which has grown increasingly solemn and self-conscious, and a few stories written in bile, Saroyan's is indeed the same voice heard in the 30s: there is grief aplenty, but man is a miracle, and merely living confirms life's miraculousness. That which seemed so distinctive to the spirit of the 30s no longer strikes us with the same relevant hopefulness, although such an observation may say more about our times than it does about Saroyan's themes, which were and still are largely prescriptions for ills which the author sees as endemic to no particular time.

(K)   James H. Justus in *The Thirties,* edited by
                              Warren French (Everett Edwards). 1967. p. 213

See *My Name Is Aram, The Human Comedy* (novels); *The Daring Young Man on the Flying Trapeze, The Assyrian* (stories); *The Time of Your Life, The Cave Dwellers* (plays); *Here Comes, There Goes, You Know Who, Not Dying* (autobiography).

SARTON, MAY (1912–   )

In *I Knew a Phoenix,* May Sarton, poet and novelist, recreates with a commingling of tenderness and reserve, the people who shaped her as she is. Autobiographical in the sense that in each of its chapters the book is concerned with either Miss Sarton's parents, her teachers, or her friends, it is not so much about herself as it is a mirror to refract the very special lights that lit her path to maturity. Because the kind and quality of her experience, rare at any time or in any country, is becoming rarer still in the political and commercial anonymity now threatening to engulf us, this modest story of a highly individual education has a nostalgic poignance all its own.

(K)   Virgilia Peterson. *NYHT.* April 26, 1959. p. 3

Poetry

A good part of Miss Sarton's poems are love sonnets. . . . To achieve the high polish which these sonnets possess it has been necessary for the poet to employ a good many pre-fabricated emotions, just as the sonnet form itself lends a ready-made gloss to the verse. The result is that the whole performance inevitably calls up Millay *et al.,* in their second April moods, and Miss Sarton's sonnets seem to stem from literary rather than personal emotions. . . . The finest piece of work in every way is a lyric in ten fluid parts, "She Shall Be Called Woman." This poem seems to me to reveal that secret access that women have into the core of their sensations and feelings. And it is certainly from that heightened consciousness that their best and unique work always comes. It is to be hoped that Miss Sarton's future writing will take its departure from this point.

Sherman Conrad. Poetry. July, 1937. pp. 229–31

Done with something of the eighteenth-century care for the sedate, unemotional line, her poems suggest the even lawns and precise gardens of the time of Queen Anne and the first of the Georges, before the turbulence of the romantic movement rushed in from the left to bewilder and overturn a strictly ordered world. Nevertheless, there is at the same time more emotion beneath the surface of Miss Sarton's dignified verses than was common in eighteenth-century poetry. The result of this slightly paradoxical combination is interesting. Let one try to visualize a butterfly imprisoned within a cake of ice and one will have a fairly good parallel to the poems.

Percy Hutchison. NYT. March 5, 1939. p. 5

May Sarton is an artist of remarkable powers. She is one of those rare poets who, in making use of simple combinations of words—and of the words of our common speech at that—has achieved a vocabulary and style as distinctly her own as any poet now writing. . . . She has drawn upon the whole stream of English literature to develop her subtle cadences and delicate, all-but-inaudible rhythms. . . . One wonders at the extreme simplicity of her statement (for such simplicity needs courage), and the more one wonders the more one is aware of the great gifts set forth. . . . Whatever life-images Miss Sarton chooses to turn into poetry become poetry. Her work is worth the admiring attention of everyone who considers himself a reader.

Martha Bacon. SR. April 17, 1948. p. 50

I suspect that what has always been considered the admirable simplicity of May Sarton's poetry is something more than that. . . . She demonstrates a great range of feeling and subject, an unusual strength in describing what comes before her eyes and touches her heart. Whether she speaks of zinnias or swans or the irradiating light of Provence, she testifies to a deep experience of reality which far surpasses purely speculative philosophy. . . . Her words . . . are never deadened by artifice or prose. The ease with which images in her poetry transpose notions provides the notions or the abstractions with their own firmness and poetic vigor.

Wallace Fowlie. NR. Dec. 14, 1953. p. 19

May Sarton's *In Time Like Air* is, to a poet at least, a book to carry in the pocket and reread with delight, the sort in which a second reading will disclose things undiscovered at first. What is the difference between this book and run-of-the-mill verse? It is partly a matter of personality, partly, perhaps, a matter of intellectual heritage, in no small degree a matter of the best kind of virtuosity. In Miss Sarton's writing there is passion, discretion, grief, joy, music and the intimation of delight. What gives her work its great distinction is its willingness to achieve its aims by simplicity when simplicity serves best and by elaboration when elaboration is proper. . . . Miss Sarton's extraordinary gift is her ability to make the actualities of physical existence and motion serve as the imaginative metaphor pointing to metaphysical reality.

Raymond Holden. *NYT*. Dec. 22, 1957. p. 4

May Sarton's *A Private Mythology* is remarkable for the savage brilliance of its poems about India, different in style from her previous work. She was offended by India; she was unprepared for it, and her response has the power of resentment and struggle. She was perhaps over-prepared for Greece and Japan; her poems about those countries have the quality of notes thought out in advance and carefully composed. . . .

Aside from the travel series, there is a resistant Lazarus, a first stanza to the Rilkean angels in the opening poem, country scenes of mowing and of pastoral Provence, and two important elegies, which have the wrathful commitment of her India poems: for a fiery child, and one of great power for a psychiatrist. Miss Sarton has moved to a new phase of sensibility with these elegies and the India poems. Considering the established range of abilities in this poet, this is a situation of the utmost promise.

(K)   Joseph Bennett. *NYT*. Nov. 13, 1966. p. 6

Novels

Only a poet and, perhaps, only a young poet could have written this beautiful and distinguished first novel (*The Single Hound*). In it May Sarton has created a little world of some half dozen people and she has given them rich, bountiful life, not only pregnant with meaning for this present instant of time in which she has placed them, but deeply rooted in that humanity which is ageless. . . . Here, as in her poems, May Sarton's aim is to arrive at what she calls "transparency." She has, also, in *The Single Hound* exemplified a way of life and enunciated a literary creed.

Jane Spence Southron. *NYT*. March 20, 1938. p. 6

Hinged on irony, *Faithful Are the Wounds* swings open onto tragedy. The movement of the book is, in its classical climbing and clearing shape, toward light and truth. It has none of that intellectual wasp sting that such a subject might afford itself. It is a quiet and ever-deepening penetration into the roiled darknesses of uncommitted passion, of jelled fervors in the cold air of doubt; it touches that reserve that jails the modern conscience in its own dubious safety from which it can utter only the cry of "Why can't love help?". . . . Miss Sarton's method, even as that of her men and women who crave the light of day against self-inflicted darkness, is to turn to light what is shadowed, raise to the level of the common ground what is half-buried underground.

William Goyen. *NYT*. March 13, 1955. p. 6

In her new novel, *Faithful Are the Wounds,* May Sarton moves from the world of purely personal relationships, brought to glowing life and examined in minute detail, to one of the most violently burning public questions of our day, democratic dissent in a time of national crisis. Yet the change is much less than the statement implies. . . . Once again the kaleidoscope of feeling is turning throughout and once again the reader feels himself constantly in the presence of a master of English fiction. There is a maturity here, a command, command of the language first of all, and of the situation, the character, the change and growth, that make one terribly impatient with much that the American novel is now bringing forth.

Frank Getlein. *Com.* April 8, 1955. p. 19

The Birth of a Grandfather is not a "woman's novel," a lending library favorite; it is much too precisely observed, truly told and serious minded. But it is limited to much the same material as these contrivances, the feminine world of family and home. What is worse, the delineation of its male characters is weakened by what may well be a conscientious scruple; a refusal (since one is not male) to try to see these characters in male terms, because such as effort would involve invention almost in the sense of falsification.

For a novelist as finely observant, as capable, as Miss Sarton, such scruples are nonsense.

Elizabeth Janeway. *NYT*. Sept. 8, 1957. p. 4

The author has long considered the difficulty of achieving personal harmony through human relationships. All her books, and much of her poetry, have shown preoccupation with the growth of personality, the ability or lack of it to communicate love, or, for that matter, to feel it in the first place, the acceptance of birth and death as cyclical parts of man's continuity. These are primary concerns, usually wrapped in the thunderclouds of *Sturm und Drang.* But Miss Sarton's style is quiet, her dialogue true and sure. She describes no scene "folkloristically" yet each has abundant authentic detail. And her situations, though low-keyed, are basic, alive with their own kind of tension, drama, and suspense.

Frances Keene. SR. Sept. 14, 1957. p. 50

"A small, accurate talent, exploited to the limit, let us be quite clear about *that!*" says F. Hilary Stevens, the seventy-year-old poet who is the heroine of poet May Sarton's latest book [*Mrs. Stevens Hears the Mermaids Singing*]. And perhaps Mrs. Stevens's definition of her own gift is the best description of her creator's as well. . . .

Miss Sarton's writing is sensitive to the point of fussiness, and totally without humor. The lack of this saving grace inevitably leads her into pitfalls of inadvertent hilarity. And there is something embarrassing about her probing of Art, as there is in the intimate obstetrical confidences of a comparative stranger. It is not that either subject is intrinsically embarrassing; but the acute self-consciousness often foundering in archness, the solemn conviction that here is revelation, make the listener uncomfortable.

(K)   Ruth L. Brown. *SR*. Oct. 23, 1965. p. 68

The style [of *Mrs. Stevens Hears the Mermaids Singing*], unguarded by irony ("It was as if she and the boy were standing in a great cleared place"); the set-up situations (the interview forces Hilary to *express* her beliefs, the guidance she gives a young apprentice tempted by homosexuality forces her to *examine* her beliefs, the interviewers demonstrate male and female sensibilities); the stagey names (Sirenica, Mar, Adrian), conversations and directions (people "rush out of the house," their eyes "twinkle," they "utter" and "mutter" such things as "Drat the boy!" or "Trapped by life!") make this novel wholly vulnerable. And yet . . . and yet it is moving, it tells the truth, if not convincingly about art, which may require more astringent expression, then at least about love, with a kind of brave disregard for the critical eye. And the critical eye is finally blinded by an integrity that shines out of the book.

(K)   Mona Van Duyn. *Poetry*. Feb., 1967. p. 333

See *Cloud, Stone, Sun, Vine, A Private Mythology* (poems); *The Single Hound, A Shower of Summer Days, Faithful Are the Wounds, The Small Room, Mrs. Stevens Hears the Mermaids Singing* (novels).

SCHISGAL, MURRAY (1926–   )

Mr. Schisgal manifests an original talent. His writing lacks distinction and his design still wants concision. But he has humor, and he has found a way of saying certain things, bitter or painful in other dramatists, which in *The Tiger* and *The Typists* are presented with a quizzical playfulness that is wholly engaging.

Mr. Schisgal's theme is by now the universal one of loneliness and alienation. . . . The "gimmick"—if you wish to call it that—in the second and longer of the two plays, *The Typists,* consists in showing us a man and a woman, typists in a mercantile office, as though their lifetime were compressed into a single day. . . . But the play has no expressionistic stress; it is obliquely sad with a suppressed tenderness.

Harold Clurman. *Nation.* Feb. 23, 1963. pp. 166–7

One thing, at least, becomes more and more clear: how right Kenneth Tynan is in his contention that if you took the Jews away from the Broadway scene, there would be no comedy left. I know, I know, but I am not resigned. . . . So it is that praise must be given Murray Schisgal for his two short plays, *The Typists* and *The Tiger,* even though the first of these does not come off at all, and the second weakens as it goes along. But Mr. Schisgal has made the decent attempt to explore the platitudes and idiosyncrasies that underlie the business of living, irrespective of clique or clan. He has found the commonplaces that are common to all, and the quirks that can crop up anywhere just as easily as somewhere.

John Simon. *HdR.* Summer, 1963. p. 271

In Murray Schisgal's merry new lampoon of the banal idiocies that attend love—or "luv," as he calls it—he has provided a challenging scenario for three inventive performers. The action of *Luv* is simple. A character named Milt sees a man about to jump off the Brooklyn Bridge. Since this is a common occurrence, he has almost passed by when he recognizes the man as Harry, a college classmate he hasn't seen in fifteen years. The traditional glad hand is in order, and it is only coincidental that their greeting requires a delay in Harry's suicide plans. Thus it is that the Schisgalian dialectic is established. We are in a comic world in which conventional responses and clichéd superficialities have their own logic and compelling force. Devastating events are to be accepted lightly as a matter of course, but trivial annoyances can evoke furious passion. . . .

That personal style is, I suspect, a reflection of Mr. Schisgal's daily irritation with the lack of connection between modern man's impulses and his means of exercising them. Neither in his Off-Broadway success of *The Tiger* and *The Typist* nor in his present Broadway hit does this lead to anything as poetic or profound as one finds in Ionesco. But it does lead to adventurous comic escapades that spring honestly and convincingly from one city-dweller's observation of an existence in which everyone seems to be voluntarily incarcerated on the wrong subway train.

Henry Hewes. *SR.* Nov. 28, 1964. p. 29

Schisgal, at present, is at an interesting (for us) and (for him) a doubtless strange and exciting moment in his career. He is no young puppy. He is not *old,* to be sure. Who thinks anyone under 57 is *old?* But he is 37, and, at 37, he stands on the threshold of what could very well be a most considerable and significant career in the American theatre. And if that sounds portentous in print, consider how it must seem to Schisgal, who has to do the threshold-standing. To date, there is no doubt that he has done some very good work. *Luv,* in fact, is very likely a "classic," a funny *serious* play which says more about Love, Money, Sex Guilt, Freud—the whole great panoply of (if you will pardon the expression) The Modern Predicament—than the last 92 pretentious, complacent, rhetorical Modern Dramas rolled into one. And how far can he go? Well, it would be downright silly to try to say. Schisgal is a very genuine talent, a serious man. He will go as far as he can, and nobody, not even he, can know how far that really is.

> M. J. Arlen. Introduction to *Fragments, Windows and Other Plays* by Murray Schisgal (Coward-McCann) 1965. p. 15

What this is, of course, is not devastating social satire, still less avant-garde theatre; it is plain and simple burlesque or vaudeville. (The fact that the avant-garde may also draw on burlesque is irrelevant: you can lead a horse to water but you can't make him a water buffalo thereby.) Indeed, *Luv* might make a perfectly acceptable fifteen or twenty-minute sketch in a jauntier nightclub or revue, but it is by no means a full-length play. The old burlesque device of repetition by way of a slow comic build-up serves a dual purpose here: it stretches out a mere playlet into the more marketable commodity of a play, and it allows the playwright's essentially commonplace mind to revel in its natural habitat. . . .

One of the troubles is that Schisgal is not quite up to what he is trying to poke fun at. . . . Another and more serious trouble is that the playwright scatters his shots in all directions, in an attempt to puncture whatever he can hit, without committing himself to any point of view. And that, in anything but a piece of unpretentious zaniness, is immoral.

> John Simon. *HdR.* Spring, 1965. p. 85

See *The Tiger, The Typists, Luv* (plays).

SCHULBERG, BUDD (1914–   )

What Makes Sammy Run? is brilliantly effective because it is completely of this time, expressing the beliefs and hopes that begin to stand out in this period, marked in it by the threat of complex defeat. The dialogue is a bit freer, less reticent than even that dialogue that shocked the dear innocent early public of Hemingway. The style is unsweated, but colorful. The story is constantly pointed up with incident. . . . It is unquestionably one of the most interesting and promising first novels to appear in several years.

Robert Van Gelder. *NYT*. Mar. 30, 1941. p. 6

If you have frequently looked with fascination at the unmistakable lineaments of big business and have tried to solve the mystery of what must have been the living transformation of the individual into the corporation, then you will follow the quest for the answer to the question posed in the title of Mr. Schulberg's book. . . . The book is uneven; the first part is badly written and developed. . . . Toward the end Mr. Schulberg does say what he wants to say, the writing is good, the plot blooms, and the form is there. Hollywood, that junction of theater and audience, is more honestly, amusingly, and instructively covered than in any other book I know.

L. P. Lazarus. *Nation*. April 19, 1941. p. 477

Budd Schulberg's new book is a hard-boiled successor to his first and tough little novel, *What Makes Sammy Run?* Just as full of heels and no-goods, and as fast, slangy and wisecracking, *The Harder They Fall* is in many ways a much better novel than *Sammy*. . . . Out of the elements of the Carnera story Schulberg has created a brilliant novel—the first of the modern prize ring, I believe, to be a worthy contender for literary honors. . . . Schulberg owes something to Hemingway, F. Scott Fitzgerald, and Jerome Weidman, and the readers of the sports pages also will recognize rhythms of sports columnist Jimmy Cannon. . . . But the final product is a Schulberg original, a switch on the American success story wherein bad boy makes good.

John Horn. *NYT*. Aug. 10, 1947. p. 3

What gives *The Harder They Fall* its impressive quality is the realism and the scientific accuracy of the deadly picture of a sordid business. Schulberg knows the atmosphere, the history and the technique of the ring and the psychology of its fighters, promoters, hangers-on and public. Even the sentimentalism, the sadness and the rare examples of bravery are credible, because the author sees not only the ugliness but the fascination of the racket that is a sport. . . . Schulberg hates the sordidness, cruelty and corruption of the so-called fight game, but he can get as sentimental as the next man about the battered and punch-drunk veterans of an earlier day and just as excited about a good battle between a couple of fighters who really fight.

Richard Watts, Jr. *NR*. Aug. 11, 1947. pp. 27–8

The Harder They Fall is the story of an American heavyweight and of how he got his. . . . Not since Hemingway's "Fifty Grand" has there been a story so idiomatic, so physically cruel, so underscored with the disgust of the corrupted. The atmosphere at Stillman's gym, the Sunday luncheon at Nick's country place, Barry Winch playing gin rummy, the sparring of George Blount—these are descriptions or bits of low comedy incomparably well done. I cannot question the tough reality of the episodes—not even the corny scenes with Shirley, a boxer's widow, who would probably be even cornier in real life. But I do wonder whether there is enough change of pace and enough high relief in the book to keep the reader coming.

Edward Weeks. *At.* Sept., 1947. p. 120

Mr. Schulberg's gamy, grimy opus is hard-fisted writing at its brass-knuckle, kidney-punching best. . . . *The Harder They Fall* is an exposé of the prize-fighting business in this country. . . . This, too, is a part of American culture, a conspicuous part; and Mr. Schulberg's combination of contemptuous hatred and reluctant fascination makes for good reading. . . . With no subtleties of characterization, but with wonderfully authentic atmosphere, he has written a scathing indictment of a so-called "sport." And in the process he has never allowed his indignation to get in the way of his story-telling.

Orville Prescott. *YR.* Autumn, 1947. p. 191

The thirty-six-year-old Mr. Schulberg is a sensitive and gentle companion. In fact, his gentleness transforms itself into an exacting concern in the modulations of an idea—such shadings and qualifications lending to Mr. Schulberg's speech a hesitant and touchingly tormented character. At the same time, within this muted atmosphere that Mr. Schulberg can't help but create, there exists an awareness in his companions that Mr. Schulberg is possessed of a remarkably powerful chest, that he is, as well, the proud possessor of a promising prize-fighter—all of which combines into a nice paradox.

Harvey Breit. *NYT.* Nov. 5, 1950. p. 28

Schulberg has moved up from the heels of *What Makes Sammy Run?* and the punks of *The Harder They Fall*. The flashy, erratic style of those novels often obscured the maturity of his implied judgements, his ability to open people up so that you can decide what makes *them* run. These gifts are more richly displayed, more fully developed in *The Disenchanted*. There are weaknesses: the book seems uneven in spots, too long, and trite and awkward when Schulberg is trying to recreate some scenes with which he appears personally unfamiliar. But there are episodes of great power and vividness, in which the thoughtful reader can discern some penetrating observations on the evils of casting stones.

Paul V. Farrell. *Com.* Nov. 10, 1950. p. 124

Because Budd Schulberg is a sound journalist who draws upon material he has lived with or authenticated, the twenty entries in *Some Faces in a Crowd* are packed with verisimilitude. Few observers know more about Hollywood . . . or about the boxing business. . . . He is suspicious of all Head Men, depicted here as uneasy end-products of a dog-eat-dog process among phonies, ingrates, bullies, eccentrics, and dreamers right out of the final scene of *The Iceman Cometh*. He believes that fame is fleeting, loyalty about as rare as the whooping crane, and moments of glory illusion.

In Schulberg land, the heels are at work, the realities are squalid, and the prognosis is dreary.

James Kelly. *SR*. May 16, 1953. p. 14

His . . . stories . . . differ from popular magazine fiction chiefly in the way they end. The characters have to take the responsibility for what they do. They have to pay moral costs and face defeats. . . . Mr. Schulberg is like the popular magazine writers, however, in his style and in the ingredients out of which his fictions are made. He obviously admires Hemingway and Lardner and Fitzgerald, but he does not feel their need to get things just right, to see the thing as what in itself it truly is. . . . Villainy is made a little too easy to be against in these stories. Villainy is, nevertheless, very clearly seen and very dramatically presented. And virtue is very clearly seen, too, especially in the war stories.

Robert Gorham Davis. *NYT*. May 17, 1953. p. 5

Schulberg . . . seems congenitally unable to see the world except through the special lenses developed by Hemingway (the sentimentalized prize fight and the brutalized deep-sea fishing stories) or Fitzgerald (the beautiful rich girl with a suicidal drive). . . . Schulberg is another of the Jewish writers like Weidman and Shaw whose work has skimmed close to the solid shores of genuine American literary achievement. These writers, in a sense which can serve only as an initial, temporary excuse, have been incapacitated from realizing their promise by a lack of a serious and active artistic tradition, something they give hints of recognizing; but, instead of seeking one, as, say, Lionel Trilling has done, in the depths of history and in the classical values, instead of dealing with the lack as part of the process of developing an authentic idiom, they have casually gone for their guidance to the popular culture heroes.

Morris Freedman. *Cmty.* Oct., 1953. pp. 389–92

See *What Makes Sammy Run?, The Harder They Fall, The Disenchanted,* and *Waterfront* (novels); also *Some Faces in a Crowd* (short stories).

SCHWARTZ, DELMORE (1913–1966)

Concerned with fundamentals, with the problem of identity, of knowledge and belief, haunted by the noise time makes, able to write wittily and movingly, Mr. Schwartz is betrayed by a failure of concentration. His diffuseness is perhaps inevitable to a sensitive person pausing before a mirror which reflects his face against the background of this distracted twentieth-century scene. . . . He shows himself open to more perceptions than he can properly control. They crowd upon him so thickly that the effect, which should be one of richness and depth is sometimes that of confusion. But at his best, and his best is very good, he exhibits a sensibility and an intelligence rare in his generation.

Babette Deutsch. NYHT. March 5, 1939. p. 21

In the story which opens *In Dreams Begin Responsibilities,* and in the lyrics which make up the third section, the author displays not only a mastery of technic that is precisely suited to his poems' intention, but also a rare sensitivity of perception, an urgent humanity, and such an honesty of expression as is rare in a day when the manners of poetry ape the sliding faithless manners of international diplomacy. It is hard to believe that this is a first book, the work of a very young man. . . . Almost without exception the short poems achieve the equilibrium between Thing Said and Way of Saying that is the mark of the finest poetry.

Dudley Fitts. SR. April 29, 1939. p. 29

Schwartz is an authoritative poet, which is to say that he is much more than a poet of the decade. His achievement is threefold. First of all, he has orchestrated the central theme of his decade more richly, more consistently, and more intelligently than any of his contemporaries. Beyond this, Schwartz differs from most of his contemporaries in having a genuinely creative attitude of mind that enables him always to project and to resolve the tensions of his poetry in terms of real experience. He rejects the easy solutions offered by ideologies; his use of ideas is always dramatic rather than didactic; he takes the hard way—to a solution in terms of poetry.

Moreover, Schwartz develops his solution in an original verse tone that modifies the English poetic tradition in using it.

George Marion O'Donnell. Poetry. May, 1939. p. 107

Much that he has done has been self-conscious rather than conscious of larger meanings than the self. He is not alone in the fault. A whole school of younger poets rely on learning rather than vision. But it is time that Mr. Schwartz find, if he is ever going to, the rhythms and images characteristic of him and of him alone, the convictions which he holds, the vision, not so narcissistic, which makes his voice worth listening to. If he does not do this he will remain one of the several bright young poets who have risen to some fame rather too easily because of their ability to handle form and to echo current ideas and patterns of belief. On a few occasions this poet has written movingly, but more often he has only composed in the more modern forms of poem, play, or short story.

Eda Lou Walton. *NYHT*. Nov. 23, 1941. p. 32

Schwartz adumbrates a theme of the first importance and value: the infinite possibilities, logically and ethically studied of human individuality. This and its uncompromising technical skill are what make the poem not only a document but positive. "You lie in the coffin of your character," one of the ghosts says . . . ; but another asks, "Who can recover actuality? And who can win his way to criticism?" In *Genesis* is a statement of this question, it creates confidence that the answer, too, will be aesthetically valid. Despite occasional garrulous aridity, it suggests as a whole a genuinely tragic view of life, which needs stating more than ever against the prevalent falsettos uttering or claiming to dispel premature indifference and despair.

Frank Jones. *Nation*. Aug. 14, 1943. p. 187

These stories (in *The World Is a Wedding*) are written, for the most part, in a monotonous, even awkward prose. For a writer with a reputation as a poet, they are surprisingly deficient in imagery, or the visual sense. But one soon notices in the explicit themes, in the abstract language, in the political references, and in the tone of polite discussion, a deliberate direction halfway between traditional fiction and the philosophical dialogue.

In a number of instances Schwartz brings it off beautifully; in any case, it's a direction along which writers, here and there, are feeling their way, and one which should have happy consequences for the form and content of fiction.

John Farrelly. *NR*. Aug. 2, 1948. p. 27

Delmore Schwartz writes fiction as a poet and not as a chronicler. For him, the history of the New York Ashkenazim from the nineties to the present is symbolic of what has happened to man everywhere. . . . I have read no fiction of late whose content seems so completely lived and comprehended—all communicated in the sparsest and barest of prose, a whole society, the generations, breathing and talking endlessly. Given this concern with most of the central anxieties of modern life, it would be easy for the author to fall into self-pity. Except for two unfortunate stories . . . , an intellectual astringency keeps Mr. Schwartz out of this kind of difficulty.

Ernest Jones. *Nation*. Sept. 11, 1948. p. 294

With a deceptive sparseness and formality of style Delmore Schwartz writes of Jewish middle class family life in New York in this century. His stories, moving from room to room inside the dry vastness of the city, show families divided against themselves, and individuals, who, though terribly interdependent, will never know each other directly in love or friendship. He describes the search for love in these people, even as they fall away from it, their feelings of guilt and self-defense even as the desire to be rid of them, and their resignation even in their frustration. . . . In a comparatively few pages some of the stories encompass generations of family tensions and frustrations without apparent strain. But the style, though quiet, has a kind of muted eloquence which testifies even more strongly to this author's talent.

John Hay. *Com.* Sept. 17, 1948. p. 551

Pleasure in reading Schwartz comes in recognition of worldly values. . . . Schwartz has long been a poet of the city. No illusions are left about it. We feel that we have been dragged through its least place in reading him, for nothing is spared in the depiction of truth. We accept, the gross, the banal, the sentimental, the sensual. . . . There is little of fury or rage, much of philosophic understanding, and a hard-worked control over what is being said. The poems erect substantial orders to mirror the actual urban world, urban life, and the foibles of both.

Richard Eberhart. *NYT*. Nov. 5, 1950. p. 2

In mercilessly identifying the sources on which he draws, and in choosing as his central theme the chasm between poetry and life and between man and man, he battles for his identity as poet. (Occasionally, when his verse gets very good, it is as if his verse had chosen him and not he it, in the very same way that Rilke became the "speaking mouth" of his visions.) In celebrating the American continent, the astonishment of the child still alive in him; in debunking America, in satirically stripping the mask of reality from its surface, and only then going on to praise its unveiled beauty and its grandeur, he struggles for his identity as an American. And in taking his origins as the point of departure for his attempt to make himself part of the world, part of the human environment and of the universe of the intellect, he battles for his identity as a Jew.

Heinz Politzer. *Cmty.* Dec., 1950. p. 568

No other young poet has realized the inadequacy of Christianity (and the Judaism from which it derives) in the modern Western world with the same appalling consciousness that he has. . . . In his own quiet American way Delmore Schwartz is the desperate counterpart of Rimbaud, whose *Une Saison en Enfer* he has translated. Both are aware that the supports of their respective cultures are tottering and new beliefs must be found to nourish the religious impulse of man. . . . Schwartz is not unaware of the literary value of his heritage. . . . Schwartz makes of Jewishness a symbol of the modern situation. The alienated man apprehends experience as the Jew lives in the modern Christian world, both through a glass darkly.

Morton Seiff. *JSS*. Oct., 1951. pp. 311–2, 316

The poet has risen from a certain moribund view of existence found in his earlier books, and like his Lazarus "thrusting aside the cold sweated linens," looks "for the first time, wonderstruck." . . .

This yielding to sensuous expression indicates that some ice-bound spring of feeling has been released. But there is danger in over-ripeness, as well as delight. In a few of the new poems Schwartz lets the happy wanderings of his imagination become too musically articulate and repetitive. But he has not lost his ironic, incisive view of character and events, or his strong philosophic vein. . . .

Schwartz matured in an age of literary self-consciousness influenced by the prevailing winds of doctrine without falling into any of the fashionable ruts. Although a product of contemporary values and techniques he is not a part of any esoteric coterie. Like Baudelaire he has a sense of his own age and its impact—depressions and war, the Marxist doctrines and Freudian theories, an urban life with its background of fervent Jewish culture. All these have kept his poetry from the dryness of intellectual abstraction.

(K) Katherine G. Chapin. *NR*. Nov. 9, 1959. pp. 24–5

Schwartz's style is the key to his stories. He casts many verbal nets for meaning, and some prove more effective than others. He catches meanings, and he also reveals the difficulty of capturing so slippery an article. (I have again fallen into Schwartz's mannerism: his favorite word is "and"; his favorite mark of punctuation is the comma that takes its place.) His characters, too, cast nets for elusive meanings, trying to encompass and to fathom life with theories that are as inadequate and as artificial as words. They carry out skilful exercises in self-deception, but they are invariably exposed by the all-wise author, who looks over their shoulders to interpret the thoughts behind the words and behind the thoughts. . . .

(K) Henry Popkin. *SR*. Dec. 2, 1961. p. 25

At first glance a comedian of alienation, Schwartz also showed a gift for acceptance, a somewhat ambiguous reconcilement with the demands and depletions of common experience. Many writers have treated similar kinds of material, but even those, like Bellow and Malamud, whose fictions are more inclusive and substantial have not captured quite so keenly as has Schwartz the particular timbre, the tangled reverberations and complications of irony within irony, that once characterized Jewish life in America. And what gave Schwartz's work its distinction was that he avoided the pieties of both fathers and sons, established community and estranged intellectuals; he worked his way past their fixed perspective, unfolding still another nuance of reflection by which to complicate and even undercut his own ironies. His poems and stories rested on what is for our time the most secure of foundations: the tempered humaneness of self-doubt. . . .

In both stories and poems his tone was deflated, as if it were looking over its shoulder to see whether it was being followed by rhetoric. It seemed to be composed of several speech layers: the sing-song, slightly pompous intonations of Jewish immigrants educated in night-schools, the self-conscious affectionate mockery of that speech by American-born sons, its abstraction into the jargon of city intellectuals, and finally the whole body of this language flattened into a prose of uneasiness, an anti-rhetoric. . . .

. . . Though not quite so good as his earlier work, the stories collected in *Successful Love* show that he chose the path of risk. Just as his recent poems represent a new development—a somewhat forced venture into lyric rhapsody over the renewed possibilities of life—so his recent stories leave the thirties behind and turn toward the prosperous confusion of post-war America.

(K)   Irving Howe. *NR*. March 19, 1962. pp. 25–6

. . . somehow a deeper necessity than merely hitting the average highbrow literary taste took hold of Schwartz, and he was faithful to a higher rule than any he flouted: namely, that an ounce of presentation is worth a pound of care; and drew what to my mind is the definitive portrait of the Jewish middle class in New York during the Depression.

How do I, knowing relatively little of this class at first hand, undertake such a verdict? Because these early stories still seem to me among the very best written anywhere at the time. They are acts of discovery and celebration such as no other group in the country at the time could have produced, and they have the great virtue of having been generated from the real, as against the ideological, preoccupations of their society, of aiming neither, like Salinger's stories, to fit the new life into the classical patterns of sentimental farce, nor, by gentle and subtle distortion, to revive lost folkish sentiments recovered from writers like Babel or Sholem Aleichem. This is New York Jewry, I venture to say, of an integrity and wholeness unmatched elsewhere in fiction, before the intellectual diaspora of the 40's began, before Leslie Fiedler began howling from Montana for an end to innocence or Karl Shapiro from Nebraska for an end to T. S. Eliot.

(K)   Robert W. Flint. *Cmty*. April, 1962. p. 336

If the oppressiveness of Schwartz's long early guilt is in some part responsible for the kinds of tactile and kinesthetic qualities in his first poems, then his latest poetry, celebrating a release from this oppressiveness, reveals qualities equally arresting. Having faced himself, explored his own history, and recognized his debts, he feels free now of all those urgent preoccupations. . . .

With this new approach to the world, Schwartz's poetry quite naturally undergoes a radical transformation. Since the dawn of the "second world" is now a major theme, light floods his poetry, replacing in large part the tactile abstractions of his former work. Auditory imagery also finds a larger place here—singing birds are obviously an essential part of any dawn. . . . But most important of all is the change from the formerly much favored blank verse and rimed iambics to the Whitmanesque cadences of these new poems. They reflect not only the release from oppressiveness we have been discussing, but a sensuous apprehension of language that is directly related to his earlier kinesthetic effects.

(K)   Jay L. Halio. *SoR*. Autumn, 1965. pp. 814–15

Though his "substratum of sensibility" is very modern, Schwartz's poetic solution is dated, goes back actually to Whitman, who sought to identify himself with everything; Schwartz tries to identify everything with himself. But this reverse-Whitman solution will not do the trick for Schwartz; it does not save his poetry from the progressive deterioration which seems to attend modern work that is ultimately and continuously romantic.

It is true that Schwartz has irony, but irony is not enough. . . .

His mode is inclusion; his key concept is "appetite." His ultimate recourse is to freedom of sensibility, the first and last reliance of the romantic. Under the guise of "giving all," he must maintain a stand of barefaced candor but behind this is self-congratulation on his ability to maintain a tension of lifelong provisionality. He remains uncommitted and arrives at truth through revelation and confession. Refusing the tools of indirection, myth, central symbol, and limits, he fights fragmentation by proudly exposing his devouring ego, tiny, hateful, and alone, as he himself often points out.

(K)   R. H. Deutsch. *SwR*. Autumn, 1966. pp. 917–18

See *The World Is A Wedding, Successful Love* (stories); *Summer Knowledge* (poems).

SCOTT, WINFIELD TOWNLEY (1910–1968)

Winfield Townley Scott is a striking poet working with an original key which was provided him by the techniques of our modern school, but one who exists in an isolated sphere in the same way that Chirico does in contrast to other surrealist painters. Scott's stark contrast to the surrealist poets like Parker Tyler, Weldon Kees, etc., is that he never builds beyond a single phenomenon, whereas they struggle to find a magnet for a series of phenomena. . . . The strange portions of his work, in concept, I feel have been affected through John Wheelwright's influence and the subtle shifting of musical phrases by simulating the poetry of Dylan Thomas. Like Wheelwright's, it is a felt poetry as well as thought, uneven and inclusive and highly original. I expect that he will grow in stature.

Maurice Swan. *NYT*. Jan. 18, 1942. p. 5

By whatever critical formulas Scott's poetry is approached and discussed, it would be an obtuse, tired reviewer who could fail to sense the genuineness of this poet's mind, the liveness of the poetic experience he records and makes. . . . For the searcher of speech patterns, they are there, not as indelible and local as Frost's perhaps, and sometimes out of control, but very close and real. The danger of prose "draining the air" is successfully overcome in almost every poem. There are enough verses presenting awareness and criticism of twentieth-century environment to meet the demands of the critic who believes modern verse must mirror the times to the last neon tube and microphone.

Marshall Schacht. *Poetry*. April, 1942. p. 47

When he is not celebrating individualists of that region whose transcendentalism enables the poets to include heaven and earth within their "regionalism," Mr. Scott is reducing the general to the individual (what John Peale Bishop called "minute particulars") in the manner of all true poets.

Mr. Scott's eye is acute; his powers of observation show to good advantage in a number of poems. In the transcendental mode he finds wide meaning in narrow corners of nature; his landscapes extend infinitely.

Gerard Previn Meyer. *SR*. Oct. 9, 1948. p. 32

The Dark Sister is a figure from the Norse saga's *Long Island Book,* the source of all we know about the discovery of America by Lief Ericson in the year 1000. . . . Winfield Scott has been accurate to the mood of the story. We forget that we know so little of our past, what ancestors we come from. . . . Scott has used a long line and diction well suited to the rough speech of his sailor characters who were under their mistress' domination throughout the voyage.

William Carlos Williams. Nation. Feb. 22, 1958. p. 171

Scott's newest book, his seventh, is The Dark Sister, a saga not only because it is about Leif Ericson's half sister, Freydis, and the Viking exploration to the new world, but because in this poet's language, narration, and sweep a saga truly rises out of Vinland. The hero is not human, but infinitely greater, the land itself bigger than all the human beings who came to it or were to come for centuries. Scott's descriptive passages of weather, forests, the sea are more the climate of the poem than "passages," but they thrust under our very feet and into our blood. . . . Scott's realization in words of that clean cold land and time is his triumph in this poem.

John Holmes. SR. April 12, 1958. p. 70

Though Winfield Townley Scott has published admirable verse for over twenty years, The Dark Sister is his masterpiece and one of the remarkable poems of recent times. It has excitement and depth. With a control of his medium that almost never falters, he handles characterization, narrative, and landscape with equal power in the flexible cadences of his verse. . . . The work is written in loose three-part measures—largely dactyls and amphibrachs with some fine spondees that have almost a quantitative effect. The form is sufficiently fluid to meet the demands of the content, and is notably satisfactory in the seaborne and windswept passages.

Robert Hillyer. NYT. March 9, 1958. p. 10

Both the conscious skill of understatement and the fine sea-rhythm (somewhat like the best of Jeffers) are present in the new long poem The Dark Sister. This is a narrative poem which—I don't know how to suggest the uncomfortable suggestion—tries to be an epic. I enjoyed reading The Dark Sister. It is an important contribution to the solution of the problem which seems to fret the good poets of Mr. Scott's generation: the long poem. Its narrative line is always clear, its characterizations are adequately distinct from one another, its heroine is a real four-square howling bitch who would plainly devour her litter. Moreover, Mr. Scott has achieved scenes which are startlingly dramatic.

James Wright. Poetry. Oct., 1958. pp. 47–8

Winfield Townley Scott is also a poet who encourages the notion that the poet's job is to walk through woods and think. Seriously. Willfully. Nor will I quarrel with this notion; it simply seems to me that Scott has, like Miss Boyle, written a few too many poems about the crocus spring, a few too many about grand and literary themes (Hamlet, Leif Ericson, Yeats). Yet Scott has a voice that, when he uses it, makes one rejoice. A few of his poems are masterpieces: "Landscape as Metal and Flowers," "Three

American Women and a German Bayonet," "The US Sailor with the Japanese Skull" and "Mr. Whittier." In such poems, he demonstrates that he has a world, one to which someone, perhaps Robinson, awakened him —a world of the local war monuments, of Grant Wood and Winslow Homer, of Methodist encampments, and memories of the Townleys—a world that is personal, intense.

(K)   David Ray. *NR*. Nov. 10, 1962. pp. 22–3

His voice is that of a reasonable man talking with an old friend. He has no desire to impress you, his friend, get you to change your mind, charm you, cozy up to you, or burden you with his secret troubles. You must pay attention to understand him, but if you do pay attention you will understand him. His voice is casual in that he is not concerned to press you into listening to him. This is not because he lacks genuine concern; it is because his greatest concern is for meaning. He wants to, and does, put what he says in such a way that you can take it if (but not as) you will. The voice is casual in that it is not oratorical or turgid, or so musical that you cease to care about the sense; especially it is casual in the way of tactfulness.

(K)   George P. Elliott. *NYHT*. Sept. 13, 1964. p. 17

Most of the poems in Winfield Townley Scott's new book, *Change of Weather,* are unambitious, which is disappointing. His style has always pleased me greatly, in itself and for the way he worked it out of the New England of Robinson and Frost into a sphere entirely his own; a strong style, flexible and modest, the best style we have, I think, for narrative verse. But it is largely wasted in the new poems, or so it seems to me. They are almost all brief lyrics on themes of declining sex, the approach of old age and death, ancestors, memories of childhood, the towns and land-scapes that give rise to these thoughts. In other words they are the poems we have come to expect from every poet who keeps going until his fifties; they are inevitable. . . . His *Collected Poems 1937–1962* is a book of great and perhaps sufficient value, as more and more people are coming to recognize. Nevertheless, without being captious we have a right to state our disappointment.

(K)   Hayden Carruth. *Poetry*. July, 1965. pp. 309–10

See *Collected Poems, Change of Weather* (poems).

SEXTON, ANNE (1928–   )

To Bedlam and Part Way Back is a remarkable book . . . , in which we feel not only the poet's experience but also something of the morality behind recalling and recording it. There is more here than a case-history or a "cruel glass."

The experience itself, though involving a stay in an asylum, is simple, moving and universal. Miss Sexton describes the loss of a child, or rather the *estrangement* of a mother from her child. Hardly born it reminds the mother unbearably of her own childhood, and continues to do so after the asylum. . . . With such a theme, developed not paradigmatically in the manner of Yeats, but directly in the manner of Lowell's life studies, did the poet have to exploit the more sensational aspect of her experience?

Geoffrey H. Hartman. KR. Autumn, 1960. p. 698

She tells stories. Her book [*To Bedlam and Part Way Back*] is full of undistinguished, unmythological people, in tensely dramatic situations which can be exploited only by an equally intense inward sympathy: a lonely empty-headed old woman, a speechless unwed mother, the author's own agonizing journey "part way back" from insanity and her complex relation to her dying mother and her unfamiliar child. Sexton's best work has qualities of the modern short story: the brutal tale like a forced confession, "better unsaid, grim or flat or predatory"; the compressed dramatic pattern of *hybris,* catastrophe, and recognition; the primitive irony of actual experience rather than the witty irony of meditation on it; the intense inward awareness of the teller; the concentration on a narrow circle of concrete persons and events; the forced brevity of narrative and lack of transition; the refusal to easily generalize. When truth bursts from the tight surface of such poems with the violence of sudden discovery, it seems the result of actual struggle.

Neil Myers. MinnR. Fall, 1960. p. 99

The most memorable poems in Anne Sexton's new book involve death and the response to death. The title of the volume is taken from the scene in *Macbeth* in which MacDuff, learning of the entire extinction of his family, cries out "All my pretty ones?" in a poignant exclamation of disbelief. How this relates to Mrs. Sexton is made explicit in the dedication to the very first poem, "The Truth the Dead Know": "For my mother, born March 1902, died March 1959, and my father, born February 1900, died June 1959." It is easy to understand how so much catastrophe coming so quickly can create crisis. Mrs. Sexton's book is a record of her crisis. . . . The sure attack, the fine use of sound, make it clear from the start that Mrs. Sexton is a lyricist of power. If one does not read carefully and accepts the hypnotic music of the lines, one can even think one is reading a conventional elegy. But of course the poem is no such thing. Earlier epochs would have found it immensely shocking. Not only does the mourner refuse to accompany the body to the grave, but she drives

off to the cape "to cultivate myself where the sun gutters from the sky."
We are in a post-Christian world where ceremonial has ceased to be important and death is something one seeks to dismiss from one's mind.

Cecil Hemley. HdR. Winter, 1962–63. p. 613

Her manner, learned from Robert Lowell and W. D. Snodgrass, is at once
confessional and understated. . . . A number of the new poems center on
the deaths of Mrs. Sexton's parents, neither yet sixty, within a few months
of one another. She evokes some of the same terror of the flesh that we feel
in [Allen Ginsberg's] *Kaddish,* and as in that poem the emphasis (with
love) is on parental weaknesses that were crucial in the poet's early unhappiness. A great difference is in the ultimately more clinical, self-
analytical character of Mrs. Sexton's elegies (or anti-elegies) and other
poems. Another is the exquisite lyric purity she achieves over and above
her energetic self-pursuit and self-exposure.

M. L. Rosenthal. Reporter. Jan. 3, 1963. p. 48

Anne Sexton is, by any standards, a bold and impressive poet. At first
glance, the unsuspecting reader may be jolted by the self-revelation that so
plainly serves as the basic raw material of her art. . . . Undisguised revelation and examination—of her parents, her lovers, her friends; of the unbelievable torment of both mental and physical illness as she has had to
endure them; of her struggles with a religious belief that eludes her but
doesn't leave her; of the face of death as she has frequently seen it—
comprise Mrs. Sexton's poetic cosmos. The eye the poet brings to bear
on these contents of her life is mercilessly lucid; yet she can be compassionate toward others and is without self-pity. Her life, as must be clear
by now, has been graced only slightly with what we ordinarily conceive
as happiness; its occasional joys and moments of tenderness are wrung
from the general pain of experience. Yet these pleasures and affections are
the more precious because of the cost involved in obtaining them, and also
because of the poet's strong love which brings them about in spite of the
odds. Mrs. Sexton has further discovered an ability to introduce order
into existence, to allow valued things to survive through the imaginative act
that in the making of a poem can create its own patterns of justice, meaning, and love.

Ralph J. Mills. Contemporary American Poetry
(Random). 1965. pp. 218–19

The literary quality of Anne Sexton's new poems, in *Live or Die,* is impossible to judge, at least in the brief time given a reviewer; they raise the
never-solved problem of what literature really is, where you draw the line
between art and documentary. Certainly her book is one of the most
moving I have read in a long time. It is the record of four years of emo-

tional illness, the turns of fear and despair and suicidal depression, a heartbreaking account. The wonder is that she was able to write any poetry at all. What she has written is strong, clear, rather simple, never repressed and yet never out of hand. Some of the poems wander a little; they are unstructured, they start up, flag, then start again, or slip into references too private for us to understand. But I do not want to give the impression that they are jottings or notes, that they are merely documentary. They are poems. They are the work of a gifted, intelligent, woman almost in control of her material.

Hayden Carruth. HdR. Winter, 1966–67. p. 698

Anne Sexton's art is particularly notable for the way it picks up the rhythms of the kind of sensibility with which she is concerned. The examples I have so far given catch the note of the self reduced to almost infantile regression (what hostile critics have called 'baby-talk'), but the mature intelligence of the speaker is ultimately that of one no longer in the literal predicament presented by the poems.

M. L. Rosenthal. The New Poets (Oxford). 1967.
p. 134

In her third volume of poetry [*Live or Die*], Anne Sexton has fashioned a brilliantly unified book. Though thematically related to *All My Pretty Ones* and to her first book, *To Bedlam and Part Way Back, Live or Die* is more passionate in its intensity and more abundant in its desperate concentration on vision. . . . This is a crazily sane and beautifully controlled work. It is the Oedipal eye; its poems are honest, terrifying! And the voice is terrifying—the voice of the human being *seeing* the nightmare and the dream that is man.

Philip Legler. Poetry. May, 1967. pp. 125–7

Miss Sexton's is a poetry of the nerves and heart. She is never abstract, never permits herself to be distracted from her one true subject—herself and her emotions. It is remarkable that she never flinches from the task at hand, never attempts to use her art as a device for warding off final perception. Unlike a poet like Frederick Seidel, she is willing to make her connections explicit. Her poems lack that hurtling momentum which keeps diverse elements in a sort of perpetual disrelation in the work of Seidel. Miss Sexton is painfully direct, and she refuses to keep her meaning at a tolerable distance. *Live or Die* projects an anguish which is profoundly disturbing precisely because its sources are effable, because the pressure of fantasy has not been permitted to distort or mediate Miss Sexton's vision.

Robert Boyers. Salmagundi. Spring, 1967. p. 62

See *To Bedlam and Part Way Back, All My Pretty Ones, Live or Die* (poems).

SHAPIRO, KARL (1913–   )

As a member of the generation that grew up between the wars, I can't help taking a certain collective pride in the poems of Karl Shapiro. They would be good poems in any generation, but for mine they express with such unusual accuracy and poignancy a set of hitherto faintly articulated attitudes that they arrive as a kind of culmination. The bitterness may be more concentrated in the poems of Kenneth Fearing. The aloof nobility of Spender . . . or the desperate humility of James Agee may not be here quite equalled. But the peculiar affirmations and negations of this generation are focused by Shapiro for the first time in a characteristic idiom. . . . Like Hart Crane, Shapiro sees life with an acute urgency. But unlike Crane, in the mirror of a well-developed social conscience. And unlike the Marxists, without wishful distortions.

Selden Rodman. NR. Dec. 21, 1942. p. 834

The manner and especially the diction of Shapiro's writing is all from Auden. . . . In Shapiro . . . the borrowed style is an aid and not an obstacle; the result is a growing originality.

The source of this originality is undoubtedly Shapiro's inexhaustible power of observation. He can see a great deal, he has taken a long, cunning, and intelligent look at the important objects of modern life, and has serious and important feelings about what he sees. Yet this strength has, like most virtues, its danger and its weaknesses. There is not only a sameness of tone and feeling in a good many of these poems but also a tendency to rely too much on dramatic observation, organized merely as a succession of items, to solve all problems and provide the insight which the subject requires.

Delmore Schwartz. Nation. Jan. 9, 1943. pp. 63–4

The notable thing about *Person, Place, and Thing* was a firmness of mood and singleness of purpose. Its well-written satires on industrial society were not great poetry or even on their way to being that; they were in the best sense "minor." And Shapiro was able to be a successful minor poet in our time because, while renouncing the larger myth-making pretensions of modern poetry, he nevertheless maintained the modernist defiance of middle-class civilization. The ground of self-assurance is now giving way, it is clear, under pressure of the war and prolonged soldiering. . . . There is in his work growing contempt for conscious artistry and intellect, an eagerness to present himself as passionately immersed in the folk life of the soldier.

F. W. Dupee. Nation. Sept. 16, 1944. pp. 327–8

Shapiro is a developing craftsman, applying himself conscientiously to problems of poetic technique and illustrating the results in his verse. Much of his work is still in the experimental stage: his technique is sometimes inept, his poems sometimes don't come off at all. But on the whole he is coming along very nicely, and has already produced a few really good poems. Let us remember, incidentally, that very few people indeed produce any really good poems, though many spend a lifetime trying. . . . Shapiro is doing all right, working his passage to salvation the hard way.

David Daiches. *Poetry*. Aug., 1945. pp. 266–7, 273

Whatever else one may conclude about the merits or demerits of Mr. Karl Shapiro's remarkable tour de force, *Essay on Rime,* and perhaps all the more because it is certain to be violently liked or disliked for an immense variety of reasons, whether esthetic, psychological, sociological or philosophic, one feels assured of one thing: this little book is destined to become a kind of literary watershed. . . . His "attack" is, one dares to use the word, masterly. As for the poem itself, and the prosody, if one finds it sometimes *too* near the prose level, and certainly oftener pedestrian than equestrian, and if it far too seldom delights the ear, nevertheless it is very cunningly calculated for its purpose: and it is questionable whether, by tightening and formalizing it further, more might not have been lost than gained. Let us be properly grateful to Mr. Shapiro. He has put himself in an enviable and dangerous position, at the head of his generation.

Conrad Aiken. *NR*. Dec. 3, 1945. pp. 752–4

He isn't a liar, he isn't an ape, he isn't just sad over the state of the world and the stars, he doesn't even bother to concern himself with humanity, or economics, or sociology or any other trio.

He's almost painfully interested in writing as it has been, masterfully, in the world and as it may be (under changed and changing conditions) in the world again. He keeps on the subject. And that's rare. More power to him. I hope he finds her rarest treasures—I am not jealous.

William Carlos Williams. *KR*. Winter, 1946. p. 125

There is something in the nature of his subject matter and his kind of diction which can easily reduce his poetry—and often does—to its lowest common denominator. . . . (Yet) Shapiro has done enough already to prove that he is much more important than the mistakes he makes. He has the personal vigor and the personal capacity—as few young poets in America have—to make his way forward through his work. . . . When you have read a good amount of his verse you are sure that he is a real poet, really feeling things and really sure that he is feeling them. He has the vocation. I say this as my last word for I am confident that in the development of Karl Shapiro as a poet this strength, this integrity, this personality will have the last word.

Henry Rago. *Com.* Jan. 16, 1948. pp. 352–3

Mr. Shapiro is a difficult poet to estimate, because whilst there are elements of technical accomplishment in his poetry which obviously command admiration, there are also elements of crudeness and insensitivity which make him vulnerable to a purist approach, and his very violence makes one uncertain of his power. Nevertheless he is a poet of rare intellectual strength, he has an exceptional power of being able to think of a poem as a single idea, and he has an interesting and perhaps passionate personality which his poetry at present partly conceals. If he were as preoccupied with the single word as he is with the stanza, he would gain enormously. At present he is too inclined to throw his words away on the wings of his stanzas. He is certainly one of the very few poets writing today whose development is an exciting subject for speculation.

Stephen Spender. *Poetry.* March, 1948. pp. 316–7

He can be tenderly emotional, savagely spiritual, and bitterly intellectual without apparently worrying over who is going to think him what.

It seems to me from his works so far . . . that Mr. Shapiro has equipped himself to handle the dark matter at the roots of the tree of poetry and the metaphysical sap of the trunk and branches as well as the mystical flower and fruit. If his apparent assumption that the poet is, in large part, an antisocial madman does not keep him too far from compassionate experience of his world, I feel that he may turn out to be that rarest of all sea-serpents, a poet whose work will be more substantial, more valid, and more perfect twenty years from now than it is today.

Raymond Holden. *SR.* March 20, 1948. p. 16

He paraphrases Descartes' famous sentence thus: *"Sentio ergo sum."* The prominence of feeling in his work is one of the elements that distinguish it from that of Auden, the cogitative contemporary from whom he learned so much. His ability to absorb and transmute this influence among others is an index of his gift. So, too, is his aptitude for making the common places of American culture in war and in peacetime come alive through his plain words and vibrant rhythms. Nor does one need to reread his lines on the "University" (of Virginia) and on "Jefferson" in the light of Warren's major work in order to appreciate that Shapiro recognizes the ambiguity that attends the human effort, even at the peak of its glory.

Babette Deutsch. *YR.* Winter, 1954. p. 281

Fortunately, the Good Lord made Karl Shapiro a genuine poet even though He skimped somewhat on the logical and critical endowment.

Despite the traumatic basis of their movement into compassion, a number of his poems reach beautiful resolution. Others explode ponderous themes—the ease with which we forget history's most dreadful lessons, the incommunicability of certain essential differences of tradition and life-principles, and so on—without losing their buoyancy and independent character as works of feeling with a design independent of doctrinal interests. Indeed, when Shapiro succeeds it is through his vibrant language and rhythm, his unabashed candor, and his irresistible emotional force that *will* bring out his true meanings even when he himself is not quite sure of them.

M. L. Rosenthal. *Nation.* July 5, 1958. p. 15

. . . I believe the [Henry] Miller essay, despite my problems with it, gives us the clue to many of the seeming contradictions and clashed textures in the book [*In Defense of Ignorance*] as a whole. For in this essay Shapiro writes: "Those poets who follow Whitman must necessarily follow Miller, even to the extent of giving up poetry in its formal sense and writing that personal apocalyptic prose which Miller does." Perhaps this is just what Shapiro himself has done. His book is not so much a sober "Defense of Ignorance" (which means innocence, uncorruptedness, unsophistication, the championing of the heart, with "its reasons the mind knows not of") though it is that in part, as it is a somewhat dionysiac and apocalyptic, canting work of art in its own right.

(K)   John Logan. *Com.* Jan. 20, 1961. p. 440

Shapiro is at his best in his satiric poems. When he feels strongly enough about a thing to attack it, he finds the right form for his thoughts. His satiric lash strikes broadly. He cites the different attitude we take toward maimed things in the animal and human worlds, pointing out how from fear and pity a mother lavishes a kindness on the deformed whereas in the animal world the mother would kill maimed offspring. His satire is sharper in his attack on those who, denying their senses, harm the world. He trenchantly depicts the emotionally and intellectually immature businessman, the organization man; nor does he show any mercy toward the pseudo-intellectual.

(K)   James G. Southworth. *EJ.* March, 1962. p. 163

He often appears Don Quixotish [in *In Defense of Ignorance*], given to rash overstatements, vexed by the static learnedness and wise-wishiness of many a don. Not all eyes are open to the view that his cause is good and vital. His cause is: (1) to ask the reader to believe in himself and therefore to assess the poems of his time on the basis of his own response, and (2) to ask that the poet believe in the poetic validity of his own experience and in his power to give new form to that experience. In other words, he asks a freshening of our view of what is original. The readers, the audience, should be able to find good things in writings, and the poets should find good things in life and art, things other than that which is established. Surely if men are to have or to do that which is fresh and unimpeded, they must value what is original and unassessed by culture— what is fresh within individual selves.

(K)   Sam Bradley. *UKCR*. Summer, 1963. p. 277

. . . Shapiro is recognizably a rebellious egotist writing in the mode of Henry Miller. He also proclaims his philosophical allegiance to Sade: he aspires to nihilistic Satanism and inveighs against order like a true Sadist (not the sadist of ordinary usage, but a person who understands the Marquis' teachings and examples). However, coming as it does in a time without authority or firm conventions and rules, Shapiro's would-be nihilism has the effect of being highly literary, derivative, and out-of-date. Sadistic rebellion is so designed as to work well against a tyrannical king, but against a permissive and floundering democracy it is at most per- niciously nasty without achieving any major destruction. . . .

The Bourgeois Poet certainly does not fail because Shapiro cannot write good enough self-prophesying incantation; on the contrary, his ear is still excellent though he abuses it, his wit is lively, his intelligence and learning are considerable, his emotions vigorous. Partly the failure is due to anachronism. But chiefly it comes from the way he confesses. This in turn is caused by defects of Shapiro's own self, defects which, in the days when he was a pro poet, he either did not have or else disguised and turned to advantage.

(K)   George P. Elliott. *HdR*. Autumn, 1964. p. 463

The Bourgeois Poet definitely has about it the air of a new imaginative release. Irony and social criticism are still there, but autobiography, in- vective, heavy doses of sexuality, often dominated by an atmosphere of the dream and of irrationality, and an occasional prophetic note are now blended together. Unquestionably, an energy and a frankness that were formerly constrained have become primary agents of this altered poetry. Because of their length—and they are ruined by presentation in bits and fragments—the prose poems must be sparingly quoted here; besides, *The Bourgeois Poet* has to be read through as a book, even though it contains no strong narrative thread. It is not a uniformly good book, but the pieces that make it up belong together and give a cumulative impression. Then again it is a book we should not try to decide about at once; it will take some getting used to.

(K)   Ralph J. Mills. *Contemporary American Poetry*
                                          (Random). 1965. pp. 119–20

The former compiler of *A Bibliography of Modern Prosody* now [in *The Bourgeois Poet*] seeks to be one with what is natural and essential in the poetic process, seeks to get in the swim, switching his old blue mantle (the-poet-as-maker) for a very loose bikini (the-poet-as-sidestroker). For him there is no question of a tension between what is to be found and what is to be formed. Mr. Shapiro's is not a dialectical spirit; as I have said, he is a terrorist, and refuses to acknowledge the possibility, let alone the value, of an exchange, a mutual tempering, between what he calls with appropriate pleonasm "the formlessness that should make you dizzy, nauseated and give you vertigo" and what for Blake was "mechanical excellence, the only vehicle of genius."

(K)   Richard Howard. *Poetry*. June, 1965. p. 228

Perhaps Shapiro's poetic irresolution grows out of this inability to "choose" either the Romantic or the Realistic faith, or to choose finally to stand between them. The "Preface" to *Poems of a Jew* seems to reveal a wish that the name be *applied* to him as a sort of arbitrary grace whether the assigner be God, history, biology, sociology or the Gentiles. I think this attitude partially explains his own religious and philosophical peregrinations, his alternation between the synagogue and the cathedral.

This is not to say that a poet cannot be religiously perplexed and still be a great poet. Indeed, Shapiro's own best productions, poems such as "Messias," "Synagogue" and "Mongolian Idiot," are great as poems because they create religious and philosophical problems through their unorthodox inquisitiveness. Unfortunately, Shapiro seems unable to live with only the "certainty of uncertainty," an inability which too often leads him to stridency in defense, or causes him to abandon the attempt to wring meaning out of large enigmas.

(K)   Richard Slotkin. *AmQ*. Summer, 1966. p. 226

See *Person, Place, and Thing, V-Letter, Essay on Rime, Trial of a Poet, Poems of a Jew, The Bourgeois Poet* (poetry); *In Defense of Ignorance* (criticism).

SHAW, IRWIN (1913–   )

He strikes a fine balance between the sentimentality of the soft-boiled and the sentimentality of the hard-boiled. The warmth of feeling, the heart, the humanity that underlies his stories is genuine and moving. The pathos is not cheap and the humor is not facile. . . . Shaw's stories are contemporary to a degree and New Yorkerish to a degree. There are in them elements that in other writers would be merely a modish despair, a modish heartbreak, a modish "social consciousness." But Shaw's genuine warmth and rightness of feeling, his mature and discriminating sensibility, gives the best of them what one feels is a solid and lasting quality.

H. N. Doughty, Jr. *NYHT*. Jan. 25, 1942. p. 6

Mr. Shaw has throughout his career been a clear spokesman of his well-meaning generation. . . . As an artist he has been an exemplary citizen—devoted, energetic, too intelligent to be too pious yet too pious to be disturbing, his talents as a writer beautifully tuned to the intellectual pitch of his society. But at last, after its long period of sounding on one note—the note of political decency—this society gives signs of having to recognize the existence of a much fuller scale of human motives and values. . . . This is the new freedom that now appears, if only by hints, in Mr. Shaw's novel (*The Young Lions*). . . . Mr. Shaw has the novelist's power—if he has the courage to release it—to overturn the conventions of truth and dig up a few of the real facts about people and the societies they create.

Diana Trilling. *Nation*. Oct. 9, 1948. p. 409

Mr. Shaw's people seem wonderfully alive, even when the author descends to caricature and burlesque. Like Dickens, Mr. Shaw has created, prodigally, a crowded gallery of memorable people. Like Dickens, too, he handles scenes superbly; from the crummy atmosphere of a third-rate New York hotel to the oppressive heat of an Army newspaper office in Algiers, his stories are firmly anchored in time and space. And he communicates experience with a narrative felicity and sincerity which redeem even a frequently far-fetched sentimental or one-sided situation.

William Peden. *SR*. Nov. 18, 1950. p. 28

I am inclined to believe that nothing Mr. Shaw might write could be wholly lacking in interest of one kind or another. For one thing, he always *does* observe and he always *does* feel, and even when he is facile in observation and sentiment he is not insincere. And then he has established himself in a position which guarantees at least the historical or sociological or cultural interest of whatever he writes. He has undertaken the guidance of the moral and political emotions of a large and important class of people, those whom he once called "the gentle people." These are men and women usually of a middling position in our society. They are involved with ideas because modern life seems to make their very existence depend upon the involvement, but they are modest in what they demand by way of ideas and are quite willing to settle for attitudes. . . . In general and almost as a function of his good will Mr. Shaw has been content to tell his audience that decency is a kind of simplicity, that modern life is ghastly because it is an affront to simplicity, and that the simple virtues are all we have for our defense.

Lionel Trilling. *SR*. June 9, 1951. p. 8

He is essentially a master of episode. . . . And it is in the short story . . . that his talents have found their most congenial scope.

Many of his stories deal with Jews. Some relate their sufferings in pogroms and concentration camps, their aspirations and agonies in Palestine. The better ones, as stories, deal with their everyday life in America. . . . Shaw's material is fresh. His people come in off the streets; they are not literary derivatives. His emotional restraint often makes them seem superficial and reduces their griefs and tragedies to an indiscriminate misery. But, where his pity overcomes his self-restraint and still evades his indignation, he has produced some of the best short stories in contemporary literature.

Bergen Evans. EJ. Nov., 1951. pp. 490–1

The group for whom he writes often appear as characters in his fiction . . . the well-heeled beneficiaries of mass communications with their regrets and "higher" yearnings. . . . It is part of Irwin Shaw's uncanny flair for what is topical in this world (which is the world of everyone, for its writers smuggle daily into their copy these bootleg ideas) that has brought him on the long journey from *Bury the Dead* to *Lucy Crown*. In a way, he is vindicating his repeated protest that he was not ever *really* a propagandist, though he wrote against war when pacificism was the reigning passion of the young (in *Bury the Dead*), then for a war against fascism when feeling had shifted in that direction (in his sadist-sentimental parable *The Gentle People*), about Nazis and non-conformists in World War II when the age demanded The Big War Book once more (in *The Young Lions*), about McCarthyism and Communism when the newspapers were trying to persuade us we could think of nothing else (in *The Troubled Air*). When no one seems to care about political subjects for the moment, or when at least they have ceased to sell, Shaw can give up politics without a quiver of regret and return to the human subject, to sex and the family, as if he had never left home. . . . At the end of this road is *Lucy Crown,* the book an author like Shaw writes when the times no longer provide him with an ostensible public subject and he must do his best with his own *Ladies' Home Journal* kind of imagination.

Leslie A. Fiedler. Cmty. July, 1956. pp. 71–3

The Young Lions

It was for this image, I suspect, that Shaw wrote his book: to tell what the army did to a nice sensitive bookish young man named Private Noah Ackerman. Noah's ordeal at the hands of his violently anti-Semitic company in Florida has haunted the reviewers into awe-stricken prose. . . . What they all mean to say, I think, is that they have gotten something really new out of a war novel; they have had a shocking emotional discovery of the cruelty in our society from a Jewish writer who is, for all his easy Broadway skill, driven by his experience as a Jew. Shaw has put into the story of Private Noah Ackerman all that Jews have felt in these last years with such particular anguish, and to see Noah there, a shy and liberal intellectual slowly petrifying into another Jew on the cross, is to awaken with horror to a victim who is more real than the millions of victims we read about, for he is familiar and yet absolutely alone.

Alfred Kazin. Cmty. Dec., 1948. p. 497

The Young Lions is a more mature work than *The Naked and the Dead* and a more complete novel than *The Gallery;* yet it shares their common weakness. On the first level, Shaw seems to be making a passionate and deeply human affirmation of the power of decency and justice to survive and even triumph amid the misery and horror of modern war. Yet if we look closely, it becomes apparent that these values do not arise out of the experience presented in the novel but remain outside and above it. Shaw, like Mailer and Burns, has seen the need for belief, but he has been able to objectify the need only and not the belief itself.

John W. Aldridge. SR. Feb. 12, 1949. p. 8

See *The Young Lions* and *Lucy Crown* (novels); also *Mixed Company* and *Tip on a Dead Jockey* (short stories).

SHERWOOD, ROBERT (1896–1955)

Plays

Reunion in Vienna is, of course, far more than another dramatization of a Vienna waltz. It is so much more that I have had moods while reading it (and it should be read as well as seen) of thinking that it is the wisest and ripest comedy ever written in America. I cannot at the moment think of another that moves with such a lively grace and still keeps an intelligent head on its shoulders. . . . Sherwood has so often been compared with Shaw that the association of their names is no longer flattering to either, and yet Shaw has done so many things with a provocative badness that it is a satisfaction to see the same things done with a graceful finality. *Reunion in Vienna* is as modern as the latest theory of the neuroses, and yet it is a modernism that is now mature enough to have languors and regrets and nostalgias.

Thomas H. Dickinson. SR. May 14, 1932. p. 728

In theatrical variety and unexpectedness of effect there is no living English-speaking dramatist the superior of Robert Sherwood. It is rare to find one of his plays which does not appeal to more than one class of people; most of them appeal to five or six. His plays are a veritable grab-bag of comedy-tragedy-melodrama-farce with always a seasoning of serious meaning. . . . Unlike most Broadway playwrights, Mr. Sherwood has both beliefs and feelings, and unlike the propaganda brethren, he has a subtle mind and a sensitivity of impression which makes him at home in the region of the ironic. Moreover, he knows the world, the great world as well as the work-a-day one.

Grenville Vernon. Com. April 10, 1936. p. 664

Reunion in Vienna (is) the first play in which Sherwood showed an aptitude for developing a good theatre situation after he had created it. From this point on, you begin to see clearly in your mind's eye the people of whom he wrote, and although you do not always see them as people walking beside you in the world, they remain with you in the shape of the actors who took part in his plays. If they are not yet people of the real world, they are real people of the theatre world, and for certain plays, such as *Reunion in Vienna,* that is quite enough.

Edith J. R. Isaacs. TA. Jan., 1939. pp. 34–7

In *Abe Lincoln in Illinois* Robert E. Sherwood is tracing the career of Lincoln from the Thirties and New Salem, Illinois, to the day he entrained for Washington to be inaugurated President. It has been called the best play about Lincoln ever written, which it probably is; the best play by Mr. Sherwood, which is a matter open to argument; and the greatest play by any living American, which it probably is not. But it is a very moving story of one of the world's great figures.

Lewis Nichols. NYT. Feb. 26, 1939. p. 18

What Sherwood most wished to tell (in *Abe Lincoln in Illinois*), I think, is summed up in a sentence Speed wrote to Herndon, "He must believe he was right, and that he had truth and justice with him, or he was a weak man; but no man could be stronger if he thought he was right." To show us the weak Lincoln, to show us the gradual infiltration of a belief in the truth and justice of the cause he was called on to lead, an infiltration which met the resistence of doubts and broodings curiously suggestive of Hamlet, and finally to show the emergence of a man who was the champion of democracy as the justice of God, was Mr. Sherwood's task. With what under the circumstances is a minimum of historical invention, this task he has brilliantly performed, brilliantly because he has given us a three-dimensional character and because he has not forgotten, also, that he is writing a play which must be effective in the theatre.

Walter Prichard Eaton. *Com*. March 3, 1939. p. 526

There Shall Be No Night is more than a good play. It is one of those events in the theatre that explain its survival and justify the faith of those who see in it one of the highest forms of human expression. . . . The play burns with passion. It is, of course, special pleading. . . . It deals with events that are not only current news but actually, in themselves, violently tragic. Yet these elements are usually obstacles rather than aids to dramatic writing. Mr. Sherwood, in undertaking this subject, dared to measure his artifices against Finland's flaming actualities. It is to the credit of his skill as a craftsman and his discipline as an artist, joined to the skill and discipline of his cast, that the attempt has proved successful.

Rosamond Gilder. *TA*. June, 1940. p. 399

Sherwood's world is very pessimistic. He hears the feet of trampling legions stamping out the vestiges of Western civilization. You cannot escape the feeling that, as in *The Petrified Forest*, he still believes that the old civilization is crumbling. The battle he proposes (in *There Shall Be No Night*) is a last ditch stand, which may leave the forces of destruction in triumph. . . . Sherwood believes in the liberal idea of freedom, the democratic ideals to which he testified in his patchwork quilt of Lincolnia, *Abe Lincoln in Illinois*. When he sees these ideals menaced by the philosophy of force, all he can say is fight. Science might save us and religion perhaps, but, anyway, we have to fight.

Robert C. Healey. *CW*. Nov., 1940. pp. 179–80

Among the personalities of the literary world none is more currently conspicuous than Robert Sherwood, and few are more representative of this age both by their revolts and by their conformities. In the theatre he is not only one of the masters of his craft, but the one playwright in the lobby or in the haunts of the after-theatre set who overshadows celebrities of the acting profession without so much as a word on his part to call attention to himself. In the political world he is, barring Archibald MacLeish, the one writer who has found a place both in the government and in the scrimmage line of public controversy. . . . And he is perhaps most significant, in the casual way in which only Sherwood can be significant, as a phenomenon of the liberal mind at work in our day.

John Gassner. *At*. Jan., 1942. p. 26

My firm conviction (is) that Mr. Sherwood's plays have always lagged one pace behind his own ever-increasing seriousness. By his own confession he wrote the highly diverting *Reunion in Vienna* in order not to think of certain things which troubled him. By the time he had got to *The Petrified Forest* and *Idiot's Delight* he could no longer wholly disregard them, and in *There Shall Be No Night* he thought that he had gone completely over to responsible seriousness. Actually, however, he has never permitted himself to go beyond journalism, and I risk the assertion that his present concern with specific political issues is as much an "escape" from deeper questions too puzzling and too painful to think about as *Reunion in Vienna* was an escape from the relatively more serious things even then struggling in his mind for recognition.

Joseph Wood Krutch. *Nation.* Nov. 24, 1945. p. 562

Written during the lull between two World Wars, *Idiot's Delight* is uncanny in its detailed forecasting of the shape the second was to take. The author was also singularly successful, it now becomes evident, in mirroring the precise attitudes of the period and their vulnerability in the face of events to come: the Marxist brotherliness which, in its fanaticism, was quickly adaptable to the needs of nationalism; the other-worldliness of science, which was to find itself not so much above politics as it had supposed; the British complacency, which was to respond so quickly, almost matter-of-factly, to any challenge to the status quo; and so on. More interesting than any of these things, however, is the sense of helplessness which pervades the play, the mood of surrender to idiocy as though idiocy were the only remaining characteristic of the human race.

Walter Kerr. *Com.* June 8, 1951. p. 213

He was a lean, tall man, six-feet-seven, who surveyed the foibles and the errors of mankind with a kindly and somewhat melancholy glance. . . . Courteous to everyone, he had a sharp tongue for isolationists. He wrote with a complete absorption and astonishing rapidity, producing five plays in two years. . . . During the years of uneasy peace and war he came to his full stature, a kindly man of impeccable honesty, courageous, eloquent in the cause of democracy, and a humorist with a touch of irony. It is often said after a man's death that "we shall not see his like again." It is true of Robert Sherwood.

Harrison Smith. *SR.* Nov. 26, 1955. p. 31

No stranger could ever encounter Bob without becoming aware that he was in the presence of a formidable brain and personality. No friend of Bob's ever found him lacking in warmth, sympathy or time when there were troubles to be met. Though he was no opportunist, though he said what he thought whenever it was useful, he made few enemies. Many stood in awe of him because of his deft and pungent tongue, but apt as he was in attack or retort, Sherwood was readier still to give mercy, happier to be tolerant than to be angry.

Maxwell Anderson. Time. Nov. 28, 1955. p. 26

Roosevelt and Hopkins—History

He writes a book that is a pleasure to read; and not the least of his merits is that being a playwright, professionally concerned with exploring the complexities of character, he knows enough about it to know how much he does not know. He attempts no "psychograph" of Roosevelt; Hopkins was a far simpler character, but Sherwood does not always explain him; he merely sets down the record—all of the record. Nothing is extenuated; what needs extenuation seems to some of us trivial beside the accomplishment, but Sherwood sets it down anyway; it happened, and he reports all that happened, good and bad.

Elmer Davis. SR. Oct. 23, 1948. p. 7

This is an amazing book Mr. Sherwood has written. It is intimate, wonderfully intimate, and yet it is history, full-scaled and far-flung. Immediately it takes its place—a high honor—on the same slim shelf with Winston Churchill's *The Gathering Storm*. The rolling periods are deliberately missing. . . . A different kind of eloquence replaces Mr. Churchill's. It is the eloquence of extreme simplicity. It is as unlike Mr. Churchill's as was Mr. Roosevelt's—a fact which is not surprising since in the preparation of his speeches Mr. Roosevelt depended so often on Mr. Sherwood's aid. . . . The prose is unembellished and swift-moving. . . . It speaks the democratic idiom, movingly, effectively, sometimes humorously.

John Mason Brown. SR. Nov. 13, 1948. pp. 54–5

See *Reunion in Vienna, The Petrified Forest, Idiot's Delight,* and *Abe Lincoln in Illinois* (plays); also *Roosevelt and Hopkins* (history).

SIMON, NEIL (1927–   )

Strictly New York in style is Neil Simon's *Come Blow Your Horn*. This new comedy follows one sound rule: When the doorbell rings it must always be the person the characters least want or expect at that particular moment. Beyond that it has, during a substantial portion of the evening, some very funny behavior by three good characters. One is a twenty-one-year-old overprotected son facing his first seduction with amusing trepidation. Another is his plump but harried and dyspeptic mother who takes all the brunt of strained father-and-son relations. And best of all is his father, a stubborn Jewish patriarch with an unbeatable technique for turn-ing all his son's reasonable arguments into disgraceful, impious assaults on his just position and his paternal generosity.

Henry Hewes. SR. March 11, 1961. p. 38

The enormous effectiveness of such facetious and arbitrary goings-on may come from the fact that we all recognize how accurately these incidents catch the flavor of starting out married life in today's mad Manhattan. Nowhere else is one called upon to adjust to so much illogical and unusual environment so quickly.

Beyond this, *Barefoot in the Park* manages again and again to achieve the special kind of humor we associate with *New Yorker* cartoons. It is a humor based upon our absurdly casual acceptance of and ways of dealing with contemporary civilization's enforced incongruities.

Henry Hewes. SR. Nov. 9, 1963. p. 32

According to Mike Nichols, who directed *Barefoot in the Park* . . . Simon's genius is for "comedy and reality, extremely distorted but recognizable, not zany behavior." . . . Simon specializes in comic suspense. Who is going to walk through the door next—and when? Even if the audience knows the answer, it savors the confrontation before, during, and after it happens. . . .

Another Simon trademark is repetition. "His humor has an almost musical rhythm," says Stanley Prager, the onetime musical comedy clown who directed *Come Blow Your Horn*. "He's as aware of the value of reprises as Richard Rodgers is. In fact, he constructs his plays the way a composer might construct a score."

Alan Levy. NYT mag. March 7, 1965. pp. 42–3

Neil Simon has followed up *Barefoot in the Park* with *The Odd Couple*, another farce that may well run forever. I find it less good; nothing much more than a joke-book tossed up on the stage. Some of the jokes are amusing, most of the acting and staging is as cleverly efficient as can be, but the plot is too specious even for farce, and the characters are militantly nonexistent.

John Simon. HdR. Summer, 1965. p. 251

This "man's" show [*The Odd Couple*] . . . is a sort of prolonged and fun-raising television sketch based on the proposition that two men living together may annoy each other just as much as any mismated husband and wife. There are other incidental sources of laughter, undoubtedly provoked by the pleasure of recognition, although when it comes down to it, *I* don't meet the fellows every Friday night for a game, nor do I often take part in or enjoy pastrami parties. Snobbish? Certainly. If *you* like it, you're welcome to it, and God bless you.

Harold Clurman. Nation. April 5, 1965. p. 373

When Simon jokes, America laughs. He is instant fodder for columnists and cocktail parties. Producers, directors, actors line up to produce, direct and act in his plays. Simon is commercial and his plays are entertainment and he wouldn't have it any other way; he likes being Neil Simon.

Nwk. Jan. 9, 1967. p. 70

See *Come Blow Your Horn, Barefoot in the Park, The Odd Couple, Plaza Suite* (plays).

SIMPSON, LOUIS (1923–   )

The work of this poet can be better understood by searching for its major themes than by trying to see it as a consistent whole. The poems have range and variety, even when they are dealing with the same subject. And, in the poems, things happen. They have a narrative, forward movement. Many of them are, in fact, narratives. "The Heroes" and "The Battle" are narratives of modern war. "Early in the Morning" retells the old story of Antony and Cleopatra. In "John the Baptist," "The Return," "Ulysses and the Sirens" and "Islanders" people have made, or are making, journeys. . . .

Throughout the book [*Good News of Death*], landscapes and seasons are the stage for the human drama. In "American Preludes," "West," "Winter," "The Return," "Mississippi," "A Lion in the Wind," they have a history and a personality of their own. In these poems, one senses time passing and yet standing still, the contemporaneity of Babylon, Rome, New York, in that blinking of an eye that we call human history.

John Hall Wheelock. Introduction to Poets of Today, II
(Scribner). 1955. pp. 12–13

A Dream of Governors . . . is his second book, and you will find in it some of the best traditional verse being written by a young American poet today. American poetry needs more than anything else a reinfusion of the narrative element, and Simpson is devoted to narrative. His book contains a long poem about World War II and the feelings of men in battle. It is, unfortunately, less a narrative poem than a short story told in well-written blank verse; its story gains little from having been told in poetic form. When it deals with a dramatic confrontation, as in the final battle when the Germans attack at Bastogne, it succeeds admirably; but it fails in conveying the passage of time, which is one of the hardest things for a narrative in verse to do.

Some of Simpson's shorter narratives do succeed: he retells myths (St. George, Orpheus, and others) in a rich aura of mysticism and moonlight. One day he will have achieved the full flavor of what he is striving for in his narratives; but this collection is uneven, and that time has not yet come. The final group of love poems, however, has things in it as whole and true as in any recent love poems I can remember.

Peter Davison. *At.* Sept., 1960. p. 92

Something of his range is indicated by the division of his book [*A Dream of Governors*] into five sections. He modernizes myths to ironic advantage, and contrasts "My America" with "The Old World." A fourth group includes some of the best poems to have come out of the Second World War, and the fifth presents love poems effective alike in their delicacy and wry strength. From this catalogue of subjects one would scarcely guess the complexity with which he realizes each, nor the variety of modes and tones his verse commands. Even his exorcisms, his phantasmagoria, his ballad of a lunatic Nazi, are lucid in organization and language, while his rationally-developed poems, such as the neo-neo-classical "The Green Shepherd" and "The Flight to Cytherea," are alive with surprises of perception and diction.

Daniel G. Hoffman. *SwR*. Autumn, 1960. p. 678

In our time, this implied story is never embodied in a complete work—a *Paradise Lost* or a *Divine Comedy*—, and apparently such an established story cannot be at this time convincingly delivered to us. But some writers do entertain hints that back of the shifting present there impends a meaning. *At the End of the Open Road* bears that kind of extra effect; the thread of the poems recurrently demonstrates the power to be derived from working near the potential of an imminent revelation. . . .

Though these poems are here collected for the first time, a number of them have been so effective in periodicals or so aptly used for touchstones that they are already more than magazine pieces; such poems are "Walt Whitman at Bear Mountain," "The Marriage of Pocohantas," "My Father in the Dark." . . . The authority of such poems helps to make this a resounding book, a solid achievement.

William Stafford. *Poetry*. May, 1964. p. 105

"It's complicated, being an American," says Louis Simpson, as if he only had escaped alone to tell us. The complications get worse as you go West. . . . I hazard a guess that Mr. Simpson wants his confrontation of New York and San Francisco to do as much for him as the confrontation of

America and Europe did for Henry James. And now that the Jamesian juxtaposition has lost much of its meaning American poets will probably drive themselves to invent new Wars between the States to replace the epic-journeys between Boston and Rome. Or Mayan remains will replace the stones of Venice. In Mr. Simpson's lower case the feeling is: if only he could find some good primitive experience beneath that Californian surface, "the aboriginal American devils" which reappear as "serious life"; if only he could feel the trembling of the veil. Meanwhile the only answers are a little Late Romantic irony and a few compensatory dreams. . . . Every decent poet is entitled to one "Gerontion," and this [*At the End of the Open Road*] is Mr. Simpson's. I hope he doesn't propose to push it to extremes; already the hum and buzz of explication are a little too audible.

Denis Donoghue. HdR. Summer, 1964. pp. 267–8

I wish I might omit from Louis Simpson's *At the End of the Open Road* the few tame, even timid poems which a lack of editorial care has allowed in. Then I might say, as I believe him to be saying, that too many modern poets are like people in apartment houses—or a "standing-room only" America—, who have been silent too long at their living in the too closely populated day and night, for fear that someone in the next room will over-hear; that, like these people, who become more silent as the next room becomes more crowded, the poets trim their fine agonies to even finer proportions, and climaxes disappear; that poetry seems to become more and more an international competition in smooth lines and innocuous statements, mostly a matter of surfaces. That people, and poets, have stopped westering.

George Scarbrough. SwR. Winter, 1965. p. 141

A poet of liberal persuasion, he is interested in public issues, in social and philosophical questions relating to the destiny of Europe and America. . . . This is a new realism that Simpson is preaching. He asks us to forget the Adamic innocence of the American past and recognize the seriousness of life in the present; we must cultivate our gardens in full awareness of the imminence of death.

Although he wrote some free verse as a young man, Simpson was deeply committed to traditional technique until 1959; he counted his accented and unaccented syllables carefully and built structures of pleasing but conventional sound, nailed with rhyme. After 1959, largely under the influence of the subjective-image poets, he changed his style drastically. The prosaism of his early work—which required metrics and rhyme in order to give it character as verse—now gave way to rich, fresh, haunting imagery. His philosophical and political speculations achieved a distinction and brilliance that they had lacked before.

Stephen Stepanchev. American Poetry Since 1945
(Harper). 1965. pp. 198–9

There are included in this volume [*Selected Poems*] all of the poems that most of us have admired over the years, but it seemed to me on re-reading them along with "The Runner" that Louis Simpson has real ability in handling a narrative form which he ought to be applying more. Some of his poems in fact seem to be truncated narratives, like "Moving the Walls," but his technique in using images and placing them in a context of some sort does not allow him the leeway he ought to have in a real narration.

The twelve wholly new poems included in this volume are neither as formalistic as some of his earlier ones, nor are they as restricted in subject matter; "Tonight the Famous Psychiatrist" is particularly well focused, as well as "The Tailor's Wedding." But there is also a kind of tiredness to these new poems—that is, as if *he* were tired. I hope he will strike out in a new direction, toward the narrative again.

Bruce Cutler. Poetry. July, 1966. p. 270

See *Selected Poems*.

SINCLAIR, UPTON (1878–1968)

The fierce and humorless intensity of Upton Sinclair's youthful masterpiece *The Jungle* has here (in *Oil!*) given place to a maturer kind of writing, with a surprising new tolerance in it for the weaknesses of human nature, and a new curiosity which fills it with the manifold richness of the American scene on every social plane. It restores Upton Sinclair to us as a novelist, and it constitutes one of the great achievements in the contemporary discovery of America in our fiction.

Floyd Dell. NYHT. June 12, 1927. p. 7

All the figures in Mr. Sinclair's world are automata except the sublime and tormented hero who is at war with them. There is only one thing in Mr. Sinclair's world that he treats with that respect which is due to reality. That is his own conception of his own mission among men. Everything else is stage properties and supers. . . . He has erected a structure of theories in front of his eyes which is so dazzling that nothing in the outer world is clearly visible to him. . . . He is a noisy and voluble saint, but none the less authentically a saint. He has consecrated himself to his own mission. He is a brave man, too, and spasmodically and spectacularly a rather dashing fighter against oppression. . . . I do not happen to admire deeply his type of saintliness, and so perhaps cannot do him full justice.

Walter Lippmann. *SR*. March 3, 1928. pp. 642–3

As art Sinclair's novel, *Boston,* is worthless; as propaganda it is superb. He has a theme and a character that ride triumphant over technical disabilities. And he has a living conscience. As he works toward a climax, the pretense of fiction gradually falls away and in the last magnificent chapters the book becomes a piece of glorified reporting. Concurrently, the heat of the author's indignation rises steadily higher until, at the end, the reader is left with the sense of having himself been cleansed and purified by fire and humbled by great tragedy.

R. N. Linscott. *SR*. Dec. 1, 1928. p. 425

The difficulty with Sinclair's characters and situations is not in recognizing them, but in *feeling* them. His characters are rational—or cerebral if you will—rather than emotive creations. One can see them—but not experience them. This is partly due to the fact that, in the main, they are types instead of individuals, types that you know. . . . Sinclair tends to portray his characters in terms of straight lines instead of in terms of all those zigzags of personality, those intricate and irrational contradictions of self, which create individuality in life as well as in fiction.

V. F. Calverton. *Nation*. Feb. 4, 1931. pp. 132–3

From *The Jungle* (1906) to date he has repeatedly thrust a sharp knife into most of the sore spots of our contemporary civilization: the packing-house filth, the newspaper racket, the oil scandal, "Massachusetts justice," etc. etc. . . . Sophisticated readers, professors and critics, hold that Mr. Sinclair's novels are not "literature"—whatever that may mean. . . . If a passionate interest in the substance of all great literature—life, if a wide acquaintance with its special manifestations of the writer's own day, if a deep conviction about the values underlying its varied phenomena and the ability to set them forth, count in the making of enduring literature, all these Mr. Sinclair has demonstrated again and again that he possesses.

Robert Herrick. *NR*. Oct. 7, 1931. p. 213

Mr. Sinclair has never pretended to be a professional literary critic. He has been a creative artist and a pamphleteer. To those readers who dislike his work he is the latter exclusively. But to the world at large he takes his place as one of the great literary men of the day. His works are almost immediately translated into French, German, Spanish, Swedish, Chinese, Japanese, and Russian, which is a testimony to his popularity, if not to his art. His books contribute to the forming of opinions about America in almost every country on the globe.

C. Hartley Grattan. *Bkm*. April, 1932. p. 61

Sinclair's moral strength has never let him escape an awareness of the degradation and humiliation that are the normal lot of the oppressed in our republic, and his honesty has never let him remain silent about them. . . . (Yet) Sinclair has scarcely attempted to interpret working-class life since *The Jungle*. His typical story is that of a rich young man who gets mixed up in the radical movement, and the drama lies in the dissolution of his ruling class dogmas.

Robert Cantwell. *NR*. Feb. 24, 1937. pp. 70–1

Because his faults are always so conspicuous and never the fashionable ones, Mr. Sinclair has been either dismissed or patronized by the majority of critics and literary historians. Yet I am willing to wager that his chances of survival are as good as those of any living American author. . . . Sinclair is a master of narrative. Like the Victorians, whose habits of underscored characterization and chatty comment he has always imitated, he has the trick of making you want to find out what happens next. . . . With his own kind of magic, Sinclair rushes you from scene to scene, and you have to go on to the end.

Granville Hicks. *NR*. June 24, 1940. p. 863

I respect him . . . because he has retained an old-fashioned and innocent love for mankind. Do you think it possible for a man to be too good to become a great novelist? . . . Sinclair . . . is so kindly and trusting—till each new disillusionment—and so convinced that men are naturally good unless distorted by the property system, that you deplore his villains instead of hating them. They are merely products of their environment. . . . Sinclair doesn't believe in Satan; at heart he doesn't even believe in Heinrich Himmler. He is a capable writer when explaining the connections between economics and politics, but he never casts much light on the connection between politics and the human soul.

Malcolm Cowley. *NR*. Jan. 11, 1943. p. 58

(*Presidential Agent*) is an extraordinary and gigantic job . . . of collation, selection, synthesis, craftsmanship, and interpretation, and one that could only have been done by a novelist as mature and practiced and experienced in thinking as its author. Desperately and nervously exciting, moreover; as desperately and nervously exciting as the desperate times in which we live. . . . Here is the first time that any novelist has had the courage to take the present monstrous shape of evil and show it in its proper proportions and in its inevitable final weakness when it meets courage, endurance, and intelligent good-will.

Struthers Burt. *SR*. June 10, 1944. p. 8

Mr. Sinclair is a major figure—and I make the statement ungrudgingly. He is a thoroughly American personality. A fluent—a fatally fluent—writer with an unconquerable desire to preach and teach, he has a heart honorably moved by human suffering. . . . His insight into society is sometimes shrewd, and his prophecies are occasionally correct. Above all, his courage is . . . the courage of American individualism, which has nothing to do with the socialism of Mr. Sinclair's dream.

But when Mr. Sinclair explicitly or implicitly demands that one's sympathy for his courage be translated into one's admiration for him as a literary artist, one can only deny the confusing plea.

Howard Mumford Jones. *At*. Aug., 1946. p. 151

The secret of Upton Sinclair nobody yet knows—except to the degree that he still represents a flourishing of those provincial rebels, free-thinkers, and eccentrics who in the 1900's, from Robert Ingersoll to Veblen, marked the climax of our earlier agrarian and mercantile society. But what is the secret of the Lanny Budd series? . . . Mr. Sinclair's familiar villains are here, to be sure, including the international bankers, the Fascists, and the military. Yet there is very little sense of evil in this entire chronicle of modern corruption and decay. Even Hitler has sense enough to listen to Lanny Budd. . . . This central view of life, which corresponds to our own earlier dreams of national destiny and to the Europeans' wildest fancy, seems to me the main element in the success of the Lanny Budd novels.

Maxwell Geismar. *SR*. Aug. 28, 1948. p. 13

See *The Jungle, Oil!, Boston,* and *The Presidential Agent* (novels).

SNODGRASS, W. D. (1926–)

Mr. Snodgrass's poems represent the increasingly sought-after effect of the journal entry, of the autobiographical report, not assembled from deep images in a kind of rhetorical patchwork, like so many of Dylan Thomas's reminiscences, for example, but written out of considered reflections, summoned up for judgment, whose preparatory motions would always have seemed to consist rather of pencil nibbling than of vocalizing. In such a form, wit is seldom an end in itself, but instead always serves to keep the open scepticism of the narrator's scrutiny clear of the attractions of abject sentimentality on the one hand, and of self-conscious posturing on the other. Poems like "April Inventory," "A Cardinal," and the title sequence, a group of poems for the poet's daughter (it takes its title from a phrase in a translation of an Old Irish story: "an only daughter is the needle of the heart"), all succeed in being openly autobiographical, intense and delicate at once, and never embarrassing.

John Hollander. *PR*. Summer, 1959. p. 504

Snodgrass's universe is about as poor a thing as you could find anywhere in America: quonset huts, zoos, a campus, debris, birds that live like vermin in the gullies beside golf courses. It sounds like a small mill town that got missed by our juggernaut prosperity. But how alive he is there! And how fluently and honestly he writes about it. . . .

Ten poems constitute a cycle of lyrics on one subject, under the title "Heart's Needle." The subject is one that has been discussed endlessly everywhere except, so far as I know, in verse. George Balanchine is said to have remarked that in a ballet you can't tell if someone is supposed to be somebody's mother-in-law. And in poetry would it seem reasonable to write about the relations of a divorced and re-married parent with a child of the first marriage? But someone must once have thought it impossibly unorthodox to write about a man's love for an unattainable woman; it would take so much explaining to make the situation clear, and then it would be so prosaic. Why not keep to the good simple themes? W. D. Snodgrass overcomes all the difficulties. The poems never leave the literal situation, yet they do not depend on appeals to it for their emotions. Each pathetic detail is given without flinching. . . .

John Thompson. *KR*. Summer, 1959. pp. 489–90

What is new in *Heart's Needle* is the poetry of divorce instead of love. The title sequence traces, in aching detail, the relationship of the divorced father to his young daughter. Other poems have to do with the uneasy relationship of the poet to the campus which gives him, but not his Muse, daily bread. Let me say at once that Snodgrass is a deft and skilful craftsman who exhibits subtle control of sound and image and fluency of movement. He has found his style—he assimilates ease and elegance along with metrics from Marianne Moore and Richard Wilbur—and practises it so consistently that no one will mistake a poem by Mr. Snodgrass for anyone else's. So we can consider the claims Mr. [Robert] Lowell makes for him. "*The* poet with content" has simply junked Pound's, Eliot's, and the imagists' dicta about the impersonality of poetry. His subject is frankly himself.

Daniel G. Hoffman. *SwR*. Winter, 1960. p. 122

You don't find Snodgrass hymning a dull Georgia boyhood or a weekend in Des Moines in the borrowed cadences of Yeats's "The Tower" or in the variegated language of Stevens' "The Comedian as the Letter C." He knows better. It is true that he owes most of what he knows about poetry to his Iowa training; he also recognizes the danger of turning that learning into dogma. In his current effort to write poetry in the larger tradition of Wordsworth, Hardy, and Chaucer, he has gone beyond his Iowa mentors, especially after working with Randall Jarrell at Colorado. Consequently, you can find in his work the unabashed presence of Midwest farmland, the deceptively simple rhythms and statements of nursery rhymes, along with many an unblushing use of such words as "loveliness" and "gentleness." This combination of hard indirection and simplicity gives a tone of dreamy precision to his work, especially in his momentary human scenes, like snowdrops in water, that are so full of implications.

Donald T. Torchiana in Poets in Progress
(Northwestern). 1962. p. 108

But [Robert] Lowell is not alone among contemporary poets in his confessional tendencies. He has said that W. D. Snodgrass used private autobiographical material before him; and Snodgrass and Lowell have contributed heavily to the personal or intimate mood in much current American poetry. Any judgment of this highly personal disclosure must be founded on the meaningfullness of the artistic object created from it—that is to say, whether it can achieve the imaginative objectivity capable of establishing it as an independent and forceful work.

Ralph J. Mills. Contemporary American Poetry
(Random). 1965. p. 156

See *Heart's Needle* (poems).

SONTAG, SUSAN (1933–   )

For me Susan Sontag's first novel, like her critical essays, beguilingly evokes an image of Lillian Gish playing Chopin on a piano to the Comanches in the shadows of her vast desert ranch in *The Unforgiven*. An alternate image might be Edna Best tending the stove on her family island in *Swiss Family Robinson*. In fact, any image suggesting a shrewd, serene, housewifely confidence in form which sustains and insulates, which reflects a sharp-edged and patient intelligence, would be applicable to Miss Sontag. In the *Benefactor*, a small, comic and charming work, she has given us a book whose protagonist, Hippolyte, tries to encompass life with just such a Sontaguesque sense of form, and whose hero *is* that sense of form. . . .

Although Hippolyte, a scholar and dilettante who runs through a great many adventures, fills pages with his personal speculations, these are nipped off by the precise, faintly inflected prose, like so many cubes snapped out of an ice tray. By the same token, the eclecticisms which embellish the story—tidbits from, among others, Gide, Rousseau, Voltaire—do not sour or oppress us nearly as much as they might: The bird-like purposefulness and persistent energy of Miss Sontag's writing infect us with her own bustling sobriety and cunning, and thus spare us the giddy sense of wayward burrowing.

Donald Phelps. New Leader. Oct. 28, 1963. pp. 24–5

The Benefactor is an intricate, ambitious fantasia on themes suggested by European literary modernism roughly up to and including Simone Weil (her speculations on grâce and pesanteur) and Jean Genet (his deliberate choice of inauthenticity as a pretext for action in a hypocritical world) as seen through the eyes of someone deeply committed to the philosophical and psychological premises of the "cool" world of the 60's, European and American. (I mean the word in no derogatory sense.) Not the mores or the latest jargon, but the idea and essence of the Cool is what she is after; her narrator's crisis straddles the war-time 40's, but she herself is closer in spirit to Robbe-Grillet and Uwe Johnson than to Weil or Genet. It is the prosy, circumstantial deliberateness of what might easily have been merely another flashy exercise in neo-surrealism that strikes one at first. Hence the peculiarly neutral "translator's English" of her by no means dull prose and her oddly spotty documentation, meticulous in many details, wholly vague in others. The novel, indeed, is very American in its combination of bookishness, philosophical literalness, and moral hypochondria.

R. W. Flint. Cmty. Dec., 1963. p. 490

The Benefactor was published with considerable fanfare and reviewed with some disappointment; it was charged with being too European, too obscure, and too fashionably involved with appearance and reality. It is all of these things, but it is more than involved with appearance and reality, it is an attempt to come to grips with this involvement—the involvement is the subject of The Benefactor. In the nameless city, very like Paris, Hippolyte has spent his life dreaming and arranging his life to correspond to his dreams. His dreams are more important to him than his life; the only object of interest in his life is a woman, Frau Anders, and she is more annoying than interesting. Hippolyte keeps trying to dispose of her, by selling her into slavery or burning down her house, and she keeps reappearing; she is a bedraggled, comical, and unexpectedly engaging representative of the external world that Hippolyte can almost, but not quite, extinguish. And it is Hippolyte and his dreams that finally triumph. With the kind of epistemological twist used by Gide in The Counterfeiters, we are left uncertain and apprehensive about what has been dream and what has not.

Geoffrey Bush. YR. Winter, 1964. p. 301

Style, dream, and banality: these notions cluster, however loosely, behind Miss Sontag's essays as they do behind her novel, *The Benefactor,* where the psychopathic narrator Hippolyte commits his life to his dreams, which are the style of his existence. Interpreting his dreams "did not relieve" Hippolyte, but only substituted irrelevant meanings for them. He detects, too, the falsity of lines "which people of taste insist on drawing between the banal and the extraordinary." Hippolyte trusts his dreams because they are at once extraordinary and banal. Today our most fantastic experiences are banalities. . . .

Obviously Miss Sontag takes positions, and she should. Above all she dreads the cliche in all its manifestations, as when she urges that religion must not be diluted to an acquiescence toward religion-in-general, or religious fellow-travelling, just as painting of a given period must not be diluted into admiration for Art, or cultural fellow-travelling. But in making these judgments she speaks for a new generation of critics who sense their distance from Culture, for they know it's foolish, or at least impoverishing, always to be requiring impressive meanings. Inevitably at a time when so much is banal, somebody had to tell us that "the discovery of the good taste of bad taste can be very liberating." Miss Sontag is a remarkably liberating writer because she has allowed herself to proceed by "immersion" in what she sees and reads. She calls it "immersion without guidelines."

Wylie Sypher. NYHT. Jan. 30, 1966. p. 2

This is a hard book [*Against Interpretation*] to like and a harder one not to admire. In a free-wheeling collection of twenty-six essays—about half of which were originally published in the *New York Review of Books* or *The Partisan Review*—Susan Sontag indicates with impressive assuredness that she knows a lot about some things and at least as much as any other authority about everything else. What puts one off more than the extravagance of her judgments ("Most American novelists and playwrights are really either journalists or gentlemen sociologists and psychologists"), or the knowing, sometimes messianic shrillness of her tone, is Miss Sontag's concern with being, above and before all, fashionably *avant-garde*. One can't resist the suspicion that "the new sensibility" she heralds in these essays is her own, and that much of her esthetic doctrine is a complicated and unconscious self-promotion. . . .

Perhaps what makes *Against Interpretation* valuable and exciting is not so much its erudition, which is considerable, or its high level of intelligence, but its passionate irresponsibility, its determined outrageousness.

Jonathan Baumbach. SR. Feb. 12, 1966. p. 33

Strangely pedantic, confused, or timid about what she would hold to, and never more so than when she produces notes and aphorisms of a fine neatness and futility, Miss Sontag comes through as someone anxious to revise what she takes to be our mistaken view of art. But her cause appears to me less momentous than she seems aware, deriving from a view of art and of persons that belongs to what is by now a quite aged modernism. It is a cause unlikely to enlist readers unacquainted with the strawman philistine—stubbornly holding to the idea of "content" in the arts—who falls regularly before her sentences; and equally those who will find her not radical enough and who are getting by various means direct access to the "eschatology of immanence" that she finds laid out in Norman O. Brown's *Life Against Death*. But no matter; it is Miss Sontag herself who proves interesting and important as she utters the incorrigible Blakean demand on an "eschatology of immanence," a celebration of the body, the flesh, the sensuous appearances of things in the world; and as she records what corresponds to this, her deep disinclination to believe any longer in the self of psychoanalysis and the academic intellectuals—in the self as the New York literary culture conceives it.

Jack Behar. *HdR*. Summer, 1966. p. 347

Like everything Miss Sontag writes, *Death Kit* has strokes of wit in its pages. . . . There are quick thrusts of imaginative perception, for example about the inward experience of the blind. The graveyard spectacular produced as a finale—a pastiche of Thomas Browne, Rider Haggard and Kafka—has passages of force.

More important than any of this, there are moments when the reader can peer through the haze of abstract, overconfident cultural critique into a highly human torment and confusion—the suffering of a writer who seems bent on transforming self-hatred into an instrument of objective analysis, yet who nevertheless knows in her deepest self that this feeling cannot be thus elevated, since it is merely another style of pride. ("He who despises himself esteems himself as a self-despiser.")

Affecting as these moments are, they are too personal and infrequent to redeem the book as a whole. The plain case—no less visible here than in *The Benefactor*—is that the author's most powerful and most valuable impulse, the impulse to rage, is thwarted by novelistic form. Damnation-dealers and ravaged consciences are swallowed up, usually, in fiction. The conventions even of so-called philosophical novels—those forgiving full-nesses of view, obligations of understanding and compassion—tend to trivialize fury.

Benjamin DeMott. *NYT*. Aug. 27, 1967. p. 2

See *The Benefactor, Death Kit* (novels); *Against Interpretation* (essays).

STAFFORD, JEAN (1915–   )

From time to time there appears on the American literary scene an exceptional and original feminine talent. Several over the past few years have exhibited brilliant facets, but Jean Stafford is the first in many years to spread before our eyes a radiant stylistic network of dazzling virtuosity.

Elizabeth Bullock. CS. Sept. 24, 1944. p. 1

There is no doubt that Jean Stafford, author of *Boston Adventure,* is a remarkable new talent. This is not to say that her first novel is a completely satisfying experience but that Miss Stafford brings to the writing of a novel an unusual native endowment; I would find it hard to name a book of recent years which, page for page or even sentence for sentence, was so lively and so clever. By the light of any one of the incandescent moments of *Boston Adventure,* it may turn out that the book as a whole is strangely disappointing, reminding us that in the final analysis no amount of skill as a writer substitutes for the total novelistic power. But for its manner, for the way in which it stands up to the literary job, Miss Stafford's novel unquestionably demands a place for itself in the best literary tradition.

Diana Trilling. Nation. Sept. 30, 1944. p. 383

Miss Stafford's remarkably fine novel (*Boston Adventure*) has been praised for its range and perception, its style, and for a distinction, as I see it, that springs from the meeting of genuine personal culture with deep independence of sight. It has also, because of certain echoes, been analyzed for its Proustian qualities. But not enough has been said of the real Proustian epic in it. . . . Here, at last, is a novel in which sensibility is not sacrificed to representation; in which the inwardness of man, at once the deposit of events and the shaper of them, is functionally related to bold and objective visual power.

Alfred Kazin. NR. Oct. 23, 1944. p. 538

(*The Mountain Lion*) is an even finer novel than *Boston Adventure,* though less brilliant. It does not have the startling wealth of anecdote which Jean Stafford offered in her first novel; but it has a deeper richness of child-myth and child-lore—charms against the adult world, rhymes, ritualistic "dialogues" and shared "jokes," intimations of mortality—and the statement it makes of good and evil, innocence and experience, is tantalizing in its possibilities of extension. In this narrower plot, the author has found, paradoxically, greater freedom of perception and utterance: her style here is cleaner and more athletic.

Henry Rago. Com. April 4, 1947. p. 618

Miss Stafford writes with brilliance. Scene after scene is told with un-forgettable care and tenuous entanglements are treated with wise subtlety. She creates a splendid sense of time, of the unending afternoons of youth, and of the actual color of noon and of night.

Refinement of evil, denial of drama only make the underlying truth more terrible.

Catherine Meredith Brown. *SR*. March 1, 1947. p. 15

The Catherine Wheel—her third and perhaps most complex novel—is supported by few of those subsidiary virtues which gave vitality and idiosyncrasy to her earlier work; for all the elaborate rendition of locale and *decor,* it never really aims—as did *Boston Adventure*—at a systematic investigation of the social fact, nor does it attempt to frame a specialized personal crisis with the masterly precision of *The Mountain Lion.* Its scope is defined by intentions at once more limited and more ambitious than these: Miss Stafford has sought to convey, through two subtly interwoven though distinct narratives, a vision of emotional anarchy assaulting a world of "traditional sanctity and loveliness"—a vision in which the individual disaster is simultaneously symptom and result of the larger social decline. . . . Miss Stafford has written a novel to compel the imagination and nurture the mind; she has also written one in which pity and terror combine to reach us in the secret, irrational places of the heart.

Richard Hayes. *Com*. Jan. 25, 1952. pp. 404–5

In her superbly controlled novel (*The Catherine Wheel*) Miss Stafford has shown a modern martyrdom; her story discloses the secret torture of two persons, a child and a woman, both caught in a tragic circumstance during a tranquil summer on the coast of Maine. . . . The village in this novel is named Hawthorne, but even without that reminder it is clear that Miss Stafford is concerned with the identical plight that Nathaniel Hawthorne pondered in his stories—the tragedy of human isolation, the devious, painful, perilous struggle for harmony and understanding. *The Catherine Wheel* is a novel of great restraint and of great beauty.

Walter Havighurst. *SR*. Jan. 26, 1952. p. 11

In each of her novels, she has begun with what her art and imagination can really create: a densely detailed, spatially narrated image of a place, some people, and their relationships, dramatizing the whole in a diffused, remembered time, rather than any too tyrannical chronological time. But then, toward the end, she seems to feel the need for a "memorable act," for some abruptly theatrical violence, which not only intrudes improbably upon the soft-grained texture she has been building up, but for which frankly she has no taste or instinct. . . . The result is false, mutilating, and unworthy of her.

Robert Phelps. *NR*. March 10, 1952. p. 21

Character is most important in these stories, but character does not play out a drama of isolated sensibility. Instead, Miss Stafford's people are seen, as it were, in a full round of experience, are set with their problems and conflicts in a milieu that is vital and charged both with intimate and external meaning. To an unusual degree, there is a significant rapport and reciprocal influence between these characters and their environments, and from this ability of Miss Stafford's to relate aspects of character with the details of scene and situation comes a major strength of these stories, their compelling believability.

Gene Baro. *NYHT*. May 10, 1953. p. 3

Maladies and misfortunes of one sort or other cause Miss Stafford's characters to retreat from the world of customary urges and responses into a never-never land of dreams and unfulfilled desires, a land where sickness is king and despair his consort. Within its boundaries, Miss Stafford writes with certainty, understanding, and beauty. Like her three novels, (her) stories within their impeccable frame-work, are meaningful and complex. They remind me of children's Japanese flower-shells which when submerged in water open silently to disgorge a phantasmagoria of paper flowers, richly colored, varied and vaguely grotesque in contrast to the bland, unrevealing walls of their temporary habitations.

William Peden. *NYT*. May 10, 1953. p. 5

These three archetypal figures—the alien, the rebel, and the freak—serve, then, as a focus for exploring the cultural condition of the modern world. That condition is given an ethical dimension through a fusion of psychological, humanistic, and Christian terms. Moral judgment is couched in the language of Freud as well as of the Bible, and the fusion is effected through imagery. The serpent, referred to in crucial scenes of each of the novels, is equally at home in the worlds of theology and depth psychology, and possession by the devil may be construed literally or metaphorically. By seeing the eternal problem of innocence and guilt, good and knowledge, from this threefold perspective, Miss Stafford gives full scope to her ironic vision while enriching and extending her material. The use of terms, concepts, and images drawn from a variety of ideologies is the language and technique of the ironist who seeks to show both the metaphoric, incomplete character of the insights they articulate and their inability to command single-minded belief.

(K)   Olga W. Vickery. *SAQ*. Autumn, 1962. p. 489

We might say that Miss Stafford knows the limits of her talent too well; neither in the Emily stories nor in any of the others does she burden her prose with a sense of personal urgency, of compulsion to speak. The stories mean just what they seem at first glance to mean; the plot itself *is* the meaning. Thus in one story we witness a beautiful lady's wasted career, and the only matter for reflection is that her career was indeed wasted. In another we see a retired professor disembarrass himself of a sycophantic disciple, and we experience relief: *that's* over with. Similarly, we share the sense of achieved freedom experienced by a young woman who deserts her provincial guardians in Colorado, and of two lovers who foil a pack of busybodies. If there is a recurrent idea in this book [*Bad Characters*] it is the idea of sheer escape, stripped of intellectual content.

(K)   Frederick C. Crews. *NYR*. Nov. 5, 1964. p. 13

Jean Stafford loves the American landscape and the American past: the Colorado desert, the coast of Maine, the old streets of Boston, Miss Pride picking her way through an ancient graveyard, Katharine Congreve wandering about her father's old mansion. Yet she always sees the relevant modern comment and fits it in exactly. She is very conscious of the deodorant in the drugstore window, the giveaway formality of the *arriviste,* the blue or pink head of the dowager. Her great gift is to be able to place the vulgar detail in the center of the picture without making the picture vulgar, making it, on the contrary, something at once more vivid, faintly humorous, accurate, and at the same time fantastic. What she does to the American scene is to show it as a landscape with a billboard in the center, a billboard that represents the human encroachment on nature, at times funny, at times sordid, at times pathetic, but at all times the reader's and the author's principal concern.

(K)   Louis Auchincloss. *Pioneers and Caretakers*
                              (Minnesota). 1965. p. 159

Some months ago the major portion of Miss Stafford's interview with the mother of Lee Oswald [*A Mother in History*] appeared in McCall's Magazine. The compelling interest of this self-portrait—for the writer let Mrs. Oswald speak for herself—was equaled only by the nature of the reader reaction to the piece. Letter after letter poured in repeating words like "disgusted," "shocked," "outraged." . . .

None were more surprised at this storm of protest than Miss Stafford herself and the editors of the magazine. For what she had done was—and is—a most valuable analysis of a woman sick with a spiritual and emotional malignancy. Like a good analyst, Miss Stafford hardly speaks at all, letting the wild, interminable flow, alternately deluded and canny, outraged and cosy, spill from the woman's lips into a tape recorder as she exonerates herself and her son from all blame, points condemning fingers at a shifting host of "Theys" and heaps scorn on the official establishment and the gullible public alike. . . .

Where Jean Stafford's great skill is manifest is in the brief interpolations, between Mrs. Oswald's copious stream, in which she describes the meticulously neat little house filled with small "decorative" objects the owner "just picked up" but empty of all roots; observes the owner's mannerisms and idioms, her bustling proffers of coffee and collaboration; tells of her own hideously hilarious struggles with the tape-recorder, of the harrowing visit with the mother to the son's grave; manages to convey the trauma of her own involvement with this woman without ever raising her voice.

(K)   Marya Mannes. *NYHT*. Feb. 27, 1966. p. 4

See *Boston Adventure, The Mountain Lion, The Catherine Wheel* (novels); *Children Are Bored On Sunday, Bad Characters* (stories); *A Mother in History* (reporting).

STEELE, WILBUR DANIEL (1886–   )

His men and women part for a day only to find the world changed upon their return. But the drama of a day arises naturally out of a long past of slowly accumulating experience, and this background of a suddenly recalled past is most often the moving force of his situation.

Few writers show such economy in the use of their material. You feel that all of Mr. Steele's stories develop from a single picture intensely realized by the artist, and that it is his spirit of inquiry brooding over the implications of this picture which has eventually constituted his story. He is a master of color, and in a few careful strokes presents the same natural background for the passion of his characters that many novelists require several chapters to reveal. . . .

It is always hazardous to prophesy the future course of an admirable writer, but it is safe to say that the rich, human embodiment of the stories collected in this volume [*Land's End and Other Stories*] assure them a permanence in our literature for their imaginative reality, their warm color, and their finality of artistic execution. Almost without exception they represent the best that is being accomplished in America today by a literary artist. But Mr. Steele will never be elected to an Academy. Such is the fate of all pioneers.

Edward J. O'Brien. Introduction to *Land's End and Other Stories* by Wilbur Daniel Steele (Harper). 1918. pp. xii–xiii

He might be a great writer, but he did not take himself seriously. He might be critically appraised as the master technician in America of the short story form, but he, Wilbur Daniel Steele, would say nothing whatever concerning it. Nor would he speak of literature or in terms of literature. Which would make him a very literary person indeed.

An authentic literary person, as I understand it, is one who writes of life in terms of life and, having done that, sits down and says humbly, "I thank Thee, Lord, and may it happen once again!" Wilbur Steele has been writing for sixteen years, and that, he says, is the only formula he knows.

Many of his stories are grim, but he himself is not grim at all. He is neither melancholy nor self centred. He reads little. When he is through with work—and four or five hours is an average day's stint—he likes to be outdoors.

Frank B. Elser. *Bkm*. Feb., 1926. pp. 691–2

Should one desire to observe a writer apparently breaking every law of the machine and actually, with a really marvelous ingenuity, availing himself of every one of them, there is Mr. Wilbur Daniel Steele. The basis of Mr. Steele's art is melodrama—but melodrama so subtly stylized and refined, so outwardly unconventional, as to be hardly recognizable. Mr. Steele has been everywhere and has picked up so many bits of color, so much realistic detail that he is capable of conveying almost any effect, be it tragedy, horror, or passion. Yet, when one thinks it over one realizes that this is exactly what he has done: given us the effect and nothing more. . . . Of the actuality, the terrifying closeness of a Katherine Mansfield he is quite incapable.

Clifton Fadiman. *Nation*. Dec. 28, 1927. p. 738

Wilbur Daniel Steele, after much successful short-story writing, has produced in *Meat* a remarkably vigorous moral tract dressed as a novel. As a tract it is so absorbing and so exciting that this reviewer, having read it through last night, has not the slightest idea if it is or is not "art." Steele's method of writing is well suited to such an exposition. His style is pruned as bare of blurring green and lacy twigs as a spring vine, and is as full of strong sap.

Frances Lamont Robbins. *Outlook*. March 14, 1928. p. 433

If I were asked to indicate the single quality by which Mr. Steele's stories rightly claim their place in American literature, I should say that it was by virtue of his sensitive fidelity to the more abiding romance of ordinary life. While it is true that his pictorial sense of atmospheric values serves to define the terms on which he is willing to render human character in conflict, the essential merit of his findings is due to the impartial view which he takes of circumstance, an impartiality as unconscious and as real as that of a child before daily happenings. It is, perhaps, this very joy in apprehending spiritual values without self-consciousness, as a child apprehends them, which has often led him to set down what he has seen in the words of a boy, to whom wonder reveals more of the truth than self-analysis, and to whom delight in a story is a sufficient preoccupation, without premature analysis of his own human relation to what he sees.

Edward J. O'Brien. *The Advance of the American Short Story* (Dodd). 1931. pp. 232–3

With *That Girl From Memphis* . . . Mr. Steele emerges as a novelist deeply serious about his material and his method of presenting it. One suspects that he has worked longer and harder on this book than on any other he has published. The result is an absorbing story that deserves to be read seriously by thoughtful people, and perhaps the most important contribution that a reviewer can make is to insist on this point—for it is a novel likely to be misunderstood. First because of the title: it is not the story of the notorious "Girl From Memphis" but of "Beulah City" in Arizona and of a man's struggle to understand himself and his life. Garnett Cannon might be called an American Parzival. . . . *That Girl From Memphis,* far from being a story of vicarious thrills, is actually a social study, an attack on the forces which have vulgarized American life.

Gay Wilson Allen. *NYT*. June 10, 1945. p. 5

Apparently Mr. Steele spends his time these days as a beachcomber operating out of Old Lyme, Connecticut, but a Coloradan he remains. No one else could have written *Diamond Wedding*.

In short, although this book is some distance this side of the best novel that will be written this year, maybe even of the best historical novel, a book more thoroughly characteristic of the people, the history, and the habits of mind which make the Coloradan a separate species in the genus Westerner is not likely to make its appearance in some years. Even in the manner of its telling *Diamond Wedding* bespeaks the country out of which it comes, the story set forth with almost maddening deliberation, all cross-grained in its structure, with a prose so knotty and gnarled that one must occasionally back away to grease the teeth of one's understanding before the meaning can be sawed out.

Dale L. Morgan. *SR*. Aug. 5, 1950. p. 15

At their best, his stories miss genuine significance primarily because of the rigidity with which he held the concept of the short story as primarily an adventure, much in the manner of Jack London, but without London's unconventionality or his vigorous social attitudes. Reading his stories today, one is still impressed by the brilliant surface glitter of them but struck, too, by what seems finally a false manipulation of material for its dramatic effect. His craftsmanship is sure—almost too predictable. And it is utilized too much for its own sake. Life gives way before it. As with O. Henry and other masters of this type of writing, once the trick is seen, too little remains to satisfy the demanding reader.

> Ray B. West. *The Short Story in America, 1900–1950*
> (Henry Regnery). 1952. p. 81

That a short story can be a poem is revealed in "How Beautiful with Shoes." Mad as the ravings of the lunatic are, they open "magic casements" for a girl who has seen little of loveliness in her life and sees even less in the life that is awaiting her.

In 1886 Wilbur Daniel Steele was born in Greensboro, North Carolina. He is a graduate of the University of Denver and has studied art in Paris, New York and Boston. He is an author whose work should be much better known today. Unlike many famous writers who appeared in the earlier volumes of *The Best American Short Stories,* the high quality of his work has not fluctuated.

> Martha Foley. *Fifty Best American Short Stories 1915–*
> *1965* (Houghton). 1965. p. 118

See *The Best Stories of Wilbur Daniel Steele.*

STEFFENS, LINCOLN (1866–1936)

Mr. Steffens describes himself as a journalist, and no doubt he is perfectly within his rights in choosing what label he will; his readers will be perfectly within their rights in wishing that all other journalists possessed Mr. Steffens's gifts for rummaging until he has found the facts, for seeing the facts as they are, and for setting them down without exaggeration. When Mr. Steffens calls himself a journalist in the composition of this book [*The Shame of the Cities*], he must mean that he has employed methods, not the manner, of journalism. He has gone to prominent men in politics and finance in each of the cities in which he was interested— St. Louis, Minneapolis, Pittsburgh, Philadelphia, Chicago, New York; he has asked them questions about their most intimate financial and personal affairs with the tranquil effrontery of an *enfant terrible* escaped from his nursery; and like the *enfant terrible* he seems to have found amongst all manner of men slaves to the direct question. They have answered him to the limits of indiscretion, and their answers are recorded in these articles.

> Alfred Hodder. *Bkm.* May, 1904. p. 302

I marvel when I reflect that he could see so clearly what most had not even the sensitiveness to feel. He went at his task quite in the scientific spirit, isolating first that elementary germ or microbe, the partizan, the man who always voted the straight ticket in municipal elections, the most virulent organism that ever infested the body politic and as unconscious of its toxic power as the bacillus of yellow fever. Then he discovered the foul culture this organism blindly breeds—the political machine, with its boss. But he went on and his quest led him to the public service corporation, the street railway company, the gas company, the electricity company, and then his trail led him out into the state, and he produced a series of studies of politics in the American cities which has never been equaled, and so had a noble and splendid part in the great awakening of our time.

Brand Whitlock. Forty Years of It (Appleton). 1925.
p. 163. [1914]

Mr. Steffens's autobiography, to be specific, is the obituary of American reformism, progressivism, liberalism; it is at once the story of and the verdict upon the whole first phase of the movement in this country against privilege, inequality, individualism—the phase that found its characteristic expression in middle-class "social work," in muckraking, in trust-busting, and in reform legislation. . . .

But he has been more than a reporter, just as he has been more than a reformer: if the word did not have too many portentous connotations for so genial a man, one would say that he has been a kind of prophet. At any rate, if to be a prophet is to have a true humility of mind and spirit, to grasp imaginatively the conflicts of one's time, to apprehend the relation between men and events, to be capable of disenchantment without bitterness or negation, then Lincoln Steffens has been something of a prophet, and this book has something of the stateliness of prophecy. I do not mean that it embraces the sum of social and personal wisdom, but I do mean that it is full of invaluable hints and intimations. It suggests how the transition can be made from a plastic liberalism to a resourceful and humane radicalism. It suggests how social movements can be given a personal and psychological as well as a collective aspect. It demonstrates, indirectly, the shabbiness of our fashionable cynicism. It is a source book for the critic, for the radical, for the man of action. But it is certainly not merely an "autobiography."

Newton Arvin. Nation. April 15, 1931. p. 416

Sure, Steffens was a dangerous radical, and this book [Lincoln Steffens Speaking] is a dangerous book. It destroys the boundaries of hatred we build about ourselves, and, worst of all, it introduces a method of thought which will keep those boundaries down. Steffens was dangerous because he didn't tell people things, but he did make them arrive at reasonably thoughtful conclusions. I have known people to leave his house aghast at what they had said and yet unable to refute themselves with their usual axioms. I expect people will leave this book aghast at themselves for agreeing with things they have been taught to believe they hated.

John Steinbeck. *NYHT*. Nov. 29, 1936. p. 6

Some of us began reading Lincoln Steffens at the time when he first reached an immense American public with his series of magazine articles on *The Shame of Cities*. We began to read him then, some of us, and we followed him on through the *Autobiography* and its postscript volume, *Lincoln Steffens Speaking*. He never once lost us as readers. Whether we said yes or no or maybe to what he was writing, we went on reading him these thirty years and more. Always he had something on the ball. You could never be sure what he was going to throw till it came. He carried an assortment of curves and a wicked straight ball. His style most often was so distinctly his own that what he put forth didn't need his signature. . . . About a million miles from being a Narcissus was Steffens. Yet how he did study himself, how he did try to fathom mankind by searching and cross-examining and spying on and carrying out counter-espionage on the single specimen piece of humanity nearest and most available, the solitary and brooding Lincoln Steffens himself.

Carl Sandburg. Memorandum to *The Letters of Lincoln Steffens*, edited by Ella Winter and Granville Hicks, I (Harcourt). 1938. pp. vii–viii

So little was he the reformer that when others were condemning and ousting corrupt politicians, Steffens was pleading for understanding of crooks, criminals, grafters; he was interested in the bosses as characters, in how they did what they did, and why; by what codes of ethics or morals they justified their behavior. He made personal friends of many of them. He turned topsy-turvy the distinction between good and bad men; "there is so much good in bad people, there must be some good in good people," ran his chuckling argument. Steffens came to disbelieve utterly in mere, piecemeal, reform. And more and more, as it became less possible to tell people what they did not know, Steffens expressed himself in paradox, irony or allegory. He wrote fables. "Only a known fool could explain [the collapse of our economic system] and be allowed to live," he said in the last paragraph he wrote. "I did it gingerly and—well, I lived." It was partly because Steffens himself was a paradox that he was allowed to live. The price he paid was that he was not well understood.

Ella Winter. Introduction to *The Letters of Lincoln Steffens*, edited by Ella Winter and Granville Hicks, I (Harcourt). 1938. p. xv

Always he sought to understand life, to see what went on behind the facades, to find the causes for the impending or the arrived collapse. Undoubtedly that weakened him so far as making the impression upon his time it was once thought he would make. He was baffled—again and again. He was always seeking some general principles to portray on a great canvas, and when he failed to find them or to picture what he did see he blamed among other things his college education. He was not one to scourge the money-changers out of the temple. His forte, and these letters prove it, was in dissecting and reporting the actions of the human beings about him. There may be bitter words in these letters; I don't seem to find them. Critical ones, yes, but not bitter. The older he grew the kindlier he became, the more forgiving, probably the more understanding. Yet it is a fact that men missed in him the clear-cut objectives which probably the reasonableness and the analytical character of his mind rendered impossible. It is perhaps true that his wit and his paradoxes, his worries and—at times—his reticences deprived him of exercising to the full the power which nature intended should be his.

Oswald Garrison Villard. *Nation.* Oct. 22, 1938. p. 426

Steffens was not likely to give his energies to a party. He had too much interest in individuals; he had too much appreciation of the human virtues as well as failings that were to be found in any man, capitalist or proletarian. Yet he knew that there must be some principle, some motive, that would induce men in the mass to work for common and progressive goals. Had Steffens been a European, his cynicism and clear view of reality might have made him a revolutionist; it all but did so years later, when he was old. But as an American he valued democracy and knew that, to have a future, democracy must be able to provide a solution for class troubles.

Louis Filler. *Crusaders for American Liberalism*
(Harcourt). 1939. p. 350

Steffens in those days was not interested in sociological or political things; the reforming or revolutionary instinct had not taken possession of him. He had been one of the best police reporters in the city, on the *Evening Post,* before going over to the *Commercial Advertiser.* His interest when he became city editor was distinctly that of the artist. He felt keenly and in great detail the picturesque and amusing side of the life of the city. He liked articles so written that the reader could see, while getting the news, the background of men behind the news. A character sketch of a Tammany official, a teamster maliciously bumping into another teamster but so gently that nothing could be done about it, was an important event in Steffens's imagination, and he would take anything of this sort—what

would be called by the other editors an eccentric story—and put it on
the first page.

> Hutchins Hapgood. *A Victorian in the Modern World*
> (Harcourt). 1939. pp. 138–9

For all his prestige and power, and for all his eagerness to improve our
democratic form of government, he remained the questioner and the critic.
He was not made of the stuff of a popular leader or of a social crusader.
The urge to right a wrong seldom impelled him to act overtly. His indignation was too often tempered by an effervescent humor: the ironist's view
of the foibles of humanity. He was more frequently impressed by the inherent decency of the unscrupulous boss than by the pinchbeck righteousness of a civic leader. It took him years to realize that what mattered was
not so much the crook as the conditions that made his crime possible. He
was equally long in learning that the key to corruption was privilege. "It
is privilege that causes evil in the world, not wickedness and not men."
Yet his attacks on corruption were written to arouse as well as to deprecate,
and few readers saw the significance of his basic conclusions. He was
satisfied to let others unsheathe their swords against the monster.

> Charles A. Madison. *Critics and Crusaders*
> (Holt). 1947. p. 405

Steffens sought in the imperfect social world for a method by which he
could improve its morals as practiced. This led him first to an inquiry
into pure ethics, both in American and European universities. The tenta-
tive conclusion at which he arrived as a result of these investigations was
that nothing decisive was known in the academic world with respect to
ethics. His marriage and return to America in search of work by means
of which he could support his family coincided with his resolution to
abandon the abstract field of academic ethics and with his attempt to discover in the hurly-burly of the social world itself just what was responsible
for its limitations. He decided, in other words, to abandon his first method
of empirical inquiry into pure ethics which could be applied, and to follow
instead the mistaken empirical method which has proved so common (but
also so fruitless) in the field of the social sciences: to study the social field
itself, empirically, in an effort to get it to yield its own hypothesis.

> James K. Feibleman. *Aesthetics* (Duell). 1949. p. 393

The bent of Steffens' interests and the nature of his opportunities leads
him inevitably to investigate the political and economic structure of society, and he becomes an actor in one exciting episode after another. As
sheer story, the document rushes on with magnificent audacity, ripping

apart the veils of hypocrisy and laying bare the secret sources of corruption. And in our travels from city to city we are led through a gallery of portraits unique and varied—portraits etched with humor and charity, to be sure, but also with unflinching fidelity. . . . He is always lucid, fluent, and utterly unaffected. The tone is conversational, and the sentences flow with a tang and vigor that make the reading both pleasant and easy even for the unsophisticated. At times, especially in the account of certain boyhood experiences, the writer's deep feeling infuses into the composition an almost poetic tenderness. His practice, moreover, of dramatizing his scenes and anecdotes, of allowing his characters to express themselves in actual speech—this method of narration imparts to the *Autobiography* the vivacity and spiritedness of a lively novel.

William H. Cunningham. Introduction to
The Autobiography of Lincoln Steffens (Abridged)
(Harcourt). 1958. pp. iv–v

Steffens prided himself upon being a scientific reformer rather than a moralist; yet the structure of his *Autobiography* depends fundamentally upon the archetypal patterns of the American myth of Eden. It follows the initiation ritual, marking Steffens' progress from innocence to a knowledge of the fruit of good and evil (Steffens first acquires a sense of guilt in adolescent sexual experience). As regards society, it builds upon the traditional polarities of America and Europe, East and West, country and city as being roughly equivalent, symbolically, to the moral conditions of Paradise and Hell. Steffens' spiritual journey takes him from the American West, which infuses him with instinctive moral character and visions of the promised land, to the corrupt eastern seaboard and thus to Europe, which becomes for him, finally, a school of worldly experience. He is as much concerned with the "sins upon the land" as the Puritan covenanter, Michael Wigglesworth, and his muckraking contributions constitute one prolonged jeremiad as he traces, in his words, "the trail of the serpent" from city to state to nation, from West to East to Europe.

Charles L. Sanford. *The Quest for Paradise*
(Illinois). 1961. p. 191

What Steffens gives is a hard ground lit by a cool, clear light: the seeing of things as things in fact *are*. This seeing is always hard to come by. It is dimmed by the fear that things are too dreadful to be seen. But when you have got it—and to the extent that you have got it—then for the first time you are truly secure. The seen reality may indeed be dangerous, as in our time a great many realities are. But all the comforts of illusion are as nothing compared to the solace of apprehended fact.

Many men, from many epochs, have taught me this; but Steffens' voice is the one I have oftenest in my ear. He is saying, perhaps, "I don't mean to keep the boys from succeeding in their professions. All I want to do is to make it impossible for them to be crooks and not know it. Intelligence is what I am aiming at, not honesty. We have, we Americans, quite enough honesty now. What we need is integrity, intellectual honesty." These words were in fact addressed to President Eliot of Harvard, who thereupon bowed politely and walked away.

> Barrows Dunham. Introduction to *The World of Lincoln*
> *Steffens*, edited by Ella Winter and Herbert Shapiro
> (Hill and Wang). 1962. p. xiv

Although Steffens would not espouse any doctrine—other than his own of applied Christianity—he found that certain institutional changes were necessary. Since privilege was a temptation to corruption, it had to be removed. The standard remedies of law enforcement and the regulation of business were not sufficient. The necessary instruments of government were not sufficiently honest and unprejudiced, and the basic evil of selfishness would still be untouched. In 1908 Steffens favored governmental ownership of public utilities. By 1914 he was talking in vague terms of taxing away unearned increment, primarily of land, and giving each man the full extent of the value that he produced. How it was to be done he did not specify.

> David Mark Chalmers. *The Social and Political Ideas*
> *of the Muckrakers* (Citadel). 1964. p. 79

Steffens . . . believed that the younger generation could see things that eluded his own. This confidence in youth became the dominant note of his later writings. However sentimental, however misplaced his confidence, it accounted for much of the serenity and charm of the last phase of his life. It rescued Steffens from the bitterness that afflicted so many of the disappointed liberals of his time. Above all, it saved him from intolerance and dogmatism, to which so many of them eventually succumbed. Even in the act of embracing a dogmatic and intolerant ideology—if he can be said to have "embraced" it—he himself came more and more to embody the liberal virtues of tolerance and intellectual modesty which some of the later defenders of liberalism so conspicuously lacked.

> Christopher Lasch. *The New Radicalism in America*
> (Knopf). 1965. pp. 280–1

See *The Shame of the Cities, The World of Lincoln Steffens* (essays); *Auto-biography*.

STEGNER, WALLACE (1909–   )

Mr. Stegner, who has not published any long fiction before this novelette (*Remembering Laughter*), has built a narrative which comes startlingly close to perfection. In many ways it will remind everyone who reads it of *Ethan Frome*. It has the same quiet strength and simplicity in structure and style. The characterizations are not as mature or subtle as those in Mrs. Wharton's novelette, but they are well-realized, and this story has dramatic relief from the tragic mood in Alec's tall tales and the opulence of the farm life.

There is no use to mention the assurance and calm competence that Mr. Stegner brings to his first book—it has to be read to be believed.

Phil Stong. *SR*. Sept. 25, 1937. p. 5

The passing generation of writers examined man with a minifying glass, made him smaller, baser, more miserable than life-size. Inevitably, the characters became too small to be seen; and new writers are returning to their only possible tool, the magnifying lens, and establishing man once more above the ground. In this tradition Mr. Stegner has written a rich and moving study (*On a Darkling Plain*). Perhaps it is in spite of himself that he is romantic, mystical, compassionate, and warm. The interbellum generation has been taught by the war generation to distrust these qualities; but in Mr. Stegner—as in Steinbeck, Wolfe, and Saroyan—they are what we value most.

Milton G. Lehman. *NR*. Feb. 26, 1940. p. 284

Stegner is prepared to give an inside view of the great Northwest as it was passing from the pioneer to the settled agricultural stage. In numerous tales he has faithfully worked this mine, without really striking pay dirt until the present moment. . . . With *The Big Rock Candy Mountain* the author takes a real hold on his subject. . . . Mr. Stegner has felt the spell of mountain and prairie, of drought, flood and blizzard; he can write of moving accidents and hairbreadth escapes which give us the feel of frontier life better than phrases about the stars and seasons.

Joseph Warren Beach. *NYT*. Sept. 26, 1943. p. 4

The Big Rock Candy Mountain is not a conscious rediscovery of American values. Mr. Stegner is as amused at small-town cussedness as was Sinclair Lewis, but he knows that satire accomplishes nothing. In a larger sense, however, his book is an extraordinary study in American folkways. The language, the psychology, the customs of his characters are essential and characteristic, largely because, knowing them, he takes them for granted and does not dissect and analyze. His, to be sure, is a masculine world, just as, despite the tenderness with which the wife is treated, this is a masculine book.

                                    Howard Mumford Jones. *SR*. Oct. 2, 1943. p. 11

Mr. Stegner is a regional writer in the usual sense that a certain geographical area engages him. Three subjects particularly intrigue him: memories of a prairie boyhood; a sudden and often belated revelation to one character of the incubi that haunt another; and what might be called the He-man pastoral, a highly American form found at its purest in the work of Sherwood Anderson and in such stories as Hemingway's "Big Two-Hearted River," and Faulkner's "The Bear."

                                    Harry Sylvester. *NYT*. Jan. 1, 1950. p. 15

Mr. Stegner writes beautifully about almost any kind of rural landscape, whether it be a birch-and-maple forest in Vermont, an apricot ranch in California, or the "endless oceanic land" of Saskatchewan. . . . At their most effective, his landscapes leap at you with a vividness that reminds you of the first time the eye doctor dropped the right lens in your test frame.

In his quiet way, Wallace Stegner is one of the most talented writers in our midst.

                                    Richard Match. *NYHT*. Jan. 1, 1950. p. 4

Stegner is always the quiet, sure workman, slipping in almost unnoticed bits of poetry and little ironies and sage observations as the story moves along, but, though almost unnoticed, the little touches dig in, take hold, do their work on the subconscious mind of the reader. But he is at his best, when he is aroused, when he gets his waters to rolling and roiling, for then he gets up on that high plateau that most of his *The Big Rock Candy Mountain* represents.

                                    Feike Feikema. *CS*. Jan. 9, 1950

Wallace Stegner is a thoroughly skilled writer who belongs to a tradition which takes the short story seriously, but not too seriously. Even his least successful stories are characterized by a well-disciplined, essentially conservative craftsmanship. Neither an entertainer nor an artist *per se,* he seldom fails to respect either his characters or his readers. In short, serious as his approach to short fiction may be, he does not allow his story to be submerged by message or overshadowed by technique.

                                    William Peden. *SR*. Jan. 21, 1950. p. 17

The psychological or regional not-at-homeness of Stegner's main characters makes the stories dominantly reflective in tone. The chances are mostly inner. What begins as condemnation of others becomes self-criticism. A deepened sense of what others are and need results in a deepened and chastened sense of self. Such detachment and reflectiveness are not likely to go with passionate commitment, and the stories do not usually drive dramatically to some final outer resolution. They are wise and humane as well as observant, however, and teach what must happen in ourselves before we can love and understand others, and by what steps we can move toward effective sympathy with those who, most needing love, are most unlovable.

Robert Gorham Davis. *NYT*. Oct. 26, 1956. p. 6

His gifts are of a distinguished, though completely unspectacular kind. They include a cool steadiness of insight into the complexities of the human condition and an extraordinary flexibility in making the idiom of the moment bespeak many subtleties of judgement. . . . Stegner always turns away from the shattering climax. When his point is made he breaks off, sometimes abruptly. This is as it must be with a writer to whom nothing is more offensive than the second-hand affirmative unless it is the garish, improbably bloody tragic resolution.

James Gray. *NYHT*. Nov. 4, 1956. p. 4

Here [in *The City of the Living*] is the commitment to life of *Remembering Laughter,* but now shaded by the sombre recognition that the affirmation must draw its strength from the tangled depths of human experience from whence it wells up. Here too is the search for understanding and identity, but now conducted with a more mature tolerance than in the earlier work. . . .

The unanswered questions at the heart of Stegner's work are: who is man and what can he affirm when he lives at dead center? It is toward this dead center that American society has been moving—the spot where the other-directed citizens practice "togetherness" and huddle in mutual anonymity. In their hands the polarities of American life are disappearing. Stegner, in refusing to make choices, speaks in the idiom of his indecisive time. Standing in the midst of his society, he has not so much seen it as experienced from it. He has tried to record the life of man and society from within the given framework. But consistent vision and true perspective, I believe, come to the artist who is outside.

(K)   Chester E. Eisinger. *CE*. Dec., 1958. p. 116

Wallace Stegner is not a major literary figure, and he can no longer be regarded as a young man of promise; but he is one of the writers, and fortunately there are many of them, who have to be reckoned with. He has written one novel of remarkable power, *The Big Rock Candy Moun-*

tain, and if his other books are not so impressive, none of them is negligible. He looks at America with a sharp eye, and he writes with precision and sometimes with beauty. . . .

As I read the novel [*A Shooting Star*], I felt that it was loosely organized, and I still think that the story of Sabrina could have been told more directly. We don't need to know as much about her ancestors as Stegner tells us, and several episodes seem to be dispensable. On the other hand, I can see why Stegner wanted to give his book breadth as well as depth, and in particular I am glad that he did so much with the MacDonalds. They are exemplary characters for our times without being in the least implausible. . . .

(K)   Granville Hicks. *SR.* May 20, 1961. p. 17

Wallace Stegner spent his young years in southwestern Saskatchewan near the Montana border in the Cypress Hills country, so named out of confusion of cypress with jack pine. Here was big country, too, then and now thinly populated. Here was a boy, like me, who got a place in his system and as a man can't get it out, no matter that he's long since moved away. He knew the distances, the animals, the Indians, the poor striving people, the smell of wolf willow, the feel of swimming-hole water, the great loneliness that is loneliness only in retrospect.

He revisited the place, in preparation presumably for his book [*Wolf Willow*], after an absence so lengthy that his connections largely were with places and memories, not men or boys he had known; and he has brought to bear on recollection the perception and confessed acknowledgment of origin of a wise and probing mind.

I have read his book twice and gone over paragraphs time after time, always with increased admiration, and I have asked myself whether others will respond as I have, no matter where their home towns. My answer is yes, for there is too much here for frontier environment alone.

(K)   A. B. Guthrie. *Reporter.* Nov. 22, 1962. p. 52

See *Remembering Laughter, On a Darkling Plain, The Big Rock Candy Mountain, A Shooting Star, Wolf Willow, All the Little Live Things* (novels); *Women on the Wall, City of the Living* (stories).

STEIN, GERTRUDE (1874–1946)

We find . . . that Miss Stein's method is one of subtraction. She has deliberately limited her equipment. . . . Obviously, any literary artist who sets out to begin his work in a primary search for music or rhythm, and attempts to get this at the expense of (the) "inherent property of words," obviously this artist is not going to exploit the full potentialities of his medium. He is getting an art by subtraction; he is violating his *genre*. . . . Miss Stein continually utilizes this violation of the *genre*. Theoretically at least, the result has its studio value. . . . By approaching art-work from these exorbitant angles one is suddenly able to rediscover organically those eternal principles of art which are, painful as it may be to admit it, preserved in all the standard textbooks.

Kenneth Burke. *Dial*. April, 1923. pp. 409–10

In her detachment, her asceticism, and her eclecticism, Miss Stein can only remind us of another American author who lived in Europe and devoted himself more and more exclusively to the abstract. The principal difference between Henry James (whom Miss Stein reads more and more these days) and Gertrude Stein is that the former still kept within the human realm by treating moral problems. . . . Moreover, what Miss Stein has in common with James she has in common with Poe, Hawthorne, Melville, and several other important and characteristic American writers: an orientation from experience toward the abstract, an orientation that has been so continuous as to constitute a tradition, if not actually *the* American tradition. Of this tradition it is possible to see in Miss Stein's writing not only a development but the pure culmination.

William Troy. *Nation*. Sept. 6, 1933. pp. 274–5

I was delighted to see that Miss Stein never mentioned her style, never said that she had a philosophy, and that her point of view was merely the natural way she had of walking and speaking English; even in her boldest creations she acted spontaneously and enjoyed the fun of amusing herself. I was surprised first because our French wits rather liked wondering at themselves and even being shocked at themselves but certainly explained to everybody how marvelous and queer they were. On the contrary this woman whose mind was so rich and so new seemed never to have time to stop, look and listen at herself. All her actions and all her attention she kept in herself. All her personality she carried inside herself, inside this space and this time which was herself.

Bernard Fay. Preface to Gertrude Stein's *The Making
of Americans* (Harcourt). 1934. pp. xii–xiii

I have never heard talk come more naturally and casually. It had none of the tautness or deadly care that is in the speech of most American intellectuals when they talk from the mind out. If sometime you will listen to workingmen talking when they are concentrating upon the physical job at hand, and one of them will go on without cease while he is sawing and measuring and nailing, not always audible, but keeping on in an easy rhythm and almost without awareness of words—then you will get some idea of her conversation.

John Hyde Preston. *At.* Aug., 1935. p. 192

She had the easiest, most engaging and infectious laugh I have ever heard. Always starting abruptly at a high pitch and cascading down and down into rolls and rolls of unctuous merriment, her hearty laugh would fill the room and then, as it gradually dwindled into chuckles and appreciative murmurs, the silence that followed seemed golden with sunlight. Her laugh was boisterous but I have never known it to offend even the most delicately attuned, for it was so straight from the heart, so human, so rich in sound.

Bravig Imbs. *Confessions of Another Young Man*
(Henkle-Yewdale). 1936. pp. 118–19

It is little surprising that the ideas of William James have influenced his pupil. It is remarkable, however, to realize that Stein has, from her first work forward, created in an aesthetics which did not have its formal doctrination until as late as two decades after her first experiments with it. It is to be understood literally that the rudiments of a pragmatic aesthetic appeared in her work before contemporary philosophers, including William James, had expounded such an aesthetic. It was, then, with the voice of annunciation that she said, in 1926, "naturally no one thinks, that is no one formulates until what is to be formulated has been made."

Robert Bartlett Haas. Foreword to Gertrude Stein's
What Are Masterpieces (Conference). 1940. p. 21

Her writing is harder than traditional prose, as a foreign tongue is harder than a native tongue; at first glance we catch a word here and there, or a phrase or two, but the over-all meaning must be figured out arduously. Yet a tension is created, a question asked and in Miss Stein at her best, dramatic context mounts to a climax and then a conclusion. It's pure creative activity, an exudation of personality, a discharge, and it can't be defined more exactly. The mysterious surge of energy which impels a boy who is idling on a corner to race madly down the street is part and parcel of the same thing. When people call it elementary, they mean elemental.

W. G. Rogers. *When This You See Remember Me*
(Rinehart). 1948. pp. 69–70

I recall having a tormented feeling when first hearing the musicians of India playing for the dancing of Shankar. The music went on and on, like the babbling of a brook, always going on, always slightly, but ever so slightly, different, but mostly always the same. One waited almost nervously for a crescendo, a period, a climax, but one waited in vain; and gradually as the expectation was thwarted, as one gave up expecting, it was a soothing music as the babbling of a brook may be soothing, and then gradually as one listened more intently it was an intensely interesting, even a revealing music. There was no blare of horns, but it was none the less interesting. Miss Stein's prose is like that.

George Haines IV. *SwR*. Summer, 1949. p. 413

"In writing a word must be for me really an existing thing." Her efforts to get at the roots of existing life, to create fresh life from them, give her words a dark liquid flowingness, like the murmur of blood. She does not strain words or invent them. Many words have retained their original meaning for her, she uses them simply. Good means good and bad means bad—next to the Jews the Americans are the most moralistic people, and Gertrude Stein is an American Jew, a combination which by no means lessens the like quality in both. Good and bad are attributes to her, strength and weakness are real things that live inside people, she looks for these things, notes them in their likenesses and differences. She loves the difficult virtues, she is tender toward good people, she has faith in them.

Katherine Anne Porter. *The Days Before* (Harcourt).
1952. p. 39

In almost all literature until Gertrude Stein, the act of composition has been used to recall, recreate, analyze, and celebrate an Object Time, the time in which the "thing seen" is happening. This is true whether this Object Time is in the historical past . . . or the historical present. . . . In Gertrude Stein, just the reverse is true. In almost everything she wrote, it is the Subject Time, the time in which she is happening as she sees and writes, which is realized. . . . When she says "The time of the composition is the time of the composition," she means exactly that. The time that goes on in her writing is *not* the time in which her "thing seen" is going on. Her complete works might very aptly be called, "A la recherche du temps présent."

Robert Phelps. *YR*. Summer, 1956. p. 601

She never relinquishes the strictest, most intimate relationship between her words and her thought. . . . The aphoristic style and the conciseness of the formulas express the energy of this writer's consciousness, which appears almost excessive. Her language is affirmed in slow tempo, with a marked degree of solemnity, as it seeks to acquire a certain weight of one-syllable words. It represents finally a summation of things felt, lived with, possessed. It is common language and yet it relates an experience of intimacy which is the least communicable of all experiences. A word used by Gertrude Stein does not designate a thing as much as it designates the way in which the thing is possessed, or the way whereby the poet has learned to live with it.

Wallace Fowlie. *SR*. Dec. 22, 1956. p. 21

If these works are highly complex and, for some, unreadable, it is not only because of the complicatedness of life, the subject, but also because they actually imitate its rhythm, its way of happening, in an attempt to draw our attention to another aspect of its true nature. Just as life is being constantly altered by each breath one draws, just as each second of life seems to alter the whole of what has gone before, so the endless process of elaboration which gives the work of these two writers (Stein and Henry James) a texture of bewildering luxuriance—that of a tropical rain-forest of ideas—seems to obey some rhythmic impulse at the heart of all happening.

In addition, the almost physical pain with which we strive to accompany the evolving thought of one of James's or Gertrude Stein's characters is perhaps a counterpart of the painful continual projection of the individual into life.

John Ashberry. *Poetry*. July, 1957. p. 252

Her "art" is one of subtraction and narrowing throughout. In her art she does not reflect, for reflection entails consciousness of identity and audience, an awareness fatal to the creative vision. She rules out the imagination because it is the hunting ground of secondary talent. She rules out logical, cause-effect relations: "Question and answer make you know time is existing." She rules out distinctions of right and wrong: "Write and right. Of course they have nothing to do with one another." She will have no distinctions of true and false: "The human mind is not concerned with being or not being true." She abjures beauty, emotion, association, analogy, illustration, metaphor. Art by subtraction finally subtracts art itself. What remains as the manner and matter of the specifically "creative" works of Gertrude Stein is the artist and an object vis-à-vis. This is not art; this is science. Miss Stein would turn the artist into a recording mechanism, a camera that somehow utters words rather than pictures.

(K)   B. L. Reid. *Art by Subtraction: A Dissenting Opinion of Gertrude Stein* (Oklahoma). 1958.

pp. 171–2

As a scientific demonstration of Gertrude Stein's belief in the final absolutism of human character, *The Making of Americans* carries the weight of its conviction and the conviction of its enormous weight. As a work of literature, it is all but swept bare of the felicities of detail, color and anecdote that beguile the attention in great books as well as minor ones. But Gertrude Stein had had enough of the picaresque trappings and sentimental diffusions that recommend novels to the insatiable reader. She wanted to come to essentials—to ideas in action rather than ideas comfortably couched in formulation, and to character as an entity alive rather than character as an identity pinned to the wall like a butterfly. Her conception would test the power of the intellect to usurp the power of the emotions in communicating living experience, yet she was ready to face the challenge. . . . The pages of *The Making of Americans* are as full of rolling and repeated cadences as the Bible, but its more prevalent sound, like that of Oriental ritual, is the music of the continuous present, always going on and always, almost always, but not quite, the same. . . . Gertrude Stein had come early to a notion that was to dominate her creative life— the notion that the "continuous present and using everything and beginning again" was the final reality in fact and thus the final reality that words could communicate. Escaping from the conventions of beginning, middle, and ending, she simply laid out a space—a space of time as big in its proportions as a canvas of Jackson Pollock—and proceeded to make sure that it would be "always filled with moving."

(K)   John Malcolm Brinnin. *The Third Rose* (Little).
                                          1959. pp. 94–5

She never had her tongue in her cheek; she genuinely believed in her own uniqueness and incomparable genius; she devoted to the prosecution of her "experiments" the single-mindedness and sense of dedication of the greatest of writers and thinkers. She was her own first victim. If her confidence was misplaced and her experiments ridiculous, she is at least to be commended for determination. . . . It also explains why she obtained a genuine *succés d'estime* denied to the glibbest of pure charlatans, and why the Forsters, Hemingways, and Eliots, though they could not possibly have brought themselves actually to read her work, still less to enjoy it, nevertheless felt constrained to praise it. . . . Nor indeed were her experimentations with language wholly without value, if only as a set of awful warnings; a wiser woman would have perceived that by their very nature they could only lead to abortions; a quicker woman would have perceived their uselessness after the first instead of the five hundredth page; a more modest, or a poorer, woman would not have published, or have been able to publish, them. The *Stanzas in Meditation* is perhaps the dreariest long poem in the world, offering the absolute minimum in reward or pleasure against somewhere near the maximum in obstruction. Let it stand as a perpetual witness against the myth of an inherent value in "experiment."

(K)   Hilary Corke. *KR*. Summer, 1961. pp. 387–8

In serious literary circles, as distinguished from the large public, Gertrude Stein's real accomplishments were always known. There, her influence was at one time considerable, though it worked in very different ways and degrees on different individuals. It was known that her writing had influenced, in certain respects, Sherwood Anderson and, later, Hemingway. It was supposed that Steinese had found echoes in Don Marquis' *archy and mehitabel* as well as in the difficult poetry of Wallace Stevens, who once wrote "Twenty men crossing a bridge,/ Into a village,/ Are/ Twenty men crossing a bridge/ Into a village." Her insistence on the primacy of phenomena over ideas, of the sheer magnificence of unmediated reality, found a rapturous response in Stevens, a quiet one in Marianne Moore.

(K)   F. W. Dupee. *Cmty*. June, 1962. p. 522

Her immediate perceptions, her thoughts about certain nagging problems, her questions about certain objects or themes that appear in her writing, the associations that a word or sound might set off in her conscious mind, all of these are for Gertrude Stein legitimate materials for her writing. Her method of composition seems to go something like this. She focuses directly on a particular subject for as long as it may stick in her mind. Then she may depart from the subject to follow an association or report something that has entered her consciousness. The subject at hand returns again and again, but the importance of this whole retrospective process is to express the continuous present on-going of her consciousness. This is, after all, the only pure knowledge according to her theory. If data other than that relating directly to the supposed subject intrude into her consciousness, then they must be recorded as a manifestation of Gertrude Stein's process of thought.

(K)   Michael J. Hoffman. *The Development of Abstractionism*
                          in the Writings of Gertrude Stein (Pennsylvania).
                                                            1965. p. 195

More extreme than Thoreau, Stein has an ideal of what we may call seeing without remembering, without associating, without thinking. She wants the eye to open to the reality of the material world as though it had never opened before: for then we catch reality at its 'realest,' unfiltered through the schemata of the sophisticated eye which is dimmed from too long domestication in the world. And even though she does not develop or push the comparison she clearly cites the child's way of looking as exemplary: naivety must be cultivated in order that we may see reality as it is and not as we remember it to be. This takes us back to the problem of how a child does in fact perceive reality. More basically, whether one can in fact see anything clearly at all without the aid of memory, the subtle reawakening of innumerable past visual experiences, is open to doubt. Certainly, words are full of memories—are perhaps pure memory—and the impressions gained by the unremembering eye could never be transmitted by the unremembering voice. For without memory there is no metaphor; and without metaphor we would never have had language. Stein avoids live metaphors but to communicate at all she has to use those dead ones we all use continually in our daily speech. Her ideal properly carried out, if it did not lead to a visual confusion akin to blindness, would certainly lead to silence.

To draw these inferences is perhaps unfair. In fact what Stein wants is to purify the eye, to break old visual habits, to initiate a more vivid commerce between the senses and the real world.

(K)   Tony Tanner. *The Reign of Wonder* (Cambridge).
                                              1965. p. 191

In "Melanctha" she simplified her diction in order to stress the developing patterns of repeated words. There too she began to stretch given moments in time to abnormal length. With *The Making of Americans,* she eliminated action, yet by using extended repetition broken by slight changes in phrasing that allowed slow conceptual accretion, she managed to conserve a dynamic subject matter. Finally in *Tender Buttons,* conventional subject matter disappeared except insofar as some single thing stimulated Gertrude Stein's mind into action. Words were arranged as objects sufficient in themselves upon the page; and both alone and in series they made their effects by the associations roused through their composition. The stylistic process was one of gradual loss of story (movement) and of subject (thing) until, at her most obscure, Gertrude Stein offered arrangements quite as abstract as those painted by her friends, Braque, Picasso, Gris, and Picabia. In so doing she emphasized the underlying structures of colloquial speech, even as the Cubists isolated and stylized the geometrical components of the human figure.

(K)   Richard Bridgman. *The Colloquial Style in America*
                                         (Oxford). 1966. pp. 193–4

See *Selected Writings;* also *The Autobiography of Alice B. Toklas;* and *Three Lives* and *The Making of Americans* (fiction).

STEINBECK, JOHN (1902–1968)

He is primarily a masculine writer. . . . He has proved himself an original and highly individualistic force. His books provoke the masculine mind because of his fearless grappling with ideas and human passions as well as sacred taboos. The dry rot of gentility has never touched him and neither sex nor a woman's honor nor romantic love loom large as a man's serious problems in his view.

                          Edmund C. Richards. *NAR.* June, 1937. p. 409

Steinbeck abhors and abjures the tag "mystic" which some critics have used in describing him. He is deeply concerned with the problem of Good and Evil, not in any conventional, moral, or philosophical sense but as phenomena in life and as animating principles in life. I have heard him use no word indicating the nature of his beliefs and intimations; but I should vaguely describe them as comprising a curious, very modern Manicheanism, derived perhaps in part from the Indians of the West Coast he has known since boyhood, from acute observation of cause and effect operating among primitive or untutored men, and from a frank facing of the evidences of his own hidden resources of mind and will.

Burton Rascoe. EJ. March, 1938. pp. 213–4

Surely no one writes lovelier stories, yielding a purer pleasure. Here are tragedy and suffering and violence, to be sure, but with all that is sharp and harsh distilled to a golden honey, ripe and mellow. Even cruelty and murder grow somehow pastoral, idyllic, seen through this amber light, as one might watch the struggles of fish and water snakes in the depths of a mountain pool. Beyond question, Steinbeck has a magic to take the sting out of reality and yet leave it all there except the sting. Perhaps it is partly the carefulness of his art, with endless pains devising and arranging every detail until all fits perfectly and smooth and suave as polished ivory. But probably it is more the enchantment of his style, of that liquid melody which flows on and on.

T. K. Whipple. NR. Oct. 12, 1938. p. 274

The variability of the form itself is probably an indication that Mr. Steinbeck has never yet found the right artistic medium for what he wants to say. But there is in his fiction a whole substratum which does remain constant and which gives it a certain basic seriousness that that of the mere performer does not have. What is constant in Mr. Steinbeck is his preoccupation with biology. He is a biologist in the literal sense that he interests himself in biological research. . . . Mr. Steinbeck almost always in his fiction is dealing either with the lower animals or with human beings so rudimentary that they are almost on the animal level; and the close relationship of the people with the animals equals even the zoophilia of D. H. Lawrence and David Garnett. . . . The chief subject of Mr. Steinbeck's fiction has been thus not those aspects of humanity in which it is most thoughtful, imaginative, constructive, but rather the processes of life itself.

Edmund Wilson. NR. Dec. 9, 1940. pp. 785–6

Handling complex material rather too easily, he has been marked by the popularizing gift—this indigenous American blessing which has, however, in the case of so many literary figures (a William Lyons Phelps, a Wooll-cott, a Louis Bromfield, as well as Steinbeck himself) become a blessing not altogether unmixed. In Steinbeck's work the false starts and turns, the thwarting problems of material and of the artist in the process of pene-trating it, which usually mark the effort to portray truth, these are singu-larly lacking. If Steinbeck has reminded us of a Thomas Wolfe rejoicing in the mournful questioning of youth which wants no answers, he has never, like Wolfe, found himself disturbed by the final enigma of existence itself. For Steinbeck, Wolfe's famous stone is a stone, a leaf a leaf, and the door is sure to be found.

Maxwell Geismar. *Writers in Crisis* (Houghton).
1942. p. 260

Much of Steinbeck's basic position is essentially religious, though not in any orthodox sense of the word. In his very love of nature he assumes an attitude characteristic of mystics. He is religious in that he contemplates man's relation to the cosmos and attempts, although perhaps fumblingly, to understand it. He is religious in that he attempts to transcend scientific explanations based upon sense experience. He is religious in that from time to time he explicitly attests the holiness of nature. . . . Nineteenth century fears that the development of naturalism meant the end of rever-ence, of worship, and of "august sentiments" are not warranted in the case of Steinbeck. . . . Steinbeck is, I think, the first significant novelist to begin to build a mystical religion upon a naturalistic basis.

Woodburn O. Ross. *CE*. May, 1949. pp. 436–7

Steinbeck illustrates vividly the kind of moral impasse to which the idea of relativity applied to the field of cultural investigation has brought us while at the same time widening the grounds of tolerance in a way we can only approve. Since what is good in terms of our culture may be a positive bad in another, we can safely apply the term "good" only to those motives which appear in common at the most primitive level. This is precisely what Steinbeck does. His paisanos in *Tortilla Flat,* Mack and the boys in *Cannery Row* and most of the characters in *The Wayward Bus* gain a certain vitality (which his less earthly characters do not have) as a result of their uninhibited response to organic drives; but this in-volves their almost complete emancipation from social responsibility and a disregard of everything which culture has added to human life.

Blake Nevius. *PS*. Summer, 1949. pp. 307–8

We have been right all along in suspecting that there are nearly two Steinbecks. There is the Steinbeck of *Grapes of Wrath,* of *In Dubious Battle,* and of a number of short stories, an angry man whose anger has put a real tension in his work; and there is also the Steinbeck who seems at times to be only a distant relative of the first one, the warm-hearted and amused author of *Tortilla Flat, Cannery Row, The Wayward Bus, The Pearl,* capable of short stretches of some really dazzling stuff but, over the length of the book, increasingly soft and often downright mushy. In other words, Steinbeck has achieved his success by working within the limitations which are perhaps self-imposed on him by his temperament. They tie him down to an exclusive preference for one type of character, which recurs with surprising consistency throughout his work, and to a maximum of two emotional attitudes, one compounded of some delight and much compassion toward the people he writes about, the other of compassion and wrath.

W. M. Frohock. *The Novel of Violence in America*
(Southern Methodist). 1950. p. 147

Those who have written about Steinbeck have disagreed far more widely— and deeply—than they have about any other important writer of our time. . . . There is at least one notable characteristic of Steinbeck's writing on which otherwise conflicting critics agree: he is a man in whom the faculty of pity is strong and close to the surface. . . . It may turn out . . . that the essence of Steinbeck-man and Steinbeck-writer lies in these two quite uncomplicated truths: he earnestly wishes to make people understand one another and he is able, like Blake, to "seek love in the pity of others' woe."

Joseph Henry Jackson. Introduction to *The Short Novels
of John Steinbeck* (Viking). 1953. pp. vii–viii

I think we have been wrong about Steinbeck. We have let his social indig- nation, his verisimilitude of language, his interest in marine biology lead us to judge him as a naturalist. Judged by the standards of logical con- sistency which naturalism demands, his best books are weak and his poorer books are hopeless. Steinbeck is more nearly a twentieth-century Dickens of California, a social critic with more sentiment than science or system, warm, human, inconsistent, occasionally angry but more often delighted with the joys that life on its lowest levels presents.

Hugh Holman. *NR.* June 7, 1954. p. 20

If Steinbeck's characters seldom achieve true novelistic reality, it is pre- cisely because they are so little individualized, so little individuals and finally so little human. Their emotions always remain obscure and some- what opaque, situated, it seems, under the diaphragm or around the solar plexus; it is hard to picture them, even in a distant time, reading a clear consciousness of themselves. . . . We may say that there is something false and suspicious, at any rate monstrous, in the very innocence of Steinbeck's heroes. . . . Because of this very amputation, Steinbeck's universe and the

artistic domain in which he can succeed will be perforce very limited. . . .
One cannot help wondering whether there are very great possibilities open
to a "novelist of animality," however perfect his art may be and however
deep the bond of sympathy between his subject and himself.

> Claude-Edmonde Magny in *Steinbeck and His Critics*,
> edited by F. W. Tedlock and C. V. Wicker (New
> Mexico). 1957. pp. 225–7

If, as Faulkner has rather perversely contended, a writer is to be measured
these days by the extent and quality of his failure, Steinbeck must inevitably be reckoned among our most sizeable novelists. Steinbeck's failure
is great, and it is incomparably more interesting and valuable than the
successes of nine-tenths of his contemporaries. For where Steinbeck has
failed is in an effort to engage, with the resources of fiction, the complex
realities, the evolving motifs, the outlines and images of things, the very
sense of life which make up the matter truly, if deeply and almost invisibly,
available to an American novelist of his generation. I am not cheaply
hinting that Steinbeck deserves, as the schoolboy saying goes, 'E' for effort.
I am saying that because of his effort and even because of its failure he
has made more visible for the rest of us the existence, indeed the precise
character, of the realities and themes and images he has not finally succeeded in engaging. This is the kind of failure which is, in the end, almost
indistinguishable from success, though we may not be sure where to
catalogue it; whether, for example, under the heading of literature or of
criticism, of art or of history.

(K)   R. W. B. Lewis in *The Young Rebel in American*
> *Literature*, edited by Carl Bode (Heinemann). 1959.
> p. 122

In spite of their philosophic shortcomings, the earlier novels are great
novels. There is much that is good in them: accurate observation, clear
and forceful writing, human sympathy, splendid insight. I am not sure
that I would except *Cup of Gold* and *To a God Unknown* (the latter is
really a remarkable book); I would certainly recommend them above
anything that Steinbeck has written since *East of Eden* (and perhaps since
Cannery Row). For in spite of beginner's faults they show a novelist on
the way up. In all Steinbeck's novels written before 1940 myth has a
dynamic function. Thoroughly integrated with the narrative theme, it
serves to interpret reality and to explode romantic illusion; in later novels
the myth is externally imposed on the material in an attempt to achieve
the same results.

(K)   John Fontenrose. *John Steinbeck: An Introduction*
> *and Interpretation* (Barnes and Noble). 1963. p. 141

A few years ago it was popular to speculate on "what had happened" to Steinbeck, and some interesting answers were proposed: Steinbeck had lost touch with the country and with California, and the new urban and urbane life of New York was insufficient to fill his well; the death of Edward Ricketts (his close friend) had been such a personal blow to Steinbeck that his creative powers were affected; Steinbeck's ideology had changed, and the new Steinbeck had nothing to say; success had "spoiled" Steinbeck. However, even though some of these answers are still being given, an increasing number of critics seem to be turning to an answer given long ago by Steinbeck's detractors: that no decline in fact exists, that Steinbeck's talents, in his earlier period, were simply overrated by those who believed in the causes Steinbeck championed. . . . Once, much of the early work—certainly *The Grapes of Wrath* and *Of Mice and Men,* and possibly *In Dubious Battle* and several short pieces—seemed certain of a place in American fiction; now, it seems necessary to restate their claim to attention. Some of these pieces—especially the "worker" novels— are still taught in the college classroom, but already (despite the work of such critics as Peter Lisca and Warren French) there is danger of their becoming known as period pieces; again (as when it first appeared) Steinbeck's work needs to be defended as art rather than sociology.

(K)   J. P. Hunter in *Essays in Modern American Literature,* edited by Richard E. Langford (Stetson). 1963. pp. 76–7

Steinbeck, to state the matter simply, is another writer who is a victim of his own success. Tragedy is not the word for it because Steinbeck still is a sensitive, skilful writer, and in his sixties he may yet surpass himself. What seems apparent in summing up the last decade of his career is that for some time there have been two Steinbecks. A comparison of his last two books, *The Winter of Our Discontent* (1961) and *Travels with Charley in Search of America* (1962), makes this clear. One Steinbeck is the older version of the artist-social critic who wrote *The Grapes of Wrath,* and the other is the pot-boiling journalist who writes for the *Saturday Evening Post* and *Holiday.* Twenty-five years ago there was only Steinbeck the writer. This was a man so determined to have his books speak for themselves that he refused to supply publicity material for Alexander Woollcott's radio program. In the recent years of Steinbeck's decline the journalist-hostage-to-royalty-statements has produced most of the books issued over the Steinbeck signature.

(K)   James Woodress. *SAQ.* Summer, 1964. p. 386

Looking over Steinbeck's career, one is forced to accept a paradox. His earlier novels, although based on an image of man almost purely biological and naturalistic, succeed in exploring and giving new significance to those aspects which in the hands of earlier naturalistic writers had resulted only in the degrading of man. Furthermore, this biological image of man created for itself techniques and aspects of form capable of conveying this image of man with esthetic power and conviction. On the other hand, when Steinbeck abandons his earlier viewpoint and attempts to project an image of man based on such more conventional notions as Christian morality and ethical integrity he cannot seem to say anything significant. And, deprived of pervasive naturalistic metaphor, the formal qualities of that fiction become no better, and in some ways inferior, to those of many writers whose endowments are not nearly so formidable as his own.

(K)   Peter Lisca. *MFS*. Spring, 1965. p. 10

As far as the central narrative about the education of the Joads is concerned, *The Grapes of Wrath* is not even truly what I have defined as a social novel. It stresses the achievement of individualism as much as the works of Thomas Wolfe and depicts the necessity of each individual's educating and reforming himself, rather than the causes of a national disaster. If the Joads had not been caught up in the events of a particular time and place that had profoundly affected Steinbeck and troubled his public, we might more easily recognize that their story belongs with Shakespeare's *The Tempest* and other masterpieces of the travail and triumph of the human spirit.

(K)   Warren G. French. *The Social Novel at the End of
                                  an Era* (Southern Illinois). 1966. p. 44

Yet even by the early 40s, certain recurring elements in his fiction had been identified and explored. A concern for common, human values, for warmth, love, and understanding, led to a view of Steinbeck the sentimentalist. The social relevance of some of his writing revealed him as a reformer. His tender evocation of the land itself, his celebration of its fertility and of his characters' concern for the bringing forth of life, implied an interest first called "primitive" and then seen as "mythic." His capacity to make both his characters and his country come alive was traced to his increasing mastery of vernacular as a counter-weight to the sonorous, almost mystical, rhythms of his frequently incantatory language. Finally, his explicit discussion, in *The Sea of Cortez,* of what he called "non-teleological thinking" confirmed what for many had been the primary motif of his fictional writing, his conception of man as a biological mechanism, purposeless as well as animal-like.

(K)   Pascal Covici, Jr. in *The Thirties,* edited by Warren
                                  French (Everett Edwards). 1967. p. 48

See *Tortilla Flat, In Dubious Battle, Of Mice and Men, Grapes of Wrath, Cannery Row, The Wayward Bus,* and *East of Eden* (novels); also *The Long Valley* (short stories).

STEVENS, WALLACE (1879–1955)

Stevens is precise among the shyest, most elusive of movements and shadings. He sees distinctly by way of delicacy the undulations of the pigeon sinking downward, the darkening of a calm under water-lights, the variations of the deep-blue tones in dusky landscapes. Quite as regularly as the colors themselves, it is their shades of difference that are registered by him. . . . Yet this fastidious, aristocratic nature possesses a blunt power of utterance, a concentrated violence, that is almost naturalistic. . . . But sensation alone is liberated to new intensity by Stevens's forms. Emotion, on the contrary, is curiously constrained by them within a small range of experience and small volume of expression. . . . Stevens's rhythms are chiefly secondary rhythms. Scarcely ever is his attack a direct and simple one. Generally, it is oblique, patronizing and twisted with self-intended mockery.

Paul Rosenfeld. Men Seen (Dial). 1925. pp. 152–5

Wallace Stevens gains elegance in large measure by his fastidiously chosen vocabulary and by the surprising aplomb and blandness of his imagery. He will say "harmonium" instead of "small organ," "lacustrine" instead of "lakeside," "sequin" instead of "spangle"; he will speak of "hibiscus," "panache," "fabliau," and "poor buffo." The whole tendency of his vocabulary is, in fact, toward the lightness and coolness and transparency of French, into which tongue he sometimes glides with cultivated ease.

Gorham Munson. Destinations (Sears). 1928. p. 81

Stevens is more than a dandy, a designer, and esthete. Each of these persons is a phase of a central person, each a mask in a masquerade at the heart of which philosophy and tragi-comedy view the world with serenity. If the earth is a tawdry sphere, America a tawdry land, the relation of human to human the most tawdry of all, Stevens refuses to despair. . . . Behind the veils there is always a meaning, though the poet employs supersubtlety for veiling the meaning as well. No one hates the obvious more. No one knows better than he that all these things have been felt and thought and known before. One can only improvise on material used over and over again and improvise for oneself alone.

Alfred Kreymborg. Our Singing Strength (Coward-
McCann). 1929. pp. 501–2

(Stevens) give us, I believe, the most perfect laboratory of hedonism to be found in literature. He is not like those occasional poets of the Renaissance who appear in some measure to be influenced by a pagan philosophy, but who in reality take it up as a literary diversion at the same time that they are beneath the surface immovably Christian. Stevens is released from all the restraints of Christianity, and is encouraged by all the modern orthodoxy of Romanticism: his hedonism is so fused with Romanticism as to be merely an elegant variation of that somewhat inelegant System of Thoughtlessness. His ideas have remained essentially unchanged for more than a quarter of a century, and on the whole they have been very clearly expressed, so that there is no real occasion to be in doubt as to their nature; and he began as a great poet, so that when we examine the effect of those ideas upon his work, we are examining something of very great importance.

Yvor Winters. The Anatomy of Nonsense (Alan
Swallow). 1943. p. 119

Wallace Stevens lives in a world from which the elemental, the supernatural, and the mythical have been drained, and in which the deeper instincts of the human race are consequently starving. Somehow, by his own mind and senses, man must find sustenance, must make terms with air and earth, must establish some relation between himself and the world about him. . . . Whether expressed in the splendor and gaudiness of *Harmonium,* or in the more restrained, more abstract verse of his latest volume, the answer is the same. It lies in the cultivation of sensibility and in the affirmation of that sensibility through works of the human imagination. . . . He is not merely the poetic dandy that he has been called. His interest in the precisions of poetic technique arises from what we might call his dedication to the mission of the poet in the modern world.

Louis L. Martz in Modern American Poetry, edited by
B. Rajan (Harcourt). 1952. pp. 94–6, 108

The liveliness of his interest, the depth of his concern, the intensity and subtlety of his connoisseurship are alike directed to what the imagination can make of our physical, factual pluriverse. "Piece the world together, boys, but not with your hands," he enjoins us. And proceeds to show us the how of it. He considers a snow man, a mountain, two pears on a dish, a man reading, a woman looking at a vase of flowers, particulars peculiar to a certain occasion in Hartford, in Florida. Speaking of these, delighting in their suggestiveness, communicating his own private exhilaration, he presents the quality of a given hour, the genius of a place, the scene and its habitants, the climates and weathers of the soul. As a result, the reader enjoys the liberating experience of a traveler: he is allowed to make the exotic to some extent his own; he learns to clothe with becoming strangeness what is native and intimate. . . . It is all a matter of words. Occasionally it is a matter of non-words. Some of Stevens's most celebrated poems are composed in traditional metrics or in free cadences to which we have long been accustomed. They are saved from monotony by his fine ear and by the fact that his vocabulary is singularly personal. It moves between colloquial speech and what he calls the "poet's gibberish," this last a dazzling medley of allusive, witty, half-foreign resonances and purely aural titillations.

> Babette Deutsch. *NYHT*. Oct. 3, 1954. p. 3

In a sense . . . Wallace Stevens has spent a lifetime writing a single poem. What gives his best work its astonishing power and vitality is the way in which a fixed point of view, maturing naturally, eventually takes in more than a constantly shifting view could get at.

The point of view is romantic, "almost the color of comedy"; but "the strength at the center is serious."

> Samuel French Morse. *NYT*. Oct. 3, 1954. p. 3

The starting point of Stevens's poems is often the aesthetic experience in isolation from all other experiences, as art is isolated from work, and as a museum is special and isolated in any modern American community. And if one limits oneself to the surface of Stevens's poetic style, one can characterize Stevens as the poet of the Sunday: the poet of the holiday, the week-end and the vacation, who sees objects at a distance, as they appear to the tourist or in the art museum. But this is merely the poet's starting point. Stevens converts aestheticism into contemplation in the full philosophical and virtually religious sense of the word.

> Delmore Schwartz. *NR*. Nov. 1, 1954. p. 16

Opulence—it is the quality which most of us, I expect, ascribe before all others to the poetry of Wallace Stevens: profusion, exotic abundance, and luxuriance. We carry in our minds an image of poems which teem with rich, strange, somehow forbidden delights, omnifarious and prodigious. . . . Stevens is Elizabethan in his attitude towards language, highhanded in the extreme. . . . Stevens is the delighted craftsman whose delight is, in part, the access of gratification which comes upon the exercise of mastery. His pleasure is endless because it is part of his work, past and present; it is transmissable because we too, in reading his poems, share that mastery.

> Hayden Carruth. *Poetry*. Feb., 1955. pp. 288–92

It is clearly too soon to estimate the value of Stevens's poems with justice, and nothing short of a detailed essay would make plausible what will surely seem personal and an over-estimation, my own conviction that the more than 500 pages of Stevens's *Collected Poems* makes a book as important as *Leaves of Grass*. The very charm and beauty of Stevens's language mislead the reader often: delighted with the tick and tock, the heigh ho of Hoon and Jocundus, "jubilating," "in the presto of the morning," the reader often missed the basic substance, the joy that for the moment at least the poet has grasped "the veritable *ding an sich* at last": for Stevens was essentially a philosophical poet, the rarest of all kinds, seeking always "in a good light for those who know the ultimate Plato," to see and possess "the nothing that is not there, and the nothing that is."

The primary philosophical motive leads to a major limitation—the meditative mode is a solitude which excludes the dramatic and narrative poet's human character and personality. But it also leads to a great access: Stevens, studying Picasso and Matisse, made the art of poetry visual in a way it had never been before, and made him the first poet to be influenced, very often in the same poem, by Shakespeare, Cubism, the Symbolist movement, and modern philosophy since Kant.

Delmore Schwartz. NR. Aug. 22, 1955. pp. 21–2

Technically Stevens was not, as were many of his contemporaries, an experimentalist. He did not write staid classroom lines that can be regularly scanned, but they lie, for all that, in regular units of 2s and 3s and 4s quite according to custom. There is an intrinsic order which they follow with a satisfying fidelity which makes them indefinably musical, often strongly stressed by Stevens, his signature.

His is not strictly speaking a colloquial diction, but there are especially in his later works no inversions of phase, "for poetic effect," no deformities of the normal syntax.

William Carlos Williams. Poetry. Jan., 1956.
pp. 235–6

One of the fascinating questions about the life and work of Wallace Stevens concerns the connection between his successful business career, as vice-president of the Hartford Accident and Indemnity Company, and his poems. At first glance it seems incredible that these particular poems . . . so full of references to painting and sculpture and music, to faraway places and figures of fantasy, should have been written by a man who spent his days dealing with the intricacies of insurance law. But a closer reading of his work suggests that there is no essential paradox after all. Stevens is a man completely at home in his environment; he lives in modern city society without any impulse to overturn or to escape. He is, indeed, the singer of suburban life.

Partly because some of his well-known early poems picture the tropical luxuriance of Cuba or Florida or Mexico, relatively little attention has been paid to the fact that he habitually refers to the New England land-

scape in writing about the nature of reality. Still less noticed is the fact
that he describes the kind of natural world enjoyed by the man who lives
in a town or suburb—who has a lawn on which crickets sing and rabbits
sit at dusk, a hedge of lilac and dogwood, a park nearby where he can
watch the swans on the lake, and a summer vacation when he can go
abroad or get to the New Hampshire hills or the coast of Maine.

Elizabeth Green. SR. Aug. 11, 1956. p. 11

O my people, burn, burn back to grace!
. . . But a light blinked and the business fronts fell past us;
a religion of chromium and plate glass windows
raising its monstrances of golden junk

called the dead poet from his imaginings:
"Soit!" he chimed back from the pixie passion
that made his belltowers tinkle as they bonged.
'Waa-wallee-waa!", the whistle learned to say.
. . .
By bong and tinkle he dwarfed back the fronts
of the age's skew and sooty imagination.
Now he is dead; one gone of the three truest*
and poverty, drowned in money, cannot care.

John Ciardi. SR. Aug. 11, 1956. p. 13

* STEVENS, FROST, W. C. WILLIAMS.

In *Harmonium,* published in the Scott Fitzgerald decade, Stevens moves
in a highly sensuous atmosphere of fine pictures, good food, exquisite
taste and luxury cruises. In the later poems, though the writing is as
studiously oblique as ever, the sensuousness has largely disappeared, and
the reader accustomed only to *Harmonium* may feel that Stevens' inspiration has failed him, or that he is attracted by themes outside his capacity,
or that the impact of war and other ironies of the autumnal vision has shut
him up in an uncommunicative didacticism. Such a view of Stevens is of
course superficial, but the critical issue it raises is a genuine one. . . . When
we meet a poet who has so much rhetorical skill, and yet lays so much
emphasis on novelty and freshness of approach, the skill acquires a quality
of courage: a courage that is without compromise in a world full of cheap
rhetoric, yet uses none of the ready-made mixes of rhetoric in a world full
of compromise. . . . It was persistence that transformed the tropical lush-
ness of *Harmonium* into the austere clairvoyance of *The Rock,* the luxurious demon into the necessary angel, and so rounded out a vision of major
scope and intensity.

(K)   Northrop Frye. *HdR*. Autumn, 1957. pp. 368–70

The predominant quality of Stevens' verse—with its extensive vocabulary, metrical dexterity, and relationship of sense and sound—is eloquence. He is the master of two styles, one epigrammatic, eccentric, teasing; the other exalted and rhetorical in the manner of Wordsworth, in which his words have the ring of authority and command. His language is written partly for its own sake, although his rhetoric always suits the mood in which it is spoken. Besides the wide variety of sound effects and his use of colors as symbols, color and sound are used also in a more general way to evoke a mood or provide a sensual background for the flights of thought. . . . Stevens' acute sense of color and sound becomes part of a larger awareness of the sensual as a principle, a force, and of physical life as the setting in which thought and imagination thrive.

(K)   Robert Pack. *Wallace Stevens: An Approach to His*
                             Poetry and Thought (Rutgers). 1958. pp. 4–5

. . . Stevens' quest for an ultimate humanism (for that surely is what it is) leads him toward a curious dehumanization. It urges (or forces) him in the end to purify his poems until they are hardly the poems of a man who lives, loves, hates, creates, dies. Rather, they are the poems of a man who does nothing but make poems; who "abstracts" living, loving, hating, creating, dying from his poems, in the hope that what will be left will be not so much poetry but the possibility of poetry. What saves the poems for humanity is the fact that such dehumanization develops in the process of searching for the ground of the very things of which they must be bereft if the search is to be carried on—their humanity. Thus the poems are incomplete, not finished but finishing, not perfected but perfecting.

(K)   Roy Harvey Pearce. *The Continuity of American*
                             Poetry (Princeton). 1961, 1965. p. 413

Accepting the condition of uncertainty and solitariness as unavoidable once man has freed himself from the gods, Stevens poses as his ultimate question not, what shall we do about the crisis of belief, but rather, how shall we live with and perhaps beyond it? And one reason for thinking of Stevens as a comic poet is that he makes this choice of questions.

How shall we live with and then perhaps beyond the crisis of belief?— it is to confront this question that Stevens keeps returning to the theme of reality and imagination. Not merely because he is interested in epistemological forays as such—though he is; nor because he is fascinated with the creative process—though that too; but because his main concern is with discovering and, through his poetry, *enacting* the possibilities for human self-renewal in an impersonal and recalcitrant age.

(K)   Irving Howe. *A World More Attractive* (Horizon).
                             1963. p. 163

One way of putting it is that Stevens, who ceased to believe in the God of Christianity and found that there was nothing left to believe, filled the void with his own inventions. Another way of putting it is that when Stevens ceased to be a Christian he lost all the valid terminologies of action and knew that he could recover them—if at all—only by playing a part in a fictive drama of his own devising. Sometimes this was a comic part, as in "A High-Toned Old Christian Woman," sometimes it was the philosopher-king, sometimes Prospero—he had a large repertoire. The greatest role he would devise for himself would be God; the most splendid drama, a new creation; and he would play all the parts himself. His play would be called "The Supreme Fiction."

(K)   Denis Donoghue. *Connoisseurs of Chaos*
                                        (Macmillan). 1965. pp. 200–1

I take it as the common experience in reading Stevens that one first finds a surface incredibly bizarre and seemingly impenetrable. Later, in the wish for simple coherence, the critic is tempted to look at Stevens' figures as an assemblage of counters in a rather abstract, doctrinal scheme. However, when the serious critic examines these figures more closely, he is aware of aspects of them which consistently undercut, in a conscious, ironic fashion, the doctrinal substance which other aspects of them are intended to bear. . . . [Stevens] passionately believed in the power of the imagination to make at least a momentary order out of chaos by means of metaphor, but he saw clearly that such an irrational order can have only transitory value. The imagination is seen as both God and fake. Thus his vital figures, almost by reflex action, have two aspects—one of value, one of nothingness.

(K)   Eugene Paul Nassar. *Wallace Stevens: An Anatomy of*
                           Figuration (Pennsylvania). 1965. pp. 13, 19

Stevens' later mode begins in the thirties in long poems like "Owl's Clover" and "The Man with the Blue Guitar," seeking to establish poetry at the center of experience and man at the center of reality; continues in the forties with ambitious examinations of the supreme possibilities of poetry in realizing the human aspiration to know beyond his world and yet to live within its vulgarity and violence; and concludes in the quiet eloquence of an almost purely contemplative poetry that illustrates how introspective exiles not only exist in the mind but create themselves there. . . . From the poems in the late thirties, which aspired to express the "idea of man" as creator of reality, to the very last ones, which seek not the surface but the very "rock" of reality, the direction of Stevens' poetry is inward.

(K)   Joseph N. Riddel. *The Clairvoyant Eye*
                                        (Louisiana State). 1965. p. 48

No one reads Stevens daily for a decade, as I have, without remarking upon the constant irony of diction and syntax as well as the more obvious irony of Stevens' personae and of his imagery. But a qualified assertion remains an assertion. . . . There are passages in "An Ordinary Evening in New Haven" that are the purest Shelley, and Stevens is at his most Romantic when he appears to be most wintry, when he qualifies and hastens the most. . . . We need to thrust aside utterly, once and for all, the critical absurdities of the Age of Eliot, before we can see again how complex the Romantics were in their passionate ironies, and see fully how overwhelmingly Stevens and [Hart] Crane are their inheritors and continuators, as they are of Emerson and Whitman as well.

(K)   Harold Bloom. *MR*. Winter, 1966. p. 37

Stevens' naturalism is immediately apparent in the basic mythic vision of nature as woman whether mother or beloved. The apparent duality of mind and world that permeates his poetry may seem, in a superficial view, to be at variance with a naturalistic conception of things; but mind in Stevens, as in Schopenhauer or Santayana, is only nature looking at itself. If the world exists as it is only in a particular experience of it, if the world that we know is a conceived world, the one who conceives is only a part of that world. His nature is her nature; or, to state the figure in an abstraction, the subject is part of the object.

(K)   Frank Doggett in *The Twenties: Poetry and Prose,*
                        edited by Richard E. Langford and William E. Taylor
                                        (Everett Edwards). 1966. p. 41

See *The Collected Poems;* also *The Necessary Angel* (essays).

STICKNEY, TRUMBULL (1874–1904)

The poems of Trumbull Stickney . . . are open to no charge of carelessness in form, the author's natural tendency and severe training in Paris . . . having led him toward the most sensitive rhythms, the most delicate choice of words, and the passionate workmanship of the artist to whom the thing done and not the intention is the mighty matter. . . . In Mr. Stickney's lines dwell all the delicacy and reticences of the New England mood, with the lovely color and flowing line of the early Italian picture makers like whom Rossetti fain would have been and like whom he never was.

NYT. April 28, 1906. p. 277

Promise rather than fulfillment is the mark of this work as a whole, for it reveals Stickney as still groping for a distinctive manner rather than as having reached a definitive expression of his powers. Reviewing his first volume, we were compelled to speak of its "jarring staccato," its "far-fetched epithets," and "its endeavor to be impressive at the cost of clear thinking and verbal restraint." The "Later Lyrics" now first printed show us the process of fermentation still at work, but serve also to deepen our sense of the poet's possibilities.

William M. Payne. Dial. Feb. 16, 1906. p. 125

He hovered—not only in the last year of his life, but always in the twelve years of writing of which we have record—constantly on the perilous balance where it is determined whether a man write sound verse or dilute his emotions in words. It is a question, often, of unconscious interest or purpose. Should he lose his emotions in words which express them adequately only because they are conventionally accepted as expressive, or should he use words to create emotions? . . . He wanted to do difficult things in the establishment of precise feelings and the presentation of sharp images. Often—and this is the search that makes long reading worth the labor—he succeeded in single lines and phrases. Even in the worst poems, the most lavishly tenuous and repetitious, the most poetic and most licensed, where *his* becomes *'s*, and *kissed* is *kisséd*, there are sudden, desperately illuminating phrases.

R. P. Blackmur. Poetry. June, 1933. pp. 159, 162

This son [George Cabot Lodge] of Senator Lodge had studied in Berlin and Paris, where he met Trumbull Stickney, who, born in Switzerland and brought up largely in Europe, later returned to Harvard as instructor in Greek. Both felt that they were Greeks born out of time. Stickney, whom Henry Adams knew in Paris, and who studied six years at the Sorbonne, was the first Anglo-Saxon who was ever awarded a doctorate in literature there. He wrote a Greek play, *Prometheus Pyrphoros,* and most of his work was distinguished, although it resounded, like Lodge's, with Victorian echoes. What, in the eighteen-nineties, could odes to Greek liberty mean except that one knew Walter Savage Landor? . . . [T]here was something autumnal and sad in Lodge's note and Trumbull Stickney's, too little native hue, too much pale thought.

Van Wyck Brooks. New England: Indian Summer
(Dutton). 1950. pp. 457–8. [1940]

This spareness and accuracy of language that carries a charge of meaning is quite unlike the decadent romanticism which reigned at the end of the century. . . . And this was what Stickney could do that was really authentic and impressive. You find often, as with Walter Savage Landor, that he will end a blurred or feeble poem with a clear minting of syllables. . . .

What is behind the best poetry of Stickney is a conflict between the desired and the possible which is felt in a more serious way than the usual wistfulness of the nineties. It is evidently one of those New England conflicts such as we get in the heroes of Henry James: the struggle of the appetite to live in resistance to cramped habits and a dead tradition. . . . And thus many of Stickney's most effective images—the soldered eyelids, the slanted door, the girl who closes her window, the desolated country of childhood —represent the poet as excluded from some source of vitality or beauty.

Edmund Wilson. *The Bit Between My Teeth* (Farrar).
1965. pp. 111–13. [*NR*. Oct. 14, 1940]

But if individual lines and stanzas revive a personality precociously gifted in its sensibility to an elegiac note in poetry (which is a classical heritage that British and American literature has carried from the past into our own day) what of the entire poems in Stickney's posthumously published volume? It is there that the shadow falls and it is there that the enthusiastic reader meets with disappointment. His poems, viewed as completed poems within themselves, show flaws of heady rhetoric and histrionic gestures that without the "beautiful gray eyes and sad, bewildered face" of their author distract the reader and leave him with the feeling that the sight of Stickney's inspiration vanished almost as soon as his pen struck paper. . . . His gifts were so lavish and his personal attractions so evident that there was apparently no need to sacrifice their immediate rewards to the demands of "a single talent, well employed." . . .

Horace Gregory and Marya Zaturenska. *A History of
American Poetry, 1900–1940* (Harcourt). 1946.
pp. 36–7

A scholar of the utmost brilliance, he took the first *doctorat ès lettres* ever given to an American or Englishman by the University of Paris; and he was described after his death by a Harvard friend as "the most cultivated man I have ever known." Stickney's *Dramatic Verses* was published in 1902. A posthumous volume, *Poems* (1905), edited by George Cabot Lodge, Moody, and others shows a poetic quality firmly his own. The melancholy of "Mnemosyne," with its subtle variation of refrain, is unforgettable; other stanzas, single lines, and complete poems must remain in the memory of the sensitive reader. Stickney broke with no traditions; but his quality is impressively pure, and, both as a man and an artist, he is the one American of his day who belongs to the world of finely tempered human beings with which, in the same period, Henry James in his last great phase was occupying himself.

Louise Bogan. *Achievement in American Poetry,
1900–1950* (Henry Regnery). 1951. pp. 31–2

The image of the earth as a dark habitation possessed Stickney. He resisted surrender to the decadent view which attracted him strongly in Paris only by cultivating assiduously an outlook derived from his classical studies, that of the Stoic. He was keenly aware of the discrepancy between the optimistic proclamations of the Social Darwinists and the actual degrading human conditions which resulted from the applications of the new technology, seeing only a bitter outcome. His observations reinforced the view of history of his friend Henry Adams, whose characteristic pessimism he shared. Since the nature of man's destiny was so bleak, Stickney the Stoic concentrated on the manner in which it was met, insisting on magnanimity even in defeat.

Large philosophical questions about the nature of man and his relation to his destiny absorbed Stickney, and he sought vehicles for their expression in classic myths or in abstractions of his own experience. He could not turn to the anti-poetic of Whitman, because this indeed was linked in his mind with the science and commerce which had smashed values. As a result he remained trapped within the house of tradition, searching for some way to make its furniture function for modern use.

Larzer Ziff. *The American 1890s* (Viking). 1966.
p. 314

Stickney had a pronounced interest—perhaps it amounted to an obsession —in time; there are only a few of his poems in which this interest is not found. It is somewhat surprising that the importance of this recurrent theme has escaped critical attention. The most conspicuous time-theme has to do with the effect of the past upon the present—its ability to provide consolation in the midst of the troubled present through recall of experiences and images; this theme develops into a romantic aestheticism and is found in some of Stickney's best poems. But the poet was too much a realist to ignore that other side of the coin: memories of past experiences can sometimes cause us sorrow in the present, because either a state of achieved happiness has been lost forever, or an opportunity for happiness has been lost. Through the uses of memory, then, the past constantly modifies the present.

Amberys R. Whittle. *SwR*. Autumn, 1966. p. 900

See *The Poems of Trumbull Stickney*

STYRON, WILLIAM (1925–   )

The brilliant lyric power of William Styron's *Lie Down in Darkness* derives from the richest resources of the Southern traditions. Although ostensibly a story of psychological and moral breakdown, it is primarily a novel of place and must be judged in terms of its successful evocation of place. Like his best older contemporaries, Faulkner and Warren, Styron possesses a poetic sensibility of the very highest order. Through it he is able to respond to and project back into language those intricate relationships between natural setting and human agony which, at least since Hardy's heath and Conrad's sea, have formed the heart of our greatest fiction.

In fact, so completely does Styron dramatize these relationships that one feels justified in saying that the Southern landscape against which the action is portrayed is the most successfully realized character in the novel.

John W. Aldridge. *NYT*. Sept. 8, 1951. p. 5

Despite its echoes of familiar authors, *Lie Down in Darkness* is satisfying work. It is planned with mature intelligence, it is written in a style everywhere competent and sometimes superb, and its slow and powerful stream is fed by insights into human beings beyond the capacity of better-known novelists. . . . Mr. Styron has fertility of imagination, he knows how to manage a long novel, and in the economy of his tale he proves himself a craftsman of the first water. . . . And though no system of morality can be explicitly drawn from these pages, Mr. Styron believes there is a moral law. Few recent writers have had the courage of this affirmation, and few have had the capacity to mingle beauty, wisdom and narrative art as he has done.

Howard Mumford Jones. *NYHT*. Sept. 9, 1951. p. 3

I should say at once that *Lie Down in Darkness* is a remarkable and fascinating novel—the best novel of the year by my standards—and one of the few completely human and mature novels published since the Second World War. . . . The story itself moves on several levels at once, as all good novels do; the characters, like images seen through a prism, are reflected from every side until the distortions of their personality are finally resolved in not their own view of themselves but the novelist's central and sympathetic view of them. But Mr. Styron is particularly good on the visual level of his craft; we are *at* all these ghastly parties, ceremonials, the festivals of a middle-class business society that has inherited the trappings of the planter aristocracy. . . . The writing itself, graceful and delicate, is rigorously controlled as the medium through which the story is revealed—not as a medium for its author's personality .

Maxwell Geismar. *SR*. Sept. 15, 1951. pp. 12–13

Lie Down in Darkness starts out a bleak and black book and it ends up as one; there is no catalyst here. That is why I have no affection for it.

I am profoundly aware, though, that in wanting to cite its perhaps inevitable defects, I have placed my criticism in an improper focus.

For example, the book is not bleakly written. On the contrary, it is richly and even (in the best sense) poetically written. . . . If . . . there exists a fugitive sense that the author has gone to Joyce for his structure and to Faulkner for his rhetoric, it is only fugitive and consequently intelligent and probably assimilated. Not least among its virtues, the novel is deeply absorbing. It is a basically mature, substantial, and enviable achievement, powerful enough to stay with you after you have shut it out.

Harvey Breit. *At.* Oct., 1951. pp. 79–80

William Styron . . . has tasted and—to his credit—very nearly digested a number of writers of what might be called the "stream of words" tradition: notably Thomas Wolfe, James Joyce and William Faulkner.

Yet from what at first appears as chaos he has subtly evolved a pattern. As form the pattern is the elaborate and skillful use of flashback: the minute advance of a funeral procession while memory strips back the life now ended. As subject the pattern clarifies once again into the theme of the sterility of modern life: this time in Tidewater, Virginia and in a family less intellectual than country club.

Ruth Chapin. *CSM*. Oct. 4, 1951. p. 15

Many of the new writers have been learning their craft from William Faulkner; that is among the leading tendencies of the day; but I can't think of any other novel that applies the lessons so faithfully, or, for that matter, with so much natural authority and talent. . . . It is a general rule that novels which stay close to their literary models have no great value of their own, but *Lie Down in Darkness* is an exception; in this case the example of Faulkner seems to have had a liberating effect on Styron's imagination. One might even say that his book is best and most personal when it is most Faulknerian.

Malcolm Cowley. *NR*. Oct. 8, 1951. pp. 19–20

Mr. Styron is twenty-six, a year or so younger than Mann was when he published *Buddenbrooks*. His first novel, *Lie Down in Darkness,* is a book of astonishing stature, as mature in conception as the work which now seems in the perspective of fifty years to have been so clear a harbinger of Mann's future achievement.

This is naturally not to say that Styron is, or will become, a great novelist—fifty years being about the shortest period in which such judgments can be hazarded. But *Lie Down in Darkness* suggests that his talents are equal to it, if he has luck and energy and capacity for growth to match. It ranks him at once as a member, and by no means the least considerable member, of that distinguished group of Southern writers whose names are generally headed by Faulkner and Wolfe.

Margaret Wallace. IW. Nov., 1951. p. 325

One would . . . welcome some insight into the expanding area . . . of comfort and complacency. . . . Is it possible to say *No* without ignoring the comfortable reality? One way is indicated by William Styron's fine story "Long March" which appeared in *discovery No. 1*. Styron focuses on the experience of several reserve officers recalled to duty during the Korean emergency, and so he manages to place our flannel-suited careers in some historical perspective. He provides only one or two quick glimpses of domestic contentment, but since they are set against a panorama of remorseless military idiocy, they take on a wonderfully delicate power. To these men suddenly back in combat dress our lives between wars seem but a childish revery—placid, mindless, comfortably unreal.

Leo Marx. NR. Oct. 31, 1955. p. 20

As one reads and ponders *Set This House on Fire,* it becomes increasingly plain, in fact, that what Styron has undertaken, and what he has in large part achieved, is nothing less than a rendition of national mood dramatized in terms of powerful characters of fiction. It is this, I think, which sets his novel above the ample shelves of those other serious-minded novels of the 1950's, so competent, so assured, so modest. What one senses as he finishes *Set This House on Fire* is an encounter with a greatly gifted writer —but there are many of great gifts—who has laboriously picked up the pieces of his gifts and his training and his torment and swept them into effective unity. There is no hedge in *Set This House on Fire*. Styron took his chances with this novel; it could have been a catastrophe, but happily it was not. Styron has undertaken the major effort which American critics have blandly urged on so many other skilful craftsmen in the past few years—O'Hara, Steinbeck, Marquand, Wescott—and which so seldom has been realized.

(K)   Charles A. Fenton. <i>SAQ</i>. Autumn, 1960. p. 475

Hailed in the press, *Lie Down In Darkness* was all but ignored by the quarterly reviews, when it was the quarterly reviews, not the Sunday book supplements, that *should* have recognized its worth. For William Styron was not and is not a "middlebrow" novelist; his work is in no way flashy and meretricious, but quite original. So that now, perhaps, the bad press he is getting in the dailies and weeklies will serve to emphasize this fact.

I had better admit my bias openly and at the start: to my mind Mr. Styron is the most impressive writer of fiction of his generation. *Lie Down In Darkness* was a remarkable novel, and *Set This House On Fire* is an even better novel. Indeed, so far as I am concerned it is like nothing else that has been written in the past decade, and deserves the respectful attention of anyone seriously interested in fiction—this despite a grievous structural flaw which in the hands of a less gifted author might have sufficed to spoil it entirely.

(K)   Louis D. Rubin. *SwR*. Winter, 1961. p. 175

Styron's characters who are destroyed or who destroy have, like the children of the Garden, fallen away from the golden age. What Styron calls the "miseries of our century" result from that "knowledge of the mechanicall arts," which is equated with civilized technology, urban areas like New York, the atom bomb and other instruments of war, and American materialism. We must endure these miseries of our time if our lives are to be anything more than meaningless vibrations lost in eternity. The children of modernity lack the strength necessary to endure because they have lost their simplicity. Endurance comes from a stoicism based upon innocence, faith, simplicity, which allows men . . . to bear their burdens. The paradox of the modern condition is apparent. The means whereby we might endure have disappeared during man's long flight into civilization, away from the bliss of the Garden of Eden or the reign of Saturn where innocent simplicity prevailed. The three novels which I shall discuss dramatize the despair of lost innocence and the hope which rises from the power to endure.

(K)   Jerry H. Bryant. *SAQ*. Autumn, 1963. pp. 540–1

"What's the matter with this world?" a nameless hillbilly singer chants dolefully at a propitious moment in *Set This House on Fire*. The singer, one of Styron's prophetic voices from other rooms, answers his own question: "Your soul's on sinking sand, the end is drawing near: That's what's the matter with this world. . . ." If anyone still wondered at this point why it had taken the author of *Lie Down in Darkness* eight years to complete his latest novel, these lines which inform the experience provide the explanation. Further indicative of Styron's attitude is that all of his sympathetic characters are alcoholics or reformed alcoholics as if he were unable to conceive of a sensitive human being who could withstand the nightmare of existence without the anesthetic of drink.

(K)   Jonathan Baumbach. *SAQ*. Spring, 1964. p. 215

Styron is, it may be concluded, no great moralist. *Set This House on Fire* is a safe and unctuous movie spectacular in the guise of a serious novel. It leaps nimbly from sensation to sensation—a bloody auto accident, a rape, a horrible disfiguring murder, a ghastly natural death in thrilling color, to mention a few—for all of which there will of course be an accounting, but oh what fun while they last, till over everything Styron can pour his shiny final lacquer of regeneration. The novel even has a part for an unutterably beautiful and virtuous Italian peasant girl, who must die so that the hero, having dallied with her (innocently!), can return to his imbecile spouse for the happy ending. It is an ignoble book.

(K)   Marvin Mudrick. *Hdr*. Autumn, 1964. p. 361

[*The Confessions of Nat Turner*] is the most profound fictional treatment of slavery in our literature. It is, of course, the work of a skilled and experienced novelist with other achievements to attest his qualifications. It is doubtful, however, if the rare combination of talents essential to this formidable undertaking, a flawless command of dialect, a native instinct for the subtleties and ambivalences of race in the South, and a profound and unerring sense of place—Styron's native place as it was Nat Turner's —could well have been found anywhere else.

(K)   C. Vann Woodward. *NR*. Oct. 7, 1967. p. 28

In literature, violence is still the sign of tragedy—of what is too much for us. This, I suspect, is why William Styron was drawn to make an imaginative narrative of his own out of Nat Turner's leadership of the 1831 slave revolt in Southampton County, Virginia; for Styron is preeminent among the "younger" American novelists in his instinct for tragedy and in his respect for the sheer force of human feeling. His first novel, *Lie Down in Darkness,* has remained with me for the expressiveness it brought to the theme of love's defeat. Although *Set This House on Fire* was too tense, and sputtered off in exasperating flights of rhetoric, it was clearly the work of a strong, serious Southern talent who had educated himself, as Southerners are still not afraid to do, to write in the language of human feeling. The Southern genius, in our time, has been to describe real defeats in a society made superficial by unreal success. . . . Othello would always have been strange to the Venetians, but what some of us want, what a Southern writer of Styron's moral urgency especially wants, is to dispel the strangeness, to show that Negro and white are kin. . . . But the real achievement of this beautiful, curious, essentially dreamlike narrative is something else. For Styron has fully imagined, he has been able to create with his honest sense of the tragic, a man whom the locked-up force of daily, hourly, constant suppression has turned into a Stranger—someone who remains single, separate, wholly other from ourselves and our notions.

(K)   Alfred Kazin. *Book World*. Oct. 8, 1967. pp. 1, 22

The message [of *The Confessions of Nat Turner*] seems to be that the Negro has every right to kill the white man, but cannot escape pollution in the process. The ending is covertly sentimental, one of those chins-up sad endings, and part of its effectiveness will be determined, as I say, by your view of the race question and the other and smaller part by whether the novel has worked with you as a novel.

And here we run into difficulties. There is no doubt that Turner is still worth writing and speculating about; but whether he can be successfully written about fictionally is another question. The historical novel is traditionally so clumsy a method of investigation that the reader usually winds up doubting whether the characters ever existed at all, in any form. And Styron has only exaggerated the difficulties by telling his story in the first person. . . .

To enrich the cramped psyche of his narrator, Styron has simply inserted endless chunks of his own nature writing—some of the best nature writing going, but largely irrelevant to the narrative and to Nat's focus at the particular moment. Important dramatic scenes are interrupted time and again for the sake of long weather and crop reports, almost as if the author's own attention had wandered. Worse, the weather is always just right for the scene: sultry for tension, cold for failure, etc. We even have clouds passing over the sun on cue. . . .

But if the book fails by default, as a novel, it does succeed in many places as a kind of historical tone poem.

(K)   Wilfred Sheed. *NYT*. Oct. 8, 1967. pp. 2–3

See *Lie Down in Darkness, The Long March, Set This House on Fire, The Confessions of Nat Turner* (novels).

SWADOS, HARVEY (1920–   )

So well is his story [*Out Went the Candle*] told, so perceptively, that is, has Mr. Swados imagined this man and devised means to place him fully before us, that we put the book down with something like a sense of knowledge. In his simplicity and complexity Herman Felton comes through to us, not just as one more character in one more novel, but as a human being, admirable, pitiable, and above all, understood.

Patrick F. Quinn. *Com*. Jan. 14, 1955. p. 412

Swados is fair, honest and gifted with insight, also he is a man of taste. This taste is apparent in his refusal to melodramatize and over-write.

His book [*On the Line*] is full of small details which reveal how much the union has accomplished positively in easing the lives of the men, men who do hard work. But his objectivity is unmarred and unbroken, and he conveys a sense of fate—the fate of those who work at de-sensitizing and psychologically-hurtful work in order that our prosperous society can maintain itself. His picture is disturbing. But what is disturbing is not a peculiarly American phenomenon: it is a disturbing feature of what we call progress. The machine has freed man from back-breaking labor. But the machine has also imposed a discipline of the clock on man which disturbs, distorts and even embitters his nature. This was one of the major insights of Thorstein Veblen in *The Instinct of Workmanship*. By artistic recreation, Swados has made emotionally comprehensible some of the best of Veblen's insights.

James T. Farrell. *NR*. Oct. 14, 1957. p. 17

Unlike many of today's able novelists, Swados does not deal with marginal figures [in *False Coin*] but introduces us to some of the giants of the age: to a philanthropist who speaks with pathos of his inherited millions; to a self-made expert on transportation, government affairs, and Vivaldi; to a manufacturer of items of feminine hygiene who is also a propagandist for women's rights; to a woman who rules a journalistic empire. The book is not, I think, a *roman à clef,* but we are reminded of people in the news, as, for the sake of verisimilitude, we should be. . . . The novel affirms not only that integrity is important but also that the artist cannot be free in our society, no matter what the beneficence of our rulers.

Granville Hicks. *SR*. Jan. 9, 1960. p. 12

Mr. Swados knows that powerful businessmen are often extremely intelligent, sociologists often impressive people, artists often weak and foolish, and up to a point [in *False Coin*] he makes his so. But at bottom he is committed to a belief in the supreme importance of artistic talent and to a conviction that the preservation of the artist's freedom is one of society's primary duties. He allows some of his characters to argue quite effectively against this view, but in the end we are to feel them wholly wrong, just as we are to feel the hero wholly right when he sacrifices his career to preserve the integrity of a work whose composer has already agreed to modify it for practical reasons. "I am buoyed," he observes when the battle is lost," "by the conviction that, although I wait in silence, I am not alone." Thus Mr. Swados' sense of life is complex only on the surface; underneath it is simple black and white. Nevertheless it is complex where a book of this kind most needs to be, and that is a considerable achievement, however much writers who fancy themselves above trying for it may scorn it.

Arthur Mizener. *SwR*. Winter, 1961. p. 156

Mr. Swados's style . . . is resolutely pedestrian. It has the metallic authority of a tape-recorder. This is how post-war men and women feel and converse during *Nights in the Gardens of Brooklyn*. Mr. Swados is an acute, scrupulous reporter of the crises of adjustment and solitude of those who came out of war to begin life and marriage in the big city. His stories deal with the moments of truth between human beings who did not quite realize when they started on love that diapers smell or that jobs can get scarce. Sometimes, the gray rectitude of Swados's vision ends in cliché: we *know* on page one of "Year of Grace" that the uneducated wife will ripen to humaneness while her Fulbright-scholar husband will wilt in the French sun. But in at least one instance, sheer directness of imagination yields a superb story. "The Letters" is a variation on the theme of Conrad's "Secret Sharer." With characteristic honesty, Swados even refers to Conrad. But his story has its own splendor and the climax leaves one numb.

George Steiner. *YR*. Spring, 1961. p. 425

A Radical's America is, as the title indicates, primarily a political and sociological book. In his Introduction, Mr. Swados mentions "the most important matters in the world, peace and racial integration," describes himself as an anti-liberal and anti-Stalinist socialist, and, preparing to denounce the first months of the Kennedy Administration, anathematizes "the professors and liberals who utilize the perversions of socialism as an excuse to capitulate to the bottomless hypocrisy of American capitalism." Fair enough (though we wince at the rhetoric) : he lets us know his exposed position, and holds it with angry consistency throughout the book. . . . Yet nobody appears in all these essays. They are written by a politician, not a novelist; they shout and grow indignant, or approve and are glad, at types, straw-men, cowardly academics, wicked critics and publishers, bad bosses, good workers.

Marvin Mudrick. *HdR*. Autumn, 1962. p. 441

A professed socialist, he is not very good as a defender of Marxist theory. The essays [in *A Radical's America*] written from a dogmatic angle for the party press are stunningly innocent of any serious doubts as to the potential rationality of human society. On most other subjects Mr. Swados is persuasive. He is good when he is contending against the complacent economics of affluence. His proofs that an authentic working class still exists and suffers are definitive. So are his studies in the malaise consequent upon non-working. As a critic of the intellectual life of America today he manages to be impressively monitory without sounding like a common scold. He doesn't cry "No in Thunder" like Leslie Fiedler and Jove. He is especially good in pointing to the historical roots of "anger," "guilt," "sex," and "self-advertisement" considered as literary staples.

F. W. Dupee. *Cmty*. Dec., 1962. p. 551

As a sensitive novelist, Swados must begin with concern for his characters; for, as he realizes, if we are to become interested in what society does to them, they, in turn, must be worth our caring. His central figure, Herman Felton, schemer, war profiteer, family man, uses the energies left over from his wheeling-dealing to shape the lives of his children. His girl, Betsy, his son, Morrow, both love and reject their father, and in their fury they seem bent on self-destruction. Joe Burley, the observer of the frightening family tensions, moves into their lives and becomes, in a positive sense, a third child of Herman's and Felton thus becomes a shabby, contemporary King Lear who must learn, too late, what he should always have known.

Out Went The Candle is Swados' best novel, and Felton is certainly his finest creation. We see him as explained by his children, as he might appear to casual observers, and, most interestingly of all, in his revealing letters to his daughter, strange cries of pain, love, arrogance, and confusion.

Charles Shapiro in Contemporary American Novelists,
edited by Harry T. Moore (Southern Illinois). 1964. p. 186

No one, reading Harvey Swados's latest novel, is likely to cry out, "Wild, man!" Sick wisdom, strange-loving burlesque, comic nihilism, hellerish fantasy, high-spirited nausea, so'thern jokes, olde-Yiddish vaudeville— these elements of recent fiction, taken in some quarters to be the last word in literary rebellion, are not to be found in *The Will*. Swados is an unfashionable writer, committed to the tradition of realism, in which it is assumed, as George Eliot remarks in *Felix Holt,* that, "There is no private life that has not been determined by a larger public life," and in which the novelist, by providing a faithful rendering of the social world, can also arrive at the elements of moral valuation. . . .

Traditional realism, to be sure, brings with it—especially at a time when the commonly shared sense of what our society is and does tends to be fuzzy—the risks of banal enumeration, passive recording, dispirited portraiture. But in *The Will* Swados has managed to show that if only the novelist is serious and humane enough, if only he is entirely committed to the terms of his enterprise, he can create versions of human existence that are binding and persuasive. Just as in Swados's journalism—he is one of the best labor reporters in the country—there is a fine gift for reaching to the human ache behind the "social problem," so in his better fiction he manages to affirm and validate the life *out there,* the experience which accumulates in perplexing and promiscuous abundance, even if intellectuals choose to ignore or dismiss it.

Irving Howe. Cmty. April, 1964. pp. 80–2

The stories [*A Story for Teddy and Others*] are in good part commemorations of youth. The one most frequent theme in them is the necessity of compassion, and the conscience of the growing boy is on every page. But not the cry of conscience grappled and possessed.

And this—this exhaustion, it must be called—is ironic because Harvey Swados manifestly is a writer who has all the honorable virtues. He is hard-working, thoughtful, sensitive, committed, and entirely serious. More than that, he is one of a very few serious novelists of the past decade who have dared even to conceive that fiction has a large moral function, that it might change society. In instances—*Out Went the Candle,* his first novel; the short stories of *On the Line;* his much-underestimated novel *False Coin* —he has all-but-uniquely discovered the mutual involvement in these times of private lives and public issues.

But you can't have a big self-sustaining issue every time out, and lacking one, Swados has obvious difficulties.

Marcus Klein. NYHT. Aug. 22, 1965. p. 9

The best stories in this collection [*A Story for Teddy*] concern the visions of youth as viewed from the vantage point of middle age. Whether describing his Coney Island Uncle or the hack writer who haunted his college days, Mr. Swados seems primarily concerned with his experience as recollected in some tranquility. The point, as in the rather touching title story, lies not in the events themselves but in the narrator's later understanding of them. . . . Unfortunately, the stories themselves *are* slight and they are saved only occasionally by our faith in the honesty and sensitivity of the author. Since the process of transformation is often left out of the stories the reader is sometimes left with the peculiar predicament of believing in Mr. Swados but not in his tales.

Paul Levine. HdR. Winter, 1965–66. p. 588

See *Out Went the Candle, False Coin, The Will* (novels); *On the Line, Nights in the Gardens of Brooklyn, A Story for Teddy* (stories); *A Radical's America* (essays).

TARKINGTON, BOOTH (1869–1946)

The Conquest of Canaan is distinctively the drama of situation, of environment on the one hand and of plot on the other; not primarily the drama of character. This is not to say that there is not real character—that there are not real characters—in the book. Admirable draughtsman that he is, Mr. Tarkington has never done more telling work than in the sketches he has given us of the group of old war-horses of town gossip who assembled daily at the "National House" in Canaan, Indiana . . . As for the judge, when he was bad, he was very, very bad, and when he was good he was horrid. You can fairly hear hisses from the gallery when he taunts the virtuous heroine with the loss of her gold. The scene in which hero Joe confronts him with his villainies is enough to send shivers of delight down the back of any reader whose wholesome tastes have not been vitiated by your decadent Ibsens and Henry Jameses.

Edward Clark Marsh. Bkm. Jan., 1906. p. 518

But if Penrod be a worthy cousin of Tom Sawyer, he is much more a worthy younger brother of Hedrick Madison, that diabolical and delightful boy of Mr. Tarkington's *The Flirt*. He lacks two years of Hedrick's age, and four or five years in the matter of literary precocity, but he has more sentiment, and every bit of Hedrick's riotous imagination. Hedrick, in his fourteenth year, aspired to *Henry Esmond,* and interspersed his conversation with fragments of French derisively intended. Penrod, at eleven, is himself a practitioner of the noble art of fiction, and his Harold Ramorez is a hero of truly epic proportions. The book would be worth while if it contained nothing but the chapter entitled "Romance."

Blair West Witherspoon. Bkm. May, 1914. p. 336

The enjoyment of good fiction is like the enjoyment of good friendship: it is a thing easy to feel, but in the last analysis hard to explain. And in the case of such a novel as Booth Tarkington's *The Turmoil* it is the "last analysis" that counts. Ultimately the charm of this tale is as real and as elusive as is the personality of a friend. One would prefer, then, to take it for granted that Mr. Tarkington is in all respects a capable story-teller—that he understands fully the kind of American life he is writing about; that he knows how to draw character convincingly; that he may be trusted to invent along the lines of probability, and to dovetail his plot with skill.

246

And, on the other hand, one would like to bring out as forcibly as possible
the fact that there is in Mr. Tarkington's novels—and especially in this
latest one, *The Turmoil*—a freshness and reality of interest such as it is
within the power of few writers to produce. . . . To write a novel of contemporary life with its scene in an unbeautiful American manufacturing
city; to portray with adequate realism, and in full daylight, the smoke, the
dirt, and the people; to refrain from romanticizing scene or psychology; to
deal with elemental, vital motives, such as love and jealousy and the driving power of modern business ambition; and through it all never to be
commonplace or depressing, but always to preserve a sense of the joy and
interest of life, even enhancing the reader's sense of life's richness, livable-
ness, worthwhileness—this would seem to be a task unmistakably requiring fertility of mind, buoyancy of temperament, that healthy and
highly developed imagination that works wonders in fiction and in life.

NAR. March, 1916. pp. 452–3

The scene of the story [*The Magnificent Ambersons*] is clearly the Middle
West, and the atmosphere is that of a newly arrived city, Indianapolis, or
Cleveland, or Omaha; but the spiritual values are no less current in Boston,
or Atlanta, or San Francisco—in short they are American. The limitation
that it is a class novel is balanced by the fact that it is the typically American class which is presented—the class which incarnates the American
ideal and to which all good Americans aspire. . . . How total is Mr. Tarkington's recall of the American Biedermeyer period is evident in the pages
of his mise en scene. . . .

. . . Readers of the *Education of Henry Adams* will remember his question—"The woman had once been supreme—why was she unknown in
America?" Mr. Tarkington's novel gives one answer. Sex in one form is
prepotent in America. "An American Virgin would never dare command,"
says Adams. True, but an American mother in her subjection is stronger
than the Virgin on her throne. It is to Mr. Tarkington's credit as an artist
that he fits this theme perfectly into the American setting and handles it
with reserve and proportion, in good faith and without cynicism. His
method is disarmingly simple and his touch gentle, with the good nature
that in America takes the place of urbanity. Above all, he gives us spiritual
values according to American standards, and professes his own artistic
belief in them.

Robert Morss Lovett. *Dial*. Jan. 25, 1919. pp. 86–7

The study of Alice [Adams] herself is masterly in its insight and the picture
of her father is just as good. Ironically enough, it has been said that Booth
Tarkington did not like *Main Street* and planned *Alice Adams* as an
answer. To be sure he has bettered the contentions of Sinclair Lewis but

nothing has been offered in rebuttal. The dinner on the hot night completes one of the most devastating pictures of American life which has ever been drawn. And incidentally no living writer can do more with temperature than Tarkington. F. Scott Fitzgerald in a short story called "The Ice Palace" made us feel almost as cold as we ever feared to be, but Tarkington cannot be matched for bringing home humidity. *Alice Adams* is a book to move the heart and wilt the collar.

Heywood Broun. Bkm. Dec., 1921. p. 395

Little reflective as he has allowed himself to be, he has by shrewd observation alone succeeded in writing not a few chapters which have texture, substance, "thickness." He has movement, he has energy, he has invention, he has good temper, he has the leisure to write as well as he can if he wishes to. . . . Why does he drift with the sentimental tide and make propaganda for provincial complacency? He must know better. He can do better.

February 1921

POSTSCRIPT.—He has done better. Almost as if to prove a somewhat somber critic in the wrong and to show that newer novelists have no monopoly of the new style of seriousness, Mr. Tarkington has in *Alice Adams* held himself veracious to the end and has produced a genuinely significant book. . . . Mr. Tarkington might have gone further than he has behind the bourgeois assumptions which his story takes for granted, but he has probably been wiser not to. Sticking to familar territory, he writes with the confident touch of a man unconfused by speculation. His style is still swift, still easy, still flexible, still accurate in its conformity to the vernacular. He attempts no sentimental detours and permits himself no popular superfluities. He has retained all his tried qualities of observation and dexterity while admitting to his work the element of a sterner conscience than it has heretofore betrayed.

Carl Van Doren. Contemporary American Novelists,
1900–1928 (Macmillan). 1928. pp. 92–4

The novel in which Tarkington's varying excellences come nearest to a complete mingling is *Alice Adams* (1921). It is a comedy, gay but penetrating, of a small-town girl who would like to impress the world that she is the petted darling of an indulgent good-mannered family. . . . At the end matters in the Adams family are much as they were at the beginning, except that Alice instead of practicing coquetry before her mirror is in a business college learning to be a stenographer. Tarkington captured the individuality of each person in the action. The story gave him the right opportunities—for good American family humor, for scalpel satire, for a little of American big business but not too much, for keenly contested struggle, and for constantly running geniality. Tarkington loved all the characters, including even the dishonest brother. The reader likewise loves them. *Alice Adams* has all the fun of *Penrod* and *Seventeen*. It has also the touch of seriousness and significance which they lack. It is fast coming to be recognized as Tarkington's masterpiece.

Vernon Loggins. *I Hear America* (Crowell). 1937.
pp. 342–3

Presented now in book form they [*Three Selected Novels*] are interesting as examples of the unfailing skill of their author as a story-teller and his genius as a reporter of the upper middle classes of the mid-West during the first third of the twentieth century. Tarkington was a gentle satirist; he realized fully the dual nature of all people, and was inclined to consider evil a temporary aberration rather than a full-time occupation of the soul. . . .

There is no denying the thinness of the material here, but it makes no difference. Tarkington could describe the inside of a vacuum cleaner and make it fascinating; reading him is like gulping ice cream on a hot night— cool and easy. He was a historian of the manners and morals of his time; he was also an entertainer. In the present volume he demonstrates a literary version of the Indian rope trick—stories which stand up without apparent foundation. No writer in his time could do half so well.

Thomas Sugrue. *NYT*. Aug. 10, 1947. p. 12

While vacationing at French Lick Springs in March and April, Tarkington began the literary exploitation of his legislative experience. Although he modestly doubted his ability to write a political novel based on his recent term of office, he set to work immediately on two of the short stories that eventually grew into the collection *In the Arena* (1905). One was "The Aliens," which he called a "story of politics in a tough precinct." This tale makes only indirect use of the legislative session, but it is a political story with a vengeance, an unrelieved little tragedy that deserves to be better known. Tarkington's observation of ward politics at their slimiest produced in this story a work of naturalistic fiction. The other story written at French Lick is identifiable only as a tale that one of Tarkington's political friends told him, but the early magazine publication date of "Boss Gorgett," a tale of machine politics in municipal government, suggests that it was one of the first stories written in *In the Arena*.

James L. Woodress. *AL*. May, 1954. p. 221

For once in his career he was guaranteed a clinical detachment. Here he felt no need for apologetics. His focus, so generally softened by fondness for the "better people," in *Alice Adams* flicked on sharply to dissect the "little people." Fortunately, Tarkington also had the gifts of humor and compassion. The Adamses are seen in the round as only an artist could have seen them and made them live with significance. By an accident of economics in real life, the Adamses represent a special American era of ambition and disaster. They are the creation of a novelist whose characteristic commercial success and literary failure arise from his conformity to the very world against which the young expatriates of Paris and Greenwich Village were rebelling. The ironic triumph in the writing of *Alice Adams* is that of conformity with a difference. The Adamses' meaning and their pathos are not limited to a calendar date; but no other novelist made quite the same contribution to the record of the 1920's.

Winfield Townley Scott. *AS*. Spring, 1957. p. 194

Although the literal mind of childhood encounters the adventures of Huckleberry Finn with an empathy never to be recaptured, it is only with maturity that one can appreciate the fine-edged irony sheathed in Huck's point of view, can become aware of the artist—the man behind the boy. "To read it young," Lionel Trilling has written, "is like planting a tree young—each year adds a new growth ring of meaning." It would be a wonderful compensation for adulthood if all the literary companions of our youth could grow as we grow, like their flesh-and-blood counterparts, gathering moral stature as we gain moral insight, but unfortunately, this is not the case. For another classic of American boyhood, Booth Tarkington's *Penrod,* has withstood the test of time, but not the demands of maturity. It remains a book for boys, and if the adult reader retreats into its pages in the afternoon hope of a delightful moral discovery, he is foredoomed to failure. Not that such an excursion is a waste of time—far from it. Discoveries are to be made in *Penrod,* as in *Huckleberry Finn,* and if they are not wonderful, at least they are fascinating.

John D. Seelye. *VQR*. Autumn, 1961. p. 591

See *The Gentleman from Indiana, Monsieur Beaucaire, Penrod, Seventeen, The Magnificent Ambersons, Alice Adams* (novels); *Clarence* (play).

TATE, ALLEN (1899–   )

Poetry

Allen Tate is a poet who seldom achieves Frost's perfection of style, but he has other qualities. He is too intelligent and cosmopolitan to find in his region, the South, the absolute satisfaction that Frost discovers in his attachment to New England. Indeed, he remains unreconciled to pretty much everything: our literature, our civilization, our wars. . . . If, then, Tate lacks Frost's repose, he also lacks his complacency. If his work is a perpetual experiment, a poetry labored out of intractable material by the naked will, it is invariably *interesting*. . . . And it is Tate, not Frost, who influences the younger poets.

F. W. Dupee. *Nation*. April 21, 1945. p. 466

Increasingly over the past quarter of a century, the name of Allen Tate has come to stand for a singular integrity of outlook. At all times he has given the impression of a poet who knows his own mind and intends to use it in his poetry. In consequence, he has been accused of a certain coldness; but hardly a line of Tate is not informed by passionate sincerity, though it may be controlled by a fine irony or educed by emotions which many readers outside the South of his fathers find inexplicable.

Gerard Previn Meyer. *SR*. March 20, 1948. p. 24

Allen Tate's poems are beautiful examples of what a hard, select intelligence can press out of rather deadly insights—but insights that are self-consistent and profound. . . . In his poetry, Tate traverses a hall of metaphysical fears and memorial pieties, at one end of which is The South and at the other The Abyss. . . . Tate's finest poems . . . are fruitless lyrics, and they impose astringent judgments upon the world and time we inhabit. Our nature as Americans is a divided nature, and if we listen carefully we may learn from this Tennessean accurate symbols of the guilt that returns and returns to us.

Robert Fitzgerald. *NR*. April 26, 1948. pp. 31–2

There are no trivia in Tate's *Collected Poems*. Every line seems to have found its inevitable final form, even if this took years of tinkering by the master workman. . . . Hart Crane once urged Tate to be true to "your language" in "so pure a way that it will be noticeable, and you will do well enough." Today Crane's prophecy has been more than fulfilled by Tate's long aesthetic asceticism, his uncompromising devotion to language.

Peter Viereck. *At*. Nov., 1948. pp. 96–8

His poems, all of them, even the slightest, are terribly personal. Out of splutter and shambling comes a killing eloquence. Perhaps, this is the resonance of desperation, or rather the formal resonance of desperation. I say "formal" because no one has so given us the impression that poetry must be burly, must be courteous, must be tinkered with and recast until one's eyes pop out of one's head. How often something smashes through the tortured joy of composition to strike the impossible bull's-eye! The pre-Armageddon twenties and thirties with all their peculiar fears and enthusiasms throb in Tate's poetry; imitated ad infinitum, it has never been reproduced by another hand.

Robert Lowell. *SwR*. Autumn, 1959. p. 559

Whatever else may be said, this much is sure: Allen Tate's accomplishments have earned him a place as one of the seminal poets of the twentieth century. His impact on the verse of his time has been far-reaching. The sources upon which he has drawn—the English metaphysicals, the classical poets—have through his example become a vitalizing force in poetry today. Reinforced by a rigorous critical foundation put forth with vigor and brilliance in a number of influential essays, his work has been example and model for the best younger poets of his day. If the best poetry of this century is firm and unified, composed in verse both texturally rich and structurally coherent, standing of its own self and making its own case, then the credit must go to Allen Tate as much as to any poet alive.

(K)   Louis D. Rubin and Robert D. Jacobs in *South:*
Modern Southern Literature in Its Cultural Setting,
edited by Louis D. Rubin and Robert D. Jacobs
(Doubleday). 1961. p. 247

Tate's style presents a specific problem; it is not mysterious and there is no need to speak of "melody" or "lyricism" or "intellectuality" in dealing with it. Let us take two words, both of which describe an aspect of Tate's poetry: "Latinity" and "Vision." Then, to avoid inventing more catch words, let us make these terms specific: "Latinity" is the formal and indeed abstract aspect of Tate's language; "Vision" is his effort to make these abstractions visible through the use of concrete adjectives, the imagery of sight, and related means. I believe we may go one step further, and make "Latinity" and "Vision" into formal images, that is, stylistic representations of an ideal classical order and a religious imagination. . . . I believe, then, that Tate's style is best seen as the method by which he brings to poetic actuality his polarized vision of the world. The tension between "Latinity" and "Vision" is an image of the dilemmas we have seen in Tate's criticism: permanent contradictions within human experience of which he is acutely aware.

(K)   R. K. Meiners. *The Last Alternatives* (Alan Swallow).
1963. p. 115

The sensible world as Tate reads it is characterized not merely by succession and change, but by a nightmare disjunctiveness. History is not synonymous with order. The "famous age" is seen in a number of poems in analogical rapport with the present, never as an undiscriminated idyll,

but inevitably with tragic irony. In "Aeneas At Washington," that time "when civilization/ Run by the few fell to the many" is now and carries with it its own destructive principle. The old soldier in "To the Lacedemonians" must say, "There is no civilization without death."
(K)   Carol Johnson. *Reason's Double Agents* (North Carolina). 1966. p. 83

Criticism

Tate . . . is a Catholic by intellectual conviction (though not by communion), he is Southern Agrarian by social background, he is a man of letters trained in the Late Romantic or Symbolist tradition—and these are three positions that cannot be reconciled anywhere short of Nirvana. The South, for example, was not in its great days hospitable either to Romantic poetry or to any other forms of creative literature . . . it was and remains hostile to Rome. Today if Tate carried his praise of traditional religion to the logical point of joining the Church, he would be alienating himself from his own people. . . . He would be forcing himself to reject many poets whom he still admires, with a divided mind. It almost seems that his essays are being written by three persons, not in collaboration but in rivalry (and we are given occasional hints of a fourth, a disciple of Schopenhauer rich in Yogi wisdom and prepared to reject the whole world as a realm of unmitigated evil).
                          Malcolm Cowley. *NR*. April 29, 1936. p. 348

Mr. Tate's method (is) . . . a method of unrelenting definition and re-definition which makes for criticism that is at once stimulating and exhausting. For it is one of the tacit assumptions of this criticism that the critic must never permit himself to become emotional, even when he is dealing with emotional subjects, and the reader must respond by pretending to remove any such suspicion from his mind. He must meet the critic on his own plane of dialectic logic, however difficult that may be, and in Mr. Tate's case it is very difficult indeed.
                          William Troy. *Nation*. June 10, 1936. p. 747

Let us return to certainties and pieties which can enlist our allegiance; let us revive the magic power inherent in tradition; let us rebuild the foundations of our ruined faith. This is substantially Tate's credo, and it is, what he intended it to be, "reactionary." . . . Whether or not Allen Tate is entitled to speak for the South, he does not represent the advanced thought of his time. He is a sectional prophet, a provincial thinker. . . . Because his call to tradition is no more than a repudiation of the present and a nostalgic flight to the past . . . and because he has lent himself to the service of economic obscurantism, he is guilty of that treason to the intellectuals which is so alarming a symptom of contemporary thought.

Charles Glicksberg. *SwR*. Summer, 1937. pp. 294–5

Mr. Tate is an earnest and subtle critic who turns his inquiring eye on past and present literature with the pure intention of perceiving it and its problems with clarity—of noting necessary distinctions, eliminating confusion and misapprehensions, and illuminating the distinctive qualities of artistic literary expression. He is often rather like a man with a powerful pair of field-glasses reporting to his friends (who lack such aids) what he sees: his friends, not being able to see through the glasses, cannot always quite make out from his description of what he sees exactly what he is describing; but they do know that he is giving an honest and careful report of what is visible to him.

David Daiches. *SR*. Dec. 25, 1948. p. 10

I do not see how to avoid saying that Allen Tate is our finest literary intelligence, though remarks like this have about them what Mr. Tate himself calls "an edifying generality": they make their subject sound remote and inhuman. . . . All we ought to mean by this "edifying generality" is that the demonstrated variety and order of Mr. Tate's awareness are greater than those of any other literary man in America. . . . Nothing could, however, be less fair to him than to make him sound remote and awful, for no one sees more clearly than him the danger of the kind of abstraction which, existing in isolation from nature, operates like a honoric hyperbole, a device for creating false gods and imaginary ghosts.

Arthur Mizener. *NR*. April 13, 1953. p. 18

The ideal, or at least the superior, conditions of the past, the South, the Feudal Age, as Mr. Tate describes them, are significant pastoral images by which to measure the insufficiencies and confusions of our own time; they are dreams of a life in which it was possible to experience things more concretely, more spontaneously, less abstractly and mechanically than perhaps we do now. They are instruments by which Mr. Tate has measured much of what our life might have been and much of what it is, and they are therefore extremely valuable. But I do think I am right in saying that the tone is valedictory and that these pastoral images therefore tell us only what we might have been, not what we ought to be. The *Collected Essays,* that is to say, are a beautiful poem about catastrophe rather than a statement of the dangers and possibilities of life. And as with any such pastoral images, there comes a moment when we ask questions about what is left out.

(K)   David Ferry. *MinnR*. Spring, 1961. p. 360

He often makes specific representations concerning, say, graduate schools or literary quarterlies. And certainly on these occasions he is mindful of a deeper and more personal issue—his defense of the contemplative against the methodical. But neither these pieces, effective as they have been, nor others which owe their permanent interest to their radical relation with the author's practice as poet, are the really great ones. In that class one thinks of "The Hovering Fly" with its urbane *progression d'effet,* the remote passion of its Fordian climax, and of the pieces in *The Forlorn Demon,* where contemplation is not a topic but a mode, and most of the rest of us (whether or no we would write like that if we had the talent) must feel like the political poets whom Tate consigns to childish voyages in Percy Shelley's paper boats. In this volume may be found the famous distinction between the symbolic and the angelic imaginations, the second characterizing an extreme humanist presumption, the hubris accompanying a desire to liberate poetry from its human limitations; I have wondered whether Tate here silently recalled the greatest of all Stevens' poetry, the passage on the angel in the last section of *Notes toward a Supreme Fiction.* Certainly to read the two together is to effect a sublime modern confrontation. In these beautiful and difficult essays Tate finds his full critical voice.

(K)   Frank Kermode. *SwR*. Winter, 1964. p. 125

By now the reader must be more and more aware that in Tate's tragic vision all problems are one vast problem. Life in modern society is hell, but hell has a variety of tortures and increasing depths of misery. Tate, like Dante, would lead us by descending circles to the very core of hell. He will not mislead "the banker and the statesman into the illusion that they have no hell, because as secularists, they have lacked the language to report it." Nor will he spare himself; he too is trapped in the modern dilemma, "his hell has not been for those other people: he has reported his own."

Part of this hell is modern man's horrible inner fragmentation. With no inner principle of unity, he is like an idiot with no values, with nothing but timeless, unrelated (because there is nothing to relate to) sense experience.

(K)   Richard J. O'Dea in *Nine Essays in Modern Literature,* edited by Donald E. Stanford (Louisiana State).
                                        1965. p. 154

When he writes that Nature is pure, inchoate Quality that threatens to overwhelm man and obliterate his identity and humanity, he is speaking obliquely of the inner disorder of sensations, impulses, tensions, random images, and abrupt and dismaying associations. (It is, as we shall see, highly significant that so many of his poems are set in the confused hours of twilight and deal with the reveries of a dazed and ill-controlled mind.) Nature, he tells us, is evil, by which he partly means that evil is centered in man, in the flux and flow of instinctual and sensual energies. . . . Good, for Tate, is the security and serenity that comes of escape from the self— the vortex of Quality—through community with others, a community so desperately needed that it cannot be taken for granted. . . . Knowledge of the universe is self-knowledge and right conduct is self-control made possible by that knowledge and by a nearly total commitment of the individual to the group which furnishes him with sustaining beliefs and guides to behavior. The danger in a society as disorderly and unstructured as that of modern America, Tate believes, is that the social forms may be insufficient; the individual cannot escape from himself and community— society—does not really exist.

(K)   John L. Stewart. *The Burden of Time: The Fugitives and Agrarians* (Princeton). 1965. pp. 312–13

Fiction

It is a curious story which Allen Tate unfolds (in *The Fathers*), subtly and delicately, all the notes muted. It is a story which lends itself readily enough to the allegorical suggestion, and the rhythm of the prose reminds us that a poet wrote it. It is concerned with imponderables, with the meanings behind the formal speeches and codes, with clashing philosophies of life symbolized by people who would never use the term. It is a psychological horror story, but it is the psychology of Henry James rather than of William Faulkner; despite the catastrophe that overwhelms all the characters it is concerned with life rather than death, with significance rather than with futility.

Henry Steele Commager. *NYHT*. Sept. 25, 1938. p. 5

Mr. Tate's prose moves with a finely balanced rhythm that is a definite aid to the narrative flow of the story, and which is almost always subtle enough not to obtrude itself into the reader's consciousness. It is a style well suited to the material, handled so skillfully that it never seems at all mannered and, while it often makes for a separate kind of beauty, it remains a part of the vital texture of the novel. . . . Of the innumerable novels that have come out of the South in the past decade or two, I think Mr. Tate's very easily challenges comparison with the best and the most penetrating.

Herschel Brickell. *NYT*. Sept. 25, 1938. p. 2

The prose is straightforward and, sentence by sentence, of the utmost simplicity. Yet the air of the narrative is charged, and behind the words, behind the imaginary narrator, who is rather a simple fellow—we are aware of a mind sharp and intense, clear as to its own situation, yet so caught in difficulties that it seems devious; secure in its own courage and yet in the midst of combat never ignorant of the imminence of defeat. . . . Mr. Tate is not unaware of the conflict in which he is involved. Because he is a poet and because it is as clear in his mind as it is confused in his emotions, he has created out of it, first in his poetry, and now in his prose, a dramatic irony, which for intensity is scarcely to be surpassed among his contemporaries.

John Peale Bishop. *NR*. Nov. 9, 1938. pp. 25–6

The central tension of *The Fathers,* like that of its design, is a tension between the public and the private life, between the order of civilization, always artificial, imposed by discipline, and at the mercy of its own imperfections, and the disorder of the private life, always sincere, imposed upon by circumstances, and at the mercy of its own impulses. We see, on the one hand, the static condition a society reaches when, by slow degrees, it has disciplined all personal feeling to custom so that the individual no longer exists apart from the ritual of society and the ritual of society expresses all the feelings the individual knows. We see, on the other hand, the forces that exist—because time does not stand still—both within and without the people who constitute a society, that will destroy the discipline of its civilization and leave the individual naked and alone.

Arthur Mizener. *SwR*. Autumn, 1959. p. 606

See *Poems 1922–1947; Collected Essays; The Fathers* (novel).

TAYLOR, PETER (1917–   )

All but two of these stories (*The Long Fourth*) concern the mores of family life in Nashville, Tennessee, but they also, except when making a tangent with the ethos of their special social and political landscape, concern all United States family mores. The tensions, affections, longings, the "shoddiness, stupidity and even cruelty" are equally true for any family confronted with the attack of modern industrial forces on inherited standards. . . . Occasionally one has the feeling that the stories are rather attenuated, perhaps because their action is not violent but quiet—almost quotidian. . . . It is a tribute to Mr. Taylor's talent that by his rendering of atmosphere, nuances of character and barely perceptible conflicts he is able to keep such episodes from rebuffing the reader.

Hubert Creekmore. *NYT*. March 21, 1948. p. 6

What Mr. Taylor is really doing, with honesty and sureness and beauty, is to experiment, both technically and psychologically, with very different approaches to extremely difficult definitions. For all its deceptively un-startling appearance, his method is quite as odd and daring as that in any of Picasso's paintings of double-headed women or seemingly capricious groupings of objects.

Mr. Taylor is inquiring into those relations through which things take on their meaning, and he makes his inquiry, not in unfamiliar language, but through connections so unfamiliar that he shakes the reader into emotional insecurity.

Marjorie Brace. *SR*. March 27, 1948. p. 18

If Taylor even remembers, he refuses to tell a story the way it was told before. He refuses, moreover, to exploit his material to the limit, to manu-facture characters, drama, suspense—in short, he won't traffic in what is known as a "strong story line." He refuses to be electric. He knows that life itself has a very weak story line. To render it truly he distils it, though again not as you might think: his work is not remarkable for its form and conciseness. He likes to take a while to get a story underway. He has a feeling for naming his characters. He has the poet's gift for finding the clichés of a nation and getting his characters to say them so that they almost sound like something else (as when one uses them oneself).

J. F. Powers. *Com*. June 25, 1948. p. 262

No description of the mere materials or events of *A Woman of Means* can indicate the particular kind of excitement it possesses. The kind of excitement is the excitement of being constantly on the verge of deep perceptions and deep interpretations. Mr. Taylor follows closely the con-tour and texture of event, and sometimes for a considerable space the reader feels that he is engaged with an ordinary realistic, objective narra-tive. However, Mr. Taylor's method is to intersperse tantalizing flashes, to break the ordinary texture of things and then quickly close the rent before the eye has caught the full significance of what lies beyond the curtain.

Robert Penn Warren. *NYT*. June 11, 1950. p. 8

What right has Mr. Taylor, one asks oneself, to be so good at drawing people, and at probing deep into the secrets of their relationships, without doing more with them? Why aren't these small kindly anecdotes, so de-lightfully told, collected more carefully into a mounting tension? They lie like pins spilled out of a box on to the floor, and one waits for the small but subtle magnet, which must surely be at work, to draw them together.

But something has gone wrong. Either the magnet is not powerful enough or else it is being held too far away.

Robert Kee. *NSN*. Dec. 2, 1950. p. 566

Peter Taylor . . . is possibly the most interesting and accomplished new writer to have come out of the South in the last ten years. . . . Mr. Taylor's comedy is quiet, his drama subtle and generally muted. Passion, violence and the more extreme aberrations are absent from his fiction. . . . And yet he fascinates, entertains and enlightens us as only a first-rate writer could. Immersed in his wonderfully lucid pages, we come to feel that this is not realism, but reality itself.

Dan Wickenden. *NYHT*. May 2, 1954. p. 4

Most of (the stories) treat family problems, the emotional relationships that make for happiness or unhappiness in domestic life, or the mutual obligations of married couples, relatives, servants and friends both to the quick and the dead. Mr. Taylor is particularly skillful in showing how the beauty of family life vanishes in the absence of free interchange in sympathy and affection among people destined to live under the same roof. . . . Mr. Taylor never preaches, but he has a message and a valuable one: If the sanctity of the home is preserved, all will be well with mankind.

Frank H. Lyell. *NYT*. May 2, 1954. p. 5

The Widows of Thornton . . . is as free of ugliness as . . . lingering nutmeg and as unpretentious as coldwater cornbread. . . . Mr. Taylor, Tennessee-born, has created a wistful, clinging but utterly non-depraved image of the Deep South that some of us, his regional contemporaries, have kept trying to recall from our childhood but were beginning, after Capote and Tennessee Williams, to doubt ever existed. . . . He has suggested that his stories may explain why a Southerner of the blood never entirely leaves home. But they are more than that, a tender and perceptive treatment of clanspeople of the same name but different pigment, drawn so close together from their beginnings that their real beauty is in each other and not in themselves.

Mack Morris. *SR*. May 8, 1954. p. 14

Peter Taylor writes of a Southern world everywhere present and tangible, but subtly, the center of his fiction is displaced in time: the mind, solaced by the wit, the elegiac temper and tender sensibility of these histories of fine consciences, is yet compelled to view them with an astonishing spaciousness of perspective. For what Mr. Taylor has achieved is the portrait of a complex society held in the most fastidious dramatic suspension; the past impinging upon and molding the present, the present rebelling against the tyranny of the past, the noisy warring of both in the abused heart.

Richard Hayes. *Com*. Dec. 17, 1954. p. 317

Mr. Taylor works efficiently and perceptively within a literary tradition which has its origins in the stories of Henry James. He examines his characters' lives and assesses their meaning in terms of the conflicts imposed by heredity and environment, by the conflicting values of past and present, by agrarian as opposed to urban values, or by the warfare between intellect and emotion. His stories succeed because his characters and their worlds are real, moving, and convincing. In each story there is always at least one character who becomes "finely aware" (the phrase is Henry James's) of the situations in which they find themselves. It is this fine awareness that gives the "maximum of sense" to what befalls them, which makes these quietly effective stories so meaningful to the reader.

(K)   William Peden. *SR*. Nov. 28, 1959. p. 33

In recent years there has been, I think, a lack of interest in Peter Taylor's fiction. At least one seldom sees his name included among those currently thought to be "our best younger writers." This decline of Mr. Taylor's literary stock may be explained in part by the thinness of his out-put (one novel, two short story collections and one play in thirteen years) and by the fact that many new young writers have appeared on the scene since 1948. But after reading *Happy Families Are All Alike,* I am inclined to think it may also be because Mr. Taylor's later stories are not as interesting nor as successful as his earliest work. . . .

But if these stories have a serious limitation—and I believe they do—it is their lack of intensity. I am not sure why this is, but even the best stories seem a trifle dull. The reason may be partly the kind of unintense people and situations Mr. Taylor usually writes about and, perhaps also, his leisurely manner of spinning a story out—both "The Other Times" and "Heads of Houses," though rather interesting, are much too long for what they *do*. Also, after reading several of these stories at one sitting, I began to tire of the smooth, unemotional style and to wish for a striking image now and then or a spark of emotion. Anything to break through the tight-lipped, reasonable flow of language and engage the reader's feelings and imagination directly.

(K)   William Stuckey. *MinnR*. Fall, 1960. p. 116

By neglecting some things, he has been able to do others supremely well. If he does not give us magnificent action scenes, he is one of the few writers to approach Tolstoy's talents in two other significant respects: (1) the ability to see in every act a man or woman performs some expression of that being's total history; (2) the ability to create real families and extremely moving scenes of family life. More than this, Mr. Taylor has achieved a third thing that we have no right to expect of a work as wide-ranging and inclusive as *War and Peace*: he has produced short stories that are perspicuous and unified gems.

Beyond this, Mr. Taylor has his own truth to tell. By showing us its roots in the small Southern town and its consequent dislocations, he has been one of the few writers of recent years who could make the everyday life of everyday members of the urban upper classes interesting, sympathetic, sometimes, indeed, dramatic. Above all, he makes it various: we know how the migration has touched the migrants—the husbands and wives, and even the maiden ladies who have sometimes gone along. But we know also the maiden ladies and the mamma's boys who have stayed behind in the dying small towns. . . .

(K)   Morgan Blum. *SwR*. Autumn, 1962. pp. 576–7

Each of his characters is solidly a person, troubled and not completely prepared for the life he must live; his past or his family or his relationship to what the present requires of him is a burden which he carries without conspicuous complaint, even when he wishes that he didn't have to. There is something of stubborn strength in almost all of them, and something queer also. The word "grotesque" inevitably comes to mind in thinking about them, more, I suspect because it is a popular word than because it describes the effect Mr. Taylor creates. If "vignette" were not old-fashioned and somehow girlish, it might do better. . . .

The principal reason for Mr. Taylor's superiority, however, is simply that he writes with such unobtrusive artistry. His is the kind of style that readers may not even notice, unless they pause to examine how he has done what he does. His mastery of gesture is subtle and delightful. . . .

(K)   Lewis Leary. *SR*. May 16, 1964 p. 45

See *A Woman of Means* (novel); *The Long Fourth, The Widows of Thornton, Happy Families Are All Alike, Miss Lenora When Last Seen* (stories).

THOMAS, AUGUSTUS (1857–1934)

None knows better than he how to use theatrical material, how to make the most of minor stage-business in order to hold and entertain his audience—a bug in a water-pipe, a little red note-book, an artist's dummy, a telegram, a bunch of violets. These are made to serve and serve well as far as they go. And in the handling of bigger situations, in getting climaxes, he is not less skillful from the stage point of view.

But his brilliance and skill are shown in a better way than by his appreciation of theatrical devices. As a careful and shrewd observer of men and manners he has given the stage more than one strong character, he has drawn more than one striking and sympathetic portrait, he has painted many true little pictures of real life. . . .

A third virtue is that Mr. Thomas writes trenchant and natural dialogue. He uses always a man's pen. Sentences full of wit, humor and a sane outlook on life, make one sit up frequently.

These are the counts we find to his credit. We quarrel with him because, knowing how to do so many things so well, he so continually overdoes them. His robustuous sense of humor, his leaning toward the theatric, lead him unconsciously or deliberately to sacrifice truth of characterization, dramatic integrity, often good taste, to gain a laugh, make a situation or complicate a plot.

Frederick M. Smith. SwR. April, 1907. pp. 193–4

Mr. Thomas always exhibits in his work qualities that place him far in advance of the ordinary playwright. He has individuality, virility, spiritual insight, independence of thought, humor, sincerity, a charming facility of apt and incisive expression, and an artistic infallibility in the writing of scenes. *The Witching Hour* is fascinatingly interesting in many of its details, but on the whole the play proves nothing and is without substance and truth.

Theatre Magazine. Jan., 1908. p. 2

Mr. Augustus Thomas's unusually successful farce entitled *Mrs. Leffing-well's Boots* was considered a failure by its producing managers until the very last rehearsals, because it depended for its finished effect on many intricate and rapid intermovements of the actors, which until the last moment were understood and realised only in the mind of the playwright. The same author's best and most successful play, *The Witching Hour,* was declined by several managers before it was ultimately accepted for production; and the reason was, presumably, that its extraordinary merits were not manifest from a mere reading of the lines.

Clayton Hamilton. The Theory of the Theatre
(Holt). 1910. p. 16

The so-called technique of this playwright is so perfect that it completely obscures his drama. Every exit and entrance, every *pince-nez* that is to be broken at a critical moment, every bandage that is to be found germ-infected and bring about a character's death, is planted with a so thorough assiduity that, once the first half of the preparation is done with, nothing remains but to hang around and watch the plants work. True, pastime may be found the while in giving ear to such of the playwright's tony Broadwayisms as "the chemistry of motivation," "the chemistry of things spiritual," and the like, and to his seriously intended love scenes wherein the hero informs the heroine, in voice a-thrill with fervour, that she is "an angelic, delectable baby" (the quotation—from *Rio Grande*—is literal!), yet in the main the evening reveals itself as a mere lecture by Thomas on "How To Write A Play," a laboratorical evening proving to the further satisfaction of the students of Professor George Pierce Baker that, with protracted schooling and practice, one may become sufficiently proficient in what is termed dramatic technique to write anything for the stage but drama.

George Jean Nathan. Comedians All (Knopf). 1919.
pp.143–4

The very heaviness of hand of Augustus Thomas is in his early plays a mark in his favor, for it is a quality of his sincerity. No man of his time had less of the theater in his works, more of native observation of life. He was always held back from the utmost of the theatrical by a native genuineness and forth-rightness.

Thomas H. Dickinson. Playwrights of the New
American Theater (Macmillan). 1925. p. 149

Mr. Thomas has technique at his finger's end; he is a man of the world, with a reporter's instinct for timely interests. As all dramatists should be, he is thoroughly familiar with American life, and, since his broad comedy period, his observation and his thought have deepened. . . . A play cannot live alone by ideas: it has an organism which must fit in with the organism of the theatre. That is something Henry James never could understand. It is a thing Mr. Thomas understood about as well as any of his contemporaries. He met these conditions with gusto; he even tried to show that the play of this character could carry idea without detracting from its workableness as a stage vehicle.

Montrose J. Moses. The American Dramatist
(Benjamin Blom). 1964. pp. 361, 366 [1925]

This play [*The Witching Hour*] is, in many respects, thoroughly American. The dialogue (or most of it) resembles the speech of everyday life; the characters, what we see of them, remind us of the men and women we see in the street, the office, and the home. The playwright is not especially interested in their philosophy of love, their sex instincts, or their ideas about God and the universe. That is his business; it is not ours to quarrel with him for not looking at life the way Hauptmann looks at it, or D'Annunzio. He was concerned chiefly with a group of persons and with "visualizing" an idea.

Barrett H. Clark. A Study of the Modern Drama
(Appleton). 1930. pp. 373–4

He stands in our drama for literary craftsmanship combined with practical knowledge of the stage and for a serious interest in the furtherance of dramatic progress. His work is not the result of accidental inspiration, but he has proceeded on a basis of logical deduction from observed facts to an establishment of fundamental principles in dramatic construction.

Arthur Hobson Quinn. *Representative American Plays*
(Appleton-Century). 1938. p. 731

An astute showman, intelligent and of high integrity, [Charles] Frohman did much to raise the producing standards in America, but within the commercial limitations of giving the public what it wanted. Or what he thought it wanted. The public takes time, sometimes, to make up its mind.

Unhappily this tardy acceptance of "the new theatre" had a crippling influence on two of the most promising talents of Frohman's day—Augustus Thomas and Clyde Fitch.

Both had admirable abilities, and in differing directions, both were capable of shrewd observation. They revealed a common interest in American locales, but Thomas had a much stronger sense of it than Fitch, whose characters and point of view, regardless of the scene of his drama, remained definitely of New York.

Neither was able to avoid altogether the lingering influences of the old melodramas, though both of them were sufficiently caught up in the movement towards realism to free their dialogue, for the most part, from the rigidities of the past. Their dialogue is less strained than any American dialogue before it, less awkward, and more to the point.

Their trouble, as both of them realized, was the star system, and its demand for the tailor-made play. With a good deal of amused urbanity, in fact, Mr. Thomas described how he cut the pattern and fitted the cloth of one of his plays to the personality of Nat Goodwin, and explained why, given such a star, the play had to take on a certain tone, and followed a certain routine.

John Anderson. *The American Theatre* (Dial).
1938. pp. 62–3

See *The Witching Hour, The Copperhead* (plays).

THURBER, JAMES (1894–1961)

Mr. Thurber's pets are, as the town knows, priceless, both pictures and prose. Here are super-beasts. Animals plus. I can stare at them over and over, acquiring new edification every minute. They are springboards to the infinite, or something like that. They run the gamut, too. For starkly sinister qualities, the bedridden cat which "follows every move I make" is almost too terrific to contemplate. . . . And surely Ibsen at his worst never thought of anything half so horribly symbolic as Mr. Thurber's night prowling horse.

Will Cuppy. NYHT. Feb. 8, 1931. p. 6

He has a style combining accuracy, liveliness, and quiet—qualities which do not often go together. He has a sense of the wildly incredible things that happen to human beings who think all the time that they are acting with the greatest prudence and common sense. It is this sense that his people imagine themselves to be moving steadily and reasonably under their own motivations when they are really being as near lunatic as you can be, unconfined, that makes Mr. Thurber an exceptionally interesting writer. . . . I think this is the reason that no matter how the extravagant situations pile up, you always have the feeling that Mr. Thurber is telling the literal truth.

Gilbert Seldes. SR. Nov. 18, 1933. p. 269

Many of Thurber's characters spend their lively existence in a state of mania. Haunted by hallucinations, they bound distractedly between the monstrous and the absurd. . . . Noting these manifestations, people who have absorbed psycho-analytic patter (by conversational osmosis rather than by study) are always sure to do a certain amount of eyebrow-raising over Mr. Thurber's themes. Obviously aware of that popular preoccupation he continues to exploit it with amiable ruthlessness. A Joyce in false-face, he strews hilarious pages with characters who take their subconscious out on a bender. . . . There's beautiful method in his madness.

C. G. Poore. NYT. Nov. 24, 1935. p. 3

Mr. Thurber's score on honesty and originality is high. In prose, he speaks his mind with a complete lack of pose not often encountered. A good many humorists get into a formula—he never has. . . . His style of drawing is completely his own. Even an unsigned Thurber is as unmistakable as an unsigned kangaroo. . . . Mr. Thurber's brand of humor lays him open to . . . ingenuous assaults. Because it has a fine cuckoo quality that is part of humor itself, it is often described as crazy. Many reviewers use words like "haywire humor," "zany" and "daffy" to describe what is a definite—and conscious—distortion of reality.

Stephen and Rosemary Benét. NYHT. Dec. 29, 1940. p. 6

In a few sentences the bold labels and solid outlines of one's fellow human beings have sagged alarmingly and nothing remains except an amoeba-like form with a startled eye in which one sees, only too plainly, one's own reflections. A sinking feeling accompanies the laughter of anyone engaged in reading Thurber; the jokes have all been salvaged from dreams. Bump!—it is oneself that has slipped on the banana skin. Whether the word for this suffering and awareness of catastrophe is humour, I don't know. Thurber does make me laugh, but I become engulfed, I am less and less sure of myself as I read on.

G. W. Stonier. *NSN*. Dec. 19, 1942. p. 414

When we view Thurber's prose as a whole, our first impression may be of rout, of frightened people, dogs and rabbits running . . . away from whatever faces them when they get up in the morning—old lettuce leaves, empty ration books, their own faces in the shaving mirror, anything familiar that haunts them. Their first impression, however, is deceptive. Man, Thurber thinks, is standing his ground, perhaps because he sees no better place to run to. . . . He tries to observe and report the fundamental disorder in the universe. Other interpreters of the modern scene attempt to suggest the truth through exaggeration, but Thurber sees that no amount of understatement can conceal the oddness of what happens.

Dan S. Norton. *NYT*. Feb. 4, 1945. pp. 1, 18

There is not much wit in Thurber's writing, although there is plenty of it in his conversation. Occasionally in a story he permits himself a relatively brilliant or sparkling metaphor . . . , but for the most part he confines himself to the almost businesslike description of incongruous situations that are often blended with pathos. . . . He writes so naturally and conversationally that it is hard to realize how much work goes into his stories. His art is in fact extremely conscious, and it is based on a wide knowledge of contemporary writing. . . . Besides learning to write with an easy flow and coherence that very few authors achieve, he also learned to omit everything inessential, including the winks, the rib-nudgings and the philosophical remarks of older American humorists. He achieves a sort of costly simplicity, like that of well tailored clothes or good conversation.

Malcolm Cowley. *NR*. March 12, 1945. p. 362

A large part of his comedy is the slow exfoliation of dilemma. It deals with people who live in a world of mist, as if they were seeing objects through a rainy windshield. Thurber's comedy not only depends on this obfuscation both of sense and value. It is part of our own obfuscation. His comedy is disturbing, therefore, because whatever else it does it identifies his people with ourselves. No one living, surely, comes so close as he does to making the personally comic shake hands with the tragic. Because this bifocal vision is our own, Thurber is able to make the stumbling of his people the stumbling of ourselves.

Francis Downing. *Com.* March 9, 1946. pp. 518–9

Thurber might be called a sprite, if sprites have sophistication. He has been repeatedly classified as a humorist. He clearly is one, though clearly also one who does not think life, even ordinary life, is a joke, nor does he find the absurdities for which he has an unfailing eye, unfailingly delicious. These essays . . . may be called roughly the prose poetry of humorous exasperation. Mr. Thurber's writing displays exasperation at once amiable and savage with all sorts of things, for instance—and repeatedly—with the pompous inefficiency of bureaucrats, both public and private. . . . We are all, Mr. Thurber seems to be saying, involved in the maddening silliness of a foolishly complicated world.

Irwin Edman. *NYHT*. Nov. 1, 1953. pp. 1, 8

Thurber's relationship to politics has never been an overt one, yet a political climate informs all his later work, either directly or by implication. . . . The early fables contained a few stories . . . which were direct attacks on the indifference with which the democratic nations faced the spreading power to the Nazis. These old fables sound just as topical today, although at the moment the foxes and the wolves . . . will sound more like the Russians than the Germans, for it is any dealers in oppression who mask their ruthlessness in fine phrases that are the target of Thurber's anger.

Gerald Weales. *Com*. Jan. 18, 1957. p. 410

When he is anatomizing the English language, or engaging in the rueful self-mockery that makes neurosis respectable and almost attractive, or reminiscing with wistful charm about his family and friends in Columbus, Ohio—then Thurber is in a class by himself, and criticism by his inferiors becomes presumptuous. . . . Thurber's great talent lies in his intuitive grasp of the unconscious (always, of course, carefully controlled by his craft); and when he deals with facts, with objective reality, he is generally reducing his powers, not expanding them.

Sydney J. Harris. *SR*. Nov. 30, 1957. p. 26

For more than a generation James Thurber has been writing stories, an impressive number of them as well shaped as the most finely wrought pieces of Henry James, James Joyce and Ernest Hemingway, as sensitively worded as the most discriminatingly written prose of H. L. Mencken, Westbrook Pegler and J. D. Salinger, and as penetrating—especially during what we can call his "major phase"—as the most pointed insights of those two large poets of our century, E. A. Robinson and Robert Frost. . . . [A]mong our living writers he is virtually our only creator of serious comedy and one of the few humanists who can make an affirmation without either a chip or a Christ symbol on his shoulder. Indeed, in Thurber's prose the individual is best off when freed of all the paraphernalia of systems, whether mechanical, social, literary or just plain transcendental.

(K)   Robert H. Elias. *AS*. Summer, 1958. p. 355

Thurber's range was extraordinarily wide. He was an admirable parodist —remember "What Cocktail Party" and the wicked lampooning of the Raymond Chandler school of penny dreadful in "The White Rabbit Caper"? He was a perceptive, if oblique, critic of literature, refracting rainbow intimations through the prism of his many essays—yes, he was a first-rate familiar essayist, too, as good a one as we have yet produced. . . . He wrote an in-between kind of essay, too—half formal, half familiar —which permitted him to work out as social historian, amateur of American murder, and definitive analyst of the curious Anglo-American cultural phenomenon, the soap opera. And all these different things got set down in a precisely elegant plain style, . . . for Thurber carried on a life-long love affair with the English language.

(K)   Charles A. Brady. *Com*. Dec. 8, 1961. p. 275

. . . some of Thurber's ideas about sex and personality are not necessarily in conflict with those of Freud. Thurber feels that the male animal is unduly repressed by his environment, an environment which includes another animal, his wife, who both abets and conceals her ruthlessness by means of more resolution, solicitude for her mate, and competence in the small matters of everyday living than he shows. Part of his environment is also a society going mad through a misapplication of technology; so-called neurosis is often merely "a natural caution in a world made up of gadgets that whir and whine and whiz and shriek and sometimes explode." Thurber differs from Freud in ignoring the Oedipus complex, whereas Freud regarded this as the major component of sex. He also differs in feeling that it is futile for man to expect to throw off his repressions or even to sublimate them satisfactorily. The civilized (or repressing and repressed) elements in the Little Man's character and environment often have the same cosmic finality as the natural traits. Thurber's people rarely succeed in changing any aspect of either their surroundings or themselves, and such "adjustment" as the male achieves usually comes only through complete withdrawal, as in the cases of Mitty, and of Grandfather in *My Life and Hard Times*.

(K)   Norris W. Yates. *The American Humorist* (Iowa
                                                   State). 1964. pp. 288–9

Although it will not do to claim Thurber for the cult of the Absurd in modern literature (Thurber having formed his view of life independently and long before the Absurd became a literary movement), the world of his later work is nonetheless close to the world as we find it in Ionesco—the apocalyptic vision, the fascination with the breakdown of communication as the primary symptom of a cosmic sickness, and the comic virtuosity are present in both.

But such parallels should not be pushed too far. The sense of modern life as too bizarre and outrageous to be presented as anything other than a grotesque comedy is, in fact, a striking characteristic of much postwar writing, and Thurber's brilliant expression of this sense is not a matter of literary fashion, but an independent response to a common cultural and philosophical situation. In any case, the world of Thurber is larger than that of Ionesco. The dark fantasies and the melancholy strain in his work are balanced by a basic sanity and a positive relish of the whole human scene. The essential quality of Thurber's imagination is the tension between a strong sense of fact (throughout his life he considered himself primarily a journalist) and a strong bias toward fantasy.

(K)   Charles S. Holmes. *YR*. Autumn, 1965. pp. 32–3

The organization of these stories [*My Life and Hard Times*] typically reflects this education; at first it may seem that there is no order—one of the narrator's recollections leads to another with little apparent method. But eventually we realize that the narration really involves a double imposture, and from this a pattern emerges. At one moment the narrator is a child, reliving the incident; at another, he is a man, looking backwards and attempting to reconcile his youthful memories and impressions with mature knowledge and judgment. In the best of these stories the isolation and alienation which seem to pervade American literature are overcome.

(K)   Stephen A. Black. *UR*. Summer, 1966. p. 258

See *The Thurber Album, Thurber Country, My World and Welcome To It, Fables for Our Time, Further Fables for Our Time, Is Sex Necessary?* (with E. B. White) (miscellany); also *My Life and Hard Times, The Years with Ross* (memoirs).

TORRENCE, RIDGELY (1875–1950)

Dedicated to Edmund Clarence Stedman, with reverence and love, and decorated by Bertram Grosvenor Goodhue, with particular felicity of invention, comes this dainty, wise, witty, malicious little book of verse [*The House of a Hundred Lights*]. The hundred lights may look out of a house in oriental style, but they look out those fivescore windows on the modern world of Western thought. The sun is center of the solar system, and life has been continuous. Man is not a finished thing. The common sense of the philosopher is put now in ironic epigram, now in fanciful fable of easy application. The homeliness and honesty of the ingredients—obtained at some moral purefood store, which by culinary sortilege have been given a delicious pungent aroma—first require praise. Why should a man writing prose have to know whereof he discourses, but the verse-maker be held unaccountable in the courts of reason? Surely it is the delightful directness of Mr. Torrence's verse, his sweet temper of statement, his gay indifference to his reader's conviction or conversion, that lend the chief charm to the third or fourth reading.

W. N. Guthrie. SwR. Oct., 1900. p. 495

Torrence and [Edwin Arlington] Robinson have the dramatic fever acutely. Torrence has just finished a three-acter which he is to read to me tonight. It is called *The Madstone*—certainly a striking title, is it not? It seems the 'mad-stone' exists among the folklore properties of his native Xenia, Ohio. It is a small porous stone supposed to possess the property of extracting poison from the human body, when placed upon an envenomed wound. He uses it as a symbol of woman. Robinson thinks the play is a big thing. He (R.) has also one in first draught, called *Ferguson's Ivory Tower,* the ivory tower, I believe, being Art. It would be wonderfully good luck if they both pulled it off. One could begin to think the American drama, long awaited and devoutly prayed-for babe, really about to be born.

William Vaughn Moody. Letters to Harriet (Houghton).
1935. pp. 319–20. [Letter of Jan. 12, 1907]

Mr. Torrence is an Ohio poet who, looking at the Negro beyond the miasma that surrounds him, has seen something so utterly different that his tenderness has occasionally got the better of him, and he has poured out his heart to the colored people like a hospitable wine. So different are the men and women and children whom Mr. Torrence has perceived for himself, it is scarcely strange that his impulse should be excessively generous, but one rejoices that this impulse enabled him to share the self-consciousness of a particular group of American citizens as it has seldom been shared before. There are three plays in the program of the Garden Theatre, the first a comedy, the second a tragedy, the third a "Passion interlude"—the incident of Simon the Cyrenian on the way of the cross. . . . One undiscovered country in emotional America is Negro country, and these productions have disclosed it in a fresh and vigorous and lovely way.

Francis Hackett. NR. April 14, 1917. p. 325

Poems by Torrence attracted immediate notice on their infrequent appearance in magazines; . . . his "Eye-Witness," "The Bird and the Tree," and "The Son," continually quoted, became contemporary classics. But Torrence remained in the peculiar position of one whose poetry was known only through anthologies, his own volume being not unprocurable but unprinted.

This strange and almost absurd circumstance has been remedied. A full quarter of a century after his advent, Torrence has published, without preamble or apology, his second collection of poems, *Hesperides*. Physically, it is not a large book—Torrence is not a voluminous writer—but in these one hundred pages is contained some of the most definite and distinguished poetry of the day. . . .

An entire article might be written concerning Torrence's firm clarity of thought and phrase. Practically every anthology of the period contains "The Son"—and yet I wonder how many of the readers of its sixteen lines are aware of the great artistry which has crowded the tragedy of a lifetime into so brilliant a condensation. Every casual line makes the revelation greater; every word is as starkly dramatic as it is inevitable.

Louis Untermeyer. *SR*. May 16, 1925. p. 756

As early as 1900, he issued *The House Of A Hundred Lights,* and then waited twenty-five years before bringing out *Hesperides*. Twelve years ago, he published a volume of negro plays, realistic and poetic, plays which ushered in the negro movement in the theatre. And, for many years past, Torrence has been the poetry editor of *The New Republic,* a position he has conducted with anonymous liberality and distinction. Despite his restraints, he is probably the most reliable of poetry editors. More important as a poet, it is a pity Torrence has devoted so little time to creative writing. He has none of the faults of the average conservative; he is too well endowed with self-criticism. Possibly the critic ultimately defeated the poet. In any event, he has written several poems distinguished for a reality of utterance and refinement of form.

Alfred Kreymborg. *Our Singing Strength* (Coward-
McCann). 1929. p. 403

Torrence had been captivated by "The Children of the Night" and, in the hospitality of his gay and expansive personality, was ready to take its author to his heart. Robinson was unprepared for this sprightly, mischievous being, this incarnation of youth, so individual, yet so free of pose, so fluid, so witty, so imaginative, yet so honest, and so loyal. He was outwardly almost the complete antithesis to Robinson, a social being to his fingertips, picking adventure from every bush; a fountain of gracefully rising and falling entertainment, giving himself with careless generosity, yet, like Robinson, wholly self-sustaining; unpossessed and unpossessable. There was a touch of St. Francis in him and of Johnny Appleseed and of Till Eulenspiegel; of Venetian color and richness and of Florentine efflorescence; and he was not wholly at home in his time.

Herman Hagedorn. *Edwin Arlington Robinson*
(Macmillan). 1939. pp. 164–5

Reading the poems in this book [*Poems*], one must admire the poet's serenity, candor, trueness, devotion. His line is always clear and musical, the tone sure, the accent right. This clarity gives Mr. Torrence's work a satisfactory timelessness; he can be modern without being modish; neither is he unaware of the bardic tradition. This tradition imputes no reproach to the poet if he is called, at times, "inspirational," at others, "visionary," or "dreamer." It is a tradition in which the general may prevail over the particular; it permits occasional vagueness, along with largeness, of mood or image; it skirts, at its lower levels, oratory or rhetoric; at its higher reaches, it approaches prophecy. It draws the poet on to raptness, exaltation.

Rolfe Humphries. *NR*. Oct. 27, 1941. p. 565

There has been more space given to *Three Plays for a Negro Theatre* in this record than will be given to anything else. Not because the plays themselves were as important dramatically as a great many things that came later, but for other reasons. They marked, it was agreed, a turning point in Negro theatre history. They broke completely with all the theatre stereotypes of Negro character. They gave Negro actors a first fine opportunity. They made Negroes welcome in the audience. They showed that Negroes could appreciate a white man's contribution to the literature of their life, if it were written in truth and beauty. They showed how a healthy criticism responds to a healthy stimulus. Above all, they showed that the *Three Plays* were not a happy accident. They were the distillation of a lyric poet's long thinking and experience of life; they were the end product of faithful training by certain actors and musicians. All of this, plus the considered intention of a producer with courage and imagination and a designer-director of unusual talent. Such things do not, in the theatre, "just happen"; but they *can* happen at any time when men and the stars will it so.

Edith J. R. Isaacs. *The Negro in the American Theatre*
(Theatre Arts). 1947. p. 60

"Heaven gives its glimpses only to those/In no position to look too close . . ." is the tribute Robert Frost paid to the genius of Ridgely Torrence a quarter of a century ago. Torrence, who took a passing glimpse at the mirror of mortality and caught its radiance in his own poetry, was slightly disconcerted by the two-edged meaning of the couplet. Did the brilliance of earth contain only in itself the brilliance of paradise? No, he never gave the imp in Frost the chance to hold an irreverent whiplash over him. He accepted the praise with the same modesty he accepted encomia from Houseman and Hodgson, his peers. Like them, he produced one book of poetry, *Poems,* a masterpiece, for posterity to judge.

A true American mystic, heir to the Transcendentalism of Emerson and Thoreau, Ridgely Torrence was of his time. Not oracular, he was a see-er, who endured the political distemper of the age, its violent world wars, its social outrages. To these themes he brought the incandescence of his rare intelligence and vision.

I. L. Salomon. *SR*. Dec. 27, 1952. p. 21

See *Poems; Plays for a Negro Theatre.*

TRILLING, LIONEL (1905–   )

Mr. Trilling has . . . , if I am not mistaken, written one of the first critical studies (*Matthew Arnold*) of any solidarity and scope by an American of his generation. And he has escaped the great vice of that generation: the addiction to obfuscatory terminology. Dealing in a thoroughgoing fashion with the esthetic, the philosophical and the socio-political aspects of his subject, he is almost entirely free from the jargons of any of these fields. I believe he has been influenced by the fashion in a little neglecting the literary aspect of Arnold as well as the biographical. . . . But if Mr. Trilling has followed the fashion, it is evidently not due to lack of competence. His observations on Arnold's style are admirably phrased as well as just.

Edmund Wilson. *NR*. March 22, 1939. p. 200

Mr. Trilling likes to move out and consider the implications, the relevance for culture, for civilization, for the thinking man today, of each particular literary phenomenon which he contemplates, and this expansion of the context gives him both his moments of greatest perception and his moments of disconcerting generalization. . . . It is civilization, we feel, that he really wants to talk about, and though, of course, all discourse about literature is and should be ultimately discourse about civilization, we sometimes feel that Mr. Trilling is stretching and forcing his literary material to allow himself to move over quickly to the larger issues.

David Daiches. *NYHT*. April 3, 1955. p. 4

As a conscious liberal Mr. Trilling is reluctant to commit himself to any single critical attitude. He cherishes a freedom to experiment, to use a combination of methods and a diversity of standards as tools at his dis-posal. . . . If there is one angle of insight which appeals to Mr. Trilling more than another, however, it is the Freudian. He even goes to the length—surely hyperbolic—of asserting that his pleasure in responding to a short treatise by Freud is difficult to discriminate from the pleasure afforded by a couplet from Yeats. Yet he also keeps his admiration this side of idolatry and on several occasions indicates his clear awareness of the limitations of Freudian concepts when applied to the interpretation of literary masterpieces.

George F. Whicher. *NYHT*. April 9, 1950. p. 5

Within his frames of knowledge and conviction his thinking is active, straightforward, and seldom clouded. Best of all, perhaps, he does not de-spise common sense as an instrument too common for an intellectual use. He does not employ jargon. He recognizes "the dangers which lie in our most generous wishes." . . . My respect for Mr. Trilling is so great that I can take no pleasure in hunting out his possible faults, but he exhibits, to my mind, one defect that should not be ignored—parochialism. He is parochial, I think, when he declares that "it is the plain fact that there are no conservative or reactionary ideas in general circulation." . . . What he is really saying here is that he cannot believe in the genuineness of any political ideas save those to which he can himself subscribe. . . . However . . . his political bias does not corrupt his literary judgments.

Ben Ray Redman. *SR*. April 15, 1950. pp. 44–5

Mr. Trilling is outstanding, in the higher ranks of criticism, for his free-dom from pedantry and his alertness to the intimate connection between the world of literature and life itself. Working with the insights of a flexi-ble, undoctrinaire modernism, he has shown himself to be a resolute and perceptive researcher into the problems of modern life. . . . To the fatuous optimism of the doctrinaire progressive, Trilling opposes the deep truth of James's moral imagination, with its awareness of disaster, and the tough psychology of Freud, which invites a more complex estimate of human motives than liberalism has made.

Charles J. Rolo. *At*. June, 1950. pp. 82–4

Lionel Trilling is not only an accomplished interpreter of the nineteenth century; he is, in his own right, a thoughtful mind of the mid-twentieth. The distance between this position and the mentality of the early twentieth century may be gauged by the very breadth of sympathy with which Mr. Trilling, Professor of English at Columbia, treats the commitments and sanctions of mid-Victorianism.

Not that his mood is nostalgia for the past; rather it is a pathos of the present, an urgent awareness of "our modern fate" well calculated to impress contemporary readers. . . . Something can be gained by revaluation—which, in these cases, means higher evaluation—of writers whose sense of individuality struggled against the encroachments of conformity.

Harry Levin. *NYT*. Feb. 13, 1955. p. 3

Mr. Trilling dares to bring scholarship into criticism; and therefore he is one of the few critics in this country who can write limpidly, humanely, undogmatically about any and every book that interests him, and who can be interested in any and every kind. While he takes care not to confuse the effects of a book upon himself with the book itself, he is not afraid to entertain relativity; he boldly sets forth a writer's intention, unperturbed by the cry of "fallacy!" So he is constantly instructive, eminently readable, always refreshing.

Perry Miller. *Nation*. March 5, 1955. p. 203

This is, in fact, real criticism, which can only be addressed to those who are directly on a level with the critic himself; they need not have read exactly the same books, but he has to assume that they have the same quality of interest in the subject as he has. Professor Trilling is a master of this procedure, for all that his tone is not conversational or intimate, but rather Arnoldian, without sharing Arnold's tendency to nag or preach. And, far more than Arnold, he has the true critic's gift of describing *exactly* the thing he is talking about. . . . His criticism, at bottom, is not technical, nor aesthetic, but moral. What makes a great book great, for him, is the spiritual and moral health it embodies.

John Wain. *Spec*. July 29, 1955. pp. 171–2

Trilling's mind will play luminously with what he knows, and what he knows is what has a *literature*. It seems hardly an exaggeration to say that it was the writings of David Riesman which led him to see American society as a *subject*. He knows London and Paris and New England and the American Frontier as they have been rendered, interpreted, discussed, projected, evoked, in innumerable books. He is at home in the world of Western culture in a positively enviable way. And yet in a sense that world of Western culture exists only in the mind of a few highly cultivated American intellectuals. In fact, it is more fragmentary, more impure, more confused, and perhaps even sometimes more exciting than the civilized and sensitive American metropolitan mind conceives it to be. Perhaps it can be said that men like Trilling (and there are all too few of them) have created Western culture, for only in their minds it lies as an ordered whole. But at least in looking on it as an ordered whole he is not looking *back* on it in Alexandrian fashion to classify and entomb: it all lives for him, vibrant with both moral and aesthetic reality; it is part of a present, or perhaps of a timeless, order, an order that is always relevant, however much one needs a sense of the past to understand it. It is this conviction of the present reality of all literature that makes Trilling such a lively and compelling critic.

(K)   David Daiches. *Cmty*. July, 1957. p. 69

The truth is, I think, that the unity of Trilling's work, if one knows where to look for it, is far more imposing than he wants to admit. It does not lie in the subjects he has dealt with. I would prefer to call it, rather, a unity of concern. About the most scattered and disparate subjects he is forever asking the same questions: about the moral implications of the arts, about the ideational substructure of politics, about the position or predicament of an intellectual class in an anti-intellectual world, about the impact of our discoveries about the irrational and subrational, about the relation of fiction to the structure of society, about the nature of culture itself. These questions come up no matter what Trilling is scrutinizing, and to such an extent that sometimes the work he criticizes seems to become only a pretext for the further elaboration of one of his favorite preoccupations. . . . Trilling's one novel, *The Middle of the Journey* (1947), treats the same matters he has worried constantly in his critical writing.

(K)   W. M. Frohock. *SWR*. Summer, 1960. p. 225

Trilling's great contribution lies in his attempt to redefine within a democratic framework the relationship between literature and politics so that we "force into our definition of politics every human activity and every subtlety of every human activity." . . .

Despite the sensitivity of his critical analysis, the mellow Arnoldian flavor of his prose, and the deep sincerity of his feelings, Trilling is ultimately a limited observer of the American scene. His inability to read the novel in any but realistic terms and his myopic sympathy for Freud's but not Calvin's image of man's limitations deprives him of any real *engagement* with American literature and culture. A striking example of the cosmopolitan provincial, he cannot conceive of an America extending beyond the confines of New York City.

(K)   Paul Levine. *HdR*. Spring, 1962. pp. 93–5

He is our one literary critic who, in a philosophical manner, unceasingly questions the categories and values of our culture. His originality resides in the way he has allied his close study of Freud with the Arnoldian dictum that literature is a criticism of life. His essays possess an air of civilized converse, a measured tone of reflection, and a tension that seems to arise from uneasiness as to where to place his critical self-assertion. The dustjacket speaks of Trilling's critical "stance," and it is this stance—half aggressive, half cautious—that has given him the authority he enjoys here and in England.

(K)   Leon Edel. *SR*. Nov. 6, 1965. p. 37

If Trilling has devoted much of his life to writing about literature when he is also very concerned with politics and sociology, it must be precisely because, as he claimed, "literature is the human activity that takes the fullest and most precise account of variousness, possibility, complexity, and difficulty." The lazy or frightened mind seeks the refuge of ideology ("ideology is not the product of thought") : those capable of "the energy of the encompassing mind" will persist in uncertainty, if only out of respect for everything that cannot be finally known about ourselves and our world. . . .

In his new collection of essays, *Beyond Culture,* Trilling returns again and again to the same preoccupations and problems. The same patient penetration and consideration are at work, though just occasionally it sounds as though the ability to live strenuously among uncertainties has slackened into a habit. There are detectable vaguenesses, and some paragraphs and essays break off or fade away just at the point one would have liked a fiercer effort at clarification. . . . He seems to feel almost imprisoned within the problems and paradoxes inherent in his rather select and oft-repeated vocabulary. There is something in the tone—between disenchantment and pessimism—which gives some of the essays an almost elegiac note.

(K)   Tony Tanner. *Encounter*. August, 1966. pp. 72–4

The Middle of the Journey—Novel

The Middle of the Journey is not a *tendenz* novel; yet it defines the tendency of our lives, and can be most easily discussed in its moral rather than its dramatic terms.

This temptation is to be resisted, for the dramatic terms are always in the fore, and sometimes almost as brightly as in a comedy of manners. Certainly it is a book of great wit, and it is difficult to think of any recent novels which are at all like it. From older writers one detects, perhaps predictably, the influence of E. M. Forster, especially in the effective combination of wit and gravity, and in the somewhat frosty detachment of style.

Mark Schorer. *NYT*. Oct. 12, 1947. p. 40

What Mr. Trilling has written is, quite overtly, a dialectical novel. . . . His language is analytical, his structure polemic, his sequence of scenes and confrontations among characters virtually syllogistic. Yet it is a remarkable testimony to his skill and sincerity and to the tenacious probity of his thinking, that he has been able to keep his plotting sharply dramatic; that as we read we lose our sense of lacking familiar fictional ingredients; and that we become profoundly absorbed in his story, not only as a brilliantly sustained argument but as the record of an essential experience and milieu of our age. . . . It is a book that brings the best critical intelligence now discernible in America into play with an absolutely honest creative talent.

Morton Dauwen Zabel. *Nation*. Oct. 18, 1947.
pp. 414–5

Because the level on which perception takes place in the novel is immeasurably higher than what is seen in most popular fiction, the writing will make considerable demands upon the reader. The reviewer for *Time,* who found the style rather too "gray," simply did not notice that Mr. Trilling's material forces him to a line of greater length and more complex contour than one finds, say, in John O'Hara or James Cain. Mr. Trilling's writing is well up to the high intelligence and peculiar tact which direct it, and in some places . . . it is literally perfect. . . . Mr. Trilling's novel stands as the testament of a real human being, struggling with the complexities of human thoughts and human feelings and moving in a journey which has meaning and purpose only as long as it remains human.

Henry Rago. *Com.* Nov. 14, 1947. pp. 121–2

Laskell [the hero of the novel] would, in every instance, employ to the best of his ability the "humanistic, critical intelligence" in endeavoring to cope with the world. This means acting "in modulation"—*but* acting. It is not acquiescence, not passivity, but it *is* moderation. Thus, as John Laskell reaches "the middle of the journey," he assumes a "middle of the road" stance, one that may, unhappily, cause alienation from his friends, but one that represents the most tenable kind of liberalism, Laskell and author Trilling agree.

In and around this ideological discussion, which serves as the core of the book, Trilling weaves various speculations about the large subjects of death and love, relating these to his political topic by virtue of the belief that undergirds his remarks in every instance, the need for human beings to adopt a responsible attitude.

(K)   Gordon Milne. *The American Political Novel*
(Oklahoma). 1966. p. 144

See *Matthew Arnold, E. M. Forster, The Liberal Imagination, A Gathering of Fugitives, The Opposing Self, Beyond Culture* (criticism); *The Middle of the Journey* (novel).

TWAIN, MARK (1835–1910)

We who remember Mark Twain when his light first rose above the horizon cannot help thinking of him as a humorist above everything else, for it was as such he rose, and as such his radiance increased. We soon came to know that he was also a philosopher and after a while that he was a story-teller, but for all that and despite our added knowledge of him, we still think first of his brightness, and often forget that his surface may be inhabited or that he has an influence upon our tides.

Frank R. Stockton. Forum. Aug., 1893. p. 677

In his books Mark Twain has set forth, and in himself he embodies, the traits, the humors, the virtues, of a distinct people. So regarded, he has in our literature no equal, and in life he has had but one superior, Abraham Lincoln. This is the explanation of Mark Twain's fame. There are few things as interesting, as attractive, as instructive, as the man who, without sacrificing a jot of his own individuality, stands out as the type of his country.

Henry Dwight Sedgwick. The New American Type
(Houghton). 1908. pp. 293–4

To accept him is almost equivalent to accepting the American flag. . . . Not by his subtlety, . . . nor his depth, nor his elevation, but by his understanding and unflinching assertion of the ordinary self of the ordinary American did Mark Twain become our "foremost man of letters." . . . When Mark Twain, robust, big-hearted, gifted with the divine power to use words, makes us all laugh together, builds true romance with prairie fire and Western clay, and shows us that we are at one on all the main points, we feel that he has been appointed by Providence to see to it that the precious ordinary self of the Republic shall suffer no harm.

Stuart P. Sherman. Nation. May 12, 1910. pp. 478–80

Mark Twain was great in many ways and especially in four—as a humorist, as a story-teller, as a stylist and as a moralist. Now and again his humor was fantastic and arbitrary, perhaps even mechanical; but at its richest it was irresistible, rooted in truth, sustained by sincerity and supported by a manly melancholy—which became more plainly visible as he broadened his outlook on life. His native gift of story-telling, the compelling power of his narrative, was cultivated by conscious art, until one could not choose but hear. . . . As a master of English prose he has not received the appreciation he deserved. . . . And his sturdy morality, inspired by a detestation of sham and of affectation as ingrained as Molière's, ought to be evident . . . to all who have meditated upon "The Man Who Corrupted Hadleyburg."

Brander Matthews. NAR. June, 1910. pp. 834–5

Mark Twain is not all of Samuel Clemens. He was much more than humorous. He was a great fictionist and a rough-hewn stylist uttering himself in his own way, which was a large, direct and forceful way. No amount of Old World contact could destroy his quaint drawl, and not all his reading nor his acquired personal knowledge of other writers could conventionalize his method. He remained the mid-Western American and literary democrat to the last. . . . Every letter of his speech was vital with the breath of his personality.

Hamlin Garland. NAR. June, 1910. p. 833

The art which premeditatively determines the scope of its venture so that one sees at every step the curvature of its rounding up—in a word the literary art—was foreign to Mark Twain's nature. . . . He always wanted room—the whole open sky—for his action. . . . Mark inherited from nobody but, if not as purposeful, he was as masterful as Rabelais, Cervantes, and Swift were. He was not learned and literary as those men, and had not their kind of conscious purpose, but there was a strain of earnestness in all his work—a Western strain. . . . Mark Twain, like Lincoln, was a native of the West and, like him, though in so different a vein, was gigantically in earnest.

Henry M. Alden. Bkm. June, 1910. p. 367

So far as I know, Mr. Clemens is the first writer to use in extended writing the fashion we all use in thinking, and to set down the thing that comes into his mind without fear or favor of the thing that may be about to follow. . . . He would take whatever offered itself to his hand out of the mystical chaos, that divine ragbag, which we call the mind, and leave the reader to look after the relevancies and sequences for himself. . . . He has not attempted to trace the threads of association between the things that have followed one another. . . . An instinct for something chaotic, ironic, empiric in the order of experience seems to have been the inspiration of our humorist's art.

William Dean Howells. My Mark Twain (Harper).
1910. pp. 166–8

One of Mark Twain's best attributes as a commentator on style, on man, on religious beliefs and on the ways of nations is his capacity for profound admiration. He has no poor provincial grudges against the souls and gifts of other peoples. He could praise well. . . . He had besides a certain essentially masculine faculty, in which no author has equaled him in many hundreds of years. . . . He could curse well. . . . To curse in a fine, forthright style and spirit seems to require at once more intensive and more extensive moral information—more knowledge of the states of Heaven and Hell and of excellence and splendor and miserableness and meanness in mortal character than has ever been acknowledged. Mark Twain will long gratify his country as a magnificent, an immortal execrator.

Edith Wyatt. NAR. April, 1917. pp. 614–5

There was a reason for Mark Twain's pessimism, a reason for that chagrin, that fear of solitude, that tortured conscience, those fantastic self-accusations, that indubitable self-contempt. . . . It is as old as Milton that there are talents which are "death to hide," and I suggest that Mark Twain's "talent" was just so hidden. That bitterness of his was the effect of a certain miscarriage in his creative life, a balked personality, an arrested development of which he was himself almost unaware, but which for him destroyed the meaning of life.

Van Wyck Brooks. The Ordeal of Mark Twain
(Dutton). 1920. p. 14

My suspicion is that it was the secondary social and conventional forces enveloping him after his early success and marriage and playing on this sympathetic, and, at times, seemingly weak humanist, succeeded for a time in diverting him almost completely from a serious, realistic, and I might say Dostoevskian, presentation of the anachronisms, the cruelties, as well as the sufferings, of the individual and the world which, at bottom, seem most genuinely to have concerned him. For, to a study of these he would have turned, had it not been, I think, for the noisy and quite vacuous applause accorded him as Genius Jester to the American booboisie. And by that I mean almost the entire American world of his time.

Theodore Dreiser. EJ. Oct., 1935. p. 621

Mark had only one discipline to which he had rigorously and successfully submitted himself—language. Mark's English is superb, his taste in diction impeccable. He boasted of it and was right. His terse, simple, effective style, his words chosen with a lively sense of values, his accuracy and his force, never fail except in an occasional purple passage when he strains after an artificial beauty which was not his forte. He writes . . . better English than Henry James, both by word and by rhythm, though with far less assistance from a flowing vocabulary.

Henry Seidel Canby. Turn West, Turn East
(Houghton). 1951. p. 191

It might be said that a humorist by temperament, for example Benjamin Franklin, is a man serenely adjusted to his environment, while a wit like Jonathan Swift is not. Clemens himself—"Mark the Double Twain," as Dreiser called him, all his engaging self-contradictions making him a "human philopena" like his extraordinary twins, Luigi and Angelo—partook of both natures. And so, while one side of his creative nature lived and moved upon the level of his boyhood, in almost perfect control of his materials, the other battled with clumsy valor upon the darkling plain of his maturity. By instinct he knew what a boy was like, from having been one himself in a river town in the golden age before the War; but to the question, What is Man? his self-taught philosophy yielded no better answers than that Man is either a knave or an illusion, "wandering forlorn among the empty eternities."

Dixon Wecter. Sam Clemens of Hannibal
(Houghton). 1952. p. 265

All that the surrealists were later to yearn for and in their learned way simulate, Twain had stumbled on without quite knowing it. . . . In the chamber of horrors of our recent fiction, the deformed and dwarfed and dumb have come to stand as symbols of our common plight, the failure of everyone to attain a purely fictional norm. Toward this insight, Twain was fumbling almost without awareness, believing all along that he was merely trying to take the curse off of a bitterness he could not utterly repress by being what he liked to think was "funny."

Leslie A. Fiedler. NR. Aug. 15, 1955. p. 17

The loneliness of Twain's childhood is reflected everywhere in his work. As has often been observed, loneliness is the peculiar quality of a great deal of American writing and comes out in many forms . . . but in Twain, loneliness almost without exception takes the form of alienation from the family. . . . With the possible exception of Poe's fantasies of being buried alive, there is no other corpus of American writing that reverts so often as does Twain's work to the nightmare of being utterly cut off.

Kenneth S. Lynn. YR. Spring, 1958. pp. 422–3

The hero who emerges in Twain's major fictions of the late '80s and early '90s is a lonesome stranger, wandering in search of a lost Paradise. Like Twain's earlier heroes, he is an "innocent," in that the ways of society are not his ways; but instead of being alienated from the group by his boyish inexperience, he is an adult who is set apart by his extraordinary knowledge. There is a familiar generosity and compassion in his spirit— and a new harshness as well; somewhere, somehow, iron has entered his soul. If he would be a liberator, he is also a destroyer, ready to tell the facts that will ruin a man's life, or even to kill him, if need be. . . .

His appearances are by no means entirely confined to fiction. Wherever one looks in Twain's later essays and correspondence, one soon comes across this man, usually standing apart from the crowd in an attitude of defiance which scarcely conceals his longing to be its leader. . . . That Twain's descriptions of this hero were projections of the crowd-defying genius whom he himself wished to be is suggested by his rueful admission in "Purchasing Civic Virtue" that he lacked the "necessary moral courage" to stand up before an audience and denounce it. The metaphorical description of the "stranger" in *Life on the Mississippi,* who brings the crowd to its feet with the volcanic fury of his invective, reveals even more about the later Twain's ambitions. For in the last quarter century of his life, Mark Twain habitually talked about himself as a volcano.

(K)   Kenneth S. Lynn. *Mark Twain and Southwest*
Humor (Little). 1959. pp. 246–7

From the beginning of his career, Twain strove for an alternation between comic and serious material in the arrangement of the episodes, relying to a large extent upon burlesque to furnish the comedy. Gradually he refined his use of the burlesque material to the point where it not only furnished an alternation with the serious material but in conjunction with it furnished foreshadowing and, as a consequence, thematic unity. Thus in *Roughing It* burlesques constitute the tenderfoot's prevision of the West and a foreshadowing of the disillusioning experiences which are to follow. A similar pattern is visible in *Huckleberry Finn.* Twain's readiness to use burlesque was a source not only of strength but also of weakness, for, accustomed to seek in burlesque answers to structural problems, he produced, for example, the incongruous Evasion to end his greatest novel.

(K)   Franklin R. Rogers. *Mark Twain's Burlesque Patterns*
(Southern Methodist). 1960. p. 156

By 1900, in short, Twain could no longer embrace all the implications of the "growth of knowledge." He dreamed again the American dream of a society liberal without being complex, politically sophisticated yet socially austere and simple—a society whose passing he had described as a young writer in *The Gilded Age*—and his dreaming heightened an already fierce nostalgia.

(K)   Roger B. Salomon. *Twain and the Image of History*
(Yale). 1961. p. 40

Clemens escaped from a dead sophisticated way of writing by evolving an alive, naive way of talking, the very virtue of which was that it never seemed to know what it was going to say next. Yet such a style cannot be detached from a certain kind of speaker: Clemens throughout his early work can be detected searching for the right mouth. Mark Twain himself is of course a life-long persona used on stage, in books and to a curious extent in Clemens's private life; but as we have seen the mere mask of Mark Twain was not enough to solve Clemens's language problem. Something, or rather some figure, more extreme, more clearly defined in his opposition to official standards, was required if Clemens was to make a clean break with the values of the official culture of his day. And since ways of speaking are inextricably involved with ways of living, it is not surprising that in searching for an anti-conventional, anti-formal mode of speech, Clemens started making use of characters whose manner of life had no respect for the conventions and forms of society. More or less anti-social figures appear in his work from the start and just as important as their freedom of action is their freedom of speech.

(K)   Tony Tanner. *The Reign of Wonder* (Cambridge).
                                                    1965. pp. 129–30

Mark Twain especially was sensitive to particulars since, joined one by one, they formed his world. He had no very strong sense of the grand design. As Edgar Branch put it, Twain's "genius was for the particular, not for the abstract or the organizational. Like Walt Whitman he was a caresser of discrete experience." His care for the individual detail made him seek the right word for the specific occasion. . . . Honesty in words was a lifelong obsession with Mark Twain. In his last years he was convinced that he was dictating such shrivelling truths into his autobiography that it could only be published posthumously. His ideal was say it out without artifice, and we can trace a common line from Mark Twain to Gertrude Stein and her preoccupation with "things as they are," to Hemingway and his search to recreate "the way it was." Although he delivers it amiably enough, there is a sharp edge to Huck's observation in *Tom Sawyer Abroad* that "the finer a person talks the certainter it is to make you sleep." He is referring to Tom, who is notably glib and fanciful, and given to putting on "style."

(K)   Richard Bridgman. *The Colloquial Style in America*
                                              (Oxford). 1966. pp. 106–9

He was, at the very least, already a double creature. He wanted to belong, but he also wanted to laugh from the outside. The Hartford literary gentleman lived inside the sagebrush bohemian. But even outwardly Sam Clemens was far different from any conventional Western journalist and rough. He had been a sickly infant, born two months prematurely, and had barely survived his first two years. He grew up sparely built, small-boned, with narrow sloping shoulders, five feet eight inches tall, a contrast with the brawny miners he knew in Nevada; all his life he liked to elaborate fantasies about small men with unsuspected gigantic strength who were always surprising people with it. His head, like a child's, seemed too large for his body. He had delicate hands, which quivered when he was stirred, and tapering fingers with pink nails. His mouth, Kipling said, was "as delicate as a woman's." . . . He was excitable, easily hurt, desperately hungry for affection and tenderness, often depressed, capable of great rage and greater remorse. He remained, in many ways, a child demanding attention in a nursery which was as large as the world; his wife was to call him "Youth" and "Little Man," and to Howells he had the heart of a willful boy.

(K)   Justin Kaplan. *Mr. Clemens and Mark Twain* (Simon).
                                                        1966. p. 18

Twain's one attempt at combining the tradition of his great earlier work with his newly deepened bitterness about the way in which the age-old evils of human nature were destroying all the promises made by nineteenth-century America was *Pudd'nhead Wilson* (1894). Here the masterful hand is evident in flashes, but on the whole there is an unresolved discrepancy between the basically pessimistic view of human nature which seems to inform the book, and the plot, which develops in contradiction to it. The oft-quoted epigraphs from Pudd'nhead's Calendar reveal an attitude which finally has not much connection with what goes on in the story. Twain in the nineties was a divided artist, humorous in familiar ways or censorious in tones of deepest pessimism, but unable to combine the two into one satisfactory work.

(K)   Larzer Ziff. *The American 1890s* (Viking).
                                                        1966. pp. 70–1

A Connecticut Yankee is the first of Clemens's novels which does not follow an important work of non-fiction. It is chiefly for this reason, I believe, that it possesses a great amount of energy: in invention, in the speed of delivery of its humor, in the multiplicity of themes, in the venom and sweep of its social criticism, in the acreage of corpses, in the ebullience of language, in the free and easy characterizations. It seems to me that this is one of the most successful of Clemens's creations, with fewer flaws than is usual in his books, and that it is one of his most important works for several reasons: the degree of success of its fancy, its coherence as a work of the imagination, the essential seriousness of its themes, and its purity and ease of language, despite the fact that the language is not the wonderful vernacular of *Huckleberry Finn*. With *Tom Sawyer* and *Huckleberry Finn* it completes the trio of Mark Twain's major novels. None of the others comes near these three in scope, in style, in characterization, in imagination and in truthful rendering of subject and scene.

(K)   Charles Neider. *Mark Twain* (Horizon). 1967.
                                                        pp. 20–1

Huckleberry Finn

Into its making went oral narrative and Washoe burlesque, practice with native characters and their speech, formulas of the journalist and lecturer, viewpoints of the westerner, and experiences of the Hannibal boy and the river pilot. In this novel humor is deepened with pathos and matured into wisdom. Here romance and realism are held in delicate balance. Men are seen and satirized with full sympathy. The heroic is balanced with the humble; the loyal and good with the selfish, craven, and false.

Edgar Marquess Branch. *The Literary Apprenticeship of Mark Twain* (Illinois). 1950. p. 199

If Mark Twain lacked art in Arnold Bennett's sense (as Arnold Bennett pointed out), that only shows how little art in Arnold Bennett's sense matters, in comparison with art that is the answer of creative genius to the pressure of profoundly felt and complex experience. If *Huckleberry Finn* has its examples of unintelligence that may accompany the absence of sustained critical consciousness in an artist, even a great one, nevertheless the essential intelligence that prevails, and from the poetic depths informs the work, compels our recognition—the intelligence of the whole engaged psyche; the intelligence that represents the integrity of this, and brings to bear the wholeness.

F. R. Leavis. *Cmty*. Feb., 1956. pp. 128–9

We can justly apply to Mark Twain's achievement what Eric Auerbach says of Dante: ". . . this man used his language to discover the world anew." Yet it would be misleading to imply that Mark Twain's break with literary tradition was all clear gain. The official culture (which we perhaps too easily dismiss by calling it the Genteel Tradition) had indeed lost its power to nourish vigorous literature; an act of repudiation was necessary. But if Mark Twain rejected the affirmations proposed by the cultural tradition, what positive value was left to sustain his work as an artist? The answer proposed by *Huckleberry Finn* is: innate, natural human goodness, which would flower into brotherhood if it could only be protected against the taint of society. The vision of innocence and happiness on the raft was exhilarating, as the book itself shows, but the affirmation of natural goodness was unsatisfactory in the long run because it was contradicted by Mark Twain's own observation of human character. There was no refuge from society, even on the River.

(K)

Henry Nash Smith. Introduction to *Adventures of Huckleberry Finn* by Mark Twain (Houghton). 1958. p. xxvi

From the start of the novel he had been of two minds about civilization and escape from it. Now his feelings were ambivalent about the things for which the shore and the raft stood: determinism on the one hand, freedom of choice on the other. Fierce though his attacks on shore folk were, his inability to condemn them brought mitigations. And his admiration for Jim and Huck was tempered by his envy of them and his skepticism about their state of grace. Both sinners and saints attracted and at the same time repelled him, and he was neither as rancorous toward the former nor as reverent toward the latter as he would have been if he were fully committed. He could make both groups comic. So the humor which makes *Huck* the funniest of all American books was vital to nuances of its meaning.

(K)   Walter Blair. *Mark Twain & Huck Finn*
                                      (California). 1960. p. 346

Mr. Eliot and Mr. Trilling agree in their readings that the River is a god, presiding over the action, its divinity everywhere implied though nowhere stated outright. But there is a more explicit supernaturalism in this book. Or, more properly, there is an exemplification and a testing of three attitudes toward the imaginative fulfillment of life, and these are largely indicated in supernatural terms. Each typifies the moral nature of those who profess it. Two of these imaginary supernatural worlds prove morally inadequate; the third—which pays homage to the river god—gives dignity to human life.

These attitudes, so compellingly dramatized by Mark Twain, are the conventional piety of the villagers; the irrelevant escape of the romantic imagination (as played by Tom Sawyer and an assorted adult cast of rapscallions and Southern gentlemen); and the world of supernatural omens which Jim, the runaway slave, best understands. Huck Finn is the sorcerer's apprentice. The superstitious imagination recognizes evil as a dynamic force; it acknowledges death. It is truer to the moral demands of life than is either the smug piety of Christian conformity or the avoidance of choice by escaping to fantasy and romance.

(K)   Daniel G. Hoffman. *Form and Fable in American*
                                      Fiction (Oxford). 1961. p. 320

Huck is given back to us at the very end in his declaration of independence, but it is significant that he is re-created primarily in the image of flight, of "lighting out for the Territory ahead of the rest." He is a character who can exist at all only outside the society that the novel allows us to imagine, who can exist in our imagination, finally, only outside the novel itself. Huckleberry Finn became for Mark Twain a kind of obsession, appearing during the years that follow in various sketches for stories and sequels to the novel. His career in this novel asks a question that Mark Twain must have urgently wanted to answer. If he must destroy Huckleberry Finn in his insistence that society cannot accommodate anything better than Tom Sawyer, then is he not in effect destroying society as a place in which the literary imagination may operate? . . . This book does in fact abandon everything it creates or depends on. And nothing is put in their place but a vague sense that—to remember Emerson once more—"Patience, then is for us, is it not? Patience, and still patience." *Huckleberry Finn* seems to me a totally revolutionary book that should not make us surprised at the later, bitterly unmodified and not very patient view of the "mysterious stranger"—that the universe is itself only "the silly creations of an imagination that is not conscious of its freaks."

(K)   Richard Poirier in *In Defense of Reading*, edited by
                             Reuben A. Brower and Richard Poirier (Dutton).
                                                            1963. pp. 308–9

See *Tom Sawyer, Huckleberry Finn, A Connecticut Yankee in King Arthur's Court, Pudd'nhead Wilson* (novels); *Short Stories; Life on the Mississippi* (autobiography and essays); *Innocents Abroad, Roughing It* (travel).

UPDIKE, JOHN (1932–   )

Leaving the contrapuntal music of the poets, the invitation is to hear a young man in a lonely pasture play the ocarina. He plays it exceedingly well; and should you wish to hear it again tomorrow you may suddenly find that his notes have overtones which at first escaped you, that his seemingly disparate little airs are somehow interrelated, and that now and then his music is coming at you from all directions, the way the sound of a winter wren in Canada will flood the valley. You should have your wits about you too, for the player is obviously an unusual individual who deserves but does not ask for an unusual audience. . . . [John Updike] has developed a maturity of technique; and in almost every instance he approaches an idea with the wariness of a sportsman after woodcock. Furthermore, he is a graceful border-crosser (light verse to poem) as Auden has been; as Betjeman and McGinley frequently are.

David McCord. *SR*. Aug. 9, 1958. p. 32

John Updike is a poet; his prose is lean and lapidary—in some cases almost engineered, like a fine, jeweled watch. Its unfragile delicacy is exactly what is needed to convey his insights whole, as in a picture or a poem. The abused word "artistry" may be here correctly applied. . . . It is a world seen neither with the brain nor the heart—or the guts—but with the understanding eye of the caring nonparticipant. It is characterized by a perceptive delicacy in which emotion is implied—as sound is implicit in a taut but unplucked string. The prime operative factor is, perhaps, a kind of genteel—almost stylish—super-awareness, with elegantly conveyed insights taking the place of events.

A. C. Spectorsky. *SR*. Aug. 22, 1959 pp. 15, 31

We are in a necessary period of non-solution in the novel, of anti-literature, which is essentially a resistance to tying neat knots, offering explanations, coming up with big solid counterweights to the miseries of life, providing alternative existences such as have come more and more to be demanded of fiction, that is to say, heroes to whom the reader can latch on and be carried right out of his mean, stifling *nonliterary* days and years. Updike, like the new French *alittérateurs*, doesn't want the novel to perpetuate itself as a compensation, a branch of philosophy or a rival of science, a *way out*. . . . *Rabbit, Run* gives off little of the air of implementing a plan which mars some of the work of Alain Robbe-Grillet or Nathalie Sarraute, for example. But it is all theorem or at least nothing else is there, no tying together of loose threads, no conclusions you can put on a shelf, no road-maps, no reinforcement of attitudes or beliefs. Only a distinguished balancing-act over a void, a major image of precarious life being true to itself.

Richard Gilman. *Com*. Oct. 28, 1960. p. 128

Updike frequently gives the impression that he has six or seven senses, all of them operating at full strength, and his writing is an attempt to register as precisely and originally as possible all the intelligence these senses send him. Struggling for a kind of hyperexpression, he mints an unceasing flow of almost invariably surprising images, which he then molds into uncluttered phrases, sentences, paragraphs, and pages that move with a sense of rhythm, timing, timbre, and volume that is impeccable. An irresistible tension is set up—a verbal rather than a narrative tension—and the reader immediately becomes a part of it, a trick dog who willingly sees, hears, smells, and feels exactly what Updike commands him to.

Whitney Balliett. *NY*. Nov. 5, 1960. p. 222

Despite the cleverness of his verse and the possibly overcivilized restraint of his fiction, Updike avoids a simple facile sophistication through his acute awareness of the "dislocations of modern life" and his religious sensitivity. A professed Congregationalist deeply familiar with theological and speculative problems, this Janus-faced writer combines a startling literacy, stylistic virtuosity, wit, and a profound melancholy in a way that is almost Joycean in quality.

Evelyn Geller. *WLB*. Sept. 1961. p. 67

Updike is not merely talented; he is bold, resourceful, and intensely serious.

His seriousness is not immediately apparent because he so often chooses to work with materials that seem slight and commonplace. . . . He is a most redoubtable explorer of the mysteries of the commonplace. . . . One of Updike's characters asks, "What is the past, after all, but a vast sheet of darkness in which a few moments, pricked apparently at random, shine?"

Updike's aim is to preserve certain of these moments, not out of nostalgia but because they give meaning to life. His Jamesian eagerness to let no experience be wasted is heightened by his sense of impermanence.

Granville Hicks. *SR*. March 17, 1962. p. 21

There is in John Updike's writing the kind of visceral understanding that can whiten a world to being in the flicker of a phrase or in a sudden crackle of speech. . . . He understands—better than foundries of socio-logical discourse can ever understand—the arcane folk rituals of ado-lescence. . . . And because John Updike writes of a more representative American experience, he tells us something other than what that fellow chronicler of the young, J. D. Salinger, tells us. For if Salinger reflects what the young would like to be, Updike tells us what they are.

Richard W. Murphy. Horizon. March, 1962. p. 84

Like the stories, the novels come close to being mere delicate restatements of the great current theme of isolation: millions of throbbing souls seek-ing fulfillment, identity, and, alas, happiness through love. Updike avoids reiterating the commonplace neurosis mainly because he is talented and intelligent. Also he is quiet and restrained. He has a commonsense per-ception of the ridiculous in things, and he is true to his personal vision. Ultimately the common thread running through all his works is the loca-tion of the human disease in the ego. But if we are all trapped in ourselves, unenlightened idealists in a real world, we are inevitably so. Except for old Hook in The Poorhouse Fair and a few matter-of-fact but terribly limited women, the people in the Updike world not only cannot communi-cate with each other, but they feel no need to.

J. A. Ward. Critique. Spring-Summer, 1962. p. 29

Updike shares with Agee a prickly, almost painful sensitivity to objects and relationships and a gift for precise and vivid prose. . . . With prose as sharp as music and jagged as rocks, Mr. Updike writes about the first furtive sexual explorations and drugstore obscenities of the adolescent. The ground is familiar enough, but the familiar is constantly undergoing transformation by his extraordinary perception. Events like a high-school basketball game or the manipulation of a pin-ball machine by a delin-quent "with an absolute purity of ambitionlessness" become, somehow, occasions of significance and even of beauty.

Updike brings to fiction unusual powers of vision and style and accom-modates these powers to a wide range of effects. Sometimes he writes in a vein of intense fantasy reminiscent of Dylan Thomas's unfinished Adven-tures in the Skin Trade, at others with the comic hypertension that is found in Kingsley Amis's novels at their best.

Peter Buitenhuis. NYT. April 7, 1963. p. 4

Now . . . it should begin to be clear how Updike is commenting not only beautifully but also meaningfully on our times. The baroque grandeur of Faulkner's world and the chivalric simplicity of Hemingway's seem far removed from the mainstream of American life as the second half of the twentieth century churns along; so indeed, do the rarefied ruminations of

J. D. Salinger's fragile Glasses. Updike, by contrast, is writing about something rather more pertinent—how most of us really live in this depressing sort of a world.

Does it follow, as *Time* and Updike's other detractors suggest, that small people necessarily have small problems?

The people Updike has written about . . . are enmeshed in the desperate facts of their condition. Their problems are just that—the desperation of their condition from which there is no ready escape. By weight of numbers alone, these problems take on a towering dimension, and one measure of Updike's achievement, it seems to me, is the quantity of joy and dignity he is able to detect in these drab existences without denying that very drabness.

Richard Kluger. *NYHT*. April 7, 1963. p. 8

In *The Centaur,* his latest novel, he gives promise of becoming a writer of considerable stature. He appears to be very knowledgeable, and it is hard to know, in reading *The Centaur,* how much he is concerned with guiding the tale or in showing us the tale as it *found* him. Mr. Updike, of course, is not the first novelist to reach out knowingly to the Greek myths for analogies, for characters, and stories. . . . Presumably Updike's *The Centaur* is an effort to get away from Shillington, Penn., or, better, to stay there and yet be able to view it from a distant time and place.

By and large, *The Centaur* is successful. *Rabbit, Run* presents a humanity that is pitiful, yet hardly pitiable; it is the foreground of a Breughel scene—with no redemptive lights in the distant valley or on a nearby river; there is no effort to justify or to redeem. *The Centaur* is a series of Breughel scenes, more heightened.

(K)   William Van O'Connor in *Contemporary American Novelists,* edited by Harry T. Moore (Southern Illinois). 1964. p. 212

Updike has chosen to give us insights into the modern world through the commonplace; he reveals to us the drama of the common man, a representative twentieth-century type who is often either dead-beat or slob, but whose significance, Updike urges, must not be slighted. His major creative problem is to encourage the reader to see this significance without resorting to the sentimental, the sensational or the sordid. It is here that his technical adroitness serves him in good stead. The refinements and subtleties of language ask us to pause over characters who would ordinarily seem undeserving of our attention, to see drama in conventional middle-class situations which would otherwise seem singularly undramatic.

(K)   David D. Galloway. *MFS*. Summer, 1964. p. 127

... implicit in the action and characterization of *The Centaur* is the feeling that a supernatural world of higher values may well exist and that the quest for it gives life meaning in this world and very possibly in the next. Being no optimist about this life and no dogmatist about the next, Updike has to be perpetually making the leap of faith. His attitude is similar to that of Miguel de Unamuno, who in *The Tragic Sense of Life* maintains that man's intuitive thirst for immortality demands a belief in God but that man's reason tells him there cannot be a God; out of this clash between reason and feeling come man's largest and noblest efforts, including genuine faith, which needs no validation other than itself. Hook [in *The Poorhouse Fair*] had this kind of faith; so does Caldwell [in *The Centaur*]. So, evidently, does their author, and he also has their kind of doubt, a skepticism which stimulates faith as certain bodily infections stimulate antibodies in the blood stream. On the other hand, *Rabbit, Run* is the fullest expression of Updike's skepticism. Doubt born of anxiety finally overwhelms faith in Rabbit, and that the spark is not completely extinguished is grounds only for pathos, not for spiritual hope.

(K)   Norris W. Yates. *CE*. March, 1965. p. 474

His latest novel, *Of the Farm*. . . , is very brief and unpretentious, but it is still a book by a deliberate stylist, and the style sometimes subsists on its own, unrelated to the simple events it is intended to serve. . . . Sometimes the preciosity is unbearable—"sere and painterly ochre," for example—but on the whole the thing works. It is the sort of thing that brings poetry back to the novel—not the poetry of action or casual close description but the poetry of digression, the only kind really admissable.

Touches like this give *Of the Farm* an intensity, as well as a relaxed quality of genuine "pastoral," very rare in contemporary letters. It does not dare as much as *The Centaur* but, in the sense that it knows almost perfectly how to encompass a foreknown and limited success, it is far more mature. What we expect from John Updike now is a book which essays margins of consciousness which will justify linguistic extravagance and a further exploitation of myth.

(K)   Anthony Burgess. *Com*. Feb. 11, 1966. pp. 558–9

John Updike's more polished, more artful, more professional epiphanies make perhaps the best short stories of our time. Such stories as "A Madman" and "Harv Is Plowing," as well as the title story, "The Music School," show an artistry and a compass of vision that I think will one day make him a major writer. He develops slowly, making slow headway against what we may call Lamb's Disease or the Blue China Syndrome: a self-conscious over-responsiveness to the charm of snow-topped branches or the round faces of children or the linked arms of strolling lovers or the merry thumping of the brass band—a slightly strained gaiety of the kind that mars the work of Katherine Mansfield and sometimes of Virginia Woolf and makes such essayists as A. A. Milne and Christopher Morley unreadable after we have passed our first youth. Logan Pearsall Smith endures by I don't know what magic, and Vladimir Nabokov by all-encompassing geniality—or, as we now miscall it, genius. But Updike's genial forces often droop under the bright load of those shiny things *The New Yorker* loves. Let us hope that he will either jettison them or develop the strength to carry them, as Nabokov does, lightly.

(K)   J. Mitchell Morse. *HdR*. Winter, 1966–67. p. 682

Even the earliest stories illustrate Updike's feeling for form and style, and the stories written in the 1960's have revealed a philosophical depth which *The Same Door* did not have. The best stories are the most recent; they are remarkable achievements in form, and their richness of meaning matches that of *The Centaur*. The themes of the recent stories echo those of the novels: the imminence of death and the threat of oblivion, yet the infinity of meaning which radiates from every human experience, and the richness of our human legacy.

(K)   Howard M. Harper. *Desperate Faith* (North
                                                          Carolina). 1967. pp. 188–9

There are good reasons for his impressiveness. Perhaps the most obvious and striking feature of his works is their poetic lavishness. Additionally there is the preoccupation with the gropings of the sensitive individual engaged in a struggle to penetrate and impose meaning upon the flux of his experiences—a concern which, especially since *The Catcher in the Rye,* has grown remarkably popular in our time. Finally there is the dazzling versatility which has enabled him to produce, in his still brief career, some fourteen-odd volumes which comprise novels, short stories, poetry, and "assorted" prose. . . . [T]he sequence of Updike's novels represents a quest for the appropriate form in which to order and best delineate his intensely subjective and impressionistic materials. Structurally he is an experimentalist, each of his novels marking a notable departure from its predecessor. But his motifs have not substantially changed—have, instead, been only modulated, varied in emphasis.

(K)   Bryant N. Wyatt. *TCL*. July, 1967. p. 89

See *The Carpentered Hen, Telephone Poles* (poems); *Pigeon Feathers, The Same Door, The Music School* (stories); *The Poorhouse Fair, Rabbit, Run, The Centaur, Of the Farm* (novels); *Assorted Prose.*

VAN DOREN, MARK (1894–   )

Poetry

We have only a few poets who have the inclination or the courage to be simple. Mr. Van Doren is one of them—his poems have that much maligned and refreshing quality of wholesomeness. They are like a lake breeze, cool milk, fresh bread and honey; though there is nothing remarkable about any of them either in subject matter or in content, almost all of them give genuine delight. . . . And though the poems have not enough individuality to win ardent admirers or vituperative assailants, they will undoubtedly and deservedly please the many who look to poetry for delicacy of feeling and charm of expression.

Marion Strobel. *Poetry*. Feb., 1925. pp. 279–80

The poetry of Mark Van Doren, an Illinois metaphysician transplanted to Connecticut, affords additional relief to readers sated with the vertigo of bookish poets. A few vital factors have saved Van Doren from growing dull: he lives on a farm and knows nature intimately; his principal masters are such commonsense Yankees as Emerson and Frost; and he has an eye and ear of his own and a style deleted of the "high-falutin," and devoted to an Anglo-Saxon rendering of concrete images. He may sound rather dry at first, but as one grows accustomed to his precision, one is moved by his passion and the wisdom of his deductions—deductions often left to the imagination.

Alfred Kreymborg. *Our Singing Strength* (Coward).
1924. p. 599

If an equivalent of these poems could be found in another medium, it would be in the art of etching. There is no music, or at most an abstract music. The tones are delicate grays and austere blacks and whites. Only a few strokes meticulously and economically drawn, are needed to suggest the bleakness of a landscape or the angularity of a person. The suasion is of the mind and not of the senses, yet the poet is concerned less to develop an idea than to suggest an evaluation. . . . If there is such a thing as a main stream of letters, they are doubtless not at its center. Yet subtlety and justness of psychological insight, precision of language, and neatness

295

of forms are qualities that are not too abundant at any time; they are particularly rare today.

Philip Blair Rice. *Nation*. Nov. 13, 1937. pp. 537–8

In his first five books of poetry, Mark Van Doren proved himself a careful craftsman with a sharp eye for the homely and a mind aware of the profound implications of the casual. . . . Yet for all the solid writing, the formal excellence, there are disturbing imperfections: monotonous verbal patterns, stanzas weakened by mannered feminine rhymes, themes overwritten. . . . But the chief defect results from an ear no longer sufficiently naive: lack of resonance. . . . However, it is easy to pick flaws in the work of a truly prolific artist. Although Mark Van Doren has written no single lyric to be compared with, let us say, Louise Bogan's "The Mark" . . . the level of his achievement has been remarkably high.

Theodore Roethke. *SR*. Nov. 17, 1937. p. 52

He is in the English tradition; his master, we can hardly doubt it, Dryden. He has the ease of Dryden, as he has the sanity; though he has always clarity, he does not have a comparable radiance. He has his own grace, but does not give that sense of inexhaustible strength which, more than anything else in Dryden, contributes to the impression of manly nobility. Mr. Van Doren is more easily resigned. He has come late to the English tradition, as he is rather belated in coming to his particular New English material. The style he has made for it is properly autumnal and dry.

John Peale Bishop. *Nation*. Dec. 23, 1939. p. 714

Mr. Van Doren thinks best through small objects seen as symbols and writes best in the short line and lyric vein.

His philosophy, also, is more attuned to the interval than the aeon. His cosmology would seem to be influenced by a conception of the universe that reduces Man to a passing and time-bound phenomenon among the slackening suns, thus increasing the importance, from the human point of view, of the small portion of life allotted him. A melancholy more delicate than pessimism evokes lost opportunities for joy and all the carnage of our years; a happiness less robust than optimism remembers the sensitiveness of childhood and takes comfortable refuge in the homely intimacies of earth.

Robert Hillyer. *NYT*. March 14, 1948. p. 6

Mr. Van Doren has somehow managed to remain undisturbed by technical revolutions, and, like Robert Frost, presents in his poetry the lively record of an individual sensibility without seeming to feel the need for any severe wrestling with language. His technical equipment is, on the whole (or at least on the surface), traditional, as far as verse forms and figures of speech go; but style and tone are often wholly original, and Mr. Van Doren is frequently able to achieve a strangely impressive significance with what seems at first sight an excessively conventional means of expression. At his best, the conventionality is superficial, and the freshness and originality of vision, which continually give new twists to traditional kinds of expression come across most convincingly.

David Daiches. *YR*. Summer, 1953. p. 629

Mr. Van Doren, hemmed in by the American world of business technology, chooses what is perhaps the most difficult strategy of all: to write poetry that employs rhyme and metre but keeps mainly within the rhetorical limits of informal prose. In this he follows Robinson and Frost, but relies less than Robinson on a strong rhythmic movement, less than Frost on colloquial effects (using no contractions, for instance, except in dialogue). He has so perfected his method that he is able to develop a highly subjective train of thought, sometimes at length, sustaining elusive figures and conceits, while keeping the alert tone and perfectly even temper of conversation.

George Dillon. *Poetry*. Aug., 1955. p. 289

His incandescent character, kindly and courageous, is as well known as his varied work of forty years' standing. It is therefore difficult to have to report that his latest book, *Morning Worship and Other Poems . . .* , disappoints by its slackness. A number of the poems first appeared in Mr. Van Doren's justly celebrated *Autobiography* and may have been included in *Morning Worship* for that reason alone. In any case, a younger poet might have omitted many of the 112 poems in this collection out of fear that the reader would not find the poet at his best. Less anxious, more tolerant, Mr. Van Doren has included them all, as one who is willing to let the reader choose for himself. His candor is admirable, but I wish he had pruned harder.

(K)   Peter Davison. *At*. Sept., 1960. p. 94

It must be plain, to the reader who has given him the attention every first-rate poet deserves, that, far from being a simple bucolic poet in the line of Crabbe or John Clare, he is an immensely learned and "literary" poet. He is not simple; he is that more difficult thing which can be pointed to with the one word *lucidity*. I am not evading what is generally supposed to be the critical task when I say he has no "method" but nevertheless is a highly conscious artist. He knows what he is doing, and if he seems to do it too often, or to publish too much of what he has done, we must remember once more what kind of poet he is. He is a formalist who is not trying in every poem to write a masterpiece; he is day by day the whole man who submits the whole range of his awareness to the forms that he has elected to use. He understands the relation of Art and Chance. If the moment of perception does not get completely into the form, that is too bad for the perception; it will have to try again. The Form is the thing.

(K)   Allen Tate. *NYHT*. Sept. 29, 1963. p. 4

Van Doren has not received, nor will he evoke, applause from the avant garde; he is solidly entrenched in the tradition of definite purpose framed in strict patterns. There is nothing spectacular about his style; he relies confidently on direct communication framed in conventional forms, although he varies his rhyme-schemes with occasional assonances and even dissonances. He avoids either extreme of the obsessively confessional and the unemotionally unaffected. Instead of a preoccupation with the lonely ego, Van Doren extends himself in various personae; yet he maintains himself in all of them with ease and penetration. Like Robert Graves and Edwin Muir he writes with clarity and force; also like these poets, Van Doren has never been slave to a vogue, and never having been in fashion will never be out of it.

(K)   Louis Untermeyer. *Poetry*. March, 1964. p. 383

Criticism

To understand the difference between these essays (in *The Private Reader*) and the run of criticism today is to discriminate not between methods but between persons, not between intentions but talents. Trying to become a science, criticism today has failed to be even a human communication. But the work in this volume is a communication, for Mr. Van Doren has the nobility that comes from discovering it in others and the wit that can define failure and pass beyond it. . . . Among good critics Mr. Van Doren has always stood out as The Great Neutral, and that neutrality is the secret and condition of his quality. For if his is an ardent mind, it is also a very tidy one; and if it is never aloof, it always lives on its own track; a mind exact and generous and often piercing in its intuitions, but very careful never to overreach, to say too much; ambitious only to stop on the necessary point made, the observation perfectly seen.

Alfred Kazin. *NYHT*. March 29, 1942. p. 2

Mr. Van Doren is a good critic in any sense of the word, for he has the ability to say interesting and illuminating things about books. He has also read deeply, so that he can fit any new book he reads into the framework of literature. And one would want to say more of all this were not one more impressed with how Mr. Van Doren can fit what he reads into

the framework of life. One always gets the feeling that a man is writing
. . . , as well as a critic. . . . His opinions, like his prose, are cool and dry;
he is masculine in his tastes, with no foolish or neurotic sensibilities.

Louis Kronenberger. *Nation*. May 16, 1942. p. 576

One of the few pieces of definitive literary criticism written in this century
during the present century (is) Mark Van Doren's *John Dryden*. . . .
Mr. Van Doren has explored the bases of Dryden's power with an industry
steadily illuminated by good sense. His book is packed with ordered information, none of which is superfluous to his intention. . . . On the first
appearance of this assured masterpiece of criticism T. S. Eliot declared:
"It is a book which every practitioner of English verse should study." The
poetry of the last quarter-century has been the poorer in that his advice
has not been taken.

George F. Whicher. *Nation*. March 2, 1946. p. 266

Nathaniel Hawthorne is quite as largely critical as it is narrative; indeed,
in the end, it is essentially a criticism of Hawthorne's work to which a good
deal of biography has been made to contribute. Criticism of the sort it is
could hardly be less perfunctory, more alert, awake, and attentive than Mr.
Van Doren's: nothing is taken for granted, and no piece of Hawthorne's
work, not even the slightest sketch, slips past Mr. Van Doren's eye in
careless companionship with some other piece to which it may bear an apparent resemblance but which in fact is of an unequal quality. . . . Criticism
of this writer's beautiful—if undeniably wavering and variable—work
will as time goes on, be more laborious and more intensive than Mr. Van
Doren's; it seems unlikely ever to be juster.

Newton Arvin. *SR*. April 30, 1949. pp. 11–2

Autobiography

Mr. Van Doren [in his *Autobiography*] writes gravely, yet with a kind of
pale, heat-lightning humor playing around the horizon of his reminiscences. He excels at some kinds of portraiture—country people, for example. He conveys an atmosphere of goodness from the academic world.
His utmost malice is a reserved portrait of Whittaker Chambers, who was
once a student of his; his utmost condemnation of anything is that "my
own opinions were called in question, though mildly as such things went"
when the Jersey City Library took his books off its shelves because he was
supposed to be a radical. And herein lies the weakness of this narrative.

For, however admirable it is in an ethical point of view to see some
good in every thing, keeping a steady eye on the Good inevitably makes
for monotony. We need salt and malice, we need some evidence that a good

man is a good hater, we need to be reminded of the vast misunderstandings possible in personal relationships, particularly in an academic community, particularly among those kittle cattle, poets and writing men. And here the book plainly fails.

(K)   Howard Mumford Jones. *SR*. Nov. 1, 1958. p. 33

See *Collected and New Poems, Narrative Poems; Collected Stories; The Private Reader, The Happy Critic, John Dryden, Nathaniel Hawthorne* (criticism); *Autobiography*.

VAN DRUTEN, JOHN (1901–1957)

If *Young Woodley* is neither a great nor a powerfully imagined play . . . it is at least a delightful and gentle thing, one of the happiest of late seasons in our theatre, one of the most lovable and memorable. Its sensitive observation, its simplicity and directness are admirable. Its picture is not so much that of youth rebellious, jazzy, ruthless, which we have been treated to so abundantly of late, but, what is more universal and poignant by far, of youth with all its passionate urgency, its surprised solitude, its brutality and confusion and rank, wild growth.

Stark Young. *NR*. Dec. 23, 1925. p. 134

After All, by John Van Druten, of *Young Woodley* renown, is a fine comedy in the proper sense of that much misused word. . . . There is nothing farcical or even melodramatic about *After All;* it is simply a keenly observant and delicately ironical study of the conflict between the generations in an upper middle-class English family. Whether you will like it or not depends on whether you believe there is a place for that sort of thing on the stage. . . . *After All* is really what in painting is known as *genre*. It depicts, or should depict, a small portion of a portion of life.

Otis Chatfield-Taylor. *Outlook*. Dec. 16, 1931. p. 502

If you can imagine a combination of the charm of Sir James Barrie, the realistic directness of George Kelly and the whimsical touch of Philip Barry, you will have a fairly good idea of what Mr. Van Druten achieves in *There's Always Juliet*. Like Philip Barry, he appreciates the importance of unspoken words, and also the significance of sheer nonsense and banter covering up much deeper emotions. He has George Kelly's particular facility for making his characters utterly natural and familiar both in speech and action. But above all he has the James Barrie trait of endowing his characters with a quite intangible and yet insistent charm.

Richard Dana Skinner. *Com*. Mar. 2, 1932. p. 495

When sex now triumphs in the theatre, it wears the trappings of romance, as did *There's Always Juliet,* in one sense the most daring production of the season. Think of the audacity required to present supposedly ultra-sophisticated Broadway with three acts of unmitigated love-making, object matrimony! Such effrontery is almost unbelievable. But the very novelty of what really wasn't a play at all, but only a duologue, resulted in a success more than justifying the iconoclasm. . . . *There's Always Juliet* was a pronounced hit, possibly because Everywoman saw in it something of her own romance, either as it was or as she wished it might have been. And romance has survived every change the world has seen.

> Louise Maunsell Field. *NAR.* Aug., 1932. pp. 174–5

Mr. Van Druten is a prolific playwright who has managed to achieve a considerable success both here and in London. . . . Nice people in their nicer—and quieter—moments he understands very well. When nothing more is required than a pleasant picture of pleasant domesticity he has a style of his own, and no one can make the tea table more genuinely agreeable than he. But he is not really at home anywhere except in the drawing room, and even there he is lost if the drawing-room atmosphere is disturbed by so much as a gentle draft from anywhere outside the walls which were built to inclose quiet affection and polite self-control. Resigned regret on the one hand, a mild determination on the other, make the limits over which his characters can move without losing all verisimilitude.

> Joseph Wood Krutch. *Nation.* April 24, 1935. p. 490

Mr. John Van Druten is one of the few men now writing for the stage who knows how to write high comedy. His touch is at once delicate and sure; his sense of comedy, particularly on the distaff side, keen and subtle; his dialogue witty, often distinguished. Perhaps the war will end this type of writing; a general leveling process will certainly end it; but if end it does, the world will be the poorer. It presupposes a certain amount of leisure, a willingness in the audience to forget for the moment social questions and to interest itself in the interplay of human character. High comedy may not be, in the critical jargon of the day, important, but it is one of the marks of a civilized society.

> Grenville Vernon. *Com.* Jan. 10, 1941. p. 303

Mr. Van Druten is a playwright who pulls no punches in exposing the shoddier aspects of his characters, but his sympathies run deep. Within the narrow confines of his play (*Old Acquaintance*) . . . he does a remarkable job of steering a group of civilized people through situations which bring out their pettiness and jealousies, without stripping them of their essential kindliness and decency. For all the smartness of the writing and sophistication of the plot, such as it is, Mr. Van Druten's play conveys a peculiarly warm conviction that humanity, even on its less rarefied levels is capable of a modest sort of nobility.

Robert Bendiner. *Nation*. Feb. 1, 1941. p. 137

The Voice of the Turtle (has) three actors, one entirely realistic set, no plot to speak of, almost no action, certainly no music and dance. And this . . . is theatre. . . . A gem of purest ray—and serene, too—set neatly, with an expert's touch, in the circlet that is to hold it; a light, deft play as winningly acted as it is wisely directed, making no greater claim than what is so amply accomplished—that of being a good example of good theatre. *The Voice of the Turtle* . . . is a pleasant study of pleasant people. Like Mr. Van Druten's earlier *There's Always Juliet,* it concerns love at first sight and has about as much or as little plot as that former excursion into the same subject. It is chiefly engaging for its amiable conversation, (and) for the discernment with which its characters are revealed.

Rosamond Gilder. *TA*. Feb., 1944. p. 73

The Voice of the Turtle, in short, is an apotheosis of the sex life and irresistible in its implications. . . . It is convincing, infinitely appealing, and beautifully indifferent to the morality held sacred by the blue-noses. Yet the latter seem to have not the slightest suspicion of the fact and not a voice has been lifted against it. That is Van Druten's triumph. For he has written it so very skillfully; he has, without the least chicanery or sub-terfuge, gone about his business with such deceptive immaculateness and simplicity; and he has so astutely avoided any slightest sense of smirk or vulgarity that he has managed to make the moralists themselves not only eat his play but digest it and like it.

George Jean Nathan. *AM*. April, 1944. p. 465

Mr. Van Druten is a dramatist who cannot write a play without some merits. In an age that has proved itself tragically uncivilized, he con-tinues to be a highly civilized talent. He is a craftsman who enjoys the challenges of his medium. He is at his best when working as a miniatur-ist. His perceptions are charming. He understands the human significance of the smallest values. . . . He wears his sophistication lightly. His wit is gentle. His audacities have a way of remaining respectable. He talks of passion in crumpet tones. He remains somewhat Victorian in tone even when in word he is the champion of the unlost weekend.

John Mason Brown. *SR*. Dec. 15, 1945. pp. 15–6

Van Druten is a kind of Katherine Mansfield among playwrights. Gen-teel, polished, mannerly, he illuminates tiny corners of middle-class life, recites a small, simple story in hushed library tones, tells us very little directly, and sends us out of the theater with disquieting reverberations echoing softly in ours ears.

Irwin Shaw. *NR*. Nov. 3, 1947. p. 36

See *Young Woodley, There's Always Juliet,* and *The Voice of the Turtle* (plays).

VEBLEN, THORSTEIN (1857–1929)

The author's theory of why fashions change is ingenious, and must be largely true. The ugliness caused by their superfluous cost renders them intolerable to behold for any great length of time, so that a change is demanded by the aesthetic sense even of the leisure class; but the new ones can be no better, because they, too, must have these marks of "reputable futility" and "conspicuous waste," that are necessarily offensive to taste, which is based on the instinct of workmanship. They must therefore also soon give way to others no better than they, and so on indefinitely. It is a perpetual conflict between pecuniary beauty and rational beauty, which are incompatible, but in which the former always prevails, and all the latter can do is to condemn the product and compel the victor to bring on another.

Lester F. Ward. *AJS*. May, 1900. p. 835

The social prophet, like the poor, is with us always, and possibly the most striking Jeremiad of the year comes in the guise of an estimate of our industrial system. The *Theory of Business Enterprise,* by Professor Veblen, is a singular instance of how economic philosophy is sometimes infected by tendencies rife in widely separated fields of thought. Through the transparent veil of this sociological essay one gets many a glimpse of the cosmic irony of Ibsen and the nihilistic doctrine of Nietzsche. A very readable quality is thus imparted to the speculation by the author, but at the cost of a most unenviable frame of mind. Professor Veblen has a preternaturally vivid insight into the pathological side of business and society; and he follows remorselessly the poisoned tract which his critical scalpel has discovered.

Winthrop More Daniels. *At.* April, 1905. p. 558

Though born, I believe, in These States, and resident here all his life, he achieves the effect, perhaps without employing the means, of thinking in some unearthly foreign language—say Swahili, Sumerian or Old Bulgarian —and then painfully clawing his thoughts into a copious but uncertain and book-learned English. The result is a style that affects the higher cerebral centers like a constant roll of subway expresses. The second result is a sort of bewildered numbness of the senses, as before some fabulous and unearthly marvel. And the third result, if I make no mistake, is the celebrity of the professor as a Great Thinker. In brief, he states his hollow nothings in such high, astounding terms that they must inevitably arrest and blister the right-thinking mind.

H. L. Mencken. *Prejudices: First Series* (Knopf). 1919. pp. 66–7

But, if a conscious effort is required fully to appreciate the outline and implications of Veblen's thought, the reader must be even more conscientious if he would discover the meanings concealed by Veblen's literary style. Veblen was inclined to use language in peculiar ways, and to be very arbitrary in the meanings which he ascribed to words. It might be possible to become habituated to his practice were he not so frequently an innovator in the use of words. In reading Veblen, the impression which remains uppermost is that he had consciously learned of the existence of a surprising range of words and saw no reason for not employing them all, but that, unfortunately for his readers, he did not heed the rule of common acceptation in determining *where* they should be used.

Yet it would be false to deny that Veblen's style has proved to be a distinct attraction to many of his readers, especially among those making up his non-academic following. The insistent redundancy of his expressions, his pungent and telling phraseology, the scope of his terminological usage, all have contributed to inspire in the minds of such readers a conviction of the erudite authenticity of his thought.

Richard Victor Teggart. *Thorstein Veblen, A Chapter in American Economic Thought* (California). 1932. pp. 39–40

From a literary standpoint the book is doubtless worthy of Ph.D. dissertations in English literature. Its extensive use of literary devices, including etymological precision, foggy language, and sharp comparisons and contrasts ever changing in form, has seldom been equalled in a study of an economic and social order. Phenomena which generally appear trivial to the ordinary intelligence are exaggerated to bring out the meaning or consequences of the dominant forces constituting the existing system. Even academic economics becomes a part of Veblen's arsenal.

The book reads as if it were a saga, as if, in accordance with saga traditions, the underlying motif constantly before the listener were the inevitable doom of the industrially advanced, democratic community, through the functioning of the heroic characters who are thrown up as

an effective leisure class by conditions supposed to make for peace, and
who go also to their destruction.

Joseph Dorfman. *Thorstein Veblen and His
America* (Viking). 1934. pp. 174–5

Veblen repudiates preaching. As an evolutionist his office is to understand; not to praise, or blame, or lead us into righteousness. From his point
of view, any notions he may entertain concerning what is right and wrong
are vestiges of the cultural environment to which he has been exposed.
They have no authority, and it would be a futile impertinence to try to
impose them upon others. There is much of the satirist in him; but it is
satire of an unfamiliar and a disconcerting kind. Professedly, he seeks
merely to describe and to explain our cultural traits in plain terms. But he
likes to put his explanations in a form that will make the commonplaces
of our daily lives startling and ridiculous to us. It is this histrionic foible
which gives his writing its peculiar flavour.

Wesley C. Mitchell. Introduction to *What Veblen
Taught* (Viking). 1936. p. xix

His *Theory of the Leisure Class* gained many readers but probably suffered loss of serious intellectual attention because of a pervasive tone of
irony conveyed in part by linguistic formalities. Though this was in a degree characteristic of most, though by no means all, of his writings, its
prominence in the earliest of his books served to give him a reputation for
humour which, though in some ways protective, postponed and even
damaged his legitimate reputation as the keenest social thinker of his time.
He did not deliberately choose and cultivate this humorous attitude. It
was inherent in the social situation as he saw it. His approach was throughout that of an interested onlooker, seeking to understand the spectacle of
American life. . . . When Veblen . . . showed how the interests of the
economic master-class drew into its gainful course, by half-conscious or
subconscious methods of attraction, the controls of politics, religion, culture, recreation, social prestige, that could give assistance and protection
to its business methods, the unmasking of such a relation between presumably independent activities and institutions was essentially humorous.

J. A. Hobson. *Thorstein Veblen* (Wiley). 1937.
pp. 220–1

To the unwary, Veblen has seemed to have created his system almost as
a by-product of something which to him was important, reaching a new
economics by way of the conspicuous consumption illustrated in women's
dress, or by way of economists' neglect for their subject matter—which,
he said, was business and the machine process—in favor of taxonomic

exercise. The studies in deliberate waste seemed to have been animated by a racial bitterness, and the undermining of economics by the need for intellectual revenge. Both have been ascribed to compensatory compulsion. Before he got through, however, it began to appear that he had done something more important than merely to exercise a complex. Those who put it all together could infer an intention to expose capitalism as an impossible mixture of mutually canceling elements, and the going economics as an inferior example of the artificial one-thing-at-a-time method. Certainly to the casual student the hypothesis was everything; to others the new institutional method had the value of release from orthodoxy and was therefore far more important.

> R. G. Tugwell in *Books That Changed Our Minds,*
> edited by Malcolm Cowley and Bernard Smith (Kelms-
> cott). 1939. p. 94

He talked a little about his own life. He had pride in his Norwegian background. I think Joseph Dorfman is right in his belief that this background, which Veblen's parents clung to in their culturally isolated Norwegian community in Minnesota, accounted for much of Veblen's philosophical detachment from American life. He was like an enlightened savage in a civilized country, or an enlightened explorer in a savage country, viewing it critically, understanding it very well but not belonging to it.

> Robert L. Duffus. *The Innocents at Cedro*
> (Macmillan). 1944. p. 58

Peerless in breadth of knowledge, Thorstein Veblen challenged the concept of normality as a qualified philosopher, a student of psychology, a trained and resourceful economist. In an important early article called "Why Is Economics Not an Evolutionary Science," the philosopher of science spoke. The concept of normality—and the kindred notions of an overruling Providence and a moral law of nature—were, to Veblen, carryovers of a primitive animism. At best, they gave rise to systems of "economic taxonomy," that is, to logically consistent propositions unrelated to life. At worst, they justified a hands-off policy with respect to the price mechanism and the market.

> May Brodbeck, James Gray, Walter Metzger. *Amer-*
> *ican Non-Fiction, 1900–1950* (Henry Regnery).
> 1952. p. 168

[*The Higher Learning in America*], along with *The Theory of the Leisure Class,* seems to me Veblen's wittiest book, the one where his shafts of satire, based on the closest observation of every scabrous detail, penetrated furthest; as an effective caricature of academia it has not been equalled (unless, perhaps, by Mary McCarthy's novel, *The Groves of Academe*). . . .

It was, as we have seen, Veblen's habit of dramatic abstraction which led him to write the world-history of predation, seeing in each age a different group of men notably gifted in exploit, or in the selling of specious but respectable intangibles. He worked his scheme of succession both forward and backward, describing for instance a period of Viking history as "An Early Experiment in Trusts," or painting the modern minister as the lineal descendent of shamans or Egyptian hieratic practitioners. Often, such comparisons were more witty than revealing. But the idea that a William Rainey Harper is "really" a Dan Drew of education—that is a discovery of some moment in understanding the nature of entrepreneurial activity in American life.

> David Riesman. *Thorstein Veblen, A Critical Interpretation* (Scribner). 1953. pp. 100–101

The career of Thorstein Veblen . . . demonstrates at least one fact: a man does not need to be born an Adams or to be descended from a line of Puritans in order to become a master of perversity, of the art of mystifying even while alluring his audience. Through his long life Veblen displayed such an independence of manner and morals as cost him his marriage, his friends, and a series of jobs, and such an independence of mind as leaves him a social theorist who defies classification and who, more than any figure of recent times, has deeply influenced a variety of followers, hardly one of whom agrees with any other. . . . To amputate portions of the *Leisure Class* (which is now available in several reprints) is to spoil a work of art. Its thesis, that in a capitalist society the creation of waste is an index of success, is in effect a standing of Herbert Spencer on his head. The mingling of serious and satiric tones make the book doubly effective, since no reader knows exactly when his leg is being pulled or whether the moral of the book should be moral indignation against an improvident society or a Pascalian compliance with folly. Veblen has inspired New Dealers and reassured reactionaries.

> Perry Miller. Introduction to *American Thought: Civil War to World War I* (Rinehart). 1954. pp. xlvi–xlviii

Certainly Veblen took nothing for granted, questioned everything, and was merciless, though his mood was only indirectly characteristic of the new century. Inscrutable and sardonic, he stood aloof from most of the currents of thought that swirled about him. Repudiating the classical economists, he refused to associate himself with the pragmatic; at war with the conservatives, he was not an ally of the radicals but cherished throughout his life a position of independent belligerency. His rebellion went so deep that it confounded even dissenters; his heresies were so profane that they baffled orthodoxy and heterodoxy alike. He invoked not only a new philosophy but a new vocabulary. . . . For he brought to the study of economic institutions and conduct not only history and anthropology but philosophy and psychology. He realized how deeply rooted in habit and custom were the economic mores of any society, and his *Theory of the Leisure Class* was the most penetrating commentary on the psychological bases of economic institutions that had yet been made.

Henry Steele Commager. *The American Mind*
(Yale). 1954. pp. 236–7, 242

. . . Veblen laughed so hard and so consistently at the servants and the dogs and the women and the sports of the elite that he failed to see that their military, economic, and political activity is not at all funny. In short, he did not succeed in relating a view of their power over armies and factories to what he believed, quite rightly, to be their funny business. He was, in my view, not quite serious enough about status because he did not see its full and intricate importance to power. He saw 'the kept classes' and 'the underlying population,' but in his time, he could not really understand the prestige of the power elite.

The heart of Veblen's conception of prestige, and even some of its terms, were set forth by John Adams in the late eighteenth century. But to know that John Adams anticipated much of Veblen's idea is in no way to deprecate Veblen, for is not his theory essentially an extended piece of worldly wisdom, long known and perhaps often stated, but stated by Veblen in magnificent form and at a time when it could take hold of a literate public?

C. Wright Mills. *The Power Elite* (Oxford). 1956.
p. 89

See *The Theory of the Leisure Class, The Theory of Business Enterprise, The Higher Learning in America, The Place of Science in Modern Civilization and Other Essays* (essays).

VIERECK, PETER (1919–   )

Poetry

With the energy, high spirits, and optimism of a young man, he has set out to conquer a space for the humane and reasonable wherever it can be found amid the encircling gloom, and he is often remarkably capable of doing it. . . . His pleasure in words occasionally leads him to dubious puns —neurosis-new roses—and neo-Swinburnian rhymes that overpower the poem. But for the most part, both in phrasing and form, the sense of craftsmanship is evident throughout the book.

Eugene Davidson. *YR*. Summer, 1949. p. 726

He is a linguist, widely read, a man of zest and wit with a beautiful control of language. . . . I enjoyed Viereck's lively historical sense, his love of fun, and the skill with which he restates the traditional and great poetic themes. Unlike most young poets, he is more impressive collected than when read in single poems. He seldom over-extends himself in the grand effect.

Edward Weeks. *At*. Aug., 1949. p. 83

Viereck has something of an insight into the tensions of poetry, into the struggles of the formative spirit, and into the spiritual area of romanticism; but he has mounted too shrilly and too athletically the stilts of "romanticism-classicism," and has taken this opposition, not so much as something from which one could learn, but as an article of faith and a source of poetry.

J. H. Johnston. *Com*. Aug. 5, 1949. p. 418

The poems are lively . . . and a few of them sustain a neat, coarse clarity and a satiric turn of fancy that is not disagreeable. . . . The appearance of these qualities, and the appeal they seem to have, are evidences of a shift long under way from visionary concentration in poetry . . . to a drier and airier attitude, a more epigrammatic vein. In Viereck's case . . . the shift is so indiscriminate that on the whole it looks more like a relapse. . . . Viereck has as yet written very little to which one could wish to return often or with serious interest.

Robert Fitzgerald. *NR*. Aug. 8, 1949. p. 17

Whatever Viereck touches takes on a freshness and excitement. He writes about the Dawn Horse and the function of the poet with an equal mixture of gravity and mockery. He puts the scrawled phrase "Kilroy was here" into rhyme with adventurous daring and epic spirit. He is amusing and arousing in the same breath. He is an experimenter who rarely yields to the speciously spectacular, a writer who respects tradition without being submerged in it, a genuine wit who is, at the same time, a poet of emotional power.

Louis Untermeyer. *Modern American Poetry*
(Harcourt). 1950. pp. 686–7

Viereck may well be described as the principal standard-bearer of the tradition of humanistic democracy in this country. . . . Combining high wit and high seriousness, Viereck has escaped the lugubriousness ever present in the work of many of his elders. His poetry, weaving together classical myths and wartime legends such as that of Kilroy, brings to the mind the aspect of Alexander Pope that appears in "The Rape of the Lock." Like (Robert) Lowell, his enemy is Satan—not the Biblical Satan, but the modern masked Satan who denies his own existence.

Anthony Harrigan. SAQ. Oct., 1950. p. 486

In opposition to one poetic fashion of the Forties—the fashion of anxious psychologizing, interrupted by metafidgets—Viereck set himself off. Ostensibly as a "classicist," but in reality as something rarer in our time and more difficult to maintain on a high level—an ambitious and intelligent romantic, one of the few new poets impatient to put the gains of the two previous generations to the service of big themes, in a style remarkable and exciting for its ability to work into one context the dramatic and the didactic, the humorous and the lyrical, the topical and the fantastic.

Maurice English. Poetry. May, 1954. pp. 89–90

It was partly Viereck's ingenuity in the use of conventional form that aroused so much interest. . . . His attack on the more arid and drooping kind of "modernism" has been frontal, and his admirers have cheered his championship of a new and rather reactionary poetic future wherein poetry, with Eliot and Pound finally vanquished in open combat, could once more "communicate" to a large and eager audience. . . . He still displays a strong belief in his own powers, both poetic and polemic, and he is still full of vigor and zest, but much of his originality seems to be stiffening into eccentricity. . . . Tricks come more and more into evidence.

Louise Bogan. Selected Criticism (Noonday). 1955.

p. 395

From the beginning he had been hard to classify. There was much that was rollicking, wild, and sometimes raucous in his initial book of verse. But half-concealed by technical fireworks and plain vitality was a quieter, more tranquil Viereck, the lyricist gravely recording the eternal flow of life and experience.

It is the lyricist who is now coming into his own. . . . The latent lyricism of the poet has become incarnate in language which evokes from the reader an equal response of mind, heart, and the wistful senses.

Chad Walsh. NYT. Oct. 28, 1956. p. 37

Viereck's star has somewhat declined since his Pulitzer Prize days, and it shouldn't have. If he isn't read, that is our loss, for he is far too volatile and perceptive to languish in old magazines. That he is a bit of a showoff and seems to some a bratty smart-aleck who knows only a little about a lot of things, and that he insists on demonstrating this to one and all, time after time, shouldn't be allowed to obscure his very real virtues, which are a perennially youthful go-for-broke recklessness, an unstudied abandon and fearlessness in the pursuit of ideas and their consequences, and a sheer bounce and linguistic *joie-de-vivre* which communicate more than a little of the "personal warmth" he posits as our salvation. He writes, in the end, a kind of poetry which, rather than seeing itself as potentially "immortal," is quite frankly ephemeral and topical, gladly (and this is a word one can hardly help applying to Viereck) sacrificing the hope of Parnassus to the more immediate one of instruction and usefulness.

(K)   James Dickey. *SwR*. Summer, 1962. p. 489

Viereck is a well-known professor of history and a professional political theorist of repute. The spill-over of his métier as historian into his poetry is unfortunate. There is endless ranting, mostly in quaint iambic pentameter and other disqualified meters, nearly all on the socio-political plane. The satire is heavily quasi-American, wrecked by thinking and an over-educated prosody.

Nevertheless a reader can comb this volume [*New and Selected Poems*] with admiration. There are poems well worth searching out, dozens of them. This reviewer would call the attention of all anthologists to the 12-line lyric "The Lyricism of the Weak," a monologue in the great American patois and a kind of elegy on the death of the English language. It is probable that the poem is intended as an assault on Incorrectness (it is hard to say), but the present reviewer knows at least 10 poets and professors who have memorized it.

(K)   Karl Shapiro. *NYT*. Aug. 6, 1967. p. 8

Prose

His aim is a foursquare blow at the standardized thinking of both the Right and the Left in contemporary America. . . . He is glib, sassy, and provocative. . . . You will have to enjoy the dexterity with which he bursts so many half-truths and slides his sword behind the arras of so many hidden fallacies.

Thurston Davis. *Am*. March 14, 1953. pp. 652–3

Mr. Viereck is full of energy, full of zest in hate and love, in fact a man who evokes . . . the word "Renaissance," not the nice humanism of an Erasmus, but a Rabelaisian piling-up of pearls and rubbish. . . . Mr.

Viereck himself is clearly a more astounding paradox than any he has written. This defender of the middle way, this classicist, this lover of French *mesure* writes most unbridled and unbuttoned books, books sewed together with all sorts of odds and ends, books that froth and foam with anger at the stupidity of the race—or at least of those of the race he knows best, his fellow intellectuals.

Crane Brinton. *JHI*. June, 1953. p. 461

In each essay Mr. Viereck arrives at the conclusion that neither of the two large opposing points of view under examination is sufficient, and he proposes a mean between them that will combine the best of both. Despite the impression of mechanical formula that such a procedure is bound to give, when Mr. Viereck speaks about specific works of poetry his taste is always good and his judgment disinterested. . . . Everywhere, in fact, his notions are sober and considered. Yet the language in which he states his moderation is neither moderate nor restrained, and sometimes not even intelligible.

Steven Marcus. *Cmty*. Aug., 1954. p. 175

As historian, Peter Viereck has an enviable catalog of data at his command. As poet, he makes such surprising juxtapositions of ideas that you are sometimes startled into accepting his thought-images for their esthetic rather than for their logical value. Viereck can't browse through old ideas without putting them back on the shelf in new positions. After reading Viereck, you might not agree with his conclusions, but it is pretty hard to say why.

Goldwater's arguments have just the edge to make liberals more self-righteous than ever. Viereck's idea-associations have the discomfiting effect of making liberals realize how conservative they are.

Both socialism and conservatism, Viereck believes, work in America as a diffusion, not a movement. They do not have a social base, a party, or a class. When they do become a movement, they become small, comical splinter groups. This diffusion will be jeopardized if the conservatives try to localize it into the apologetics for any one class. Viereck speaks of a "diffusion" because he thinks conservatism is essentially an ethical and cultural force. It may seem strange to ignore the obvious economic factors and think of both conservatism and socialism as ethical and cultural forces, but this is the way Viereck plays it.

(K)   Edward Cain. *They'd Rather Be Right* (Macmillan).
1963. pp. 111–12

See *New and Selected Poems, The Tree Witch;* also *Dream and Responsibility, The Unadjusted Man* (prose).

WALLANT, EDWARD LEWIS (1926–1962)

This brief first novel is done in tones of gray, with occasional blood splotches. It is the story of the life and grief of Joe Berman, plumber. The grief is the framework within which, starting with the death of Joe's wife, flashbacks intermittently fill in his European, Jewish childhood, his growing up, his marriage, his friends, his children, his simple and yet full life.

Yet the grief is more than the framework: it becomes the central theme, really. For Joe at fifty-nine is inconsolable for the loss of his wife. . . .

The trouble with *The Human Season* is that, having detailed Joe's misery, Mr. Wallant has nowhere to go except around and around again. Getting up, going to bed, eating or not eating, pacing the floor, watching TV; these repetitions, despite the author's development of new situations—despite even the interruption by flashbacks—become monotonous.

Winfield Townley Scott. NYHT. Dec. 25, 1960. p. 34

Like Bernard Malamud, Edward Lewis Wallant has made contemporary Jewish life the focus of his work. He was the author last year of *The Human Season,* a deeply compassionate study of a Jewish plumber grieving for his dead wife. Now, in *The Pawnbroker,* Mr. Wallant attempts a fuller, richer orchestration of human experience. His interest in Jewish life broadens out into the festering world of New York's Harlem, where Jewish businessman and ghetto Negro confront each other over a pawnshop counter. And framing the somber events of this novel is the dark apocalypse of Nazi Europe. Mr. Wallant has written an ambitious, unparochial novel that says something about man's responsibility to man.

David Boroff. SR. Aug. 26, 1961. p. 16

The Tenants of Moonbloom . . . is a remarkable tour de force in which this gifted writer takes the elements of several "Street Scenes," and spins them faster and faster like a deranged merry-go-round. Norman Moonbloom, the pivot of Mr. Wallant's off-center carousel, is a perpetual student . . . who has finally matriculated as renting agent for his slum-lord brother Irwin. . . . His apotheosis, in a heroic burst of filth and renovation, is depicted by Mr. Wallant with great wit and style.

Martin Levin. NYT. Aug. 18, 1963. p. 30

Far from being one of our best novelists, as a number of reviewers have belatedly claimed, Wallant did not have the time to become even a fully competent one. All four of his novels were clearly written under the spell of a deep view of life to which his developing powers as an artist were only beginning to be adequate. *The Children at the Gate* is alternately crude and sensitive, thin and dense, obvious and subtle; its chief significance, like that of Wallant's other novels, lies in the vision that he was struggling to clarify and expand. . . .

His perspective, largely a psychoanalytic one, came from his understanding of what a man goes through in the course of altering his character, of breaking down his defenses in order to live his life rather than to merely survive in it. Instead of writing about Madison Avenue analysands, though, Wallant chose to reach into the dark, marginal pockets of urban existence, usually in the ethnic slums, and to find his heroes among their lost souls, men living alone and unto themselves, whose habits of deprivation and repression are suddenly torn apart by the engagement of circumstances without and deeply within.

Theodore Solotaroff. NYHT. April 5, 1964. p. 5

Wallant's themes are more or less constant. His central character is a Jew, who is sensitive to life's sufferings; he wants to hold himself back from the harshness, cruelty, senselessness and pain of life. But he cannot. Something always happens to bring him back. The plumber, after a sordid clutching after a slattern, is ashamed of himself but recognizes the welling up of lust as a return to life and its desires. The pawnbroker, after his assistant is murdered in a hold-up, finds himself mourning the death of the boy and, in weeping, discovers that life has new meaning for him, although he thought that after the concentration-camp experiences, he had been cut away from passion and emotion. Norman Moonbloom, afraid of life's realities, is liberated by a sexual experience, and discovers the high passion of doing something for his repressed, suffering and poverty-stricken charges.

Harold U. Ribalow. JF. June, 1964. p. 27

All of Wallant's novels have a similar, ritual structure: a man cut off from the source of himself, in a delicate truce with the nightmare of survival, slowly, terrifyingly, at the risk of everything, rediscovers the possibility of feeling. Whereas *The Human Season, The Pawnbroker,* and *The Children at the Gate,* are almost airlessly intense, *The Tenants of Moonbloom,* Wallant's next to last novel (actually, in fact, the last to be written), is an attempt at treating the same dark concerns, the same human dislocations, with something like comic perspective. Where the others are indebted in tenuous ways to the fiction of Malamud and Bellow (and Dostoevsky), *The Tenants of Moonbloom* is, in the only way the term is meaningful, an original achievement. And since it shows another aspect of the resources of Wallant's vision, I think it worth the attention of close analysis. *Moon-bloom* is also the most beautifully written of the four novels, an uncannily funny and discomforting book.

Jonathan Baumbach. *The Landscape of Nightmare*
(NYU). 1965. p. 146

One must wonder what film director Sidney Lumet's initial reaction was as he read, for the first time, Edward Lewis Wallant's novel, *The Pawn-broker*. Wallant had created a story about Sol Nazerman, a forty-five-year-old Jewish pawnbroker conducting his underworld-financed trade in the Harlem slums. Nazerman, once a professor at the University of Cracow, lost his family, and his humanity, in the Nazi concentration camps. Now, twenty years after the war, he moves with zombie-like purpose between the relatives he supports in Mount Vernon, the hysterical wife of an exterminated friend, and his dingy shop. His is dedicated to isolating himself from any feelings of hope or compassion; of existing, one day after the other, in a carefully maintained vacuum which allows neither love, hatred, nor involvement of any kind. Yet every year, in August, the precarious equilibrium sustaining this vacuum is threatened by the anniversary of his family's death. As the day approaches it evokes desperately suppressed memories of the camp, and of the wife and children who were butchered there. To expose the torment these memories inflict on Nazerman, Wallant employs vivid and merciless flashbacks, and Lumet, in plotting his translation of the novel into a film, must deal with this most unwieldly of cinematic techniques as the crucial expository and dramatic vehicle of the story. For while the plot may hold together if these memories were simply to be narrated, the dramatic impact of the horror that has driven this man to deny all his former values and aspirations would be lost, and the story, *in toto,* would abrogate its considerable power.

Joseph Lyons. *WHR*. Summer, 1966. p. 243

See *The Human Season, The Pawnbroker, The Children at the Gate, The Tenants of Moonbloom* (novels).

WARREN, ROBERT PENN (1905–   )

The poetry of Robert Penn Warren can best be studied as the esthetic expression of a mind in which tradition and the forces destroying tradition work in strong opposition to each other—ritual and indifference to ritual; self-knowledge and indifference to or inability to achieve self-knowledge; an inherited "theological" understanding of man and the newer psychological or social understanding, illustrated perhaps in the religious concept

of evil and the liberal belief in man's ultimate power to control "evil"
forces. There are two major pulls at work in shaping his idiom, the older
belief in a morally integrated human being and the naturalist belief in a
being formed by ill-understanding forces. The former pull expresses itself
in a body of poems, and in some of his prose, as a provincial, homogeneous
and consistent view that in another age might have achieved the epic
proportions we associate with poetry as vision, the latter pull expresses
itself in fictional characters of a low order and in a poetic idiom of a considerably less imaginative vitality.

William Van O'Connor in *A Southern Vanguard*,
edited by Allen Tate (Prentice-Hall). 1947. p. 92

Trite as it is nowadays to stigmatize an author as a dual personality, I
cannot help pointing to a duality in Warren that may well constitute his
major problem: it is his combination of critical and creative power. I am
far from suggesting that the critical and the creative are of their nature
antipathetic and I am fully ready to grant that what makes Warren remarkable among American writers is his double endowment. The problem lies precisely in his being so two-sidedly gifted; he evidently finds it
difficult to combine his two sorts of awareness. There is Warren, the critic,
the cosmopolitan, the scholar, the philosopher; and there is Warren, the
raconteur, the Kentuckian, the humorist, the ballad maker. . . . Warren is
a faulty writer, but he is worth a dozen petty perfectionists. Though commonly associated with "formalists" and "classicists" in criticism, he is
close to the type of romantic genius: robust, fluent, versatile, at his worst
clever and clumsy, at his best brilliant and profound.

Eric Bentley. *KR*. Summer, 1948. p. 424

Warren, as he is in the pristine sense a religious and moral writer, has
worked directly towards the centre of the "modern problem," the fundamental nature of our guilt. The probing of that cancerous tissue is done
solely in terms of imagery and dramatic situation. Even Warren's attitude
to the craft of poetry reflects one facet—the deathly divorce between
metaphor and statement—of the disintegration theme; for his poetry is
dedicated to the wedding of concept and image. Shying from abstract
analysis of the conflicts within the world, he has approached his material
in the structural terms of tragedy. . . . Warren's form is the tragedy and
the vision which informs and bloods the drama (for his method is invariably dramatic rather than discursive) is a stark but sympathetic one
of the "divided man." . . . Many of the poems, one might say, are explorations of the problem of knowledge. They receive much of their force from
the ironic contrast between the purity of experience and man's commentary
upon it. Man is consistently relating himself to Nature, but man's peculiar

position is that, if only from his ability to suffer regret and attempt definition, he is over and above Nature.

> Frederick Brantley in *Modern American Poetry*,
> edited by B. Rajan (Dobson). 1950. pp. 66, 75

Mr. Warren draws the themes for his books from historical incidents in
the South. . . . His novels are crammed with blood and thunder in the
tradition of historical fiction, but his stories take on the depth and universality of a parable, because the characters seek to learn the causes of
their plight, the reasons for the rules of society, and the philosophical ideas
which seem tenable in a morally, politically, and economically confused
world.

> Harry R. Warfel. *American Novelists of Today*
> (American). 1951. p. 442

The wide range of his subjects, the treatment of problems that touch
upon the fundamentals of human existence, the vitality of his characters,
the skill with which he creates suspense and atmosphere, and the richness
of his language, are characteristics that one does not often find together
in a modern writer. . . . Like Hemingway and Steinbeck, he believes in
the principle of solidarity as an essential value, but different from them,
he stresses its inevitable clash with other elements of human behavior,
above all with those of ambition, love of power, physical desire. He stands
for the fundamental honesty that is so vital an issue for the generation
between the two wars, but he realizes that the process of arriving at some
truth may have devastating effects on the seeker.

> Heinrich Straumann. *American Literature in the
> Twentieth Century* (Hutchinson). 1951. pp. 114–5

(Warren's poems) use an aristocratic and slightly archaic diction comparable to Ransom's, and they may have learned from him some of their
suave irony. But, more essentially, they show how much a poet can still
profit from Marvell. They are as different as possible from Cummings.
Despite Cummings's distaste for abstractions, his lyrics hardly more than
name the wonders of love and beauty, and thus, except for their eccentric
syntax, are little thicker in texture than the songs of tin-pan alley. Warren,
on the contrary, has devoted his whole attention to crowding his lines with
the greatest specific gravity they will bear, so that they will not merely
assert the uniqueness of an experience but will convey the actual burden
of that experience, both as it has been felt and as it has been thought about.

> F. O. Matthiessen. *The Responsibilities of the Critic*
> (Oxford). 1952. p. 121–2

I find all of the novels of Robert Penn Warren to be variations on a single theme, symbolized in the polarities of violence and order. He could not have chosen two concepts more arresting to the modern reader or more deeply imbedded in the history of his country and his region. . . . Robert Penn Warren has uncovered the historical sources of American violence and made them available for literary purposes, all four novels taking off from violent episodes in history that are used to illuminate modern meanings. But in writing tragedy, though the downward plunge into action takes up the most space and provides the greatest interest, violence alone is not enough. The tragic note cannot be struck without a positive world view. . . . For Warren murder, rape, and arson are simply the most effective dramatic means of developing one half of his theme: that *violence is life without principle.* Nor, to illustrate the other half, does he use orderliness for its own sake (there are no police chiefs or private detectives among his heroes); to him *order is living by principles,* even when the particular effort to do so falls far short of perfection.

Charles R. Anderson in *Southern Renascence,* edited
by Louis D. Rubin, Jr., and Robert D. Jacobs (Johns
Hopkins). 1953. pp. 207–9

Both the rhetoric and the "smart-aleck" commentary of *All the King's Men* have been roundly condemned by critics, usually without reference to their functional significance. . . . The cynical smart-aleck pose is Jack's defense against an alien world, the "fancy writer" the smothered and hence exaggerated ideal of himself. The two continually warring elements are further overlaid by the retrospective reflections of the mature philosophic Jack of the book's end. . . . Warren's ear is uncommonly acute, but the most valuable faculty he possesses is human insight, a shrewd and at the same time sympathetic ability to penetrate imaginatively into the inner life of his characters. In the most caustic vignette offered through Jack Burden's squinted eyes, the pity of human wastage is never lost. Warren's sense of "irreducible evil" and of human frailty permits an extremely wide range to a natural sympathy that is completely devoid of sentimentalism—ironic in the Richards sense that it is immune to irony.

John M. Bradbury. *Accent.* Spring, 1953. pp. 87–9

I think highly of Mr. Warren's poetry. There is a subtlety about it that is not readily apparent. I said earlier . . . that his rhythms resembled those of Mr. Ransom with the graciousness squeezed out of them. That is not literally true. The oftener one reads the poems—not all of them to be sure—the more aware he becomes of a new music. There is graciousness in the rhythms, but it is less obvious. The reader who has not freed himself from a subservience to the music of the iambic foot will find some of his rhythms strange. He, however, who joys in the fact that English and American poetry is returning to the rhythms natural to English, before the leaden-eared nineteenth century critics uttered inanities about the dominance of the iambic line, particularly the iambic pentameter, will delight in the subtle music of Mr. Warren's verse.

James G. Southworth. *More Modern American Poets*
(Blackford). 1954. pp. 118–9

Beneath the dulled-rust-red, short-clipped hair his face was astonishingly compact: slits of eyes almost lashless, taut skin over hard cheekbones, spare modeled nose, straight line of mouth—the "entire consort" a sculpture in granite. The hard-knit, barrel-chested torso added more if that were possible, to the impression. But when Mr. Warren talked, the shock was the discovery in each subsequent moment of how much warmth and wit and wisdom, of how much humanity, there issued from that stony image.

Harvey Breit. *The Writer Observed* (World).
1956. p. 131

What he has managed to create (in *All the King's Men*) is a work of literature that is a fully realized "concrete universal," a work which presents particulars everywhere concretely imaged yet having together a kind of universal relevance or reference—a work of the order of *Crime and Punishment* or Pope's satires or the *Oedipus Tyrannus*. . . . Such creation always depends upon a unified, integral imaginative grasp which apprehends reality in many dimensions or on many levels simultaneously. A concrete-universal cannot be schemed into existence; it issues from a sensibility aware of the implication of the universal in the concrete and a narrative skill or felicity which is able to exhibit, not merely assert or weakly suggest, their fusion. It is Warren's particular distinction to have created such a work in these times of fragmented sensibility.

Neal Woodruff, Jr. *All the King's Men: A Symposium*
(Carnegie Institute of Technology). 1957. p. 62

The need to accept the consequences of eternity's terrible intrusion on time has always been Warren's major theme, just as the place he has always seen it with the fullest particularity is the South, at some point where the contemporary life of football games and state cops, political manipulation and television exploitation tangles with the older life of the red-necks and the hunters, the Baptist ministers and the ballad singers. With this novel (*The Cave*) he has come back to the life of *Night Rider* and *All the King's Men,* where there is never world enough and time to love in but God's plenty of both to die in.

Arthur Mizener. *NYT.* Aug. 23, 1959. p. 1

In reading Warren's fiction and poetry I often have the sense that this theme of "the true life," of the necessary contradiction between man's nature and man's values, offers an image of stoical struggle that is necessary to Warren. He refuses the sanctions of orthodox Christianity, which proclaim spiritual values as absolute truths, and the naturalistic interpretation of values as pragmatically necessary to man. For Warren values are something that man *insists* on heroically and arbitrarily in the face of everything. There is no *system* of values that he believes in; there is only the last-ditch faith in values themselves as they emerge through the activity of literature. At the heart of literature is the essential faculty of poetic imagination, which works through symbols that are recollections of our ancient connections with a spiritual world.

Alfred Kazin. *PR*. Spring, 1959. p. 315

Warren's right to be regarded as an intellectual is indisputable; he is a formidable and influential critic; he has won general recognition as a poet; he has taught at some of our best institutions. Moreover, from the point of view of either structure or style, his novels could serve as texts in writing courses. . . . Even the most skeptical of his critics, I suppose, would agree that Warren's fundamental intentions as a novelist are completely serious. He simply tries, as nineteenth-century novelists commonly tried and twentieth-century novelists commonly don't try, to entertain the reader who is looking merely for entertainment and at the same time to reward one who is willing to make some effort of intellect and imagination. . . . He tells a story and the story is fascinating in its own right, but it is not for the story's sake that he tells it. All his skill as a story-teller— his mastery of narrative form, his wonderfully racy style—serves his real purpose. He is concerned with the deepest realities of the human spirit.

Granville Hicks. *SR*. Aug. 22, 1959. p. 13

The theme that has principally exercised his imagination is that of the "incompleteness" of man, the struggle to reconcile the idea and the need of unity with the facts of multiplicity in human experience. He has, on the one hand, an immense fascination with the varieties of human possibility, with man becoming. But, opposed to this—Warren's formulation of the problem is, I think, basically a moral one—there is the old Hawthornian, post-Puritan hatred of hypocrisy, the profound feeling that man, a man, should be what he seems. And it is from this opposition that the peculiar tension of his fiction derives—the conflict between the psychological and merely sensual, human richness of the story, with its endless complications of mere plot, that threatens continually to get out of hand, and the continually and rather desperately reimposed philosophical order, the precarious balancing of antinomies.

John Edward Hardy. *VQR*. Autumn, 1960. pp. 587–8

Warren's typically personal view rejects the state worship and general dehumanization which he associates with giantism in industry and pyramided cities. Yet his special agrarianism cannot abide either that naïve optimism, kin to the frontier dream of perpetually renewed innocence, which sprang from Jeffersonian neglect of man's dark ancestry.

These broad themes emerge with all the conviction that fullness of style at once intense and delicate can provide. They have been grounded by Warren in everyday particulars of a South which lends itself to metaphor and metaphysical expansion. . . . The excruciating self-consciousness and willful complexity of the South, its ferment of tensions, its acceptance of complicity (even its rejection of the Negro often seems motivated less by denial of guilt than by fear of retribution)—these provide Warren with handy symbols for the fate of the modern self, subsectioned by Freud and indexed in depth by Jung. The malices of society are used to dramatize the inward twist of shadows in any man, anywhere.

> Leonard Casper. *Robert Penn Warren: The Dark and Bloody Ground* (U. of Washington). 1960. pp. 6–8

The poetry, the fiction, and even the critical essays of Robert Penn Warren form a highly unified and consistent body of work. But it would be impossible to reduce it, without distorting simplifications, to some thesis about human life. The work is not tailored to fit a thesis. In the best sense, it is inductive: it explores the human situation and tests against the fullness of human experience our various abstract statements about it. But Warren has his characteristic themes. He is constantly concerned with the meaning of the past and the need for one to accept the past if he is to live meaningfully in the present. In this concern there are resemblances to Faulkner, though Warren's treatment is his own. Again, there are resemblances to W. B. Yeats in Warren's almost obsessive concern to grasp the truth so that "all is redeemed / In knowledge." Again, as with Yeats, there is a tough-minded insistence upon the facts, including the realistic and ugly facts—a fierce refusal to shield one's eyes from what is there.

(K)   Cleanth Brooks. *The Hidden God* (Yale). 1963. p. 98

There is no real development in a collection of Warren's critical essays, only expansion. The choice of terminology may shift a little. But we do no injustice in taking the body of Warren criticism as one extended discourse, from any part of which we may justly derive a hint or a word or a quotation to fill out the following exposition. Equally in treating fiction or poetry, Warren's end is to discover, to unfold, or to reconstruct the thematic center around which a work has unity and symbolic validity. He seeks to hold clearly before himself and his reader the operative symbol by means of which a story or a poem illuminates for the reader some vital awareness: not a set of abstractions or allegories, but an immediate intuition with massive and multiple implications—in other words, "the value as a celebration of life."

(K)   John Hicks. *SAQ*. Autumn, 1963. p. 509

In novel after novel there is some public issue—the Civil War and Reconstruction, an effort of social reform, crime in a high place—in which the protagonist is directly or indirectly involved and which in some crucial way reflects or comments upon the protagonist's inner conflict. The availability of such an issue seems to be, in fact, one of the important conditions determining Warren's choice of subjects. The technical advantage derived from such a practice is evident: texture is enriched thereby. But, as always with matters of technique, it is more than that. Concern with the balance or relationship between private and public worlds, between self and other than self, is that which inspires the technical practice. Warren's view is the classic one, conceiving of the purely private self as incomplete, and of the community as analogue or projection of the individual. By this view, one illuminates the other.

(K)   Madison Jones. *SAQ*. Autumn, 1963. p. 489

What I am groping for here is a statement adequate to describe Warren's work; all of it, the historical and critical commentary as well as the purely creative. Such a definition, very tentatively offered, would be something like this: Great art is dramatic, not didactic, and is humanly centered. Behind it is the insistent presence of a world, a cosmos, which is full and complete in its multiplicity, containing a simultaneous awareness of past history, the hopes of the future, and the incessant demands of the present moment—the *nowness* of God's will. Often a particular example of dramatic showing will employ a character in pursuit of some fanatic abstraction: power, personal purity, political ideals, or a specious self-created image of the self without which life is unthinkable. Such fragmentation is the particular disease of our time and must be documented, but always against a cosmos seen unfragmented and whole. The potentialities of such a creative strategy are extensive, and can be employed without risking a journalistic flattening of the conceptual vision.

(K)   John Lewis Longley. *SoR*. Autumn, 1965. p. 972

The fable has a place in Warren's writing comparable to the parable of the innocent abroad in Henry James's or the tale of the lonely egotist learning to survive in the destructive element in Conrad's. Like these two novelists, Warren returns again and again to certain types: whining older women who think they deserved better of the world, indulged and selfish girls, fathers whose awkward devotion annoys the beloved child, exuberant shouters and doers, monomaniacal idealists, sentimental cynics, and older men saddened by the weight of their wisdom. . . . [T]he people of Warren's fable reach adulthood ill prepared for its risks and responsibilities for they have not yet outgrown the dependencies and self-centered daydreams of childhood and adolescence. Wavering between thinking themselves too good for the world and too weak and unworthy to cope with it, they want to return to the pre-experiential innocence. . . . The climax of the fable comes when the protagonist prepares to act upon this knowledge and achieve his identity within the human communion. He may not make it, but, as Warren says in *Brother to Dragons,* there is a glory and meaning in the effort.

(K)   John L. Stewart. *The Burden of Time: The Fugitives*
                       and Agrarians (Princeton). 1965. pp. 487, 491, 494

What *Brothers to Dragons* does in relation to Warren's total body of poetry is to restate, with admirable power and eloquence, the main themes of Warren's earlier poetry. The black abyss without—the dark night of naturalism as seen in *Thirty-six Poems*—and the black abyss within—man's dark, innermost self as sought in *Eleven Poems:* both of these themes recur in *Brother to Dragons,* embodied in this poem's beast-metaphor and in its winter setting. Moreover, the ideal of a united self, predicated on the hope of reestablishing the lines of communication between conscious and unconscious, is the recurrence of a theme (not widely understood) from "The Ballad of Billie Potts." In witnessing the reconciliation of conscious and unconscious, of Jefferson and Lilburn, the reader may well feel a sense of *déjà vu,* recalling a similar reunion between Billie (the conscious self, made desperate by emptiness and lack of identity) and his father (like Lilburn, a hatchet-wielder, "evil and ignorant and old").

(K)   Victor H. Strandberg. *A Colder Fire* (Kentucky).
                                                              1965. p. 168

[In *Who Speaks for the Negro?*] Warren assails segregationist myths: i.e., that the colored folks invariably just love the white folks, and that just a few "bad niggers" and "Jew Communists" are making all the trouble. He admonishes the Northern liberal to re-examine his attitude for its self-righteous irresponsibility; debunks the liberal notion of Negro "betterness," as a form of the Noble Savage myth; would expunge of some of its morbidity the claim that the Negro is to redeem our society; warns Southerner and Northerner, alike, of condescension in their attitude toward the Negro. Indeed, Mr. Warren covers the categories of sentimentality over the race issue more fully and impartially than I have ever before found them considered. . . .

No other culture offers us a model, he says. We must go it alone, except for the non-white American: the Negro. "But if the Negro is to redeem America, he will do so as a creative inheritor of the Judeo-Christian and American tradition." Mr. Warren would proclaim this redemptive Negro the " 'existentialist' American" whose "role is to dramatize the most inward revelation of that culture."

(K)   Brainard Cheney. *SwR*. Spring, 1966. p. 549

Even in the beautiful 1954–1956 poems from *Promises,* some of them set in Italy and addressed to the poet's son and daughter, though dazzlement is present, and blazing is often high, glimmer still modulates the tone down to itself and a kind of positive uncertainty. But in the first section of this volume [*Selected Poems*], the one which is taken from the most recent work and called *Tale of Time* (1960–1966), *glimmer,* which appears altogether more than a score of times throughout the three hundred pages of the book, now occurs in three instances only, and *dazzle* in six, while *blaze* goes on to ten. The latest poetry of Robert Penn Warren abounds in light. At highest intensity it becomes light. . . .

"What of the darkness, is it very fair?" Sometimes not very. Besides being a poet, a novelist, a critic, a dramatist, a cultural recorder of North as well as South, Mr. Warren is a philosopher. He is a philosopher of the unfair darkness of the childhood out of which light will spring. He continually goes back to his own childhood even in his latest poems, trying to find the child that is father of the man who must become a child to be a father.

(K)   Elliott Coleman. *Poetry*. Sept., 1967. p. 417

See *Night Rider, At Heaven's Gate, All the King's Men, World Enough and Time, Band of Angels, The Cave, Wilderness* (novels); *Selected Poems, Brother to Dragons* (poetry); *Who Speaks for the Negro?* (journalism).

WELTY, EUDORA (1909–   )

She proceeds with the utmost simplicity and observes with the most delicate terseness. She does not try mystically to transform or anonymously to interpret. The parallel forced upon us, particularly by those of Miss Welty's stories which are based on an oblique humor, is her likeness to Gogol. . . . Like Gogol, Miss Welty opens the doors and describes the setting, almost inch by inch. . . . Miss Welty's method can get everything in; nothing need be scamped, because of romantic exigencies, or passed over, because of rules of taste. Temperamentally and by training she has become mistress of her material by her choice of one exactly suitable kind of treatment, and—a final test of a writer's power—as we read her, we are made to believe that she has hit upon the only possible kind.

Louise Bogan. Nation. Dec. 6, 1941. p. 572

Now I happen to think that to make a ballet of words is a perversion of their best function and I dislike—because it breeds exhibitionism and insincerity—the attitude toward narrative which allows an author to sacrifice the meaning of language to its rhythms and patterns. . . . Miss Welty constantly calls attention to herself and away from her object. . . . This is the sin of pride—this self-conscious contriving—endemic to a whole generation of writers since Katherine Mansfield and most especially to the women of that generation. . . . I have spoken of the ballet quality of Miss Welty's stories: in this connection I am reminded of the painter Dali and—via Dali—of the relationship between the chic modern department store and much of modern fiction.

Diana Trilling. Nation. Oct. 2, 1943. pp. 386–7

It is her profound search of human consciousness and her illumination of the underlying causes of the compulsions and fears of modern man that would seem to comprise the principal value of Miss Welty's work. She, like other best writers of this century, implies that the confusion of our age tends to force individuals back upon conscience, as they have not been since the seventeenth century; for in the intervening centuries, values were more closely defined, behavior was more outwardly controlled. Miss Welty's prose fiction, like much of the poetry and fiction of this era that seeks to explore the possibilities of the imagination, is comparable to the rich prose of Sir Thomas Browne; and reminiscent of the poetry of the seventeenth century.

Eunice Glenn in A Southern Vanguard, edited by
Allen Tate (Prentice-Hall). 1947. pp. 89–90

From her earliest stories, Miss Welty's writing has had a high degree of individuality. Her memory for colloquial speech is unbelievably accurate, and her antic imagination, coupled with her profound compassion and understanding, gives us people much realer than real, stranger, yet more believable than the living.

Herschel Brickell. SR. Aug. 27, 1949. p. 9

Amongst the younger generation, there are very few novelists indeed whose work is plainly based on the conception of the absolute autonomy of imagination. In fact, Eudora Welty, a Southern writer, appears to be the only one with an undisputed talent for this kind of writing, and she is also the most promising one, because, unlike James Branch Cabell's and Gertrude Stein's, her fantasies appear entirely normal and her style practically without mannerism. The reason for this achievement lies undoubtedly in the fact that Eudora Welty possesses the faculty of moving imperceptibly from the world of fantasy into everyday life and back.

Heinrich Straumann. American Literature in the
Twentieth Century (Hutchinson). 1951. p. 125

Let us admit a deep personal preference for this particular kind of story, where external act and the internal voiceless life of the human imagination almost meet and mingle on the mysterious threshold between dream and waking, one reality refusing to admit or confirm the existence of the other, yet both conspiring toward the same end. This is not easy to accomplish, but it is always worth trying, and Miss Welty is so successful at it, it would seem her most familiar territory. There is no blurring at the edges, but evidence of an active and disciplined imagination working firmly in a strong line of continuity, the waking faculty of daylight reason recollecting and recording the crazy logic of the dream.

Katherine Anne Porter. The Days Before
(Harcourt). 1952. pp. 107–8

There is one young woman who is accepted as "different" and "authentic" even by the best celebrants of the black mass in Taos and Carmel and Greenwich Village and Norfolk: the Eudora Welty who, with her two recent volumes of short stories, *A Curtain of Green* and *The Wide Net,* has become possibly the most distinguished of the new story-tellers. Oh yes, she has heard of Symbolism, but her writing is as clear—and free of obscenity—as the Gettysburg Address.

Sinclair Lewis. A Sinclair Lewis Reader
(Random). 1953. p. 212

The best of Eudora Welty's fiction bears little direct resemblance to that of any other writer. In it the reader feels the form and pressure of a coherently organized view of the world in which the author lives, and perhaps she has inherited that view from Faulkner; but the deep, inward response of her characters to the conditions of existence is her unaided achievement. If we began by wondering how her gift would thrive in Faulkner's gigantic shadow, we end by deciding that it has grown and flourished all the more for being rooted in prepared ground.

Robert Daniel in Southern Renascence, edited by
Louis D. Rubin, Jr., and Robert D. Jacobs (Johns
Hopkins). 1953. p. 315

Miss Welty revels in working in terms of conscious ambiguity; she leaves the last word unsaid, the ultimate action unconsummated. Writing with swift, sure, and often devastating understanding of her characters, and indulging a humor which is at times like the despairing cry of a child being swallowed up by quicksand, she has created out of artifice and artistry a world unmistakably her own and authentically real.

William Peden. *SR*. Jan. 16, 1954. p. 14

Miss Welty's writing is "feminine" in both the best and the worst senses: it is sympathetic, generous and intuitive; it is also fragile, verbose and hypersensitive. The author, it could be said, rarely gets to the heart of her material, but is very good around the smaller veins.

Jean Holzhauer. *Com*. April 29, 1955. p. 109

Miss Eudora Welty . . . deals in overtones and moments of implication; she . . . compels our acceptance by the spell of words and symbols. The significance of her characters and scenes lies as much in the past behind them and in the future before them as in the moment snatched from the moving reel and set before us in a vivid "still." . . . The unsaid and the implied are essentially human, and human sophisticated at that, for although the characters of her creation are usually simple folk the reader is never for a moment unconscious of Miss Welty's sophisticated eye. Here is a wonderfully clear vision, humorous, tender, and always shaping the raw experience before her to our satisfaction. Nevertheless, as I read each successive book of Miss Welty's, I am less and less satisfied. She is so entirely successful on her own home ground, but she hardly ever wins an away match.

Angus Wilson. *NSN*. Nov. 19, 1955. p. 680

From her earliest published work to her latest collection of stories Miss Welty has drawn heavily upon the worlds of myth and folklore and, while handling many of the same motifs again and again, has consistently absorbed them more and more fully into her own meaning, so that in her most successful work it is impossible to say that here is Cassiopeia and here Andromeda. The reader can only be aware that these legendary figures, along with similar ones from Germanic, Celtic, Sanskrit, and numerous other folk sources, are suggested by the characters that Miss Welty is drawing. . . . Quite consciously Miss Welty has taken the characters common to several mythological systems and translated them into present-day Mississippians. Although a faintly fantastic element remains in her stories, her characters and her atmosphere are too thoroughly

Southern to be mistaken for those of Siegfried's Germany or Perseus's Greece. So typically Southern are they, in fact, that many critics damn her for her provincial approach to life.

By patterning her characters closely after folk heroes Miss Welty has avoided exactly such a strictly regional approach as that for which she has been blamed. Since her first published story she has been working toward a fusion of the universal mythic elements embodied in various culture-heroes with the regional world that she knows first-hand. The effect of this attempt on her work and her degree of success with it may be followed throughout her work.

(K)   William M. Jones. *Southern Folklore Quarterly.*
                                                    Dec., 1958. pp. 173–4

Her problem as an artist has been to find words to convey the mysteries, the elusive and subtle inner states of mind and feeling for which most people (and certainly the people of her fiction) have no words at all: she must be articulate about what cannot be articulated. . . . Her language cannot always be adequate to the difficulty of what must be conveyed, which is perhaps the reason why she has often been accused of being coy, arch, perversely subtle, or precious. . . . In observing and recording the mysteries, Miss Welty creates a response of wonder, terror, pity, or delight, which is strangely and sometimes unnervingly amoral in its effect. Her characters are never roundly judged or emphatically "placed" morally; they are often delighted in (there is obvious relish in much of her description), but they are never sympathized with to the point of indulgence. They are usually just *seen,* inside and out, with that relentlessly clear vision, which records but does not judge, and which seems, at times, almost to reduce experiences of good and evil, joy and sorrow, to the same thing.

(K)   Ruth M. Vande Kieft. *Georgia Review.* Fall, 1961.
                                                            pp. 355–7

Eudora Welty is an imaginative writer. With her, nothing comes out of stock, and it has been impossible for her to stand still. Her art is a matter of contemplation, susceptibility, and discovery: it has been necessary for her to evolve for herself a language, and to arrive, each time she writes, at a new form. . . .

[*The Golden Apples*] is great, tender, austere stuff, shot through from beginning to end with beauty. . . . In *The Golden Apples,* Miss Welty would seem to have found, for her art, the ideal form. But, for a writer of her stature, nothing is conclusive—what comes next? American, deliberately regional in her settings, she "belongs," in the narrow sense, to no particular nation or continent, having found a communication which spans oceans.

(K)   Elizabeth Bowen. *Seven Winters & Afterthoughts*
                       (Knopf). 1962. pp. 216–18

Her imagination is essentially poetic; her fiction is clearly centripetal, structured like poetry with an intuited center and everything subdued to the demands of this central insight. As her art develops, so her fiction accumulates a more profound sense of human suffering and dignity and it covers a wider area of human activity without losing any of its original power. She continues to affirm the beauties and terrors inherent in the human situation while asserting the right to love and the need to dream. Through dream, as through art, man can express and realize his secret self: through love, as through art, he can communicate that secret self to others; for art, she believes, is the power to convey love. . . . The tragedy of man is to be separate and lonely, his glory is to be capable of dissolving his loneliness in love.

(K)   Alun R. Jones in *The Creative Present,* edited by
                       Nona Balakian and Charles Simmons (Doubleday).
                       1963. p. 182

When Miss Welty says that she is "touched off by place," she suggests a journey beyond the region of the touching off. And indeed her imagination molds her material into beautifully symmetrical essences and shapes. She participates in the life around her with such perception and fidelity that she catches it exact, and then she colors it and carves it into an entity beyond the realism of daily life, which is just what the people of her region have done with the often shallow and monotonous basic material of their lives. The result is an ironical tension between form and content, in which prosaic experience is enveloped in a mist of rhetoric, and irrational action is reported in the most attractive of verbal forms.

(K)   Robert B. Holland. *AL.* Nov., 1963. p. 357

With her wide range in style, point of view, subject matter, and fictional modes, Miss Welty has thoroughly investigated the possibilities inherent in the short story form, enriching and extending the potential of this demanding genre. Through her constant experimentation she has literally defied the genre's limitations and boundaries, and in exploring the mysteries of the inner life she has used dream and fantasy in a manner that has enabled her to produce a heightened realism. Her vision of relationship as a "changing and pervading" mystery is consistent throughout her fiction, and her characters are continually probing into these mysteries, trying to surmount the separateness existing between themselves and others, and undergoing experiences in which they are "initiated" or "reborn" into the world.

(K)   Alfred Appel. *A Season of Dreams: The Fiction of Eudora Welty* (Louisiana State). 1965. p. 256

See *A Curtain of Green, The Wide Net, The Golden Apples,* and *The Bride of Innisfallen* (short stories); also *The Robber Bridegroom, Delta Wedding,* and *The Ponder Heart* (novels).

WESCOTT, GLENWAY (1901–   )

(*The Apple of the Eye*) is a book almost exclusively of emotional propulsion. Indeed, it even becomes a drenching in emotions, those softer, readier emotions which we designate usually as "feminine," an experience purely of "delight and tears" (to borrow one of his chapter heads) and is thus a kind of revival in letters, an atavism, albeit a revival which is done with such force, such conviction, that one is caught unawares and before he knows it is deeply involved in these partings (by death and locomotion), this girl like a wilted flower left to perish, these stutterings of love, the sleep-walking in the moonlight, the call, or lure, of the city over hills and plains. . . . In method, Mr. Wescott's chief contribution is the bringing of a greater and more sensitive vitality to a type of book in which the typical novelist would feel very much at home.

Kenneth Burke. *Dial*. Dec., 1924. pp. 513–4

About *The Grandmothers* I feel it difficult to remain calm. Its appearance at this time is comparable to the occasions when *The Spoon River Anthology* and *Winesburg, Ohio* were first given to the public. Indeed, it bears some superficial likeness to both of those books. . . . *The Grandmothers* is a novel not only with its roots in the American soil, but it is a novel of those roots and of that soil. It is a novel that gives a new significance to American life. It should inculcate a finer patriotism and a deeper sense of pride of country than all the Fourth of July orations ever delivered.

Burton Rascoe. *Bkm*. Sept., 1927. pp. 86–7

(*The Grandmothers* is) altogether a magnificent record of failure, a stately elegy on lives too fine for success, but in no real sense a novel. A scheme which gives to each life a chapter and to each chapter the import of the whole permits neither movement nor design. But as autobiography, the book provides a not unworthy complement to *The Education of Henry Adams*. The prose, though less spontaneous than in his first novel, is Mr.

Wescott's principal accomplishment. He lavishes on the sad and wasted figures in his collection a sort of valedictory elegance, which more than anything else should compensate them for the many losses, the many humiliations.

William Troy. *NR*. Sept. 14, 1927. p. 105

Glenway Wescott opens a family album and out of its portraits he makes a book (*The Grandmothers*). From its stained pages ghosts emerge, each with a story. History repeats itself to him—the history of a group of people all bound by ties of blood or marriage, settlers in Wisconsin. The scene has the strong quality of those early days, there is that somber sense of the land, of the growth of the soil and of those who took root there.

Each ghost becomes in turn the shadow of an earlier wraith who left a heritage of energies and impulses. Each life yields its hidden drama; the past gives up its secret. Out of the cross threads of passion is woven the material of this novel. Out of it the author cuts the pattern of the race.

Halle Schaffner. *Survey*. Nov. 1, 1927. p. 161

His is a vision that may be at times extravagant and is certainly open to the charge of cloudy mysticism—but it is a vision, moving and troubling, of a wide, brooding land that (we are at last realizing it) calls not for a Dreiser but for a Dostoevsky. . . . More important than any individual story is the sense they all give of a beautiful and trained style, a style at times over-poetic and at times over-mannered, but which bears within itself many of the qualities of greatness. It is not too much (and certainly not much) to say that Mr. Wescott's prose is among the most beautiful being written in America today.

Clifton Fadiman. *Bkm*. Oct., 1928. pp. 220–1

The Wisconsin of Glenway Wescott is more than a geographical region with natural boundaries of hills and rivers, a landscape of highways and farms. He sees it also as a symbol of narrowness because the old pioneer spirit has dwindled to the restlessness of discontent. . . . Wescott seems to write while remembering, his mind filled with images of places and people seen but half-forgotten, stories heard long ago and recalled in tranquil recollection. . . . He saw the late twilight of the pioneering epoch and he has watched with moving, troubled gaze the effects of those factors that are transforming rural Wisconsin into an urban landscape. . . . He is always the observer, watching, remembering, attempting to explain the implications of a national birthright.

Dayton Kohler. *Bkm*. April, 1931. p. 143

The intimate routines of the family, love's power to survive its own abuses, to arrest the flux and establish continuity, filled the younger Wescott with frank wonder and curiosity. And he used to astonish the sophisticated twenties by exhibiting all this, the stuff of average human experience, as something very rare, almost a mystery. He was the poet of the family album; a repentant Ishmael, to whom his artist's exclusion from the tribe had become a burden. . . . But Wescott the emergent artist has become Wescott the mature spectator, coolly ironic where he used to be impassioned and devout. Clearly he has set out to transcend the nostalgic lyricism of his early work and to bring to bear upon his favorite themes a more complex experience and a more objective method. . . . One hopes . . . that he will not permit his newly acquired irony to dissipate the intensity and peculiar visionary idealism which have always been his strength.

F. W. Dupee. *NR*. Dec. 9, 1940. pp. 807–8

The Pilgrim Hawk, with which Glenway Wescott returns to fiction after a twleve-year absence, is less a story of love than a fable. . . . The dramatic substance of his scenes and characters does not manage to sustain the elaborate commentary he has imposed on it. The annotation becomes too elaborate, strained, ingenious, and self-conscious. A tendency toward a worrying preciosity of inference and analysis is never genuinely subdued to the natural volition of events and personalities, and the result becomes too patently contrived and at times almost desperately *voulu*. This is not to minimize the beauty of many of its pages, the great superiority of its style and feeling to the general ruck of fiction, and its always subtly considered, often brilliant observations.

Milton Dauwen Zabel. *Nation*. Dec. 21, 1940. p. 636

In *Apartment in Athens* Glenway Wescott writes fiction transcendentally, aware that, whatever their ultimate reality, events are known only in individual consciousness, and that social and political developments can be fully understood, fully responded to, fully shared, only as they are related to archetypes, partly unconscious, within the individual. What Wescott is doing imaginatively is so important that we don't mind the failures in surface realism or in information about Greece. But on a higher level the lack of convincing Greekness is still a defect.

Robert Gorham Davis. *NR*. April 16, 1945. p. 526

We don't expect a writer of Mr. Wescott's caliber to use his talents in the service of propaganda, and I especially didn't expect him to propagate hatred. To the writer of real creative power there is usually something deeply antipathetic in the act of subordinating free creativity to indoctrination, and where there is as much critical awareness of style as in all of Mr. Wescott's work, I would have expected—though, I now see, mistakenly—to find enough critical awareness of self to save an author from guilty gestures. We are told that Mr. Wescott calls *Apartment in Athens* his war work. It is the kind of war work we commonly look for, not at the head or heart of intellectual and artistic life, but at its fringes, where conscience seems to exist only to be uneasy.

Diana Trilling. *Nation*. March 17, 1945. p. 312

In *Apartment in Athens* (1945), Wescott's latest book, Wisconsin is not mentioned at all, just as the world outside Wisconsin does not appear in his first novel. The characters are all European and the scene is Greece during the last world war. Here, then, Wescott has reached the extreme in his travel from West to East. At least as regards literal fictional material, his last work totally abandons the region from which he sprang. It completes a trend of his writing with all the regularity of a linear mathematical equation. Here, too, the respect accorded family and country are quite different from that shown in earlier works. The plot is a thorough fulfillment of the promise that character may be proved under duress, that the stress of invasion may turn marital life into rich understanding and produce both a true family spirit and a proper realization of national humanist ideals.

(K)   C. E. Schorer. *CE*. March, 1957. p. 324

For some years middlebrow critics have been pleading for literary criticism based on personal delight, outright enthusiasm, instead of cold, intellectual analyses of structures, symbols, images, textures, etc. Here [*Images of Truth*] are six literary studies (of Katherine Anne Porter, Somerset Maugham, Colette, Isak Dinesen, Thomas Mann, and Thornton Wilder) which are based on subjective experience and expressed with uninhibited candor. This "old-fashioned" critic not only uses biography where it can lead to appreciative understanding, but he also draws upon his personal knowledge and varying degrees of friendship (in descending intimacy: with Porter, Maugham, Wilder, Colette). . . .

Although Mr. Wescott is well aware that a novel must give pleasure if it is to have many readers, he does not regard entertainment as a worthy objective of the novelist. For his own part, when he reads for amusement he chooses a fairy story, "Arabian Nights," or one of Isak Dinesen's stories. With Samuel Johnson he agrees that "the only end of writing is to enable readers better to enjoy life, or better to endure it."

(K)   Gay Wilson Allen. *SR*. Oct. 6, 1962. pp. 41–2

Bent on sharing his enthusiasm with his readers, Wescott manages now and then [in *Images of Truth*] to lift the veil, so to speak, on the mysteries of creative writing. He is also to be complimented on a highly perceptive and elaborately detailed analysis of the different texts under consideration.

. . . Furthermore, an old hand at storytelling, Wescott has wisely livened his somewhat lengthy expository sections with chatty *memorabilia* and, perhaps best of all, "informal portraiture." . . . The volume contains little or no adverse comment. On the contrary, such negative matters are left to Wescott's harsher critics, who are apt to seize on the fact that he believes in playing safe, since there is not a loser in the group he backs. . . . Still, there is no law that says he cannot write testimonials to his fellows if he wishes to. Besides, is it not quite a rarity nowadays?

(K)   Richard McLaughlin. *Com.* Oct. 12, 1962. pp. 78–9

To a really extraordinary degree, the positive values of the self have remained fixed for Wescott from 1940 on, but the search for a form has gone on. However, unlike many other writers, as the self became fixed in its values, it became less and less creative: from 1920 through 1940 (*The Pilgrim Hawk*) Wescott wrote nine books of varying lengths, a ballet libretto, plus numerous book reviews and essays; from 1941 through 1963 he has written three books, and the last of these (*Images of Truth*) is a collection of nearly everything he has published since 1945. Of equal importance is the fact that Wescott has published no fiction since 1945; this would suggest that, contrary to what almost everyone has said, the search for the self rather than the regional material was the motivating creative force. Fiction seems to have been an active and passive (retrospective) part of that search, something compulsive and necessary as long as the search continued. The basic movement in all of Wescott's fiction is toward knowledge of the principal character. . . .

(K)   William H. Rueckert. *Glenway Wescott* (Twayne).
                                        1965. p. 151

A principal question for mankind, according to Glenway Wescott, is the way home, a theme recurring from Homer's *Odyssey* to contemporary novels. Wescott's own fiction can be seen as illustrating this theme; from his stories about Americans in his home state of Wisconsin, to one of an American's experience in Europe, to a story of Greece and its traditions of heroic manhood, his work reflects a journey home, a movement from the place of birth to the place of affinity. Although Wescott has been praised more for his style than for his substance (he once called himself a fussy stylist), in his theme of going home, he has written a kind of Odyssey of an American that deserves attention for itself as well as for its embodiment in his fine prose.

(K)   Patricia Kane. *Critique.* Winter, 1965–66. p. 5

See *The Apple of the Eye, The Grandmothers, The Pilgrim Hawk, Apartment in Athens* (novels); *Good-bye, Wisconsin* (stories); *Images of Truth* (criticism).

WEST, NATHANAEL (1906–1940)

It is easy enough to indicate the materials which Mr. Nathanael West has used in his grotesquely beautiful novel, *Miss Lonelyhearts*. But it is a far more difficult matter to convey some notion of the intensely original incandescence of spirit which fuses these simple elements. Chapter after brilliantly written chapter moving like a rocket in mid-flight, neither falls nor fails. The book itself ends with the sudden, swift delumination of a light going out.

Florence Haxton Britten. NYHT. Apr. 30, 1933. p. 6

Mr. West pierces beneath the surfaces of his material. The tragic lives of his characters impress us even more powerfully because they are made to seem stupid and comic. We may laugh with the author at these people, but we recognize the essential seriousness which has given his writing its impetus. . . . Mr. Dreiser would have made a tragedy out of this material; Mr. West, in making a satiric comedy of it, has perhaps given a more adequate rendering of men whose warped lives do not offer any theme considerable enough for tragedy.

T. C. Wilson. SR. May 13, 1933. p. 589

His new novel, *The Day of the Locust,* deals with the nondescript characters on the fringe of Hollywood studios. . . . And these people have been painted as precisely and polished up as brightly as the figures in Persian miniatures. Their speech has been distilled with a sense of the flavorsome and the characteristic which makes John O'Hara pedestrian. Mr. West has footed a precarious way and has not slipped at any point into relying on the Hollywood values in describing the Hollywood people. . . . The doings of these people are bizarre, but they are also sordid and senseless. Mr. West has caught the emptiness of Hollywood; and he is, as far as I know, the first writer to make this emptiness horrible.

Edmund Wilson. NR. July 26, 1939. p. 339

Here is a book (*The Day of the Locusts*) that attempts to do a great deal more than just pillory the foibles and flimflammery of the movie industry. While its setting is Hollywood and the miasma of the studio naturally permeates the lives of the people concerned, Mr. West has sketched an acidulous melange of Southern Californian grotesques, including . . . some samples of the queer folk you don't read so much about: the Middle Westerners who have saved up a few thousand dollars and moved to California to end their days basking in its vaunted sun. These people, mostly middle-aged, often semi-invalid, invariably bored with their self-chosen life of idleness, inhabit an appalling spiritual wasteland. . . . There is abundant material here for scathing satire or careful social study, and the principal objection to *The Day of the Locusts* is apt to be that it merely scratches the surface.

Louis B. Salomon. Nation. July 15, 1939. pp. 78–9

West's contemporaries were realists; he was a kind of superrealist. He often used enormous incongruities to make his points, which gave him a kinship with French writers of the school of Rimbaud and with the later surréalistes; but instead of documenting his perceptions with magnifying-glass clarity, he preferred to distill them into images and situations painfully barren of minutiae. He was an extreme pessimist, which may have been the reason why he never reached a wide audience while he was alive.

Richard B. Gehman. At. Sept. 19, 1950. p. 69

West's Hollywood is made up of degeneracy and brothels, of failure and sexual desire, of cock-fighting and third-rate boarding houses. But more than anything it is made up of significant boredom, of an etiolated ennui: the whole canvas on which the motiveless actions take place acquires a Breughal-like stillness, as if all the monstrous things going on were part of a very ordinary pattern. And, indeed, the pattern of all West's books is ordinary; it is only the extraordinary stylized grotesques on the edge, the narrative logic that touches the rim of fantasy, that charge it with the nervous garishness, the disproportionate perspective that, like the beautiful hunchbacks in *Balso Snell,* mock normality with their own freakishness.

Alan Ross. Introduction to The Complete Works of
Nathanael West (Farrar). 1957. pp. xxi–ii

West's symbols and grotesques are perhaps more disturbing even than Kafka's, because they more strongly resemble the real. His satire never loses its sting because it is always more real than satirical. He delves more deeply than Melville into the ingrained confidence game of American civilization, the ever-widening split between aspiration and actuality that keeps our public statements, from school days on, from corresponding with the way things are. . . . West treats serious subjects flippantly; but that is better than treating trivial subjects, such as the "romance of business," seriously. He is like a perky little wind that blows, now this way, now that, until all the fog of illusion is dispelled from the land.

William Bittner. Nation. May 4, 1957. pp. 394–6

The recognition grows that West wrote about something more than pseudo-surrealist characters inside the Trojan horse, a demented writer giving advice to the unloved, a bumpkin determined to act out all the Horatio Alger stories, a group of Hollywood grotesques. He had to write about something. He could not simply and starkly proclaim: here in America is a great emptiness, a vacuum sucking us all in and forcing us to die of spiritual bends. He did not tell, he showed. . . . He sensed what Paul Tillich calls "the shaking of the foundations." Like an expressionistic artist, he saw the breaking up of life's surface, and in his prose he drew the fragments.

Richard L. Schoenwald. Com. May 10, 1957.
pp. 162–3

Nathanael West's saving grace was that, as a man and as a writer, he practiced the fine art of detachment. Although he was as concerned as his colleagues with the ills of Depression America (once he was arrested for joining a picket line in front of a New York department store), he rarely permitted the period's numerous teapot tempests to intrude on his serious writing. As a writer, his preoccupation was with the moral bankruptcy that underlay the surface ills. Specifically, he wrote of the dreams by which man attempts to live and of the violence which perverts these dreams.

Roger H. Smith. SR. May 11, 1957. p. 13

He had the gift of a grotesquely accurate imagination, so much admired in the Nineteen Twenties, but the chief reason why his work is remembered is simply that he could write. He wrote as carefully as if he were chiselling each word in stone, with space around it. He wrote as if he were composing cablegrams to a distant country, with the words so expensive that he couldn't waste them, and yet with the need for making his message complete and clear. In rereading his works one is always surprised to find how short they are. The proof of their value is that they occupy more space in one's memory than they do on the printed page.

Malcolm Cowley. NYT. May 12, 1957. p. 5

Although West's style and ideas are refined in his later novels, his outlook and method do not, in my opinion, undergo any fundamental changes. For West, the old gods are dead; no miraculous loves or births occur among men any more: at our slightly ridiculous births, "instead of the Three Kings, the Dove, the Star of Bethlehem, there was only old Doctor Haasenschweitz who wore rubber gloves and carried a towel over his arm like a waiter." Yet we destroy ourselves by holding up an idealized image of mankind that can never be. We indulge in a "terrible competition" that demands our "being more than animals." Our idealized notion of ourselves derives from our worshiping false gods, cultural as well as religious. West's antidote for this corrupting poison would seem to be his scoffing, humorous vernacular style and his hard, derisive, realistic look at the world without the illusive veil of religion, culture, or art.

(K)   Edward G. Schwartz. *Accent*. Autumn, 1957. pp. 255–6

West does not seem finally a really achieved writer; certainly, no one of his books is thoroughly satisfactory, though there are astonishing local successes in all of them. His greatness lies like a promise just beyond his last novel, and is frustrated by his early death; but he is the inventor of a peculiar kind of book, in which the most fruitful strain of American fiction is joined to the European tradition of avant-garde, anti-bourgeois art, native symbolism to imported *symbolisme*. The Westian or neo-gothic novel has opened up possibilities, unavailable to both the naturalistic semi-documentary and the over-refined novel of sensibility, possibilities of capturing the quality of experience in a mass society—rather than re-treating to the meaningless retailing of fact or the pointless elaboration of private responses to irrelevant sensations. Putting down a book by West, a reader is not sure whether he has been presented with a nightmare endowed with the conviction of actuality or with actuality distorted into the semblance of a nightmare; but in either case, he has the sense that he has been presented with a view of a world in which, incredibly, he lives!

(K)   Leslie Fiedler. *Love and Death in the American Novel* (Criterion). 1960. p. 465

Such psychological tension—in which a man hates the thing he loves and loves the thing he hates—is at the center of every novel West wrote. In *Balso Snell* the repulsion-identification is associated with the entire world of Western mentality. In *Miss Lonelyhearts* it is associated with the modern Christ figure and also with the hordes that the modern—and futile—Christ would save through love. In *A Cool Million* the repulsion-identification is with the American dream and the mob of gullibles deluded by its falsities. In *The Day* the psychological tension is associated with the great unwashed beast—its culture and its political system. . . . Finally, one should note a basic result of this psychological tension: the need to resolve it. Thus at the very center of West's fiction there is the quest for order—security—and the desperate knowledge that the search for order is doomed to failure.

(K)   James F. Light. *AmQ*. Spring, 1960. pp. 53–4

The motive power of West's work from first to last was a fascinated disgust with the processes of the body and an accompanying obsession with physical violence. His virtues, his limitations; his scabrous wit, effective social satire, his compulsion to shock and his lapses into self-pity all spring from the same source. The passionate feeling in this fiction streams from West, not from his individual characters. It animates the inanimate. The helplessness of his individuals to communicate with fellow beings is heightened to nightmare proportions in the gulf of non-communication in which people move like somnambulists. But the inability of the individuals in the novels to communicate is compensated in West by the extreme lucidity of the prose. West's coming to terms with incomprehensible emotional forces is counterbalanced by his own strenuous efforts at rigorous control of language.

(K)   Josephine Herbst. *KR*. Autumn, 1961. p. 614

His books should, I think, be classified as Cautionary Tales, parables about a Kingdom of Hell whose ruler is not so much the Father of Lies as the Father of Wishes. Shakespeare gives a glimpse of this hell in *Hamlet,* and Dostoievsky has a lengthy description in *Notes from the Underground,* but they were interested in many hells and heavens. Compared with them, West has the advantages and disadvantages of the specialist who knows everything about one disease and nothing about any other. He was a sophisticated and highly skilled literary craftsman, but what gives all his books such a powerful and disturbing fascination, even *A Cool Million,* which must, I think, be judged a failure, owes nothing to calculation. West's descriptions of Inferno have the authenticity of first-hand experience: he has certainly been there, and the reader has the uncomfortable feeling that his was not a short visit.

All his main characters suffer from the same spiritual disease which, in honor of the man who devoted his life to studying it, we may call West's Disease. This is a disease of consciousness which renders it incapable of converting wishes into desires. A lie is false; what it asserts is not the case. A wish is fantastic; it knows what is the case but refuses to accept it. All wishes, whatever their apparent content, have the same and unvarying meaning: "I refuse to be what I am." A wish, therefore, is either innocent and frivolous, a kind of play, or a serious expression of guilt and despair, a hatred of oneself and every being one holds responsible for oneself.

(K)   W. H. Auden. *The Dyer's Hand* (Random). 1962. p. 241

There is humor but little joy in West's novels, obsessive sexuality but few consummations (except for that sit-up-and-lie-down doll Betty Prail). The world West shows us is for the most part repulsive and terrifying. It is his genius to have found objective correlatives for our sickness and fears: our maimed and ambivalent sexuality, our terror of the idiot mass, our helpless empathy with suffering, our love perverted into sadism and masochism. West did this in convincing present-day forms of the great myths: the Quest, the Scapegoat, the Holy Fool, the Dance of Death. His strength lay in his vulgarity and bad taste, his pessimism, his nastiness. West could never have been the affirmative political writer he sometimes imagined, or written the novels that he told his publisher, just before his death, he had planned: "simple, warm and kindly books." We must assume that if West had lived, he would have continued to write the sort of novels he had written before, perhaps even finer ones.

In his short tormented life, West achieved one authentically great novel, *Miss Lonelyhearts,* and three others less successful as wholes but full of brilliant and wonderful things. He was a true pioneer and culture hero, making it possible for the younger symbolists and fantasists who came after him, and who include our best writers, to do with relative ease what he did in defiance of the temper of his time, for so little reward, in isolation and in pain.

(K)   Stanley Edgar Hyman. *Nathanael West* (Minnesota).
                                                        1962. pp. 45–6

So important and redeeming an aspect of West's characters is aspiration that one is tempted to say that it is only the lack of it in Shrike which makes him such an ugly character and which sets him apart from the rest of West's major characters. . . . Unfortunately, aspirations have a tendency to ennoble people—often unduly. West did not want such ennoblement; at least, he never permitted aspiration to have this effect. By selecting goals which are degrading or unattainable, and by making the pursuit of these goals absurd and comical, he has emphasized his characters'—and man's— insignificance; and he has largely done it by focusing on inadequacies of character as well as on defects in society. . . .

For West, entrapment was a fundamental issue: man is trapped, and any pretension at being otherwise leads to tragic frustration and destruction. Yet man's very nature seems to demand ideals, for in West's world, man seems to be unable to exist without dreams. When these dreams are thwarted, as they inevitably are, the result is the boredom of those who "came to California to die"; the violence of Shrike, Miss Lonelyhearts, Homer, and the crowd in *The Day of the Locust;* or the insanity of Miss Lonelyhearts. For West, man's lot is a miserable one, and only ignorance of that fate can permit one to go on; West makes it clear, however, that he has no sympathy with such ignorance.

(K)   Victor Comerchero. *Nathanael West, The Ironic
                                        Prophet* (Syracuse). 1964. pp. 164–5

At his most authentic, West is the "universal satirist." His humor is savage and sad, in contrast to [S. J.] Perelman's brash spoofing, and it springs, I think, from his tragi-comic view of the world, from his wry awareness of the disparity between secular facts and his suppressed religious ideals.

His slapstick ends in a scream; the self-hatred of his characters, their efforts—sometimes grotesque and always painful—to find answers or relief, only curdles his pity. In *A Cool Million,* as in his other novels, the real culprit is not capitalism but humanity.

(K)   Daniel Aaron. *MR.* Winter-Spring, 1965. p. 316

In a world that is crass and ugly, then, a dream of grace and beauty will only betray the dreamer. The compassionate, unfortunate, suffering good man is turned back upon himself. Being Jewish, or a creature of Jewish imagination, he cannot simply acknowledge that the world is evil and become evil himself. He is committed to ethical behavior. If he despairs in the manner of West, he will discover self-ridicule, one of his oldest resources, at the heart of his tormenting dreams. . . . Both *Miss Lonely-hearts* and *Day of the Locust* are also told as deephearted "jokes": nothing bitter but is laughed at.

(K)   Maurice Kramer. *Works.* Autumn, 1967. pp. 106–7

See *The Complete Works of Nathanael West.*

WHARTON, EDITH (1862–1937)

I take to her (Mrs. Wharton) very kindly as regards her diabolical little clevernesses, the quality of intention and intelligence in her style, and her sharp eye for an interesting *kind* of subject. . . . She *must* be tethered in native pastures, even if it reduces her to a back-yard in New York.

Henry James. *Letters,* edited by Percy Lubbock
(Scribner). 1920. v. 1, p. 396

One of Mrs. Wharton's greatest distinctions is that she is not sentimental; when she succeeds in awakening an emotion in the reader, it is a legitimate one; and she accomplishes it by her art, not through parade of her own feelings. . . . She is detached from her plot. She can stand over and away from her structure and let the story tell itself, absorbing all our attention with a few light touches, and giving finality to all of them. The tenseness of her style and the manner in which she combines eagerness with discipline, poise, and perfection of phrase with lack of mannerism, are the tangible bases of her talent. She plots her stories, sees in her mind's eye the persons who participate in them, how they look, dress, and act, what their background is. She seeks to tell the truth about them, impartially and unemotionally.

Joseph Collins. *Taking the Literary Pulse* (Doran).
1924. pp. 54–5

Despite her artistry . . . Mrs. Wharton has failed as the eighteenth century failed, by her insistence upon definitions of life in terms of the artificial, in terms of civilization rather than in the fundamentals of Nature. Of the great, quivering, suffering, laboring human mass, she knows little. . . . Nature unadorned she views with all the horror of an Addison or a Pope.

Fred Lewis Pattee. The New American Literature
(Century). 1930. p. 253

Mrs. Wharton . . . has been far too much the professional novelist to sustain the qualities which first and very justly brought her fame. These were . . . an unflagging distinction of manner and a very high and very penetrating wit. Nor was this all. Her people were very much alive and several of her earlier books at least have that virtue so immensely rare in our letters: architectonic beauty, beauty of inner structure. Yet her work is fading and crumbling and will probably be almost forgotten until a time so detached from the present arises that people can go back to a little of it as to something quaint and sweet and lavendered, wondering that at so late an age a woman as intelligent as Edith Wharton could have taken seriously the conventions of a small and unimportant social group, could have in ultimate judgement identified herself with these futile and fugitive notions and confronted the moral world with the standards of a silly and cruel game.

Ludwig Lewisohn. Expression in America (Harper).
1932. p. 466

Nothing was ever more unmistakable in Edith than the quality of the foundations of her culture. She was never delayed in trifling with the easy, the showy, the quickly and cheaply rewarding; she went straight for the best, and no time lost; and she set up her standards once for all, to serve her lifetime. She seemed to be excused the long labor of trying the wrong turnings, following the wrong leads, discarding misfits, such as most of us have to worry through with patience; and this was fortunate, for she had no patience at all or any time for second thoughts and anxious renewals, only an eagerness, never exhausted, for further exploration and acquisition. . . . She was all that was right and regular in her smooth clan-plumage, but the young hawk looked out of her eyes. . . . She actually grasped what she was about, this one, as she settled down to her work and stuck to it; and on fire as she was with her ambition, her head was cool, she knew her place, and her pride in it was as sound as her modesty. The sagest and sternest of the craftsmen must admit that she meets them on their ground.

Percy Lubbock. Portrait of Edith Wharton (Appleton-
Century). 1947. pp. 13, 244

In the stories of Mrs. Wharton, men are condemned for their paucity of understanding. The lament which sounds from Mrs. Wharton's fiction is not that women must inhabit a man's world, but that, because of man's unperceptiveness, each sex is consigned to a different world. . . . Men are the visitors who never arrive. Women wait for them their life long, women who demand neither the vote nor economic equality, women who seldom clamor for a single standard of sex morals. What the women of Edith Wharton's novels crave is an understanding presence, and that man is never able to accord. . . . For the man of Edith Wharton's conceiving, woman is always walled away, by his own blindness; so that she, unbeheld, finally ceases to behold.

> Josephine Lurie Jessup. *The Faith of Our Feminists*
> (R. R. Smith). 1950. p. 80

Especially in her earlier work, Edith Wharton is chiefly concerned with the overpowering effect of social and tribal conventions on the individual. She adheres to the assumption that the reality of these conventions is stronger than Man, who, though he may not always perish in this conflict, will be fatally injured in his happiness. If, in addition to this conception, the role played by blind chance is taken into account, the criteria of a determinist attitude are obvious. It may, however, be necessary to point out that for those readers to whom the cruelty of social conventions is not a reality, a good deal of Edith Wharton's art will be lost.

> Heinrich Straumann. *American Literature in the*
> *Twentieth Century* (Hutchinson). 1951. pp. 54–5

There was something odd in the resentment with which she seemed to exaggerate the vulgarity of the vulgar and the illiteracy of those whom she disliked. It was as if, in some way, she felt that she was menaced by them, as if she was in some fashion on the defensive, and certain it was that, as a writer, she was not at ease with American life when she left the small magic circle of her old New York. As a rule she could not yield herself to her native world as it actually was, she felt obliged to see it in terms of England, so that she constantly suffered lapses in which her people and scenes no longer corresponded with the reality they assumed to present.

> Van Wyck Brooks. *The Confident Years* (Dutton).
> 1952. p. 278

It is interesting to see how Henry James's insistence on "form" in the novel was simplified by his friend and follower, Mrs. Wharton, into mere adherence to plot. The plot must proceed, through all its ramifications, even though characters be wrenched out of shape to serve it. Minor figures, put in purely to prop up the plan, soon are shuffled away, and are featureless from the beginning. The long arm of coincidence snaps up the roving actors and places them down neatly in surroundings cleverly arranged to suit their situation. . . . Mrs. Wharton's work formed a bridge from the nineteenth-century novel to the magazine fiction of the present where, in a superficially arranged scene, manners, clothes, food, and interior decoration are described carefully and at length; how she contained in herself, as it were, the whole transitional period of American fiction, beginning in the bibelot and imported-European-culture era of the late nineties, and ending in the woman's-magazine dream of suburban smartness.

Louise Bogan. *Selected Criticism* (Noonday).
1955. p. 84

To be haunted by George Eliot is a fine, but awesome experience. That great moralist (who was also a great artist) is a convenient ghost at anyone's writing desk, but a formidable presence at the dinner table. Moving as she did in both the literary and the social world, Mrs. Wharton may have felt (other writers have done so) that putting pen to paper was in itself a moral act. This may be one explanation for the unevenness of her writing. She could be sharp and she could be dull; this was true of her not just in her later years but throughout her career.

(K)   Wayne Andrews. Introduction to *The Best Short Stories of Edith Wharton* (Scribner). 1958. p. xiii

The technique for her major characterizations moves, as it were, in two directions, both inward and outward. The theory of morality helps her to get at the inner truth of personality, the unique quality which individualizes and sets apart. Convention supplements morality in two ways: first, by providing a basis for contrast, a standard or norm by which the divergences from the usual and/typical may be underlined; second, by serving as a control or guide rope for keeping morality within the bounds of the familiar and away from mere eccentricity. Thus Mrs. Wharton's basic technique for creating her central figures is to endow them with certain qualities which fail to fit into the established social pattern but are yet related to it, in this way giving them a greater value and interest than the generality of persons possess. Often the most trivial details are sufficient indication of individuality.

(K)   Marilyn J. Lyde. *Edith Wharton: Convention and Morality in the Work of a Novelist* (Oklahoma).
1959. p. 150

. . . Ethan Frome, when he plunges towards what he considers certain death, is a failure but not a mystery. His behavior is not unmotivated; the tragedy is not contrived. The very heart of the novel is Frome's weakness of character, his negation of life. Behind that is his true, unfulfilled, relationship with Zeena. Wharton's economy of language in the novel is superb. There is hardly a word unnecessary to the total effect. Her final economy is the very brevity of the book. It fits the scene and character. There were depths to plumb; her people were not simple. To overcome the deficiencies of their natural reticence (and perhaps her own), to retain the strength of the severe and rugged setting, particularly the "outcropping granite," she resorted to a brilliant pattern of interlocking imagery and symbolism. . . .

(K)   Kenneth Bernard. *CE*. Dec., 1961. p. 184

Within these traditional limits, and despite her coolness to modernist innovations, Mrs. Wharton was a restless writer, forever seeking new variations of tone and theme, and in her several important novels after *The House of Mirth* rarely troubling to repeat a success. In *The Reef* (1912) she composed a subtle though tenuous drama of personal relations, Jamesian in manner and diction, which deals largely with the price and advantage of moral scruple. In *The Custom of the Country* (1913) she turned to—I think it fair to say, she was largely the innovator of—a tough-spirited, fierce and abrasive satire of the barbaric philistinism she felt to be settling upon American society and the source of which she was inclined to locate, not with complete accuracy, in the new raw towns of the mid-West. Endless numbers of American novels would later be written on this theme, and Sinclair Lewis would commonly be mentioned as a writer particularly indebted to *The Custom of the Country;* but the truth is that no American novelist of our time, with the single exception of Nathanael West, has been so ruthless, so bitingly cold as Mrs. Wharton in assaulting the vulgarities and failures of our society.

(K)   Irving Howe. *Encounter*. July, 1962. p. 46

Because of reticence and the mark of scars on her own tissue, she kept on pretending that her imaginary life showed in it little if anything of herself. Yet her imaginary Vance [*Hudson River Bracketed*] could have told her that it was out of her tissue that, as an artist, she fed her visionary offspring. Her great excitement in fantasy was not unrelated to her joys and sorrows in real life, or the theory she devised to account for artistic creation would fall apart. The happiness she knew in watching shy, strange creatures emerge and speak was her happiness, and was shared by them, too. And the control visible in their comings and goings, as they took their journey through a tale, revealed only too vividly the nature of her own precise and judging temperament. The two worlds she would fain have believed isolated from each other were, in not so secret ways, one and the same.

(K)   Alexander M. Buchan. *NEQ*. Sept., 1964. p. 362

Ethan Frome, I have no doubt, will always be read, but it is out of the main stream of her work. I believe that she will be remembered primarily for her two great novels of manners: *The House of Mirth* and *The Age of Innocence.* In these she succeeded in re-creating an unadventurous and ceremonious society, appropriately sheltered behind New York brownstone, looking always to the east rather than to the west, and the impact upon it of the winds that blew from both directions. There were plenty of minor writers who attempted to delineate this society, but among those of the first rank Mrs. Wharton, at least in the first decade of our century, had it to herself. . . . The reason Mrs. Wharton succeeded where so many others have failed is that in addition to her gifts as an artist she had a firm grasp of what "society," in the smaller sense of the word, was actually made up of. She understood that it was arbitrary, capricious, and inconsistent; she was aware that it did not hesitate to abolish its standards while most loudly proclaiming them. She knew when money could open doors and when it couldn't, when lineage would serve and when it would be merely sneered at. She knew that compromises could be counted on, but that they were rarely made while still considered compromises. She knew her men and women of property, recently or anciently acquired, how they decorated their houses and where they spent their summers. She realized that the social game was without rules, and this realization made her one of the few novelists before Proust who could describe it with any profundity.

(K)   Louis Auchincloss. *Pioneers and Caretakers*
                                      (Minnesota). 1965. pp. 53–4

Her inordinate shyness—what Mrs. Wharton often spoke of to her intimates as her "long, cold agony of shyness"—grew a shell about the child. Within it already were the seeds of everything that makes up the woman. The shell was never quite dissolved. It lasted to the woman's last day. Mystification enters only because the shell changed its contours, its consistency and its coloration. For the child it was soft, vulnerable, amorphous, dull-hued. For the woman it was tenacious of its form, impervious, brilliantly glazed, iridescent. But it was the same shell. For the child it was symbolized by a deserted library, for the woman by a crowded drawing room. Dim library or salon bright with the rainbow lights of prismed chandeliers—they can be equally retreats.

(K)   Grace Kellogg. *The Two Lives of Edith Wharton*
                                      (Appleton-Century). 1965. p. 42

Mrs. Wharton writes two distinct versions of the naturalistic novel, corresponding to her double vision of the possibilities of human tragedy. In her first kind of novel, "things" encumber the individual, binding him to a permanently indifferent universe. Fundamentally a novel of self or psyche, this version delineates the tragedy of aspiration. Inevitably held and defeated by his alien surroundings, the protagonist nonetheless aspires, imaginatively and intellectually, to strike through the bondage of things into the personal freedom and fulfillment that he can only suppose might be his. . . .

In her second kind of novel not the natural, but the human "things" of a hollow society are so devoid of meaning that the individual drifts aimlessly among them. People are defined by their clothes or houses; they are spoken of, usually, in terms of the machine culture that they mentally exemplify, as "a screw or a cog in the great machine." . . . In the midst of a society filled with human automata, Mrs. Wharton sets seekers after human fulfillment. Here she writes a picaresque novel of manners in which the individual seeks satisfaction in collectives as far apart as vulgar parvenu parties and "republics of the spirit." Again and again, however, he is alienated by the indifference or emptiness of society; he can find no satisfactory way of penetrating social things, and so wanders vaguely across the changing surface of society.

(K)   Jay Martin. *Harvests of Change* (Prentice). 1967. p. 266

See *The House of Mirth, Ethan Frome, The Custom of the Country, The Age of Innocence* (novels); *Best Short Stories; A Backward Glance* (autobiography).

WHEELOCK, JOHN HALL (1886–   )

He acknowledges the message of Whitman, even as every musician must feel the impress of Wagner, every sculptor the force of Rodin. . . . It is just because Mr. Wheelock is so much in touch with today that he seems so often to be speaking with the accents of Whitman. But, though he too insists on the glory of the commonplace . . . , he strikes out for a freedom of style and utterance entirely his own. . . . At its best Mr. Wheelock's poetry is clear, revealing and full of that high realism which is the color of life. He has something of the vision which uplifts sensuality, and enough of the realist's passion to save mysticism from itself, and humanize it.

Louis Untermeyer. *NYT*. Dec. 29, 1912. p. 800

At its best the poetry of John Hall Wheelock has been notable for a gravity in feeling and reflection which has given it, at times, a sober romantic beauty quite its own in character. . . . Abstaining from experiment is his privilege, probably his advantage. . . . The grandiose, the ingenious, the clever and exciting elements of the art are not for him. With a firm lonely sobriety he now addresses a life sombrely shaded. . . . In his ripe unbaffled sincerity there is still a true, if uneventful, meditative beauty.

Morton Dauwen Zabel. *Poetry*. Feb., 1927. pp. 280–2

Mr. Wheelock knows how to be alone and how to make friends with humanity and the distant suns in the vast silence that is himself. . . . This poet can trace the line in the marks a mouse's feet make in the dust or in the rays of a star in outer space, and can see them as foliations of the same scroll. He can handle the mystic magnitudes, yet he can be private in his tenderness as well. Without the ancient theological designs, he can find deity.

Robert P. Tristram Coffin. *NYHT*. Dec. 13, 1936. p. 18

His eclecticism is enormously wide; but if ghosts as dissimilar as Wordsworth, Matthew Arnold, Tennyson, Blake, and even Sydney Lanier, sometimes rise from his pages, they are conjured before us by the magic of a genuine intuition; and their intrusion cannot dissipate the conviction we have of witnessing the impact upon a man of sensibility and surcharged feeling of a world physically real. . . . His most marked virtues are due to his amazing instinct for representing moods with appropriate cadences; and to capacities which have prolonged through years those excitements in physical living, that élan from tragedies, which, in most of us, escape after youth.

Evelyn Scott. *Poetry*. May, 1937. pp. 102–3

John Hall Wheelock shows himself a devoted and sincere disciple of the art, but more notable for the sense of exaltation with which he writes than for his actual performance on the page. . . . Mr. Wheelock's whole poetical stock seems to consist of rapturous but undifferentiated, unparticularized feeling; and as the emotion is undefined, so the expression is indistinct, putting up with all manner of phrases from the common sentimental store. . . . At times the genuineness of his emotion proves communicable, and then the reader comes on a passage in which a sense of exalted participation in the sum of things is truly given. This is Mr. Wheelock's poetry at its best; at its all too frequent worst it is a poetry of pink mist.

Theodore Morrison. *At.* June, 1937. Unpaged

He sings; his concept of poetry is ecstatic, vatic; even in his latest work the grand public manner of his youthful poems compels though less overtly, the gesture of composition.

Because the manner is grand, and because the purity of the emotion finds, at moments of greatest intensity, modes of declamation that are just and persuasive, we find from the very beginning poems and parts of poems that have the definitive rightness. These are the passages that establish Mr. Wheelock—not in the vatic tradition, where I suspect he would like to be, but in the soberer tradition of poets who enforce a more human response. The less oratory, the more conviction.

Dudley Fitts. *NYT*. Sept. 9, 1956. p. 10

It is, of course, not simply his preference for accepted forms that makes Mr. Wheelock a traditionalist. He writes about the human condition not as it has been affected by such thinkers as Marx, Freud, and Einstein, by the dazzle that the hydrogen bomb and the IBM diversely provide, but in terms that would have been understood by men living in Jerusalem in the first century of our era or in Athens five centuries earlier. Recent ideological and technological revolutions have not been big enough, however, to silence the old questions about the half-known self and the great unknown Other. . . . Poems that speak feelingly of these matters, with candor and with the force bred of economy, have a durable value. Mr. Wheelock's most carefully wrought lyrics belong.

Babette Deutsch. *Poetry*. Feb., 1957. pp. 320–1

John Hall Wheelock's career as poet is a curious one. It is not exceptional for a lyric poet to be prolific in his youth—as Wheelock was—and then run thin and dry in his forties—as Wheelock did. . . . But what is really curious, and all but unique, is the revival of his talent in the past ten years; better still, the improvement of it. . . . The effort is to bring the language into a simpler, more natural tone; and to make, one can say, better sense. It is this effort—to abandon rhetoric, to walk without the embroidered coat—which makes the . . . new poems . . . so much more meaningful reading, so much more *real*. One can say "against" some of the recent poems that the pulse is low and the language meandering, but on the whole their fresher vocabulary guarantees an immediacy and poignancy never achieved in the earlier work.

Winfield Townley Scott. *SR*. March 2, 1957. p. 20

Wheelock comes into his old age with exhilaration, a philosophical reach of perspective that has nothing to do with academies, and a craftsman's hand still firm enough to register exactly what he sees and feels. Acceptance—not to be confused with resignation—is his muted theme. . . . His late look at the world has the freshness of his earliest, to which have been added all the meanings of being intelligent and human. Yeats raged openly at the burden of his many years; Eliot carries his with a tired smile and a drooping wing. But Wheelock accepts his advanced age as a point of vantage from which he continually examines wonder and comes upon delight. He does not have the corrosive passion of the septuagenarian Yeats, nor the power of both Yeats and Eliot to isolate from the language a seam of expression that is in each case theirs alone. Wheelock's passion is less a passion for poetry as the art of difficult song than for poetry as a kind of metaphysical reportage. In his case, the report is a long account of joy, sophisticated, qualified—even, in some cases, alloyed with darker elements—and for these reasons thoroughly convincing.

(K)   John Malcolm Brinnin. *SR*. Nov. 4, 1961. p. 24

Like Wordsworth, Mr. Wheelock is a first-person poet. He offers us his interpretation of man's place in the scheme of things, and the interpretation seems, at least, to grow out of his private experience: his sense of the joy of consciousness, his celebration of the life-force, these balanced by a sense of the tragic absurdity in being conscious, the meaning death has for him, the sources of the creative spirit, his memories of family and influential occasions, the things he loves. In short, this book [*The Gardener*] is a sort of poetic biography—the biography of a sensitive and philosophical human being, who offers himself to us for whatever we may find of value.

(K)   Edwin S. Godsey. *SwR*. Spring, 1962. p. 254

Fortunately for Mr. Wheelock's book [*What Is Poetry?*], the personality that emerges is noble. He has written and read a great deal of poetry for poetry's sake, and has done more—especially through his publications in the Scribner's "Poets of Today" series—to encourage poetry in this country, than anyone else I can think of. His views of poetry are large and serious.

(K)   Louis Simpson. *NYHT*. Oct. 27, 1963. pp. 6, 25

Death and the thoughts suggested by its closeness are, as it were, one more string on the same board over which Wheelock has dwelled some twenty years—a string which he now chooses to pluck almost exclusively. His penchant has always been for the occasional poem; and more specifically, for the meditation on occasions. Even his short lyrics and sonnets (well represented here [in *Dear Men and Women*]) are sustained by a bold detachment from their subjects, so that persons and places mentioned in them, against a backdrop of accomplished or imminent death, become real in the emblematic sense. . . . In all the summations of experience, the profits and losses, which these new poems attempt, Wheelock's way of telling a story, of positioning details, might be termed a graceful reticence.

(K)   David Galler. *Poetry*. May, 1967. p. 124

John Hall Wheelock has learned nothing from Pound or Williams, is not out to influence younger poets, and titles his latest book, unembarrassedly, *Dear Men and Women*. Without becoming J. Donald Adams and using him as a stick to beat other contemporaries, it should be said that Mr. Wheelock, at age 80, has looked back on his life and written some wholly affecting, totally genuine songs of experience.

(K)   William H. Pritchard. *HdR*. Summer, 1967. p. 312

See *Poems, Old and New, The Gardener, Dear Men and Women* (poetry); *What Is Poetry?* (criticism).

WHEELWRIGHT, JOHN BROOKS (1897–1940)

Despite their mathematical whiskers, Wheelwright's unconventional sonnets are patently integral, the forms of an experience. Long, in instances singing, in other instances staccato breaths or periods sustained by an individual, racy, infrequently exalted idiom harmoniously compose them; and these harmonies—in some cases somewhat cryptically but in others clearly and fully—convey a fresh grasp of life, particularly of the ways, fortunes, and tragedies of friendship.

Paul Rosenfeld. *Nation*. Oct. 15, 1938. p. 386

He is called hag-ridden, exhibitionist, skillful, dignified like a Greek, a leader of a revolutionary school; it is further stated that he has no ear and that his language is bald. Some make of him a mystic; others are satisfied that he comes from New England—and that almost as an accusation. . . . He seems a poet, for he infuses and infuriates. He is skillful, for he is called a heretic. In brief, he claims attention for his Christian attitudes as well as for his Marxist politics; and both, fused into his poetry, easily run riot with the critical fanciers of the laissez-faire in verse. . . . It is to the accomplished Deed that Wheelwright gives his strange allegiance and his stranger art.

Harry Roskolenko. *Poetry*. August, 1940. pp. 278–81

Technically, Wheelwright . . . was a most versatile poet. He was equally adept at handling a metaphysical conceit and a dramatic monologue. In some of his shorter poems he even appears as the terrible man—there is no adequate, single word to describe him—who deliberately mixed his metaphors. . . . In all capacities, however, he was a precise writer, one who avoided unnecessarily expansive language and who achieved his effects by sharp contrasts, clever juxtapositions.

E. Reed Whittemore. *NYHT*. Aug. 17, 1941. p. 13

John Wheelwright was not able or not willing to practice the necessary insincerities of communication; this absolute honesty sanctioned the bewildering, misleading, and seemingly captious items that fill his poems, underneath which the reader will often look in vain for the directive logic, poetic or otherwise, that should organize and sustain them. . . . The short satirical and epigrammatical poems are particularly good of their kind. There the poet, being forced to revolve his poem around a single point, hasn't the pretext for divagation and must concentrate what he says into one small, but very sharp, bite. The gnomic flavor of Wheelwright's poetry makes the bite all the sharper—once it is felt.

Clement Greenberg. Nation. Aug. 30, 1941. p. 186

On the technical side, John Wheelwright is a genuinely advanced poet; he has thoroughly explored the tradition, and the recent extensions of the tradition, and his final products are by and large richly original, formally ambitious, and modern in a mature and respectable sense. His themes and perceptions spring typically from the operation of a well-sharpened intellect upon the objective world, with the result that the poems never try to lift themselves by their own platitudes, nor do they ever open their hearts to the amateur of emotions of the good-old-fashioned kind. . . . Wheelwright is an intellectual poet, and by this I mean not merely that he is an intelligent poet, but that the themes of his poetry are quite often the propositions of philosophical argumentation.

E. S. Forgotson. Poetry. Oct., 1941. pp. 45–6

Wheelwright had sense, satire, sensibility and the salt of literature that made him one of the best of the recognizable minor poets. Had he lived, he would have perfected his New England acerbity, his tart sort of common sense that we badly need, but, as he writes in another context:

Then I departed as I came, tearing roses
and trampling the gooseberries and the strawberries.

Peter Monro Jack. NYT. Dec. 14, 1941. p. 5

Very nearly all of Wheelwright's verse lacked the presence and the unforced control of a "melodic ear," and unlike Marianne Moore, he had yet to find a "light rhyme" or its equivalent with which to define his particular art of writing verse. Some of his effects were "experimental" and inventive, others seem to have been studiously premeditated, still others had an air of seeming accidental, and the great majority were dominated by a prose rhythm that had yet to achieve its maturity. But at the center of the verse where a number of Wheelwright's epigrams remained half-formed and half-concealed, a personality that had created its own speech emerged: the speech was often critical and it welcomed controversy, and it was persistent in its effort to write poetry with ideas and not with words.

Horace Gregory and Marya Zaturenska. *A History of American Poetry* (Harcourt). 1947. pp. 348–9

It is part of Wheelwright's integrity, of course, that he gave no palm to halfway measures. He hounded Truth. Therefore the didactic note in all his poetry, his effort to objectify and dramatize. The image is never for its own sake: sense must be made of it—a thing said. His obituary poems on Hart Crane, Crosby, and Miss Lowell say definitive things; like all his best poems, they survive with a remarkable solidarity. Where his thought attained the vigor of eloquence, neither matter nor manner damaged by the other, he wrote poems which repeatedly reward attention and which should give him a yet unsuspected importance in the history of American poetry.

Winfield Townley Scott. *NMQ.* Summer, 1954. p. 195

See *Rock and Shell, Mirrors of Venus, Political Self-Portrait,* and *Selected Poems* (all poems).

WHITE, E. B. (1899–   )

Mr. White—known to the readers of the Conning Tower and the *New Yorker* as E. B. W.—in addition to being a skilful versifier with a rare sensitiveness for words, shows in this book [*The Lady Is Cold*] flashes of poetic distinction. He possesses much of the bite and sting of Dorothy Parker with none of her sardonic bitterness, and his lighter verses have all of the fantastic whimsicality and none of the mawkishness of A. A. Milne. He is a poet who will bear watching.

Nation. Aug. 14, 1929. p. 177

The clever editorial paragraphs under "Notes and Comment" on *The New Yorker's* first page are written by one of the most brilliant men on its staff, one E. B. White, co-author with Jim Thurber of *Is Sex Necessary?* and author of much delightful verse, some of which you will find in *The Lady Is Cold. Every Day Is Saturday* is a selection from those same hebdomadal paragraphs.

Most of us have marvelled that one man could conduct the procession of those paragraphs every week with such sapience and humor as Mr. White has evinced. Now, in the "Acknowledgement" of his book, he modestly calls attention to how other people in some degree have constantly contributed to the ingredients of his columns. No contemporary commentator of the kind is methodical. He gathers his material "from a thousand mysterious and unremembered sources." Quite true; but the force of Mr. White's comments has not depended so much upon his material as upon his way of using it. . . . It is his civil way of presenting some of the most astonishing phenomena of our time that has endeared Mr. White to his audience.

William Rose Benét. SR. Oct. 27, 1934. p. 240

People discovered E. B. White for a thousand reasons, all good. The news got out, and E. B. White got out, too, out of New York. He is now in Maine. But he is the same, or better. His prose is still as pinched as ever, and its temper, bland insouciance itself, has echoes and overtones of hurt introspection and cosmic solicitude. He has still an unerring eye (a cliché of which he would never be guilty) for the minor madnesses of the age. He brings as the measure of madness his own genial but inexorable reason. By faint clues and indirections he gives us a moral philosophy, for he asks almost desperately, but always quietly, what the minor madnesses add up to.

Irwin Edman. SR. March 18, 1939. p. 7

. . . White's pieces take anything of interest for their subject matter, from the brooder stove on his saltwater farm in Maine to a personal plan for world peace, and distill it down to a moral conclusion. The touch is always light, but the punch can be heavy and full of conviction. . . .

White's style is the essence of what gets called "New Yorker style." Its ingredients are a meticulous ear for sound (his chapter on Maine Speech is something to make a phonetician's recording blush for shame) and a fresh use of words that always looks effortless and almost never is. An example is the much-discussed phrase, "the unspeakably bright imploring look of the frustrated," in his great short story, "The Door." Change the "unspeakably" to its uncle "terribly" and you have reduced a perfect and momentous expression to a merely good one.

Stanley Edgar Hyman. NR. July 20, 1942. p. 91

The record of his adventure [<i>One Man's Meat</i>] shows not the slightest trace of being directed against <i>you:</i> peculiar among literary farmers, Mr. White didn't leave the city in order to leave you behind, nor is it any part of his effort to outsmart you on new territory. He will respect you and leave you alone as long as you respect him and leave him alone; this would be his definition of democracy, and he is ready to die for democracy. Vulgarity is something Mr. White takes into account by the way; he helps fumigate it out of existence with his fine aseptic prose.

The kinship with Thoreau is explicit throughout this book but there is also Mr. White's implicit kinship with Montaigne. Obviously, compared to the great humanist, Mr. White's powers are on a minor scale; in the matter of style, real as his gifts are, we question whether his felicity has not sometimes been achieved by going around rather than over intellectual hurdles. But as we read the diary he kept in the First World War, we recognize how compellingly the humanistic tradition had already claimed him, even as a young man.

Diana Trilling. Nation. Aug. 8, 1942. p. 118

These monthly reports of Mr. White's doings, collected [in *One Man's Meat*] from *Harper's* and other magazines, are in the office they perform like the intimate letters of the eighteenth century, say, of Cowper or Gray, and occasionally they resemble those of Lamb. When the reader closes the book, he feels that he knows the author exceedingly well; he has suffered summer catarrh with him, has lived in his house, has made a pilgrimage with him to the lake of his boyhood, has voted in town meetings, and has hunted coons with him in the season of the year, has read farm papers, heard Maine speech, gone lobstering, and whiled away Sundays. The reader is taken into the thick of things, and likes what he sees. All these things would be dull indeed in the journal of a dull man. Happily, Mr. White is not dull. He is a personality of a rare sort, and has the gift of engaging us in his practicalities, his generosities, his sympathies and prejudices, and in his contagious enthusiasm for individual liberty. The most engaging quality of all is his quick-turning humor which, though expected, always surprises.

William C. DeVane. YR. Autumn, 1942. p. 164

Little Stuart is a very engaging hero, and *Stuart Little* is an entertaining book, whether for children or their parents. If I also found it a little disappointing, perhaps that is because I had been expecting that E. B. White would write nothing less than a children's classic. He has all the required talents, including a gift for making himself understood. He never condescends to his readers: if they happen to be younger than the audience he reaches through *The New Yorker,* he merely takes more pains to explain his story. Style is even more important in children's books than in those for adults because one often reads aloud to children, and a bad style wearies the reader, not to mention what it does to the listeners. Within his own range of effects, Mr. White has the best style of any American author: clear, unhackneyed and never tying the tongue into knots.

He has, moreover, a talent for making big things small and homely, as if he saw the world distinctly through the wrong end of a telescope. . . . But the garden that Mr. White describes in his essays is the world as a whole, and the effect of smallness is deceptive—just as the effect of big-ness is deceptive in the authors who imitate Walt Whitman; they describe a world that is really bare and simple, whereas Mr. White's world merely gives, through art, the effect of simplicity.

Malcolm Cowley. *NYT*. Oct. 28, 1945. p. 7

White's prose nears the ideal style defined by Hazlitt, except that White makes freer use of words which have not taken out their final papers with the lexicographer. His colloquialism, an aspect of his independence and informality, can give students of English a model, too, in that it is always a precise diction, and never trite. Actually he is a purist in the best sense, and not least in that he is helping to fix meanings of words that will appear in future editions of dictionaries. Moreover, it is all done without flourish or groaning; White has the true artisan's unaffected dexterity. . . .

Out of his work emerges a spare but striking profile. It is that of the ironic spectator, the minority report personified, the man with eyebrows raised but never harshly supercilious, the uncompromising individualist who would as lief split a hair with himself as with anybody else, and a still, small, humane voice through two troublesome decades, when to be at the same time a sensitive, serene, incorruptible, polite, rugged, and charitable person has been the rarest of achievements. White's geniality and fancy, detectable in his briefest jottings, are more generally recognized than his penetration and virility.

Warren Beck. *CE*. April, 1946. pp. 368–9

He has done much toward preserving the essay from death. The essay, the genial, reflective, personal essay of Addison and Steele, Montaigne, Lamb, so much honored in English courses, has almost disappeared in America. Perhaps our civilization is too hard on the individual; perhaps few individuals are interesting enough to hold readers with their small doings and large thoughts. But E. B. White, almost alone in our time, has captured and held his readers. He has done so, I think, chiefly because he has brought the poetic spirit as well as verbal felicity into popular journalism. Or, to say the same thing over (always good pedagogical practice), he has made of the editorial an art form. . . .

He has made bourgeois idealism reputable. In the twenties and thirties of this century most young writing men were rebels against their time, their civilization. E. B. White did not rebel. He liked his time; he enjoyed living and watching life; he respected his fellow men, whether New York intellectuals or Maine farmers and fishermen. While certainly he finds many aspects of our civilization ridiculous or repellent, he does not reject it. He sees that it breeds the fundamental virtues: honesty, courage, fidelity, sympathy. He is in favor of these virtues. He accepts life, whereas many of the superior young men seem to hate and fear life.

Morris Bishop. Introduction to One Man's Meat
by E. B. White (Harper). 1950. p. x

He is not one of those peripatetic philosopher-essayists who plod about, armed with walking-stick, pipe and rucksack, forever seeking new bistros or bazaars about which to write whimsical "papers": he has found his best in the doorways and the pastures and range shelters (for chickens) that he knows so well and he doesn't need to look elsewhere, except in the daily papers, for all the material he'll ever need. . . .

The sense of melancholy which has always been evident in his writings, even the funniest ones, increases as the world in which he lives becomes more and more exasperating (as he says, he cultivates "a disconsolate attitude which has some slight literary value"). But there is nothing passive about his melancholy, as has been the case with other gentle writers who have been content to take it lying down. The answer to E. B. White's occasional tendencies toward despair is E. B. White's persistent and zestful capacity for indignation. Is there a phony in the house, or a demagogue or a dogmatic pedant or an officious bureaucrat? White will handle him. The best thing about E. B. White is that he is alive—very much so—alive and kicking, and (I confess I know him only through his work) he never seems to grow a day older, or less in love.

Robert E. Sherwood. NYHT. Jan. 17, 1954. p. 1

In 1957 Mr. White wrote a piece for The New Yorker about Professor Strunk, who was a teacher of his at Cornell forty years ago, and about the manual Strunk had prepared for the use of his classes in writing. White brought this manual up to date and wrote an essay for it on some of the larger problems of style. The result is not a substitute for such a work as H. W. Fowler's Modern English Usage, but its seventy-one pages are full of good sense. . . .

Even without the assistance of those who have their own reasons for greasing the skids, the language is always slipping into imprecision, and most of us, no doubt, are guilty of at least contributory negligence. We need to be reminded from time to time that we too have a responsibility for resisting the process of attrition and decay, and The Elements of Style is a worthy and practical sort of reminder. As White says, "Clarity, clarity, clarity."

Granville Hicks. SR. Aug. 1, 1959. p. 13

E. B. White has tried to live in society. He has had, and still has, a wife; one can almost say that he has also had a magazine, The New Yorker, much of whose best prose is either his or reflects his own wryly committed spirit. But the burden of grafting a Thoreauvian blend of stoical abstention and poetic concern onto *The New Yorker*'s peculiarly discreet diction has weighed heavily on White. *The New Yorker* dislikes strong emotion strongly expressed, sustained argument argumentatively put forward. It is as if emotion and argument might keep the commuters reading past their stops on the train. White has been one of the architects of *The New Yorker*'s style, and also one of its victims. Nevertheless, his real quality as a man and a writer has managed to survive. He has felt strongly about various matters, from the atomic bomb to urban noise. Wit and under-statement and a contained rage result in a considerable achievement in this new collection, *The Points of My Compass,* which is brilliant sentence by sentence, convincing paragraph by paragraph, but occasionally fades out into whimsy over the long stretch of an essay.

Herbert Gold. *SR.* Nov. 24, 1962. p. 30

Throughout *One Man's Meat* White was trying to stimulate the ordinary man's awareness of world-wide social problems (as the Progressives had tried to do) and to reawaken his sense of relationship with the earth as part of the cosmos. White was also trying to make him feel the inter-relatedness of the social and natural realms and the significance of that relatedness for the average man's fate: ". . . a man's free condition is of two parts: the instinctive freedoms he experiences as an animal dweller on a planet, and the practical liberties he enjoys as a privileged member of human society . . ." Without either, true freedom is impossible. The need for stressing freedom through harmony with nature at a time when the admittedly important struggle for political freedom was getting all the headlines was the justification White offered for writing mostly about farm and household chores while "Countries are ransacked, valleys drenched with blood."

Norris W. Yates. *The American Humorist* (Iowa
State). 1964. p. 312

Though White is the co-author of a celebrated guide to style, he is too humble before the elusive miracle of the written word to pose as a solemn expert on it. He is a professional writer, not a rhetorician; his voice is authoritative, not authoritarian.

William W. Watt and Robert W. Bradford in *An E. B.
White Reader* (Harper). 1966. p. 4

See *Is Sex Necessary?* (with James Thurber), *Every Day Is Saturday, Quo Vadimus?, One Man's Meat, Wild Flag, Here Is New York, The Second Tree from the Corner, The Elements of Style* (with W. Strunk), *The Points of My Compass* (essays); *Charlotte's Web, Stuart Little* (children's stories).

WHITTEMORE, REED (1919–   )

Skeptical of Providence and man alike, Mr. Whittemore depicts a melancholy world. In a world without established values, he asks indirectly, What is law? What is order? But fickle values do not keep him from pondering the problem of evil. Dogged by a compassionate interest in society, he looks at cruelty and evil in its other forms. . . .

Heroes and Heroines, however, is far from being a melancholy book. Despite their seriousness, many of the poems are in the tradition of light verse, a light verse that owes something to Auden. A man of tough, observant mind and mocking merriment looks at pomposity, love of power, stupidity, avarice, ruthlessness, etc.; records what he sees; and refuses to be undone by it. His buoyancy is manifested primarily in his vigorous, flexible, subtle cadences, his use of irony and paradox, and his remarkable virtuosity in language.

> R. L. Lowe. *Poetry.* Nov., 1947. p. 99

The poems in Reed Whittemore's second collection, *An American Takes a Walk,* have the reliable but sometimes unresilient honesty of a street corner seen in the Midwestern summer sun. They are revealing in the way a man might unconsciously reveal himself in his talk while standing on that corner. They are bookish poems, some of them, but without caring. Many are slangy. They are necessary in the way that only the poems of poets are necessary. They have their work to do and they know, though they might wish it were not so, that that work is of the mind and the guts. Thus they flow from a sense which is not especially Midwestern. Or contemporary.

The poems never risk ecstasy, fearing perhaps that vulgar monster the dishonest bliss. In fact they seldom risk music in the more ambitious pieces, though there is plenty of it in some of the very beautiful short poems such as "Naples" and "Capri."

> John Logan. *SR.* July 28, 1956. p. 10

As a poet with certain very obvious and amusing gifts, Reed Whittemore is almost everyone's favorite. Certainly he is one of mine. Yet there are dangerous favorites and inconsequential favorites, and favorites like pleasant diseases. What of Whittemore? He is as wittily cultural as they come, he has read more than any young man anybody knows, has been all kinds of places, yet shuffles along in an old pair of tennis shoes and khaki pants, with his hands in his pockets, saying to every head-down, hustling graduate student he meets, "Shucks, fellow, don't take all this so seriously. Learn, as I was born to know, that all literature, all life, is secretly funny." . . . Whittemore is wickedly delightful, deft as Willie Hoppe, as good in spots as Auden himself, and a great deal more fun. Yet, as I have been suggesting, something else keeps grazing these poems, and the mind that reads them: something more valuable, more difficult than the poems themselves would have you believe anything is.

James Dickey. *Poetry*. Nov., 1956. pp. 115–16

The poetry of Reed Whittemore has not, so far as I know, had the attention it deserves at the hands of serious readers. It is occasionally, in reviews, acknowledged to be good work, and otherwise is rather neglected than objected against; its rare candor and integrity of purpose have not been valued as they ought to be.

For this neglect I think there are two reasons: that he is often funny, and that he is often literary. People who either have no faculty of independent judgment or perhaps rightly distrust what they do have, are suspicious and even resentful of new poetry which is funny (the word "wit" has been made safe for democracy, but does not include the idea of actually laughing), because they are afraid of being caught admiring something which will turn out to be light verse. . . .

I said before that the impulse to poetry is regarded as immediate and given in Whittemore's work, where many of the poems begin simply with that situation, the poet's impulse to write; what stands in the way becomes, often, the subject of the poem. I say further that this impulse, with Whittemore, is to a heroic, representative poetry, a poetry synoptic of history, of culture, making the same claims as the major poems of the past; the evidence for this is his persistent preoccupation with heroism in action, matched, on the technical side, by a preoccupation with epical devices, which he employs, however, chiefly in a mocking or critical sense.

Howard Nemerov. *KR*. Spring, 1959. pp. 260, 267

Mr. Whittemore is invincibly and delightedly a Professor of English; but the gown is worn with an exuberant grace, the allusive wit is as light as it is sharp. There is no intensity here [*The Boy from Iowa*], and the satiric intelligence is less somber and considerably less shaking than Mr. [John] Hollander's; but the loose, sprawling cantos of the two "Writer's Epics" (a new kind of Browning) hit hard in spite of their dead-pan slap-dash, their deceptively innocent air. The more conventional poems are less effective, not because they are more serious—a useless distinction: Mr. Whittemore's giddiest comedy is caustically, even therapeutically, serious —but because the power of the prevailing tone distorts them in this context. They would be better printed apart. Here it is the satire that matters, the gay and definitive assault.

Dudley Fitts. *SR*. Aug. 4, 1962. p. 23

Now Mr. Whittemore is at his best a good poet. He is at his best a rare poet as much of his fine work manifests such a gayety, such a vivacity, such a real charm—I do not mean "cuteness"—and an intelligence and precision of wit that I am inclined not to complain. I do complain because Mr. Whittemore must know that poetry is not judged on a basis of bulk. He must know that every poet should publish only those poems which seem to him his very best work. Then, too, the more poems anyone writes in a fixed manner, the more likely it is that the style will limit the scope until, alas, the poet has little more to offer than a style the years of practice and habit have polished to a blank perfection.

Roger Hecht. *SwR*. Winter, 1963. p. 106

When a man is represented by a piece of fiction or a small selection of poems in a magazine, he puts himself forth as a story writer or a poet and he is judged as such. Attention is drawn to and captured by the writing itself, and without conflict. But when he shows all his wares, the reader is tempted, as I was, to use, say, the essays to judge the verse, the personal recollections to gain insights into the fiction, and all of it together to discover what the man himself is like. This can be an interesting game, as it was in reading *The Fascination of the Abomination,* but it can prejudice one against the writer's accomplishments in the separate fields. . . .

This is not the whole story. Whittemore's long, ambitious essay on Browning's poems made me search out and dust off my own Modern Library edition. "A Letter to Karl Shapiro," which appeared originally as a review of Shapiro's terrible-tempered *In Defense of Ignorance,* is an eloquent message to a fellow-writer that he had inadvertently given aid and comfort to the enemy—to his own enemy, to Whittemore's enemy, to the real yahoo, the real square, the guy who ends his review with "Nonetheless, many will find. . . ."

Charles Simmons. *SR*. June 8, 1963. p. 28

In any reading of Reed Whittemore's essays and poems two qualities stand out: clarity and engagement. The man is urbane yet committed, ironic yet *present*. The voice in Whittemore's poems, maundering and casual as it may seem, constantly surprises with what it yields: the faintly, even deliberately, tired comic self-indictment of a man of that generation that now finds itself approaching middle age. And this coupled with an accurate and beautifully playful vision of literary America, 1940–1960.

Robert Sward. *Poetry*. Sept., 1964. p. 380

See *Heroes and Heroines, An American Takes a Walk* (poems); *The Boy from Iowa, The Fascination of the Abomination* (poems, stories, essays).

WILBUR, RICHARD (1921–   )

Wit of the kind he is aiming at—the Swiftian or Eliotesque kind—demands more intellectual incisiveness and emotional "blackness" than Mr. Wilbur is at present able to muster. His true domain is the borderland between natural and moral perception, his special gift for the genteel, non-metaphysical conceit which illuminates the hidden correspondences between natural and moral phenomena. Characteristically, two of Mr. Wilbur's favorite devices stem from Marianne Moore: the lingering over minute particulars and the sudden introduction of anecdotal units into straight narrative or meditative sequences . . . where the "anecdote," so far from merely winding up the poem, both climaxes and clinches it.

F. C. Golffing. Poetry. Jan., 1948. pp. 221–2

His poems are full of affirmation, delight in the shapes and colors of the visible world; water and light are favorite symbols. Mr. Wilbur's turn of mind is philosophic as well as sensual; his epithet is neither the fashionably verbal nor the obsolescent conventional; he has considerable variety of manner and a meet sense of proportion in the way he fits manner to theme. The danger he may face . . . is that of finding things a little too easy, of having forms come facile, however quick, to suit the demands of the not quite deep, really, levels of emotion.

Rolfe Humphries. Nation. Dec. 9, 1950. p. 536

Some of these poems are pieces of pure gaiety, some present uncrossed felicity. Most of them are about gratifying objects. All of them are charged with responsiveness to the lusters, the tones, of the physical world, and show the poet alert to less apparent matters. The scenes are alive with light, be it the light coined by "the minting shade of the trees" that shines on clinking glasses and laughing eyes, or one of a wintrier brightness. They shiver and sway happily with the sound of winds and waters. Yet they are apt to close upon a somber chord, to admit an intrusive shadow.

Babette Deutsch. NYT. Feb. 11, 1951. p. 12

Mr. Wilbur always keeps firm control over the shape of his poems, and it is a shape determined jointly by the ear and by the mind, so that the poems resolve themselves to a conclusion both musically and intellectually. He is at his best with the longer line and the slower cadence, in subjects which take their origin in scenes observed or remembered. Occasionally observation gives way too readily to exclamation. . . . But this is not a common fault, and for the most part he moves from description to comment so subtly yet naturally that the texture of the poem remains even and a descriptive poem has become a meditative or even a philosophic one before the reader is aware.

David Daiches. *NYHT*. Feb. 18, 1951. p. 4

The precise quality of the poems is a delicate suspension. He performs an extraordinary feat of balance. His poems are strong and yet are sensitively wrought so that in general the reader gets a fine, real sense of the world.

There is a sense of mastery but of struggle, of order claimed from chaotic forces never allowed to assume disproportion, yet valued as formative. . . . One returns to the idea of balance, of orderliness, of excellence, of elegance, of a good centrality, nothing excessive, nothing divisive, which is to say that Wilbur has achieved a natural and full harmony in his poetry.

Richard Eberhart. *NYT*. June 24, 1956. p. 5

Now with *Things of This World,* his enormous gifts grown into their mature assurance, Wilbur certainly emerges as our serenest, urbanest, and most melodic poet. To say Wilbur has matured is not to imply that he will not accomplish finer things yet, and I would suggest for instance that in his search for a serene diction he might place less reliance on such adjectives as "clear," "pure," "calm," and "graceful." It is exactly the qualities described by these adjectives that best describe the best Wilbur poems, but it is very much to the point, I believe, that in those best poems the clarity, purity, calm, and grace emerge thing-wise and self-living, not by adjectival assertion.

John Ciardi. *SR*. Aug. 18, 1956. p. 18

Imagination as a word has tended to associate with the bodiless. "Imaginary" and "fictional" are synonyms. In Wilbur's previous work, the attempt is to divest objects of being or relevance and create a world of the imagination independent of objects. Here we find imagination in another function, applied to things not to uncover an inner reality superior to the outer, but to present their gaudiness and to celebrate sensuous enjoyment of them. If we "imagine excellence" it is in order to "try to *make* it." . . . There has been a steady intellectual growth, and a movement away from the destitution of formalism into the beginnings of something else; from a self-delighted loveliness (and the poems, let it be insisted, really *are* lovely) not to any "affirmation" as Life editors would have it, but toward the discovery of some "things of this world."

Donald Hall. *Poetry*. Sept., 1956. p. 403

Mr. Wilbur used to be a kind of backward-looking, forward-aspiring fellow. If it were a spring day, he perversely wanted it to be an autumn one. . . . But all is changed now. In his newest work he stands squarely in the midst of the things of this world and likes all of what he sees, smells, hears, touches, and tastes. . . . If *Things of This World* is marked by Wilbur's new-found sense of reality, it still exhibits what have come to be the trademarks of his work—formal elegance, unusual although never grotesque imagery, control, quiet gaiety, and an agile imagination. Now that Wallace Stevens is dead, Williams seems headed toward being the dandy of American verse.

Leah Bodine Drake. At. June, 1957. p. 78

Nor does Wilbur wear a mask all the time. He gives the game away in "Juggler" and "Mind," both of which treat of his artistic aim. The aim is to do his work so skillfully, the first of these says, that it will "shake our gravity up" and we shall, for the moment, have "won for once over the world's weight." He recognizes the self-deceptiveness of this ideal in the image of the juggler who gets tired and puts his marvelous paraphernalia back "in the dust again" so that they resume their normal heaviness in "the daily dark." . . . But in the poems that move with a weary splendor to the full assumption of their Existential burden ("Marginalia," for instance, and "Beasts," "After the Last Bulletins," and "Merlin") we feel, if still no irresistibly new perceptions, the breath of a true diver into his own meanings. And curiously enough, we feel it as strongly in those poems which, with a joyous connoisseurship, give praise to beauty and to the variety of worldly possibility.

(K)   M. L. Rosenthal. *The Modern Poets* (Oxford). 1960.
p. 255

As Ortega y Gasset says . . . , "Everything in the world is strange and marvellous to well-open eyes." Unquestionably, Wilbur would meet with the Spanish philosopher's approval. For he discovers the strange and the marvellous in the commonest objects. Like the painter, Pieter de Hooch, whom he admires ("Objects" and "A Dutch Courtyard"), he is entranced by the way in which a courtyard seems to burn in the sun, finds pleasure in "true textures," "true integuments," magic in "the weave of a sleeve." Even the lowly potato inspires a lyric ("Potato") ten stanzas long.

Yet he is aware, as Wordsworth earlier was aware, that when he invests the commonplace with magic, he half perceives and half creates the objects of his vision.

(K)   Frederic E. Faverty in *Poets in Progress,* edited by
Edward B. Hungerford (Northwestern). 1962. p. 70

. . . Richard Wilbur's *The Beautiful Changes* . . . was the peak of skilful elegance. Here was the ability to shape an analogy, to perceive and develop comparisons, to display etymological wit, and to pun six ways at once. It appealed to the mind because it was intelligent, and to the sense of form because it was intricate and shapely. It did not appeal to the passions and it did not pretend to. . . . Many poets after Wilbur resembled him, and some of them were good at it, but the typical *ghastly* poem of the fifties was a Wilbur poem not written by Wilbur, a poem with tired wit and obvious comparisons and nothing to keep the mind or the ear occupied. (It wasn't Wilbur's fault, though I expect he will be asked to suffer for it.)

(K)   Donald Hall. Introduction to *Contemporary American Poetry* (Penguin). 1962. p. 20

. . . even in this book [*Advice to a Prophet*], which is not Wilbur's best, there is, underlying the grace and negligent mastery, the thing that should eventually make him the truly important poet that he deserves to be: the thing which his superlative manipulation of verse forms, his continuous and unobtrusive skills never fully state but never lose sight of. This is the quietly joyful sense of celebration and praise out of which Wilbur writes: the kind of celebration that is done, usually, without anyone's being told, and of the things that cause joy to rise unexpectedly, excessively and almost always voicelessly in the human breast. This sense underlies Wilbur's work as the sea underlies a ship, or rather a garlanded Shelleyan boat which we admire so much that we forget that the sea makes its movement possible. Wilbur's celebration is sweet-natured, grave, gentle, and as personal to him as his own breath, a praise of small moments in which there is profound and intense life, and in his best poems (such as the one a few years back about burying the pet dog) it rises as it deserves to rise.

(K)   James Dickey. *SwR*. Summer, 1962. p. 490

Though there is little of the ascetic mystic in Wilbur's temperament, he is—at least some of the time—a religious poet. But he is not religious in any strict or doctrinal sense of the word; rather, he is deeply concerned with an experience of life and of the universe as sacramental—as possessing a spiritual worth that shines on surfaces but also hides in recesses.

(K)   Ralph J. Mills. *Contemporary American Poetry* (Random). 1965. p. 167

See *The Beautiful Changes, Ceremony, Things of This World, Advice to a Prophet* (poems).

WILDER, THORNTON (1897–   )

Before we read him, we are likely to think that he is one of those contemporary writers who seem still to date from the nineties—that he is simply another "stylist," another devotee of "beauty"—that we shall, in fact, find him merely a pretty or a precious writer; but Wilder, when we come to read him, turns out to be something quite different. He certainly possesses that quality of "delightfulness" of which Saintsbury has said that Balzac didn't have it, but that Gérard de Nerval did. But he has a hardness, a sharpness, a precision, quite unlike our Cabells, our Dunsanys, our Van Vechtens and our George Moores. He has an edge which is peculiar to himself and which is never incompatible with a consummate felicity.

Edmund Wilson. *NR*. Aug. 8, 1928. p. 304

The Bridge of San Luis Rey can be sacrificed without loss. . . . Its fatalism seems specious, trivial, and even dishonest, as though consistency in the Maker's ways were trumped up to serve the ends of plot. *The Cabala* is much better, though questionable in that general air of selectness which it has in common with the society novels of writers like Marcel Prévost . . . and Paul Bourget. . . . And the work is vitiated at the close by that superficial coquetting with the mystic which mars *The Bridge* as a whole.

Kenneth Burke. *Bkm*. Aug., 1929. p. 562

That so exquisite a writer and so intense an inventor should devote his arts entirely to moral, as distinct from political, purposes is an admirable but, in the present state of things, a rare characteristic. . . . Through a combination of qualities almost unheard of in England but not uncommon in France, all Mr. Wilder's virtues, even the tidy flamboyance of his prose and the pagan revels of his intellect, arise from this smack of the evangelist in him.

E. G. Twitchett. *LM*. May, 1930. p. 32

Wilder has concocted a synthesis of all the chambermaid literature, Sunday school tracts and boulevard piety there ever were. He has added a dash of the prep-school teacher's erudition, then embalmed all this in the speciously glamorous style of the late Anatole France. He talks much of art, of himself as Artist, of style. He is a very conscientious craftsman. But his is the most irritating and pretentious style pattern I have read in years. It has the slick, smug finality of the lesser Latins; that shallow clarity and tight little good taste that remind one of nothing so much as the conversation and practice of a veteran cocotte.

Michael Gold. *NR*. Oct. 22, 1930. p. 267

He was a dramatist before he became a novelist, and his prose has always shown the discipline of the theater. His novels were never completely satisfactory in form: they were panel novels—long, vivid character sketches linking dramatic scenes. The quality of his imagination and his interest in character portrayal were both dramatic in spirit.

Dayton Kohler. EJ. Jan., 1939. p. 4

Thornton Wilder possesses several distinctive virtues as a creative literary artist, but unfortunately none of them has much to do with his actual skill as a writer. He has an adventurous mind, which makes him try new and interesting fields without resting comfortable on already won laurels. He is of an independent nature, which leads him to write as he pleases without being intimidated by critics or public. He is ambitious, which makes him do difficult and arresting things, even if not always seeming too well equipped for them. He has versatility, which results in his knowing his way about in both the novel and the drama. And he knows the advantage of leisure, which enables him to take his time about polishing his work, even to the extent of allowing fourteen years to elapse between novels.

Richard Watts, Jr. NR. March 1, 1948. p. 22

Mr. Wilder has been unfairly ignored by serious literary critics. . . . He is a humorist who knows the underlying seriousness of comic events, a satirist who loves the human race. True, his style has sometimes been pretentious, and his stories slow-paced; but he deserves our respect as an artist. The bold attempt of his whole career has been nothing less than the re-establishment of human values in a world which, he believes, desperately needs them. Consistently he has attempted to write literature which, having a value of its own, would still not be an end in itself. He deserves our admiration for accepting as his task the difficult artistic problem of suiting fable to idea and sound to sense, producing thus an integrated whole.

Joseph J. Firebaugh. PS. Autumn, 1950. p. 438

Though Wilder, when we look closely, has a mark of his own, his work strikes one as that of an "arranger" rather than a creator. His arrangements are artful, attractive, scrupulously calculated, and unmistakably gifted. They are delightfully decorative patterns created from the raw material dug up by other men. To put it another way, he arranges "flowers" beautifully, but he does not grow them. In this sense, he resembles certain modern Frenchmen rather than one of our own playwrights.

What is American in Wilder's plays are their benign humor, their old-

fashioned optimism, their use of the charmingly homely detail, the sophisticated employment of the commonplace, their avuncular celebration of
the humdrum, their common sense, popular moralism, and the simplicity
—one might almost say simple-mindedness—behind a shrewdly capti-
vating manipulation of a large selection of classic elements.

Harold Clurman. Nation. Sept. 3, 1955. p. 210

Mr. Wilder's play is, in a sense, a refutation of its thesis. Our Town is
purely and simply an act of awareness, a demonstration of the fact that
in a work of art, at least, experience can be arrested, imprisoned, and
preserved. The perspective of death, which Mr. Wilder has chosen, gives
an extra poignancy and intensity to the small-town life whose essence he
is trying so urgently to communicate. . . . The perspective is, to be sure,
hazardous; it invites bathos and sententiousness. Yet, Mr. Wilder has
used it honorably. He forbids the spectator to dote on that town of the
past. He is concerned only with saying: this is how it was, though then
we did not know it.

Mary McCarthy. Sights and Spectacles (Farrar).
1956. p. 28

I think that if the play (Our Town) tested its own theme more remorselessly, the world it creates of a timeless family and a rhythm of existence
beyond the disturbance of social wracks would not remain unshaken. . . .
I think, further, that the close contact which the play established with its
audience was the result of its coincidence with the deep longing of the
audience for such stability, a stability which in daylight out on the streets
does not truly exist. . . . To me, therefore, the play falls short of a form
that will press into reality to the limits of reality, if only because it could
not plumb the psychological interior lives of its characters and still keep
its present form.

Arthur Miller. At. April, 1956. p. 39

He is our great unsocial and antihistorical novelist, the artist of the
anachronism. . . . Wilder does not think of history as an irreversible process
of a river in flood; he thinks of it as a series of recurrent patterns, almost
like checkerboards set side by side. . . . Wilder has written a dozen books,
each strikingly different from all the others in place and time, in mood,
and even more in method, yet all the books embody or suggest the same
feeling of universal experience and eternal return. Everything that happened might happen anywhere, and will happen again. That principle
explains why he is able to adopt different perspectives in different books,
as if he were looking sometimes through one end of a telescope and sometimes through the other.

Malcolm Cowley. SR. Oct. 6, 1956. pp. 50–1

Although Wilder has been hysterically popular in Germany since the end of the war, when the State Department sent *Our Town* on tour as a "representative example" of "modern American theatre" . . . , his star has risen even higher since he received the Peace Prize at the Frankfurt Book Fair in 1957. . . . The vitalistic cosmic optimism of *The Skin of Our Teeth* provides the contemporary German with the psychological reassurance he demands. Shocked and terrified by the situation in which he finds himself as the primary European target of bombs dispatched from opposite directions, the middle-class German reader flees to the lap of Wilder.

Paul Fussell, Jr., Nation. May 3, 1958. pp. 394–5

When we examine the nature of Wilder's humanistic affirmation, what do we discover? His plays celebrate human love, the worth and dignity of man, the values of the ordinary, and the eternity of human values. From the little boy in Wilder's first play who says: "I am not afraid of life. I will astonish it!" to Dolly Levi and her cohorts in adventure in *The Matchmaker,* Wilder has always been on the side of life and life is seen to be most directly affirmed through love. Love, then, is his most persistent theme and it has been for him an inexhaustible subject. Of its worth he is convinced, but it is interesting to note that Wilder has never been able to make any commitments as to the reasons for its worth. Wilder can deal with life and love directly and concretely; but when he moves to the edges of life, the focus becomes less sharp.

(K)   Robert W. Corrigan. *ETJ.* Oct., 1961. p. 168

He is a man of singular temperament, often delighting in paradox, willing and able to challenge us and disturb us. But he likes things to seem traditional, that is, to be stated within the traditional frame of reference, though they may be somewhat new or idiosyncratic. He likes every present expression to hark back to the entirety of beloved accumulated literature, and constantly shows or suggests that every current thought is based on someone else's thinking, every day of our lives is rooted in olden time.

The moderation and correctness of Wilder's way of writing are so reposeful that at times one can imagine them lulling us too much, but they never do. His definiteness and dispatch and his natural popular touch, and the bravery of his sudden little assertions every so often—as though for percussiveness, for punctuation—animate his every page and every scene. Verily, as he himself tells us, what he offers a good deal of the time is only fantasy and spirituality, illusion and hypnosophy. But we dance in his dream, throughout; it is active and bright. It is an art on the side of Apollo, though ever respectful of Dionysus.

(K)   Glenway Wescott. *Images of Truth* (Harper). 1962.

p. 308

Thornton Wilder's plays have an inverse-Antaean quality: the closer down to earth they get, the weaker they are. Whenever Wilder attempts to achieve imaginative reality and tell us "truths" about human beings, we get a sentimentalization of the little guy that is as unbelievable as it is indigestible.'. . . . [O]f *The Bridge of San Luis Rey,* D. H. Lawrence noted, "I found [it] a dull dough-nut with artificial jam in it." But let the subject-matter get away from reality—let it be, for example, what goes on in the rarefied minds of babies, as in *Infancy,* the best of the three new *Plays for Bleecker Street*—and Wilder can be enormously convincing.

(K)   John Simon. *HdR*. Summer, 1962. pp. 268–9

The eyes behind the horn-rimmed spectacles have probed into the values of life, and under the colloquial language which he has employed for its appeal to the minds of Americans can be heard an urgent call to reason. The small number of carefully made works which he has issued over four decades have made their point, and it is doubtful that any of them save *The Cabala* and *The Woman of Andros* will drop into oblivion. *Our Town,* in all likelihood the most widely produced play in the entire history of American drama, and *The Skin of Our Teeth* have deserved the prizes bestowed on them by the Pulitzer committee as surely as any of the other plays granted the same award; and if *The Bridge of San Luis Rey* is not the best novel to have won the Pulitzer Prize, Wilder's five novels as a group have justly earned the Gold Medal for fiction given to him by the American Academy of Arts and Letters in 1952.

Being a conscientious craftsman, Wilder has grown steadily in strength and taste.

(K)   Malcolm Goldstein. *The Art of Thorton Wilder*
(Nebraska). 1965. p. 165

Wilder's efforts since *Heaven's My Destination* have all been directed toward expressing "the sublime in the pedestrian." Alcestis is the knight of faith, but who can understand her? The audience can only watch her and do their best with their own lives. *The Alcestiad* is unqualifiedly and unwaveringly, with no "concession to a contemporary standard of good manners," a religious play. The meaning of life that Wilder has cherished so carefully throughout all his work finally found its clearest expression through the philosophy of Kierkegaard. . . . Although *The Alcestiad* is clearly religious, it provides no answers; it does not seek to comfort the audience with soothing reports of rewards waiting for the good or anyone else. It is religious in the sense of Gertrude Stein's cooking pots, of Goethe's reading of the *Iliad,* or Kierkegaard's understanding of the stories of Job and Abraham and Isaac. Existence is difficult, painfully so; but it is available and better than anyone can realize.

(K)   Donald Haberman. *The Plays of Thornton Wilder*
                        (Wesleyan). 1967. pp. 51–2

Today, though the novelist-playwright is stouter and has lost some of the bristling bounce of his middle years, he retains the restless vitality that helps explain his infinite curiosity, his capacity for endless renewal. His voice has lost none of the earnest courtesy and considerateness so vividly recalled by those who have known him. And though he has long since forgone the company of other writers, having become more solitary, more *private* a person, Wilder retains his interest in experimentation, best exemplified in his celebrated explications of James Joyce and Gertrude Stein. . . .

What one recognizes beneath Wilder's genial exterior, within the essential being of the man and his work is the impulse, the peculiarly American capacity, to evoke and celebrate the meditative, the serene, the reverential sense of life. Never fully expressed in our national literature, it has been manifested in the achievements of social philosopher Bronson Alcott, painter Thomas Eakins, composer Charles Ives. It is that ultimately Vergilian pathos concerning itself with the tears of things that provides the thrust from which Wilder's latest work emerges.

(K)   Richard H. Goldstone. *SR*. April 1, 1967. p. 28

Thornton Wilder has been, in his day, a daring gamester. In every aspect of literary form: a very playboy of point-of-view (see *The Ides of March*), an inventor—with others—of the fluid, unboxed stage that was to become the International Theater. . . . But in matters of ethical and even epistemological substance, Wilder is highly traditional—not precisely a new humanist in the Babbitt-More model, but far closer to these daylight types than to any known underground man. . . . Everywhere in Wilder's books . . . , the Author appears as an admirer of decorum, self-restraint, disciplined goodness—and as an enemy of misrule, comic reversal, indulgence of personal (i.e., selfish) feeling. . . .

And, as should quickly be added, the values in question have become more visible, not less, as Wilder's career has progressed. *The Eighth Day* —the new book at hand—is a family novel, expansive, meditative, and surprisingly conventional in method and structure. . . . From *The Cabala* (1926), Wilder's first novel, a tale of an aristocratic order fallen into decline, to *The Eighth Day,* a steady ho-hum of condescension—curious suggestions of a faint personal disdain even for those whom the author is, on the face of it, celebrating—meets the reader's ear. The overview in this artist is, in short, not only cosmological, it is somehow social as well; the sense of time inhibits the imagination, but so too does a sense that The Others are inferior, not clubbable, not finally chic enough. People are held off without ill will, yet also without the remotest thought that a surrender of one's own ego to the other person could ever in this world occur. Self-regard, self-respect, self-absorption obliterate the possibility.

(K)   Benjamin DeMott. *NYT*. April 2, 1967. pp. 1, 53

So his career remains a puzzle, not to be explained by sheer deterioration. Let us forget the young stylist of *The Cabala;* what happened to the valid Americanist of *Heaven's My Destination,* the prober of true mysteries in *The Ides of March,* the effective heart-tugger of *Our Town?* Possible explanations occur for his failure to realize his promise, but they all falter. Is it because he has spent much of his life as a wanderer and observer, unintegrated for long with any society or community? So did Ibsen and Strindberg. Is it because, admittedly, he derived much of his story material from literature rather than from life? Whisper the names of Shakespeare and Racine. Is it because he has remained aloof from 20th-century currents in sociology, politics, psychology? So—quite deliberately—did Nabokov and Waugh. And if these are high names against which to posit Wilder's, that only aggravates the puzzle, because it was on a high level that he was first hailed.

(K)   Stanley Kauffmann. *NR*. April 8, 1967. p. 46

Mr. Wilder is so devoted to the ordinary universe that he is content to be its witness. In his own behalf he claims so little that it does not count as a claim. He assumes that life is a carpet with a figure in it. The figure begins in the past, as far back as lore and memory can reach. We are the sum of many generations. As a chronicler, the novelist is thrilled by the grandeur of the carpet, after all, and by the dramatic power of its figure. Lest this power be slighted, he allows the Deacon, in *The Eighth Day,* to recite a heavy sermon upon its text, for the benefit of young Roger.

This is to say that *The Eighth Day* is one of those old-fashioned things called novels, stories with truth in them. The trouble with books of this kind is that they claim to tell All, and the claim is difficult to sustain. As Mr. Wilder's book proceeds, his narrative voice becomes more obtrusive, insisting, as if this were our last chance to study the carpet. At the same time the reader has the impression that the Stage-Manager sees more in his drama than anyone else can see. . . .

A big novel, then, impressive in its scale, *The Eighth Day* is touching in its regard for truth, that great lost cause. It is grand to know that there are still writers who believe that the world is a real garden with real toads in it. If the novel does not quite, as we rudely say, "come off," the reason is that it lacks variety.

(K)   Denis Donoghue. *NYR*. Aug. 24, 1967. p. 12

See *The Cabala, The Bridge of San Luis Rey, Heaven's My Destination, The Ides of March, The Eighth Day* (novels); *Our Town, The Skin of Our Teeth, The Matchmaker, The Alcestiad, Plays for Bleecker Street* (plays).

WILLIAMS, TENNESSEE (1914–   )

No play can be truly flawless and certainly *The Glass Menagerie* is not so. Mr. Williams has replaced action in his script with the constant flow of human attitudes, relations and ideas across the stage; there are bound to be a few slow moments in the parade. There is one particular instance of too-obvious symbolism. . . . For every flaw, however, there are twenty brilliancies, even in the matter of symbolism.

Otis L. Guernsey, Jr. *NYHT ts*. Apr. 8, 1945. p. 1

A Streetcar Named Desire emerges as the most creative American play of the past dozen years. . . . What *A Streetcar Named Desire* has is the abundance of a good novel. . . . Life has density in this drama of a woman's tragic effort to clothe her nakedness. . . . The author's viewpoint combines a sharp sense of reality, a naturalistic fearlessness in the face of what is gross in individual life and society, and a just compassion. The handling of the dramatic elements is remarkably astute, since the author keeps wave after wave of revelation hurtling through the play. . . . But what stands out as most contributory to the making of a memorable play is the over-all effect of humanity seen in the round.

John Gassner. *Forum*. Feb., 1948. pp. 86–7

There are a number of superficial resemblances between the two plays (*The Glass Menagerie* and *A Streetcar Named Desire*) that have established Tennessee Williams as one of the finest of modern dramatists: both deal with the grotesque, an anachronistic refinement of a moribund Southern society; both make incidental mention of Moon Lake Casino and other names from the landscape of his memory. . . . Williams says that Southern women are the only remaining members of our populace who can speak lyrical dialogue without sounding highflown.

Paul Moor. *Harpers*. July, 1948. p. 71

Although Tennessee Williams writes a gentle style, he has a piercing eye. . . . The insight into character is almost unbearably lucid. Although it derives from compassion, it is cruel in its insistence on the truth. . . . He is a writer of superb grace and allusiveness, always catching the shape and sound of ideas rather than their literal meaning. As its title suggests, *Summer and Smoke* deals in truths that are unsubstantial. But as Mr. Williams sees it, these are the truths that are most profound and most painful, for they separate people who logically should be together and give life its savage whims and its wanton destructiveness.

Brooks Atkinson. NYT tp. Oct. 7, 1948. p. 33

Williams is, of course, one of two or three good playwrights writing today. . . . But why does he arrange his dramas like inquisitions, with torture preceding the confession and death following? Why is his world recognizable only fitfully, and why does he flagellate his heroines so? Does Mr. Williams mean that the original sin they have committed is that they are women? . . . One understands and is moved by his tragedies and his luckless people, and is sympathetic to his sense of the disaster that lies at the heart of our world; one understands and even partially accepts—but why does it seem all wrong?

Alfred Hayes. NYHT. Oct. 22, 1950. p. 14

Tennessee Williams, to come right out with it, seems to me not only the finest playwright now working in the American theatre but in one very strict sense the *only* playwright now working in the American theatre. Alone among his contemporaries he works as an artist and a poet: he makes plays out of images, catching a turn of life while it is still fluid, still immediate, and before it has been sterilized by reflection. Arthur Miller, for instance, builds a better play, but he builds it out of bricks; Williams is all flesh and blood. He writes with his eyes and his ears where other men are content to pick their brains—poetry with them is an overlay of thought, not a direct experience—and his plays emerge in the theatre, full-bodied, undissected, so kinetic you can touch them.

Walter Kerr. Com. Feb. 23, 1951. p. 492

With a pen that smokes and burns, Mr. Williams has created some horribly memorable chapters in the history of what one of his characters calls the "mad pilgrimage of the flesh." . . . He began as a poet, and perhaps it is as the poet of the blasted, the doomed, and the defeated that he will be remembered. . . . At his best . . . Tennessee Williams is in a class by himself. Even at his worst he creates magical, terrifying, and unforgettable effects; his only limitations appear to be self-imposed.

William Peden. SR. Jan. 8, 1955. p. 11

Living vitally in illusion is the substance of nearly all the important people in nearly all of Williams's work. . . . Williams explores in fiction and the theatre the *true* world behind the apparent one. . . . He pushed aside the great iron door and discovered there, behind the pulsating machine of modern technology, the throbbing human heart. It is this care for the individual man and woman and child and cornered cat which warms the lines of his plays and stories, which makes each example of his writing useful and moving. . . . The more he illuminates that inner and contrived world, however, the more he actually reveals of the brutal daylight outside.

Paul Engle. *NR*. Jan. 24, 1955. p. 27

He has said that he only feels and does not think; but the reader's or spectator's impression is too often that he only thinks he feels, that he is an acute case of what D. H. Lawrence called "sex in the head." And not only sex. Sincerity and Truth, of which he often *speaks* and *thinks,* tend to remain in the head too—abstractions with initial capitals. His problem is not lack of talent. It is, perhaps, an ambiguity of aim: he seems to want to kick the world in the pants and yet be the world's sweetheart, to combine the glories of martyrdom with the comforts of success. If I say that his problem is to take the initial capitals off Sincerity and Truth, I do not infer that this is easy, only that it is essential, if ever Mr. Williams's great talent is to find a full and pure expression.

Eric Bentley. *NR*. Apr. 11, 1955. p. 29

The crises of Williams are never common. They are the creation of a very strange and very special imagination, potent enough to impose itself on an audience and hold it in a common trance. He is a theater magician, invoking the lightning of emotion, releasing the doves of instinct, holding in fanlike suspension a brilliant pack of cards peopled with symbols and specters. . . . And I doubt whether the emotional exhaustion that is the residual effect of seeing a play by Tennessee Williams . . . is either illuminator or catharsis. It is a shock treatment administered by an artist of great talent and painful sensibility who illumines fragments but never the whole. He illuminates, if you will, that present sickness which *is* fragmentation.

Marya Mannes. *Reporter*. May 19, 1955. p. 41

Mr. Williams's plays involve, in a most vexing and intimate way, the problem once defined by Stark Young as that of "scraping back to the design." The early works, with their slight yet audible music, elude the charge, but in the later plays—ambitious statements about personality and suffering and society—one has somehow the insupportable sense that life is being obscurely practiced upon, the substance of feeling coerced into new and bizarre patterns. Not alone Mr. Williams's emphases nourish this unease, but the gathering awareness of his startling omissions, too. Yet subtly, this consciousness of nullity is modified by the curious presence of an impulse, the burden of some serious concern and intention making itself felt through layers of modish sensibility and gratuitous shock.

Richard Hayes. *Com.* June 3, 1955. p. 230

It occurs to me that we might well now regard Tennessee Williams as perhaps our great expert today in *Realpsychologie*. For, in such theatricals as *The Rose Tattoo* and *Baby Doll,* what he has undertaken is to strip the human animal of all moral refinements and to present the "true" animal, the "fine, wild" animal at whom we laugh, however, because for all the wildness the animal functions like a kind of clock, automatically, that is, giving heed to the promptings of natural impulse. But the major point to be made, it seems to me, is that the ribaldry, unsalacious as it really is, is utilized for the sake of what it is often Williams's major purpose to do; namely, to laugh at the very notion that human life might have a dimension of tragic significance.

Nathan A. Scott, Jr. *CC*. Jan. 23, 1957. p. 112

In his continued self-analysis Williams makes use of standard dream symbols—largely sexual. Added to these are personal symbols. The playwright is at his best when he is creating symbols out of situations rather than superimposing them or hauling in irrelevant or traditional ones. One of Tennessee Williams's outstanding talents is his ability to see his life and his world metaphorically. The most exciting Williams symbols are those fashioned from his own experience.

The author's enthusiasm for metaphor and symbolism comes partially from modern psychology and partially from an enduring regard for the French symbolist poets. . . . The use of symbolist atmosphere and musical accompaniment provides stimulating contrasts to the realism of his characterization and dialogue. Because his sense of theatre restricts him to a basic realism, he seldom allows the atmosphere of his plays to thin out into a symbolist fog. It has been hard for Williams to use other influences effectively, but in his use of symbolism his talent and his literary tastes are happily united.

Nancy M. Tischler. *Tennessee Williams:*
Rebellious Puritan (Citadel). 1961. pp. 294–5

The universe is the great antagonist in Tennessee Williams. It is as malignant as it is implacable. It has, through time, destroyed a way of life and a tradition that once meant civilization and has evolved a society that is grasping, repressive and destructive. Anything that was honorable is gone and the codes of the past have become anachronistic and ridiculous in the present. The standard bearers of this tradition are hopelessly inadequate in a world which calls for Jim O'Connor's "zzzzzzzzzp!" and yet if there is to be any meaning in life it will have to come, Williams is saying, from the codes and traditions which his ragged cavaliers and tattered ladies are waving in the face of impending darkness.

This is the credo of the romantic, the cry of Don Quixote charging the windmills and Lord Byron making his final stand for Greek independence. But if Williams devoutly believes in the romantic revolt against the Philistines, he has no illusions about the triumph of this insurrection. While sympathizing with his romantics he is at the same time able to see and understand the futility of their quest. Williams is the romantic and the realist, and his best work is marked by this important juxtaposition of beliefs.

Benjamin Nelson. *Tennessee Williams: The Man and His Work* (Ivan Obolensky). 1961. pp. 288–9

It is from [the] conflict between the need to condemn and the desire to pardon that the weakness of Williams's work stems, for it is ironically the strength of his moral temper that forces him to censure what he wishes to exalt. Williams is passionately committed to the great Romantic dictum inherent in his neo-Lawrentian point of view, that the natural equals the good, that the great natural instincts that well up out of the subconscious depths of men—and particularly the sexual instinct, whatever form it may take—are to be trusted absolutely. But Williams is too strong a moralist, far too permeated with a sense of sin, to be able to accept such an idea with equanimity. However pathetic he may make the martyred homosexual, however seemingly innocent the wandering love-giver, the moral strength that led Williams to punish the guilty Blanche impels him to condemn Brick and Chance. But because he is condemning what he most desires to pardon, he must sometimes in order to condemn at all, do so with ferocious violence.

Arthur Ganz. *AS*. Spring, 1962. p. 294

Though Williams has not, so far as I know, delivered himself of a single pronouncement on the question of integration, though his signature is never to be found on a petition or a full-page ad in the New York *Times,* he seems to have located the trouble spots more precisely than Arthur Miller, for instance, who deals so conscientiously with social questions. Williams is American in his passion for absolutes, in his longing for purity, in his absence of ideas, in the extreme discomfort with which he inhabits his own body and soul, in his apocalyptic vision of sex, which like all apocalyptic visions sacrifices mere accuracy for the sake of intensity. Intensity is the crucial quality of Williams's art, and he is perhaps most an American artist in his reliance upon and mastery of surface techniques for achieving this effect.

Marion Magid. *Cmty*. Jan., 1963. p. 35

The cannibalism in *Suddenly Last Summer,* I conclude, is not merely sensational. It is symbolic of man's place in the "ravening maw" of nature. Williams is saying that men are no exception to the rule of life; they, like plants and animals, eat one another. It is no accident that Williams refuses to condemn Sebastian, for Sebastian is his hero. He is the poet, in whom the way of the world is transformed, misunderstood, and destroyed. Even Mrs. Venable is in a sense justified; bizarre as she is, she is nevertheless on the side of the saints in a world of merely wolfish mediocrity.

(K)   William E. Taylor in *Essays in Modern American*
                         Literature, edited by Richard E. Langford (Stetson).
                                                              1963. p. 96

A study of the whole range of Williams' drama shows the gradual development of a comprehensive moral structure. If his early works are concerned primarily with ethical implications within art—with the need for the integrity of self-expression—this playwright's later works have been increasingly concerned with the exploration of moral problems which are more comprehensive in nature. Williams' development as a moralist seems to have experienced three main phases of growth. His early plays are concerned with the struggle of the individual for self-realization. In the middle period of his development the playwright begins to equate his accounts of individual crisis with more universal phenomena, especially to trace their effect on society at large. In his later works Williams seems to relate these personal crises to the timeless progress of mankind in the moral universe.

It is significant to note that Williams' later works have taken on more and more of the apparatus of the orthodox Christian search for God. Gradually Williams' anti-hero—his symbol for modern man—has begun to assume the visage of the "negative saint," the great sinner, toiling up the steep ascent to God.

(K)   Esther M. Jackson. *The Broken World of Tennessee*
                                  Williams (Wisconsin). 1965. p. 154

In general, we might reasonably think of Williams as experiencing a tension between fantasies of catastrophe and fantasies of salvation. Fantasies of catastrophe produce dramas of disaster; those of salvation may lead him to the basic structure of melodrama—twice, we note, with a *dea ex machina.* In *Milk Train,* of course, Williams works in another manner, that of the allegory; here his interest is not in catastrophe or in the success or failure of the savior type, but in the complex attitudes of the affluent society toward the equivocal figure who is both pensioner and alleviator. If the dramatic focus is on the sick or disintegrating character who simply follows his sad downward course, or whose strongest act is to be the beneficiary of someone else's supporting clasp or cool hand on fevered brow, then the direction is not a tragic one. Nevertheless Williams shows himself also able to imagine the relatively well or strong person or that in-between figure who has had to struggle for wellness or strength. The last of these, Hannah Jelkes in *The Night of the Iguana,* is moving toward dramatic centrality. If such a character gains the center of the stage, it will be a move away from dramas of disaster (without drifting into drama of easy triumph). So far, the occasional moves have been toward comedy. They could also be toward tragedy.

(K)   Robert Heilman. *SoR.* Autumn, 1965. p. 790

Williams reveals, for better and sometimes worse, areas of thought, feeling, and imagination that extend above, below, and frequently beyond the literal details of any man's daily life. He is not always strictly modern in his technique, though with *Camino Real,* he tried to build—not always successfully—a romantic abstraction into a sustained drama; and in his latest work, *Slapstick Tragedy* (two short plays), he aims for what he calls "vaudeville, burlesque and slapstick, with a dash of pop art thrown in." But whether he is "current" with any given play, whether he succeeds or fails with technical experiment, he is surely modern in temperament, though never making a sound quite like anyone else's.

(K)   Gordon Rogoff. *TDR.* Summer, 1966. p. 85

His stories still emit the troubling poetic atmosphere of his plays, but in this latest collection [*The Knightly Quest*] Williams has exorcised the most destructive of his devils. Cannibalism, cancer and castration give way to concerns equally horrible but more objective and general—the shadow of nuclear annihilation, the rape of already shabby Southern charm by drive-ins and motels, and the planing down of personality by the machines of a mass-production age. . . . Williams is less concerned with ethics than with the survival of the poetic and romantic in a monstrous society.

(K)   Paul D. Zimmerman. *Nwk.* Feb. 27, 1967. p. 92

See *The Glass Menagerie, A Streetcar Named Desire, Summer and Smoke, Orpheus Descending, Camino Real, Cat on a Hot Tin Roof, Suddenly Last Summer* (plays); *The Roman Spring of Mrs. Stone* (novel); *One Arm, The Knightly Quest* (stories); *In the Winter of Cities* (poems).

WILLIAMS, WILLIAM CARLOS (1883–1963)

He can give himself, William Carlos Williams, such as he is, without either simple or inverted pride; give himself in his crassness, in his dissonant mixed blood, in absurd melancholy, wild swiftness of temper, man-shyness; Americano, Jerseyite, Rutherfordian; give himself with a frankness, a fearlessness, a scientific impersonality, that is bracing as a shock of needle-spray. . . . And, in moments, of felt power, in moments of conscious toughness and sharp will, he breaks "through to the fifty words necessary," and briskly, laconically, like a man with little time for matters not absolutely essential to the welfare of the universe, brings into clarity the relation existing between himself and the things seen by him.

Paul Rosenfeld. *Port of New York* (Harcourt). 1924.
pp. 109–11

Surely Williams's savagery is a unique essence in modern American letters. He has perceived his ground, he has made a beginning, he is riding the forces of his locality. Determinedly, he seeks to be a Daniel Boone of letters, a Sam Houston in method, and an Aaron Burr in personal psychology. What threatens him—be it puritanic pressures or the hard exigencies of combining literature with medicine—he barks at it: the dog with a bone in its throat is symbolic of his attitude toward all that might interrupt or diminish his poetic pursuit.

Gorham Munson. *Destinations* (Sears). 1928. p. 134

For the most part, so completely in fact that one must search out the rare exceptions, Williams's verse has been unrhymed; in temper it has been at the furthest remove from "professional" verse; it has been protestant, yet formal, and the virtues of even his slightest pieces have been those of presenting definite objects and scenes before the eye of the reader. . . . Williams's search for "an honest man," as well as an instruction to others "to stand out of my sunlight," are the kinds of truth that Williams sought in verse. The search may at times seem wantonly naive, and at times it has resulted in incomplete and "experimental" poems, but we may be certain that Williams has never falsified his language; and he has made an ethical distinction between the uses of artifice and art. Craftsmanship, not artifice, has been his concern, and perhaps no writer of the twentieth century has yielded so little to the temptations that mere artifice places within his path.

Horace Gregory and Marya Zaturenska. *History of
American Poetry* (Harcourt). 1947. pp. 208–12

Although his lines rarely descend to slang, they are full of the conversational speech of the country; they express the brusque nervous tension, the vigor and rhetoric of American life. Even when they are purposely unadorned and non-melodic they intensify some common object with pointed detail and confident, if clipped, emotion.

Louis Untermeyer. *Modern American Poetry*
(Harcourt). 1950. p. 275

Life is more than art for Dr. Williams, as the object is prior to the word. He is no goldsmith making timeless birds. Part of the exhilaration in reading his poetry comes of its formal and logical incompleteness (this is at the same time its greatest drawback). Many of his poems seem notes to a text—to the dense and fluid text of reality; they seem gestures and exclamations in appreciation of something beyond the poem, insistences that we use our senses, that we be alive to things.

Richard Wilbur. *SwR*. Winter, 1950. p. 139

Examined from the perspective of an ideal academic poet like say, Bridges, Dr. Williams appears to be groping about under a very low ceiling indeed. . . . Truthfully pleading his inability to handle traditional coin traditionally, Williams improvises, issues a fluid currency of his own. . . . Incoherence, then, is the principal "cost," to use a favorite word with Williams, incoherence raised to a level where it corresponds to Eliot's diffidence or Pound's tactlessness, a quirk which can sometimes reveal the poetry, sometimes conceal it, sometimes ruin it altogether, but which is also absorbed into the success of passage after passage, poem after poem.

R. W. Flint in *Kenyon Critics,* edited by John Crowe
Ransom (World). 1951. pp. 335–40

Williams has found his end in his beginnings. He has devoted himself to the American scene as it met the eye of a doctor practicing in the provinces. . . . He gives the inner quality of things not by transferring to them his feeling about them, nor by a kind of damp sentiment from which even so inward a poet as Rilke was not wholly free. He gets at the essence, as apprehended not *behind* but actually *by means of* the phenomenon: the reality grasped by devoted concentration on its manifest being.

Babette Deutsch. *Poetry in Our Time* (Holt). 1952.
pp. 109–10

It is necessary to love this man because he teaches life the richness of its own combinations. The world is his mistress, made beautiful by his love. The fact of her is his passion. No poet since Donne has banged so avidly at Things, at the hammer and take of the world upon the senses. Everything, even his own aesthetic, has been shattered in the name of Things.

John Ciardi. *Nation*. April 24, 1954. p. 368

He is one of the most tensile, dynamic, and kinaesthetically engaging of poets; his quick transparent lines have a nervous and contracted strength. Often they move as jerkily and intently as a bird, though they can sleep as calmly as a bird, too; they do not have the flowing and easy strength, the rhythmic powers in reserve, the envelopment and embodiment of some of the verse of old poets. But sometimes they have a marvelous delicacy and gentleness, a tact of pure showing; how well he calls into existence our precarious, confused, partial looking out at the world—our being-here-looking, just looking! And if he is often pure presentation, he is often pure exclamation, and delights in yanking something into life with a galvanic imperative or interjection. . . . He loves to tell the disgraceful or absurd or obscene or piercing or exhilarating or animally delightful truth. He is neither wise nor intellectual, but is full of homely shrewdness and common sense, of sharply intelligent comments dancing cheek-to-cheek with prejudice and random eccentricities; he is somebody who, sometimes, does see what things are like, and he is able to say what he sees more often than most poets.

Randall Jarrell. *Poetry and the Age* (Knopf). 1955.
pp. 236–7

After more than thirty books and at his present age Williams exercises his whole personality to unlock a remarkable lyrical lore of love. His love is inclusive of many things, attitudes, and feelings. It has the qualities of sincerity, knowledge, and acute perception. It is mature man speaking direct truth. Yet I do not mean that there is not a great deal of strategy in the way he makes his verses.

Richard Eberhart. *SR*. Feb. 18, 1956. p. 49

I have emphasized William's simplicity and nakedness and have no doubt been misleading. His idiom comes from many sources, from speech and reading, both of various kinds; the blend which in his own invention is generous and even exotic. Few poets can come near to his wide clarity and dashing rightness with words, his dignity and almost Alexandrian modulations of voice. His short lines often speed up and simplify hugely drawn out and ornate sentence structures. I once typed out his direct but densely observed poem, "The Semblables," in a single prose paragraph. Not a word or its placing had been changed, but the poem had changed into a piece of smothering, magnificent rhetoric, much more like Faulkner than the original Williams.

Robert Lowell. *HdR*. Winter, 1961–2. p. 534

In Williams we have a poet who refuses to belittle the American genius for mechanical inventiveness; who developed the concept of a poem machine to achieve artistic expression in the American idiom; but who sees at the same time the moral and spiritual toll it has exacted from our culture because we have made a machine-world geared to such high speed and efficiency that we are losing our ability to see and touch the simple, the natural. It is for this reason Williams would make St. Francis of Assisi our patron saint. He asks us to realize our humanity in the scientific age. He sees the objective poem, in which the poet like the linguistic scientist has put his speech to the test of human need, as a means toward that goal. "But before I extol too much and advocate the experimental method," he warns, "let me emphasize that, like God's creation, the objective is not experimentation but *man*. In our case, poems!"

Mary Ellen Solt. *MR*. Winter, 1962. p. 317

It is Dr. Williams's distinction that he is willing to incur time and again the enormous risk of dispensing with the protections poetry has traditionally devised for itself. Eschewal of safety, in fact, has come to seem to him a matter of honour. He will have no special vocabulary, around which common speech has learned to tiptoe; he will not suffer attention to be lulled by a metric of recurrences; there are not even privileged subjects to which the poem addresses itself, or approved planes of consciousness on which it functions. The Williams poem at the first word takes its life in its hands and launches itself from a precipice, submitting itself to accelerations it does not seek to control, and trusting its own capacity for intimate torsions to guide it into the water unharmed. It is not surprising that so many of his poems get shattered; the miracle is that he succeeds with half his attempts, that indeed he ever succeeds. For the gravitational field to which he entrusts his poems is the enveloping tug of impassioned daily speech, which precipitates into a void whatever it gets hold of.

Hugh Kenner. *MR*. Winter, 1962. p. 328

William Carlos Williams may well turn out to be one of the most significant writers of our time. . . . It would be easy to say, as some have already said, that Williams, like Walt Whitman, loves life—sees all that his eyes will let him see and shrinks from none of it, lovingly presenting the whole in inconspicuous language. But this would be to talk sentimentally about a writer who is almost never guilty of sentimentality. . . . Williams simply has no sense of a capacity for contamination. He treats the flesh with respect because he seems to believe that flesh, even at its worst, has a capacity for dignity; and under the term *flesh* he would include not only people but dogs, chickens, rocks, pine trees, and wet ferns.

Yet if this were all Williams had, he would be neither a good writer nor a good physician. He would merely be avoiding the other kind of sentimentality that those writers are guilty of who speak glibly of the autonomy of the word. In fact, one gets the impression from reading these stories that one liberates the other: the word becomes respectable for serving as the matrix by which the object is made knowable, and the marriage of the two means a generation of love for both.

J. A. Bryant, Jr. *SwR*. Winter, 1963. p. 121

William Carlos Williams, poet and physician. Trained to crises of sickness and parturition that often came at odd hours. An ebullient man, sorely vexed in his last years, and now at rest. But he had this exceptional good luck: that his appeal as a person survives in his work. To read his books is to find him warmly there, everywhere you turn.

In some respects, the physician and the poet might be viewed as opposites, as they certainly were at least in the sense that time spent on his patients was necessarily time denied to the writing of poetry. But that's a superficial view. . . . The point is this: For Williams any natural or poetic concern with the body as a sexual object was reinforced and notably modified by a professional concern with the body as a suffering or diseased object. . . . The same relation to the human animal in terms of bodily disabilities led him to a kind of democracy quite unlike Whitman's, despite the obvious influence of Whitman upon him.

Kenneth Burke. *NYR*. Spring, 1963. p. 45

From the mid-twenties until very recently, American poetry has functioned as a part of the English tradition. The colloquial side of American literature—the side which valued 'experience' more than 'civilization'—was neglected by the younger poets. . . .

The only contrary direction which endured throughout the orthodoxy was the direction I will inadequately call the colloquial, or the line of William Carlos Williams. Williams himself has been admired by most new American poets, of whatever school, but the poets of the orthodoxy have admired him for his descriptive powers; they learned from him a conscience of the eye rather than a conscience of the ear; for Williams the problem of native speech rhythm was of first importance.

This poetry is no mere restriction of one's vocabulary. It wants to use the language with the intimacy acquired in unrehearsed unliterary speech. But it has other characteristics which are not linguistic. It is a poetry of experiences more than of ideas. The experience is presented often without comment, and the words of the description must supply the emotion which the experience generates, without generalization or summary. Often too this poetry finds great pleasure in the world outside. It is the poetry of a man in the world, responding to what he sees: with disgust, with pleasure, in rant and in meditation. Naturally, this colloquial direction makes much of accuracy, of honest speech. 'Getting the tone right' is the poet's endeavour, not 'turning that metaphor neatly,' or 'inventing a new stanza.' Conversely, when it fails most commonly it fails because the emotion does not sound true.

(K)   Donald Hall. Introduction to *Contemporary American Poetry* (Penguin). 1963. pp. 19, 21–2

Through his half century of writing, Dr. Williams believed firmly in "the local." The poem was to re-create significant elements of contemporary life as found in the poet's immediate surroundings—his local. This was his concept, far removed from that of the "local colorists" with whom critics regularly associated him. What Williams championed was the use of familiar materials as the means of general truths, not an emphasis on local culture for its own sake. The relevance of scenes like the small child trying to escape her parents' surveillance or the dog lying injured in a street is broader than the poet's New Jersey "local." . . . Although his roots are in his local, however, man need not exist in a vacuum. The local itself has history, literature, art, and science; all are legitimate subjects for the contemporary poem. The only thing twentieth-century artists must remember, according to Dr. Williams, is to use traditional subjects not for effect or pretension, but for their elements still meaningful to man.

(K)   Linda Welshimer Wagner. *CE*. March, 1964. pp. 427–8

The first remarkable feature of the poetry of William Carlos Williams is the sheer clarity of his images of parts of the world. He respects these images too much to blur their edges for the sake of the grand poetic gesture. To a great degree he continuously invents and renews his world in the poetry; and he does so, to a great degree, in order to create himself within it and to wonder at the product. This, I think, is the major fact about his poetry, and it cannot be better summarized than in Roy Harvey Pearce's phrase: "Brave new world . . . that has me in it!" And yet at the same time, beyond the real world into which he has created himself there is another one, no less real, which remains virginal to his approaches. . . . Within the invention, the reverence for particularity is clear enough; but our sense of it is doubled by the presence in the poems also of raw materials that the poetry cannot, or cannot yet, or will not, encompass. I wish to show in this essay how Williams' work, especially that of his last years, both invents the world and also looks outward beyond what it has invented and is thus romantic, incomplete, and heuristic.

(K)   A. Kingsley Weatherhead. *ELH*. March, 1965. p. 126

The first principle of objectivism—that "associational or sentimental value is false"—and the second—that the objectivist poet must have "earthy tastes" ("God, if I could fathom / the guts of shadows!")—have profoundly influenced Williams' portrayal of human subjects no less than they have his treatment of objects in nature. The poems in this manner are offered without comment and usually without implication. . . . When the response is not wholly aesthetic, it is generally ironic—the irony, with exceptions, not being blatant.

(K)   L. S. Dembo. *Conceptions of Reality in Modern American Poetry* (California). 1966. pp. 57–8

Williams always sees himself as handling the units of a dance. His tools, especially in the beginning, are personal sensitivity, fascination with natural order in the seasons and in human self-assertion, and love of precision, elegance, and experiment in the formal relationships of images and words. Against him is something destructive if uncontrolled by the mind forced against it. The opposition of contending forces penetrates every aspect of Williams's poetry.

(K)   Neil Myers. *AL*. Jan., 1966. p. 466

By contradicting Whitman's myth of plenitude with the myth of sterility, Eliot prompted Williams to identify his own informing myth—the discovery of plenty lodged, as it must be in the modern world, in barrenness. In the first few years of the twenties Williams' work grew out of his own experience of postwar disillusionment. . . . The feeling in Williams' work of the period is not quite one of despair, but of life buried, maintaining itself underground, in a kind of hell, but powerless to assert itself. In *Sour Grapes* (1921), Williams constantly gives us images of life buried but persisting in winter or old age. . . . The constant subject of the poems in *Spring and All* is the emergence of life out of death, ecstasy out of despair, poetry unexpectedly blossoming in a parched industrial landscape. The shift in the outer world, as Williams' identification with the spring suggests, corresponds to an inner change—and so the real subject of these poems is the re-creation of the self.

(K)   James E. Breslin in *Literary Criticism and Historical*
                              Understanding, edited by Phillip Damon (Columbia).
                                                                    1967. pp. 161–3

Paterson

A man spends Sundays in the park at Paterson, New Jersey. He thinks and looks about him; his mind contemplates, describes, comments, associates, stops, stutters, and shifts like a firefly, bound only by its own milieu. The man is Williams, anyone living in Paterson, the American, the masculine principle. . . . The park is Everywoman, any woman, the feminine principle, America. . . . "Paterson" . . . is about marriage. . . . Everything in the poem is masculine or feminine, everything strains toward marriage, but the marriages never come off, except in the imagination and there, attenuated, fragmentary, and uncertain.

                              Robert Lowell. *Nation.* June 19, 1948. pp. 692–3

It may be simply the effect of time, but at this writing "Paterson I" seems to me better than "Paterson II" and both of them better than "Paterson III," though the difference is small. What cannot be enough insisted on is that in this poetry, which operates by what Crane called "metaphorical logic," the whole is always greater than the sum of the parts. "Paterson" is planned, though more loosely than *Ulysses,* "Four Quartets," or the "Cantos." Successive books have worked fresh material into the mythic, rhythmic, and metaphorical pattern established in the first, so that the effect, though cumulative, is not oppressively so. We don't feel the clouds of a portentous Greatness gathering over us.

R. W. Flint in *Kenyon Critics,* edited by John Crowe
Ransom (World). 1951. p. 335

If "Paterson" is rarely as good as Pound's work at his best, it is far more alive than the drearier sections of the "Cantos." Both poets are concerned with communication, and with the forces obstructing and debasing it. The great difference is that for Williams the time is not antiquity or the renaissance, but now (he sees its old roots): the scene is no foreign country, but is the provincial factory town on the Passaic in all the sordidness of its abused beauty and energy.

Babette Deutsch. *Poetry in Our Time* (Holt). 1952.
pp. 104–8

The organization of "Paterson" is musical to an almost unprecedented degree: Dr. Williams introduces a theme that stands for an idea, repeats it over and over in varied forms, develops it side by side with two or three more themes that are being developed, recurs to it time and time again throughout the poem, and echoes it for ironic or grotesque effects in thoroughly incongruous contexts. . . . Everything in the poem is interwoven with everything else, just as the strands of the Falls interlace: how wonderful and unlikely that this extraordinary mixture of the most delicate lyricism of perception and feeling with the hardest and homeliest actuality should ever have come into being!

Randall Jarrell. *Poetry and the Age* (Knopf). 1955.
pp. 203–9

Ultimately, of course, in *Paterson,* the poem in which he has attempted to unite and articulate fully all his beliefs about both the actual world and art, Williams presents the dissociation of things as the primary evil in the world. Here, where a man is a city and the city paired with, but separated from, the fecundating giant female counterpart, the mountain and her natural world, the divorce is stated: men from nature, from what they have made, and from each other. Not only are the three classes of existence broken apart, but even within them things are separated. And the language that might save men, might make them (and the world) whole again, is divorced from the things it represents, just as it is gone from men's mouths. . . .

. . . for Williams the poem must stand in a direct, easily discernible relationship to the language of common speech, it must partake of that language and not stray too far from it. At the same time, however, the poem must make something uncommon of the common, it must formalize that inherently amorphous mass, must purify it by measuring it, must impose upon the freedom—even irresponsibility—of speech a structure that will reproduce the poet's understanding of the rhythm, the measured pattern, of the life of his world. This is, for Williams, the poem's prime need. (K)   Alan Ostrom. *The Poetic World of William Carlos Williams* (Southern Illinois). 1966. pp. 46, 105

See *Collected Earlier Poems, Collected Later Poems, Paterson, Pictures from Brueghel* (poems); *Autobiography; Selected Essays; The Build-Up* (novel); *Make Light of It* (stories); *Many Loves and Other Plays; Selected Letters.*

WILSON, EDMUND (1895–   )

The distinction of Edmund Wilson's critical writing, at a period of low pressure in this field, resides in his skepticism, his candor, and his boldness. Where most other professional critics, in America, are content to remain journalists, timid or compromised through intangible connections with the literature-business, Wilson is a widely read, laborious, and willing adventurer into the forest of modern art. Here, amid these shadows, the others may remain ignorant or bewildered, conceiving or relating nothing to any recognizable suite of ideas—or simply grow humoristic, like Mencken; Wilson attacks his chosen material with intelligence and with high energy, scrutinizing the product, demanding of it insistently, almost clamorously, what is its meaning and what is its intention.

Matthew Josephson. *SR*. March 7, 1931. p. 642

The ability to tell what a book is about remains Mr. Wilson's greatest distinction, his almost unrivaled skill, among living students of literature. His explorations have steadily widened; he has risked the formulations but surmounted the limitations of historical, sociological, and psychiatric method; he has brought the rich sympathies and recognitions of his earlier investigations to a steadily sounder and more penetrating use. . . . He writes criticism of one kind and one of the best kinds, but it continually requires supplementing and extension by specifically aesthetic analysis and normative evaluation. But there are only two or three other contemporaries who have been as scrupulous in making the matter of modern literature available, in defining historical and categorical relationships, and in arriving at the sense of the elements and complexities of creative genius which must be realized before the full scope and richness of books can be determined by whatever keener instruments or methods of dissection.

Morton Dauwen Zabel. Nation. Oct. 11, 1941. p. 350

Honesty is perhaps the most admirable of all Edmund Wilson's gifts. He is as sympathetic and just as he can be: where his sympathy fails him, as it does when he approaches Paul Elmer More in a tone of continued flippant severity, and where his justice fails him, as it does in his estimate of the narrow scholarship of Housman, it is because, like every man he is held within the bonds of his temperament, and within those of the social pressures about him. The reader is sure that the critic has done his utmost to release himself from such bonds, that he has never wantonly tightened them, as almost all of his contemporaries have done. He has never asked himself what the party-line would be—Marxist, or Freudian, or bohemian —and he has never allowed a scruple for abstract logic (if one said such and such about Henry James in 1938, must one say this and that about Edith Wharton in 1941?) to come between him and his material.

E. K. Brown. UTQ. Oct., 1941. pp. 110–1

Edmund Wilson has a genuine feeling for the chthonic, the underground aspects of a literature. He has learned to hold his Freudianism like a gentleman. Dislike of people, despair of life, the cultivation of private values, and other trappings of romantic individualism are fashionable today; and Edmund Wilson has successfully kept two jumps ahead of the fashion. A technique which mingles the methods of fiction with those of criticism, and a willingness to subordinate inconvenient facts in the interest of an interpretation have helped him in this project. The prose style of Edmund Wilson is sensitive though sesquipedalian, his reporting is accurate and perceptive, he has read more than most journalists, and he is not afraid to use his reading.

Robert Adams. SwR. Spring, 1948. p. 286

Sometimes Wilson is guilty of gratuitous waspishness and sometimes he is glaringly condescending. Occasionally he employs a tank attack against a molehill (the syntax of Mission to Moscow), and once or twice, notably in Maugham's case, he carries depreciation to very questionable lengths (granted Maugham's lifelong love affair with the cliché, some of his work is surely not completely second-rate). But by and large, Wilson tellingly points up the failings and limitations in the work of well-known writers— O'Hara, Saroyan, and Steinbeck, for instance—without losing sight of their qualities. His loathing of commercialism and championship of the nonpopular; his respect for writers who toil for the mot juste; the slightly romantic feeling he projects of the glamour and dignity in the calling of letters—all this I find admirable and it outweighs Wilson's crotchets.

Charles J. Rolo. At. Nov., 1950. p. 98

How Wilson gets time to do anything but sit and read, one marvels. What keeps him from being merely an omnivorous reader is the intensity of his passion for literature. And he can find it in the most unlikely places, because in his view literature has little or no relation to the so-called "subject matter." . . . The great works of our time, he asserts, may and must express the despair and anguish of these years, but instead of discouraging they fortify. . . . His passion for literature is definitely not aestheticism: his chase has an end in view. . . . If Wilson makes anything that may be called mistakes—he says that all critics have failings—it is out of excess of devotion to the ideals which he feels came into their own with the rationalists of the twenties.

Perry Miller. Nation. Jan. 27, 1951. pp. 87–8

If it is a crime for a critic of literature to be also a good writer then by all means let us shoot him, or at least ban his books; but if it should happen to be a virtue then, if only in a whisper, perhaps we should honor it. It seems likely that Mr. Wilson had to sweat over his early writing just in order to beat out his competitors, win magazine-space for himself, and earn a living. This is simply not true of the formal or college-professor critics: not dependent on writing for a living, concerned with criticism as an extension of knowledge rather than as an art, they were never called upon to compress or season their thought for *practical* reasons, as was Wilson. The result is that while several of these critics are more original than Wilson, the results of their thinking are rarely consolidated with his tested generalship and authority.

Seymour Krim. HdR. Spring, 1951. p. 152

Wilson was always bringing fascinating and profitable writers to our attention, and he never made us feel that he was displaying his own subtlety and wit and invention at their expense. In these later days a good many critics seem to be yielding to the vice of ostentation; criticism has exfoliated until the work of art is sometimes smothered beneath it, like a tree covered with fox grapes and Virginia creeper. Wilson kept trying to strip off the critical misconceptions and reveal the tree in its proper form. He kept inviting his readers to join him in a search for intellectual heroes, since—as he told us time after time—the existence of such men gives meaning and value to our lives.

Malcolm Cowley. NR. Nov. 10, 1952. pp. 17–8

I suppose literary history will class Wilson as a social critic, and recently there has been a tendency, mostly on the part of the younger formalist critics, to brush him aside as an extra-literary critic, who has not done enough to illuminate immediate literary texts and problems. . . . I think the criticism of him on this score has been very unfair and represents a sectarian judgment. For, if Wilson, like Parrington and other social critics, has taken literature as a part of history, unlike most of them he has not dissolved literature into history. . . . Actually his method has been to find the basic mood and intention of a literary work, and then to connect it with the pattern of the author's life, and literary tradition and social history. . . . On purely literary grounds, it is amazing to see how many of Wilson's judgments have stood up, which is, I am sure, the final test of a critic's accomplishment.

William Phillips. AM. Nov., 1952. pp. 106–7

I cannot think of any other critic who would be capable of writing intelligently about Faulkner, Sartre, Tolstoy, and Shakespeare, about such eccentricities as manuals of conjuring and the biography of Houdini, about both burlesque shows and Emily Post, about both best sellers and obscure difficult authors, and—here is a peculiar and rather touching speciality of Wilson's—about interesting near-failures like John Jay Chapman. . . . He writes about so many things because he has a multitude of active and growing ideas, and because he chooses the new intellectual experiences that will feed them. . . . He believes in the mind, and the taste, and the fancy. He dislikes the tyrants who try to throttle them or starve them or exploit them, and he enjoys every activity which sends blood through them, lets them expand, gives them hope and laughter, precision and purpose.

Gilbert Highet. People, Places, and Books (Oxford).
1953. pp. 33–5

The high place of Edmund Wilson in modern American literary criticism has been slow of recognition because he has always seemed to play the role of counselor, interpreter and friend to his fellow writers and readers rather than that of lawgiver or of chronicler. . . . Yet he has been from the twenties down to the present, a leading voice among those critics who cling to the conception of art as an expression of its own creator and of the culture which produces him. An historical critic rather than a literary historian, he has done more than anyone else in his time to make the master works of his contemporaries intelligible to their own readers and to assign to them the values which posterity in many cases must accept.

Robert E. Spiller. Nation. Feb. 22, 1958. p. 159

His extraordinary gift for turning every assignment into a superb literary article is a symbol of his inability to lose himself, as so many writers did, in a purely human situation. The reins are always tight, and the horses always go the same way. On the other hand, Wilson's detachment certainly never made him incurious. The secret of his durability as a writer is his patient, arduous effort to assimilate, to clarify for himself and others, subjects from which he feels excluded by temperament. . . . Amid the laziest minds in the world he is the most Puritanical of intellectual students, the most exacting in the correctness of his language and his learning.

Alfred Kazin. Reporter. March 20, 1958. p. 44

At its heart then *Patriotic Gore* . . . is an act of patriotism, a historical reminder not only of the great hopes of the original Republic but of the great men who lived its ideals. If these men are draped with robes that glow with a kind of supernal light, that is all right too because this is what an epic is supposed to do: to present the national life and purposes at their highest pitch and enveloped in poetry. Further, as *Patriotic Gore* demonstrates, the traditions *were* real too; Sherman himself said that the Southern "knight" was not a myth: "they are the most dangerous set of men that this war has turned loose upon the world. They are splendid riders, first-rate shots, and utterly reckless."

So far as I know, there is nothing else in American literature quite like *Patriotic Gore*. Whatever its inconsistencies or irrascibilities or impossibilities, it stands, in all its fine prose and wide range, as an eloquent rebuke to the poor writing and the narrow specialization of so much current literary and historical studies. . . . What a relief to read a book that is beautifully written, that you can argue with all the way through, and that poses some national ideals.

(K)   John Henry Raleigh. *PR*. Summer, 1962. pp. 435–6

Emotionally Mr. Wilson seems to see the war of the North against the South in somewhat the same way that he saw the war of the Power Authority of New York against the Tuscarora nation. Mr. Wilson hates the modern state with its arbitrary exercise of power and its denial of the individual's limited responsibility for the direction of events. He hates bureaucracy, governmental anonymity, the absorbent power of the Federal authority. He hates these things because they produce Power Authorities and arrogant public servants that think God created man for them. It is difficult not to hate with him. But despite the brilliance of *Patriotic Gore,* it seems doubtful if the Civil War can really be judged in a frame this narrow.

As I have already said, this book is not conventionally pro-South in the way some have suggested. In dividing the honours between the two sides Mr. Wilson is remarkably bipartisan, and those chapters are best in which he deals with persons, whether of the North or of the South, whose understanding of issues is comprehensive enough to confer a dialectical centrality on their thought. . . . Taking the book as a whole, Mr. Wilson is not *for* the South as much as he is *against* the whole disastrous fact of the Civil War. In dealing with the men and women who were the leaders of thought and action, he measures out honours and demerits with a superbly bipartisan hand, while he sees both the North and the South falsifying equally the image of itself under which each fought the war. . . . The picture of the Civil War world [*Patriotic Gore*] gives is so vivid, its rendering of personality so dramatic, that it is easily his most entertaining work.

(K)   Marius Bewley. *HdR*. Autumn, 1962.
                                                    pp. 432, 435, 439

He is *the* American, relegating himself willingly and proudly to the semi-posthumous position that he had protested against in 1943 when the Princeton Library asked him for a bibliography of his work. At that time he had said that the literary worker of the 20's seemed to the teachers of English and the young writers who grew up in the 30's "the distant inhabitant of another intellectual world" who belonged "to a professional group, now becoming extinct and a legend, in which the practice of letters was a common craft and the belief in its value a common motivation." Today, when the process has gone much further, Wilson—and the group of which he is the best and most impressive representative—seems more distant than ever, and the two possible ways of dealing with him, now as then, are apparently either to make him an object of veneration or to ignore him altogether. But these are not really the only alternatives. We can recognize the element of myth and simplification in his sense of America, in his Whiggish interpretation of the nation's history, and in his image of himself without thereby denying that what he stands for—faith in the importance of the things of the spirit and the responsibility that rests with writers and thinkers to maintain that faith—is the only principle on which, in the long run, civilization can be maintained, or by which intellectuals can be immunized against a sense of futility.

(K)   Norman Podhoretz. *Doings and Undoings* (Farrar).
                                                    1964. p. 50

Edmund Wilson's *Protest* is a document of no mean interest. The author has one of the best literary minds of our generation. He has developed a limpid and casual prose in the great tradition of essay writing in English. His criticism exhibits a rare combination of qualities. He has humor and a very personal sensitivity to whimsical human nuances. Besides being a historical critic and an able journalist of literature he is a scholar; as John Adams said of Jefferson: "a great rubber-off of dust."

There can hardly be a subject more appealing and timely than the misadventure of a man of talent caught in the bureaucratic web of the Internal Revenue Service. It is one of those situations that Kafka prophetically foresaw. Vivian Kellems told the story from the point of view of small business. Now we have it from the point of view of the absent-minded professor who is also one of our ranking men of letters.

He tells the sad tale of *lèse-majesté* towards the bureaucratic state and of the retribution that followed. The recital is clear and brief, uncloyed by self pity. . . . The final note is of a despair that seems unnecessarily helpless. One is reminded of the black nihilism of some of Mark Twain's last writings.

(K)   John Dos Passos. *National Review*. Jan. 28, 1964.
                                                                     pp. 71, 73

An even more interesting aspect of the organization of the book [*Patriotic Gore*] is the clue it provides to Wilson's present assessment of his role as man of letters. The two parts of the book are joined in a way that has the deepest meaning for him, and the impression that the movement of the book makes is related to this. The Civil War, in its scale, technique, brutality, is "modern"; the Southerners remind us of war's time-honored but foresaken rules. But in spite of the parallels this permits Wilson to draw to more recent enormities, and in spite of the verbal equivalents that call to mind his favorite Callot's *The Miseries of War,* we are struck by his vicarious excitement over its action and, especially in the portraits of Grant, Sherman, and Mosby, by the extent to which he identifies with the men of action who are making history. He remarks of Henry James that he liked to read military memoirs and books about Napoleon, envied the qualities of "'the brilliant man of action,'" and planned his literary career as if it were a military campaign; and we feel that he, too, would like to experience, as he says of Sherman, "the real exaltation of leadership." Still unsatisfied with the role of sayer, he would be a doer—and it is not fortuitous that one remembers in reading *Patriotic Gore* how he had dramatized once before in *To the Finland Station* a glorious imperative to action.

(K)   Sherman Paul. *Edmund Wilson, A Study of Literary
                                        Vocation in Our Time* (Illinois). 1965. p. 205

Professors who may well have formed their taste on *Axel's Castle* and their politics on *To the Finland Station* are now sufficiently wise to call Wilson superficial. It is not a simple case of ingratitude; in a limited sense the professors are right. Wilson's talent has always been more for introducing men and movements than for analyzing them. He has rarely tried to do more than register the encounter of his sympathetic and judicious mind with alien materials—to jog a pleasant mile with the bit between his teeth. This latest book makes explicit his affinity with Van Wyck Brooks and Newton Arvin and Mario Praz—civilized, omniverous impressionists who are largely unencumbered by theory. His patient recitals of bio-graphical facts, his plot-summaries, his assurances that the work under discussion is good bedtime reading have always been characteristic of his method. . . . In his best work we see that his frank interest in the social and emotional vicissitudes of writers has led him back into an awareness of the immediate psychological quality of literary texts—that pervasive atmosphere which somehow eludes the formalist and the moralist and the historian of ideas.

(K)   Frederick C. Crews. *NYR*. Nov. 25, 1965. pp. 4–5

The example of Wilson—discipline, persistence, self-involvement, a will-ingness to acquire the means with which to practise an effective criticism—has been followed, but not adequately acknowledged, by younger Ameri-cans. To make possible an American criticism that would be strong enough for its job, to provide for it the strength, range and subtlety of the French, was the vast undertaking. Wilson himself saw that it meant good reviewing in the periodicals. The job begins there. . . . And so the task of providing America with a criticism was difficult even on the mundane level of simply finding time to do it. You had to review a lot but your reviewing would be useless unless you did other things on another level. Sometimes it wasn't possible to do both; during the years when he was reading for *To the Finland Station* Wilson, as he says, lost touch with what was going on. But by working enormously and being provident in the choice of subjects he succeeded remarkably in his attempt to do everything at once. Because he did so there *is* in America literate unacademic criticism.

(K)   Frank Kermode. *Encounter*. May, 1966. pp. 65–6

This row on the Edmund Wilson shelf, sturdy as bricks, now numbers nearly two dozen: fiction, poetry, drama, scholarship, memoirs, travel, anthropology, history, reporting, political pamphleteering; but it would scarcely do to arrange the books in this way. They are all Wilson, and all probably at last criticism. Even though many of them are not examina-tions of texts, but firsthand reports or original creations, they are all formed by the way the critical mind works. They note the provenance and the surface manner of whatever is being examined, person, place, or thing, and then rapidly, clearly, without any sparring or hesitation or qualifica-tion, the underlying structure is exposed and articulated, and its signifi-cance stated. This is as true of the slightest book review as of major works of literary history like *Axel's Castle,* in which the "Modern Literature" of our century and its roots in Symbolism were first and probably best expounded.

(K)   John Thompson. *NYR.* Sept. 28, 1967. p. 8

See *Axel's Castle, To the Finland Station, The Triple Thinkers, Classics and Commercials, The Wound and the Bow, The Shores of Light, Patriotic Gore, The Bit Between My Teeth* (criticism); *Memoirs of Hecate County* (stories); *A Prelude* (autobiography); also *Apologies to the Iroquois* and *The Cold War and the Income Tax: A Protest.*

WINTERS, YVOR (1900–1968)

Poetry

His poetry is gaunt, gray and harsh. It is also cold, with that burning cold that belongs to ice. . . . There is an integrity about it which derives from the poet's metaphysical passion—a passion colored by his sharp apprehension of physical things, and having its issue in a profound disenchantment with the world. He conveys it by means of a few spare, precise images. In some thirty words he will give you the essence of a moment. But these moments are an effectual screen for eternity. Time, Space, and the mind that spins them are Mr. Winters's ultimate concern.

Babette Deutsch. *Bkm.* June, 1928. p. 441

Mr. Winters remains one of the best of the imagist school, but limited by that school. He is afraid to trust himself in any extension of language beyond absolute clarity and precision, and he therefore loses much in power. He remains one of the most interesting and contemporary of our poets, despite the fact that his critical mind does his poetic mind some injury. He states more clearly than any other poet the modern dilemma: the gradual loss of feeling through too much of "print."

Eda Lou Walton. *Nation.* Dec. 17, 1930. p. 680

Mr. Winters's work is precise, scrupulous and taut; no syllable is wasted: the intellectual element does not exclude emotion, though it controls it. The metrics are formal, the rhymes strict; seldom does a word seem rhyme-fetched, rather than intended. The poet's ear is good. If his poems seem cold—or, anyway, cool—it is worth remembering that it can be with poems as with women: some like them so, at least sometimes.

Rolfe Humphries. *NYT.* April 23, 1944. p. 24

In his own generation he has the eminence of isolation; among American poets who appeared soon after the first world war he is, Crane being dead, the master. If he has been neglected—when he has not been ignored—the reasons are not hard to find. He has conducted a poetic revolution all his own that owes little or nothing to the earlier revolution of Pound and Eliot, or that goes back to certain great, likewise neglected Tudor poets for metrical and stylistic models. . . . He is a Renaissance humanist of the pre-Spenserian school of metaphysical rhetoricians, the school of Greville and Raleigh: a poet whose moral imagination takes, without didacticism, the didactic mode, striving for precision in language and, in verse, for formal elegance.

Allen Tate. *Nation*. March 2, 1953. pp. 17–8

His best poetry is "occasional." It takes off from something observed or remembered, or from a contemporary occasion, and by a combination of perception and mediation wrings some human meaning out of it. This meaning is often oblique, often delicate, quite different from the great commonplaces of the Victorian or eighteenth-century poets. Nor does it reach out through deliberate symbolic echoes and ironic parallels to include all of civilization, as the early Eliot so often did. Winters works by limitation; the meaning which each of his poems achieves is precise and restricted; and perhaps his most remarkable technical accomplishment is his control, his ability to stop (not only in terms of length but also in terms of depth) when he has said enough.

David Daiches. *YR*. Summer, 1953. p. 629

When I was the poetry consultant at the Library of Congress in 1947 and '48, I had the luck to listen frequently to records of Winters reading a dozen or more of his best poems: "Time and the Garden," "John Sutter," "The Marriage," "Heracles," and others. His voice and measures still ring in my ears. They pass Housman's test for true poetry—if I remembered them while shaving, I would cut myself.

Winters likes to declare himself a classicist. Dim-wits have called him a conservative. He was the kind of conservative who was so original and radical that his poems were never reprinted in the anthologies for almost twenty years. Neither the *avant-garde* nor the vulgar had an eye for him. He was a poet so solitary that he was praised adequately only by his pupils and by Allen Tate. Yet Winters is a writer of great passion, one of the most steady rhetoricians in the language, and a stylist whose diction and metric exemplify two hundred years of American culture.

(K)   Robert Lowell. *Poetry*. April, 1961. pp. 40–1

Reading through the *Collected Poems,* you sense that Winters shares none of the wishy-washy reverence for the artistic or the ecstatic experience that has destroyed the later work of so many of his contemporaries; his manner is gruff, his language direct; he resists prettyness and he has been known to express his disgust for the involuted literary world about him in a blunt, irascible way.

But when these same elements of temperament and conviction are turned loose in a shorter lyric poem of unadorned language, the result is a strong, masculine poetic statement. This is a traditional poetry that is not anachronistic; it seems as engaged with human experience as the most robust spiritual noisemaking of his contemporaries; and it is much less arbitrary in its devices. Potent with meanings yet impeccable in its diction as his verse is, Winters does his poetry a disservice when he calls it "the definition of a style," for it is also the record of particular experiences and the expression of a particular personality that is uniquely suited to the timbres and movements of that plain speech style.

(K)   Richard M. Elman. *Com.* July 14, 1961. pp. 401–2

If, however, no poem of Winters was ever fished at random from the subconscious, neither is it likely that—having eliminated that sort of richness along with that redundance—any poem of his should surrender in its purposeful simplicity to a record of an event. His poetics evidently intends the ultimate reduction of highly conscious experience to its most inclusive terms. . . .

It is his skill in placing feeling and the conviction from which this work proceeds, far more than his almost archaic strictness of form, that I think allies Winters most fundamentally to classicism. . . . Memory, I believe, considered as a gift of language, in its deeper rhythms functions as the source of form in the shaping of these poems. Not memory vulgarized and distorted by sentiment, but that memory which Pascal said is necessary for all the operations of reason.

(K)   Carol Johnson. *Reason's Double Agents* (North
                       Carolina). 1966. pp. 99–101

Criticism

Mr. Winters started with a basis of ideas which he has never found reason to abandon, either creatively or critically. His is a centrifugal progress. He has had the courage to work outward from hard absolutes of meaning and intuition toward the surfaces of sense, and thus toward the periphery of a complete and comprehending sensibility. To express this sensibility perfectly is to achieve style. Mr. Winters's difficulties have been chiefly of two kinds: in communication because the initial meaning or intuition has not always found a genuine sensible embodiment; and in persuasion, because, even when it has, the requisite passion and conviction of style have too often been lacking.

Morton Dauwen Zabel. *Poetry*. Jan., 1931. p. 226

Yvor Winters, writing like a combination of a medieval scholastic and a New England divine, is a critic of a type that one has become accustomed to regard as practically extinct. . . . Evidently Mr. Winters began with a temperamental distaste for the general atmosphere of distress, the hectic experimentation with forms and with style, that has characterized so much contemporary verse. But to this situation he responded with that mechanism of the mind which consists in reacting to any phenomenon by celebrating its opposite. . . . Mr. Winters is narrow, dogmatic, parochial; and these are all the defects of his method. But it would be unjust not to mention the virtues of these defects: the sharpening of focus on important problems, the formulation of useful distinctions, and the construction of definitions that at least provide a springboard for discussion.

William Troy. *Nation*. Feb. 20, 1937. p. 216

When Mr. Winters is actually talking about the work of the American experimental poets, how it failed and even how it could have been improved, when he talks about meter and convention or any technical matter, he makes only normal mistakes and produces a great many pertinent and stimulating facts. . . . Mr. Winters's system of absolutes, his coinage of intellectual counters, is not much better than other systems or much worse; but it is more bare-faced, candid and uncompromising than most; hence more irritating and I should say easier, in a good cause, to ignore. When he translates his absolutes back into the genuine but ultimately provisional elements of his feeling for poetry, he will always be at the level of his best.

Richard P. Blackmur. *NR*. July 14, 1937. p. 285

To watch him taking a critical misjudgment apart gives the same kind of pleasure that we get from seeing a first-rate woodman split a log— the great secrets being merely to start the opening wedge in the right place and then to hit it hard enough. Mr. Winters has no lack of sharp, smooth wedges to start where they will do the most good, and his style can be on occasion a two-handed sledge to sink them home. . . . Those who perceive how much Mr. Winters has as a critic cannot well help wishing that he had everything. What he does not at present seem to have in normal measure is the rounded man's appreciation of writing that is consummate in a small way. His canons are serious to severity and he is little tolerant of the playful, the trifling, the frankly artificial, the droll, the merely mellifluous.

Wilson Follett. *NYT*. Dec. 4, 1938. p. 36

To his earlier perversities . . . Winters adds an intemperate denigration of the poetry and criticism of T. S. Eliot. . . . This seems to me not only mistaken but ungenerous, since I cannot help but feel that Winters shares both Eliot's literary and religious traditionalism and his method of employing arresting *obiter dicta* which contain valuable insights even when the essays in which they blossom are elaborately wrong-headed.

What I find of value in Winters's criticism is precisely what I have found (but in a larger measure) in Eliot's: a love of good writing and an occasional articulation of that passion, despite theories and posturing.

George Mayberry. NR. July 12, 1943. pp. 51–2

Winters is what Kierkegaard said *he* was—a corrective; and Winters's case for the rational, extensive, prosaic virtues that the age disliked, his case against the modernist, intensive, essentially romantic vices that it swallowed whole, have in his late criticism become a case against any complicated dramatic virtues. Winters's tone has long ago become that of the leader of a small religious cult, that of the one sane man in a universe of lunatics; his habitual driven-to-distraction rages against the reprobates who have evidenced their lunacy by disagreeing with him go side by side with a startled, giant admiration for the elect who in a rational moment have become his followers.

Randall Jarrell. NYT. Aug. 24, 1947. p. 14

Although Winters' description of the good life, and even his estimate of the good in art, has what we might call a psychological center, he consciously avoids purely psychological discourse on the grounds that his proper business is literature. The same may be said of ethical theory, for his critical approach does invite him to go off into a general evaluation of ethical systems to discover which might help a man adjust most happily; but, in the main, he leaves that sort of treatment for the more special occasion and deals solely with the relevant literary consequences of the artist's moral perception. Aside from those two possible points of departure, his critical theories tend to carry him directly to the works. If the rational structure of a poem is obscure, then there can be no appropriate emotion; or, if the emotion is not clearly motivated by the meaning, then again we have obscurity. In either case, the critic must attend to the art, and, whatever else he is, Winters is impressive as a close and imaginative reader.

(K)   Keith McKean. *UKCR*. Winter, 1955. p. 133

. . . he is unquestionably one of the most distinguished and brilliant of living critics, a master of lucid, precise and superbly turned English prose. He is immensely persuasive, a ready and telling wielder of invective; his seriousness, as he reminds us occasionally, is complete. There is no doubt that he loves the kind of poetry that he admires. . . . [H]e is also, considered in relation to the writers of our time, or indeed of the past two hundred years, one of the most eccentric of contemporary critics. He is, by sympathy, conviction and long practice, a rationalist; one of the worst things he can say about a work of literature is that it is romantic; he can detect romanticism, of the kind he most deplores, in most of the writing of the last two hundred years, and in his view its presence there renders the greater part of our literature since the mid-eighteenth century not only sadly imperfect but wrong.

(K)   W. S. Merwin. *NYT*. July 21, 1959. p. 10

In Winters' critical system everything fits together. It is a many-armed body with one head, and that head is the concept of a poem as an evaluation of experience and therefore a moral judgment. It is a pervasive concept, running through every part of the poem, determining the efficacy of every device and the acceptability of every phrase.

This objection to poems whose viewpoint is disapproved of is an objection made from the moralist position—Winters says "theoretic moralists," but I do not know what that means, so I will not try to use it. The point is that if anything will clarify for us what Winters is talking about whenever he talks about poetry, it is an understanding of this concept of poetry as moral judgment.

In my opinion Winters sees two ways in which a poem can fail on moral grounds. These are: by a false wedding of emotion and the object or idea which is supposed to evoke that emotion; and by expressing a theme or general philosophical viewpoint which is morally or rationally unacceptable.

(K)   Miller Williams in *Nine Essays in Modern American*
                 Literature, edited by Donald E. Stanford (Louisiana
                                     State). 1965. pp. 163–4

Winters prefers books of poems in which moral theme predominates. It is extremely curious that he prefers *Macbeth* to either *King Lear* or *Hamlet,* and the reason is not far to seek: the morality of *Macbeth* can be more simply abstracted from the play.

If Winters' theory is true, then literature can offer us no more nor other kind of human and moral understanding than ethical generalization. What literature does, according to his theory, is to convey the feelings appropriate to the understanding which is itself totally paraphrasable and essentially abstract. But to use one of Winters' favorite sorts of arguments, this is false because it is contrary to all our experience. Literature has the full resources of the meaning of ordinary and extraordinary language, a language from which concept and feeling do not neatly sift out. The experience is not opposed to, but it is more than reasoning.

That is as true of Winters' poems as of others. His poems are strengthened by his theory and limited by it; in good ways they go beyond it.
(K)   Paul Ramsey. *SwR*. Summer, 1965. pp. 456–7

See *Collected Poems;* also *In Defense of Reason* (criticism).

WOLFE, THOMAS (1900–1938)

Some of Mr. Wolfe's material is not subordinated to the intention of the book. What is his intention? On what is the mass of material focussed? What is to give it form? His novels are obviously autobiographical. This means that the binding factor should be, at least in part, the personality of the narrator, or since Mr. Wolfe adopts a disguise, of the hero, Eugene Gant. . . . The hero is really that nameless fury that drives Eugene. The book is an effort to name that fury and perhaps by naming it to tame it. But the fury goes unnamed and untamed. Since the book is formless otherwise, only a proper emotional reference to such a centre could give it form. Instead, at the centre there is this chaos that steams and bubbles in rhetoric and apocalyptic apostrophe, sometimes grand and sometimes febrile and empty; the centre is a maelstrom, perhaps artifically generated at times; and the other tangible items are the flotsam and jetsam and dead wood spewed up, iridescent and soggy as the case may be.
Robert Penn Warren. *AR*. May, 1935. pp. 199–202

Mr. Wolfe has power, passion, a singular fearlessness, the ability to create individual scenes of brilliant truth, a genius for lyrical prose unequalled in contemporary letters, insight into certain types of characters and problems. But Mr. Wolfe the artist has advanced scarcely a step since *Look Homeward, Angel*. He is full of self pity. If he is a genius, he is still an adolescent genius. His universe is utterly or mainly subjective, and the result is a transcript of experience curiously true in some particulars, curiously false in others.
Howard Mumford Jones. *SR*. Nov. 30, 1935. p. 13

His imagination has provided him with a great theme and his accurate memory flashes infinite exact detail of the life which he intends to make his book. But he cannot control the theme or reduce his substance to a medium. He will write neither poetry nor prose, but both. He will not be content with the literal autobiographic description of men and events which his journalistic sense supplies so readily but must intersperse with passages of sheer fantasy or poetical uplift. He will stick neither to fiction nor to fact. Hence the reader never enters into that created world of the real novelist which has its own laws, its own atmosphere, its own people, but goes from here to there in Mr. Wolfe's own life, seeing real people as he saw them, and often recognizing them . . . not as created characters but as literal transcripts from the life. So that the effect is always of being in two worlds at one time, fiction and fact, until curiosity takes the place of that ready acceptance of a homogenous life in the imagination which a fine novel invariably permits.

Henry Seidel Canby. *Seven Years' Harvest*
(Rinehart), 1936. p. 168

Something of the homefolk's first resistance to the book about the home town may lie behind the criticism of Wolfe's books as undisciplined and formless. I suspect in some such criticism a wish, like Asheville's, to have a native story a little nicer, a trifle neater, more ordered and patterned in delicacy and decorum. And now at his death I expect that the suggestion will be strenuously stirred that had he lived Tom Wolfe's big, sprawling, powerful, pouring prose would have been served in neater packages of sweeter stuff. It is possible to say anything about the dead. In Wolfe's case, they may even make him a classicist who might have been. But our loss will remain the unbounded vitality, the uncaptured power which made his books and his world and all his Gants and Pentlands alive. Form and discipline undoubtedly in important respects he lacked; it is lacking also in the confusion which is as much a part of American life as Tom Wolfe was.

Jonathan Daniels. *SR*. Sept. 24, 1938. p. 8

Wolfe wrote *great* American novels, he wrote great *American* novels, and, loosely speaking, he wrote great American *novels*. But he fails to measure up in the fourth respect: he did not write *the* great American novel. . . . Wolfe was not of the artistic temperament to write such a work. The author of The Great American Novel must be dramatic and omni-present; Thomas Wolfe was lyrical and uni-present. For him there was only one world and he was at the center of it. . . . But his . . . gravest limitation was his genius. . . . The genius of Thomas Wolfe was too much. He was driven by a restlessness which kept him from achieving that cool perfection which often comes easy to lesser men.

Thomas Lyle Collins. *SwR*. Fall, 1942. p. 504

The career of Thomas Wolfe is the spectacle of a novelist who began with the sole concern to transfer to others his fascination with his own family as material for fiction, who turned thereafter in the same simplicity of intention to his own relationships with persons outside his family, but who poured into these relationships all the disorders of the contemporary world until he was forced at the end to attempt their solution in a letter to his editor on social views, in which his work as a writer culminated and, it may be said, his life concluded.

Edwin Berry Burgum. *VQR*. Summer, 1946. p. 421

Even among the most famous representatives of the more serious contemporary literature that I know, Thomas Wolfe, it seems to me, is the only one endowed with the prophetic Ethos and the poetic Pathos of the true genius. He is the only one consciously transmuting his own discovery of life and of the world into a message of religious intensity. He had consented to be "God's lonely man." He knew from the start that "genius can bring death." There must have been in him from his early youth this feeling of being consecrated, fated, and inevitable.

Even beyond his own artistic testimony, it is a most poignant human experience to witness this Pilgrim's Progress from the exalted rhapsodic lyricism, the youthful turmoil and ecstasy of his first book to the manly composure, the profound ethical awareness of his "Credo" in the last chapter of *You Can't Go Home Again*.

Franz Schoenberger. *NYT*. Aug. 4, 1946. p. 1

Wolfe's poetry is not calmly and quietly intense; his main theme is the theme of being lost in America, and it is treated by a poet who is still lost. His perspective of America itself is out of joint: distances and spaces are magnified, a trip from New York to North Carolina becomes a journey "down the continent"; much of his America is an abstraction. He has some of the naturalistic pantheism, the feeling that man and soil are intensely bound together in essence which marks so much Western literature since Zola and which makes him sound occasionally like Jean Giono, just as he shows at times some of the enthusiasm for being American, if not the faith democratic, of Walt Whitman. Now and again he reveals a feeling for, though not much knowledge of, the history of our people— the feeling that this land is something apart because the dust of his ancestors is mixed with its dust. But mostly his complaint is that these things do not mean more to him than they do, that he really has no place and "no door where he can enter," and that meanwhile he is being swept along by the stream of life. The answer to his eternal question is not the answer of Whitman and Crane and Paul Engle. The one thing that he can be sure of, the one door that must open for him, is death.

W. M. Frohock. *SWR*. Autumn, 1948. p. 357

Disillusionment, the hindsight of the self-deluded and the half-blind, was not one of Thomas Wolfe's qualities. No one ever accused him of being blind in any degree. His fault, if fault it was, was that he saw too much. Till the day he died he retained that luminous gift which all bright children seem to possess up to a certain age: the ability to look at life and see it as it really is, with all its many and ever-changing faces, its mystery and wonder, its exhilaration and stark terror, its endless contrasts of beauty and ugliness, its haunting interplay of good and evil, its flashing colors and subtly shifting shadows.

Edward C. Aswell. *SR.* Nov. 27, 1948. p. 34

In the style of Wolfe is his essence. It is for this that we read him—not for his narrative, not for philosophy, not for the desire to study more intently the nature of human thought and behavior. The narrative is dictated by the circumstances of his own life, and he runs wild as an unsheared hedge. The philosophy is half-baked—a sequence of ideas held today because of yesterday's impressions, and just as likely to be altered tomorrow. . . . We read Wolfe primarily for his rhetorical poetry, which he delivers from his great height with the authority of a prophet who has seen the clouds open to reveal a calligraphy of fire upon the white spaces of the air.

Pamela Hansford-Johnson. *Hungry Gulliver*
(Scribner). 1948. p. 20

It is largely through his effort to find permanence in flux that the novels of Thomas Wolfe may be considered "modern" in their treatment of time. In Wolfe's novels time becomes a rushing all-erosive river, which, nevertheless, may be arrested or turned back by the memory. Like Proust, Wolfe seeks to recapture the past through memory, including unconscious memory, and to show the sensations and moods that recollections of the past evoke in the present. Or again, like Joyce in *Finnegan's Wake,* he opposes a linear conception of time with a cyclical one, wherein the eternal is repeated through apparent change.

W. P. Albrecht. *NMQ.* Autumn, 1949. p. 320

The four novels of Wolfe's tetralogy echo the voice of time. Like the great railroad sheds, they harbor its sound. For Wolfe was secure only when he was in motion and never so sure of himself as when he was on a moving train. His books came from the huge railroad stations of his mind where "the voice of time remained aloof and imperturbed, a drowsy and eternal murmur," and where the train whistle "evoked for him a million images: old songs, old faces, and forgotten memories." Involved with Proustian metaphysics Wolfe was not, but as the taster of life and time his experience was much the same as Proust's. And for both of them the sudden and vivid resurrection of the lost moment, through a present sensory impression, was the central time-experience.

Margaret Church. *PMLA*. Sept., 1949. p. 638

His aim was to set down America as far as it can belong to the experience of one man. Wolfe came early on what was for him the one available truth about this continent—that it was contained in himself. . . . He could— and it is the source of what is most authentic in his talents—displace the present so completely by the past that its sights and sounds all but destroyed surrounding circumstances. He then lost the sense of time. For Wolfe, sitting at a table on a terrace in Paris, contained within himself not only the America he had known; he also held, within his body, both his parents. They were there, not only in his memory, but more portentously in the make-up of his mind. They loomed so enormous to him that their shadows fell across the Atlantic, their shade was on the cafe table under which he stretched his long American legs.

John Peale Bishop in *Kenyon Critics*, edited by John
Crowe Ransom (World). 1951. pp. 3–4

These antagonisms of Wolfe's, which have been dubbed "provincial," are in actuality national and American—historically, traditionally so. In his aversion from either extreme—great wealth or deep poverty—Wolfe is at one with the cosmopolitan William Dean Howells; and, as with Howells, his at-homeness, his central core of concern, is with the people of the middle-income groups. His middle-class characterizations, however, far exceed those of Howells in vividness of realization, in adventurousness, and above all in variety.

(K)   Walter Fuller Taylor. *SAQ*. Oct., 1953. p. 547

Thus when we examine the plots of the four novels, we see that to varying degrees they mark stages along the way toward responsibility. *Look Homeward, Angel,* the most compact of the four, represents the artist's birth into a particular home and community and the successive stages of his alienation from it. At the end the young Eugene leaves the town for the city. In *Of Time and the River* he tangles with the world of art, then flees his country to go abroad, and there discovers his unescapable ties with his country. In *The Web and the Rock* he has his romance with the city and a love affair, and then he flees both—the woman's love and the city's ways. In *You Can't Go Home Again* he realizes that neither town nor city, woman or fame, but only his mind can give him peace, and that the direction of flight must not be away from reality but toward the creation of his artistic reality—and that this artistic reality is not one of proud romantic isolation and the storming of heaven by frontal assault, but a reality grounded in morality and personal human responsibility.

(K)   Louis D. Rubin. *Thomas Wolfe: The Weather of His Youth* (Louisiana State). 1955. pp. 24–5

Wolfe's error in creation was the failure to associate the type and the individual. When, for example, he created a character and fitted his personality into the pattern and framework of one of his books, he did so because in life he had known such a real person. Seldom, indeed, did he weave a figure mainly from the fabric of his imagination and use threads from the lives of many people. Frequently, and especially in the later books, he created a character on the basis of one prototype but selected additional traits from other people. His memory for the specific enabled him to portray characters that are supremely vivid, yet the same quality also perhaps caused his failure to select details he wanted from many sources. To generalize and combine, he seems to have thought, would be to lose particularity.

(K)   Floyd C. Watkins. *Thomas Wolfe's Characters: Portraits from Life* (Oklahoma). 1957. p. 181

He was completely ignorant of how to shape a piece of writing and make it publishable, but he had a deep instinctive feeling for his work which rarely played him false. He was fascinated by the concept of time in all its aspects, but he always was an hour or more late to his appointments. . . . He had what he called "a mountaineer's suspicion of people from outside," which sometimes made him accuse even his best friends of "betraying" him, but he was the most naïve and trusting man on earth and wanted everyone to be his friend. He had "black moods" so deep that he sometimes was afraid of going crazy, but he also had periods of the greatest hope and joy. He had a humorless self-pity, but a sense of humor that was superb. He had the greatest difficulty in making decisions, but when he made one, he did it utterly, irrevocably, and with a bang. He had a ruthlessness in breaking free from too smothering relationships, but he had depths of loyalty which never changed. He was driven wild with exasperation at his family, but he worried endlessly about them and gave them hundreds of his own much-needed dollars during hard times. He was in many ways an adolescent boy, but he had the philosophy, the hope, the resignation of a great man.

(K)   Elizabeth Nowell. *Thomas Wolfe: A Biography* (Doubleday). 1960. pp. 12–13

In the final analysis, . . . Wolfe's success or failure rests on his adventure with the American Dream, as this Dream was developed from the time of Jefferson on through Emerson and Whitman up to the first quarter of the twentieth century. The Dream encompassed the hopes of young men everywhere for democracy and liberty and equality and individuality. It was an ideal and a promise. Wolfe was an American writer, not only because his problems were those of an American within America, but because his youth demanded fulfillment in a land where individual fulfillment was possible. In this Dream, it was Whitman who was his nearest spirit. Each of them spoke poetically out of his loneliness for all the young artists—and every young man is an artist to himself—across the sweep and breadth of the great land.

Before he completed his investigation into the nature of permanent acceptance in America, Wolfe had won within himself the struggle which is the essence of all human drama. With courage and honor, he had discovered through experience that his lot was common to that of all men. Out of his life and out of this discovery came the books.

(K)   Richard Walser. *Thomas Wolfe: An Introduction and Intrepretation* (Barnes and Noble). 1961. p. 143

To Wolfe, the notion that you can't go home again applies specifically to *art* in two principal ways: in its essentially moral statement that you can't use art itself as an escape from reality; and, more important for its complete reversal of Wolfe's former views, in its essentially aesthetic statement that you can't create worthwhile art through the particular escapes of Time and Memory. . . . Wolfe's statements are not specific enough for us to be able to tell the extent to which he consciously intended his new position as a criticism of all that he himself had so far written, but it is natural that his readers look at it in terms of the light it sheds upon Wolfe's accomplishments. One's attitude toward it necessarily involves an evaluation of Wolfe's entire career; in so far as one regards the view taken at the end of *You Can't Go Home Again* as valid, then so much lower must his estimate be of all of Wolfe's novels, for that view rejects their very basis: the assumption that you can return to the past. But it is not a perfectly simple matter to judge the validity of Wolfe's notion that he had been wrong to try to go home again, for though his memory produced some of the most glaring of his artistic defects, it often contributed much of the value and uniqueness his novels do have. It was at times his strength and at times his weakness.

(K)   Morris Beja. *MFS*. Autumn, 1965. pp. 312–13

His works are encyclopedic because he sought to embrace the diversity of American life. But to recognize diversity is not to integrate all the diverse elements, and Wolfe was able only occasionally to achieve the integrity that we think of as artistic wholeness. His best work is his first novel. In later work his plans were so complex and his scope so broad that he did not accomplish what he wished before he died. Perhaps too, his difficulty in accepting the diversity of human life in America contributed to his artistic uncertainties. Whether he ever would have brought his mammoth work about George Webber under control or not we will never know. But we certainly must respect his aim and ambition to create an American prose epic. We should also feel some admiration for a writer who, beset with neurotic difficulties, was still able to marshal his energies sufficiently well to achieve a partial success in his epic attempt.

(K)   Richard S. Kennedy. *MFS*. Autumn, 1965. pp. 232–3

Faulkner and Wolfe shared many things—being "Southern," verbal power, intensity, probing introspection—but they differed in significant ways. For Faulkner was the novelist of the rural South and its traditions of social order, and Wolfe was the spokesman of the New South, the South which was embracing the future of industrialism and capitalism and whose sons dream of great cities and the vast nation. Thus, where Faulkner used a rural county and the material around it to write a cosmic tragedy, Wolfe sought in his pages to show through the experience of one man what it meant to be American. Faulkner's characters are embedded in history; Wolfe's are dramatizations of attitudes that are national and epic rather than sectional and mythic. Wolfe's fiction was determined by the Piedmont middle-class world which he knew. When he moved from it, he moved outward to embrace the nation and to attempt to realize the promise of America.

(K)   C. Hugh Holman. *Three Modes of Modern Southern Fiction* (Georgia). 1966. p. 70

See *Look Homeward Angel, Of Time and the River, The Web and the Rock,* and *You Can't Go Home Again* (novels).

WOUK, HERMAN (1915–   )

Behind the rosy anachronisms of *Aurora Dawn* there would seem to be a nice talent for light fiction; and a talent for light fiction is no drug on our market. Of course, the reason we have no decent light fiction in this country is because we respect no literary work that is not heavy with portent or pretension. Mr. Wouk gives us plenty of evidence that he could write simple colloquial English if he thought it desirable. He is naturally witty. He is well educated. It is the sad mark of our times that he should nevertheless find it necessary or favorable to roll in the full periods of a bygone prose and display his book learning like a sophomore.

Diana Trilling. *Nation*. May 24, 1947. p. 636

There are three themes which the novelist has woven together for his story [*The Caine Mutiny*]. First, the life aboard ship with the community frictions and loyalty, with its pecking order as the strong men assert themselves, and with its instinctive reaction to the skipper. . . . The second theme is an ironic scrutiny of the whole Naval system as it is mocked, hated, but obeyed by the civilian officers who did not graduate from the Academy. . . . And the third theme, and the most personal, is the development of men at sea, particularly the character of Willie Keith. Willie at first is so casual that for three days he forgets to decode an action dispatch which he thrust into a hind pocket in a moment of excitement. But it is a different Willie who emerges from the long ordeal under Queeg. In the process of his self-possession Willie frees himself from his mother's domination and comes to value his affection for May Wynn, an Italian night club singer, but these are minor incidents in a story of men, one of the best designed and best developed novels of the war yet published by an American.

Edward Weeks. *At*. Aug., 1951. p. 79

What the new middle class wanted—and found in *The Caine Mutiny*—was an assurance that its years of discomfort and hardship in the Second World War were not in vain, and that its sacrifices in a permanent war economy and its gradual accommodation to the emergence of the military as a dominant element in civil life have been not only necessary but praiseworthy. More than this, it requires such assurance in a sophisticated form, allowing it to feel that alternatives have been thoughtfully considered before being rejected: in *The Caine Mutiny* ample space is given over to consideration of "psychoanalytic" motivations in Queeg and in Keefer too, and even in Cain-Abel analogy is mentioned as evidence that the title is not an unmotivated slip of the pen.

Harvey Swados. *PR*. March-April, 1953. p. 256

One might view this straightforward portrait of a young girl [*Marjorie Morningstar*] as the counterpart of the wry and oblique *Adventures of Augie March,* for while in Augie we see the formation of a man through his series of occupations, in Marjorie we see the formation of a woman through her series of courtships. But Saul Bellow retained a bitterness toward his background, satirizing the vulgarity of Augie's well-to-do connections. Wouk writes with the warmth he displayed in *The City Boy*. He has respect for his people, but he is hardly uncritical. His folkloristic scenes have more tenderness than ire. His satire is directed against those who have lost the traditional values, like the young parents who nearly wreck a Passover seder with their psychoanalytic jargon and their permissive pampering of a spoiled brat. Within this irony is a grotesque hilarity stemming from Wouk's early days as a radio gag man, for the brat has to have a satchelful of toy airplanes brought along wherever he goes—even to a seder. What happens is sheer Milton Berle.

Meyer Levin. *SR*. Sept. 3, 1955. p. 9

The moral is: if one's destiny is suburbia, there is no point in seeking to "be an actress" rather than "a fat dull housewife with a big engagement ring." The moral is also that a man who has written an interesting book from a masculine point of view (*The Caine Mutiny*) shouldn't push his luck too far by trying to reverse the procedure. At one point in her life, Marjorie Morgenstern finds that she is "very bored with the problems of being a girl." Herman Wouk's problem is plainly that he has never been one, and he cannot quite manage to tell a girl's story from a girl's point of view. *Marjorie Morningstar* is soap opera with psychological and sociological props. . . .

The environment Wouk creates is vivid and enormously complex. It touches on economic mobility—the moves from the Bronx to the Upper West Side to the suburbs, the compromises at Hunter between the Jewish and the Christian sororitites for political control, and the relationship of City College to Ivy League students; the conflicts between the older, immigrant generation—sweet, squashed, and loving—and the younger, growing up in a world that includes Freud and pork and the Unitarian Church; the flight from and to Jewishness.

The fascinating cultural scene is, however, backdrop to the banal love story.

Nora Magid. *NR*. Sept. 5, 1955. p. 20

In the Age of Wouk, the new writing will certainly have the impulse of revolt, but not the act; just as Marjorie Morgenstern—the "American Everygirl," as we are told—must first rebel against her environment in order properly to conform to it. There will be a little, or quite a lot of sex, so long as it is never fulfilled and has no meaning. There will be the usual periods of doubt, heart-searching, and despair in the lives of these new folk-figures of the American Way—in order to have a happy ending. Marjorie will always marry the man in the gray flannel suit in the typical configuration of the classless—and mindless—society. Well, what does it all really mean? I suspect that the final impact of the atomic age has had the effect of a lobotomy upon the national spirit. Don't look now, but we're all dead.

Maxwell Geismar. *Nation*. Nov. 5, 1955. p. 400

Herman Wouk stands at the very crossroads of modern literature. As the old American dream of perfect freedom faded, mature disillusion replaced it. "The lost generation" became "The Disenchanted" until the wisdom of disillusion produced "The Mature Mind." The dim light of Marjorie Morningstar faded, and the dream died: came the Aurora Dawn and Herman Wouk. Even the author's name seems allegorical.

Much of the interest of these novels comes from their treatment of basic American problems. Much of their excellence comes from the vivid characters they create to explore these problems. But much of their weakness comes from the black and white answers which they suggest. For, although Wouk protests that he takes no sides and plays no favorites, all his readers have disagreed. Tom Keefer is a heel and Noel Airman is a heel; but Barney Greenwald is a hero and Mike Eden is a hero. Always romantic rebellion is bad, but clear-eyed disillusion is good, and salvation is achieved by renouncing the foolish dreams of youth.

Frederic I. Carpenter. CE. Jan., 1956. p. 215

I was fascinated by *The Caine Mutiny* in all three forms, and unlike the jaundiced critic of *The New Yorker* I did not find *Marjorie Morningstar* "a damp and endless tale." The hunt for the missing strawberries is, I believe, a permanent addition to the literature of the sea, the account of more serious hostilities is lucid and exciting, and the breakdown of Commander Queeg under court-martial examination is a genuinely dramatic moment. In the later novel, the scenes of Jewish life seem to me authentic and good-natured. The description of the Bar-Mitzvah, the religious and social celebration of Seth Morgenstern's thirteenth birthday, is a skillful blend of solemnity and comedy. Marjorie's stage-struck progress through her late teens and early twenties can be shrugged off as uninteresting, I believe, only by those who have really lost interest in youth. . . .

Yet there is a common weakness in these two successful novels which bodes ill for the future. I refer to the sudden reversal near the end, the injection of conservative values in a manner which is structurally weak and at odds with the character values established in the first nine-tenths of each novel.

B. R. McElderry. AQ. Summer, 1959. p. 128

We do not share the indignation of some of the theologically sophisticated neo-ascetics of our day who have criticized *This Is My God* because Judaism appears in it as a pleasurable experience. It is well to remember that in spite of the manifold hazards and disabilities from which the Jew was never free, he always found his tradition a source of light and joy. . . . One misses not only the perspective of the historian, but the forward thrust of the prophet. One listens in vain for the passionate cry for justice, the revolt against the tyranny, want and cruelty of the world. One does not sense the unshakable faith in the advent of the Messianic age in which the Jew must be not only witness, but participant. We do not hear the yearning of the individual soul for God of which the Psalmist sings; the doubts and fears, the hopes and passions of the human situation are all lacking. Instead, this attractive book gives us a still-life portrait of Judaism—it is Judaism in one tense; only the comfortable present is here; the past and the future are absent.

Robert Gordis. *Midstream.* Winter, 1960. pp. 83, 89

Herman Wouk is the only living nineteenth century novelist. He glories in the fact and so do his ten million readers, including me. It is strange, as a matter of fact, that Dickens, our greatest English novelist, has been so little emulated. His genius may indeed have been inimitable but certainly his techniques were simplicity itself. And yet he has had no lineal descendants. Wouk is a late-rising avatar, not up to the original, but a contender. One way he falls short is in the matter of conviction. Dickens was sublimely self-confident. All his melodrama, all his wild coincidences, the sentimentality, the simplistic morality gave off a sense of absolute conviction. Wouk, on the other hand, is defensive, he invites patronizing and he gets it. He is continually looking over his shoulder, saying, "Can I get away with this?"

And he plods. Sometimes he plods so doggedly that you begin to admire him more for his stamina than his story-telling. Again he is defensive. "I may not be a poet," he says, "and I may not get very far off the ground, but I go slugging along with my story." This is true, and more power to him for it. Dickens did get off the ground, to be sure, but then he did a bit of plodding too.

William James Smith. *Com.* June 29, 1962. p. 355

See *Aurora Dawn, The City Boy, The Caine Mutiny, Marjorie Morningstar, Youngblood Hawke, Don't Stop the Carnival* (novels); *This Is My God* (essay).

WRIGHT, JAMES (1927–   )

Even more striking than its attitude toward nature and time is the kind of person whom modern poetry chooses to speak of. Aside from love poems and poems addressed to relatives, the persons who have stimulated Mr. Wright's imagination include a lunatic, a man who has failed to rescue a boy from drowning, a murderer, a lesbian, a prostitute, a police informer, and some children, one of them deaf. Common to them all is the characteristic of being social outsiders. They play no part in ruling the City nor is its history made by them, nor, even, are they romantic rebels against its injustices; either, like the children (and the ghosts), they are not citizens or they are the City's passive victims.

His one poem to a successful citizen is, significantly, to a singer, that is to say, to someone whose social function is concerned with the play of the City, not with its work.

W. H. Auden. Foreword to The Green Wall by
James Wright (Oxford). 1957. p. xiii

James Wright has reported that he has taken Edwin Arlington Robinson and Robert Frost for his masters, and has attempted as a working principle to "say something humanly important instead of just showing off with language." With such a choice of masters one could hardly quarrel, and he has followed them wisely—he approaches the human scene with something of Robinson's warmth and charity, and has something of Robinson's gift of narrative economy, with little of his embarrassing reluctance to turn loose of an effect before he has worked it to exhaustion. With Frost he finds some of his most fruitful occasions in the natural scene, which he can regard like Frost with accuracy and sympathy and without too much in the way of sentimentality—and also without so far very much of that archness which Frost can affect in his playful moods. These qualities of course are not peculiar to Robinson and Frost, and I am not sure that if Mr. Wright had not acknowledged their influence I would have thought it sufficiently pronounced to bring them into the discussion. Here they are, however, and in my opinion Mr. Wright need not feel too unworthy to share their company.

J. E. Palmer. SwR. Autumn, 1957. p. 693

"After the first death, there is no other." Individually, many of James Wright's poems give the impression that he would agree with that statement. Taken collectively, or reconsidered, the poems seem to make compulsive use of the deaths they describe; and mourning . . . becomes a means for quieting guilt so that the dead in the poems are scarcely celebrated. Indeed, the author is seldom willing that they even find rest; some of them speak, others seem always about to appear in the landscape—but more of this later. Mr. Wright is a supple writer who wears the minister's black veil. It is almost as if the emotion of loss in the poems, valuable in itself, is nourished to give rise to the more valuable emotion of guilt; and guilt is used frequently to effect a situation of self-depreciation, seemingly the most valuable of all.

David Galler. Poetry. June, 1960. pp. 185–6

The condemned, the lost, the disfigured, the loved, the guilty Americans in James Wright's poems move through his stanzas as presences who make the poet speak and in speaking define himself by his reactions to them. The questions which summoned them to him, he tells us, are moral ones. . . . Mr. Wright calls up his hapless ghosts in order that he may find words to describe them, pity them, love them. Many of his poems succeed because in them these separable actions are in fact made so interdependent as to seem inseparable; insofar as his moral questions are answered in those poems the answers are discovered, rather than proclaimed.

Daniel G. Hoffman. *SwR*. Autumn, 1960. pp. 674–5

James Wright's new book [*The Branch Will Not Break*] has moved away from a poetry of explanation to a poetry of suggestion; image rather than comment is intended to do the work. . . . The book depresses me, because of its sense of failure and loss, of a defeated life in which, if happiness is to exist, it will do so only briefly. The world of man shown here seems largely horrible, and only the uncomplicated world of animals, of physical nature, offers relief. . . . From his first book, Wright's poetry struck me as extraordinary and beautiful, as containing the sudden moments of pure excitement that I spoke of at the beginning of this review. The moments are still there, but now they are muted by the sadness, diminished, brought down. Wright has the clear vision, the exactness, the pure language of poetry; I would give him happiness, if I could.

William Dickey. *HdR*. Summer, 1963. p. 315

As soon as we put Wright's poetry in the company of the nostalgic Pastoral, difficulties of judgment begin. There is, in this collection, nothing to compare with Keats's "Ode to Autumn," Heine's "Aus alten Märchen winkt es" (which the poet quotes on the title page), or even with Thoreau's prose. As a new note (in concert with Robert Bly) in contemporary American poetry, it is certainly healthy and purgative: we have had too many of what Salinger's Franny calls "syntax droppings." *The Branch Will Not Break* is at most, however, a sketch-book of verses, a new beginning which wants to be criticized, rather than a consummation.

Geoffrey H. Hartman. *KR*. Autumn, 1963. pp. 751–2

In telling us how poems of inwardness voice their opposition to the status quo, [Robert] Bly implies, among other things, a love for the rural mode of existence which both he and James Wright juxtapose with the urban environment augmented by our contemporary technological and industrial gains. The two settings are plain in the city images and in the pastoral qualities and meditative lyricism of *The Branch Will Not Break*. Moral passion, which generated an ample part of Wright's earlier writing, has been assimilated by the new poetic method. His criticisms now submit themselves to the ruling influence of the imagery rather than depend upon any declared moral purpose. The total effect of this imagery is slow and cumulative; it is in accord with the actual movement of the poems, with their free but apt rhythms, their shifting but calculated emphases.

Ralph J. Mills. *Contemporary American Poetry* (Random). 1965. p. 214

At first a typically edgy poet of the age, disturbed by the terror in the air and finding a half-masochistic release in projecting it, he has turned the unease into several channels. The first is political—for instance, "Eisenhower's Visit to Franco" or "Two Poems about President Harding." The irony and bitterness of these pieces and others like them do take to a certain degree, though there is a facile, unearned quality to the emotion. The second is quietistic, the speaker deriving strength by "turning to nature" in the good old-fashioned way. . . . A third channel is the continuation of his earlier mode of thought, but in a simplified style that stresses the naked pain and fear of natural existence and brings social criticism into the poem almost incidentally. This is Wright's most sympathetic vein, because closest to the state of his own sensibility.

M. L. Rosenthal. *The New Poets* (Oxford). 1967. pp. 324–5

See *The Green Wall, Saint Judas, The Branch Will Not Break* (poems).

WRIGHT, RICHARD (1908–1960)

Story Magazine offered $500 for the best book-length manuscript submitted by anyone connected with the Federal Writers' Project. The prize was awarded to Richard Wright, a young, serious, quiet-spoken Negro born in Natchez and haphazardly educated in Chicago. His book (*Uncle Tom's Children*) published last week, consists of four long stories. . . . I found them both heartening as evidence of a vigorous new talent, and terrifying as the expression of a racial hatred that has never ceased to grow and gets no chance to die.

Malcolm Cowley. *NR*. April 6, 1938. p. 280

Violence has long been an important element in fiction about Negroes, just as it is in their life. But where Julia Peterkin in her pastorals and Roark Bradford in his levee farces show violence to be the reaction of primitives unadjusted to modern civilization, Richard Wright shows it as the way in which civilization keeps the Negro in his place. And he knows what he is writing about. . . . The essential quality of certain phases of Negro life in the South is handled here vigorously, authentically, and with flashes of genuine poetry.

Sterling A. Brown. *Nation*. April 16, 1938. p. 448

Mr. Wright has laid bare, with a ruthlessness that spares neither race, the lower depths of the human and social relationships of blacks and whites; and his ruthlessness so clearly springs not from a vindictive desire to shock but from a passionate—and compassionate—concern with a problem obviously lying at the core of his own personal reality that while the reader may recoil he cannot escape from the conviction that this problem is part of his reality as well.

Margaret Marshall. Nation. March 16, 1940. p. 367

Wright does not see the whole of life steadily and thoroughly: he sees only a segment of life, and even this limited part he views in its most violent and horrible aspects. To this restricted perspective may be traced the battering redundancy, the morbid melodrama, the overwrought excitement and the inflated calamities that sometimes appear in his work. In his limited field, nevertheless, he is generally a realistic analyst and thoughtful interpreter of social ills and, above all other American novelists, is the sensitive painter and perspicacious spokesman of the inarticulate black millions of this century.

Hugh M. Gloster. Negro Voices in American Fiction
(North Carolina). 1948. p. 234

All through *The Outsider,* Mr. Wright keeps telling us that the least important thing about his hero is that he is a Negro. . . . He is trying to portray modern man in his existential loneliness . . . but in fact, instead of "universalizing" the Negro, he simply denies the Negro's experience and reality. . . . Mr. Wright, it turns out, is unable to say anything at all about being a Negro except that to be a Negro is to be incoherent, and to do violence and murder. . . . Emptying his hero's life of all content except that existentialist content which evades reality through the pretence of trying to grapple with it on its "deepest" level—he has left us with only the familiar old black chasm.

Steven Marcus. Cmty. Nov., 1953. pp. 457–8

(Gertrude Stein) had never heard of Wright until her return to Paris after its liberation from the Nazis. Her book *Wars I Have Seen* was published soon after that, and among the reviews she saw was a laudatory one by Wright in *PM*. Asking a G.I. friend who this admirer of hers was, she was given a copy of *Black Boy* from the army library.

"I was very excited and wrote for the rest of his stuff," she told me. "I found Wright was the best American writer today. Only one or two creative writers like him come along in a generation. Every time he says something it is a distinct revelation."

Ben Burns. Reporter. March 8, 1956. p. 23

Many literary men has fought crusades; Wright is a crusader who fights with words. It makes a difference and it accounts for the special quality of his fiction. *The Long Dream* is not a badly-made book, as you will discover if you try to pull it to pieces. It is very strong, but its workmanship is careful only where care is needed for Wright's purposes. Elsewhere the book is boldly hammered together—not as a work of art but as the scaffolding for an idea. . . . He writes now with much more control than he once showed; his ear is wonderfully acute and his judgment of emotional degree and balance is subtle, varied, and exciting.

> Robert Hatch. *Nation.* Oct. 25, 1958. p. 297

But now that the storm of Wright's life is over, and politics is ended forever for him, along with the Negro problem and the fearful conundrum of Africa, it seems to have been the tough and intuitive, the genuine Richard Wright, who was being recorded all along. It now begins to seem, for example, that Wright's unrelentingly bleak landscape was not merely that of the Deep South, or of Chicago, but that of the world, of the human heart. . . .

This violence, as in so much of Wright's work, is gratuitous and compulsive. It is one of the severest criticisms that can be leveled against his work. The violence is gratuitous and compulsive because the root of the violence is never examined. The root is rage. It is the rage, almost literally the howl, of a man who is being castrated. I do not think that I am the first person to notice this, but there is probably no greater (or more misleading) body of sexual myths in the world today than those which have proliferated around the figure of the American Negro. This means that he is penalized for the guilty imagination of the white people who invest him with their hates and longings, and is the principal target of their sexual paranoia. Thus, when in Wright's pages a Negro male is found hacking a white woman to death, the very gusto with which this is done, and the great attention paid to the details of physical destruction, reveal a terrible attempt to break out of the cage in which the American imagination has imprisoned him for so long.

In the meantime, the man I fought so hard and who meant so much to me is gone. First America, then Europe, then Africa failed him.

(K)   James Baldwin. *Reporter.* March 16, 1961. pp. 53–5

. . . for all of the bland notations of achieved progress that may be offered by the social scientist, there is still an *agonia* here whose gall partakes of the "extreme situation"—and this was the perspective by which Richard Wright was consistently guided in all his efforts to shape the story of the American Negro into something whose tragic sorrow might quicken the conscience of our time.

Though he had numerous minor predecessors, Mr. Wright was the first American Negro writer of large ambitions to win a major reputation in our literary life. *Uncle Tom's Children,* his first collection of stories, achieved a limited currency in the late '30s among readers of leftist social sympathies, but it was not until *Native Son* burst upon the scene in 1940 that he won access to the kind of forum that Sunday supplement reviewers and a national book club could give. And the publication in 1945 of his autobiography, *Black Boy*—which is, I believe, his finest book—brought him to the zenith of his success. Thereafter his fiction and his political criticism, though no different in tone and emphasis from his earlier work, seemed to be nettling in their effect, and the reputation of the early '40s— if these things are susceptible of measurement by an impressionistic mathematic—has today, one feels, shrunk to a quarter of its original size. This is in part, I suspect, but a particular case of the more general demise of the naturalism of the American 1930s.

(K)   Nathan A. Scott. *KR*. Spring, 1961. pp. 338–9

Then he read James, and James was later supported by the professional social psychologists. It is revealing to quote the passage that Wright quotes: "No more fiendish punishment could be devised . . . than that one should be turned loose in society and remain absolutely unnoticed by the members thereof. . . ." . . . It is scarcely to be doubted that from the moment he read it, groping through it toward the knowledge of its empirical truth and listening to its mournful echoes in the still locked chambers of his soul, Wright became a man with a message and a mission. Long before he wrote *White Man, Listen!* the message was addressed to a white audience, and the mission was to bring awareness to that audience and perhaps thereby to save the world.

Both the message and the mission were particularized by Richard Wright's conception of a world where men "still cling to the emotional basis of life that the [old] feudal order gave them," and by his supra-consciousness of being Negro in that world. Translated into creative terms, this necessitated the rendering of Negro life with greater circumstantiality than had ever before been attempted. Oh, what psychological detail, what analysis of external influences, what precise attention to physical minutiae! He was in the naturalistic tradition, but without the naturalistic writer's aesthetic theories, abstract knowledge, and controls. Wright put everything in to arouse an audience which he hoped would be white, as principally it was.

(K)   Saunders Redding in *Soon, One Morning,* edited by
                                 Herbert Hill (Knopf). 1963. pp. 56–7

The mood of the emergent Negro radicalism is akin to the mood of the 1930's, and many a young seeker is going beyond Martin King only to go back to Richard Wright. The transition is not so abrupt as one might think. In theory, no two ideologies could be more different than King's Christian non-violence and Wright's angry, poverty-centered atheism. But King in action, as we observed, accepts and uses coercion, and the Wright of *Lawd Today,* written before *Native Son,* had not yet identified the cross of Jesus with the fiery cross of the Klan. Above all, King and Wright are at one in their consciousness of suffering.

(K)   Staughton Lynd. *Cmty.* Sept., 1963. p. 255

As a writer, Richard Wright has outlined for himself a dual role: To discover and depict the meaning of Negro experience; and to reveal to both Negroes and whites those problems of a psychological and emotional nature which arise between them when they strive for mutual understanding.

Now in *Black Boy,* he has used his own life to probe what qualities of will, imagination, and intellect are required of a Southern Negro in order to possess the meaning of his life in the United States. Wright is an important writer, perhaps the most articulate Negro American, and what he has to say is highly perceptive. Imagine Bigger Thomas projecting his own life in lucid prose, guided, say, by the insights of Marx and Freud, and you have an idea of this autobiography. . . .

. . . along with the themes, equivalent descriptions of milieu and the perspectives to be found in Joyce, Nehru, Dostoievski, George Moore and Rousseau, *Black Boy* is filled with blues-tempered echoes of railroad trains, the names of Southern towns and cities, estrangements, fights and flights, deaths and disappointments, charged with physical and spiritual hungers and pain. And like a blues sung by such an artist as Bessie Smith, its lyrical prose evokes the paradoxical, almost surreal image of a black boy singing lustily as he probes his own grievous wound.

(K)   Ralph Ellison. *Shadow and Act* (Random). 1964.
pp. 77–9

Essentially, of course, Wright was and remained not only an American but a Southerner. Negroes have a special fondness for that old saw, "You can take the boy out of the country, but you can't take the country out of the boy." The saying could be paraphrased and pointed up in Dick's case. His deepest roots were in the folk culture of the bottom—not *deep* but *bottom*—South. The lore of that milieu was such an intimate part of his background he sometimes treated it as if it had all originated in his own family. . . .

In the sense of his being a product of the Southern environment and of the Negro's situation, Dick's case is . . . clear. He was untouched by the redeeming influences sometimes present on campuses of colleges for Negroes in the region or even in the high schools. His was a total exposure to the callousness and cruelty of the closed society. Despite these odds, however, a delicate sensitivity survived. A major talent began to grow. There is a rumor that he wrote and published a story in a local Negro newspaper before he left Mississippi. He had completed no more than eight grades—such as they were down there at that time. He was so much an American with very deep roots in Southern Negro life that the effort of the Sartre crowd to take Dick over was bound to fail. Although he was definitely influenced by them over a period of two or three years it was not lasting, it really didn't take.

(K)   Arna Bontemps in *Anger and Beyond,* edited by
                             Herbert Hill (Harper). 1966. pp. 207–9

Wright said that he felt identified with the migrant Negro worker, and his typical protagonist comes from that group. The Wright hero continually endeavors to define his existence and to achieve his identity. The struggle for a "human life" and a genuine identity is particularly sharp for Wright's characters since the cultural and social definition of the American Negro has a built-in tension which demands resolution. In the Christian and democratic traditions, the sources of Wright's values, the individual is regarded as having inherent worth, and yet for the American Negro this worth is everywhere denied by racial discrimination. For most of Wright's characters, like Bigger Thomas, the two worlds of "thought and feeling, will and mind, aspiration and satisfaction" are never united, or are united only briefly through violence.

(K)   Clifford Hand in *The Thirties,* edited by Warren
                             French (Everett Edwards). 1967. p. 83

Native Son

Its swift rise to murder, its ruthless staging of a scene where race prejudice and palpable injustice capture the reader's sympathy, and the refusal of its author to make his chief character anything but a criminal, dangerous to society, all reveal a creative mind of unusual power, discipline, and grasp of large ideas. The question, which first concerns vice and viciousness and crime, slowly becomes ethical, political, and psychological without once separating itself from an intensely human content.

Henry Seidel Canby. *SR.* March 23, 1940. p. 8

Native Son, the most perdurable and influential novel yet written by an American Negro, is at the same time one of the masterpieces of modern proletarian fiction. Taking as its leading character a traditional "bad-nigger" stereotype usually accepted as a representative Negro by misinformed whites and frequently viewed with nausea by supercilious blacks, the book seeks to show that the individual's delinquency is produced by a distorting environment rather than by innate criminality. Having this purpose, *Native Son* may rightly be regarded as the most significant probing of the plight of the lower-class Northern urban Negro in contemporary American literature.

> Hugh M. Gloster. *Negro Voices in American Fiction*
> (North Carolina). 1948. p. 233

Elements of heredity, of social environment both black and white, of blind chance and misdirected attempts on the part of the whites to break down the colour bar, are brought together to drive the coloured hero of *Native Son* to the murder of a white girl and of his own sweetheart until he is caught, brought to trial, and sentenced to death. The dramatic development and straightforward characterization, as well as the absence of any false sentiment or propagandistic tone, make the novel more effective than most writing in this field. The book gives one of the rare examples of what can be achieved by the technique of pure reporting applied with a consistent attitude and an adequate subject matter.

> Heinrich Straumann. *American Literature in the*
> *Twentieth Century* (Hutchinson). 1951. p. 50

The most impressive feature of *Native Son* is its narrative drive. From the outset the novel assumes a fierce pace which carries the reader breathlessly through Bigger's criminal career. Wright allows as little interruption of the action as possible, with no chapter divisions as such and only an occasional break to mark a swift transition or change of scene. At the same time, he writes with great economy, breaking with the comprehensive and discursive tradition of the naturalistic novel. He provides only three brief glimpses of Bigger's life prior to the main action of the novel: his relationship with his family, with his gang, and with his girl, Bessie. The reader must supply the rest, for Wright's presentation is not direct but metaphorical.

On a literal level *Native Son* consists of three Books, dealing with a murder, a flight and capture, and a trial. But the murder and the circumstances which surround it are in reality an extended metaphor, like the whale hunt in *Moby Dick*. The novel is not to be read merely as the story of a gruesome crime, though it is that. It is the hidden meaning of Bigger's life, as revealed by the murder, which is the real subject of *Native Son*. The novel is a modern epic, consisting of action on the grand scale. As such, it functions as a commentary on the more prosaic plane of daily living.

(K)   Robert A. Bone. *The Negro Novel in America* (Yale).
                  1958. pp. 144–5

See *Uncle Tom's Children* (short stories); also *Native Son, The Outsider,* and *The Long Dream* (novels) and *Black Boy* (autobiography).

WYLIE, ELINOR (1885–1928)

A lyric voice slight, but clear and fine, may be heard in this book [*Nets to Catch the Wind*], the voice of a free and lightly ranging spirit. The sound of it is now gay, now grave, but always it holds a little aloof—one detects that something "austere, immaculate" for which the poet herself holds her Puritan ancestry responsible. . . . But always the emotion is shy and delicate, as of a cool small wild-flower growing, by some whim of Nature, not in the woods, but in the protected area of a garden. The flower is very simple and of quiet color, but it has an individual vitality nevertheless.

Harriet Monroe. Poetry. Jan., 1922. pp. 220–1

The apparent coldness in Elinor Wylie's work has been misunderstood by readers who were looking for the ruddy stupefactions of sentimentalism. Here is neither a case of cold nor warmth, but rather one of rhythms, and by rhythms I mean the curious capacity of thought for circumscribing static points of passion with melodic and luminous nuances. This is partially an *amor intellectualis,* but because it burns with a steady lambency and a concentrated fierceness, instead of flaring into ragged flames, there is no reason to doubt its intensity. Mrs. Wylie's best poems are jeweled instances in the fluctuating toils of Time. They are abstractions given a body and a shape and accoutred in armour. . . . I should say that she is cerebral in the sense that Dr. John Donne was cerebral. More than any woman of this generation she may claim to be a spiritual daughter of Donne. Through an intellectual chemical process, she crystallizes her emotions and yet retains their vitality.

Herbert S. Gorman. NAR. May, 1924. pp. 680–1

The despair and disillusionment setting in after the World War found its most tragic voice abroad in T. S. Eliot. On this side the Atlantic, it found a feminine counterpart in the marvelous brain of Elinor Wylie. Her work was not a direct reaction to the aftermath, but was raised on the private life of an aristocratic nature in no wise akin with the mob or democracy. Among the new aristocracy of intellects rearing ivory towers out of independent domiciles, Eliot was the prince, Elinor Wylie the princess. Each has had a long line of retainers and imitators. The despair of the woman was a positive thing; it was composed, not of self-pity, but of heroic acceptance.

Alfred Kreymborg. Our Singing Strength (Coward-
McCann). 1929. p. 459

We may grant, nevertheless, that this kind of romance writing is a poetry—a "making"—to which the unhappy contribute. They contribute so widely and so very variously that where a wastrel like Marlowe from out of his pot-house squalor may augment this branch of literature with a *Hero and Leander,* a restrained schoolmaster like Charles L. Dodgson, from out of the forlorn stuffiness of that atmosphere which is thought most suitably to develop the minds of the young, will bring forth an *Alice in Wonderland.* We may grant also that this is a branch of literature to which, through plain enough reasons, do belong *Jennifer Lorn* and *The Venetian Glass Nephew.*

I must here of necessity approach to matters which as yet stay delicate. It suffices to remark that the corporal life of Elinor Wylie was but too often at odds with her circumstances. The nature of this very beautiful and tragic woman was not ever in all adapted to that makeshift world in which perforce moved her superb body. She had found, after marrying several of them, that this world was over full of disappointments. She, who possessed the needed ability and an urgent need to use it, created therefore quite another sort of world, building amid desolation a baroque pagoda to be the sanctuary of wounded dreams and unfed desires. She created, in brief, a retreat wherein the rebuffed might encounter no more inglorious fiascos of the spirit and of the affections.

James Branch Cabell. *VQR.* July, 1930. p. 340

An agile wit was the factor which propelled her from charm to charm in her choice of materials: from historic themes of the most ingenious fragility and inaccessibility, to familiar encounters rendered desirable by the humor and elegance of imagination she brought to them. Thus seventeenth-century Venice had no riches to strike envy in the heart of a pioneer farmer on the Chesapeake: for each of them she conjured an experience of equal splendor. There was a prodigality in her verbal invention which certainly stemmed from something deeper than museum catalogues or encyclopedias; if we are to praise phonetic dexterity in Byron and Browning, we must praise it in her. The pictorial and impressionistic efforts of the 'nineties wilt feebly in comparison with the brittle imagery of her designs. In the tradition of *Émaux et Camées* she is, on first acquaintance at least, an austere and distinguished disciple.

Morton Dauwen Zabel. *Poetry.* Aug., 1932. pp. 276–7

. . . she was born to welcome the most intensely arduous mental labour in passionate exploration of the utmost resources of the English language in order to express every finest shade of thought and feeling that she experienced. She was abnormally sensitive to the powers latent in language. She had an altogether unusual intuition for the exact word, and had assimilated a large vocabulary. She was unusually erudite, and had her life led her in another direction, might have been a great scholar. . . .

Elinor Wylie wrote with extraordinary precision; but it was a precision that never for a moment sacrificed the incalculable turn of phrase, the spontaneously felicitous expression, that intuitive visitation of words that seems to us who have it not as a gift from the gods. Her subconsciousness was constantly preoccupied with the shape, look, colour, and sound of words; just as the rhythms of poetry were matters to her of second nature, and her sometimes intricate interior rhyming, art concealed by art, in the same kind.

William Rose Benét. *The Prose and Poetry of Elinor
Wylie* (Wheaton College). 1934. pp. 12–13

She was again writing poetry and had prepared *Trivial Breath* for summer publication, her first book of verse to be published since *Black Armour* in 1923, five long years. She loved talking to Edna Millay when that lovely creature paid one of her rare visits to town. She would show her the new poems or a Shelley manuscript and, in her own words, watch "the green eyes of a high lyrical poet fill with tears at the evocation of a spirit."

Writing poetry, which was to her the breath of life, had become almost a luxury now that she was so busy with prose. She could still find time to compose it in the tub or on one of her weekly expeditions to the hairdresser which an earthquake or any other act of God could not have persuaded her to forego. Why genius should be supposed to be untidy I don't know, since my most intimate acquaintance with it led me to find it fanatically fastidious. Elinor adored having her tawny thick hair washed and waved and brushed.

Nancy Hoyt. *Elinor Wylie, The Portrait of an
Unknown Lady* (Bobbs-Merrill). 1935. p. 152

She could not bear being less than first in any company. Nothing on earth would do but that a few of her close friends should join her in another room and hear her read some poems—say some poems, as she always put it. Her friends humored her in such tantrums of vanity and went to all lengths in flattering her. She liked flattery as a lizard likes the sun. . . .

. . . I remember her best for these perfect sonnets ["One Person"] and her broken commentary. What she and the sonnets together said was that this final love had come to her like first love, and had dissolved her to her youngest elements, but that she was no less a poet than before, and she could instinctively find ripe, skilful words for emotions which ordinarily go no farther than sighs and tears, timid raptures and pitiful despairs. For once in the world, youth knew and age could. The heart of sixteen spoke with the tongue of forty.

Carl Van Doren. *Harper*. Sept., 1936. pp. 365–6

The sonnets to "One Person" are generally accepted as the consummation of Elinor Wylie's poetry. There certainly is no other group among her poems that leaves so much satisfaction on so many counts. There is a warmth of feeling and directness of thought that is not usual in her work and the circle of experience that is touched upon has a much more general appeal than formerly. Technically the sonnets show a complete mastery of the form. Her experience in handling words in fanciful moods and in light, quick cadences stands her in good stead and she moves perfectly at her ease within the narrow limits of the sonnet structure. But she does not allow it to dissolve in the easy flow of the lines.

H. Lüdeke. *English Studies.* Dec., 1938. p. 248

Elinor Wylie's closest literary kinship, which began in early childhood and lasted throughout her lifetime, developing as an obsession in her life and work, was Percy Bysshe Shelley. The best and the greater part of her prose and poetry reflect his subtle influence. Seven of her eleven essays and sketches in *Fugitive Prose* are a key to her sources and methods in regard to Shelley. In her four novels there is a progression of interest in the same poet: *Jennifer Lorn* contains a background resembling that of the Shelley family; *The Venetian Glass Nephew* stems from some of Shelley's thought and the philosophy of his age; *The Orphan Angel* brings Shelley to life again; and *Mr. Hodge and Mr. Hazard* is a composite picture of Shelley and Elinor Wylie. Of her four volumes of verse, the last two books *Trivial Breath* and *Angels and Earthly Creatures,* which contain her finest poetry, also show an increasing preoccupation with Shelley himself and with his thought.

Julia Cluck. *PMLA.* Sept., 1941. p. 841

Once devoted to the rococo, the artist can break its spell only by shattering himself: what is required is a clean break, a fresh start, a new confronting, however painful and terrified, yet humble and thankful, of reality. The risk of this necessity Miss Wylie's integrity could not have long postponed. She might have shirked it for a while, because, like everybody else, she had her peculiar foolishness; and rather more than most, she might have been spoiled by adulation. Against these risks her besetting sin was her saving virtue, that fierce fine pride. . . .

It is good to hear this voice again, not only because it is familiar, but because even when it is being fantastical or fancy, it is always firm and fine. Apprehensive, yes, but gloomy never; amused, amusing, ironical, exquisite, precise, and proud.

Rolfe Humphries. *Nation.* April 3, 1943. p. 494

If Elinor Wylie's self-absorption may be defined in terms of what the eighteenth century called a "ruling passion," like all overwhelming and consuming emotions it carried with it the conviction of having an importance beyond the mere reflection in a glass; and she conveyed her "passion" with all the art her skill could master. To this day we have unconsciously amusing parodies of her style, poems that speak of proud boys running in the wind, poems of equally proud, fastidious, well-dressed, good-looking women who yearn to possess the "hard heart of a child," to own things that contain the qualities of quicksilver and of crystal—but it is the attitude and not the essence that her imitators have caught—and she, like many a good artist before her, cannot be held responsible for all the inept vanities and empty gestures of the school which followed her.

Horace Gregory and Marya Zaturenska. *A History of American Poetry* (Harcourt). 1946. pp. 284–5

The gifts of Elinor Wylie . . . brought to the feminine lyric a mature emotional richness, as well as an added brilliance of craftsmanship. Mrs. Wylie early caught the note of Eliot's shorter poems. *Nets to Catch the Wind* (1921) revealed, as well, a first-hand apprenticeship to Donne, Herbert, and Marvell. For a time she seemed overwhelmed by her own virtuosity; but she became more tellingly controlled as time went on, and in her last volume achieved a power that was directly structural. Although an undertone of rather inflated romanticism was constantly in evidence, her work as a whole was far more complex than that of any feminine predecessor.

Louise Bogan. *Achievement in American Poetry, 1900–1950* (Henry Regnery). 1951. p. 80

It is in *Angels* . . . that Mrs. Wylie comes into full richness of statement, which ranges from the opening sequence of unusual sonnets entitled "One Person" to the touchingly simple and lovely conclusion of "Little Elegy." This sequence, in which she protests most humbly her love and her sense of her lover's superiority (an idea in a sense foreshadowed in the "Little Sonnet" of *Black Armour* and recurrent in her later work), consolidates her distinction in a form in which she was from the beginning capable. . . . Succeeding poems . . . proceed to broaden her claim to a warmer humanity, a clearer logic, and a greater naturalness than previously evident; even mere technique invites increasing admiration. . . .

Actually, Mrs. Wylie flaunted an individual gift from the first mature volume onward. Initially, she seemed in some respects like a super-sophisticated Blake, though she opened no doors on the chaos he exposed. Unfortunately, manner largely degenerated into mannerism in *Black Armour* and *Trivial Breath,* with intelligence resolving itself into superficial cleverness time and again, so that much of this material suggests unconscious parody of earlier self. Like much shortly succeeding verse which it foreshadows, a great deal of the work has an air of significance which close examination does not justify.

George Brandon Saul. *BNYPL*. Nov., 1965. pp. 619–20

Judging from one of her poems, she longed to be freed from hardness, liberated from marble: "Sleeping Beauty," published after her death, shows a strong man carving the "living rock" and releasing, not the angel that Michelangelo is said to have set free, but "a lady like a lioness." This is Elinor Wylie, for her friends compared her bronze hair to a lion's mane, and she identifies herself with lions in several poems—"Pity me," "Unfinished Ballad," and "A Proud Lady." The image of herself as sculptor's work recalls her way of comparing her characters to dolls. She admired the miniature in art: at the British Museum her principal reading matter was the labels on the Tanagra figurines (or so she assures the readers of her essay "The Pearl Diver").

Celeste Turner Wright. *TCL*. April, 1966. pp. 22–3

See *Collected Poems; Collected Prose* (novels, essays).

YOUNG, STARK (1881–1963)

Nature is one source of Mr. Young's inspiration [in his poems]; man is another. He is not content to seclude himself as a worshiper of nature, a devoted high priest of "these beauteous forms," and allow them to lead him to "the still, sad music of humanity" and to the "something far more deeply interfused." He loves the society and fellowship of man and courts the discipline which comes from the struggle for survival. He loves his solemn, melancholy nature musings, and, like Wordsworth, he often goes apart to sit "the length of half a day" upon some "old gray stone," or lie for hours upon some stubble hill with his face upturned to heaven. But he loves the strife and strain of real life as well. He is so young in years and buoyant in spirit, that he thinks never to grow old. He seeks to sound the joys of enthusiastic youthful friendships, of love, of society, of life in all its relations, even unto death. The "Ode in Mississippi's Troubled Hour," read before the Alumni Society of the University of Mississippi, June, 1904, amply illustrates his interest in questions of the times.

L. W. Payne. *SAQ*. Oct., 1909. p. 319

Something is going on in all of the creative arts in America, and the dawn of creative flowering is always preceded by statement of art principles and close questioning of art technic. Stark Young's *The Flower in Drama* is marked by calmness of judgment, which suggests to me that he has come to the theater as critic after his aesthetic philosophy has been shaken and enriched by the theories of design and form and color introduced into the realm of modern painting by Cézanne, Matisse, and others. In other words, he gives us creative criticism, and, as his book is composed of thoughts that are worth while, yet hung on the very casual moment of the current theater in New York—however high the spots may be according to the general average of our American production—meeting with such lucid understanding of what art comprises, makes us welcome Young in the theater as one of the few who will help the new movement immeasurably by interesting his readers simply, and with no propaganda motive, in reaching a deeper appreciation of the finest things in art.

Montrose J. Moses. *Outlook*. May 9, 1923. p. 853

Acting is of all the arts of the theatre the most difficult to catch and re-create in writing. Generally it eludes the phrase as music escapes it. In

429

the essays brought together in *Glamour,* however, Mr. Young seizes upon its essentials with such an uncanny comprehension of the actor's problems and the actor's art, and writes of them in a style at once so glamorous, revealing and precise, that the volume is lifted to that lean shelf reserved for the few permanently contributive books on the theatre. Behind the strong coloring and "resistant flexibility" of his prose there is a poet's vision and a philosopher's insight. At times he is tempted by his own rhythms, and succumbs to a Southern gift for sound. But more often, and especially in the essay on Duse, and the "Letters from Dead Actors," he writes with a beauty and a penetration unrivaled in the host of books treating the actor's art. At his best, and he is at his best in almost all of *Glamour,* Mr. Young surpasses all contemporary critics when he writes of acting.

John Mason Brown. TA. June, 1925. p. 417

The perception of the characteristic qualities underlying an art is, as Stark Young says, the most useful and constructive aspect of criticism. Especially is this true when such perception is joined to a gift of lucid and stimulating expression. It is this double endowment that makes Stark Young's writings on the theatre not merely important but absorbingly interesting. Not only does he see the point, but he makes it luminously clear and inevitable. His discussions of acting, directing, the wearing of costume, and other aspects of theatre practice are "useful and constructive" and at the same time they fall within Plato's definition of art as the discussion of one thing in terms of another out of which "something appears which was not there before." The something in this case is a sort of celestial text book [*Theatre Practice*] which actually succeeds in the main function of education, that of spurring the mind of the reader into at least a mild activity, in arousing in him a sense of the possibilities of theatric art and in elucidating some of those fundamental points of technique and craftsmanship so generally ignored or forgotten.

Rosamond Gilder. TA. Sept., 1926. p. 647

In *River House* Mr. Stark Young makes a very penetrating study of the Southern tradition. John Dandridge, educated at Princeton and trained for business in St. Louis, marries an ultramodern girl after his mother's death and returns to his ancestral estate, there to live with his father and his aunts. He is well aware of the common tendency to abuse the Southern tradition, to show the only defects of its qualities. But John Dandridge desires a better understanding of the fine old tradition that he and his generation are losing, and this really explains the purpose of Mr. Young's book.

Mr. Young is aware that the ideals and tendencies of our time seem to move in opposition to certain instincts or principles that are deeply rooted in the Southern character. A man's instincts and principles can be changed only slowly, "and as they change they must find some way of harmonizing themselves with the new belief and direction."

Abbott Martin. *SwR*. Jan.-March, 1930. pp. 114–15

Stark Young's *River House* and Thomas Wolfe's *Look Homeward, Angel* are both novels about the South written by Southerners. But a foreigner would not readily discover in the two books reflections of the same civilization. *River House* is a backward glance at a dying culture submerged and overwhelmed not merely by America but by its own Americanized youth. *Look Homeward, Angel* is the saga of a human soul, the soul of a boy who happened to grow up in North Carolina.

Many of Mr. Young's most ardent admirers have doubted whether the novel was his true métier: it has been in his dramatic criticism, his "encaustics," his vignettes that they felt most the force of his personality, a personality rich in artistic sincerity, in restraint, in spiritual discretions. But I think that in *River House* Mr. Young has done a valuable piece of work and one that could have been done in no other form. Who else in America is so well fitted to portray the conflict between the older South and its Americanized offspring? And how surely he has placed his finger on the real tragedy of that conflict: not that—as Major Dandridge of *River House* would have put it—the South was defeated but not beaten, but that Major Dandridge's daughter-in-law did not know how many years it took to get from Fort Sumter to Appomattox.

Stringfellow Barr. *VQR*. April, 1930. p. 310

In much modern prose, even the finest, there is a suggestion of those Japanese flowers that are rooted in no element more stable than water; but in the writing of Stark Young I never lose the feeling of solid substance, of clinging tendrils and rich, dark soil, beneath. I am brought back again and again to the truth that life as a sum and a whole reaches far below the fragmentary surface we call human experience. . . . In these latest stories [*The Street of the Islands*], which are scarcely stories so much as transmitted impressions, the scene is not confined to the old South of the earlier novels. One is tempted to say that the spirit of place has become, for the moment, a rover. Yet underneath all the changing images of the visible world, the antiphonal life is reflected in a multitude of inarticulate lives. The recurring *motif* winds like a strain of music through almost every tale. Life at its best and its worst is more than mere living.

Ellen Glasgow. *SR*. Sept. 7, 1930. p. 157

Stark Young's *So Red the Rose* is a study of the effects of the Civil War on a small civilian segment of the old South. Mr. Young tells of the planter society of Mississippi, a comfortable, highly developed, eccentric lot of people, and his account of them is one long, slow caress. He perhaps imagines that he has written a dispassionate account of the ways and feelings of these cultivated individuals; he does, in fact, make every attempt to be fair, to see all sides of the case. Nevertheless, his story of the Mc-Gehees of Montrose and the Bedfords of Portobello is not truly a history or a novel, but a poem of glorification. He presents us with a group of highly varied individuals, full of quirks, and full of character. If Mr. Young were to be believed, it would appear that even the bores of old Mississippi were amusing. . . . The first glimpse one has of these people is tremendously exciting. For a moment, one thinks that Stark Young has been given miraculous penetration, that he will recreate a dead world in true and living terms. But it is soon evident that he is not interested in truth, but in romance. He quickly gives up the fascinating business of creating people for the more routine job of pleading their cause. After a magnificent two hundred pages, there is no development of character.

Mary McCarthy. Nation. Aug. 8, 1934. p. 167

Stark Young transports us again into the recreated charms of his beloved Southern parishes in most of the short stories that make up his new book, *Feliciana*. The more captious critics try to tell us that the grace of the Feliciana parishes was probably never quite as Mr. Young sees it. They say, more or less boldly, that he is romanticizing the persons and places his ancestors loved. . . . Yet if no such civilization ever graced the earth as that which Mr. Young describes, for example, in "Shadows on Terrebonne," it is a comfort to feel that it could exist even in the mind of an artist of today. That, I think, is of the essence of Stark Young's literary contribution. When the realists are busily examining their internal anatomy or the intricate convolutions of their brains, there is small chance for beauty to emerge in literature unless someone like Mr. Young appoints himself its guardian.

Richard Dana Skinner. Com. Oct. 25, 1935. pp. 645–6

The utmost reach of theatrical experience, the absolute in Mr. Young's critical "system," was suggested in the title of two of his early collections of criticism: *Glamour* and *The Flower in Drama*. *Glamour* is a quality strongly felt, indubitably *there,* which one would find it hard to derive from the mere facts of the situation, just as, by looking at a root and a stalk one would scarcely derive from them, by logical extension, all the glory of a *flower*. What mystics say of their supposed communing with the divine, what we all know of ecstasy in love, seems similar. It is experience that any of the arts might convey, but which Mr. Young has encountered—a few times—in the theatre and in peculiar ways. . . .

A moment of greatness—and greatness comes to us in moments—is a moment when we are brought into a feeling of harmony with all things. Such being Mr. Young's highest expectation it is natural that he praises works and performances in the degree to which they approach such moments. Hence his emphasis upon emotional quality. He speaks of being "stirred and swept and shaken." He uses expressions like "the beat of instincts," "lustre and relief," "the quiver and pulse, the rush and pause," "glow and shimmer and lyric brightness." Such phrases are not scientific terminology. They are based, I should think, on a feeling that in this field supposedly scientific terminology would turn out to be pseudo-scientific jargon. Call Stark Young's writing impressionistic or mannered, if you will. It is an attempt to come closer than criticism usually does to the definition of our responses to works of art.

Eric Bentley. KR. Winter, 1950. pp. 140–1

These reminiscences [*The Pavilion*] by the drama and art critic and author of *So Red the Rose* might be read as a new landscape of the Faulkner country, painted with a more romantic brush. Stark Young's memory has reached back to a childhood spent at Como and Oxford, Mississippi, in the latter part of the nineteenth century, and he has put his emphasis upon white columns rather than upon white tragedies. His book, which carries on a running, interlinear debate with what might be called Manhattan values, is really a defense of the intangibles that departed with the Old South, the tacit agreed-upons that made for gentle living in the distinguished family to which he was born. . . . *The Pavilion* suffers from concretism, an almost adolescent incapacity to abstract realistically from experience, and it also suffers from self-congratulation, but it invokes traditional graces and hard-headed classical insights that no one with culture or imagination would wish to see vanish from the world.

Gerald Sykes. NR. Oct. 22, 1951. p. 19

The death of Stark Young at the age of 81 is an occasion which we have special cause to mourn. As a writer on *The New Republic* for more than 25 years, he initiated, almost singlehandedly, a tradition of serious American theater journalism which set the highest standards of style, sensibility and judgment for contemporaries and for those who were to follow. Young's writings were animated by a fierce, uncompromising love of art. Confronting a fundamentally impure medium still in its puling infancy in America, he continually elbowed aside the artless and the false, to seek the shimmering and the true, emerging like a diver from a sea of meritriciousness, with a pearl in his hand, and proceeding to describe it in delicate, gracious, emotionally eloquent prose.

NR. Jan. 26, 1963. p. 6

See *The Flower in Drama, Glamour, Theatre Practice, Immortal Shadows* (essays); *River House, So Red the Rose* (novels); *The Street of the Islands* (stories); *The Pavilion* (reminiscences).

BIBLIOGRAPHIES

The bibliographies list the major books and plays of the authors included in this work; the dates are of first publication or, in the case of plays, usually of first production. Pamphlets, one-act plays, juveniles, contributions to multi-authored collections, and other minor publications are included only selectively. Stories and articles in periodicals are not included.

GENRE ABBREVIATIONS

a	autobiography	n	novel
b	biography	p	poetry
c	criticism	pd	poetic drama
d	drama	r	reminiscence
e	essay	rd	radio drama
h	history	s	short stories
j	journalism	sk	sketches
m	memoir	t	travel or topography
misc	miscellany	tr	translation

DOROTHY PARKER
1893–1967

(with George S. Chappell and Frank Crowninshield) *High Society,* 1920 (sk); (with Franklin P. Adams) *Men I'm Not Married To,* 1922 (sk); (with Elmer Rice) *Close Harmony,* 1924 (d); *Enough Rope,* 1926 (p); *Sunset Gun,* 1928 (p); *Laments for the Living,* 1930 (s); *Death and Taxes,* 1931 (p); *After Such Pleasures,* 1933 (s); *Collected Poems: Not So Deep As a Well,* 1936; *Here Lies* (collected stories), 1939

V. L. PARRINGTON
1871–1929

Sinclair Lewis: Our Own Diogenes, 1927 (c); *Main Currents in American Thought,* I, 1927; II, 1927, III, 1930; one volume edition, 1939 (h)

KENNETH PATCHEN
1911–

Before the Brave, 1936 (p); *First Will and Testament,* 1939 (p); *The Journal of Albion Moonlight,* 1941 (m); *Teeth of the Lion,* 1942 (p); *The Dark Kingdom,* 1942 (p); *Cloth of the Tempest,* 1943 (p); *Memoirs of a Shy Pornographer,* 1945 (n); *An Astonished Eye Looks Out of the Air,* 1945 (p); *Selected Poems,* 1946 (enlarged edition, 1958); *Outlaw of the Lowest Planet* (selections), 1946 (p); *Sleepers Awake,* 1946 (e); *A Letter to God,* 1946 (e); *Pictures of Life and Death,* 1947 (p); *They Keep Riding Down All the Time,* 1947 (p); *Panels for the Walls of Heaven,* 1947 (p); *See You in the Morning,* 1948 (n); *Red Wine and Yellow Hair,* 1949 (p); *To Say If You Love Someone,* 1949 (p); *The Famous Boating Party,* 1953 (p); *Fables,* 1953 (s); *Orchards, Thrones and Caravans,* 1955 (p); *Glory Never Guesses,* 1955 (p); *A Surprise for the Bagpipe Player,* 1956 (p); *Poems of Humor and Protest,* 1956; *Poemscapes,* 1956; *Hurrah for Anything,* 1957 (p); *When We Were Here Together,* 1957 (p); *Because It Is,* 1959 (p); *Selected Love Poems,* 1960; *But Even So,* 1965 (p); *Doubleheader (Poemscapes* and *Hurrah for Anything),* 1966 (p); *Hallelujah Anyway,* 1966 (p); *Like Fun I'll Tell You,* 1966 (p); *Collected Poems,* 1968

WALKER PERCY
1916–

The Moviegoer, 1961 (n); *The Last Gentleman,* 1966 (n)

KATHERINE ANNE PORTER
1894–

Outline of Mexican Popular Arts and Crafts, 1922 (e); *Flowering Judas*, 1930 (s); *Hacienda*, 1934 (s); *Flowering Judas* (enlarged edition), 1935 (s); *Noon Wine*, 1937 (s); *Pale Horse, Pale Rider* (with *Old Mortality* and *Noon Wine*), 1939 (s); *The Leaning Tower*, 1944 (s); *The Days Before*, 1952 (e); *The Old Order*, 1955 (s); *Ship of Fools*, 1962 (n); *Collected Stories*, 1965

EZRA POUND
1885–

A Lume Spento, 1908 (p); *A Quinzaine for This Yule*, 1908 (p); *Exultations*, 1909 (p); *Personae*, 1909 (p); *Provenca* (selected poems), 1910 (p); *The Spirit of Romance*, 1910 (c); *Canzoni*, 1911 (p); *Ripostes*, 1912 (p); *The Sonnets and Ballate of Guido Cavalcanti*, 1912 (tr); *Canzoni & Ripostes*, 1913 (p); *Personae & Exultations*, 1913 (p); *Cathay*, 1915 (tr); *Lustra*, 1916 (p); *Gaudier-Brzeska*, 1916 (b); (with Ernest Fenellosa) *Certain Noble Plays of Japan*, 1916 (tr); (with Ernest Fenellosa) *'Noh,' or, Accomplishment, A Study of the Classical Stage of Japan*, 1916 (c); *Lustra, with Earlier Poems*, 1917 (p); *Dialogues of Fontenelle*, 1917 (tr); *A Study of French Modern Poets*, 1918 (c); *Pavannes and Divagations*, 1918 (e); *The Fourth Canto*, 1919 (p); *Quia Pauper Amavi*, 1919 (p); *Hugh Selwyn Mauberley*, 1920 (p); *Umbra* (collected early poems and translations), 1920; *Instigations*, 1921 (c); *Poems, 1918–1921*, 1921; *The Natural Philosophy of Love* (by Remy de Gourmont), 1922 (tr); *Indiscretions*, 1923 (e); *Antheil and the Treatise on Harmony*, 1924 (e); *A Draft of XVI Cantos*, 1925 (p); *Personae* (collected poems), 1926; *A Draft of the Cantos 17-27*, 1927 (p); *Selected Poems* (edited by T. S. Eliot), 1928; *Ta Hio*, 1928 (tr); *A Draft of XXX Cantos*, 1930 (p); *Imaginary Letters*, 1930 (e); *How To Read*, 1931 (c); *Prolegomena I*, 1932 (c); *ABC of Economics*, 1933 (e); *ABC of Reading*, 1934 (c); *Eleven New Cantos, XXXI-XLI*, 1934 (p); (English edition, *A Draft of Cantos XXXI-XLI*, 1935); *Homage to Sextus Propertius*, 1934 (tr); *Make It New*, 1934 (e); *Jefferson and/or Mussolini*, 1935 (e); *Social Credit: An Impact*, 1935 (e); *The Fifth Decad of Cantos*, 1937 (p); *Polite Essays*, 1937; *Culture*, 1938 (e) (English edition, *Guide to Kulchur*); *Cantos LII-LXXI*, 1940 (p); *The Unwobbling Pivot* and *The Great Digest*, 1947 (tr); *If This Be Treason*, 1948 (e); *The Pisan Cantos*, 1948 (p); *Cantos* (1-71, 74-84), 1948 (p); *Personae: Collected Poems* (revised edition), 1949; *Selected Poems*, 1949; *Section: Rock-Drill: 85-95 de los cantares*, 1949 (p); *Money pamphlets*, 1950–1952 (e); *Letters*, 1950; *Patria Mia*, 1950 (e); *Translations*, 1954; *Liter-*

ary Essays, 1954; *The Classic Anthology Defined by Confucius,* 1954 (tr); *Women of Trachis,* 1956 (tr); *Thrones: 96-109 de los cantares,* 1959 (p); *Impact,* 1960 (e); *A Lume Spento and Other Early Poems,* 1965; *Cavalcanti Poems,* 1966 (tr, e); *Pound/Joyce,* 1967 (letters, e); *Drafts and Fragments of Cantos CX-CXVI,* 1968 (p)

J. F. POWERS
1917–

The Prince of Darkness, 1947 (s); *The Presence of Grace,* 1956 (s); *Morte D'Urban,* 1962 (n)

THOMAS PYNCHON
1936–

V., 1963 (n); *The Crying of Lot 49,* 1966 (n)

PHILIP RAHV
1908–

(co-editor with William Phillips) *The Partisan Reader,* 1946; *Image and Idea,* 1949 (c); *The Myth and the Powerhouse,* 1965 (c)

JOHN CROWE RANSOM
1888–

Poems About God, 1919; *Armageddon,* 1923 (p); *Chills and Fever,* 1924 (p); *Grace After Meat,* 1924 (p); *Two Gentlemen in Bonds,* 1927 (p); *God Without Thunder,* 1930 (e); (with others) *I'll Take My Stand,* 1930 (e); *The World's Body,* 1938 (c); *The New Criticism,* 1941 (c); *Selected Poems,* 1945; *Poems and Essays,* 1955; *Selected Poems* (revised and enlarged edition), 1963

MARJORIE KINNAN RAWLINGS
1896–1953

South Moon Under, 1933 (n); *Golden Apples,* 1935 (n); *The Yearling,* 1938 (n); *When the Whippoorwill,* 1940 (s); *Cross Creek,* 1942 (a); *Cross Creek Cookery,* 1942 (cookbook); *Jacob's Ladder,* 1950 (n); *The Sojourner,* 1952 (n); *The Marjorie Rawlings Reader,* 1956

JOHN REED
1887–1920

Insurgent Mexico, 1914 (j); The War in Eastern Europe, 1916 (j); Tamburlaine, 1917 (p); Ten Days That Shook the World, 1919 (j); Daughter of the Revolution, 1927 (s, sk)

KENNETH REXROTH
1905–

In What Hour, 1940 (p); The Phoenix and the Tortoise, 1944 (p); The Signature of All Things, 1949 (p); The Art of Worldly Wisdom, 1949 (p); Beyond the Mountains, 1951 (pd); The Dragon and the Unicorn, 1952 (p); One Hundred Poems from the Japanese, 1955 (tr); Thirty Spanish Poems, 1956 (tr); In Defense of the Earth, 1956 (p); One Hundred Poems from the Chinese, 1956 (tr); Bird in the Bush, 1959 (e); The Phoenix and the Tortoise, 1959 (p); Assays, 1961 (e); Poems from the Greek Anthology, 1962 (tr); Natural Numbers, 1963 (p); The Homestead Called Damascus, 1963 (p); An Autobiographical Novel, 1966 (n); The Collected Shorter Poems, 1967; The Heart's Garden the Garden's Heart, 1968 (p); Collected Longer Poems, 1968

ELMER RICE
1892–1967

On Trial, 1914 (d); The Home of the Free, 1917 (d); For the Defence, 1919 (d); (with Hatcher Hughes) Wake Up, Jonathan! 1921 (d); The Adding Machine, 1923 (d); (with Dorothy Parker) Close Harmony, 1924 (d); (with Philip Barry) Cock Robin, 1928 (d); Street Scene, 1929 (d); The Subway, 1929 (d); See Naples and Die, 1929 (d); A Voyage to Purilia, 1930 (n); The Left Bank, 1931 (d); Counsellor-at-Law, 1931 (d); The House in Blind Alley, 1932 (d); Black Sheep, 1932 (d); Plays, 1933; We the People, 1933 (d); Judgment Day, 1934 (d); Between Two Worlds, 1934 (d); The Passing of Chow-Chow, 1934 (d); Three Plays Without Words (Landscape with Figures, Rus in Urbe, Exterior), 1934; Not for Children, 1935 (d); Two Plays (Between Two Worlds, Not for Children), 1935; Other Plays and Not for Children, 1935; Imperial City, 1937 (n); American Landscape, 1939 (d); Two on an Island, 1940 (d); Journey to Jerusalem, 1940 (d); Flight to the West, 1940 (d); A New Life, 1943 (d); Dream Girl, 1945 (d); The Show Must Go On, 1949 (n); Seven Plays, 1950; The Grand Tour, 1951 (d); The Winner, 1954 (d); Cue for Passion, 1958 (d); The Living Theatre, 1959 (e); Love Among the Ruins, 1963 (d); Minority Report, 1963 (a); Three Plays, 1965

ADRIENNE RICH
1929–

A Change of World, 1951 (p); *The Diamond Cutters,* 1955 (p); *Snap-shots of a Daughter-in-Law,* 1962 (p); *Necessities of Life,* 1966 (p)

CONRAD RICHTER
1890–1968

Brothers of No Kin, 1924 (s); *Human Vibration,* 1925 (e); *Principles in Bio-Physics,* 1927 (e); *Early Americana,* 1936 (s); *The Sea of Grass,* 1937 (n); *The Trees,* 1940 (n); *Tacey Cromwell,* 1942 (n); *The Free-man,* 1943 (n); *The Fields,* 1946 (n); *Smoke Over the Prairie,* 1947 (s); *Always Young and Fair,* 1947 (n); *The Town,* 1950 (n); *The Light in the Forest,* 1953 (n); *The Mountain on the Desert,* 1955 (e); *The Lady,* 1957 (n); *The Waters of Kronos,* 1960 (n); *A Simple Honorable Man,* 1962 (n); *The Grandfathers,* 1964 (n); *A Country of Strangers,* 1966 (n); *The Awakening Land (The Trees, The Fields, The Town),* 1966 (n); *The Aristocrat,* 1968 (n)

ELIZABETH MADOX ROBERTS
1886–1941

In the Great Steep's Garden, 1915 (p); *Under the Tree,* 1922 (p); *The Time of Man,* 1926 (n); *My Heart and My Flesh,* 1927 (n); *Jingling in the Wind,* 1928 (n); *The Great Meadow,* 1930 (n); *A Buried Treasure,* 1931 (n); *The Haunted Mirror,* 1932 (s); *He Sent Forth a Raven,* 1935 (n); *Black Is My True Love's Hair,* 1938 (n); *Song in the Meadow,* 1940 (p); *Not by Strange Gods,* 1941 (n)

KENNETH ROBERTS
1885–1957

Europe's Morning After, 1921 (t); *Sun Hunting,* 1922 (t); *Why Europe Leaves Home,* 1922 (t); (with others) *The Collector's Whatnot,* 1923 (sk); *Concentrated New England,* 1924 (b); *Black Magic,* 1924 (e); *Florida Loafing,* 1925 (t); *Florida,* 1926 (t); *Antiquamania,* 1928 (sk); *Arundel,* 1930 (n); *The Lively Lady,* 1931 (n); *Rabble in Arms,* 1933 (n); *Captain Caution,* 1934 (n); (with Robert Garland) *The Brother-hood of Man,* 1934 (d); *For Authors Only,* 1935 (e); *It Must Be Your Tonsils,* 1936 (sk); *Northwest Passage,* 1937 (n); *Trending into Maine,* 1938 (e); *Oliver Wiswell,* 1940 (n); (with Anna M. Roberts) *Moreau de St. Méry's American Journey,* 1947 (tr); *Lydia Bailey,* 1947 (n); *I*

Wanted To Write, 1949 (m); *Henry Gross and His Dowsing Rod,* 1951 (e); *The Seventh Sense,* 1953 (e); *Boon Island,* 1956 (n); *The Battle of Cowpens,* 1958 (h); *Water Unlimited,* 1957 (e)

EDWIN ARLINGTON ROBINSON
1869–1935

The Torrent and the Night Before, 1896 (p); *The Children of the Night,* 1897 (p); *Captain Craig,* 1902 (p); *The Town Down the River,* 1910 (p); *Van Zorn,* 1914 (d); *The Porcupine,* 1915 (d); *The Man Against the Sky,* 1916 (p); *Merlin,* 1917 (p); *Lancelot,* 1920 (p); *The Three Taverns,* 1920 (p); *Avon's Harvest,* 1921 (p); *Collected Poems,* 1921; *Roman Bartholow,* 1923 (p); *The Man Who Died Twice,* 1924 (p); *Dionysus in Doubt,* 1925 (p); *Tristram,* 1927 (p); *Sonnets 1889–1927,* 1928; *Cavender's House,* 1929 (p); *Collected Poems,* 1929; *The Glory of the Nightingales,* 1930 (p); *Selected Poems,* 1931; *Matthias at the Door,* 1931 (p); *Nicodemus,* 1932 (p); *Talifer,* 1933 (p); *Amaranth,* 1934 (p); *King Jasper,* 1935 (p); *Collected Poems,* 1937; *Selected Letters,* 1940; *Letters of Edwin Arlington Robinson to Howard George Schmitt,* 1943; *Untriangulated Stars,* 1947 (letters); *Tilbury Town,* 1953 (p); *Selected Early Poems and Letters,* 1960; *Selected Poems,* 1965; *Letters to Edith Brown,* 1968

THEODORE ROETHKE
1908–1963

Open House, 1941 (p); *The Lost Son and Other Poems,* 1948; *Praise to the End!* 1951; *The Waking: Poems 1933–1953,* 1953; *Words for the Wind* (collected poems), 1957; *I Am! Says the Lamb,* 1961 (p); *Party at the Zoo,* 1963 (p); *Sequence, Sometimes Metaphysical,* 1964 (p); *The Far Field,* 1964 (p); *On the Poet and His Craft,* 1965 (e); *Collected Poems,* 1966; *Selected Letters,* 1968

OLE RÖLVAAG
1876–1931

Giants in the Earth, 1927 (n); *Peder Victorious,* 1929 (n); *Pure Gold,* 1930 (n); *Their Fathers' God,* 1931 (n); *Boat of Longing,* 1933 (n)

HENRY ROTH
1906–

Call It Sleep, 1935 (n)

PHILIP ROTH
1933–

Goodbye, Columbus, 1959 (n, s); Letting Go, 1962 (n); When She Was Good, 1967 (n)

CONSTANCE ROURKE
1885–1941

Trumpets of Jubilee, 1927 (b); Troupers of the Gold Coast, 1928 (b); American Humor, 1931 (c); Davy Crockett, 1934 (b); Audubon, 1936 (b); Charles Sheeler, Artist in the American Tradition, 1938 (b); The Roots of American Culture, 1942 (e)

MURIEL RUKEYSER
1913–

Theory of Flight, 1935 (p); U.S.1, 1938 (p); A Turning Wind, 1939 (p); Wake Island, 1942 (p); Willard Gibbs, 1942 (b); Beast in View, 1944 (p); The Children's Orchard, 1947 (p); The Green Wave, 1948 (p); Orpheus, 1949 (p); The Life of Poetry, 1949 (e); Elegies, 1949 (p); Selected Poems, 1951; One Life, 1957 (b); Houdini, 1957 (b); Body of Waking, 1958 (p); The Speaking Tree, 1961 (p); Poems Selected and New, 1961; Sun Stone (by Octavio Paz), 1962 (tr); Waterlily Fire (collected poems), 1962; Selected Poems of Octavio Paz, 1964 (tr); The Orgy, 1965 (n); The Speed of Darkness, 1968 (p)

DAMON RUNYON
1880–1946

Tents of Trouble, 1911 (p); Rhymes of the Firing Line, 1912 (p); Guys and Dolls, 1931 (s); Blue Plate Special, 1934 (s); Money from Home, 1935 (s); Best of Runyon, 1938 (s); Take It Easy, 1938 (s); Omnibus, 1939 (s); My Old Man, 1939 (e); My Wife Ethel, 1940 (s); Runyon à la Carte, 1944; In Our Town, 1946 (s); Runyon First and Last, 1949; A Treasury of Damon Runyon, 1958

J. D. SALINGER
1919–

Catcher in the Rye, 1951 (n); Nine Stories, 1953 (s); Franny and Zooey, 1961 (s); Raise High the Roof Beam, Carpenters, and Seymour—an Introduction, 1963 (s)

CARL SANDBURG
1878–1967

In Reckless Ecstasy, 1904 (misc); *Chicago Poems,* 1916; *Cornhuskers,* 1918 (p); *The Chicago Race Riots,* 1919 (e); *Smoke and Steel,* 1920 (p); *Rootabaga Stories,* 1922 (juvenile); *Slabs of the Sunburnt West,* 1922 (p); *Rootabaga Pigeons,* 1923 (juvenile); *Selected Poems,* 1926; *Abraham Lincoln: The Prairie Years,* 1926 (b); (editor) *The American Songbag,* 1927; *Good Morning, America,* 1928 (p); *Steichen the Photographer,* 1929 (b); *Potato Face,* 1930 (juvenile); *Mary Lincoln, Wife and Widow,* 1932 (b); *The People, Yes,* 1936 (p); *Abraham Lincoln: The War Years,* 1939 (b); *Bronze Wood,* 1941 (p); *Storm over the Land,* 1942 (h); *Home Front Memo,* 1943 (j); (with Frederick Hill Meserve) *The Photographs of Abraham Lincoln,* 1944 (e); *Remembrance Rock,* 1948 (n); *Lincoln Collector,* 1949 (b); (editor) *The New American Songbag,* 1950; *Complete Poems,* 1950; *Always the Young Strangers,* 1953 (a); *Abraham Lincoln* (condensed and revised), 1954 (b); *The Sandburg Range,* 1957 (misc); *Harvest Poems, 1910–1960,* 1960; *Six New Poems and a Parable,* 1961; *Honey and Salt,* 1963 (p); *Letters,* 1968

GEORGE SANTAYANA
1863–1952

Sonnets and Other Verses, 1894 (enlarged edition, 1896); *The Sense of Beauty,* 1896 (e); *Lucifer,* 1899 (pd) (revised edition, 1924); *Interpretations of Poetry and Religion,* 1900 (e); *A Hermit of Carmel,* 1901 (p); *The Life of Reason,* 1905–1906 (e) (revised edition, 1954); (with Emily Shaw Forman and Marie Agathe Clarke) *The Complete Writings of Alfred de Musset,* 1907 (tr); *Three Philosophical Poets,* 1910 (c); *Winds of Doctrine,* 1913 (e); *Egotism in German Philosophy,* 1916 (e) (revised edition, 1940); *Character and Opinion in the United States,* 1920 (e); (with others) *Essays in Critical Realism,* 1920; *Little Essays* (selected from the works), 1920; *Soliloquies in England,* 1922 (e); *Poems,* 1923; *Scepticism and Animal Faith,* 1923 (e); *Dialogues in Limbo,* 1926 (e); *Platonism and the Spiritual Life,* 1927 (e); *The Realm of Essence,* 1927 (e); *The Realm of Matter,* 1930 (e); *The Genteel Tradition at Bay,* 1931 (e); *Some Turns of Thought in Modern Philosophy,* 1933 (e); *The Last Puritan,* 1935 (n); *Obiter Scripta,* 1936 (e); *The Philosophy of Santayana* (selections), 1936; *Works,* 1936–1940; *The Realm of Truth,* 1938 (e); *The Realm of Spirit,* 1940 (e); *Realms of Being (The Realm of Essence, The Realm of Matter, The Realm of Truth, The Realm of Spirit),* 1942 (e); *Persons and Places: The Background of My Life,* 1944 (a); *The Middle Span,* 1945 (a); *The Idea of*

Christ in the Gospels, 1946 (e); *Dialogues in Limbo* (enlarged edition), 1948 (e); *Atoms of Thought* (selected passages), 1950; *Dominations and Powers*, 1951 (e); *My Host the World*, 1953 (a); *The Poet's Testament: Poems and Two Plays*, 1953; *Letters*, 1955; *Essays in Literary Criticism*, 1956; *The Idler and His Works and Other Essays*, 1957; *Persons and Places* (*The Background of My Life, The Middle Span, My Host the World*); 1963 (a); *George Santayana's America*, 1967 (e); *The Genteel Tradition*, 1967 (e); *Selected Critical Writings*, 1968

WILLIAM SAROYAN
1908–

The Daring Young Man on the Flying Trapeze, 1934 (s); *Inhale and Exhale*, 1936 (s); *Three Times Three*, 1936 (s); *Little Children*, 1937 (s); *Love, Here Is My Hat*, 1938 (s); *The Trouble With Tigers*, 1938 (s); *Peace, It's Wonderful*, 1939 (s); *My Name Is Aram*, 1940 (s); *Three Plays* (*My Heart's in the Highlands, The Time of Your Life, Love's Old Sweet Song*), 1940; *Three Plays* (*The Beautiful People, Sweeney in the Trees, Across the Board on Tomorrow Morning*), 1941; *Razzle-Dazzle*, 1942 (d); *The Human Comedy*, 1943 (n); *Dear Baby*, 1944 (s); *Get Away Old Man*, 1944 (d); *The Adventures of Wesley Jackson*, 1946 (n); *Jim Dandy*, 1946 (d); *Don't Go Away Mad*, 1946 (d); *The Saroyan Special*, 1948 (s); *Don't Go Away Mad and Other Plays*, 1949; *The Assyrian*, 1950 (s); *Twin Adventures* (*The Adventures of Wesley Jackson* and *Diary*), 1950 (n, m); *Rock Wagram*, 1951 (n); *Tracy's Tiger*, 1951 (n); *The Bicycle Rider in Beverly Hills*, 1952 (a); *The Laughing Matter*, 1953 (n); *The Whole Voyald*, 1956 (s); *Mama, I Love You*, 1956 (n); *Papa, You're Crazy*, 1957 (n); *A William Saroyan Reader*, 1958; *The Cave Dwellers*, 1958 (d); *Here Comes, There Goes, You Know Who*, 1961 (a); *Not Dying*, 1963 (a); *Boys and Girls Together*, 1963 (n); *After Thirty Years: The Daring Young Man on the Flying Trapeze*, 1964 (s); *One Day in the Afternoon of the World*, 1964 (n); *Short Drive, Sweet Chariot*, 1966 (t); *I Used to Believe I Had Forever. Now I'm Not So Sure*, 1968 (misc)

MAY SARTON
1912–

Encounter in April, 1937 (p); *The Single Hound*, 1938 (n); *Inner Landscape*, 1939 (p); *The Bridge of Years*, 1946 (n); *Underground River*, 1947 (d); *The Lion and the Rose*, 1948 (p); *Shadow of a Man*, 1950 (n); *A Shower of Summer Days*, 1952 (n); *The Land of Silence*, 1953 (p); *Faithful Are the Wounds*, 1955 (n); *The Fur Person*, 1957 (n); *In Time Like Air*, 1957 (p); *The Birth of a Grandfather*, 1957 (n); *I Knew a Phoenix*, 1959 (a); *Cloud, Stone, Sun, Vine*, 1961 (p); *The Small*

Room, 1961 (n); *Joanna and Ulysses*, 1963 (n); *Mrs. Stevens Hears the Mermaids Singing*, 1965 (n); *Miss Pickthorn and Mr. Hare*, 1966 (fable); *A Private Mythology*, 1966 (p); *Plant Dreaming Deep*, 1968 (m)

MURRAY SCHISGAL
1926–

Knit One, Purl Two, 1963 (d); *The Typists*, 1963 (d); *The Tiger*, 1963 (d); *Luv*, 1965 (d); *Fragments, Windows, and Other Plays*, 1965; *Jimmy Shine*, 1968 (d)

BUDD SCHULBERG
1914–

What Makes Sammy Run? 1941 (n); *The Harder They Fall*, 1947 (n); *The Disenchanted*, 1950 (n); *Some Faces in the Crowd*, 1953 (s); *Waterfront*, 1955 (n); *A Face in the Crowd*, 1957 (screenplay); *Across the Everglades*, 1958 (screenplay); (with Harvey Breit) *The Disenchanted*, 1959 (d); (editor) *From the Ashes: Voices of Watts*, 1967

DELMORE SCHWARTZ
1913–1966

In Dreams Begin Responsibilities, 1939 (misc); *A Season in Hell*, 1939 (tr); *Shenandoah*, 1941 (pd); *Genesis*, 1943 (p); *The World Is a Wedding*, 1948 (s); *Vaudeville for a Princess*, 1950 (p); *Summer Knowledge*, 1959 (p); *Successful Love*, 1961 (s)

WINFIELD TOWNLEY SCOTT
1910–1968

Biography for Traman, 1937 (p); *Wind the Clock*, 1941 (p); *The Sword on the Table*, 1942 (p); *To Marry Strangers*, 1945 (p); *Mr. Whittier and Other Poems*, 1948; *Dark Sister*, 1958 (p); *Scrimshaw*, 1959 (p); *Exiles and Fabrications*, 1961 (e); *Collected Poems*, 1962; *Change of Weather*, 1964 (p); *New and Selected Poems*, 1967

ANNE SEXTON
1928–

To Bedlam and Part Way Back, 1960 (p); *All My Pretty Ones*, 1962 (p); *Live or Die*, 1966 (p); (with Thomas Kinsella and Douglas Livingstone) *Poems*, 1968

KARL SHAPIRO
1913–

Person, Place and Thing, 1942 (p); *V-Letter*, 1944 (p); *Essay on Rime*, 1945 (p, c); *Trial of a Poet*, 1947 (p); *Poems 1940–1953*, 1953; *Beyond Criticism*, 1953 (e); *Poems of a Jew*, 1958 (p); *In Defense of Ignorance*, 1960 (e); *The Bourgeois Poet*, 1964 (p); *Primer for Poets*, 1965 (c); *Selected Poems*, 1968; *This Age of Betrayal*, 1968 (e); *The Abolished Children*, 1968 (e)

IRWIN SHAW
1913–

Bury the Dead, 1936 (d); *Siege*, 1937 (d); *The Gentle People*, 1939 (d); *Quiet City*, 1939 (d); *Sailor Off the Bremen*, 1939 (s); *Retreat to Pleasure*, 1940 (d); *Welcome to the City*, 1942 (s); *Sons and Soldiers*, 1943 (d); *The Assassin*, 1945 (d); *Act of Faith*, 1946 (s); (with Peter Viertel) *The Survivors*, 1948 (d); *The Young Lions*, 1948 (n); *Mixed Company* (collected stories), 1950; (with Robert Capa) *Report on Israel*, 1950 (j); *Brooklyn*, 1950 (t); *The Troubled Air*, 1951 (n); *Lucy Crown*, 1956 (n); *Tip on a Dead Jockey*, 1957 (s); *Two Weeks in Another Town*, 1960 (n); *Selected Short Stories*, 1961; *In the Company of Dolphins*, 1964 (t); *Children From Their Games*, 1965 (d); *Voices of a Summer Day*, 1965 (n); *Love on a Dark Street*, 1965 (s)

ROBERT SHERWOOD
1896–1955

The Road to Rome, 1927 (d); *The Love Nest*, 1927 (d); *The Queen's Husband*, 1928 (d); *Waterloo Bridge*, 1930 (d); *This Is New York*, 1930 (d); *Reunion in Vienna*, 1931 (d); *The Virtuous Knight*, 1931 (n) (English edition, *Unending Crusade*, 1932); *The Petrified Forest*, 1935 (d); *Idiot's Delight*, 1936 (d); *Tovarich*, 1937 (d, tr); *Abe Lincoln in Illinois*, 1939 (d); *Revelation*, 1941; *There Shall Be No Night*, 1941 (d); *The Rugged Path*, 1946 (d); *The Best Years of our Lives*, 1946 (screenplay); *Roosevelt and Hopkins*, 1948 (h); (with Moss Hart) *Miss Liberty*, 1949 (d); *Small War on Murray Hill*, 1957 (d)

NEIL SIMON
1927–

(with Daniel Simon) *Come Blow Your Horn*, 1961 (d); *Barefoot in the Park*, 1963 (d); *The Odd Couple*, 1965 (d); *The Star-Spangled Girl*, 1967 (d); *Plaza Suite*, 1968 (d); *Promises, Promises*, 1968 (d)

LOUIS SIMPSON
1923–

The Arrivistes, 1950 (p); Good News of Death, 1955 (p); A Dream of Governors, 1959 (p); At the End of the Open Road, 1963 (p); Selected Poems, 1966; An Introduction to Poetry, 1967 (c)

UPTON SINCLAIR
1878–1968

Springtime and Harvest, 1901 (n) (also published as King Midas, 1901); The Journal of Arthur Stirling, 1903 (n); Prince Hagen, 1903 (n); Manassas, 1904 (n) (also published as Theirs Be the Guilt, 1959); A Captain of Industry, 1906 (n); The Jungle, 1906 (n); What Life Means to Me, 1906 (e); The Industrial Republic, 1907 (e); The Overman, 1907 (n); The Metropolis, 1908 (n); The Moneychangers, 1908 (n); (with Michael Williams) Good Health and How We Won It, 1909 (e) (English edition, The Art of Health); Prince Hagen, 1909 (d); Samuel the Seeker, 1910 (n); The Fasting Cure, 1911 (e); Love's Pilgrimage, 1911 (n); Plays of Protest, 1912; Damaged Goods, 1913 (n); Sylvia, 1913 (n); Sylvia's Marriage, 1914 (n); King Coal, 1917 (n); The Profits of Religion, 1918 (e); Jimmie Higgins, 1919 (n); The Brass Check, 1919 (e); 100%, The Story of a Patriot, 1920 (n) (English edition, The Spy, 1921); Mind and Body, 1921 (e); They Call Me Carpenter, 1922 (n); Love and Society, 1922 (e); Hell, 1923 (d); The Goose-Step, 1923 (e); The Millenium, 1924 (n); The Pot Boiler, 1924 (d); The Naturewoman, 1924 (d); Singing Jailbirds, 1924 (d); The Goslings, 1924 (e); My Life and Diet, 1924 (e); Mammonart, 1925 (e); Bill Porter, 1925 (d); What's the Use of Books, 1926 (e); The Spokesman's Secretary, 1926 (sk); Oil!, 1927 (n); Money Writes, 1927 (e); Boston, 1928 (n); Oil!, 1929 (d); Mountain City, 1930 (n); Mental Radio, 1930 (e); What Is Socialism and Culture? 1931 (e); Roman Holiday, 1931 (n); The Wet Parade, 1931 (n); American Outpost, 1932 (r) (English edition, Candid Reminiscences); I, Governor of California and How I Ended Poverty, 1933 (e); Upton Sinclair Presents William Fox, 1933 (e); The Way Out, 1933 (e); An Upton Sinclair Anthology, 1934; The EPIC Plan for California, 1934 (e); The Book of Love, 1934 (e); I, Candidate for Governor: and How I Got Licked, 1935 (e); Depression Island, 1935 (d); Co-op, 1936 (n); Wally for Queen, 1936 (d); What God Means to Me, 1936 (e); Little Steel, 1938 (n); Our Lady, 1938 (n); (with Eugene Lyons) Terror in Russia? 1938 (e); Marie Antoinette, 1939 (d); World's End, 1940 (n); Between Two Worlds, 1941 (n); Dragon's Teeth, 1942 (n); Wide Is the Gate, 1943 (n); Presidential Agent, 1944 (n); Dragon Harvest, 1945 (n); A World to Win,

1946 (n); *Presidential Mission*, 1947 (n); *One Clear Call*, 1948 (n); *A Giant's Strength*, 1948 (d); *O Shepherd, Speak!*, 1949 (n); *Another Pamela*, 1950 (n); *The Enemy Had It Too*, 1950 (d); *A Personal Jesus*, 1952 (e); *The Return of Lanny Budd*, 1953 (n); *What Didymus Did*, 1954 (n) (American edition, *It Happened to Didymus*, 1958); *Cup of Fury*, 1956 (e); *My Lifetime in Letters*, 1960 (letters); *Affectionately, Eve*, 1961

W. D. SNODGRASS
1926–

Heart's Needle, 1959 (p); *After Experience*, 1968 (p)

SUSAN SONTAG
1933–

The Benefactor, 1963 (n); *Against Interpretation*, 1966 (e); *Death Kit*, 1967 (n)

JEAN STAFFORD
1915–

Boston Adventure, 1944 (n); *The Mountain Lion*, 1947 (n); *The Catherine Wheel*, 1952 (n); *Children Are Bored on Sunday*, 1953 (s); *Bad Characters*, 1964 (s); *A Mother in History*, 1966 (j)

WILBUR DANIEL STEELE
1886–

Storm, 1914 (n); *Land's End*, 1918 (s); *The Shame Dance*, 1923 (s); *Isles of the Blest*, 1924 (n); *The Giants' Stair*, 1924 (d); *The Terrible Woman and Other One Act Plays*, 1925 (d); *Taboo*, 1925 (n); *Urkey Island*, 1926 (s); *The Man Who Saw Through Heaven*, 1927 (s); *Meat*, 1928 (n) (English edition, *The Third Generation*, 1929); *Tower of Sand*, 1929 (s); *Undertow*, 1930 (n); *Diamond Wedding*, 1931 (s); (with Norma Mitchell) *Post Road*, 1935 (d); *Sound of Rowlocks*, 1938 (n); *That Girl from Memphis*, 1945 (n); *Best Stories*, 1946; *Diamond Wedding*, 1950 (n); *Their Town*, 1952 (n); *The Way to the Gold*, 1955 (n)

LINCOLN STEFFENS
1866–1936

The Shame of the Cities, 1904 (j); *The Struggle for Self-Government*, 1906 (e); *John Reed: Under the Kremlin*, 1920 (b); *Moses in Red*, 1926 (e); *Autobiography*, 1931; *Lincoln Steffens Speaking*, 1936 (misc); *Letters*, 1938; *The World of Lincoln Steffens*, 1962

WALLACE STEGNER
1909–

Remembering Laughter, 1937 (n); *The Potter's House*, 1938 (n); *On a Darkling Plain*, 1940 (n); *Fire and Ice*, 1941 (n); *Mormon Country*, 1942 (t); *The Big Rock Candy Mountain*, 1943 (n); *Second Growth*, 1947 (n); *The Women on the Wall*, 1950 (s); *The Preacher and the Slave*, 1950 (n); *Beyond the Hundredth Meridian*, 1954 (h); *The City of the Living*, 1956 (s); *A Shooting Star*, 1961 (n); *Wolf Willow*, 1962 (n); (with others) *Four Portraits and One Subject: Bernard DeVoto*, 1963 (b); *The Gathering of Zion*, 1964 (n); *All the Little Live Things*, 1967 (n)

GERTRUDE STEIN
1874–1946

Three Lives, 1909 (s); *Tender Buttons*, 1914 (e); *Geography and Plays*, 1922; *The Making of Americans*, 1925 (n); *As a Wife Has a Cow*, 1926 (s); *Composition as Explanation*, 1926 (e); *Useful Knowledge*, 1928 (misc); *A Village*, 1928 (d); *An Acquaintance with Description*, 1929 (e); *Lucy Church Amiably*, 1930 (n); *Dix Portraits*, 1930 (sk); *How To Write*, 1931 (e); *Operas and Plays*, 1932; *Matisse, Picasso, and Gertrude Stein*, 1933 (e); *The Autobiography of Alice B. Toklas*, 1933 (a); *Four Saints in Three Acts*, 1934 (libretto); *Portraits and Prayers*, 1934 (sk); *Lectures in America*, 1935 (e); *Narration*, 1935 (e); *The Geographical History of America*, 1936 (e); *Everybody's Autobiography*, 1937 (a); *Picasso*, 1938 (c); *The World is Round*, 1939 (s); *Paris France*, 1940 (t); *What Are Masterpieces*, 1940 (c); *Ida, A Novel*, 1941; *Wars I Have Seen*, 1944 (r); *Brewsie and Willie*, 1946 (m); *Selected Writings*, 1946; *Four in America*, 1947 (b); *Last Operas and Plays*, 1949; *Things As They Are*, 1951 (n); *Two: Gertrude Stein and Her Brother*, 1951 (m); *Mrs. Reynolds*, 1952 (n); *Bee Time Vine*, 1953 (misc); *As Fine as Melanctha*, 1954 (e); *Painted Lace*, 1955 (misc); *Stanzas in Meditation*, 1956 (p); *Alphabets and Birthdays*, 1957 (juvenile); *A Novel of Thank You*, 1958; *Selected Writings*, 1962

JOHN STEINBECK
1902–1968

Cup of Gold, 1929 (n); *The Pastures of Heaven*, 1932 (s); *To a God Unknown*, 1933 (n); *Tortilla Flat*, 1935 (n); *In Dubious Battle*, 1936 (n); *Of Mice and Men*, 1937 (n); *Of Mice and Men*, 1937 (d); *The*

Long Valley, 1938 (s); *Their Blood Is Strong*, 1938 (e); *The Grapes of Wrath*, 1939 (n); *Sea of Cortez*, 1941 (t) (published as *The Log from the Sea of Cortez*, 1951); *The Moon Is Down*, 1942 (n); *Bombs Away*, 1942 (e); *The Red Pony*, 1945 (n); *Cannery Row*, 1945 (n); *The Portable Steinbeck*, 1946; *The Wayward Bus*, 1947 (n); *The Pearl*, 1947 (n); *A Russian Journal*, 1948 (t); *Burning Bright*, 1950 (d); *East of Eden*, 1952 (n); *Sweet Thursday*, 1954 (n); *The Short Reign of Pippin IV*, 1957 (n); *Once There Was a War*, 1958 (j); *The Winter of Our Discontent*, 1961 (n); *Travels with Charley*, 1962 (t); *Short Novels*, 1963; *America and Americans*, 1966 (t)

WALLACE STEVENS
1879–1955

Harmonium, 1923 (p); *Ideas of Order*, 1935 (p); *Owl's Clover*, 1936 (p); *The Man with the Blue Guitar*, 1937 (p); *Parts of a World*, 1942 (p); *Transport to Summer*, 1947 (p); *The Auroras of Autumn*, 1950 (p); *The Necessary Angel*, 1951 (e); *Collected Poems*, 1954; *Opus Posthumus*, 1957 (misc); *Selected Poems*, 1959; *Letters*, 1966

TRUMBULL STICKNEY
1874–1904

Dramatic Verses, 1902 (p); *Poems*, 1905

WILLIAM STYRON
1925–

Lie Down in Darkness, 1951 (n); *The Long March*, 1955 (n); *Set This House on Fire*, 1960 (n); *The Confessions of Nat Turner*, 1967 (n)

HARVEY SWADOS
1920–

Out Went the Candle, 1955 (n); *On the Line*, 1957 (s); *False Coin*, 1960 (n); *Nights in the Gardens of Brooklyn*, 1961 (s); *A Radical's America*, 1962 (e); *The Will*, 1963 (n); *A Story for Teddy*, 1965 (s)

BOOTH TARKINGTON
1869–1946

The Gentleman from Indiana, 1899 (n); *Monsieur Beaucaire*, 1900 (n); (with E. G. Sutherland) *Monsieur Beaucaire*, 1901 (d); *Samuel Brohl and Company* (by Victor Cherbuliez), 1902 (tr); *The Two Vanrevels,* 1903 (n); *In the Arena,* 1905 (s); *The Beautiful Lady,* 1905 (n); *The Conquest of Canaan,* 1905 (n); *His Own People,* 1907 (n); (with Harry Leon Wilson) *The Guardian,* 1907 (d) (published as *The Man from Home,* 1908); *The Guest of Quesnay,* 1908 (n); *Beasley's Christmas Party,* 1909 (n); (with Harry Leon Wilson) *Your Humble Servant,* 1909 (d); *Cameo Kirby,* 1909 (d); (with Harry Leon Wilson) *Getting a Polish,* 1910 (d); *Beauty and the Jacobin,* 1912 (d); *The Flirt,* 1913 (n); *Penrod,* 1914 (n); *The Turmoil,* 1915 (n); *Penrod and Sam,* 1916 (n); *Seventeen,* 1916 (n); (with Julian Street) *The Ohio Lady,* 1916 (d) (revived as *The Country Cousin,* 1921); *Mr. Antonio,* 1916 (d); *Works,* 1918–1928; *The Magnificent Ambersons,* 1918 (n); *Clarence,* 1919 (d); *Ramsey Milholland,* 1919 (n); (with Harry Leon Wilson) *The Gibson Upright,* 1919 (d); (with Harry Leon Wilson) *Up from Nowhere,* 1919 (d); *Poldekin,* 1920 (d); *Alice Adams,* 1921 (n); *Harlequin and Columbine,* 1921 (n); *The Wren,* 1921 (d); *The Intimate Strangers,* 1921 (d); *Works,* 1922–1932; *Gentle Julia,* 1922 (n); *Rose Briar,* 1922 (d); *The Midlander,* 1923 (n); (with Harry Leon Wilson) *Tweedles,* 1923 (d); *Magnolia,* 1923 (d); *The Fascinating Stranger,* 1923 (s); (with others) *The Collector's Whatnot,* 1923 (sk); *Women,* 1925 (n); *Looking Forward,* 1926 (e); *Selected Stories,* 1926; *Growth,* 1927 (n); *The Plutocrat,* 1927 (n); *The World Does Move,* 1928 (r); *Claire Ambler,* 1928 (n); *Penrod Jashber,* 1929 (n); *Young Mrs. Greeley,* 1929 (n); *Mirthful Haven,* 1930 (n); (with Harry Leon Wilson) *How's Your Health,* 1930 (d); *Colonel Satan,* 1931 (d); *Penrod, His Complete Story,* 1931 (n); *Mary's Neck,* 1932 (n); *Wanton Mally,* 1932 (n); *Presenting Lily Mars,* 1933 (n); *Little Orvie,* 1934 (n); *Mr. White,* 1935 (s); *The Lorenzo Bunch,* 1936 (n); *Rumbin Galleries,* 1937 (n); *Some Old Portraits,* 1939 (e); *Kate Fennigate,* 1943 (n); *The Show Piece,* 1947 (n); *Three Selected Short Novels,* 1947; *Your Amiable Uncle,* 1949 (letters); *The Gentleman from Indianapolis* (selections), 1957; *On Plays, Playwrights and Playgoers,* 1959 (letters)

ALLEN TATE

1899–

Mr. Pope and Other Poems, 1928; *Stonewall Jackson,* 1928 (b); *Jefferson Davis,* 1929 (b); (with others) *I'll Take My Stand,* 1930 (e); *Ode to the Confederate Dead,* 1930 (p); *Poems: 1928–1931,* 1932; *Robert E. Lee,* 1932 (p); *The Mediterranean and Other Poems,* 1936; *Reactionary Essays,* 1936; *Selected Poems,* 1937; *The Fathers,* 1938 (n); (with A. Theodore Johnson) *America Through the Essay,* 1938 (e); *Sonnets at Christmas,* 1941 (p); *Reason in Madness,* 1941 (e); *Vigil of Venus,* 1943 (tr); *The Winter Sea,* 1944 (p); *Poems: 1920–1945,* 1946; *On the Limits of Poetry,* 1948 (e); *Poems: 1922–1947,* 1948; *The Hovering Fly,* 1949 (e); *Two Conceits for the Eye To Sing, If Possible,* 1950 (p);

The Forlorn Demon, 1953 (e); *The Man of Letters in the Modern World,* 1955 (e); *Collected Essays,* 1959; *Poems,* 1960; *Essays of Four Decades,* 1968

PETER TAYLOR
1917–

The Long Fourth, 1948 (s); *A Woman of Means,* 1950 (n); *The Widows of Thornton,* 1953 (s, d); *Tennessee Day in St. Louis,* 1956 (d); *Happy Families Are All Alike,* 1959 (s); *Miss Lenora When Last Seen,* 1963 (s)

AUGUSTUS THOMAS
1857–1934

Alone, 1875 (d); *The Big Rise,* 1882 (d); (with Edgar Smith) *Combustion,* 1884 (d); *The Burglar,* 1889 (d); *Reckless Temple,* 1890 (d); *Alabama,* 1891 (d); *A Night's Frolic,* 1891 (d, tr); (with Clay M. Greene) *For Money,* 1891 (d); *Colonel Carter of Cartersville,* 1892 (d); *Surrender,* 1892 (d); *In Mizzoura,* 1893 (d); *New Blood,* 1894 (d); *The Capitol,* 1895 (d); *Chimmie Fadden,* 1896 (d); *The Jucklins,* 1897 (d); *The Hoosier Doctor,* 1897 (d); *Don't Tell Her Husband,* 1898 (d) (also produced as *The Meddler*); *Colonel George of Mount Vernon,* 1898 (d); *Arizona,* 1899 (d); *Oliver Goldsmith,* 1899 (d); *On the Quiet,* 1901 (d); *Champagne Charley,* 1901 (d); *Colorado,* 1901 (d); *The Earl of Pawtucket,* 1903 (d); *The Other Girl,* 1903 (d); *Mrs. Leffingwell's Boots,* 1905 (d); *The Education of Mr. Pipp,* 1905 (d); *DeLancey,* 1905 (d); *The Embassy Ball,* 1905 (d); *The Ranger,* 1907 (d); *The Member from Ozark,* 1907 (d); *The Witching Hour,* 1907 (d); *The Harvest Moon,* 1909 (d); *As A Man Thinks,* 1911 (d); *The Model,* 1912 (d) (also produced as *When It Comes Home,* 1912); *Mere Man,* 1912 (d); (with George Scarborough) *At Bay,* 1913 (d); *Indian Summer,* 1913 (d); *Three of Hearts,* 1913 (d); *The Battle Cry,* 1914 (d); *The Nightingale,* 1914 (d); *Rio Grande,* 1916 (d); *The Copperhead,* 1918 (d); *The Cricket of Palmy Days,* 1919 (d); *Speak of the Devil,* 1920 (d); *Nemesis,* 1921 (d); *The Print of My Remembrance,* 1922 (a); *Still Waters,* 1925 (d)

JAMES THURBER
1894–1961

(with E. B. White) *Is Sex Necessary?* 1929 (sk); *The Owl in the Attic,* 1931 (s); *The Seal in the Bedroom,* 1932 (sk); *My Life and Hard Times,* 1933 (a); *The Middle-Aged Man on the Flying Trapeze,* 1935 (s); *Let Your Mind Alone!* 1937 (sk); *The Last Flower,* 1939 (illustrated parable); *Cream of Thurber*, 1939; *Fables for Our Time*, 1940 (sk); (with Elliot Nugent) *The Male Animal*, 1940 (d); *My World—and Welcome to It*, 1942 (e); *Many Moons*, 1943 (s); *Men, Women and Dogs*, 1943 (sk); *The Great Quillow*, 1944 (s); *The Thurber Carnival*, 1945 (s); *The White Deer*, 1945 (s); *The Beast in Me and Other Animals*, 1948 (sk); *The Thirteen Clocks*, 1950 (s); *The Thurber Album*, 1952 (s); *Thurber Country*, 1953 (s); *Thurber's Dogs*, 1955 (sk); *A Thurber Garland*, 1956; *Further Fables for Our Time*, 1956 (sk); *The Wonderful O.*, 1957 (s); *Alarms and Diversions*, 1957 (sk); *The Years with Ross*, 1959 (r); *Lanterns and Lances*, 1961 (sk); *Credos and Curios*, 1962 (sk)

RIDGELY TORRENCE
1875–1950

The House of a Hundred Lights, 1900 (p); *Plays for a Negro Theater*, 1917 (d); *Hesperides*, 1925 (p); *Poems*, 1941; *Last Poems*, 1944; *The Story of John Hope*, 1948 (b); *Poems*, 1952

LIONEL TRILLING
1905–

Matthew Arnold, 1939 (c); *E. M. Forster*, 1943 (c); *The Middle of the Journey*, 1947 (n); *The Liberal Imagination*, 1950 (e); *Freud and the Crisis of Our Culture*, 1955 (e); *The Opposing Self*, 1955 (e); *A Gathering of Fugitives*, 1956 (e); *Beyond Culture*, 1965 (e); *The Experience of Literature*, 1967 (c)

MARK TWAIN
1835–1910

The Celebrated Jumping Frog of Calaveras County, 1867 (s); *The Innocents Abroad*, 1869 (t); *Mark Twain's (Burlesque) Autobiography and First Romance*, 1871 (sk); *Roughing It*, 1872 (t); (with Charles Dudley Warner) *The Gilded Age*, 1874 (n); (with G. S. Densmore) *The Gilded Age*, 1874 (d); *Sketches, New and Old*, 1875; *The Adventures of Tom Sawyer*, 1876 (n); *A True Story and The Recent Carnival of Crime*, 1877 (s); (with Bret Harte) *Ah Sin*, 1877 (d); *Punch, Brothers, Punch!* 1878 (sk); *1601*, 1880 (sk); *A Tramp Abroad*, 1880 (t); *The Prince and the Pauper*, 1882 (n); *The Stolen White Elephant*, 1882 (sk); *Life on the Mississippi*, 1883 (m); *The Adventures of Huckleberry Finn*, 1885 (n); (with William Dean Howells) *The American Claimant*, 1887 (d); *A Connecticut Yankee in King Arthur's Court*, 1889 (n); *Merry Tales*, 1892; *The American Claimant*, 1892 (n); *The £1,000,000 Bank-Note*, 1893 (s); *Tom Sawyer Abroad*, 1894 (n); *The Tragedy of Pudd'n-*

head Wilson, 1894 (n); *Personal Recollections of Joan of Arc*, 1896 (n); *Tom Sawyer Abroad, Tom Sawyer, Detective, and Other Stories*, 1896; *How To Tell a Story*, 1897 (e); *Following the Equator*, 1897 (t); *Writings*, 1899–1910; *The Man That Corrupted Hadleyburg*, 1900 (s, e); *English As She Is Taught*, 1900 (sk); *Edmund Burke on Croker and Tammany*, 1901 (sk); *A Double Barrelled Detective Story*, 1902; *My Debut as a Literary Person*, 1903 (s, e); *A Dog's Tale*, 1904 (sk); *Extracts from Adam's Diary*, 1904 (sk); *King Leopold's Soliloquy: a Defense of His Congo Rule*, 1905 (sk); *Eve's Diary*, 1906 (sk); *The $30,000 Bequest*, 1906 (s); *Christian Science*, 1907 (e); *A Horse's Tale*, 1907 (sk); *Is Shakespeare Dead?* 1909 (sk); *Captain Stormfield's Visit to Heaven*, 1909 (n); *Speeches*, 1910 (revised edition, 1923); *The Mysterious Stranger*, 1916 (n); *Letters*, 1917; *What Is Man?* 1917 (e); *The Curious Republic of Gondour*, 1919 (sk); *The Mysterious Stranger and Other Stories*, 1922; *Europe and Elsewhere*, 1923 (t); *Writings*, 1923–1925; *Autobiography*, 1924; (with Bret Harte) *Sketches of the Sixties*, 1926 (enlarged edition, 1927); *The Adventures of Thomas Jefferson Snodgrass*, 1928 (sk); *Works*, 1929; *Notebook*, 1935; *Slovenly Peter*, 1935 (tr); *The Washoe Giant in San Francisco*, 1938 (sk); *Letters from the Sandwich Islands*, 1938; *Letters from Honolulu*, 1939; *Travels with Mr. Brown*, 1940 (sk); *Mark Twain in Eruption*, 1940 (misc); *Letters to Will Bowen*, 1941; *Republican Letters*, 1941; *Letters in the Muscatine Journal*, 1942; *Washington in 1868*, 1943 (e); *The Letters of Quintius Curtius Snodgrass*, 1946 (sk); *Mark Twain in Three Moods*, 1948 (misc); *Mark Twain to Mrs. Fairbanks*, 1949 (letters); *Love Letters*, 1949; *Report from Paradise*, 1952 (t); *Mark Twain-Howells Letters*, 1960

JOHN UPDIKE
1932–

The Carpentered Hen, 1958 (p); *Hoping for a Hoopoe*, 1959 (p); *The Poorhouse Fair*, 1959 (n); *The Same Door*, 1959 (s); *Rabbit, Run*, 1960 (n); *Pigeon Feathers*, 1962 (s); (with others) *Five Boyhoods*, 1962 (m); *The Centaur*, 1963 (n); *Telephone Poles*, 1963 (p); *Olinger Stories*, 1964 (s); *Assorted Prose*, 1965 (e); *Of the Farm*, 1965 (n); *The Music School*, 1966 (s); *Couples*, 1968 (n)

MARK VAN DOREN
1894–

Henry David Thoreau, 1916 (c); *The Poetry of John Dryden*, 1920 (c); *Spring Thunder*, 1924 (p); (with Carl Van Doren) *American and British Literature since 1890*, 1925 (c); *7 P.M. and Other Poems*, 1926; *Edwin Arlington Robinson*, 1927 (c); *Now the Sky*, 1928 (p); *Jonathan Gentry*,

1931 (p); *The Transients,* 1935 (n); *A Winter Diary,* 1935 (p); *The Last Look,* 1937 (p); *Shakespeare,* 1939 (c); *Collected Poems, 1922–1938,* 1939; (with Theodore Spencer) *Studies in Metaphysical Poetry,* 1939 (c); *Windless Cabins,* 1940 (n); *The Mayfield Deer,* 1941 (p); (with Huntington Cairns and Allen Tate) *Invitation to Learning,* 1941 (e); *Our Lady Peace and Other War Poems,* 1942; (with others) *The New Invitation to Learning,* 1942 (e); *The Private Reader,* 1942 (e); *The Seven Sleepers,* 1942 (p); *Liberal Education,* 1943 (e) (revised edition, 1959); *Tilda,* 1943 (n); *The Country Year,* 1946 (p); *The Noble Voice,* 1946 (c) (published as *Great Poems of Western Literature,* 1962); *The Careless Clock,* 1947 (p); *New Poems,* 1948; *Nathaniel Hawthorne,* 1949 (b); *Humanity Unlimited,* 1950 (p); *The Witch of Ramoth,* 1950 (s); *Short Stories,* 1950; *Introduction to Poetry,* 1951 (c); *In That Far Land,* 1951 (p); *Mortal Summer,* 1953 (p); *Nobody Say a Word,* 1953 (s); *Spring Birth,* 1953 (p); *Selected Poems,* 1954; *Man's Right to Knowledge and the Free Use Thereof,* 1954 (e); *Home with Hazel,* 1957 (s); *Autobiography,* 1958; *Don Quixote's Profession,* 1958 (e); *The Last Days of Lincoln,* 1959 (d); *Morning Worship,* 1960 (p); *The Happy Critic,* 1961 (e); *Collected Stories,* I, 1962, II, 1965; *Collected and New Poems, 1924–1963,* 1963; *Narrative Poems,* 1964; *Three Plays,* 1966; *Collected Stories,* III, 1968; *100 Poems,* 1968

JOHN VAN DRUTEN
1901–1957

The Return Half, 1924 (d); *Chance Acquaintances,* 1927 (d); *Young Woodley,* 1928 (n); *Young Woodley,* 1928 (d); *Return of the Soldier,* 1928 (d); *Diversion,* 1928 (d); *After All,* 1929 (d); *A Woman on Her Way,* 1930 (n); *London Wall,* 1931 (d); *There's Always Juliet,* 1931 (d); *Somebody Knows,* 1932 (d); *Behold, We Live!* 1932 (d); *The Distaff Side,* 1933 (d); *Flowers of the Forest,* 1936 (d); *Most of the Game,* 1936 (d); *And Then You Wish,* 1936 (n); *Gertie Maude,* 1937 (d); *The Way to the Present,* 1938 (a); *Leave Her to Heaven,* 1940 (d); *Old Acquaintance,* 1941 (d); (with Lloyd R. Morris) *The Damask Cheek,* 1943 (d); *The Voice of the Turtle,* 1944 (d); *I Remember Mama,* 1945 (d); *The Mermaids Singing,* 1946 (d); *The Druid Circle,* 1948 (d); *Make Way for Lucia,* 1949 (d); *Bell, Book and Candle,* 1951 (d); *I Am a Camera,* 1952 (d); *I've Got Sixpence,* 1953 (d); *Playwright at Work,* 1953 (m); *The Vicarious Years,* 1955 (n); *The Widening Circle,* 1957 (a)

THORSTEIN VEBLEN
1857–1929

The Theory of the Leisure Class, 1899 (e); *The Theory of Business Enterprise,* 1904 (e); *Imperial Germany and the Industrial Revolution,*

1913 (e); *The Instinct of Workmanship*, 1914 (e); *An Inquiry into the Nature of Peace*, 1917 (e); *The Higher Learning in America*, 1918 (e); *The Vested Interests*, 1919 (e); *The Place of Science in Modern Civilization*, 1919 (e); *The Engineers and The Price System*, 1921 (e); *Absentee Ownership and Business Enterprise in Recent Times: The Case of America*, 1923 (e); *Essays in Our Changing Order*, 1934; *What Veblen Taught* (selections), 1936; *Thorstein Veblen* (selections), 1963; *Writings*, 1964

PETER VIERECK
1919–

Metapolitics, 1941 (e) (revised edition, 1961); *Terror and Decorum*, 1948 (p); *Conservatism Revisited*, 1949 (e); *Strike Through the Mask*, 1950 (p); *The First Morning*, 1952 (p); *The Shame and Glory of the Intellectuals*, 1953 (e) (revised edition, 1965); *Dream and Responsibility*, 1953 (e); *The Unadjusted Man*, 1956 (e) (revised edition, 1962); *Conservatism: From John Adams to Churchill*, 1956 (e); *The Persimmon Tree*, 1956 (p); *Inner Liberty*, 1957 (e); *The Tree Witch*, 1961 (pd); *Conservatism Revisited and the New Conservatism*, 1965 (e); *New and Selected Poems*, 1967; *God and the Basket Cases*, 1967 (pd)

EDWARD LEWIS WALLANT
1926–1962

The Human Season, 1960 (n); *The Pawnbroker*, 1961 (n); *The Tenants of Moonbloom*, 1963 (n); *The Children at the Gates*, 1964 (n)

ROBERT PENN WARREN
1905–

John Brown, 1929 (b); (with others) *I'll Take My Stand*, 1930 (e); *Thirty-Six Poems*, 1935; (with Cleanth Brooks) *Understanding Poetry*, 1938 (c); *Night Rider*, 1939 (n); *Eleven Poems on the Same Theme*, 1942; *At Heaven's Gate*, 1943 (n); *Selected Poems*, 1944; *All the King's Men*, 1946 (n); *The Circus in the Attic*, 1948 (s); *World Enough and Time*, 1950 (n); *Brother to Dragons*, 1953 (p); *Band of Angels*, 1955 (n); *Segregation: The Inner Conflict of the South*, 1956 (e); *Promises*, 1957 (p); *Selected Essays*, 1958; *The Cave*, 1959 (n); *All the King's Men*, 1960 (d); *You, Emperors, and Others*, 1960 (p); *The Legacy of the Civil War*, 1961 (e); *Wilderness*, 1961 (n); *Flood*, 1964 (n); *Who Speaks for the Negro?* 1965 (j); *Selected Poems*, 1966

EUDORA WELTY
1909–

A Curtain of Green, 1941 (s); The Robber Bridegroom, 1942 (n); The Wide Net, 1943 (s); Delta Wedding, 1946 (n); Music from Spain, 1948 (n); The Golden Apples, 1949 (s); Short Stories, 1950 (e); The Ponder Heart, 1954 (n); The Bride of the Innisfallen, 1955 (s); Place in Fiction, 1957 (e)

GLENWAY WESCOTT
1901–

The Bitterns, 1920 (p); The Apple of His Eye, 1924 (n); Native of Rock, 1925 (p); Like a Lover, 1926 (s); The Grandmothers, 1927 (n); Good-bye, Wisconsin, 1928 (s); The Babe's Bed, 1930 (n); Fear and Trembling, 1932 (e); A Calendar of Saints for Unbelievers, 1932 (sk); The Deadly Friend, 1933 (sk); The Pilgrim Hawk, 1940 (n); Apartment in Athens, 1945 (n); Twelve Fables of Aesop, 1954 (tr); Images of Truth, 1962 (e)

NATHANAEL WEST
1906–1940

The Dream Life of Balso Snell, 1931 (n); Miss Lonelyhearts, 1933 (n); A Cool Million, 1936 (n); The Day of the Locust, 1939 (n); Complete Works, 1957

EDITH WHARTON
1862–1937

(with Ogden Codman) The Decoration of Houses, 1897 (e); The Greater Inclination, 1899 (s); The Touchstone, 1900 (n) (English edition, A Gift from the Grave); Crucial Instances, 1901 (s); The Valley of Decision, 1902 (n); The Joy of Living (by Hermann Sudermann), 1902 (tr); Sanctuary, 1903 (n); The Descent of Man, 1904 (s); Italian Villas and Their Gardens, 1904 (e); The House of Mirth, 1905 (n); Italian Backgrounds, 1905 (t); The Fruit of the Tree, 1907 (n); Madame de Treymes, 1907 (n); The Hermit and the Wild Woman, 1908 (s); A Motorflight Through France, 1908 (t); Artemis to Actaeon, 1909 (p); Tales of Men and Ghosts, 1910 (s); Ethan Frome, 1911 (n); The Reef, 1912 (n); The Custom of the Country, 1913 (n); Fighting France from Dunkerque to Belfort, 1915 (j); Xingu, 1916 (s); Summer, 1917 (n);

The Marne, 1918 (n); *French Ways and Their Meaning*, 1919 (e); *In Morocco*, 1920 (t); *The Age of Innocence*, 1920 (n); *The Glimpses of the Moon*, 1922 (n); *A Son at the Front*, 1923 (n); *Old New York: False Dawn, The Old Maid, The Spark, New Year's Day*, 1924 (n); *The Writing of Fiction*, 1925 (c); *The Mother's Recompense*, 1925 (n); *Here and Beyond*, 1926 (s); *Twelve Poems*, 1926; *Twilight Sleep*, 1927 (n); *The Children*, 1928 (n) (reissued as *The Marriage Playground*, 1930); *Hudson River Bracketed*, 1929 (n); *Certain People*, 1930 (s); *The Gods Arrive*, 1932 (n); *Human Nature*, 1933 (s); *A Backward Glance*, 1934 (a); *The World Over*, 1936 (s); *Ghosts*, 1937 (s); *The Buccaneers*, 1938 (n); *The Best Short Stories*, 1959; *The Edith Wharton Reader*, 1965; *Collected Short Stories*, 1968

JOHN HALL WHEELOCK
1886–

(with Van Wyck Brooks) *Verses by Two Undergraduates*, 1905 (p); *The Human Fantasy*, 1911 (p); *The Beloved Adventure*, 1912 (p); *Love and Liberation*, 1913 (p); *Dust and Light*, 1919 (p); *The Black Panther*, 1922 (p); *The Bright Doom*, 1927 (p); *Poems, 1911–1936*, 1936; *Happily Ever After*, 1939 (s); *Poems Old and New*, 1956; *The Gardener*, 1961 (p); *What Is Poetry?* 1963 (c); *Dear Men and Women*, 1966 (p)

JOHN BROOKS WHEELWRIGHT
1897–1940

Rock and Shell, 1934 (p); *Mirrors of Venus*, 1938 (p); *Political Self-Portrait, 1919–1939*, 1940 (p); *Selected Poems*, 1941

E. B. WHITE
1899–

(with James Thurber) *Is Sex Necessary?* 1929 (sk); *The Lady Is Cold*, 1929 (p); *Ho Hum*, 1931 (sk); *Another Ho Hum*, 1932 (sk); *Every Day Is Saturday*, 1934 (e); *The Fox of Peapack*, 1938 (p); *Quo Vadimus?* 1939 (e); *One Man's Meat*, 1942 (e); *Stuart Little*, 1943 (juvenile); *The Wild Flag*, 1946 (e); *Here Is New York*, 1949 (t); *Charlotte's Web*, 1952 (juvenile); *The Second Tree from the Corner*, 1954 (e); (with William Strunk) *The Elements of Style*, 1959 (c); *Points of My Compass*, 1962 (e); *An E. B. White Reader*, 1966

REED WHITTEMORE
1919–

Heroes and Heroines, 1946 (p); *An American Takes a Walk*, 1956 (p); *The Self-Made Man*, 1959 (p); *The Boy from Iowa*, 1962 (p, e); *The*

Fascination of the Abomination, 1963 (p, e, s); *Poems, New and Selected,* 1967; *From Zero to the Absolute,* 1967 (e)

RICHARD WILBUR
1921–

The Beautiful Changes, 1947 (p); *Ceremony,* 1950 (p); *The Misanthrope,* 1955 (tr); *Things of This World,* 1956 (p); *Advice to a Prophet,* 1961 (p); *Tartuffe,* 1963 (tr)

THORNTON WILDER
1897–

The Cabala, 1926 (n); *The Bridge of San Luis Rey,* 1927 (n); *The Angel That Troubled the Waters,* 1928 (d); *The Woman of Andros,* 1930 (n); *The Long Christmas Dinner,* 1931 (d); *Heaven's My Destination,* 1935 (n); *Our Town,* 1935 (d); *The Merchant of Yonkers,* 1938 (d) (published as *The Matchmaker,* 1955); *The Skin of Our Teeth,* 1942 (d); *The Ides of March,* 1948 (n); *The Alcestiad,* 1955 (d); *Three Plays (Our Town, The Skin of Our Teeth, The Matchmaker),* 1957; *Plays for Bleecker Street,* 1962; *The Eighth Day,* 1967 (n)

TENNESSEE WILLIAMS
1914–

(with others) *Five Young American Poets,* 1944 (p); *Battle of Angels,* 1945 (d); *The Glass Menagerie,* 1945 (d); *Twenty-Seven Wagons Full of Cotton,* 1946 (d); (with David Windham) *You Touched Me!* 1947 (d); *A Streetcar Named Desire,* 1947 (d); *One Arm and Other Stories,* 1948 (s); *Summer and Smoke,* 1948 (d); *American Blues: Five Short Plays,* 1948; *The Roman Spring of Mrs. Stone,* 1950 (n); *The Rose Tattoo,* 1951 (d); *I Rise in Flame, Cried the Phoenix,* 1951 (d); *Camino Real,* 1953 (d); *Hard Candy,* 1954 (s); *Cat on a Hot Tin Roof,* 1955 (d); *Four Plays (The Glass Menagerie, A Streetcar Named Desire, Summer and Smoke, Camino Real),* 1956; *In the Winter of Cities,* 1956 (p); *Baby Doll,* 1956 (d); *Orpheus Descending,* 1958 (d) (published as *The Fugitive Kind,* 1958); *Suddenly Last Summer,* 1958 (d); *Sweet Bird of Youth,* 1959 (d); *Three Players of a Summer Game,* 1960 (s); *Period of Adjustment,* 1960 (d); *The Night of the Iguana,* 1961 (d); *The Eccentricities of a Nightingale;* and *Summer and Smoke,* 1964 (d); *The Milk Train Doesn't Stop Here Anymore,* 1964 (d); *Slapstick Tragedy,* 1967 (d); *The Knightly Quest,* 1967 (s); *The Seven Descents of Myrtle,* 1968 (d) (published as *Kingdom of Earth*)

WILLIAM CARLOS WILLIAMS
1883–1963

Poems, 1909; *The Tempers,* 1913 (p); *Al Que Quiere!* 1917 (p); *Kora in Hell: Improvisations,* 1920; *Sour Grapes,* 1921 (p); *Spring and All,* 1923 (p); *The Great American Novel,* 1923 (n); *In the American Grain,* 1925 (e); *A Voyage to Pagany,* 1928 (n); *Last Night of Paris* (by Philippe Soupault), 1929 (tr); *A Novelette and Other Prose,* 1932 (misc); *The Knife of the Times,* 1932 (s); *Collected Poems 1921–1931,* 1934; *An Early Martyr,* 1935 (p); *Adam and Eve and The City,* 1936 (p); *White Mule,* 1937 (n); *Life Along the Passaic River,* 1938 (s); *Complete Collected Poems 1906–1938,* 1938; *In the Money,* 1940 (n); *The Broken Span,* 1941 (p); *Trial Horse No. 1,* 1942 (d) (also produced as *Many Loves*); *The Wedge,* 1944 (p); *Paterson, Book One,* 1946 (p); *First Act* (*White Mule* and *In the Money*), 1946 (n); *Paterson, Book Two,* 1948 (p); *A Dream of Love,* 1948 (d); *The Clouds,* 1948 (p); *The Pink Church,* 1949 (p); *Selected Poems,* 1949; *Paterson, Book Three,* 1949 (p); *Make Light Of It: Collected Stories,* 1950; *The Collected Later Poems,* 1950; *The Collected Earlier Poems,* 1951; *Paterson, Book Four,* 1951 (p); *Autobiography,* 1951; *The Build-Up,* 1952 (n); *The Desert Music,* 1954 (p); *Selected Essays,* 1954; (with Raquel Héléne Williams) *A Dog and the Fever* (by Don Francisco de Quevedo), 1954 (tr); *Journey to Love,* 1955 (p); *Selected Letters,* 1957; *Paterson, Book Five,* 1958 (p); *I Wanted To Write a Poem,* 1958 (m); *Yes, Mrs. Williams,* 1959 (r); *The Farmers' Daughters* (collected stories), 1961; *Many Loves and Other Plays,* 1961; *Pictures from Brueghel,* 1962 (p); *Collected Later Poems* (revised edition), 1963; *Paterson,* 1963 (p); *The William Carols Williams Reader,* 1966

EDMUND WILSON
1895–

(with John Peale Bishop) *The Undertaker's Garland,* 1922 (s, p); *Discordant Encounters: Plays and Dialogues,* 1926; *I Thought of Daisy,* 1929 (n); *Poets, Farewell!* 1929 (p, sk); *Axel's Castle,* 1931 (c); *The American Jitters,* 1932 (e); *Travels in Two Democracies,* 1936 (t); *This Room and This Gin and These Sandwiches,* 1937 (d); *The Triple Thinkers,* 1938 (c) (revised and enlarged edition, 1948); *To the Finland Station,* 1940 (h); *The Boys in the Back Room,* 1941 (c); *The Wound and the Bow,* 1941 (c); *Note-books of Night,* 1942 (p, sk); *The Shock of Recognition,* 1943 (c); *Memoirs of Hecate County,* 1946 (s); *Europe Without Baedeker,* 1947 (t) (revised edition, 1966); *The Little Blue Light,* 1950 (d); *Classics and Commercials: A Literary Chronicle of the Forties,* 1950 (e); *The Shores of Light: A Literary Chronicle of the*

Twenties and Thirties, 1952 (e); *Eight Essays*, 1954; *Five Plays*, 1954; *The Scrolls from the Dead Sea*, 1955 (e); *Red, Black, Blond and Olive*, 1956 (e); *A Piece of My Mind*, 1956 (e); *A Literary Chronicle: 1920–1950*, 1956 (e); *The American Earthquake: A Documentary of the Twenties and Thirties*, 1958 (e); *Apologies to the Iroquois*, 1960 (e); *Night Thoughts*, 1961 (p, sk); *Patriotic Gore*, 1962 (c); *The Cold War and the Income Tax*, 1963 (e); *O Canada*, 1965 (e); *The Bit Between My Teeth*, 1966 (e); *A Prelude*, 1967 (m); *The Fruits of the MLA*, 1968 (e)

YVOR WINTERS
1900–1968

The Immobile Wind, 1921 (p); *The Magpie's Shadow*, 1922 (p); *Notes on the Mechanics of the Poetic Image*, 1925 (e); *The Bare Hills*, 1927 (p); *The Proof*, 1930 (p); *The Journey*, 1931 (p); *Before Disaster*, 1934 (p); (with Frances Theresa Russell) *The Case of David Lamson*, 1934 (j); *Primitivism and Decadence*, 1937 (c); *Maule's Curse*, 1938 (c); *Poems*, 1940; *The Giant Weapon*, 1943 (p); *The Anatomy of Nonsense*, 1943 (c); *Edwin Arlington Robinson*, 1946 (c); *In Defense of Reason*, 1947 (c); *To the Holy Spirit*, 1947 (p); *Collected Poems*, 1952 (revised editions, 1960, 1963); *On Modern Poets*, 1957 (c); *The Function of Criticism*, 1957 (e); *The Poetry of William Butler Yeats*, 1960 (c); *The Poetry of J. V. Cunningham*, 1961 (c); *Early Poems, 1920–1928*, 1966; *Forms of Discovery*, 1967 (c)

THOMAS WOLFE
1900–1938

Look Homeward, Angel, 1929 (n); *Of Time and the River*, 1935 (n); *From Death to Morning*, 1935 (s); *The Story of a Novel*, 1936 (m); *The Web and the Rock*, 1939 (n); *The Face of a Nation* (selections), 1939; *You Can't Go Home Again*, 1940 (n); *The Hills Beyond*, 1941 (s); *Letters to His Mother*, 1943; *The Portable Thomas Wolfe*, 1946; *Mannerhouse*, 1948 (d); *A Western Journal*, 1951 (t); *The Correspondence of Thomas Wolfe and Homer Andrew Watt*, 1954; *Letters*, 1956; *Short Novels*, 1961; *The Thomas Wolfe Reader*, 1962

HERMAN WOUK
1915–

Aurora Dawn, 1947 (n); *The City Boy*, 1948 (n); *The Caine Mutiny*, 1951 (n); *Marjorie Morningstar*, 1955 (n); *Nature's Way*, 1958 (e);

This is My God, 1959 (e); *Youngblood Hawke,* 1962 (n); *Don't Stop the Carnival,* 1965 (n)

JAMES WRIGHT
1927–

The Green Wall, 1957 (p); *Saint Judas,* 1959 (p); *The Branch Will Not Break,* 1963 (p); (with Robert Bly) *Twenty Poems of Pablo Neruda,* 1968 (tr); *Shall We Gather at the River,* 1968 (p)

RICHARD WRIGHT
1908–1960

Guide to Harlem, 1937 (t); *Uncle Tom's Children,* 1938 (s); *Native Son,* 1940 (n); *Twelve Million Black Voices,* 1941 (h); *Black Boy,* 1945 (a); *The Outsider,* 1953 (n); *The Long Dream,* 1958 (n); *Eight Men,* 1961 (s); *The Lawd Today,* 1963 (n)

ELINORE WYLIE
1885–1928

Nets To Catch the Wind, 1921 (p); *Jennifer Lorn,* 1923 (n); *Black Armour,* 1923 (p); *The Venetian Glass Nephew,* 1925 (n); *The Orphan Angel,* 1926 (n); *Mr. Hodge and Mr. Hazard,* 1928 (n); *Angels and Earthly Creatures,* 1929 (p); *Collected Poems,* 1932; *Collected Prose,* 1933; *The Novels of Elinor Wylie,* 1934; *Last Poems,* 1943

STARK YOUNG
1881–1963

The Blind Man at the Window, 1906 (p); *Guenevere,* 1906 (d); *Addio, Madretta and Other Plays,* 1912; *Three One-Act Plays,* 1921; *The Twilight Saint,* 1921 (d); *The Queen of Sheba,* 1922 (d); *The Flower in Drama,* 1923 (e); *The Colonnade,* 1924 (d); *The Three Fountains,* 1924 (t); *The Saint,* 1925 (d); *Sweet Times and The Blue Policeman,* 1925 (d); *Glamour,* 1925 (e); *Heaven Trees,* 1926 (n); *Theatre Practice,* 1926 (e); *Encaustics,* 1926 (e); *Mandragola,* 1927 (tr); *The Theater,* 1927 (e); *The Torches Flare,* 1928 (n); *River House,* 1929 (n); *The Street of the Islands,* 1930 (s); (with others) *I'll Take My Stand,* 1930 (e); *So Red the Rose,* 1934 (n); *Feliciana,* 1935 (s); *The Sea Gull,* 1939 (tr); *Immortal Shadows,* 1948 (e); *The Pavilion,* 1951 (r)

COPYRIGHT ACKNOWLEDGMENTS

465

by L. S. Dembo, © 1960 by Cornell University. Used by permission of Cornell University; for the excerpt from *The Theory of American Literature* by Howard Mumford Jones, © 1965 by Cornell University. Used by permission of Cornell University.

DOUBLEDAY & COMPANY, INC., from E. B. White's Introduction to *the lives and times of archy and mehitabel* by Don Marquis. Introduction copyright 1950 by Doubleday & Company, Inc. Reprinted by permission of the publisher: excerpt from *O Rare Don Marquis* by Edward Anthony. Copyright © 1962 by Edward Anthony. Reprinted by permission of Doubleday & Company, Inc.; excerpts by Robert Gorham Davis, Alan R. Jones, and David L. Stevenson, from *The Creative Present*, edited by Nona Balakian and Charles Simmons. Copyright © 1963 by Nona Balakian and Charles Simmons. Reprinted by permission of Doubleday & Company, Inc.; excerpt from *The Theatre of the Absurd* by Martin Esslin. Copyright © 1961 by Martin Esslin. Reprinted by permission of Doubleday & Company, Inc.; excerpt from *Thomas Wolfe: A Biography* by Elizabeth Nowell. Copyright © 1960 by Doubleday & Company, Inc. Reprinted by permission of the publisher.

DOVER PUBLICATIONS, INC., for the excerpt from George Barkin's Preface to Ambrose Bierce: *Sardonic Humor of Ambrose Bierce,* Dover Publications, Inc., New York, 1963. Reprinted by permission of the publisher.

TOM F. DRIVER, for the excerpt from his article on Edward Albee in *The Reporter* (Jan. 2, 1964), reprinted by permission of the author and his agent, James Brown Associates, Inc. Copyright © 1964 by The Reporter Magazine Company.

E. P. DUTTON & CO., INC., for excerpts from "Lewis Mumford: American Prophet" (*Harper's,* June, 1952) by Van Wyck Brooks and Introduction to *The History of a Literary Radical and Other Papers* (by Randolph Bourne, published by Russell & Russell) by Van Wyck Brooks, permission is granted by E. P. Dutton & Co., Inc. on behalf of Mrs. Gladys Brooks.

EVERETT/EDWARDS, INC., for excerpts from six essays in *Essays in Modern American Literature,* edited by Richard E. Langford, published by Stetson University Press in 1963.

EYRE & SPOTTISWOODE LTD., for permission for the British Commonwealth for excerpts from *The Theatre of the Absurd* by Martin Esslin.

FABER AND FABER, LTD., for permission for world rights excluding the U.S.A. and Canada for excerpts from *The Dyer's Hand* by W. H. Auden.

FARRAR, STRAUS & GIROUX, INC., for excerpts reprinted with the permission of Farrar, Straus & Giroux, as follows: from *Babel To Byzantium* by James Dickey. Copyright © 1956, 1957, 1958, 1959, 1960, 1961, 1962, 1963, 1964, 1965, 1966, 1967, 1968 by James Dickey; from *The King of the Cats* by F. W. Dupee. Copyright © 1963 by F. W. Dupee; from *The Collected Works of Jane Bowles.* Introduction copyright © 1966 by Truman Capote; from *A Reader's Guide to William Faulkner* by Edmond L. Volpe. Copyright © 1964 by Edmond L. Volpe; from *The Magic of Shirley Jackson,* edited by Stanley Edgar Hyman. Copyright © 1965, 1966 by Stanley Edgar Hyman; from *Doings and Undoings* by Norman Podhoretz. Copyright © 1958, 1964 by Norman Podhoretz; from *The Myth and the Powerhouse* by Philip Rahv. Copyright © 1949, 1950, 1951, 1952, 1953, 1954, 1955, 1956, 1957, 1958, 1960, 1963, 1964, 1965 by Philip Rahv.

SAMUEL FRENCH, INC., for the excerpt from *New Theatres for Old*: copyright, 1940,

1962, by Mordecai Gorelik, reprinted by special arrangement with Samuel French, Inc.; for the excerpt from the Introduction to *Peace on Earth*: copyright, 1933, by George Sklar and Albert Maltz, reprinted by special arrangement with Samuel French, Inc.

THE GRIFFIN, for the excerpt from "Habit and Promise" by R. P. Blackmur, p. 7 of *The Griffin*, March 1961, Volume 10, No. 3, The Readers' Subscription, Inc., Publishers, New York, 1961.

HARPER'S MAGAZINE, INC., for the excerpt from "The Riddle of John Dos Passos" by Daniel Aaron, copyright © 1962 by Harper's Magazine, Inc. Reprinted from the March, 1962 issue of *Harper's Magazine* by permission of the author; for the excerpt from "Lewis Mumford: American Prophet" by Van Wyck Brooks, copyright © 1952 by Harper's Magazine, Inc. Reprinted from the June, 1952 issue of *Harper's Magazine* by permission of Mrs. Gladys Brooks; for the excerpt from the review of *Nova Express* (by William Burroughs) by Robert Hatch, copyright © 1964 by Harper's Magazine, Inc. Reprinted from the January, 1965 issue of *Harper's Magazine* by permission of the author; for the excerpt from the review of *The House of Five Talents* (by Louis Auchincloss) by Paul Pickrel, copyright © 1960 by Harper's Magazine, Inc. Reprinted from the October, 1960 issue of *Harper's Magazine* by permission of the author; for the excerpt from the review of *In Cold Blood* (by Truman Capote) by Rebecca West, copyright © 1966 by Harper's Magazine, Inc. Reprinted from the February, 1966 issue of *Harper's Magazine* by permission of the author.

HARPER AND ROW, PUBLISHERS, INC., for excerpts from *American Poetry Since 1945* by Stephen Stepanchev. Copyright © 1965, by Stephen Stepanchev. Reprinted by permission of Harper and Row, Publishers.

RUPERT HART-DAVIS LTD., for permission for the British Commonwealth for the excerpt from *William James* by Gay Wilson Allen.

HARVARD UNIVERSITY PRESS, reprinted by permission of the publishers as follows: from Albert J. Gelpi, *Emily Dickinson: The Mind of the Poet*, Cambridge, Mass.: Harvard University Press, Copyright © 1965, by the President and Fellows of Harvard College; from Thomas H. Johnson, *Emily Dickinson: An Interpretive Biography*, Cambridge, Mass.: The Belknap Press of Harvard University Press, Copyright © 1955, by the President and Fellows of Harvard College; from J. Hillis Miller, Jr., *Poets of Reality: Six Twentieth-Century Writers*, Cambridge, Mass.: The Belknap Press of Harvard University Press, Copyright © 1965, by the President and Fellows of Harvard College; from Walter Bates Rideout, *The Radical Novel in the United States, 1900-1954,* Cambridge, Mass.: Harvard University Press Copyright © 1956, by the President and Fellows of Harvard College; from Moses Rischin, *The Promised City: New York's Jews, 1870-1914,* Cambridge, Mass.: Harvard University Press, Copyright © 1962, by the President and Fellows of Harvard College; from Ernest Samuels, *Henry Adams: The Major Phase*, Cambridge, Mass.: The Belknap Press of Harvard University Press, Copyright © 1964, by the President and Fellows of Harvard College; from Theodora Ward, *The Capsule of the Mind: Chapters in the Life of Emily Dickinson,* Cambridge, Mass.: The Belknap Press of Harvard University Press, Copyright © 1961, by the President and Fellows of Harvard College.

WILLIAM HEINEMANN LTD, for permission for the British Commonwealth excluding Canada for the excerpt from *Emily Dickinson's Poetry: Stairway of Surprise* by Charles R. Anderson.

THE HUDSON REVIEW, for the quotations from *The Hudson Review*, which are copyrighted © 1957, 1958, 1959, 1960, 1961, 1962, 1963, 1964, 1965, 1966, 1967, 1968 by the Hudson Review, Inc.

MRS. RANDALL JARRELL, for the excerpt from the review of *The Diamond Cutters* (by Adrienne Rich) by Randall Jarrell in *The Yale Review* (Autumn, 1956).

JOHNS HOPKINS PRESS, for excerpts from *ELH*, cited in the text, all quotations reprinted by permission of The Johns Hopkins Press.

HUGH KENNER, for the excerpt from *The Invisible Poet: T. S. Eliot*.

LIFE MAGAZINE, for the excerpt from "A Cry of Loss: Dilemma Come Back" by Tom Prideaux, *Life* Magazine © 1966 Time Inc.

LITTLE, BROWN AND CO., for excerpts from books published by them, cited in text as Little; for the excerpt from *The Third Rose* by John Malcolm Brinnin, published by Atlantic-Little, Brown and Company; for the excerpt from *The Thought and Character of William James* by Ralph Barton Perry, published by Atlantic-Little, Brown and Company.

MCINTOSH AND OTIS, INC., for permission for the British Commonwealth for the excerpt from *Ambrose Bierce* by Richard O'Connor, and for the excerpt from *Jack London* by Richard O'Connor.

THE MASSACHUSETTS REVIEW, for the quotations from *The Massachusetts Review,* which are copyrighted © 1965, 1966, by The Massachusetts Review, Inc.

THE UNIVERSITY OF MICHIGAN PRESS, for the excerpt from *The Poetic Themes of Robert Lowell* by Jerome Mazzaro, copyright © 1965 by the University of Michigan; for the excerpt from *The Major Themes of Robert Frost* by Radcliffe Squires, copyright © 1963 by the University of Michigan; for the excerpt from *The Loyalties of Robinson Jeffers* by Radcliffe Squires, copyright © 1963 by the University of Michigan; for the excerpts from *The New England Conscience* by Austin Warren, copyright © 1966 by the University of Michigan.

MODERN LANGUAGE ASSOCIATION OF AMERICA, for excerpts from the following articles, reprinted by permission of the Modern Language Association: from Julia Cluck's "Elinor Wylie's Shelley Obsession," *PMLA*, LVI (Sept., 1941); from Stanley Greenfield's "The Unmistakable Stephen Crane," *PMLA*, LXXIII (December, 1958); from James G. Hepburn's "E. A. Robinson's System of Opposites," *PMLA*, LXXX (June, 1965); from Benjamin T. Spencer's "Pound: The American Strain," *PMLA*, LXXXI (December, 1966).

ELLEN MOERS, for the excerpt from her article on Theodore Dreiser in the *American Scholar* (Winter, 1963-64), to be published in her book, *Two Dreisers* (Viking).

WILLIAM MORROW & COMPANY, INC., for the excerpt from *Stephen Crane* by John Berryman, copyright © 1950 by William Sloane Associates, Inc.; for the excerpt from *Margaret Mitchell of Atlanta* by Finis Farr, copyright © 1965 by Finis Farr and Stephens Mitchell.

THE NATIONAL COUNCIL OF TEACHERS OF ENGLISH, for permission to use excerpts from articles in *College English,* cited in text; for permission to use excerpts from articles in *English Journal,* cited in text.

NATIONAL REVIEW, for excerpts from articles by John Dos Passos and Hugh Kenner,

Robert Sklar. Reprinted by permission of Oxford University Press, Inc.; from *The Poetry of W. H. Auden* by Monroe K. Spears. Copyright © 1963 by Monroe K. Spears. Reprinted by permission of Oxford University Press, Inc.; from *The American Historian* by Harvey Wish. Copyright © 1960 by Oxford University Press, Inc. Reprinted by permission.

PARTISAN REVIEW, for excerpts from reviews and articles, cited in text, © 1941, 1947, 1951, 1959, 1961, 1962, 1964, 1965, 1966, 1967 by Partisan Review.

LAURENCE POLLINGER, LTD., for permission for the British Commonwealth for the excerpt from *The Third Rose* by John Malcolm Brinnin, published by George Weidenfeld & Nicholson, Ltd.

PRENTICE-HALL, INC., for excerpts, as follows: from the Introduction to *O'Neill: A Collection of Critical Essays* by John Gassner, © 1964. Reprinted by permission of Prentice-Hall, Inc., Englewood Cliffs, New Jersey; from *Harvests of Change* by Jay Martin © 1967. Reprinted by permission of Prentice-Hall, Inc., Englewood Cliffs, New Jersey; from the Introduction to *Ezra Pound: A Collection of Critical Essays* by Walter Sutton © 1963. Reprinted by permission of Prentice-Hall, Inc., Englewood Cliffs, New Jersey.

PURDUE RESEARCH FOUNDATION, for excerpts from *Modern Fiction Studies*, cited in text, reprinted by permission of the Purdue Research Foundation, Lafayette, Indiana.

RANDOM HOUSE, INC., for the excerpt from *The Dyer's Hand* by W. H. Auden © Copyright 1962 by W. H. Auden. Reprinted by permission of Random House, Inc.; for the excerpts from *A Piece of Lettuce* by George P. Elliott. Copyright © 1960 by George P. Elliott. Reprinted by permission of Random House, Inc.; for the excerpt from *Shadow and Act* by Ralph Ellison, Copyright © 1945 by Ralph Ellison. Reprinted by permission of Random House, Inc.; for excerpt from the Foreword by Clark Kinnaird to *A Treasury of Damon Runyon*. Copyright © 1958 by Random House, Inc. Reprinted by permission of Random House, Inc.; for excerpts from *Contemporary American Poetry* by Ralph J. Mills. © Copyright 1965 by Random House, Inc. Reprinted by permission; for excerpts from *Postscript to Yesterday* by Lloyd Morris. Copyright © 1947 by Lloyd Morris. Reprinted by permission of Random House, Inc.; for excerpt from *Father's Footsteps* by Damon Runyon, Jr. Copyright © 1953 by Curtis Publishing Co. Copyright © 1954 by Damon Runyon, Jr. Reprinted by permission of Random House, Inc.; for excerpt from the Introduction by Mark Schorer to *Selected Writings of Truman Capote*. © Copyright 1963 by Random House, Inc. Used by permission of Random House, Inc.; for excerpt from *The Autobiography of Alice B. Toklas* by Gertrude Stein. Copyright © 1933 and renewed 1961 by Alice B. Toklas. Reprinted by permission of Random House, Inc.

PAUL R. REYNOLDS, INC., for permission for the British Commonwealth for *O Rare Don Marquis* by Edward Anthony.

THE RONALD PRESS COMPANY, for the excerpt from *The Course of American Democratic Thought* by Ralph Henry Gabriel. Copyright © 1940, renewed 1968. The Ronald Press Company, New York.

ROUTLEDGE & KEGAN PAUL, LTD., for the excerpt from *Poetry and Belief in the Work of T. S. Eliot* by Kristian Smidt and for the excerpt from *T. S. Eliot and the Idea of Tradition* by Sean Lucy; for permission for the British Commonwealth for the excerpt from *Ezra Pound: Poet as Sculptor* by Donald Davie.

INDEX TO CRITICS

Names of critics are cited on the pages given.

Himes, I, 92; Macdonald, R., II, 257, 259

BOURNE, Randolph
More, II, 370

BOWEN, Elizabeth
Saroyan, III, 143; Welty, III, 329

BOWER-SHORE, Clifford
Bierce, I, 107

BOWRA, C. M.
Lattimore, II, 191

BOWRON, Bernard
Matthiessen, II, 307

BOYD, Ernest
Lewis, II, 207

BOYERS, Robert
Sexton, III, 167

BOYLE, Kay
Baldwin, I, 67; Nabokov, II, 395

BOYNTON, Percy
Bierce, I, 106; Cabell, I, 181; Cather, I, 207; Hearn, II, 58; Masters, II, 300; Robinson, III, 81; Rolvaag, III, 95

BRACE, Marjorie
Taylor, III, 258

BRACKER, Jon
Morley, II, 380

BRADBURY, John M.
Warren, III, 318

BRADFORD, M. E.
Baldwin, I, 69; Faulkner, I, 366

BRADFORD, Robert W.
White, III, 358

BRADLEY, Sam
Shapiro, III, 172

BRADLEY, Sculley
Fitch, I, 394; Moody, II, 358

BRADY, Charles A.
Capote, I, 195; Thurber, III, 268

BRADY, Mildred Edie
Miller, H., II, 346

BRANCH, Edgar Marquess
Farrell, I, 359; Twain, III, 286

BRANTLEY, Frederick
Roethke, III, 88; Warren, III, 317

BREIT, Harvey
Agee, I, 11; Bellow, I, 86; Capote, I, 195; Hemingway, II, 68; Jackson, II, 118; Patchen, III, 11; Schulberg, III, 154; Styron, III, 237; Warren, III, 319

BRENNER, Conrad
Nabokov, II, 397

BRESLER, Riva T.
Levin, II, 206

BRESLIN, James E.
Williams, W. C., III, 386

BRETT, G. S.
More, II, 373

BRICKELL, Herschel
Fisher, V., I, 389; Green, II, 32; Tate, III, 256; Welty, III, 325

BRIDGES, Horace James
Lewisohn, II, 214

BRIDGMAN, Richard
Hemingway, II, 73; James, H., II, 129; Lardner, II, 190; Stein, III, 218; Twain, III, 284

BRINNIN, John Malcolm
Eberhart, I, 327; Fitzgerald, R., I, 407; Rukeyser, III, 113; Stein, III, 216; Wheelock, III, 350

BRINTON, Crane
Viereck, III, 312

BRITTEN, Florence Haxton
West, III, 335

BRODBECK, May
Veblen, III, 306

BROMFIELD, Louis
Rawlings, III, 51; Richter, III, 69

BRONSON, John
Fisher, V., I, 388

BROOKS, Cleanth
Auden, I, 55; Bishop, J. P., I, 116; Faulkner, I, 365; Hemingway, II, 71; Warren, III, 321

BROOKS, John
Auchincloss, I, 45; Kerouac, II, 172

BROOKS, Robert C.
London, II, 223

BROOKS, Van Wyck
Bierce, I, 105; Bourne, I, 131; Chopin, I, 218; Dreiser, I, 315; Hemingway, II, 67; Howells, II, 102; James, H., II, 122; James, W., II, 134; Jewett, II, 153; Lowell, A., II, 233; Mencken, II, 312; Millay, II, 336; Mumford, II, 393; Robinson, III, 81; Stickney, III, 233; Twain, III, 281; Wharton, III, 343

BROSSARD, Chandler
McCarthy, II, 242

BROUN, Heywood
Connelly, I, 228; Ferber, I, 374; Tarkington, III, 248